PROGRESS IN CYBERNETICS AND SYSTEMS RESEARCH

Volume II

Socio-economic Systems
Cybernetics of Cognition and Learning
Systems Education
Cybernetics in Organization and Management
Special Aspects

PROGRESS IN CYBERNETICS AND SYSTEMS RESEARCH
Volume II

Socio-economic Systems
Cybernetics of Cognition and Learning
Systems Education
Cybernetics in Organization and Management
Special Aspects

Edited by

ROBERT TRAPPL

Professor of Biocybernetics and Bioinformatics
University of Vienna Medical School

and

F. de P. HANIKA

Austrian Society for Cybernetic Studies

WITH INTRODUCTION BY
STAFFORD BEER

HEMISPHERE PUBLISHING CORPORATION

Washington, D.C.

A HALSTED PRESS BOOK

JOHN WILEY & SONS

New York   London   Sydney   Toronto

Hemisphere Publishing Corporation
1025 Vermont Ave., N.W., Washington, D.C. 20005

Distributed solely by Halsted Press, a Division of John Wiley & Sons, Inc., New York.

Library of Congress Cataloging in Publication Data

Main entry under title:

Progress in cybernetics and systems research.

    Vol. 2 edited by Robert Trappl and F. de P. Hanika.
    "Symposium was organized by the Austrian Society for
Cybernetic Studies."
    Sponsored by the Bundesministerium für Wissenschaft
und Forschung, and others.
    "A Halsted Press book."
    Includes bibliographical references.
    1. Cybernetics—Congresses. 2. System theory—
Congresses. I. Trappl, Robert. II. Pichler, Franz
III. Hanika, Francis de Paula. IV. Austrian Society
for Cybernetic Studies. V. Austria. Bundesminister

ium für Wissenschaft und Forschung. VI. Title.
Q300.E87 1974   001.53   75-6641
ISBN 0-470-88476-2

This Symposium was organized by the Austrian Society for Cybernetic Studies
in cooperation with
Society for General Systems Research

International Association of Cybernetics

PATRON

Dr. Hertha Firnberg
Austrian Federal Minister of Science and Research

CHAIRMAN

Professor Robert Trappl
President, Austrian Society for Cybernetic Studies

SPONSORS

Bundesministerium für Wissenschaft und Forschung*
Gemeinde Wien**
Bundeskammer der Gewerblichen Wirtschaft***
Honeywell Bull
IBM
Verband Österreichischer Banken und Bankiers****

ADVISORY COMMITTEE

Professor A. Adam, Kepler University, Linz
D.J. Bamber, Institute for Management Sciences (UK Chapter)
Dr. Bela H. Banathy, Far West Laboratory for Educational Research and
Development, Berkeley, USA.
Dipl.Ing. G. Chroust, IBM Laboratory, Vienna.
Professor F. de P. Hanika, Austrian Society for Cybernetic Studies (Chairman)
Dr. Maria Holzer, Austrian Society for Cybernetic Studies
P. Martin, Society for General Systems Research.
G. Nauer, Austrian Society for Cybernetic Studies.
Dr. Ingomar Poschik, Austrian Society for Cybernetic Studies.
Professor F. Pichler, Kepler University, Linz.
Dr. N. Rozsenich, Federal Ministry of Science and Research
Dkfm. V.D. Vesper, Free University of Berlin.
Irmgard Wenko, Austrian Society for Cybernetic Studies (Secretary).

*Austrian Federal Ministry of Science and Research.
**The Vienna Community City Hall.
***Austrian Federal Chamber of Trade and Commerce.
****Society of Austrian Banks and Bankers.

Contents

Contents

List of authors

Báger, Gustáv, Institute of Economic Planning, Budapest, Hungary.

Bamber, D.J., Beecham Pharmaceuticals, Brentford, UK.

Banathy, Bela H., Program Director, Far West Laboratory for Educational Research and Development, Berkely, California, USA.

Bojórquez, Luis, Laboratory of Physiology and Biophysics, Facultad de Ciencias, Universidad Nacional, Autónoma de México, México 20, D.F. México.

Brown, D.J.H., Polytechnic of Central London, UK.

Carroll, John M., Computer Science Department, University of Western Ontario, London, Canada.

Checkland, P.B., Department of Systems Engineering, University of Lancaster, Lancaster, UK.

Conn, J.J., Director, Manpower Analysis, Operational Research and Analysis Establishment, Ottawa, Ontario, Canada.

Cornock, Stroud, Leicester Polytechnic, Leicester, UK.

Coulter, N.A., Jr., Curriculum in Bioengineering and Mathematics, Department of Surgery, UNC Medical School, Chapel Hill, North Carolina 27514, USA.

Dal Cin, M., Institute of Information Sciences, University of Tübingen, 74 Tübingen, Germany.

Darvas, György, Institute for Science Organization, Hungarian Academy of Sciences, Budapest, Hungary.

Della Vigna, P.L., Istituto di Elettrotecnica ed Elettronica, Politecnico di Milano, Italy.

Dorow, Wolfgang, Freie Universität, Berlin, Germany.

Dubois, Daniel M., Université de Liège, Institut de Mathématique, 15 Avenue des Tilleuls, B-4000 Liège, Belgium.

Fleissner, Peter, Institute for Socio-economic Development & Research, Austrian Academy of Sciences, Vienna, Fleischmarkt, 20, A-1010, Austria.

Fu, K.S., Purdue University, West Lafayette, Indiana, USA.

Garstka, Hansjürgen, University Regensburg, Germany.

Gasparski, W.W., Department of Praxiology, Institute of Organization, Management and Control of the Polish Academy of Sciences and Ministry of Science, Higher Education and Technology, Warsaw, Poland.

Gergely, T., Central Research Institute for Physics of the Hungarian Academy of Sciences, Budapest, Hungary.

Ghezzi, C., Istituto di Elettrotecnica ed Elettronica, Politecnico di Milano, Italy.

Grolmusz, Vince, Institute for Science Organization, Hungarian Academy of Sciences, Budapest, Hungary.

Gutiérrez, Andrés E., Universidad de Carabobo, Valencia, Venezuela.

Gutiérrez, Andrés F., Universidad de Carabobo, Valencia, Venezuela.

Gutiérrez, Manuel, Universidad de Carabobo, Valencia, Venezuela.

Hagen, J.J., Universität Salzburg, Austria.

Hajnal, Albert, Institute of Economic Planning, Budapest, Hungary.

Hanson, O.J., The City University of London, UK.

Hoedl, Erich, Institut für Makro- und Strukturplanung, Technische Hochschule, D-61 Darmstadt, BRD.

Holstein, Hans Jürgen, Research Group on Socio-cybernetics, c/o Computer Science Laboratory,

Uppsala University, Sweden.

Horváth, György, Ganz Measuring Instrument Works, Budapest, Hungary.

Hough, Robbin R., School of Economics and Management, Oakland University, Rochester, Michigan 48063, USA.

Ince, F., The Scientific & Technical Research Council of Turkey, Turkey.

Kostić, Živko K., Faculté Economique de l'Université de Belgrade, Zmaj Jovina 15, Belgrade, Yugoslavia.

Kühlwetter, J., Fachgebiet Übertragungstechnik im Fachbereich Nachrichtentechnik der TH Darmstadt, Merckstr. 25, Bundesrepublik Deutschland.

Leonov, Arch. P., Dr. A. Schwartz & Co., Acoustical Consultants Ltd., 6 Zerubbabel Stairs, Haifa, Israel.

Lim, Fang-Ning, Computer Science Department, University of Western Ontario, London, Canada.

Locker, A., Biophysics Unit, Institute for Biology, Austrian Research Center, Seibersdorf-Vienna, Austria.

Maffioli, F., Istituto di Elettrotecnica ed Elettronica, Politecnico di Milano, Italy.

Mago, G.A., Computer Science Department, University of North Carolina, Chapel Hill, N.C. 27514, USA.

Mairlot, Fernand E., Université Catholique de Louvain, Faculté de Médecine, 18 Regentiestraat, B-2700 St. Niklaas, Belgium.

Maitra, Amit K., Regional Science Department, The Wharton School, University of Pennsylvania, Philadelphia, Pennsylvania, USA.

Martin, Paul E., INDUSTRA G.m.b.H., Zug, Switzerland.

Mayerhöfer, Josef, Österreichische Nationalbibliothek, Vienna, Austria.

McCaul, G.J., McCaul Associates (Pty) Ltd., Johannesburg, South Africa.

Németi, I., Central Research Institute for Physics of the Hungarian Academy of Sciences, Budapest, Hungary.

Owen, Philip James, University of Illinois, Urbana, USA.

Piccoli, Mary Louise, Purdue University, West Lafayette, Indiana, USA.

Prautsch, Werner F., Technische Universität Berlin, Fachbereich Kybernetik, Berlin, Germany.

Rees, S.J., Department of Electrical & Control Engineering, Liverpool Polytechnic, UK.

Reisinger, Leo, University of Vienna, Austria.

Russell, D.W., Department of Electrical & Control Engineering, Liverpool Polytechnic, UK.

Sandblom, Carl-Louis, Department of Econometrics & Social Statistics, Faculty of Commerce and Social Science, The University of Birmingham, Birmingham B15 2TT, UK.

Schwartz, A., Dr. A. Schwartz & Co., Acoustical Consultants Ltd., 6 Zerubbabel Stairs, Haifa, Israel.

Seeger, Claus, Technische Universität Berlin, Fachbereich Kybernetik, Berlin, Germany.

Stalberg, Lennart, Research Group on Sociocybernetics, c/o Computer Science Laboratory, Uppsala University, Sweden.

Steinmüller, Wilhelm, University Regensburg, Germany.

Strebl, Laurenz, Federal Ministry of Science and Research, Vienna, Austria.

Streit, Max, Institut für Wirtschaftstheorie an der Universität Graz, Halbärthgasse 8, A-8010 Graz, Austria.

Taschdjian, Edgar, 109-50 117th Street, New York, N.Y. 11420, USA.

Vesper, Volker D., Freie Universität Berlin, West-Berlin, Germany.

Watson, H.D.D., IBM UK Scientific Center, Peterlee, County Durham, UK.

Whinston, Andrew B., Purdue University, West Lafayette, Indiana, USA.

KEYNOTE INTRODUCTION

On heaping our science together

STAFFORD BEER

Just two years ago I should have introduced the first symposium on Cybernetics and Systems Research. Most unfortunately, all I could do on that occasion was to send a telegram from the other side of the world regretting my unavoidable absence. Ten days ago, Professor Hanika summoned me again. And so he has made good the prophecy he may not remember making those two years ago: 'aufgeschoben ist nicht aufgehoben'.

The reason for my defection on the last occasion was in fact an urgent recall to Santiago from the late President Salvador Allende of Chile. We had embarked six months earlier upon a program so ambitious as to have had at least a chance of revolutionizing the form of government on a cybernetic basis that would match the revolutionary political intentions of that democracy. This endeavor took precedence with me for two years, and I emerged from the experience very much changed. I changed in my awareness of myself, of my fellow men and of political realities; but these are not the topics that I shall discuss today. I changed also as a technologist, in terms of confidence. For I now know that it is possible to do what I have advocated for so many years—things which many used to say, and some still do say, are impossible.

But the changes that bear upon the nature of this symposium have to do with cybernetic insights themselves. There is of course no way of changing the laws by which large systems operate; but there can be a change in one's perception, and a change in the depth of understanding of principles we have known about all the time. It is of these matters that I speak today, because I know more clearly now what I am trying to say, and because I also know more about the direct practical relevance of these things to society at large.

We have all found it very difficult, I suspect, to convey the relevance of our kind of science to senior managers and to ministers of government. If this were not so, we should have changed the world by now. After all, we deal in organizational science, and the contemporary world is one in which modes of organization that are at the same time effective and freedom-preserving are virtually inknown. Moreover, the notion of effective management or government has become almost synonymous in people's minds with the idea of tyranny. And there is good reason for this, as one looks around the world. But in my opinion the confusion is leading steadily toward a disastrous error: namely, that everyone concerned to preserve freedom may automatically eschew effectiveness—finding it too dangerous a commodity to approach at all. And then we encounter the opposite fallacy, which is to say that what is ineffective is necessarily free. On the contrary, I believe, confusion and muddle are excellent cloaks for exploitation; and even where there is no

Progress in Cybernetics and Systems Research, Volume 2
Copyright © 1975 by Hemisphere Publishing Corporation

sinister intent, the instabilities created through organizational deficiencies are everywhere a danger to survival.

The technical concept that we people have which points most surely to a resolution of this dilemma is the concept of a selforganizing system. A self-organizing system is by definition one on which organization is not imposed. And yet it must be designed so that it *is* selforganizing. There is an apparent contradiction in this which caused me a great deal of difficulty inside Chilean politics, and even worse difficulty with hostile critics elsewhere. But the contradiction is not real; and considered as a technical problem in cybernetics the difficulty is easy to resolve. That is, one designs a free, self-organizing system by using a language of logically higher order than that of the system designed; and our mathematical apparatus for doing this leads us to talk of 'metalinguistic' criteria and 'metasystemic' regulators. Now it is perfectly clear that talk of this kind is wholly unacceptable to people who do not really understand it. The message that comes through to them is undoubtedly a confession that everything is being secretly manipulated by shadowy figures in high places. But this is not at all the intention, not at all the reality, and we must find better words with which to explain ourselves. Let me use my first Chilean example.

Consider the workers' committee that is trying to run a factory. What do they need to know? Now of course if our anxiety about effectiveness and freedom is real, the immediate response to this question is: what they need to know is entirely a matter for them—let them find out. Some would say that to give that answer leaves us innocent; I would call it downright oppressive. Who are we to deny to the workers' committee the tools of modern science? So, right from the start, we began an active campaign to explain to the people that science is simply order-ed knowledge which can be communicated, and which is part of their cultural inheritance. To make that communication effective, the knowledge obvi-ously must be conveyed in terms that people can understand. And we confront the cultural absurdity that no real attempt has ever been made to do it. When I say 'real', I do not mean the lucrative sale of pot-boiling books nor the patronizing display of miraculous scientific fireworks delivered to an amazed public on television. I mean something founded in the reality of people's own experience, and in this case the factory itself.

We wanted to show workers how they could them-selves make a model of their factory; therefore there is simply no sense in conceiving of the type of model which has to be expressed by differential equations. Instead, we developed a set of rules for devising iconic representations of the dynamics of the busi-ness, which we called quantified flowcharts. To set them up in the first place, operational research teams visited all the firms, creating the rules as they went along. The important point was to create a tech-nique that anyone could learn, and that would make the relative importance of different flows and the critical measurements which govern their dynamics instantly recognizable by anyone *who actually knows the business.* So we gave them the rules; we gave them initial flowcharts; we marked initial sets of key indicators; and we explained how to express the numerical quantities in the form of indices.

Why the rules, and why the indices, and why hand over charts and create initial indicators? It is obvious that all these things are specified by the logical design of some metasystem. But in truth this is no more than to specify a language that people are asked to use inside the industrial economy so that everyone can understand everyone else. If every factory were to develop a different set of linguistic conventions, there would be no effective communication. But having made this start, we were careful to say that the quantified flowchart could be elaborated, or totally redrawn, by the workers' committee at any time; that they could add to the list of indicators as they pleased, not even saying what the new daily figures referred to, so long as they were formulated as indices—pure numbers ranging between 0 and 1; and that they could do anything else they wished provided they spoke the language provided.

Now the most interesting point about this is that if they were to find the language itself defective, then obviously they would be able to propose its elabora-tion too. In this way there is nothing whatever to stop a self-organizing system that is also self-aware from joining in the process of specifying its own metasystem. Indeed, each of us does this as a human individual, insofar as he exercises choice over his environment. Note the word 'insofar'; no individual has the chance *totally* to specify his metasystem, much of which is a genetical inheritance, more of which is socio-economically restrained. For identical reasons, it seems to me, no unit of society—such as a workers' committee—can expect to operate without any constraint from some metasystem. But it can demand maximum freedom within it, and it can claim a democratic share in its specification. To argue for greater freedom than this, seems to me a plea for anarchy; to accept less freedom than this is to abdicate responsibility and embrace dependency.

Let me now complete the example, and reveal —against this background—a feature of the Chilean work which has frightened some observers. We wanted to make science available to that workers' committee, and with it the tools of science—especially the electronic computer. There was no way of purchasing more computers, because of the economic stranglehold in which the entire country was held by the rich world—which cut off its supplies, its spare parts, and its credit. There was no way of training workers in their instant use. So we set out to link up all the factories down the three thousand mile length of Chile to a single computer in Santiago. Again, we could not afford a genuine real-time system, because there was no teleprocessing equipment available. But using Telex and existing microwave links, we had seventy five per cent of the social economy in touch with this computer on a daily basis inside four months. 'Centralization', opponents have screamed. Not at all. If there is only one computer available, you have to use it.

Into this computer came a daily flow of indices reported from each factory. What should the computer now do with these data? Add them up? Report them? File them away in a massive data bank? Certainly not. Think of all the work that cybernetics has put in over a quarter of a century to questions of artificial intelligence. Is it not about time that managements and governments used a little human intelligence in deploying computers as the logical engines which men like Leibnitz and Babbage intended them to be, and not as glorified adding machines? This is what we set out to do, in a modest but potent way, and again—for the same reasons as before—it meant specifying a metalanguage. This, in brief, was a computer program that automatically undertook the following examination of every index from every plant every day.

The first question answered by the program suite called Cyberstride was this: has the value arrived, and is it statistically plausible? Secondly, if so, is it to be viewed as a statistically random sample from the population from which it is supposed to be drawn? If it is not, that is to say if there is a strong probability that the inspected value does not lie within the normal limits of variation about the average, then someone must be told. Who must be told? Why, the workers' committee running the factory concerned, of course—AND NO-ONE ELSE. We are making progress, because we are providing people with a service notifying them *immediately* of likely deviations from standard values. Most firms cannot

do that on a weekly basis, still less a daily basis; and we were doing it over a three thousand mile long country. But there is more to come.

Even immediate notification that something may have gone wrong is too late for corrective action to be taken: I mean that yesterday lies as much in the past as does last year. What intelligent machinery ought to do is to use the information it has to predict that something may go wrong in the future. And this is just what the Cyberstride program went on to do. It would inspect every index against the background of the time series of which it was a part, and assign probability to the likelihood that whatever this index was measuring was changing. To be precise: it calculated four probabilities: that the new point showed no change, that it showed a transient pulse in the time series, that the series was developing a slope, and that the new point indicated a step change. In the latter two cases the computer would automatically notify the plant concerned, thereby (I feel entitled to say) breaking the time barrier and showing some intelligent anticipation of events. All this analysis was done using Bayesian probability theory. [1]

So there, in the shape of the Cyberstride program, was a metasystemic brain-like activity which the workers' committee had no chance to modify. In fact, this is just like my saying that I have a brain whose basic functions are determined by the genetic code of my own DNA. But my brain is a service to me; and I do not think of it as being oppressive—although there are ways of discussing this matter which surely make it so. In the Chilean example, I think the only way in which this service to the workers' committee could possibly have become oppressive would have been if the closed loop flowing from the factory through the computer program back to the workers' committee was subject to invigilation by some 'higher authority'. The system laid down that this would not happen; but I do not for a moment pretend that this system—like any other system whatsoever—could not have been perverted by a malevolent régime. Then, say the anarchists, do not instal it. And to this I reply: there is no way of building freedom into a system of government that oppression backed by force cannot overthrow in any case.

I will leave the Chilean experience there for the time being, with the remark that if one can devise a self-organizing system in this sense for every firm that belongs to the economy, then one can presumably do it for other social units as well. These are of two kinds. First of all there are other social units than firms, such as neighbourhoods. And this way of looking at society will create a total system, called the country, which contains many sub-systems of similar size and evincing a fairly similar degree of organization, which are sub-systems of the total-system—all interconnected, all adjusting to each other in a self-organizing way. For example, we may expect neighbourhoods of a city to be supplied with quite a high proportion of their consumer requirements from factories also located in the city. The second kind of development we should expect is hierarchical. Factories belong in some sense to an industry of which they see themselves as representatives. Industries in turn become larger sections of the economy —whereby, we speak, for example, of light and heavy industry. It is to this problem of hierarchy that I next turn attention, because I think it has been left in a very, very confused state in our literature.

If we take any viable system we shall certainly find that it is broken down into sub-systems, and that these sub-systems are in turn broken down into sub-sub-systems, and so on. I am describing the primitive notion of hierarchy, and do not take your time to attempt extremely formal definitions because this has been done so well by other cyberneticians —notably, in their different ways, by Mesarovic and Pask. May we please take their work as given. I do not seek to criticise it: on the contrary, it provides us all with extremely powerful theoretic foundations for hierarchical analysis. The confusion to which I refer in this case has nothing to do with theoretical cybernetics, but with the domain of social applications. In this area we inherit a long-standing tradition of analysis by use of the tool called the organization chart. It is very easy to make fun of this device, and I often do so myself, on the grounds that it does not at all depict a dynamic self-organizing system, but a machine for apportioning blame. If something goes wrong, you can consult the organization chart to discover whose fault it is. Now that is the kind of complaint that I make to business men and to civil servants, on the ground that we need a better account of what is dynamic, what is self-regulatory, what is self-organizing, what is adaptive and evolutionary, than this kind of chart can possibly provide. But in speaking to you as cyberneticians and systems scientists, I have something very much more fundamental to say. In saying it, I wish to use the technical term, due to our greatly missed teacher Ross Ashby—the term 'Variety', meaning precisely the possible number of states of a system.

When we address ourselves to the analysis of any real social system, we are confronted with gigantic variety at the level of humanity itself. Vast numbers of men, women and children live on the territory of our social system, their feet on the ground, their arms outstretched in love and hate, in need and aggression, their heads anywhere between firm implantation in the sand and the clouds above. They proliferate variety on a scale that I think we cannot possibly imagine, although—thanks to logarithmic functions—we may be able to put some sensible numbers to it. If, as before, we demand a base in people's own reality, here it is that we must start. And if we develop a hierarchical analysis we shall agglomerate these people, by some criterion, into units, which we shall then aggregate into larger units, and so forth. If we are being at all meticulous about this, we shall not—in any real social situation, whether a firm or a whole country—make a very useful hierarchical classification having less than seven levels. There is no proof for the assertion of this number seven: I can only say that in practice a lesser number conceals too much, while a larger number probably exceeds the brain's discriminatory capacity to tell them apart or to hold them together synoptically.

I am entirely convinced that a hierarchical model based on this approach, using any of the scientific techniques that I know to be available, will not work. The problem is this. If we start at the top of such a structure, we specify (at least) a seventh order meta-language and metasystem. By the time that the rules have been elaborated through the remaining six orders of hierarchy, the total system cannot possibly operate effectively—because it has seized up; and those actual living people at the bottom cannot possibly be free—because everything about their behaviour will by now be totally constrained. The fact is that every hierarchical level on the way up the pyramid is, because it must be under this model, a variety attenuator; whereas, on the way down, the whole apparatus is a kind of megaphone, the amplifications of which will flood the people with sheer noise. As I said, I know of no scientific approach to this monstrosity that would predict a society that is both free and effective. Perhaps the most obvious model to employ would be an electrical model. Given that we are dealing with a high variety network, rather than with the idealization proposed by the hierarchic tree laid down in the representation, then it seems fairly clear that the impedance of the system would be such as to close it down altogether.

Quite apart from the models that reveal to us the impossibility of tackling the societary problem in this way, I myself consider that theoretical analysis poses an insoluble problem. In 1960, I propounded a model of the brain (in which the variety-handling difficulties seem to be of similar order to the societary problem) which postulated a law that I called 'the indeterminacy of configuration structure'. [2] This declared that in a very complex hierarchical network of the kind we are considering in a social system (as in the brain) the configuration of the network would be indeterminate. That is, if it retained its identity through time, then it could not be denoted by a general algebraic function; whereas if it could be so denoted it would not retain its identity. In the fifteen years since I proposed this law, no-one has either assented to it or denied it: as for me, I still believe it. But if the law is true, we must expect not to be able to handle the variety of a system of this kind by hierarchical formalizations on their own. Indeed Mesarovic [3] himself has not concealed this limitation of his work. Most of it considers optimizing systems, whereas I do not consider that society—even in the shape of a business concern—much concerns itself with optimization. He also says 'we found it convenient to assume that the decision problems of the sub-systems are relatively well defined and simple; otherwise, we might have been bogged down with the intricacy of individual unit behaviour and not have the chance to study the proper hierarchical questions at all'. We must take this disclaimer seriously, because the high variety, which he calls 'the intricacy of individual unit behaviour', is exactly the problem with which any societary system has to deal; its sub-systems are not relatively well defined—and certainly not simple; and as far as I can see they put the intention to survive in front of optimization every time. In fact, optimization is an extremely precarious strategy for any viable system to adopt, because the maximal value of any complex objective functional turns out typically to be unstable. Any sensible manager would rather sit securely on a plateau of reasonable profit than to climb a further two per cent in payoff, only to perch on the brink of a precipice leading to bankruptcy.

So here is our second dilemma. It is clear that all complex viable systems do have an hierarchical structure; but it is equally clear that some kind of pyramid involving an endless succession (or even merely seven) levels of sub-system and sub-sub-system will not serve as an analytical device for resolving the cybernetics of any such organization.

My answer to this problem lies in the concept of recursion, not of hierarchy. I base my use of the term 'recursion' in the mathematical usage of recursive number theory—not merely in the loose and idiomatic usage of ordinary language. Recursive number theory is interested in examining the process of *counting*; and indeed we are counting when we look at a society through various levels of aggregation. Then, at each level, we are looking at some kind of collection; this being admitted, the counting process explicitly 'consists in overlooking the individual idiocyncracies of the elements of the collection and regarding them as being all alike (but not identical) for the purpose in hand'. [4] In expressly mathematical terms, 'a function $f(n)$ is said to be defined by recursion if, instead of being defined explicitly (that is, as an abbreviation for some other expression), only the value of $f(0)$ is given, and $f(n+1)$ is expressed as a function of $f(n)$',

The argument, then, is that we have to define exceedingly complex probabilistic systems, such as societies, by recursion rather than by hierarchy. You may have noticed that I have been using the words 'viable system' rather a lot. It is possible to define a viable system, namely a coherent whole that is capable of independent survival, at only *two* levels of hierarchy. The lower level has a sub-system consisting of any number of viable systems. The upper level is metasystemic to that set of sub-systems, and itself consists of four sub-systems. Because the lower level sub-system consists of viable systems, we now have a recursive definition that we can handle.

It took me more than twenty years to validate in practice, that is to say in application to societary systems, this model of a viable system. I have found that there is no limit to the number of levels of recursion that can be accommodated in a societary model. And I firmly believe that because the nest of systems that results is connected together only by the process of nesting itself, which is specified in the metalanguage of the whole, the *operational* freedom of each viable system can be totally preserved. And so I have stated a Recursive System Theorem, which says: 'If a viable system contains a viable system then the organizational structure must be recursive'. [5] I might better have said: 'If we decide to define a social system by recursion, we shall find that every viable system contains a viable system'.

What all this adds up to is a way of modelling a society, not as a hierarchy looking like a family tree with so many branches that all the cousins could not possibly know each other's names, never mind interact, but as a series of Chinese boxes. Every box is a viable system containing a viable system; every box is contained within a viable system. Continuity is given by the boxiness of the boxes, rather than by their explicit contents—for as we have read recursion regards the collections as being all alike, but not identical, for the purpose in hand. The purpose in hand is the design of a metasystem that can be both effective and free at the same time. To be free, each box is its own viable system--untrammelled. To be effective, each box is enclosed in its metasystemic box, which is also a viable system. And to maintain freedom, ultimately, we shall take note of the endowment that every box is entitled to participate in the specification of the metalanguage used by its enclosing box.

To bring this theoretical disquisition back to reality, I turn to my second Chilean example. You may remember that I said that the firms using the system I earlier described could be aggregated into industries—or, as the Chileans called them, sectors. Then the firm is a viable system, and so is the sector. This means we need a model of the sector. And if we adhere to our rules about the language that is spoken within this total system, then the sector must be describable in terms of a quantified flowchart, and must be quantified in terms of indicators relating not to the firm but to the sector—yet still expressed as indices. Then if you can tolerate the notion of this second Chinese box, a viable system enclosing a set of firms that are themselves viable systems, you will see that both the model of the sector and the quantification of its indicators will be given at a *higher level of recursion* than the elementary data themselves define. This leads to a process of aggregation of models and of data, which is quite unlike the process of aggregation familiar in economic controls throughout the world.

The systemic model of the sector looks exactly the same as the systemic model of the firm: both are viable systems. But the quantified flowchart of the sector looks nothing like any one of the flowcharts of the firms; obviously not, we are looking at a different (though still viable) animal altogether. But when we come to quantify the model of the sector, we shall want to use the basic data of the firms—not as totals or as averages, but as defining whatever functions are necessary for us to define in the *metasystemic* model. Then once again freedom is preserved, because the data available at the sector level reveal nothing of the individual idiocyncracies obtaining at the level of recursion below. Because the mathematical concept of recursion is not violated, the political concept of freedom is not violated either—and this is what so many critics have totally failed to understand.

Having set up a sector model, at a second level of recursion which is not to be confused with a second level of hierarchy, we observe how the agglomerated data—agglomerated (not totalled, not averaged)—become susceptible to treatment through the Cyberstride computer program for the artificially-intelligent handling of facts. Because each sector model is expressed as a quantified flowchart, and because its indicators are expressed as indices, there is no difficulty whatsoever in channelling daily *agglomerated* information through the same suite of programs. And whatever signals emanate from that daily process are fed back to the committee of workers responsible for the sector, in exactly the same way as indicators belonging to the lower level of recursion were fed back to the factory. Please note that this does not make itemized information about factory performance available to the sector committee. Each level of recursion is its own self-organizing system; they are linked by recursive transformations of data founded (where else should they be founded?) in shop floor reality.

Now to continue with this second Chilean example, what applied to the second level of recursion—the sector—also applied to the third level of recursion, which is a branch of the industrial economy. In the case of Chile, these were categorized as light industry, heavy industry, consumer industry and 'materials' industry—which in round terms meant 'the rest'. And everything I have said about modelling and quantifying the second level of recursion, applies at this third level; as indeed it does at the fourth level of recursion—total industry itself. This means that when the President's economic committee came to consider the performance of the total industrial economy in the social area, it would be looking at quantified flowcharts linking together the elements of the next level of recursion downwards, quantified by variables appropriate to that level, *but processed through Cyberstride just the same.* So here is the massive variety reduction that of course we must have to obey Ashby's Law. The machinery designed to apply artificial intelligence to sensory inputs works identically at every level or recursion.

I wish to emphasize this point. As long as we have organization-chart models of societary systems, and as long as we insist on treating them as multi-level hierarchies, so long shall we compel ourselves to devise data-handling routines that are specific to every separate cell of this beehive. Then no wonder that all we have so far managed to do with our computers is cybernetically trivial, and no wonder it is done at prodigious expense.

Let us now turn to the next fundamental cybernetic concept, so often debated among us, which I believe to have been illuminated in the context of

Chilean reality. This is the problem of man-machine interfaces: how does the brain behave when operating as a decision node in an informational network? As neurocyberneticians, a great duty lies upon us to persuade people that the brain itself does *not* behave as the electronic data processing culture which civilization has developed over the last twenty years would have us believe. The vast data bank that potentially contains whatever information a manager may want, the foot thick pile of computer readout which must hold the alarm signal the manager ought to have, the streams of data crudely aggregated by totals and sub-totals.... Such things are epiphenomena of the management scene, generated by computer sales campaigns. The decision-taker cannot possibly handle this variety; we know from theoretical considerations that his brain does not deploy the requisite variety to do it. And the verdict is confirmed by observation, enquiry, experiment and even personal experience. If this proliferation of variety is in truth the raw material of management processes, then by Ashby's Law of Requisite Variety, corporate and state machinery of equivalent variety must handle it. This is exactly what happens, and we call it bureaucracy. And while that bureaucratic machinery churns on, the decision-taker proceeds with his decisions—using his own brain as the only filter that he has.

Now the Cyberstride program suite is an example of a brain-like filter that is handed to the manager as a tool. It can demonstrably perform better than the human brain in predicting likely change. So can other brain-like artefacts which have been studied in our general field. The most notable of these, perhaps, is the technique of simulation, which performs the brain-like function of running through assorted strategies and assessing their likely impact on events for a range of possible futures. As you know, both the brain and the simulation undertake such exercises in panic-free time—that is to say a time that runs much faster than the clock, and without the pressures of insistent stimuli demanding urgent responses. The technique has been widely and most successfully used by operational research for a quarter of a century, a fact obscured in the public mind by the notoriety accorded to recent ecological simulations. The criticism one hears of these is primarily concerned with the validity of the data used to generate them. The answer of the simulators is of course to say that input variables can be allowed to range over a wide spectrum, so that sensitivity analyses can be performed to cover this point. But the fact remains that we should not acquiesce in the cultural dictat that economic data must necessarily be months out of date. If,

for direct regulatory purposes, a societary system is accepting virtually real-time input and filtering it by some such program as the Cyberstride suite I have described, then of course simulations can be fed with these real and filtered inputs, and can be continuously updated.

Returning then to the question of the man-machine interface, I have now outlined three quite different and very basic cybernetic approaches to variety attenuation as managerial data approach the manager's brain. To recapitulate: the first was the quantified flowchart, which uses iconic conventions to permit human insights through relative size, relative shape, relative colour, and relative speed; the second was the kind of 'importance filter' called Cyberstride— which is also predictive; the third was the use of simulation with real-time inputs to provide a forecasting capability. All of these use the concepts of machine intelligence to enrich the brain's capacity to be the brain that it immanently is, rather than to engulf it in the electronically processed data that enhance historical archives but generate no wisdom.

Next, to facilitate the operation of all this, we designed a decision environment in which a group of human beings could use these new tools. This is a room in which the dynamic, quantified model of the relevant viable system (that is to say, the two-hierarchy five-part model appropriate to this particular level of recursion) is continuously displayed as a psychological backdrop. On the next wall are the computer alerting signals deriving from Cyberstride. If we now imagine the group of decision-takers faced with these alerting signals, we shall realize that they need more information. This is provided in the prototype room by three back projection screens coupled to an index mechanism which is called Datafeed. Each of the three screens is driven by five back projectors, each containing 80 slides of iconic information. These screens are commanded, through a five-bit code displayed on the index screen, from buttons planted in the arms of the chairs of the decision-takers. Finally, a wall is devoted to the display of an animated systems diagram of a simulation appropriate to this level of recursion, which can be used experimentally and in real-time by the group. They can propose experimental changes in their strategy, and obtain ten-year projections of critical variables from the computer on an adjacent screen.

Such an operations room as this can of course be set up to operate at any level of recursion, by supplying it with background information and the various sensory inputs appropriate to that level. The information provided includes statements about other levels of recursion, so that the role of each level in relation to the total nest is clear to it; but there is no scope for intervention in the autonomous responsibilities of these other levels, so long as they are operating homeostatically. There does however need to be a system for altering the next higher level of recursion to any homeostatic failure as such. This requirement is an instance of what I have elsewhere labelled an algedonic loop. 'Algedonic' means 'pertaining to pain and pleasure'; and the cry of pain emitted by a viable system if its homeostatic, self-organizing machinery fails to deal with a serious perturbation will be heard at the next level of recursion.

This was done in the Chilean system by a meta-systemic subroutine in Cyberstride capable of recognizing the failure of any sub-system to react within its normal relaxation time. Of course, this procedure has been represented as a betrayal of autonomy, because people who do not study cybernetics think they see a higher level of command in the hierarchical sense poking about in the contents of boxes at a lower level of command. The truth is that the meta-system is keeping watch on the stability of the self-organizing homeostat, and that statements about this stability are metalinguistic statements. If the debate about freedom and effectiveness is to be kept sane, such cybernetic distinctions will have to enter into the political vocabulary.

A prototype room complete with all these facilities was actually built in Chile. It was 'live'; but of course—given that this whole project lasted just under two years from start to finish—it was operated only in an experimental mode. Our plans included the intention to mass-produce such rooms, to equip all levels of recursion in the social economy with a cybernetically sound decision environment. But it was not to be. The last instruction we received from President Allende was to move the prototype room right into the government palace, La Moneda. Three days later, La Moneda stood in ruins: the 'Chilean Experiment' was over.

I have dealt, in this address much too briefly, with six key cybernetic issues as they were reflected in the practical context of the Chilean work: the problem of autonomy, freedom versus effectiveness; the problem of requisite variety, iconic presentations versus EDP; the problem of artificial intelligence, brain-like filtration and simulation versus routine tabulation and analysis; the problem of organizational impedance, the theory of recursion versus proliferating hierarchy; the problem of control, algedonic loops versus authoritarian invigilation; the problem

of the man-machine interface, designed decision environments versus traditional boardrooms. There is yet a seventh fundamental cybernetic concept, the most real of all in terms of the Chilean experience, to which I must refer. It was taught to us by the great Warren McCulloch: the concept of redundancy of potential command. According to this concept, brains and brain-like systems take their decisions wherever the information relevant to those decisions comes together. Therefore it is unphysiological to appoint permanent centres where the decisions must lie. Any concatenation of logical elements may acquire the information relevant to the decision, therefore any such concatenation is potentially in command. And since the combinatorial properties of a brain or a brain-like regulator are exponentially explosive, such potential command is highly redundant. Cyberneticians know the theory. Managers very well know the practice. It is only the culture that tells us we are all wrong. The culture says that the responsibility for decision lies inside a room whose doors bear the legend 'Production Director' or 'Sales Director' or 'President'. The culture encourages the people in those rooms to beat the bounds of their estates of responsibility, keeping out trespassers, and declaring 'this is where the buck stops'. Not for nothing has the culture produced highly placed executives who write letters headed: 'From the desk of So and So'. The friend I have who replied to such a letter: 'Dear Desk' produced his own cultural reaction; in fact he was making a profound cybernetic point.

Decisions do not lie on this desk in this room, nor hang like an albatross around the neck of this man. As McCulloch disclosed, decisions really *are* taken where information collects in a concatenation of informed nodes. Now I have explained how we set up a virtually real-time informational network in Chile, and how we were teaching its use as a nervous system of societary management. It quickly became clear that this facilitated potential command in quite unexpected ways, and also that the nodal redundancy provided a flexibility in handling problems that no-one concerned had ever experienced before. This was a revelation, and indicates that we should take our cybernetics seriously—believing what we discover as scientists, and not hesitating to apply our results in the real world.

As I said at the start, our science is an organizational science. Our studies of the brain or any other animal system, our studies of automata or any other artefacts, our studies of society itself, and the studies of everyone in this Symposium—all have relevance to the nature of effective organization. Therefore I would like to make a personal appeal to everyone here. It is to ask you to take the trouble to survey your own work from the standpoint of the world's need—political and socio-economic—for better organizational modes. I have read all the titles under which the speakers are speaking. In some cases people are working directly on this problem, but in most they are not. To them I say: can it be that you have not asked that larger question, can it be (if you have) that you see no relevance, can it be (if you do) that you see no outlet? I do not believe that there is no relevance between your work and the world's problem of effective organization. I could easily believe that there is no outlet. But in that case we must all get together and find one. We simply must find a way to assemble all our contributions into a critical mass that will effect substantial, life-saving change.

Three organizations are involved in sponsoring this symposium. I was a founder-member of one; I am past president of another. And I wonder why it is that we who study effective organization, who can effectively organize a meeting of friends to *talk* effectively *about* effective organization, seem unable to organize ourselves effectively to assault the ineffectiveness of organizations throughout the world—at every level of recursion. For we have much to say, and much to do.

As I also said at the start, we have not changed the world so far because managers and ministers do not understand what we are talking about. They would not understand this address, which does not matter—because I am not talking to them, but to you. This is one of those rare and amiable occasions when our own jargon ought to be admissible. But here comes the second appeal: please consider whether you cannot explain what you personally cybernetically know to the people who desperately need those insights, in words that they can understand. Some of you I know are good at this; some

of you apply yourselves to the study of this very problem; but mostly we do not bother.

I suggest to you that bothering about this, in a world that has become wildly unstable in almost every dimension of its organization, is now an ethical imperative for all of us cyberneticians. To use my last example from Chile: we were setting out to make films, to publish booklets, to paint slogans on the walls, and to sing songs about the scientific inheritance that belongs to the people, *and* about the effective organization of a free state, in words that all could understand. In saying 'all', I mean *all*; not simply the élite, but the people themselves—with whom decisions ought to lie, but alas in Chile, finally, did not.

To them, their loved Chilean folklore singer and my friend used to sing a song called 'Litany for a Computer and a Baby about to be Born'. Its chorus said:

"So let us heap all science together
before we reach the end of our tether."

I can say no better to you, today, and once again,

"Hay que juntar toda la ciencia
Antes que acabe la paciencia."

References

1. HARRISON, P.J. and STEVENS, C.R., 'A Bayesian approach to short-term forecasting', *Operational Research Quarterly* 22(4), (December 1971).
2. BEER, Stafford, 'Set-theoretic formulation of the brain model', in: 'Toward the Cybernetic Factory', *Principles of Self-organization* (edit. by Von Foerster and Zopf), Pergamon Press (1962).
3. MESAROVIC, M.D., MACKO, D., and TAKAHARA, Y., *Theory of Hierarchical, Multilevel Systems*, Academic Press (1970).
4. GOODSTEIN, R.L., *Recursive Number Theory*, North-Holland Publishing Company (1957).
5. BEER, Stafford, *Brain of the Firm*, Allen Lane the Penguin Press (1972).

SOCIO-ECONOMIC SYSTEMS

Choice functions and social preference orderings modelled by heuristic grammatical inference

MARY LOUISE PICCOLI, ANDREW B. WHINSTON, and K.S. FU
Purdue University, Indiana, USA

1. Introduction

The concept of grammar is reviewed and shown to model the social choice process. With grammars, the processes themselves, the interdependencies which characterize economics, are modeled. The problem in modeling economic processes with grammars, however, is selecting the best grammar to represent the process, and this is exactly the problem of grammatical inference.

The heuristic application of grammatical inference is shown to be useful in social choice to state the choice function concept explicitly in terms of formal language. Specifically, it is shown that non-Independent-of-Path choice functions can be modeled by context-sensitive grammars and Independent-of-Path choice functions are not only context-free, but may be modeled by finite state grammars. The grammar inferred corresponds to the process used by society when the results of voting decisions are given by a choice function. Results of choice functions of a society may be considered strings in a language of the society. With grammatical inference, the decision process can be modeled and much insight gained into the workings of society. Using Plott's result making Independence-of-Path and

Extension axioms sufficient conditions for rationalization of social preferences by a total, reflexive binary relation which defines a transitive social preference ordering, a language translation system is suggested which uses the results of choice functions to construct the social preference relations representing the society.

2. Grammars and languages

In ordinary usage, a language must follow the rules of the grammar for that language. For example, the construction of an English sentence may be described as shown in Fig. 1. The bracketed expressions may be considered nonterminals and the non-bracketed words are terminals. The language is formed by the concatenation of terminals following the rules of the grammar, called the productions. One production here would be

<noun phrase> $\longrightarrow$ <adjective> <noun phrase>

Generalizing, the formal definition of a grammar, G, is a 4-tuple [1]

Progress in Cybernetics and Systems Research, Volume 2
Copyright © 1975 by Hemisphere Publishing Corporation

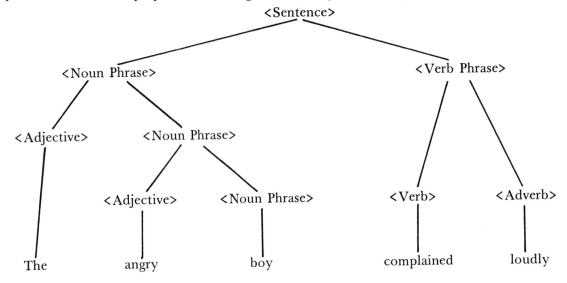

Fig. 1

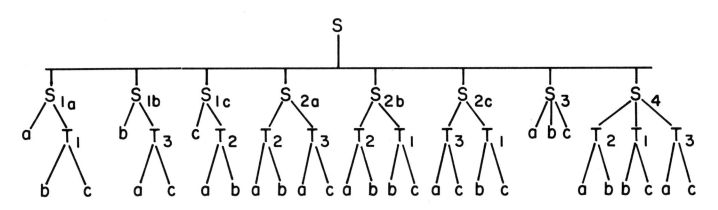

Fig. 2

$$G = (V_N, V_T, P, S)$$

where V_N are nonterminal variables (usually upper case letters), V_T terminal variables (usually lower case letters), P = set of productions, and S = start symbol.

We define the language generated by G, $L(G)$, to be

$$L(G) = \{\,|\,w \in V_T^* \text{ and } S \overset{*}{\underset{G}{\Rightarrow}} w\,\}$$

meaning that $w \in L(G)$ if and only if
1. w, a string, consists solely of terminals,
2. w can be derived from S by a series of productions in G.

J^* is the notation referring to the set of all concatenations of $j_i \in J$.

For example, $G = (V_N, V_T, P, S)$ where

$$V_N = \{S\}, \quad V_T = \{0, 1\}, \quad S = S,$$

$$P: \; S \to 1S$$
$$S \to 0$$

We use the notation j^n to refer to a string of n j's so

$$L(G) = \{1^n 0 \,|\, n \geqslant 0\}$$

To model social choice procedures with grammars, consider Farquharson's example of a social choice process [2]. The possible alternatives are acquittal, banishment, or condemnation, abbreviated *a, b, c*. Farquharson begins by recognizing the various ways in which the alternatives can be considered, the voting sequence. Graphically, these procedures may be represented as in Fig. 2, where S_{1a}, S_{1b}, S_{1c} are Successive Procedures, S_{2a}, S_{2b}, S_{2c} are Amendment Procedures, S_3 is Plurality Procedure, and S_4 is Elimination Procedure.

Farquharson describes his procedures as [2, pp 61-62]:

Successive S_{1a} "The first poll is taken between *a* and the rest, only if *a* is rejected is a second poll taken between *b* and *c*."

Amendment S_{2a} "The first poll is taken between *b* and *c*; the second poll is taken between *a* and the winner of the first poll."

Plurality S_3 "A single poll is taken between *a, b,* and *c*. The outcome with the greatest number of votes wins. The first voter has an additional casting vote."

Elimination S_4 "The first poll is held between the pairs *(a,b), (a,c),* and *(b,c)*. The pair with the greatest number of votes wins; the second poll is taken between the two members of the winning pair. The first voter has an additional casting vote."

Let us try to represent the acceptable procedures in a society whose policy is: a suspect is innocent until proven guilty. Its acceptable procedures may only be procedures S_{1a}, S_{2a}, S_3, S_4, procedures where the chance of getting an "*a*" verdict for acquittal is high. We can construct a grammar to represent this society as:

$$G = (V_N, V_T, S, P)$$

where

$$V_T = \{;, a, b, c\}$$

$$P: \quad S \to S_{1a} \quad S \to S_{2a} \quad S \to S_3 \quad S \to S_4$$

$$S_{1a} \to a; T_1 \quad S_{2a} \to T_2; T_3 \quad S_3 \to abc$$

$$S_4 \to T_2; T_1; T_3$$

$$T_1 \to bc \quad T_2 \to ab \quad T_3 \to ac$$

This grammar forms a language, $L(G)$, whose members are:

$$\{a; bc, ab; ac, abc, bc; ab; ac\}$$

where the semicolons separate results from different nodes and so show the previous choices.

Thus we have illustrated one use of grammars to model the social choice process and the interdependencies which characterize it.

3. A brief description of grammatical inference

The heuristic application of grammatical inference is shown to be useful in social choice to state the choice function concept explicitly in terms of formal language. The grammar to be inferred corresponds to the process used by society when the results of voting decisions are given by a choice function. Results of choice functions of a society may be considered strings in a language of the society. With grammatical inference, the decision process can be modeled and much insight gained into the workings of society.

The grammatical inference process searches for a grammar which can be used to derive strings in a language L and will not produce strings which are not in L. A grammatical inference machine or algorithm may be viewed as making guesses about the grammar at each time t as it receives more information about the language L (more strings in L and in L complement) until it successfully describes the grammar G_t such that $L = L(G_t)$. This model of grammatical inference is shown in Fig. 3 [3, p. 39].

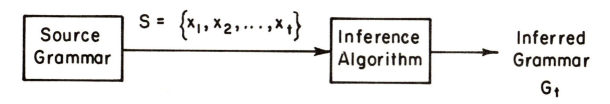

Fig. 3 A basic model of a grammatical inference machine

Heuristic procedures for recognizing grammar structures likely to generate the given language are useful in cutting search time for an inferred grammar. For example, consider the problem of finding a context-free grammar for the set of strings:

$aaabbb, aabb, ab, aaaabbbb \in L(G)$
$aaabb, aabbb, abb, aabbbb \notin L(G)$

It seems the language requires that strings have an equal number of a's and b's. A parse of the strings known to be in $L(G)$ is:

$a(a(ab)b)b$
$a(ab)b$
(ab)
$a(a(a(ab)b)b)b$

A structure to achieve this is $S \to aSb$, $S \to ab$, and the grammar $G_1 = (V_N, V_T, P, S)$ where

$V_N = \{S\}$; $V_T = \{a,b\}$; $S = S$
$P: S \to aSb, \quad S \to ab$

can be used to infer G. The search for G_1 is much simplified by our heuristic recognition of the structure of the language. Because the grammars used here will be based on choice functions, the choice function structure will provide a foundation for heuristic grammatical inference.

4. Use of grammars in economics

Grammars explicitly model processes and the interdependencies inherent in them. Since economics focuses on the problem of the allocation of limited goods among unlimited wants, the economist must understand and cope with the interdependent results of any allocation decision and the processes by which those results become evident. In the discussion of grammars, it was shown that a grammar can be used to model a society's acceptable voting procedures. That grammars can be used to model economic processes should be obvious by the nature of grammars; the choice of a grammar to accurately model specific economic systems is not so obvious. For this latter task in modeling choice functions, we must apply heuristic grammatical inference.

We shall illustrate the uses of heuristic grammatical inference to facilitate economic modeling of social choice using choice functions. With this rather esoteric application, however, we remain in the mainstream of economic theory, since social choice is concerned with allocation of resources in a public choice, or voting, context.

5. Grammatical inference in social choice

5.1 The choice function

In social choice, grammatical inference can be applied to state the concept of a choice function explicitly in terms of formal language and automata. The choice function gives the results of a decision made over a set of possible alternatives; the possible alternatives are the arguments of the function. Thus the choice function

$C(a,b,c) = a$

is interpreted as society's choosing alternative a when a, b, and c were the possibilities available. When expressed in a choice form as "a," choice functions for a society may be considered strings in a language of the society. The grammar to be inferred for this language, beginning with a start symbol defined on the set of available alternatives, corresponds to the process, or the social preferences, used by society in making its choices on the issue. Economics, concerned with constrained optimization, has viewed the social choice problem as optimization of social benefit subject to fairness conditions to individuals and coalitions. The usual mathematical framework, however, makes no explicit provision for the social decision *process*. Using grammatical inference to apply formal language and automata theory to social choice, concepts designed specifically to provide formal descriptions of processes, much insight may be gained into the workings of society.

5.2 The Independence-of-Path axiom

The ethical axiom, Independence of Path, may play a role in the grammatical formulation of a choice function. Independence of Path is the mathematical expression for the ethic by which society deems that the results of an acceptable voting method should not depend on the order in which the alternatives are voted upon, or the way in which a large set of alternatives is divided to allow voting over smaller sets. Plott writes that Independence of Path means:

> One should be able to "split up" the alternatives into smaller sets, choose over each of these sets, collect the chosen elements, and choose over them. This done, he should be assured that the outcome

did not depend upon the arbitrary way he initially divided the alternatives for consideration [4, p. 7].

This ethical consideration is especially significant for voting methods which are only defined for small sets; for example, majority rule is only defined over two-element sets. The Independence-of-Path ethic requires that choice over larger sets, by repeated application of such a choice method to smaller sets, is unambiguous, in that it does not depend on the way the larger set was divided into smaller sets, the voting sequence.

Plott formally defines Independence of Path as follows:

Assume E is a finite set of conceivable alternatives. Let $V = \{V_1, ..., V_m\}$ be a family of subsets (agendas) of E. For all $S \subset E$, define
$V_S = \{V : \bigcup_{v \in V} v = S\}$.

Assume that $v \subset E$ and $v \neq \emptyset \Rightarrow C(v) \neq \emptyset$, where C refers to the choice function.

Independence of Path:

$$(\forall S)_{S \subset E} \{V \in V_S \ \& \ V' \in V_S \Rightarrow C(\bigcup_{v \in V} C(v)) = C(\bigcup_{v \in V'} C(v'))\}$$

and he gives examples of choice functions which satisfy the Independence-of-Path axiom and which are non-Independent of Path.

Example 1 (Independent-of-Path Choice Function):

$C(a) = a$ for $a \in \{x, y, z, x,y, x,z, y,z\}$ and

$$C(x,y,z) = x,z$$

Example 2 (Non-Independent-of-Path Choice Function):

Consider the cyclical majority situation where 3 individuals use the majority rule method to vote on 3 alternatives. The individuals' preferences, respectively, are:

$x > y > z$
$y > z > x$ where ">" is read "is preferred to"
$z > x > y$

and the choice function defined on the 2-element subsets is:

$$C(x,y) = x \quad C(y,z) = y \quad C(x,z) = z$$

The reader may easily verify that the choice over the 3 alternatives depends on the way the alternatives were originally divided into subsets so that the cyclical majority choice function is non-Independent

of Path.

5.3 Grammars representing Independent-of-Path and Non-Independent-of-Path choice functions

We assert that an unrestricted choice function, specifically one not satisfying the Independence-of-Path axiom, may be represented by a context-sensitive grammar and a choice function which is Independent of Path is context-free and may, in fact, be represented by the more restrictive finite state-type grammar. We will first define context-sensitive and context-free grammars and explain this assertion intuitively. Then examples will be given of grammars modeling such choice functions.

A context-sensitive (Type 1) grammar is defined to have productions of the form $\alpha \rightarrow \beta$, where $|\beta| \geq |\alpha|$, when $|x| =$ number of symbols in the string x. An alternate description, motivating the name "context-sensitive", is that the productions have the form $a_1 A a_2 \rightarrow a_1 \beta a_2$, where a_1, a_2 and β are in V^* and $\beta \neq \epsilon$, and $A \in V_N$. ϵ refers to the empty string, the string with no elements. The language in this formulation may be termed context-sensitive since A can be replaced by β whenever A appears in the context of a_1 and a_2. Similarly, it is clear that under the first definition, α can be greater than 1, so that the set of nonterminals, α, can be replaced by β as a totality.

A context-free grammar (Type 2 grammar) is restricted to productions of the form $A \rightarrow \beta$, where A is a single variable and β is any string other than ϵ. Thus the single variable A is replaced by β regardless of the context in which A appears. In our choice function application of context-sensitive and context-free grammars, the difference between them which will be most frequently employed is that, if $|\alpha| = 2$ and $|\beta| \geq 2$, the grammar is context-sensitive. And if the productions of the grammar cannot be rewritten such that $|\alpha| = 1$, the grammar cannot be considered context-free.

A general choice function, as a process, may be modeled by a grammar, and the grammar will be at least context-sensitive since

1. The results of a subdivision of the agenda may give two or more subsets and in such a case $1 = |\alpha| < |\beta|$, where $|\beta| \geq 2$; and
2. The results of a vote over alternatives will result in at least one choice, so that $1 = |\alpha| \leq |\beta|$, where $|\beta| \geq 1$.

Consider an Independent-of-Path choice function. No matter what the voting sequence and intermediate division of alternatives into subsets, the choice over all alternatives will be the same. Thus the final choice is independent of previous choices, and any choice does not depend on concurrent alternatives. In a formal language framework, the choice is independent of the context in which it occurs and, as we shall show, an Independent-of-Path choice function may be modeled by a context-free grammar. In fact, an Independent-of-Path choice function may be modeled by the more restrictive finite state grammar.

An unrestricted choice function, specifically one that is not Independent-of-Path, can only be represented by a context-sensitive grammar and not a context-free grammar, since the non-Independent-of-Path choice function will result in various final choices, depending on the way the alternatives were subdivided. Thus a choice at any stage may depend on concurrent alternatives, or previous subdivisions. In grammatical terms, the choice will depend on the context in which the choice is made. In particular, a choice over two alternatives may depend on exactly what those competing alternatives are, so that the left-hand side of such a production cannot be reduced to 1 variable and must have length of at least 2. We thus appeal to the fact that $|\alpha|$ may equal 2 if $|\beta| \geqslant 2$ for the grammar to be context-sensitive and not context-free, since $|\alpha|$ cannot be reduced to 1.

5.3.1 Examples of grammars representing Independent-of-Path and Non-Independent-of-Path choice functions

To make the preceding intuitive explanation clearer, we illustrate how the Independent-of-Path and non-Independent-of-Path choice functions would be modeled by context-free and context-sensitive grammars. We shall later show that the Indpendent-of-Path choice functions may actually be modeled by finite state grammars. Note here, however, that the non-Independent-of-Path choice function cannot be represented by a context-free grammar.

In the following examples, the subscripted S variables describe groups of alternatives which may be either further subdivided or voted upon. Subscripted S variables will also describe those further subdivisions. Upper case alternatives give the results of voting over a subset (even trivial voting of a 1-element set) when another subset is voted upon concurrently; the upper case alternatives are thus not the final choice but are themselves nonterminals describing alternatives available in the final choice process. The lower case alternatives are terminals giving the results of the final choice process. The reader will note that $\$$ is a dummy terminal neces-

sary to satisfy the requirements of the two types, context-free and context-sensitive, grammars, but unnecessary to describe the salient aspects of the choice functions.

We give the general plan for the heuristic grammatical inference scheme used here to model choice functions by a grammar. The nonterminal and terminal variables are formally defined as:

$S_{ABC...Z}$ = nonterminal denoting the start of the voting process, where the subscripts show all alternatives considered. This symbol is the start symbol of the grammar.

S_{ABD} = nonterminal showing that the alternatives are divided into subsets for the subsequent vote over the subset, where the subscripts are a proper subset of the full set of alternatives considered.

A = result of a vote over a subset, these nonterminals are used when the final choice is not yet determined.

a = terminal denoting one element contained in the final choice.

$\$$ = dummy terminal contained in final choice string but meaningless in terms of the set of alternatives in the final choice.

Productions of the grammar have the form:

$$S_{ABC...Z} \to S_{ADE}BS_{CFG}E...S_{VWXYZ}$$

where the symbol on the left is the start symbol and the symbols on the right are nonterminals denoting voting in process. These productions are used to divide the alternatives into all possible subsets.

$S_{ABD} \to A$ is a production used to illustrate a choice function of the form $C(a,b,d)=a$. Productions of this form model each statement of the choice function.

$A \to a$ is a production used when a is in the final choice set.

$A \to \$$ is a production used to derive the final choice string when a is not in the final choice set.

$ABD \to a$ is also a possible production when final choice depends on other available alternatives so that the grammar is context-sensitive.

Such a grammar describes the choice function and the voting process used to choose over a set of alternatives.

Consider the Independent-of-Path choice function

did not depend upon the arbitrary way he initially divided the alternatives for consideration [4, p. 7].

This ethical consideration is especially significant for voting methods which are only defined for small sets; for example, majority rule is only defined over two-element sets. The Independence-of-Path ethic requires that choice over larger sets, by repeated application of such a choice method to smaller sets, is unambiguous, in that it does not depend on the way the larger set was divided into smaller sets, the voting sequence.

Plott formally defines Independence of Path as follows:

Assume E is a finite set of conceivable alternatives. Let $V = \{V_1, ..., V_m\}$ be a family of subsets (agendas) of E. For all $S \subset E$, define $V_S = \{V: \underset{v \in V}{\cup} v = S\}$.

Assume that $v \subset E$ and $v \neq \phi \Rightarrow C(v) \neq \phi$, where C refers to the choice function.

Independence of Path:

$$(\forall S)_{S \subset E}\{V \in V_S \ \& \ V' \in V_S \Rightarrow C(\underset{v \in V}{\cup} C(v)) = C(\underset{v \in V'}{\cup} C(v'))\}$$

and he gives examples of choice functions which satisfy the Independence-of-Path axiom and which are non-Independent of Path.

Example 1 (Independent-of-Path Choice Function):

$C(a) = a$ for $a \in \{x, y, z, x,y, x,z, y,z\}$ and

$$C(x,y,z) = x,z$$

Example 2 (Non-Independent-of-Path Choice Function):

Consider the cyclical majority situation where 3 individuals use the majority rule method to vote on 3 alternatives. The individuals' preferences, respectively, are:

$x > y > z$
$y > z > x$ where ">" is read "is preferred to"
$z > x > y$

and the choice function defined on the 2-element subsets is:

$$C(x,y) = x \qquad C(y,z) = y \qquad C(x,z) = z$$

The reader may easily verify that the choice over the 3 alternatives depends on the way the alternatives were originally divided into subsets so that the cyclical majority choice function is non-Independent

of Path.

5.3 Grammars representing Independent-of-Path and Non-Independent-of-Path choice functions

We assert that an unrestricted choice function, specifically one not satisfying the Independence-of-Path axiom, may be represented by a context-sensitive grammar and a choice function which is Independent of Path is context-free and may, in fact, be represented by the more restrictive finite state-type grammar. We will first define context-sensitive and context-free grammars and explain this assertion intuitively. Then examples will be given of grammars modeling such choice functions.

A context-sensitive (Type 1) grammar is defined to have productions of the form $\alpha \rightarrow \beta$, where $|\beta| \geq |\alpha|$, when $|x| =$ number of symbols in the string x. An alternate description, motivating the name "context-sensitive", is that the productions have the form $a_1 A a_2 \rightarrow a_1 \beta a_2$, where a_1, a_2 and β are in V^* and $\beta \neq \epsilon$, and $A \in V_N$. ϵ refers to the empty string, the string with no elements. The language in this formulation may be termed context-sensitive since A can be replaced by β whenever A appears in the context of a_1 and a_2. Similarly, it is clear that under the first definition, α can be greater than 1, so that the set of nonterminals, α, can be replaced by β as a totality.

A context-free grammar (Type 2 grammar) is restricted to productions of the form $A \rightarrow \beta$, where A is a single variable and β is any string other than ϵ. Thus the single variable A is replaced by β regardless of the context in which A appears. In our choice function application of context-sensitive and context-free grammars, the difference between them which will be most frequently employed is that, if $|\alpha| = 2$ and $|\beta| \geq 2$, the grammar is context-sensitive. And if the productions of the grammar cannot be rewritten such that $|\alpha| = 1$, the grammar cannot be considered context-free.

A general choice function, as a process, may be modeled by a grammar, and the grammar will be at least context-sensitive since

1. The results of a subdivision of the agenda may give two or more subsets and in such a case $1 = |\alpha| < |\beta|$, where $|\beta| \geq 2$; and
2. The results of a vote over alternatives will result in at least one choice, so that $1 = |\alpha| \leq |\beta|$, where $|\beta| \geq 1$.

Consider an Independent-of-Path choice function. No matter what the voting sequence and intermediate division of alternatives into subsets, the choice over all alternatives will be the same. Thus the final choice is independent of previous choices, and any choice does not depend on concurrent alternatives. In a formal language framework, the choice is independent of the context in which it occurs and, as we shall show, an Independent-of-Path choice function may be modeled by a context-free grammar. In fact, an Independent-of-Path choice function may be modeled by the more restrictive finite state grammar.

An unrestricted choice function, specifically one that is not Independent-of-Path, can only be represented by a context-sensitive grammar and not a context-free grammar, since the non-Independent-of-Path choice function will result in various final choices, depending on the way the alternatives were subdivided. Thus a choice at any stage may depend on concurrent alternatives, or previous subdivisions. In grammatical terms, the choice will depend on the context in which the choice is made. In particular, a choice over two alternatives may depend on exactly what those competing alternatives are, so that the left-hand side of such a production cannot be reduced to 1 variable and must have length of at least 2. We thus appeal to the fact that $|\alpha|$ may equal 2 if $|\beta| \geqslant 2$ for the grammar to be context-sensitive and not context-free, since $|\alpha|$ cannot be reduced to 1.

5.3.1 Examples of grammars representing Independent-of-Path and Non-Independent-of-Path choice functions

To make the preceding intuitive explanation clearer, we illustrate how the Independent-of-Path and non-Independent-of-Path choice functions would be modeled by context-free and context-sensitive grammars. We shall later show that the Indpendent-of-Path choice functions may actually be modeled by finite state grammars. Note here, however, that the non-Independent-of-Path choice function cannot be represented by a context-free grammar.

In the following examples, the subscripted S variables describe groups of alternatives which may be either further subdivided or voted upon. Subscripted S variables will also describe those further subdivisions. Upper case alternatives give the results of voting over a subset (even trivial voting of a 1-element set) when another subset is voted upon concurrently; the upper case alternatives are thus not the final choice but are themselves nonterminals describing alternatives available in the final choice process. The lower case alternatives are terminals giving the results of the final choice process. The reader will note that $\$$ is a dummy terminal neces-

sary to satisfy the requirements of the two types, context-free and context-sensitive, grammars, but unnecessary to describe the salient aspects of the choice functions.

We give the general plan for the heuristic grammatical inference scheme used here to model choice functions by a grammar. The nonterminal and terminal variables are formally defined as:

$S_{ABC...Z}$ = nonterminal denoting the start of the voting process, where the subscripts show all alternatives considered. This symbol is the start symbol of the grammar.

S_{ABD} = nonterminal showing that the alternatives are divided into subsets for the subsequent vote over the subset, where the subscripts are a proper subset of the full set of alternatives considered.

A = result of a vote over a subset, these nonterminals are used when the final choice is not yet determined.

a = terminal denoting one element contained in the final choice.

$\$$ = dummy terminal contained in final choice string but meaningless in terms of the set of alternatives in the final choice.

Productions of the grammar have the form:

$$S_{ABC...Z} \rightarrow S_{ADE}BS_{CFG}E \ldots S_{VWXYZ}$$

where the symbol on the left is the start symbol and the symbols on the right are nonterminals denoting voting in process. These productions are used to divide the alternatives into all possible subsets.

$S_{ABD} \rightarrow A$ is a production used to illustrate a choice function of the form $C(a,b,d)=a$. Productions of this form model each statement of the choice function.

$A \rightarrow a$ is a production used when a is in the final choice set.

$A \rightarrow \$$ is a production used to derive the final choice string when a is not in the final choice set.

$ABD \rightarrow a$ is also a possible production when final choice depends on other available alternatives so that the grammar is context-sensitive.

Such a grammar describes the choice function and the voting process used to choose over a set of alternatives.

Consider the Independent-of-Path choice function

given in Example 1. It may be represented by the context-free grammar, $G_1 = (V_N, V_T, P, S)$, where $S = S_{XYZ}$; $V_N = \{S_{XYZ}, S_{XY}, S_{YZ}, S_{XZ}, X, Y, Z\}$; $V_T = \{x, y, z, \$\}$; and P:

1. $S_{XYZ} \rightarrow ZS_{XY}$ 4. $S_{XY} \rightarrow XY$ 7. $X \rightarrow x$ 10. $S_{XYZ} \rightarrow xz$

2. $S_{XYZ} \rightarrow XS_{YZ}$ 5. $S_{YZ} \rightarrow YZ$ 8. $Y \rightarrow \$$

3. $S_{XYZ} \rightarrow YS_{XZ}$ 6. $S_{XZ} \rightarrow XZ$ 9. $Z \rightarrow z$

The reader may easily verify that G_1 is a context-free grammar. We should note that production 10 shows it is not necessary for choice over alternatives to be reduced to binary choice when the choice process is modeled by a grammar. Extension, an axiom to be introduced subsequently, however, is an axiom of social choice defined on binary choices and so is a concept for which binary choice is important.

In contrast, examine the non-Independent-of-Path choice function, the cyclical majority situation given in Example 2. It may be represented by $G_2 = (V_N, V_T, P, S)$, where $S = S_{XYZ}$; $V_N = \{S_{XYZ}, S_{XY}, S_{YZ}, S_{XZ}, X, Y, Z\}$; $V_T = \{x, y, z, \$\}$; and P:

1. $S_{XYZ} \rightarrow ZS_{XY}$ 4. $S_{XY} \rightarrow X$ 7. $XZ \rightarrow z\$$

2. $S_{XYZ} \rightarrow XS_{YZ}$ 5. $S_{YZ} \rightarrow Y$ 8. $XY \rightarrow x\$$

3. $S_{XYZ} \rightarrow YS_{XZ}$ 6. $S_{XZ} \rightarrow Z$ 9. $YZ \rightarrow y\$$

The left-hand side of productions 7, 8, and 9 cannot be reduced to a single variable, since final choice depends on the other alternatives which result from choices over earlier subdivisions of the alternatives. Thus the grammar representing a non-Independent-of-Path choice function cannot be context-free.

As an additional example, *Example 3*, consider a choice function of majority rule with noncyclical underlying individual preferences, as:

$x > y > z$
$y > z > x$ where ">" is read "is preferred to".
$x > z > y$

The majority rule choice function here may be represented by the context-free grammar $G_3 = (V_N, V_T, P, S)$ where $S = S_{XYZ}$, $V_N = \{S_{XYZ}, S_{XY}, S_{YZ}, S_{XZ}, X, Y, Z\}$; $V_T = \{x, y, z, \$\}$; and P:

1. $S_{XYZ} \rightarrow ZS_{XY}$ 4. $S_{XY} \rightarrow X$ 7. $X \rightarrow x$ 10. $S_{XYZ} \rightarrow x$

2. $S_{XYZ} \rightarrow XS_{YZ}$ 5. $S_{YZ} \rightarrow Y$ 8. $Y \rightarrow \$$

3. $S_{XYZ} \rightarrow YS_{XZ}$ 6. $S_{XZ} \rightarrow X$ 9. $Z \rightarrow \$$

In this Independent-of-Path, majority rule choice function, all productions, including 7, 8, and 9, are context-free, since x wins in a final choice no matter what alternatives, resulting from previous choices, oppose it.

While the contrast between context-sensitive and context-free in relation to Independent-of-Path choice functions was useful, it can further be shown that an Independent-of-Path choice function can be modeled by a grammar even more restrictive than a context-free grammar, a finite state grammar. A finite state grammar is defined by the allowable productions of the form $A \rightarrow aB$ and $A \rightarrow a$, where A and B are nonterminals and a is a terminal. With slightly different productions, we can show that the Independent-of-Path choice functions given here in Examples 1 and 3 may be modeled by finite state languages. The basic difference is that in the finite state productions, the nonterminal upper case alternatives are deleted and replaced by their resulting lower case terminals when those lower case terminals will be in the final choice set; otherwise, they are replaced by the terminal $\$$. As another slight correction to conform to the definition of finite state grammars, a new nonterminal, S_z, is introduced in Example 1. In this way, the 2-element final choice may be represented by only one terminal appearing at a time in the productions forming it so that the productions have the form of the allowable finite state productions. Thus Example 1 has finite state productions of the form:

1. $S_{XYZ} \rightarrow zS_{XY}$ 4. $S_{XY} \rightarrow x$ 7. $S_Z \rightarrow z$

2. $S_{XYZ} \rightarrow xS_{YZ}$ 5. $S_{YZ} \rightarrow z$ 8. $S_{XYZ} \rightarrow xS_Z$

3. $S_{XYZ} \rightarrow \$S_{XZ}$ 6. $S_{XZ} \rightarrow xS_Z$

And Example 3 has finite state productions of the form:

1. $S_{XYZ} \rightarrow \$S_{XY}$ 4. $S_{XY} \rightarrow x$ 7. $S_{XYZ} \rightarrow x$

2. $S_{XYZ} \rightarrow xS_{YZ}$ 5. $S_{YZ} \rightarrow \$$

3. $S_{XYZ} \rightarrow \$S_{XZ}$ 6. $S_{XZ} \rightarrow x$

The fact that Independent-of-Path choice functions are not only modeled by context-free grammars but may be modeled by finite state grammars increases the range of grammatical results which may be applied to Independent-of-Path choice functions. Since a finite state language may be recognized by a finite state automaton, the views of a society which holds the Independent-of-Path ethic may be chosen from a larger set of possible choices (resulting from unrestricted choice functions) by the construction of an automaton which only recognizes the results of a finite state grammar modeling such a society. For a more detailed explanation of the formal language and automata representation of the social choice process, see [5].

5.4 Extension axiom

Plott discusses another axiom of social choice, Extension [5, p. 11], which combined with Independence of Path, gives sufficient conditions for the social preference to be rationalized by a total, reflexive binary relation defining a transitive social preference relation. Informally, the Extension axiom insures that if a certain alternative, x, is chosen each time it is compared in binary choice with all other alternatives, x should be among the alternatives selected from the full set of alternatives. In mathematical notation, Extension may be expressed as

$$(\forall S)_{S \subset E} [\{x \in S \text{ and } (\forall y)_{y \in S} \ x \in C(x,y)\} \Rightarrow x \in C(S)]$$

In formal language terms, Extension may be stated as

If $S_{X\alpha} \to \beta$, where x or $X \in \beta$, for all $\alpha \in E$ are productions in G, a grammar representing a choice function, then $x \in L(G)$.

The Extension axiom is independent of the Independence-of-Path axiom.

Before discussing Plott's result linking Extension, Independence of Path and a binary rationalizing the social preferences of the society, we must discuss binary relations and their properties. Binary relations are of the form aRb, binary meaning defined over 2 alternatives at a time, as a and b. A total binary relation is defined over all possible pairs of alternatives. A reflexive binary relation includes relations of the form xRx, for all $x \in E$. aRb may be interpreted as "a is at least as preferred as b". "a is preferred to b", or aPb is defined as aRb and not bRa. If aPb and bPc imply aPc, P is called a transitive preference ordering.

Plott shows that a choice function which satisfies both the Independence-of-Path and Extension axioms

can be rationalized (the social preferences can be explained) by a total, reflexive binary relation R such that the preference relation, P, defined on R is transitive. Since verification of the Extension axiom requires the choice function to be defined on all 2-element subsets, all pairs of alternatives, the R which rationalizes the choice function may be defined as

For all x, $y_{x,y \in E}$ $xRy \Leftrightarrow x \in C(x,y)$

The following theorem shows that a grammar modeling a choice function which satisfies both the Independence-of-Path and Extension Axioms has a transitive property, in terms of its productions.

Theorem: Given a grammar satisfying the Independence-of-Path and Extension axioms, if $S_{AB} \to \alpha$, where A or $a = \alpha$, and $S_{BC} \to \beta$, where B or $b = \beta$, then $S_{AC} \to \alpha$.

Proof: Consider two possible derivations of the final choice string from the alternatives a, b, and c.

I: $\quad S_{ABC} \overset{1}{\to} AS_{BC} \overset{2}{\to} AB \overset{3}{\to}$

II: $\quad S_{ABC} \overset{1}{\to} S_{AB}C \overset{2}{\to} AC \overset{3}{\to}$

The first and second transitions are straightforward applications of the choice function grammar scheme and the assumptions. Recalling that an Independent-of-Path choice function is modeled by a context-free grammar, the third derivation used in I must use one of the following:

a) $A \to a$, $B \to \$$
b) $A \to \$$, $B \to b$
c) $A \to a$, $B \to b$

Similarly, the third derivation in II must be either

a) $A \to a$, $C \to \$$
b) $A \to \$$, $C \to c$
c) $A \to a$, $C \to c$

By Independence of Path, the terminal letters (disregarding the dummy terminal, $\$$) in strings derived in both I and II must be the same, so derivations b and c cannot be used. Thus the a derivations are the only possibilities, and $AC \to a\$$, meaning that a is chosen in a choice between a and c, or $S_{AC} \to \alpha$.

While the preceding theorem assures that the social preference relation, P, defined by a grammar satisfying the Independence-of-Path and Extension axioms is transitive, the theorem was stated in terms of the productions of the grammar itself. Alternatively, the binary relation may be considered explicitly.

In the language framework, the binary relation R may be considered a social preference translation of the choice function satisfying Independence of Path and Extension, modeled by a grammar. Such a translation system [6] would follow the derivation of a choice over a set of alternatives by itself explicitly designating the preferences shown in the choice sequence. The language of the social preference grammar may be said to define the preference relation which rationalizes the choice function. The correspondence between the productions in the choice function and the preference relation grammars is shown below:

(for G_P, V_N = {upper case letters, not R}, V_T = {lower case letters, R})

T: G_C, Choice Function Grammar, expressed as context-free G_P, Preference Relation Grammar

1. $S \to \alpha S_{AB} \beta$ $S = AB$

2. $S_{AB} \to a$ $AB = aRb$

3. $S_{AB} \to A$ $AB = aRb$

4. All other productions   No corresponding production

The preference relation grammar is context-sensitive, since preference is a *binary* relation and the preference ordering is thus dependent on the exact *two* elements compared.

A translation is an ordered pair; the first term is the expression in the original grammar, the second term is the translation. We illustrate such a translation for Example 3, which satisfies both Extension and Independence of Path:

$$(S,S) \xrightarrow{1} (ZS_{XY},XY) \xrightarrow{4} (\$S_{XY},XY) \xrightarrow{3} (\$X,xRy) \xrightarrow{4} (\$x,xRy)$$

$$(S,S) \xrightarrow{1} (XS_{YZ},YZ) \xrightarrow{4} (xS_{YZ},YZ) \xrightarrow{3} (xY,yRz) \xrightarrow{4} (x\$,yRz)$$

$$(S,S) \xrightarrow{1} (YS_{XZ},XZ) \xrightarrow{4} (\$S_{XZ},XZ) \xrightarrow{3} (\$X,xRz) \xrightarrow{4} (\$x,xRz)$$

It should be noted that such a translation scheme translates the *process* of choice into a preference relation rather than strictly translating a string in one language to a string in another language. Also, the total social preference ordering which rationalizes a choice function, designated i, is given by the language G_{Pi}, the language giving all its possible translations.

6. Summary

This Chapter has used heuristic grammatical inference to model choice functions in a formal language framework. It was shown that non-Independent-of-Path choice functions may be modeled by context-sensitive grammars, while Independent-of-Path choice functions are not only represented as context-free but may be modeled by finite state grammars. Plott showed that a choice function which satisfies both the Independence-of-Path and Extension axioms may be rationalized by a total, reflexive binary relation which defines a transitive preference relation. The construction of such a rationalization of a choice function was represented as a translation from the grammar modeling the choice function to another grammar representing the social preference ordering.

References

1. HOPCROFT, John E. and ULLMAN, Jeffrey D., *Formal Languages and Their Relation to Automata*, Addison-Wesley Publishing Company, Reading, Mass. (1969).
2. FARQUHARSON, Robin, *Theory of Voting*, Yale University Press, New Haven (1969).
3. FU, K.S., 'A Survey of Grammatical Inference', TR-EE 72-18, Purdue University, School of Electrical Engineering (June 1972).
4. PLOTT, Charles R., 'Social Choice and Social Responsibility', Purdue University, unpublished (1971).
5. PICCOLI, Mary Louise and WHINSTON, Andrew B., 'Social choice and formal language theory', *Journal of Cybernetics* (forthcoming).
6. AHO, Alfred V. and ULLMAN, Jeffrey D., *The Theory of Parsing, Translation and Compiling*, Prentice Hall, Englewood Cliffs, N.J. (1972).
7. BIERMAN, A.W. and FELDMAN, J.A., 'A survey of results in grammatical inference', *Frontiers of Pattern Recognition* (edit. by S. Watanabe), Academic Press, New York (1972).

Organisational aspects of social planning

GUSZTÁV BÁGER and ALBERT HAJNAL
Institute of Economic Planning, Budapest, Hungary

A view over the recent states

Stages of scientific and technical development can be well measured on which of the results of development have been realized through careful planning and which may be considered as a result of spontaneous social activities. Within the sphere of results achieved through careful planning, how the complexity of the planned results have grown is to be considered an important indicator of development. In our time a considerable number of countries of the world have arrived at the stage where they plan the development of the whole national economy. However, in recent years the view has strengthened that *planned development can be less and less limited to only the economy of a country.* In more favorable terms the situation can be described in that the requirement has come to the foreground that the planned development of the national economy must be extended so as to cover the planned development of the society of the country. Such a change in the subject of planning is, however, not to be conceived as a sudden step. Transition will probably be continuous and last for quite a long time. Certain intermediate stages of this transition are already taking shape, and these can be described partly by changes in the subject of planning and partly by the framework of approaches in planning. The following stages may be identified:

1. The planned development of the national economy.
2. The planned development of the national economy in such a way that the main social aspects affected by economic development are consciously considered.
3. Society-orientated planning of economy.
4. The planned development of society in such a way that the national economy is described as a prominent part of society.

This identification of stages is, of course, arbitrary to a certain extent but there are a number of facts to indicate that these stages represent the natural transition. It can be said of the First Stage that it has been done in many countries. The Second Stage is seen in the formulation: "social aspects of economic planning". The Fourth Stage is seen as the ultimate aim in various works of the special literature and, what is more, it appeared as the main subject of discussion at the Seventh Sociological World Congress held in Varna (Bulgaria) in 1970. The Third Stage had to be included in the line because it is not possible to transfer immediately from the stage of "social aspects of economic planning" into that of "social planning". This is because however natural it seems *that social development must also be planned, the idea is rather intuitive.* If we examine it thoroughly what is exactly meant by the planned development of society, what it is that must be or can be planned, what future perspectives of develop-

Progress in Cybernetics and Systems Research, Volume 2

ment the plans ought to cover, on which criteria it can be found out whether such plan is feasible, what scientific information should be used in the elaboration of the plans, who should be the planners, what institutional framework and forms may guarantee the good quality of plans, etc.—a multitude of problems suddenly arise from the basic thought. And, beside all this, we have an experience of basic importance from the initial period of economic planning, which is that in the transition from spontaneous to planned development, such planning can easily entail several harmful effects as does not count with the varied and complex nature of national economy. It is, of course, not to be expected for some time yet that social planners take into account the varied and complex nature of the national economy to the required extent, or the tasks of the same nature involved in planning. There exists, however, a remarkable—although rather neglected—feature in the development of humanity. The phylogenetic and ontogenetic experience, accumulated in man, has largely contributed to that man. And, as social experience has accumulated, there has also been more of the spontaneous than of the conscious. It is also true that the knowledge presented by modern sciences has almost suddenly changed a number of the development characteristics of humanity. All the same, spontaneous experience—as regards the resultant of its general effect—has still, doubtlessly, a bigger ordering force than scientifically conscious knowledge.

All considered, the idea of a planned development of society ought to be evolved and led to the practical direction by coordinating two approaches. One is the conscious approach of modern sciences, which is grounded on *what we know*. The other counts with *what we do not know*, at least not consciously and rationally, but what our instincts and automatisms know, and which has a lot of heuristic value of favorable effect in that we know or rather feel what is to be avoided. It has been in fashion for a long time to depreciate instinctive knowledge; its values are just beginning to be recognized again.

The transition from the planned development of the economy to the planned development of society can be described, in a first approach, by the *objectives* and *strategies* of their realization. In this approach the objectives may be represented by the plan-model used by the planners. In the First Stage the plan-model is that of the national economy. In the Second Stage the plan-model is that of the national economy in which social aspects are represented by conditions built into the model. In the

Third Stage the plan-model is a nondetailed model of society, developed on our conscious and scientific social self-knowledge, in which the economic model has more details, because we have better knowledge of it. In the Fourth Stage the plan-model is that of society developed on the enlarged field of our knowledge matured also scientifically. Socialist countries have practically always planned their economy in the sense of the Third Stage, since there the Marxist society-model has been the theoretical regulator of economic development, although it is also true that the formal plan-model is still *only* an economic model. Therefore, socialist countries are also only at the Second or Third Stage of the transition.

If the final objective of a long-range development is defined as a society of planned development, there will be seen in our time—only very roughly described —*two varieties of strategy*.

FIRST STRATEGY—its approach and value system are based on the technical-economic rationality which sees advanced society through the indicators of a highly developed mechanical civilization (mass production, the quickest possible increase of production and economic efficiency, belt technology, etc.)

SECOND STRATEGY—its approach and value system are human-orientated, i.e., it approaches society in a way in which an individual has a possibility for selfrealization, i.e., he can accomplish his personality, and this feature will always be given priority as opposed to merely technical-economic rationality.

Socialist countries follow intentionally the second strategy, since it is in the fundamental idea of socialism, yet in the course of following this strategy the heuristic line of experiments had to be several times adaptively corrected. In these corrections the spontaneously accumulated experience on society was used in the way described above. The reason therefore is obviously that our present scientific knowledge about society does not cover as yet all details of the extreme complexity of society.

If we consider the problems of social planning in the terms of the situation as described above, an interpretation will present itself, which may grasp a most important aspect of the development tendency of the near future. This interpretation may be conceptualized by the following train of thought.

The plan of the economy of a country is today such a complex intellectual product that it can be created only by the co-operation of a large number of institutions. The system of these planning institutions is characterized by an intense differentiation of the intraorganizational and interorganizational labour division. Labour division is necessary not only because of the "size" of the plan. The variety of comptetences† activated in planning is also growing. *In socialist countries, such as Hungary, this planning system is organically built into the still larger system of state administration.* This system, consisting of specialized competences, is of course very sensitive and selective in relation to all social phenomena that are screened by competence and professional experience. This system gave rise to a rather peculiar situation. The small group of competent planners plan such results of development as affect the larger part of society, which latter consists of the noncompetent. Or, more succinctly expressed: *the competent decide the questions affecting the noncompetent.* But, since the noncompetent are competent in the field of other problems, this is a mutual relationship.

Experience shows that on account of the extremely complex nature of society this *competence-oriented planning system cannot, as a matter of course, fully grasp and foresee in all details the results of the plans that have been deemed correct.* This characteristic and also limit of the planning system may be counterbalanced to a certain extent by *drawing, in some form, the noncompetent into the planning,* with the consideration that they might recognize and indicate, by a more direct sensitivity, the results that are going to affect them. Such participation already exists in certain forms. These, however, have not proved efficient enough. The main reason for this is that they do not fit organically into the planning system so far developed, because it has not been expressly organized to which plans they should contribute and according to which programme.

In the following the concept of such a system will be outlined as must satisfy at least the criteria listed below:

a) to guarantee, formally and organized, the participation of the noncompetent and/or of their representatives in the solution of development problems that affect them;

b) to fit organically into the functional order of such a planning system as plans the development of the national economy and takes into account the main social aspects (second stage);

c) to cooperate, not only seemingly but with well identifiable results, in the planning and in the control of the implementation of the plans.

Such a system is, of course, extremely complicated in its real form. Here only its most important theoretical characteristics are outlined. In order to give an idea of the theoretical characteristics in their practical variation *the organizational system of the Hungarian national economy has been taken as an example.* It is to be emphasized that this is *only as an example,* since the conception is but imaginary. The idea will be developed whereby first the existing organizational system of the national economy will be presented, then within its framework the main features of the cooperation of the noncompetent will be described and, finally, the proposed conception of the system will be drawn up.

The competence-oriented organization of the national economy

Although the state organization of the different countries is imilar in many respects, the socialist countries have a specific feature. It is that in the organizational system of the state a dominant role is played by such a subsystem whose main task is to accomplish the planned economic development. This subsystem has a formal organizational framework, which has been organically built into the organizational system of the state. This characteristic is specific also of Hungary. This organizational system of the Hungarian economy will be presented in what follows with the aid of a highly simplified model (Fig. 1).

First of all, it is stated that *in the organizational system of economy, labour division and spheres of activity are competence-oriented.* This aspect of the system will be referred to in the following by the word COSY (Competence-Oriented SYstem).

The most important theoretical attributes of the system are summarized below. In the description the language of the systems theory is used [1].

1. The national economy is the ensemble of continuously developing organizations. According to the general systems typology it is a self-evolving system and, as such, a creative system.

2. The whole society of the country and the whole organizational system of the state in which the former is organically fitted are interpreted as the internal environment of the system. The external environment is represented by the other countries.

3. As a creative system, it has a readily definable

---

† In order to avoid misunderstanding, competence is interpreted here as scientifically grounded or based on long practical experience.

product within a plan period, which is the difference generated by economy between the initial and the final state of the plan period.

4. It has three basic subsystems, each of them including many smaller organizational units:
   i. *Central planning organizations.* They plan on the national level.
   ii. *State-administrative organs.* They contribute to the planning work on the national level and actively control the implementation of the national plans within their scope.
   iii. *Economic units* (enterprises, institutions, local governmental organs, etc.). They supply products, provide services, and plan their own development within the frames of the national plans.

Consequently, the results and the process of the selfevolution of the economy are planned on two levels, i.e., on the national level and on the level of the economic units.

5. In consideration of the fact that the economy is developing continuously, the plans of a period are elaborated on the national level according to a special program. The program may be described by the series of documents (see Fig. 1). At the start of the procedure an analytical picture of the present state of the economy (document A) is needed. The end-document is represented by the national economy plans (document P).

6. The central planning organizations make two kinds of plans, i.e., *goal-plans* P^g and *action-plans* P^a.

7. Both the P^g and the P^a plans divide into further types of plans. Development results of national importance are planned directly in the national plans (P_d). Results of less importance are planned only in an aggregated form and in an indirect way (P_i); economic regulators belong to this type of plans.

8. The plans P^g–P^a and P_d–P_i present reference bases for the operative control subsystems.

9. There exists a national subsystem of information, which has two subfunctions. One is to supply the central planning organizations with such information as they need in their planning work on the national level. The other is to supply the state-administrative organs with feedback information. The center of this subsystem of information is the Central Statistical Office.

Upon interpretation of the above-described features of the system, how this organization of COSY character functions theoretically can be conceived.

It is to be added here that in the organizational system of the Hungarian economy *a few such functions exist at present as represent the noncompetent.* One is the country's Parliament, the other consists of the party organizations covering the whole country, and the third is represented by the trade unions. The function of Parliament must be stressed, because in the procedure of approval of the national economy plan it is an important event when Parliament discusses, approves and incorporates the plan in law. In Hungary the middle-range five year plan is approved by Parliament in the form of law.

In the following the construction of COSY character will be evaluated as to *how much it can guarantee participation of the noncompetent* and it will be outlined, on which systems criteria this participation can theoretically be increased.

Review, forecast and problems

The thought of a society planning its own future has a great generative power. The process has started, irreversibly, at the end of which this thought will be realized. Since our knowledge with regard to society is rather deficient and even what we know has only a slight predictive and innovative power, the majority of the problems to be solved in the course of the process are also unexplored. Therefore, the work that can be done with a view to realizing the idea carries primarily a heuristic value. This study is an enterprise of such a kind. In the following it will investigate what problems may arise at the Second Stage, within the second strategy. Among the components and interrelations of the model drawn up previously there are numerous such invariant aspects by which the existing situation can be described. The not too distant future can be forecast and, the

---

See page 28.

Fig. 1 Key: A—analytical picture of actual states, PR—preconceptions of the potential futures, EP—acceptable variants consistent with economic policies, C—plan conceptions, P—final plans, P_d—plans of national importance (direct), P_i—regulators (indirect), P^g—goal plans, and P^a—action plans.

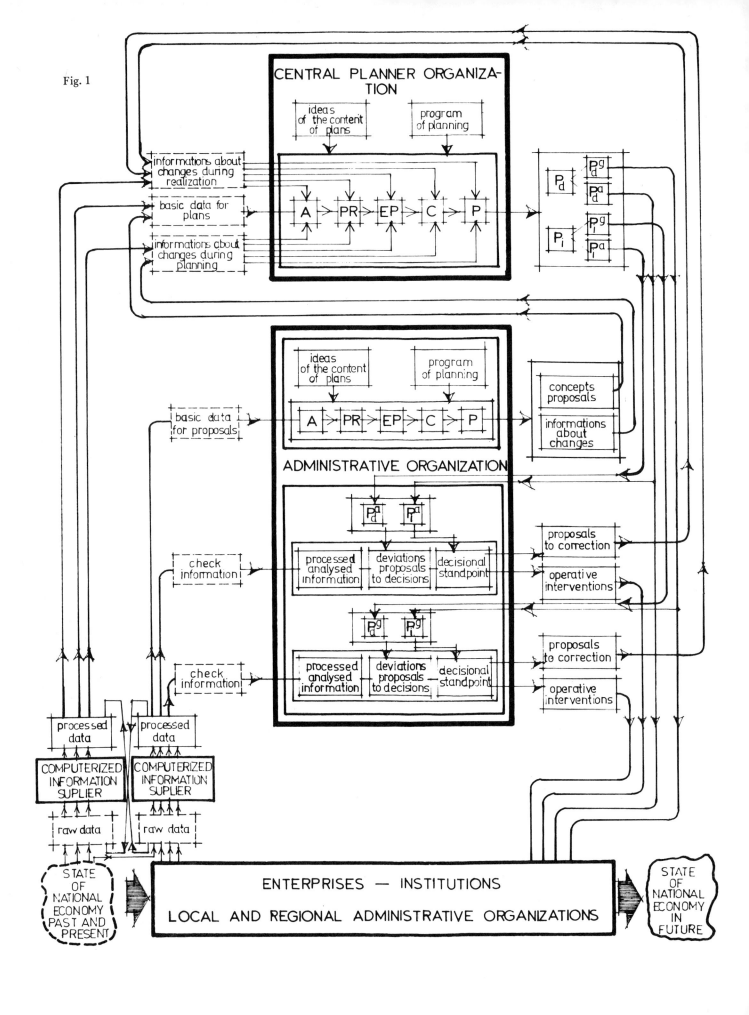

Fig. 1

two compared, such problems can be identified as will have to be solved in the course of the process. In what follows only those problems will be treated which are connected with the improvement of participation of the noncompetent.

Practical planners present the social aspects of the economy by indicators which, although connected with economic development, are yet the direct marks of the developmental state of society. The main groups of indicators are the following: general educational and professional standards, living standards, health and recreational services, working conditions, mode and way of life, environment, etc., and the interrelated system of institutions. These groups of indicators show that *the variety of sensitivity of planners has grown.* This means that they have contributed to the extension of the sphere of aspects planned on the national economy level as compared to the earlier sensitivity centered on industrial products and on the economy. However, the new indicators carry a heavy burden as opposed to those concerned only with the economy. They are not suitable for generating a complex model structure, which would show, in explicit form, also the inter-relations between the indicators. From economic indicators models of practical value can be developed already. As opposed to them, social indicators today constitute only a huge mass of unrelated statistical data. Even in a favorable case they can be arranged only into a few particular forms. Such are the classes (or clusters), time series, vague correlations without cause-effect connections, i.e., the forms of the statisticians' world view. It is known from the planning experience of socialist countries that the world view of planners increasingly deviates from the world view—otherwise pragmatically justified—of statisticians. In other words: *the plan of the future cannot be a statistics of the future.* The economic models (already at a well advanced stage) are given, but there are as yet no formalized society models. Therefore, the transitional version may be considered to embed the social indicators in economic models. The question is, however, which indicators of which aspects of society ought to be included. Should selection rely on the sensitivity of the competent or of the noncompetent? Planner organizations of the COSY character, on a national level, use the data of statistical institutes. On the other side, statistical institutes supply information almost exclusively to state organizations of COSY character. Therefore, the indicators of statistics are selected in the COSY view.

The national economy has been interpreted here as a creative organization. Its products can be described in terms of plan models. The actual starting state is represented by Document A and the end state by Document P. The former is the plan model of the present, while the latter is the plan model of what is qualified as feasible. Following this train of thought it is possible to have social aspects represented in these plan models by indicators selected according to the view of the competent or of the noncompetent. What is more, the two kinds of indicator can be combined. In the Second Stage this latter is considered as desirable.

The ideas treated above are closely connected to the framework of Fig. 1. By them one of the most important problems of the Second Stage has practically been explained in more exact terms: at present there exists no such plan model of the economy in which indicators selected according to the competent and the noncompetent view together represent the social aspects, although this is desirable.

For the national economy plans, social indicators are basic data just the same as the other variables of the plan model. According to Fig. 1 such data are needed in the organizational system of the national economy according to two aspects. First, for Document A at the beginning of the planning work, and later for the series of Documents PR, EP, C, P in the course of work (so that plans should rely always on the latest data); secondly, at the time of implementing the plans—but then in the form of negative feedback information. If the organizational system of the national economy is sufficiently adaptive and is capable of continuous planning, the two aspects can be combined and *the basic data can be interpreted as the current latest information about the present states of the economy.* For this, however, such an evaluating and analyzing function is needed as can judge selectively whether—regarding present conditions—an operative control-intervention is necessary, or modifying of the plans, or there is no need for intervention. This selectivity in the judgement of consequences is on the one hand *present-orientated* (when it triggers control-intervention), on the other hand it is *future-orientated* (when it demands modification of plans). Acknowledging the necessity for social indicators selected according to both competent and noncompetent sensitivity and in a form and manner coordinated with the operational order of the organizational system of the economy, another very important problem of the Second Stage will be arrived at on the basis of the preceding argumentation. The problem may be exposed in the following: in the economic organization of COSY character there are today no institutionalized functions to enable social indicators including the sensitivity of the noncompetent to be supplied for the current state of affairs both in the sense of Document A and of the feedback, although this would be required by enlarged social participation.

In the preceding, two dominenat problems have been presented. One is concerned directly with *what can/must be planned in the Second Stage.* The other is the relation between *the information about the current state of the economy* and the *two subsystems* (planner and operative controller). A few further dominant problems may be revealed if the method of planning and the operational order of the planner system are analyzed separately and in their interrelations.

As the economy transforms itself into a future state planned on the basis of the currently existing state, so the planners map the model of the future (Document P) from the model of the present (Document A). In Hungary a specific order of the A→P mapping has developed, in which invariant features of large ordering power are latent. A→P is a multiple-stage transformation whose milestones are a series of documents: A→PR→EP→C→P. The content and operational aspects of this series are rather complex. Among others, it has a *rational* and a *value* implication. These can be described shortly in what follows:

The *rational* feature of the series consists in that image A is necessary, from which the existing and unsolved problems can be defined. The use of the stage PR is that the more variations are conceived of the preconception of the possible future, the more open will be the planner's work. Stage EP is a screen in the terms of economic policy, so that what is not in coordination with economic policy (social policy is in the background) will be eliminated from the variations. Stages C and P reduce the number of variations so that only one should remain in the end—the plan itself. The *value* implication of the series is that selection must be made in all the five steps and all must be preceded by evaluation. In the value system an important role is played by what is described as the problem, what is considered as the desirable future and its feasible variations, and according to what gradation of value/preference selection is made until the one final plan is accepted.

Would the series A→PR→EP→C→P be quite otherwise if influenced also by the view and scale of values of the noncompetent? Obviously, it would be otherwise. The rational aspect of the problem is known from the theory of problem-solving—when the train of thought must go through a maze. And the value system may influence selection at every node of the branch structure of the maze. Although it is not the custom to stress it, there are two aspects of the value system that may influence the choice. This is because each feasible state of the future has a value charge, as they are results of economic development. But the variations of ways leading to only one result have also a value charge. In short, the *value system has a result-orientated aspect and an action- or strategy-orientated aspect.* In the policies (social, economic, education, health, etc., policies) their formalized variations are seen. There exist also other representatives, less consciously recognized but having a very strong influence. *When talking about the new, improved variations of participation, these value implications will play a particularly important role in the participation of the noncompetent.* And, if social participation is activated in planning, the question arises naturally as to how much the existing COSY organization, with its operational order, can receive the participants representing quite a heterogeneous world of values. The situation is complicated by the fact that all kinds of socioeconomic development necessarily entail the changing of views and of the value system. Taking into account the irrational climate prevailing in the formal system of the COSY organizations, as well as the fact that there is still too much of the accidental in their operational program and that they often try to solve conflicts between partial problems by simplification, *the third dominant problem* can be formulated: the operational system of the COSY organizations is not activated and sensitive enough in the identification, handling and solution of value-charged problems, although improved participation would require such quality of the organization.

The *fourth dominant problem* considered essential in the Second Stage is concerned with the self-innovation of the COSY organizations. Innovation is interpreted very generally as the production of new products by new procedures in possession of new scientific results. In other words, *an organization can be innovative in the sense of "know what" and of "know how",* relying on sufficiently matured new scientific knowledge. Organizations are also the results of institutional work, therefore the idea is obvious that *organizations themselves can be subjects of innovation.* Within the framework of the Second Stage—taking into account the three dominant problems discussed—the *desirable result of such innovation* can be already outlined: an organizational system of the economy which, by its formal architecture and operational system, organically embeds the functions of the noncompetent. Within the framework of the Second Stage such an organization can be interpreted also in such a way that the COSY organization so far developed has to be enriched by new features and abilities. This interpretation follows also from the fact that in the Second Stage a new criterion appears as compared to the First Stage: social aspects in the economic plans. This interpretation of pragmatical simplification will, however, not diminish the extent and complexity of the task, but only make the desirable result more tangible. This is because it seems most likely that the task is so complex that this result cannot be achieved, or only in a very long time, without a "mission-oriented research". There exist already such scientific results as can be activated and only have to be innovatively matured for this purpose. Such knowledge is supplied by not only one branch of science but by many. Even the beginning of the work need not be entirely without a pattern. The organizations of space research offer a number of generalizable experiences for such organizations as are the results of innovation. The problem is, however, made more difficult by the fact that in the formation of the existing COSY organizations there were much more spontaneous instances than scientifically based ones. Therefore, quite an important attitudinal breakthrough will be needed to achieve a COSY organization with selfinnovative ability. In consideration of the preceding, the *fourth dominant problem can be* formulated: COSY organizations are not yet selfinnovative or at least not according to requirements generated by the Second Stage, although the new demand for social participation necessitates the selfinnovative ability.

Relying on the draft analysis, four such dominant problems have been presented as will have to be solved, with a view to the planned development of society, already at the initial stage of realizing the final objective, more exactly, at the Second Stage. Putting it concisely, the four dominant problems can be connected to the following subjects:

a) such a plan model of the national economy in which social indicators selected with competent and noncompetent sensitivity can be formally included;

b) the institutionalized participation of the noncompetent in that—within the organizational system of the economy—adequate information on plans and feedback information should supply the grounds for plans and control-inter-

ventions;

c) such an organizational system of the economy as is sensitive also to the value aspects of development problems (in both the result-orientated and strategy-orientated sense of values), whose formal operative system is able to handle and solve such problems and, in this formal system, the noncompetent would participate in some institutionalized form;

d) a selfinnovative organizational system of the economy, in which the organization itself is a subject of innovation, in order that it can become capable of solving the problems of the Second Stage.

Although the above-mentioned dominant problems are determinant, they do not represent all the problems of the Second Stage. In any case, they are suitable for the outlining of criteria that ought to be satisfied by an organizational system which plans the social aspects of economic development as well. These criteria are, of course, in multilateral interrelation with each other. Before drawing up the concept of a suggested system, i.e., of a modified organization of COSY character, these criteria and their more important interrelations will be described in detail.

The development plans of the economy and society can be elaborated today only by strictly organized planner organizations competent in the given subjects. This fact is one of the most important criteria. Therefore, members of society outside these organizations *can only contribute* to the planning work *but cannot replace* these COSY organizations.

Planned creative work requires, also in the frame of the national economy, that operative control organs be present in the organization of the economy. Competence is the criterion in the case of these organs just the same as in the case of planners. Therefore, they can also be completed by the noncompetent but not replaced.

The complementary contribution of the noncompetent can be described in more exact terms in the following. The *noncompetent should raise the sensitivity of the planner system to social indicators* to be built into the plan model not only in the rational sense but also in such a way that *the value-charge of the indicators should become explicit* so that the exploration, recognition and elimination of the inner sources of conflicts of society should be facilitated. It is important that the institutions of the noncompetent should—with their operational system—organically adjust themselves to the stages

A–PR–EP–C–P of the planning, according to the tasks following from the nature of each stage. They should similarly adjust themselves to the operational order of the operative control organizations; within this criterion it is possible to a certain extent to judge selectively whether the answer of the system to the feedback information should be control-intervention, or adaptively modified plans. Another important criterion originates in that the system of economic and social policies accepted in the country is formally also determinant for the COSY organizations, since this is what renders their decisions coherent in relation to both results and action program. By their participation the noncompetent should help to reveal hidden inconsistencies in the system of policies. In a longer period it occurs that the system of policies must be refined, with adaptive adjustment to unforeseeable and uncontrollable, but already manifested conditions. This is a special task for the planner organizations, because it can be interpreted in such a way that they plan also the system of policies. The institutions of the non-competent can usefully complete the work of the COSY organizations also in this respect; they can increase the variety of the problem-sensitivity of the latter.

These criteria could be derived primarily from the formal system of the model of Fig. 1. Another group of criteria must also be mentioned, the source of which is one of the basic characteristics of the general social development. This characteristic can be shortly defined in that *the development of the society of a country necessarily implies the self-realization of each of its members.* In other words, it is a basic condition of social development that *members of society can accomplish their potential personality.* It follows from this basic characteristic of society that the members of the collectivity want to have their part in the activities of planning their common future. The followers of the narrow-minded technical-economic rationality (i.e., those of the first strategy) cannot fit this criterion into their own system of conditions. However, it is already known —as an information of predictive force—that *a special price has to be paid for it if a complex system wants to increase its degree of freedom: there will be more constraints, and more criteria will have to be ful-filled than in the case of a smaller degree of freedom.* The society whose members accomplish their potential personality undoubtedly involves a more complicated system of criteria than the society in which such aims are not fulfilled, but the degree of freedom of the former is higher. This state of a higher

degree of freedom can, of course, be approached step by step, while we are at the Second Stage of the way of development interpreted here as a work concept. At this stage the nearest aim of this approach—for which a general social demand has grown active—can be made tangible, as a so-to-speak heuristic step, in a special form: an enlarged and improved social participation in the planning of the economy and of its social aspects. But, since planning tasks will require even in the near future a more highly activated competence, social participation can hardly be a planner function. The roles to be played by social participation and COSY organizations are to be conceived rather in a way that together they should encompass a larger scope than the COSY organizations alone; not only in that they satisfy the demand for social participation but also in that they must render the whole of the planning work more efficient and more fruitful.

Relying on the four dominant problems formulated above and on the main criteria to be satisfied in their solution a proposition may be set forth for such a further developed version of the existing COSY organizations as will play *the role of "variety-amplifier" for COSY organizations in several aspects.* The concept of variety-amplifier is interpreted in the sense of Ashby's "intelligence-amplifier" concept. The variety-amplifier differentiates problem-sensitivity for both planner and control organizations, because it indicates, in time and sensitively, if something is not in order. It gives a picture of the value system of society and of its changing, which is concomitant with development. It channels so far unused social experience purposefully and programmed, primarily in the PR stage of planning, in which it is desirable that planners think in as many varieties as possible; this amplifier role may be interpreted as a kind of extensive brainstorming function. For the denomination of a system offering the institutional framework for such participation the English word "audit" was selected. In one of the dictionaries (The Advanced Learner's Dictionary of Current English): the meaning of the word is explained as follows "official examination of accounts to see that they are in order". The word has been used recently in management literature in a wider sense than the original meaning. In the suggested system concept the meaning of the word was further extended. The system concept itself will be called *National Audit System*—NAS. In the following the most important characteristics of NAS will be outlined and summarized. The further developed system, desirable at the Second Stage, will be referred to by the abbreviation

COSY+NAS.

A form of improved participation: National Audit System

A number of details have been given of the National Audit System in the analysis of the necessity and problems of social participation. Those considerations are now going to be connected with the COSY organization of the national economy, and will be completed by a few more relevant details. For the representation of COSY and NAS combined, the use of a flow chart is sensible because, in this way, the various partial functions of NAS and its connections with the existing COSY parts may be clearly localized. The structure of the Figure is theoretically the same as that of Fig. 1.

Figure 2 shows the very simplified architecture and operational characteristics of the system concept COSY+NAS. NAS has been broken down into five partial functions. They are as follows:

NAS–I is directly connected to the central planning organization. At step A of the planning it makes proposals as to which social indicators should be built into the national economy plans, it explores which unsolved problems must be counted with and where there are such hidden tensions as escaped the attention of planners.

NAS–II is directly connected to the units of state administrative organs that make proposals, within their own sphere of authority, for the national economy plans. This function is very similar to NAS–I, only much more specific.

NAS–III is directly connected to the central planning organization as well as to each intermediate step of the planning, primarily to steps PR, EC and P. *The cooperation of central planners and NAS–III must be made programmed,* adjusted to the particular problems to be solved at each step. At step PR this function would enrich the number of feasible variations of the future. At step EP its main task may consist in exploring the subtle inconsistencies of the policy system, and in rendering explicit the consequences of envisaged decisions. At step P it may contribute to the discussion of plans. This NAS function could be *cyclically* manifest in the course of the continuous planning, in cases when, because of unexpected events, the plans must be revised, and thus *it could increase the adaptivity of the planner system.*

NAS–IV is connected directly to the operative control organizations. It would improve sensitivity to feedback information in the sense of the "requi-site law of variety". Besides—and this would be also an explicit condition of this function—it may accelerate the flow of information in a way that it bypasses long official channels.

NAS–V is connected directly to the part of the central planner organization that plans the policy system. This function has a long tradition in Hungary (the Parliament, party organs, trade unions). However, with a more formalized cooperation of COSY+NAS the contribution and efficiency of this function could be increased.

The above-described tasks of the five NAS functions indicate merely the most important features, in an analytical approach. It is, however, desirable to treat the COSY+NAS system as an integral whole. Therefore, the individual NAS functions must be coordinated so that the NAS can be a uniform subsystem within the COSY+NAS system. The uniform aspect of NAS can be described by a few such common features as differentiate it from COSY. These will be illustrated by a few examples in tabular form (see Table 1).

Finally, a few ideas will be given about the *direction in which* the rather abstract system concept of COSY+NAS *must be broken down* if we want to reveal the practical details of a living system. *A number of equivalent taxonomies* offer themselves for the break-down. The need for such a number of taxonomies must be especially stressed in the case of such a complex system as is the organizational system of the economy of a country. Therefore, *the systematization of practical taxonomies is also necessary.* An important help in this can be given by all such master models for which Figs 1 and 2 are two examples. In the course of investigations it has been found that, in the first approach, it is useful to group the directions of the break-down according to two points of view. One group can represent the *planned spheres* of the economy. The other group can comprise the *organizational subsystems* (state administrative organs, local and regional government, enterprises, etc.), in the competence sphere of which the planned spheres belong. Then, between the taxonomically ordered components of the two groups, interrelations can be revealed, systematized and in model form. In the end it can be made explicit also, to which level (national, regional, local, etc.) the planned development results belong from the point of view of the whole national economy.

The planned spheres can be interpreted as products of economic development. For the first group of the break-down the following important partial

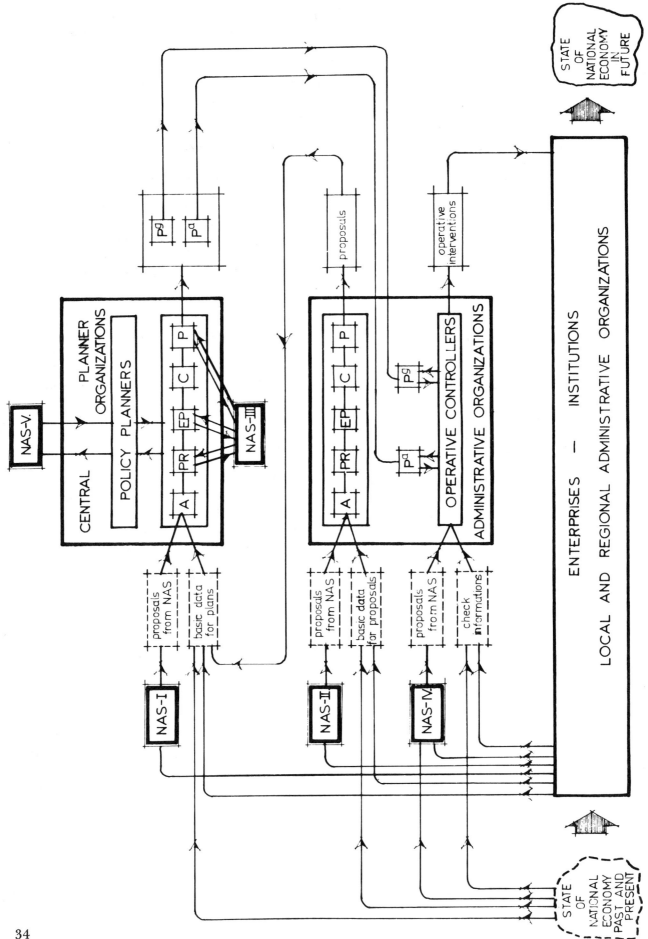

Fig. 2

34

TABLE 1

COSY	NAS
Sensitivity to variables of the plan models of the national economy.	Sensitivity to indicators of the state of subcultures and groups.
Systems view in goals, strategies, policies, and plans.	Variety-amplifier of sensitivity to the state-indicators of society.
Inclination to rational judgement.	Inclination to emotional judgement.
Regular conflict-eliminator.	Conflict-generator.
Highly organized, within a permanently existing institutional framework.	Loosely organized, within the framework of ad hoc established or activated groups.
Rigidity in changing situations.	Helps to become open-minded in changing situations.
Slows down the flow of ideas through the system (low conductivity).	Accelerates the collection of ideas and their forwarding to the competent place.

groups can be identified:
  a) Industrial and agricultural products and services (production means, consumption, etc.).
  b) Health and cultural services.
  c) Civilized environment and developed regions.
  d) Educated and qualified persons.
These spheres may be important ordering ones in that the concrete representatives of the five NAS functions can be precisely drawn up.
The suggested COSY+NAS is rather a complicated system. Our civilization, however, also tends to be increasingly complex. In this study a detail of this increasing complexity has been analyzed in an aim to identify at least the main aspects of problems within the process in the course of which the important objective to be realized is the planned development of society.

Bibliography
1. BÁGER, G. and HAJNAL, A., 'On the Organizational System of the Hungarian Economy', Systems Approaches to Developing Countries, Proceedings of the Symposium May 28-31, 1973, Algiers, Algir. A publication of the IFAC Instrument Society of America, Pittsburgh, Pennsylvania (1973).
2. BÁGER, G. and HAJNAL, A., 'The Growing Complexity of Plans and Planning' (in Hungarian), Közgazdasági Szemle, Part I and II, No. 4 and 5 (1972).
3. CHERNIAK, Y., 'Economic Systems and Economic Information' (in Russian), *Economica i Matematicheskie Metodi*, Vol. 3, No. 1 (1967).
4. HAJNAL, A., 'Organizations for vs. against creativity', Paper at Second European Meeting on Cybernetics and Systems Research, Vienna (1974). In this book.
5. MAIMINAS, Y., 'On Logical Schemes of Information Simulation (in Russian), Lectures of the Seminar on Systems of Economic Information, Academy of Sciences, USSR, Moscow (1963).
6. RAIATSKAS, R., *An Integrated System of Planning of the Economy of a Federal Republic* (in Russian), Wilnius, "Mintis" Publ. House (1972).

Optimization in simulation

H.D.D. WATSON
IBM UK Scientific Centre, Peterlee, Co. Durham, UK

1. Introduction

In very many (perhaps the majority) of simulation studies the purpose of the work is to find the 'best' design, or at least a 'good' design for the system under study. Decisions are to be made as to the optimal choice of the parameters entering the problem, e.g., for an aircraft engine (physical dimensions, compression ratios), for a freight depot (numbers of loading bays, fork lift trucks, storage areas, manpower), for a chemical process (rates of flow of feedback), or for a transportation system (number, frequency and type of vehicle).

At the present time such problems are usually solved by means of the analyst repeatedly running his simulation model under varying assumptions, and 'feeling' his way towards an acceptable solution. However, this mode of operation is slow in elapsed time, and limited by the analyst's ability to understand the interactions between the system variables. Consequently, the last few years have seen the increasing use of various pieces of code designed to put the search for optimal parameters under the complete control of the simulation program. These codes may take advantage of some special property of the system under study, or perhaps require explicit calculation of derivatives, and for such reasons are usually of limited applicability. Furthermore, the construction is often distinctly 'unfriendly' to the user.

In view of the significance of the problem and the evident requirement for such a facility, we believe that it is appropriate to investigate the introduction of a general purpose, easy to use optimization facility into a high-level simulation language. We believe that the current state of the art in both simulation and nonlinear optimization makes such an investigation timely both from the technical viewpoint and from the viewpoint of the simulation user.

We have chosen to work with the IBM continuous simulation program package CSMP III. However, the objectives which we have tried to satisfy are applicable in general:

1. Modifications of the simulation system which the user is required to carry out should be few in number and easy to implement.
2. The user should have complete flexibility in his choice of optimizing routine.
3. In making use of the simulation-optimization system, no more should be required of the user than would be the case in conventional 'stand alone' optimization applications.

Given some familiarity with internals of the CSMP III system, it turns out that it is not difficult to meet these objectives. Consequently the system which we describe is simple to create and to use, which we take to be a virtue. The orientation of the Chapter is somewhat pedagogical, in that we hope that the reader who is faced with the problem of finding optimal parameters in a continuous system, but who knows little about the internal structure of CSMP or of the optimization techniques which are available, could proceed from this point to a solution of his problem.

Progress in Cybernetics and Systems Research, Volume 2

2. Nonlinear optimization

The optimization facility which we wish to build into a simulation package has for many years been available as a stand alone technique with wide applicability *outside* the field of simulation. The general problem is that of nonlinear optimization (NLOP), and a variety of algorithms and computer codes have been evolved to solve the very many problems which arise in practice.

The general problem of NLOP may be stated as follows:

Given a function $F(\underline{x})$ of n variables $(x_1,x_2,...,x_n)$, determine the minimum value of F, say F^*, and the corresponding values of x_i, say x_i^*.

The variables x_i may in general be subject to constraints, though we shall consider only the unconstrained case. However, the constrained case may frequently be reduced to an unconstrained problem, either through transformations of the independent variables or by using a penalty function (see, for example, Fiacco and McCormick [1]). The maximisation problem may, of course, be solved by minimizing $(-F)$.

Note that $F(\underline{x})$ is an *explicit algebraic function* and we may therefore directly and immediately calculate its value for any given $\underline{x}$.

Problems which fall into this class arise very frequently, e.g., in design studies (minimize the material or cost needed to achieve a desired structural strength), in determination of the equilibrium composition of a chemical mixture (determined by minimizing the free energy), or parameter estimation in curve fitting (nonlinear regression, maximum likelihood estimation).

An NLOP routine of this type is conveniently referred to as 'an optimizer'. In use the function F is programmed in a subprogram (say CALC) under call to the optimizer (say OPTIM) which carries out systematically a series of evaluations of F by means of calls to CALC for different values of the arguments (the search parameters) and continues iterating in this fashion until an optimum is detected.

The computer linkage is straight-forward and is indicated in Fig. 1(*a*).

In this type of 'conventional' use of NLOP the objective function, $F(\underline{x})$ is explicitly given and is capable of direct and immediate algebraic calculation. We wish to extend the use of optimization to the case where $F(\underline{x})$ can only be evaluated by invoking a run of the simulation model. What we require is an interface which will put the simulation model under the control of an optimizer.

The choice of an optimizer is extremely important in simulation applications. Apart from the obvious desirability of working with a routine which has been well tested and is robust and reliable, it is extremely important to have an *efficient* optimizer, since each call for a function evaluation involves a complete run of the simulation model, and the number of such calls will increase rapidly with n.

The field of nonlinear optimization has seen intensive development in the last 15 years or so, and there are now a great number of algorithms and codes which address the problem. For an introduction to the field the reader is referred to Fletcher [2]. Much of the literature contains comparisons between different methods, but unfortunately the nature of the problem (where the results are dependent on the test functions used, the starting point chosen for the search, the criteria used for termination, and the dimensionality of the problem) makes it practically impossible to draw general conclusions.

Many users will find suitable optimization routines available in their installation libraries; others, not new to the field, will have their own preferences. Here we confine ourselves to mentioning a few of the better known techniques. The user should bear in mind that a FORTRAN implementation is required to interface with the CSMP system.

i. Variable metric or quasi-Newton methods

Much of the current literature relates to work in this area, of which perhaps the most widely known algorithm arises from the work of Davidon [3] and Fletcher and Powell [4]. However, these techniques require calculations of the gradient vectors. The latter will not be provided by a simple simulation run, and though they may be obtained by finite difference methods, we have found that this is not a reliable process on a machine of finite word length, even with the use of double precision arithmetic. We would therefore recommend the use of a direct search technique, of which ii, iii, and iv below are examples.

ii. Powell's method

This is by now almost a classical method, and is the method which we have used in the examples given in this Chapter. The particular code used was basically that of Powell's [5] own version (VAO4A), with a few diagnostic messages added. We tested the routine on four sample problems, where the dimensionality was varied between 1 and 25, and the routine did not fail in a single case to reach the opti-

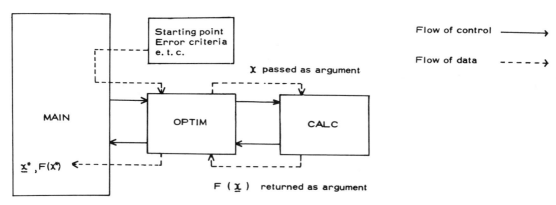

Fig. 1(*a*) Stand alone optimization

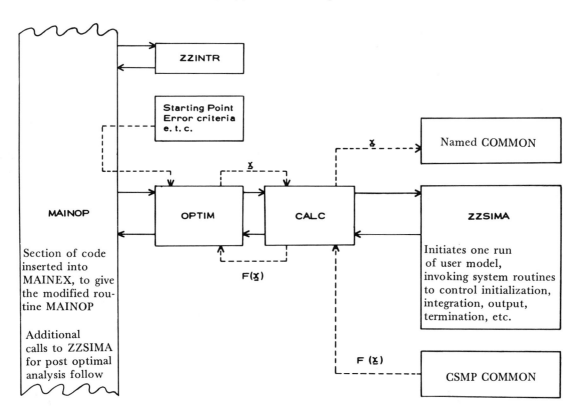

Fig. 1(*b*) CSMP III—optimization interface

mum. The routine also seemed to us to be efficient.

iii. The simplex method
This is originally due to Nelder and Mead [6], though there are now many variants. It is known, however, that the number of function evaluations

required by the method increases rapidly with n.

iv. Random search methods
There is some evidence that methods of this type may be computationally advantageous for large n. See, e.g., Yvon [7].

3. Implementation in CSMP III

To interface the optimizer to CSMP we require that each time CALC is called by OPTIM, the appropriate values should be assigned to parameters in the simulation model, a run of the model should then be invoked, and the value of the objective F should be returned to CALC. Thus CALC becomes a linkage routine which accepts values of the search parameters from OPTIM, and after invoking the simulation model, returns a value of the objective back to OPTIM.

We have adopted the naming conventions of F for the objective function, and a dimensional array X in a named COMMON block (MINE) which is accessed by both CALC and the CSMP program to contain the current values of the search parameters.

The action of CALC, an example of which is shown in Fig. 2 is as follows:

1. On entry to CALC OPTIM passes as arguments the values of the search parameters. These are placed in COMMON/MINE/. If the optimizer is coded in double precision, the search parameters may be conveniently converted to single precision at this stage to correspond with the CSMP system.

2. A call is made to the CSMP routine ZZSIMA. This is a system routine which initializes the model, controls the integration, calls output routines as appropriate and in general performs the necessary 'house keeping' and monitoring tasks to conduct one run of the simulation model.

3. When control returns to CALC, the value of F is obtained from CSMP (blank) COMMON using the symbol table for locating F.

4. The value of the objective function is passed back to OPTIM in appropriate precision.

5. CALC may be used to write out an iteration log, i.e., values of the objective and the search parameters for each call to the model. Such an iteration log is of use in a variety of ways, for example, in checking the progress of the optimization where some limit has been placed on either the computer time or the maximum number of iterations.

Little of this is 'seen' by the problem programmer. He must declare a COMMON block MINE containing the array X; he must assign the values in this array to his search variables; and he must define an objective function F.

```
      SUBROUTINE CALC(N,DX,DF)
      COMMON/ZZSYMB/SYMB(1)
      COMMON/ZZPOIN/ID(8),NOSYMB
      COMMON/MINE/X(30)
      COMMON C(1600)
      DOUBLE PRECISION DX(N),DF,CHARF
      DATA CHARF/'F'/
      NOUT=20
      IF=1
      CALL CSTORE(CHARF,1,SYMB,NOSYMB,K,IF)
      IF(K.EQ.1)GO TO 101
      DO 1 I=1,N
    1 X(I)=DX(I)
      REWIND 13
      REWIND 15
      CALL ZZSIMA
      F=C(IF)
      DF=F
      WRITE(NOUT,100)DF,(DX(I),I=1,N)
  100 FORMAT(24X,E21.14,(T56,E20.10,5X,E20.10))
      RETURN
  101 WRITE(NOUT,102)
  102 FORMAT(//' OBJECTIVE FUNCTION NOT DEFINED IN CSMP PROBLEM'//)
      RETURN
      END
```

Fig. 2 An example of a linkage routine, CALC

```
      SUBROUTINE MA1NOP
      COMMON/ZZSYMB/SYMB(1)
      COMMON/ZZHIST/KEEP,NALARM,IZ0000,IZ0001,HIST(1)
      COMMON/ZZPOIN/NOINTG,NISTO,IINT,IPARM,IFUNC,IOUT,IARRA,IARRI
     .,NOSYMB,ILAST,NMEMRY,NFUNCT,NPOINT,NFIXED
      COMMON/ZZEXIN/TIMEX,TNEXT,TPRINT,TPLOT,TLAST,H,TIMER(8),DTIME
     1,IEND,IFIRST,IPLOT,IPRINT,IERR,ISTEP,JTEM,KKGRAF,KFIXED
     2,OPT,DPL,ISTINT,INTYPE,KLOCK,KRERUN,KTERM,KGRAPH,NGRAPH,KPROUT,K14
     2,KPOINT,KABS,KREL,ALAST,RLAST,KPRINT,KTITLE,KFINIS,KRANGE,KRANG
     3,K2R,LINK,LINE,LINE1,IDEBUG,NLINES,KLINE,IFCOUN,KPOIN,ILFUN
     4,IDXFAM,NFAM,KFAM,FAM(50),INAME(220),INDEXG(220),RANG(440)
      COMMON/ZZINTP/WORD,A(12),ISTART,LETERS(73),KA(6),ITYPE,IPAREN
      REAL*8 TIMEX,TNEXT,TPRINT,TPLOT,TLAST,H,TIMER,WORD,A
      INTEGER*2 INAME,INDEXG
      COMMON C(2),DELT,DELMIN,FINTIM,PRDEL,OUTDEL,DELMAX
      REAL*8 TIME,DELT,FINTIM,PRDEL,OUTDEL,DELMAX,DELMIN,D(7)
      EQUIVALENCE(D(1),TIME,C(1))
      EQUIVALENCE (IWORD,DWORD,VALUE)
      DOUBLE PRECISION X(30),S(30),ESCALE,F,E(30)
C
C *** SYSTEM EXECUTION CONTROL STATEMENTS
C
C
C *** INITIALISATION OF RESERVED WORDS AND COUNTERS FOR JOB
C
      CALL ZZINIT
C
C*********************************************************************
C
C          OPTIMISING SECTION
C
C          CONTROL PARAMETERES FOR OPTIMISING ROUTINE ARE READ FROM
C          CARD INPUT AND PRINTED.
C          CONTROL IS THEN PASSED TO OPTIMISING ROUTINE
C
C*********************************************************************
C
      CALL ZZINTR
      GO TO(9,1050,1050),IERR
    9 CONTINUE
C
C *** SET I/O UNIT NUMBERS
C
      NIN=5
      NOUT=20
      READ(NIN,3,ERR=999)N,IPRINT,ICONV,MAXIT,ESCALE
    3 FORMAT(4I5,E12.4)
      READ(NIN,2)(E(I),I=1,N)
      READ(NIN,2)(X(I),I=1,N)
    2 FORMAT(E10.2)
      WRITE(NOUT,8)N,IPRINT,ICONV,MAXIT,ESCALE
    8 FORMAT(1H1,' N  = ',I5,' IPRINT= ',I5,' ICONV = ',I5,' MAXIT = ',
     *I5,'  ESCALE = ',E12.4)
      WRITE(NOUT,5)
    5 FORMAT(' PRESCRIBED ERRORS')
      WRITE(NOUT,200)(E(I),I=1,N)
  200 FORMAT(2X,E10.4)
      WRITE(NOUT,6)
    6 FORMAT(' INITIAL COORDINATES')
      WRITE(NOUT,200)(X(I),I=1,N)
      WRITE(NOUT,7)
    7 FORMAT(//10X,21H ITERATION SEQUENCES //)
      CALL OPTIM(X,E,N,F,ESCALE,IPRINT,ICONV,MAXIT)
C
C*********************************************************************
C
C          END OF OPTIMISING SECTION.RERUNS FOLLOW
C
C*********************************************************************
C
C
C *** READ INPUT/OUTPUT CONTROL AND RUN OR CASE SIMULATION CONTROL
C *** READ CSMP DATA STATEMENTS
C
 1000 CALL ZZINTR
C
C *** TEST FOR JOB END OR ERROR EXIT
C
      GO TO(1010,1050,1000),IERR
C
C *** BRANCH DEPENDING ON INTEGRATION TYPE
C *** PERFORM INTEGRATION OUTPUT
C
 1010 CONTINUE
      CALL ZZSIMA
      GO TO 1000
  999 WRITE(NOUT,998)
  998 FORMAT(//'    ERROR IN DATA SUPPLIED TO OPTIM')
 1050 CONTINUE
      RETURN
      END
```

Fig. 3 Example of modified MAINEX routine

To invoke the optimization facility the user takes advantage of the CSMP structure to substitute the main line execution phase program, MAINEX, with a special purpose program, MAINOP. This routine is invoked by the 3 FORTRAN statements CALL MAINOP, RETURN, END placed immediately after the STOP card. The routine MAINOP reads numeric data which is delineated by the CSMP statements INPUT and ENDINPUT and placed in the input card stream. This data consists of control information such as the starting point for the search, the accuracy required, the maximum step length, the maximum number of iterations permitted, etc. MAINOP then passes control to OPTIM. As OPTIM searches for a minimum, according to its algorithmic strategy, each time it requires a 'function' evaluation it calls CALC, which invokes a run of the model and returns the required value, in the manner described above. When the optimum is detected, control is returned to MAINOP, which reads in CSMP output control or other execution time statements separated by END cards in the usual manner, so that output describing the behavior of the system at the optimum may be obtained.

The complete linkage is illustrated in Fig. 1(*b*), and the close correspondence with Fig. 1(*a*) will be apparent.

MAINOP differs from MAINEX (which is distributed in source form with the CSMP III system) only in that an extra section of code is inserted to read the type of control data which any optimizer will require (such as has been described above), and (optionally) to write this data on the printer for record and verification purposes before passing control to OPTIM.

An example of the coding additions necessary in MAINOP is given in Fig. 3. In this case the optimizer was a version of Powell's [5] well known method, (which we have used in the examples discussed in this Chapter), and the control data which is to be read in corresponds to this routine.

As we have seen, there is considerable variety possible in the choice of an optimization routine. It is the author's experience that different institutions frequently have strong preferences for one 'favorite' routine, and MAINEX can be modified accordingly, so that the user is not restricted in his choice of optimizer.

The routines MAINOP and CALC may be included in the input stream following the STOP card, or, particularly when the system is operational on a production basis, compiled into a user library.

4. Example 1: The rate constants of a chemical reaction

The first example, which we describe in considerable detail in order to give a clear understanding of the use of the optimization system, is a problem in reaction kinetics discussed by Herbold [8]. It is an example of the use of the optimizer in parameter estimation in differential equations.

In this class of problem one is given a set of differential equations containing certain undetermined parameters, and some measurements of the behavior of the system. The problem is to determine those values of the parameters for which the best fit to the data is obtained—i.e., the problem is a type of regression analysis.

The system we consider here is the reaction

$$A + B \rightleftharpoons C + D$$

where A, B, C, and D ($A = A(t)$, etc.) represent the amounts of four species present at time t. The system is described in terms of unknown rate constants k_1 and k_2 by the equations

$$\dot{A}(t) = -k_1 AB - 0.01 A - k_2 A$$

$$\dot{B}(t) = -k_1 AB - 0.05 BD$$

$$\dot{C}(t) = k_1 AB$$

$$\dot{D}(t) = 0.01 A + k_2 A - 0.05 BD$$

where the initial conditions are $A(0) = 1$, $B(0) = 1.03$, $C(0) = D(0) = 0$. Experimental measurements of $A(t)$ and $C(t)$ are available. The problem is to determine the unknown reaction constants from this data.

The problem is shown in Fig. 4 programmed for CSMP. The experimental data is entered as functions. Trial values for k_1 and k_2 are picked up from named COMMON as described in the previous section, and loaded into the locations K1 and K2 from the vector X using the CSMP SCALAR function. The system of equations given above is solved. The CSMP PROCEDURE calculates a value for F, the objective, which is the sum of squares of the differences between the calculated values (A, C) and the observed values (AU, CU) taken at the times to which the data relates, $t = 0, 10, 20, ..., 60$. (The variable I is used as a counter to indicate when time has been incremented by 10 units, or 50 integration steps.)

Because MAINOP has been invoked the program automatically minimizes the objective F as a function of k_1 and k_2, i.e., k_1 and k_2 are determined by a least squares fit to the data. The data between the

```
£££CCNTINUOUS SYSTEM MODELING PROGRAM  III   V1M1   TRANSLATOR OUTPUT£££

/      COMMON/MINE/X(30)
FIXED I
INITIAL
    I=49
    F=0.0
AFGEN AA=0.0,1.0,10.C,0.483,20.0,0.281,30.0,0.191,...
      40.0,0.134,50.C,0.0S7,60.0,0.C65
AFGEN CC=0.0,0.0,10.0,0.419,20.0,0.563,30.0,0.629,...
      40.0,0.666,50.0,0.6E9,6C.0,0.708
    K1,K2=SCALAR(X(1))
TIMER CELT=0.20, FINTIM=60.0, PRDEL=1C.0, OLTDEL=2.0
METHCD RKSFX
DYNAMIC
    A=INTGRL(1.0,-K1*A*B-0.01*A-K2*A)
    B=INTGRL(1.03,-K1*A*B-0.05*B*D)
    C=INTGRL(0.0,K1*A*B)
    D=INTGRL(0.0,0.01*A+K2*A-0.05*B*D)
    AU=AFGEN(AA,TIME)
    CU=AFGEN(CC,TIME)
PROCEDURE  F =FCN(AU,A,CU,C)
    IF(KEEP.NE.1) GO TO 1
    I=I+1
    IF(I.NE.50)GO TO 1
    I=0
    F = F +(AU-A)*(AU-A)+(CU-C)*(CU-C)
  1 CONTINUE
ENDPRO
END
INPUT
    2     1    1   9S9+01.0000E+03
+01.00E-04
+01.00E-04
+01.00E-02
+05.00E-02
ENDINPUT
OUTPUT K1,K2,A,AU,C,CU
OUTPUT A,AU,C,CU
END
STOP

OUTPUT VARIABLE SEQUENCE
I      F      K1     K2     ZZ1002 A      ZZ1005 B      ZZ1008 C
ZZ1011 D      AU     CU     F
```

```
£££ TRANSLATION TABLE CCNTENTS £££        CURRENT        MAXIMUM

MACRC AND STATEMENT OUTPUTS               21             600
STATEMENT INPUT WORK AREA                 64             1900
INTEGRATCRS+MEMORY BLCCK OUTPUTS          4 + 0          300
PARAMETERS+FUNCTION GENERATORS            4 + 2          400
STORAGE VARIABLES+INTEGRATOR ARRAYS       0 + 0/2        50
HISTORY AND MEMORY BLOCK NAMES            21             50
MACRO CEFINITIONS ANC NESTED MACROS       6              50
MACRO STATEMENT STORAGE                   13             125
LITERAL CONSTANT STORAGE                  2              100
SORT SECTIONS                             2              20
MAXIMUM STATEMENTS IN SECTION             16             600


    CALL MAINCP
    RETURN
    END
```

```
£££END OF TRANSLATOR OUTPUT£££
```

Fig. 4 Formulation of Example 1 in CSMP III

INPUT and ENDINPUT cards is the control data for the optimizer-starting point, termination criteria, etc.

As the optimization search proceeds an iteration log is recorded (Fig. 5). When the optimum is detected, the problem is run once more (because of the inclusion of the second END card) to print the optimal values of k_1 and k_2, and to compare the observed values (AU, CU) with the calculated best fit values (A, C) (Fig. 6). It will be seen that the values

```
ITERATION    3            71 FUNCTION VALUES

    OBJECTIVE BELCW                    SEARCH VARIABLE VALUES BELOW

      0.136454691528340D-03         0.76061703310D-01      0.39077263960D-02
      0.219560373807330D-03         0.75033876360D-01      0.38196281150D-02
      0.143270313856190D-03         0.76418836560D-01      0.38776213770D-02
      0.136172835462280D-03         0.76126066740D-01      0.39023007960D-02


ITERATION    4            74 FUNCTION VALUES

    OBJECTIVE BELCW                    SEARCH VARIABLE VALUES BELOW

      0.136172835462280D-03         0.76126066740D-01      0.39023007960D-02
      0.142339355079460D-03         0.75943751940D-01      0.37671297360D-02
      0.136200396869730D-03         0.76087657150D-01      0.38738023328D-02
      0.136104907142C0D-03          0.76108421500D-01      0.38892183430D-02


ITERATICN    4            77 FUNCTION VALUES

    OBJECTIVE BELOW                    SEARCH VARIABLE VALUES BELOW

      0.136104907142C0D-03          0.76108421500D-01      0.38892183430D-02
      0.136414921144020D-03         0.76155139700D-01      0.38707102900D-02
      0.136872142320500D-03         0.76208421500D-01      0.38807887110D-02
      0.136104717967100D-03         0.76110554730D-01      0.38890385190D-02


ITERATION    5            80 FUNCTION VALUES

    OBJECTIVE BELCW                    SEARCH VARIABLE VALUES BELOW

      0.136104717967100D-03         0.76110554730D-01      0.38890385190D-02
      0.138380462685830D-03         0.76010554740D-01      0.38148969510D-02
      0.136090937303380D-03         0.76112286650D-01      0.38903225930D-02
      0.136289585498160D-03         0.76138766460D-01      0.39059551420D-02
      0.136115224449900D-03         0.76118681210D-01      0.38950636190D-02


ITERATICN    5            84 FUNCTION VALUES

    OBJECTIVE BELOW                    SEARCH VARIABLE VALUES BELOW

      0.136090937303380D-03         0.76112286650D-01      0.38903225930D-02
      0.136106682475660D-03         0.76116151800D-01      0.38914268440D-02


OPTIMUM REACHED
```

Fig. 5 Example 1—iteration log

we obtained are (to 3 significant figures) $k_1 = 0.0761$, $k_2 = 0.00389$, in complete agreement with Herbold.

Note that the equations treated here are nonlinear.

We have gone through this rather simple example in some detail so that it may be quite clear just how little is required of the user in invoking the optimization facility.

5. Example 2: A servo control system

We now consider an example which consists in the design of an optimal control system. Such systems are widely studied by simulation, and are of two types. In regulatory control we are concerned with taking action to keep a variable (speed, concentration, temperature, etc.) as close as possible to some set-point. In servo control we are concerned with the manner in which a variable responds to a change in set-point. In both cases we are interested in the response of the controlled variables to a disturbance such as a step change in one of the variables of the system. The general requirement is that the response of the controlled variable should be as 'good' as possible. Different measures of the 'goodness' of response (or indeed a combination of measures) may be taken, such as the maximum error arising, the time taken before the error stabilizes within some defined limit, or the integral of the square of the error (ISE). In all cases we would like to choose parameters in a control system to minimize whichever of the above variables seems most appropriate.

We consider here an example of such a control

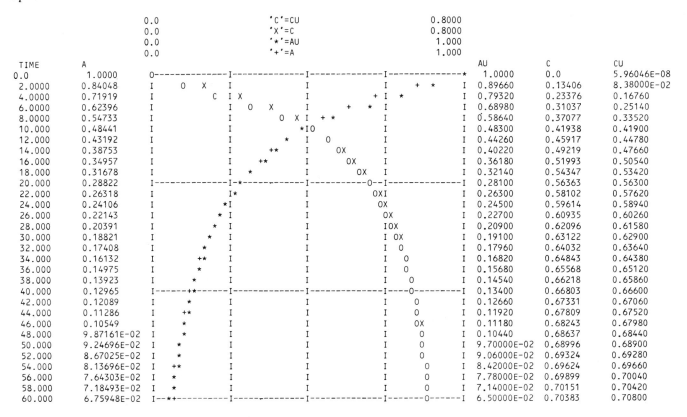

Fig. 6   Example 1—output of results

system given by Syn and Wyman [9]. It represents the servo control of the output temperature from a heat exchanger by proportional, integral and differential control signals. This type of 3 mode control system (or a 2 mode system where the differential term is omitted) is extremely common, and only the dynamics of the system under control will change.

In our example it is required to control the temperature of the output flow of a heat exchanger, T_{out}, to a set point T_s. The complete system is shown in Fig. 7. The output temperature is measured by a thermocouple which gives a response T_m, which of course, lags behind T_{out}. The difference $(T_s - T_m)$ provides an error signal e to actuate the controller. The controller output, V_c, actuates a heating system and determines the temperature, T_{in}, of the controlling input stream of the heat exchanger. This in turn determines the temperature T_{out}.

We have not bothered to specify in detail the dynamics of the process (heating system, heat exchanger, or thermocouple). For our purposes this is irrelevant. The process can be regarded as a 'black box', the dynamics of which may be highly non-linear.

The control signal V_c is made up of three components

$$V_c = V_p + V_i + V_d$$

and three corresponding parameters k_p, k_i, and k_d as follows:

i) $V_p = k_p e$. This represents a signal which is proportional to the present state of the system.

ii) $V_i(t) = k_i \int_0^t e(t)\, dt$. This represents a signal determined by the past behavior of the system. If e remains nonzero for a significant time, V_i builds up correspondingly to a large value which will force e back to zero. Unlike the other two terms, V_i can remain nonzero when the system is in the steady state with e zero. It will in fact settle out to a value which gives the correct steady state control signal, V_c.

44

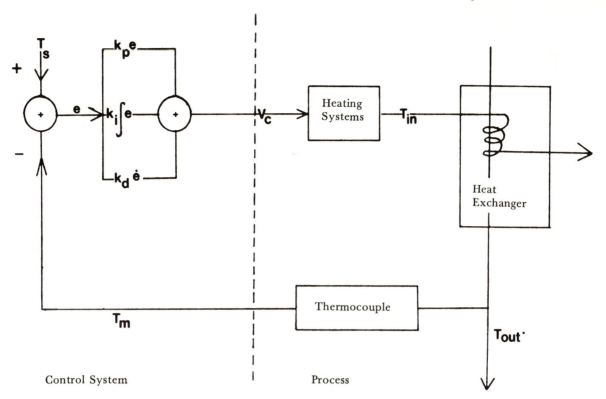

Fig. 7 Three mode control system

iii) $V_d = k_d \dot{e}$. This is a 'look ahead' term. If T_m is falling $(\dot{e} > 0)$ or rising $(\dot{e} < 0)$ very rapidly, this term comes into play to counteract such rapid changes, which might otherwise lead to a large overshoot of the set-point.

It is required to determine optimal values of the parameters k_p, k_i, and k_d so that the response of T_{out} to a step change in T_s is optimal, where the criterion is that the objective

$$F = ISE = \int_0^T e^2 \, dt$$

should be a minimum, where T is the run time of the simulation, and is large compared with the settling time of the system.

With initial values of 2.0 for k_p, k_i, and k_d, and a request for accuracy of ± 0.05 in each of the k's (which in fact implies that iteration of the search continued until the modular difference between two successive values of all the k's was less than 0.005, a considerably smaller tolerance), the search terminated after 58 calls to the simulation model, giving

optimal values for the k's which contained errors of less than 5 parts in 1000.

To give an indication of the cost and ease of use of the approach, the entire model was programmed and run, and the solutions verified, in one day. The CPU time used was less than 15 min on a 360/44, which is not a fast machine by current standards.

There is little point in showing the response of system in detail. As T_s is stepped from 20° to 25°, T_{out} and T_m rise rapidly and overshoot the new set-point, with a damped oscillatory behavior. The proportional term follows $(T_s - T_m)$; the differential term leads T_m by 90° before settling out at the current steady state value.

6. Example 3: Corporate investment planning

The third example which we discuss is a problem of optimal investment sizing in an industrial organization, and is included to bring out several points of general methodology in the areas of model formulation, validation, and in the use which is made of 'optimized' results.

45

Gutierrez and Brennan [10] have described and discussed in detail a model of a firm competing for orders in an open market. The system is viewed as consisting of four sections (Fig. 8). The *order* section models the degree to which the firm is successful in obtaining orders against the background of an assumed total marked demand for its products. The *production/distribution* section models the operational function of the firm, and the constraints imposed by the availability of such resources as machinery, space, and office capacity. These resources may be augmented by decisions initiated in the *planning*

section, and the manner in which they come into productive use (after allowing for the delays inherent in procurement, construction, commissioning and training) is represented in the *capital equipment* section. The model involves over 150 variables, though this complexity is somewhat masked by the elegant formulation of the authors, who make extensive use of nested MACRO functions.

We postulated a specific economic environment for the model, and posed the question as to the *optimal* investments in the differing resources, discarding the planning section of Gutierrez and

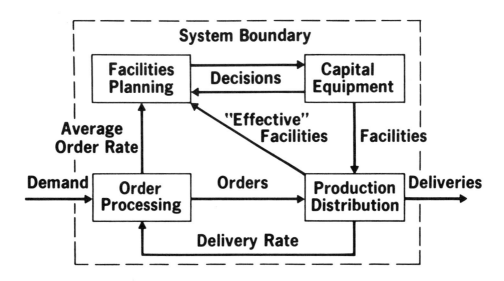

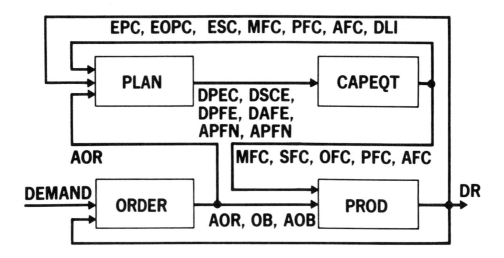

Fig. 8 Facilities planning model—conceptual overview and corresponding model structure

Brennan. Specifically, we made assumptions as to the behavior of market demand (such as might be forecast in practice), and ascribed costs and revenue to activities. A profit function thus derived was maximized within an assumed planning horizon.

The optimization procedure did indeed give optimal magnitudes for acquisitions of machinery, inventory capacity and office accommodation, together with consequent plant and land requirements. However, this study highlighted certain general points which deserve consideration.

The first concerns the validation of results. In the model outlined above, the introduction of new capacity gave rise to an oscillatory behavior in most of the system variables, such as order rate, production rate and inventory level. These predictions could not be accepted without further analysis. (They are, in fact, accurate within the assumptions of the model, and arise from strong feedback between the production/distribution and order sections.) This leads us to emphasize that however convenient may be the use of an automated procedure, results so obtained must sill be validated, which remains a matter for the analyst's intuition and skill.

Secondly, an automated search procedure may force a model into abnormal conditions which the author did not anticipate, and he should be alive to this possibility. For example, the present model could have contrived to manufacture products at a great loss, and make a profit by selling negative quantities. This was precluded by imposing the necessary positivity constraints.

Finally, results obtained are only optimal within the framework of the model, and there will often be extraneous factors to take into consideration. It is very doubtful if the fluctuations in activity described in the present model would be judged acceptable on a variety of grounds, and one would want to explore how they could be mitigated. However, this by no means reduces the utility of the 'optimal' solution, which remains as a base case against which other solutions can be quantitatively compared.

References

1. FIACCO, A.V. and McCORMICK, G.P., *Nonlinear Programming: Sequential Unconstrained Minimization Techniques*, Wiley, New York (1968).
2. FLETCHER, R. (Ed.), *Optimization*, Academic Press, London (1969).
3. DAVIDON, W.C., AEC Research and Development Rep. No. ANL-5990 (Revised) (1959).
4. FLETCHER, R. and POWELL, M.J.D., *Computer Journal* 6, 163 (1963).
5. POWELL, M.J.D., *Computer Journal* 7, 155 (1964).
6. NELDER, J.A. and MEAD, R., *Computer Journal* 7, 308 (1965).
7. YVON, J.P., *Minimization Algorithms, Mathematical Theorems, and Computer Results* (edit. by G. Szego), Academic Press, London (1972).
8. HERBOLD, R.J., Proc 1970 SCSC, p. 73 (1970).
9. SYN, W.M. and WYMAN, D.G., DSL/44 Users' Manual, IBM Corporation (1968).
10. GUTIERREZ, L.T. and BRENNAN, R.D., IBM Technical Publication No. GE20-0349 (1971).

The control of complex systems

Professor ROBBIN R. HOUGH
School of Economics and Management,
Oakland University, Michigan, USA

Introduction

The purpose of the work discussed herein is the further development of a class of intelligent population models which promises to substantially alter users' perceptions of appropriate economic, ecological, and social policies. The models so described are based upon a restatement of General Systems Theory which has been developed by the writer over the course of the past five years. It is beyond the scope of this Chapter to provide an outline of that work. However, the work is far enough along to allow a description of the framework for analysis which the restatement makes available to the user.

The central thesis of the work is that the social behaviors adopted by any population are based on patterns of process deficiencies. It will be seen to follow from the thesis that conventional engineering-type controls exert no visible influence on social behavior. However, they do result in system behaviors which are the *unintentional* consequences of the engineering control. A class of educational policies will be defined, and these policies, if utilized, lead to the change of social behaviors.

A class of population models

It has long been recognized that populations confront their environments as organized wholes. Such diverse writers as Boulding [1], von Bertalanffy [2], Hawley [3], and Ardrey [4] have made this observation. Miller [5] has suggested that as we move from universe to particle, distinguishing systems within systems, we may treat the elements of a system themselves. By his analysis, it can be concluded that a distinction should be drawn between the behavior of a population and the behavior of elements of that population.

Social behavior

The literature on the characteristic behavior forms of populations is extensive and need not be quoted here; however, it is useful to simply list a number of the more predominant forms. These forms are migration, conflict, mutualism, parasitism, mitosis, commensalism, miniaturization, and reproduction. For the purposes of the present Chapter, these behaviors will be called *social behaviors* and will be seen to play an important role in the development of the population as a whole. Migration, as has been discussed by Christian [6], may serve to reduce the pressures on the well adapted members of a population, while forcing the least-adapted to find an alternative habitat. Violence, as discussed by Hough [7], may serve to reduce population pressure or to accelerate the division of labor and a variety of other social processes. Similar relevant observations have been made on each of the other behavior forms listed.

Life-styles

The social behaviors of a population may be con-

Progress in Cybernetics and Systems Research, Volume 2

trasted with the *life-styles* of the population elements; that is, specialization and division of labor characterize the internal organization of the population. The impact of that organization is to determine an array of tasks to be carried out by the population elements. Rappaport [8] explicitly defines the range of activities to be carried out by the population elements in a simple agricultural society and the allocation of human energy to each of those tasks. Similarly, Mintzberg [9] describes the allocation of managerial time to a series of less clearly defined but equally characteristic tasks in the context of a modern industrial organization.

Process

Now, consider a means for describing such a population or the elements of a population which allow us to treat the population or the elements as essentially independent from but occasionally reacting to environmental change. The population or element is an energy-consuming organization which obeys the laws of thermodynamics; that is to say, it must continuously take in more energy than it produces or it will be subject to entropic decay. Two forms of organization will be evident at either level of analysis.

Process and temporal organization

Temporal organization will be evident. Much of the earlier discussion of the temporal organization of populations has centered on birth and death processes. An insistence that the population is subject to the laws of thermodynamics suggests that we must be concerned with changes in the *outputs* and the *structure* of a population as well as the *mass* of a population. Quite simply, the intake of nutrients and information requires that the population be organized to (1) receive those energy inputs and to store and metabolize them, and (2) produce certain outputs, including structural elements, and to store and transport them. As the literature of operations research amply testifies, temporal organization cannot be adequately described solely in terms of birth and death processes. Fredericksen [10] and others have only of late begun to point out the pitfalls inherent in the simpler approach.

Process limits and spatial organization

Spatial organization will also be evident. Each of the temporal processes involved has implicit spatial requirements. Thus, a temporal description will inadequately capture those dimensions of population organization which are dictated by spatial constraints. The works of Schelling [11] and others [12] alert

us to the potential importance of spatial organization in the construction of systems models. Some of the more interesting implications of spatial organization are discussed in Christian [6], Galle [13], and Ardrey [14]. MacArthur's [15] seminal studies are also of great importance.

Spatial and temporal organization can be seen to have implications for both the behavior of the population and that of the elements of the population. By the simple description above we may think of the population or its elements as organized along the lines suggested by Fig. 1. Temporally, energy flows from A to B; spatially, channels, processors, and storage require space. Channel, storage, or processing deficiencies or overloads may be viewed as imperatives which demand behavior changes. By our description, social behavior would result only when energy flow or capacity bounds were transgressed. Such a point of view is consistent with Ashby's [16] observations on complex systems; that is, no variation in the functioning of the population would be observed until such time as one or more of a range of limits had been broached.

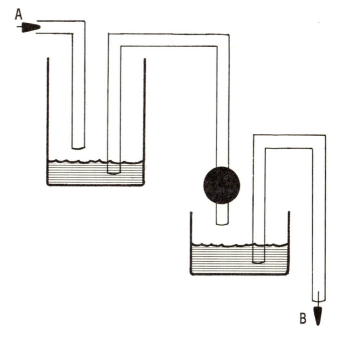

Fig. 1

The implications of energy process population models

The macro-policy implications of an energy process

population model can be easily illustrated with reference to the current food-price inflation. The demonstration associated with a model of caloric-price determination by Hough [17] allows us to conclude that under normal conditions the real demand for food is calorically determined. The money demand will fluctuate also according to the level of income. It follows that the equation of exchange may be altered from

$$Y = MV = PQ$$

to

$$Y = MV = P_1 Q_1 + P_2 Q_2$$

where $P_1 Q_1$ expresses the level of food prices and the total caloric production, while $P_2 Q_2$ expresses the level of prices and production of all other goods. In both cases, Y stands for the level of income, M stands for the level of the money supply, and V stands for the velocity of circulation. It follows from this formulation that food-induced price inflation cannot be controlled by a restrictive monetary policy without causing unemployment in the non-food factor. The seemingly paradoxical behavior of the U.S. system since about 1960 and the beginnings of Food for Peace can be explained, therefore, in a straightforward and simple way. If examined carefully, food-price behavior in the 1934-1937 period followed a similar pattern. In the latter case, the problems were induced by fertilizer and weather-related shortages rather than by export-generated caloric deficiencies. Not surprisingly, however, these periods were both characterized by substantial changes in birth rates and internal migration.

In general, earlier descriptions provided the basis for models of populations in direct functional relationships of one kind or another. At best, these models imply a kind of simple thalamic governance of social behavior. The type of model described above provides the basis for an entirely different class of models. The link between the energy-driven population model and an intelligent population model is a model of cognition, to which we now turn.

A model of cognition

A problem which is shared by the information-retrieval theorist and the cognitive theorist is that of developing an adequate model of the description and manipulation of data. In the case of the information-

retrieval theorist, the job is the retrieval of a document most relevant to the query generated by the system user. In the case of the cognitive theorist, the problem may be described in quite analogous terms. An appropriate behavior must be retrieved with respect to each pattern of deficiencies and overloads which confronts the population or population element. As will be seen, a model which appropriately defines the boundaries of the retrieval problem is most suggestive in terms of the outlines of the cognition problem.

A simple model of information retrieval

Assume that there is a collection of messages and that each message is described by a list of words. Consider an easily applied set of rules which might be utilized to search the collection for those messages most relevant to a given query stated in the vocabulary of the collection. The rule is, count the number of words that appear in the query and that also appear in the message. The score for each message will then be represented by the count for the message. Having provided a count for each message in the collection, the collection may be rank ordered according to the counts and their relevance to the query thus determined.

The preceding model of the retrieval process may be stated in more formal terms. Suppose a set of messages, $D = d_i$ $(i=1,...,d)$ is indexed by a set of terms, $T = t_i$ $(i=1,...,t)$. The indexed set of messages may be represented by a $d \times t$ matrix (C) where each of the d rows represents a message, each of the t columns a term, and all matrix cells contain 1 or 0, according to whether or not the corresponding term appears in the message.

A simple model of information retrieval may now be represented by

$$R = CW \qquad (1)$$

where R is a $d \times 1$ vector of weights on messages and W is a $t \times 1$ vector of weights on terms. A weight of, say, 1 might be assigned to each term in W in which the searcher is interested and 0 to each term of no interest. The multiplication of the matrix C by the vector W so defined then yields the vector R such that the message containing the largest number of terms receives the highest weight.

The model above is a generalization of the majority of information-retrieval models now in use. It covers the class of so-called coordinate systems and assumes, of course, that the weight to be applied to a given message is a linear function of the weights on the terms contained in the message.

A linear associative retrieval model

The basic model may be improved by allowing previously received messages to alter the retrieval order of messages so as to reflect relations of synonymy and contiguity between terms. Suppose that, for W in Eq. (1), we substitute the following equation:

$$W = \lambda C^T R + Q \qquad (2)$$

Substituting in Eq. (1), we get

$$R = C[I - \lambda C^T C]^{-1} Q \qquad (3)$$

where Q is the original query and λ is a constant which may vary between 0 and 1. Equation (3) lies at the heart of the class of linear-associative retrieval systems defined by Guilliano [18].

If the row elements in the matrix C are normalized so as to sum to 1 before the indicated operations are carried out, the inverse matrix is a $t \times t$ matrix, each cell of which contains the value of an associative bond of the form $f(ij)/f(i)f(j)$. Thus, each row may be interpreted as a thesaurus of terms relating to the row term. The cell values may range from 0 to 0.99 where 0 represents the absence of a relationship and 0.99 represents either perfect complementarity or perfect substitutability.

The thesaurus so constructed thus makes possible the weighting of an incoming message so as to reflect "meanings" previously established. Four factors will thus come to determine the relevance of a previously stored message to the query. These are

1. The number of terms in the query which match the terms in previously stored messages.
2. The relative frequency with which terms in the query appear in the entire collection of previously stored messages.
3. The number of terms in the collection which are associated with the terms in the query.
4. The strength of the associations between the terms in the query and the terms of the collection.

The control of intelligent population models

By combining the two classes of model discussed above, we may define a class of intelligent population models. The chief properties of these models are

1. The current state of a model is defined in terms of information or nutrient flow, storage, or processing deficiencies or overloads.
2. The behaviors of a model are defined in terms of their impact on energy flows to population elements.

Table 2

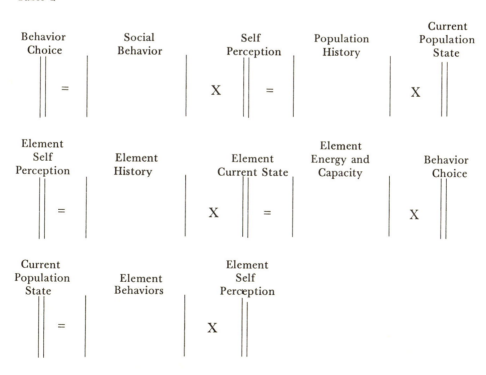

Table 3

Bank

Holding	.14
Regulations	.13
Loans	.12
Discount	.12
Regulation	.08
Mergers	.07
Commission	.06
Company	.06
Empirical	.06
Rate	.06

Consumer

Decomposability	.17
Elasticities	.12
Price	.12
Functions	.10
Insurance	.09
Prices	.08
Chances	.07
Level	.07
Index	.07
Buying	.07

Entrepreneur

Sociological	.09
Firm	.06
Models	.04
Economic	.03
Social	.02

Firm

Size	.36
Product	.11
Inputs	.09
Oligopoly	.09
Monopolistic	.09
Jurisdiction	.09
Output	.07
Nationalized	.07
Rate	.06
Opportunity	.06

Table 4

Bank

Central	.82
Reserve Requirements	.70
Banks	.55
Ceiling	.52
Treasury	.49
Money Supply	.45
Loan	.43
Credit	.40
Velocity	.37
Reserve	.36

Consumer

Utility	.59
Maximization	.33
Income Taxes	.28
Income	.27
Maximum	.24
Property	.20
Relief Payments	.20
Per Capita	.18
Education	.17
Demand	.15

Entrepreneur

Attitude	.32
Conflict	.32
Activity	.24
Commercial	.22
Formation	.22
Legal	.22
Budget	.18
Creation	.18
Economic	.18
Export	.18

Firm

Output	.37
Profit	.35
Profits	.33
Maximization	.29
Inputs	.28
Long-run	.25
Investment	.24
Plant	.23
Product	.23
Returns	.23

3. The history of the model is described as the collection of current states encountered in previous time periods.

4. The current behavior choice of the model depends upon the current state and the history of the model.

In dynamic overview, the elements of the population pursue a life-style in which the role of an element is identified by the allocation of its time to tasks. The movement of an element from task to task is dependent upon the process deficiencies or overloads generated by the current task and the restorative power of the alternative tasks to be engaged in the next time period. The impact of a chosen social behavior of the population may be defined in terms of the energy and capacity returns to tasks performed by the elements. Table 2 describes the dynamic impact of a change in current state from T to $T+1$.

Influencing intelligent population models

A decision maker who confronts a population can be seen to face rather interesting control problems; that is to say, conventional engineering-control techniques are aimed at influencing flow rates or capacities. If the decision maker expands all of the limits which constrain the population, the system may continue to operate under the influence of the new and more generous limits. However, other attempts to directly influence the system will either have no effect at all or will produce social behavior which is directed at countering the control influence. On the other hand, an awareness of the rules which govern behavior choice will allow a decision maker to design a control policy. A control policy may be defined as a social behavior which allocates energies to tasks so as to produce the desired current state of the population.

By the earlier discussion, there are two requirements for such a policy

1. The policy must be specified in terms of process limits which can be recognized by the population.
2. The sum of the weights on the policy must exceed the weights on the alternative policies available to the population.

The control problem illustrated

The problem can be illustrated with reference to classroom teaching policy, as in Hough [19]. In some cases, the classroom teacher can be said to be seeking the adoption of a point of view, or, in the current context, a social behavior. In other cases, the classroom teacher may be simply attempting to

report the findings which have resulted from working within a particular point of view. For example, the economist is often seeking to get his students to adopt the idea that the world is populated by decision makers, as in Hough [20]. In the context of the model, *adoption* implies that under a range of future circumstances the student will use the idea of a decision maker to organize the circumstances at hand. At such a time, it is also implied that the decision-maker idea will outweigh associatively all other frames of reference available to the student. On the other hand, the journal literature of economics contains a wide range of materials which has been prepared by persons working with the idea that the world is inhabited by decision makers.

As a practical matter, the distinctions between simply reporting the findings of work within the frame of reference and seeking the adoption of the point of view can be seen by comparing the term thesauri found in Tables 3 and 4. Table 3 contains a thesaurus $[I - \lambda C^T c]^{-1}$ constructed from a Key Word in Contest Index of about 1,000 abstracts in the *Journal of Economic Literature*. Table 4 was constructed by an identical procedure *except* that individual terms were identified as referencing *decision makers*, *instruments* over which the decision makers had control, *variables* over which the decision makers had no control, or *goals* sought by the decision makers. Though the overall frequency distributions of terms in the two samples were virtually identical, the thesaurus resulting from the second procedure clearly provides a superior conception of the referenced decision makers. Unguided reading by a novice in the literature of economics could be expected to produce a set of results similar to those in Table 3. A carefully tutored experience would lead to results similar to those in Table 4.

From the policy maker's perspective, we are thus led to conclude that both the explicit policy and the frame of reference from which that policy was constructed must be conveyed if the policy is to have a fair prospect for adoption.

References

1. BOULDING, Kenneth E., 'General systems theory: the skeleton of science', *Management Science*, pp. 197-208 (April 1956).
2. Von BERTALANFFY, Ludwig, *General Systems Theory*, Brazilier, New York (1962).
3. HAWLEY, Amos H., 'Ecology and population', *Science*, 179, 1196-1200 (23 March 1973).
4. ARDREY, Robert, *The Territorial Imperative*,

Atheneum Publishers, New York (1966).

5. MILLER, J.G., 'Living systems: basic concepts', *Behavioral Science*, 10, 212-213 (1965).

6. CHRISTIAN, John J., 'Social subordination, population density and mammalian evolution', *Science*, 168, 84-90 (3 April 1970).

7. HOUGH, Robbin R., 'War and economic development', *What Economists Do*, pp. 105-111, Harper and Row, New York (1972).

8. RAPPAPORT, Roy A., 'The flow of energy in an agricultural society', *Scientific American*, pp. 117-132 (November 1971).

9. MINTZBERG, Henry, 'Managerial work: analysis from observation', *Management Science*, pp. 897-910 (October 1971).

10. FREDERIKSEN, Harold, 'Feedbacks in economic and demographic transition', *Science*, 166, 837-847 (14 November 1969).

11. SCHELLING, Thomas C., 'The ecology of micromotives', *Public Interest*, pp. 61-98 (Fall 1972).

12. GARDNER, Martin, 'Mathematical games', *Scientific American*, pp. 120-123 (October 1970).

13. GALLE, Omer R., 'Population density and pathology', *Science*, 179, p. 430 (2 February 1973).

14. Same as [4] above.

15. MacARTHUR, R.H., *Geographic Ecology*, Harper and Row, New York (1972).

16. ASHBY, Ross, *Design for a Brain*, Chapman and Hall, London.

17. This as yet unpublished work will be described in *Systems*, a volume which is currently being written with a target of July 1974. In essence, the average price received by farmers from 1910 through 1970 is shown to be a function of total caloric output, income, and the difference between the calories available per capita and a calorically adequate diet.

18. GUILLIANO, V.E., 'Automatic language processing', a report prepared for Arthur D. Little Company Inc., and Harvard University, appearing in the Proceedings of the Institute of Electronics and Electrical Engineers.

19. HOUGH, Robbin R., 'A study to extend the development and testing of a systems model of the classroom', a final report to the Office of Education (1968).

20. Same as [7] above.

Multi-levelled causal simulation modelling of socio-economic systems

HANS JÜRGEN HOLSTEIN and LENNART STALBERG
Research Group on Sociocybernetics,
c/o Computer Science Laboratory,
Uppsala University, Sweden

Contemporary attempts at computer modelling socio-economic phenomena tend to be rather limited in scope, namely either predominantly macro-economical, or micro-economical, or sociopolitical, but very rarely combining two or three of these realms. These models are usually numerical, having the form of sets of equations. Practically all are based upon aggregate data and used for predictive purposes; the *explanation* of socio-economic phenomena is not their concern (cf. [1-6]).

Why are there so few computer models that combine the three above-mentioned realms? Is it because their predictive power has been found not to increase sufficiently to justify such combinations? Or is it because only few single-model users could afford the additional costs and labor of continuously collecting the data required for valuating a much larger model? And are social scientists quite disinterested in the explanatory potentials inherent in multi-levelled simulations? Or have integration attempts surrendered to the difficulty of the task?

At least from the sociologist's point of view this segregation is dissatisfactory. Reliable sociological data are increasingly difficult to obtain, quite in contrast to the trend in economics. Social micro-processes accumulate, after all, into the economic givens which so evidently constrain social behavior in return. If economic data are relatively easy to obtain, it makes, of course, little sense to try to infer them from the underlying sociological level as long as one has no explanatory ambitions. But fruitful inferences the other way around could, by a model which integrates the economic and sociological levels, be made both easily and inexpensively.

It is a common objection against detailed causal modelling that it is impossible to simulate millions of persons as individuals. Memories could not suffice, computer times would be too costly, we could not supply the empirical data necessary to valuate such models, and such models would also be as unserveillable as reality itself (Bonini's 'paradox') and therefore impossible to handle and to cope with. Abstract models which focus upon only a few variables and their interrelationships are therefore claimed to be a necessity; we shall call such models 'behavior models'.

One obtains results from behavior models, of course, but what do we know about their validities? What is the use of predictions if we do not know to what extent they are trustworthy? That is why we ask ourselves how we can validate behavior models. It is not sufficient to prove that their results are logically consistent with their premises, and neither does it suffice to point to the fact that a given model's predictions have been adequate in the past. To reason in this manner means that we regard the behavior model as a material implication; the truth value or validity of this implication is exclusively dependent on the truth value of the consequence and completely independent of the validity of the premises. Few would surely wish to take this extreme view; most would rather agree that the use of a model is only justified if the truth of the consequent depends on the validity of the model. Because one might otherwise as well generate random results.

This means that we must try to validate the assumed premises without making reference to the truth values of conclusions drawn from them. We must instead seek to derive the premises from assumptions which we believe to be more obviously valid. But the same argumentation is applicable to the new assumptions, and we are thus recursively led to the point where assumptions are such basic constituents of our common-sense world-view which we cannot imagine to reject.

Complete validation implies thus reverse axiomatization. We know that social reality has not yet been given an axiomatic description, and that high-level premises can therefore not simply connect to such a description; they float in the air as yet. In other words: Complete validation of a behavior model requires its transformation into a deterministic causal model. Validation must be based upon an explanatory model, and we seek explanatory models for the sole purpose of validating other models.

Let us now look at the problem from a less theoretical and more practical point of view. It is indeed plausible to assume that a model which consistently has yielded correct predictions in the past most probably also will predict correctly the next time. But few social models, at least, are as reliable and well tested. Social reality changes fast nowadays, and macro-social models need regularly to be put 'back on the track' by fresh empirical data.

Comprehensive causal models can, where they are adequate, predict reality changes and adapt to them. They need therefore to be put back on the track less often. This is a way of using a model's validity and comprehensiveness for reducing modelling costs.

Another reason for causal modelling is that such models are less 'distorted' than analytical models; models constructed by different persons can therefore more often and more easily be coupled. Knowledge accumulation is therefore easier to achieve with causal models.

And finally: A number of futurological studies, to take a popular example, have pointed out that mankind will approach doomsday unless certain trends are changed. But it is not always obvious from the fact that a particular parameter value must be reduced from 0.9, for instance, to 0.5, what we are to change in our everyday lives in order to achieve the necessary adaptation. Causal models are necessary here for enabling us to plan our actions, irrespective of whether the predictions are correct. The prediction model has only been able to indicate goal-achievement criteria.

But the question remains how the simulation of very large deterministic causal models is to be made possible. We have tried ourselves for several years and naturally met serious difficulties, but we are at present engaged in the implementation of a model, the principles of which we shall describe in short in the following. Its details are specified in [7].

Our supreme design principle has been that we must be able to reason fuzzily, sketchily, and incoherently about the total prototype phenomenon, as we usually do when we try to develop a model about something we do not yet know sufficiently well. But we wish to increase coherence and precision little by little as we learn, without the need for reprogrammings. That means that we let our model be *modular, incremental, selforganizing*, and *multi-levelled*. Modularity implies that model parts can easily be replaced by more differentiated ones. Incrementality implies that not all model components need be specified from the start but can be added in the course of time. Selforganization implies that we do not determine the ordering of all processes and the structuring of all aggregates in detail; it means also that we seek to be able to *generate* structures instead of explicitly defining them. Multi-levelled modelling, finally, implies that we make use of descriptions and rules available at several levels of aggregation; these are often complementary and cannot always be projected upon each other.

Deterministically causal modelling is to a great extent non-numerical. Computation is non-algorithmic, but instead often heuristic. It is thus basically non-deterministic after all, but only from the programmer's point of view, since the system seeks to translate his fuzzy advices into concrete configurations of determinate mechanisms. These mechanisms can be regarded as 'information-processing modules' which interact as if they were simple robots or demons.

The 'information-processing modules' operate within, and on, the framework of a database. We define the intial state of this database intensionally; a special monitor generates the extensional definition from the intensional one. We call the intensional definition 'morphology of the system'. It is much more concise than the corresponding extensional definition because it only specifies constraints but not exact and concrete values. The latter are to be found by the monitor within the prescribed limits. The same morphology can therefore give rise to a great multitude of different concrete databases.

The morphology speaks of aggregates of various kinds and indicates orderings. Families cannot be subsystems of organizations, for instance, but they can be of households. They consist of persons, not groups or firms, and they are usually spatially located. Et cetera. Much heuristic information can thus be supplied which gives the resulting database a plausible form.

Although we regard persons as the 'real' agents in our system, we allow the focus to shift from the person level to aggregate levels of different orders. Groups interact thus according to their own behavior rules, formal organizations according to theirs, et cetera. These behavior rules make reference to the aggregate's properties, of course. These properties have not been ascribed by us a priori, but are instead derived from detailed simulation of the aggregate. They are what is called 'emergent' properties.

When simulating very large systems we can always distinguish classes of similar subsystems. It is in these cases unnecessary, if not impossible, to compute the 'emergent' properties of each and every one of the subsystems. Since they are similar, it is sufficient to micro-simulate a representative sample only, and then to let each of the remaining class members 'pick' a prototype from that sample in random fashion. When all agents on a certain level of aggregation thus have been assigned their properties, we can again let them interact and generate the next level's 'emergent' properties. Et cetera.

Our present theoretical simulation aim is to define mechanisms which minimize the recurrent needs of empirical data for setting macro-sociological models back on their tracks. Morphologies and models can be regarded as 'canned and condensed' data. We suggest therefore that common-sense knowledge and morphology-constrained random data plus a comprehensive causal and multi-levelled simulation model can generate macro-level data which are at least as reliable as empirically obtained data. We mentioned before that sociological data are increasingly difficult to collect, therefore also probably less reliable and more expensive. Considering the decreasing trends in computer costs, it is therefore possible that simulated macro-social data are less expensive and more reliable than 'real' data. Simulated data could also become of particular value in those third-world countries where official statistics still are very dissatisfactory.

References

1. DUTTON, John M. and STARBUCK, William H. (eds.), *Computer Simulation of Human Behavior*, Wiley, New York, N.Y. (1971).
2. FORRESTER, Jay F., *Industrial Dynamics*, MIT, Cambridge, Mass. (1961).
3. FORRESTER, Jay F., *Urban Dynamics*, MIT, Cambridge, Mass. (1969).
4. FORRESTER, Jay F., *World Dynamics*, Wright-Allen, Cambridge, Mass. (1971).
5. GUNZENHÄUSER, Rul (ed.), *Nicht-numerische Informationsverarbeitung*, Springer-Verlag, Wien and New York (1968).
6. NAYLOR, Thomas H., *Computer Simulation Experiments with Models of Economic Systems*, Wiley, New York, N.Y. (1971).
7. HOLSTEIN, Hans Jürgen, *Homo Cyberneticus*, Sociografica, Uppsala (1974).

A simulation model of the Austrian medical care system

PETER FLEISSNER
Austrian Academy of Sciences, Vienna, Austria

1. General remarks

The simulation model presented here is only one element of a larger interdisciplinary project on "Long-term medical care in Austria". It was carried out at the Institute for Advanced Studies, Vienna, in connection with the Institute for Research in Socio-economic Development of the Austrian Academy of Sciences. The project had a duration of nearly two years. The members of the project-team were physicians, economists, political scientists, sociologists, mathematicians and systems analysts. Professor Naschold, now president of the University of Konstanz, was in charge of the team.

Conventional projects in the health sector are usually short- or medium-term oriented. They optimize one or two subsectors, e.g., the hospital system, the financing system; as a side condition they take the existing social order for granted and their results therefore are more or less nice adaptations to it. They do not deal with the different modes of illness formation in different social structures. They look at the health system as a highly professionalized and bureaucratically controlled subsystem of society—but in general they are not aware of this fact, with once and for all fixed goals, a repair-shop for the working capability, governed by the laws of private enterprise (medical industrial complex, or the system of private general practitioners).

The task of this project is

1. To show the performance of the health system in dependence on the prevailing capitalistic structure of the Austrian economy.
2. To compare different countries with different social orders with respect to the influences on the health system and vice versa.
3. To analyze the Austrian health system in terms of political economics.
4. To initiate public discussion to promote the evolution of a qualitatively changing health system in Austria.

To draw a clear picture of the ideas and the philosophy of the team we decided to develop a mathematically formulated model of the health system and its connected subsystems. First we started with causal loop diagrams in rather qualitative terms, but step by step we tested our hypothesis by empirical data and, if they were statistically by means of econometric methods accepted, we translated them into mathematical or logical expressions. We finished the model by connecting the single equations together and combining them into a large-scale hierarchical, modularized (by subroutines) simulation model, which at the moment consists of more than 500 linear or nonlinear equations. More than 50 of them have simultaneous structure and are solved by a specially developed algorithm, a combination of Gauss-Seidel and Aitken's Delta square method. The

Progress in Cybernetics and Systems Research, Volume 2
Copyright © 1975 by Hemisphere Publishing Corporation

equations were translated into FORTRAN IV (for IBM 370/155) and FORTRAN V (for UnIVAC 1106). By coupling the equations to Input and Output routines similar to Dynamo, but homemade, a computer run, simulating year by year from 1961 to 1995, needs about two minutes CPU-time.

2. Applications and results

According to the project philosophy the model is illustrating the increasing misery of medical care in Austria under the two alternative political developments—a conservative, and a reformistic way. It shows decreasing life expectancies for different social classes, an increasing use of the hospital and a fast rise of prices of medical goods, while the material standard of living is growing. The gaps between the standards of medical care with respect to social classes in Austria are widening and the introduction of large-scale reform programs will lead to a large cost explosion of this sector, followed by a partial paralysis of the medical system as a whole.

Using the model it is possible to study the influence of change in the health care system on the rest of the model, to explicate the powers of the different interest groups of the medical system, and to analyze the generation of immanent change and the resulting behavior inside the health care system.

For our model it was necessary to compose four subsectors to give only some of the interesting information to the health planners:
1. The health maintenance sector.
2. Its political sector.
3. The Austrian economic sector.
4. The population subsystem.
Of course, this model is a very restricted and rough mirror of the philosophies of the whole team. Better technique, perhaps another type of mathematical language, is needed to pack all the information available into the model.

3. A short description of the submodels

3.1 The health maintenance sector
If the empirical data base did allow it, we divided the population into subsets to characterize the different health care conditions. We chose the following categories: industrial workers, clerical employees, farmers, older people and children, male and female (a partition by age, occupational status and sex). For these groups in the health system we derived subjective/objective indicators of well-being. We

used the pre-professional concept of "morbid episodes (ME)". Some empirical evidence in Austrian surveys told us that with the increasing material standard of living, indicated by labor-productivity, ME are increasing. Our hypothesis was strengthened by the fact that life expectancy is stagnating or decreasing in nearly all countries with high productivity and high living standards. Only one quarter of ME is handled by professional health institutions as a regular disease. Therefore such professional indicators as sick-leave statistics or hospital-stays are more or less filter-indicators. They do not reflect health conditions, but social pressure, accessibility, and in the best case the dominant health paradigm. Nevertheless we found that workers are twice as much on sick-leave as employees in their offices, although conditions for sick-leave are worse for workers. Sick leaves for workers/head are changing with the growth-rate of the GNP, giving evidence for the heavy influence of the economic system on health behavior. The number of beds in Austrian hospitals was found to influence the average duration of a hospital stay.

For general practitioners, physicians, paramedical professionals such as nurses and medical-technical assistants, a forecasting model was built, depending on population, average time of study, drop-out rates, etc.

A wide field of the public and private spending on the health services was included in the model, e.g., spending on gp's, on hospital care and investment, and on drugs.

3.2 The political subsystem of the health sector
In this sector we tried to embody "soft" data and information on health-politics. We represented the conflicts by means of a very simple mathematical model

$$I_{t+1} - I_t = \left(\sum_{k=1}^{m} w_k \cdot P_k \right) \cdot (1 - |I_t|)$$

I_t ....Indicator of the level of the political issue investigated (range 0...1).

P_k....Political power of interest group k with respect to the issue investigated, represented by (transformed or weighted) social indicators, endogenous variables of the model.

w_k ...Weights of the powers according to the over-all situation.

m ....Number of conflicting groups.

The damping factor $(1-|I_t|)$ holds I between -1 and $+1$, in general.

The five interest groups of our model are
1. General capitalists.
2. Medical-technical capitalists.
3. Medical doctors and pharmacists.
4. Social-bureaucracy.
5. Health interests of the people.

Usually a change of I_t will change the structural coefficients of the model, weighted in its influence by the team, by experts or public declarations of ministries, etc. Changed coefficients are followed by changed values of social indicators, changed indicators are followed by changed powers of the interest-groups. In consequence of this change the indicator I, e.g., "preventive-therapeutic care", "public-private financing of the health sector" is changing.

Of course, this concept of political indicators can be generalized. One could widen it to more than one dimension, one could alter the behavioral assumptions of conflict, but for us it seemed complicated enough to estimate the weights and coefficients for the one-dimensional case for the political issues. This concept is leading to a very interesting tendency of this type of model: If one is changing exogenously the value of a structural coefficient of the economic or the health model the internal logic of the whole system is able to correct or to increase the changed value of this parameter, depending on the stabilizing behavior of the model.

3.3 The economic model

This subsector is of the type of income-distribution/consumption-investment models, but there are some features which are going across usual econometric models. By the introduction of the approximate Marxian rate of profits (net-profits divided by constant and variable capital of the economy) as central variable there was a nice combination of short- and medium-term effects possible. The rate of profits influences prices, governmental expenditures, invest-

ment, and the labor market. The state deficit is an endogenized variable of the model. Therefore one can investigate influences of changed economic policies with respect to public consumption, transfers, public investment, etc.

The labor market is differentiated into four parts: male workers, female workers, male and female office employees and male and female officers, the average incomes of each of these groups are summed up to the general wage sum (besides taxes). The number of employees and workers is corrected by the number of sick-leave-days per year and the social group. Every equation was estimated by OLS on the database 1954-1970. The submodel is non-linear and simultaneous.

3.4 The population model

On the basis of Austrian census data (1961), a simple dynamic population model was developed. It includes birth and death rates and is disaggregated to one year classes. The average birth rate of women between 20-40 is correlated to the economic growth rate. The death-rates are computed in two ways: On one side the ongoing trends of the last 10 years were estimated, on the other side the death rates are corrected by an increase in mortality, trickling down from older people to younger, as do heart diseases nowadays. The output of the population model is used as input for the different health institutions included in the model.

4. Conclusion

We do not think that this model will describe the future exactly, but we have learned by building the model to do a structured analysis of the problems of medical care. Our results are not that incrementalistic reforms will solve the health crisis but a structural change of society as a whole.

Incorporating social justice in the optimal space-time development process

AMIT K. MAITRA
Regional Science Department,
University of Pennsylvania, USA

Introduction†

This Chapter is the second in a series of papers on regional systems. In the first, presented last year at Washington, D.C., an attempt was made to

1. Show the interrelation of diverse processes of social, economic, and political systems.
2. Present some ideas of time sequence useful in the study of regional growth.
3. Explore the practical application of the concept of 'time' and notions of dynamic interrelationships of social, political, economic subsystems in projecting outcomes in the future.
4. Analyze several processes at play in decision situation involving a behaving unit such as a political leader.

†Many of the ideas contained in this Chapter emerged in discussions with my colleagues at the Regional Science Research Institute. I would particularly like to thank Drs Titus Podea (United Nations), Thomas Reiner (University of Pennsylvania), Robert Holt (University of Minnesota), and John Murray (Rutgers University), and Elena Yandola (Regional Science Research Institute) and Najma Davis (University of Pennsylvania) for helpful discussions in the earlier stage of writing this Chapter.

Progress in Cybernetics and Systems Research, Volume 2

Specifically, the paper outlined a framework within which decision-makers would normally function. Generally speaking, the main ideas were derived from some theories of economics and also from a simulation model of a complex social system developed by Jay W. Forrester in his book, *World Dynamics*. It was pointed out that the different rates of change (growth and decay of relevant magnitudes) and *change* in these rates would lead decision-makers to measure the growth phenomena quite differently, and to attach different weights to variables (like capital, natural resources in the form of raw materials, and labor in the form of raw and skilled labor) at play in decision situations. The growth in the model was represented in terms of economic cycles. The dynamics of the model were characterized by the flow of economic goods in both directions (flow and counterflow) and it was shown how this typical cycle would create a situation which results in

1. Some form of accumulation.
2. Some form of socio-economic-ecological imbalance in any growing region at any specific point in time.

The primary task of the regional growth model would be to satisfy initially the basic human needs

—food, shelter, education, etc.—and to increase the economy's capability for doing so in the future. When most basic needs have been taken care of, an economic system can begin to satisfy the preferences of its consumers for more discretionary goods and services.

Keeping these basic human needs in perspective, an index formulation was suggested for enabling the decision-maker to evaluate his future choices. The index was defined as the 'Quality of Life due to Production' (QLP). It was implicit in this kind of formulation that the decision-maker would be guided by such an index (which might change from one time period to another because of variations in production of goods and other related factors) to formulate development strategies in ways harmonious with the physical environment. The formulation was based on the analysis of economic variables. This is not meant to imply that the quality of life consists exclusively of material satisfactions. In the course of the discussion, an attempt will be made to extend and refine the previous notion of the quality of life index. The point of departure for this Chapter is, therefore, to see what develops as a result of adopting a broader definition of the quality of life.

In general terms, we can say that incomes differ markedly among parts of a state, among cities of different sizes within the state, among smaller population groups within the cities. As a consequence, the pace of development in most parts of the world today is unacceptable—and growing more so. It is unacceptable because of two important factors, which indicate that

1. Developments have been directed largely at gross economic goals.
2. Developments have failed to insure that all groups within states or cities have shared equitably in economic advance.

It is, therefore, possible that while the quality of life due to production would improve in certain situations, this definition is not explicit enough to include distributive measures of environmental, social, and economic quality on an overall population basis.

In recent years social scientists from around the world have raised interesting questions relating to the uneven distribution of goods, wealth, resources, and opportunities. Improvement in the quality of life in any particular point in time and space generally indicates more goods, resources and opportunities at hand for effective utilization. Unequal command of goods, wealth, resources, and opportunities by any social group, therefore, immediately raises some issues of equity or justice. Our newer

and broader definition of the quality of life should ideally include the idea of distribution of wealth, resources, and opportunities. A new definition gives us an opportunity to study and to develop models with the end of defining the nature of social preferences for alternative configurations of external conditions. It can lead us to some conclusion as to how similar populations will value environments with not too dissimilar dimensions.

The concept of social justice has both a political and economic dimension. We would be essentially dealing with the economic aspect. This should enable us to establish a principle by which the 'assessment' of alternative possible distributions can be carried out. After defining adequately the notion of social justice, our next step would be to examine how the optimal space-time development model could be modified with the incorporation of social justice criterion. In attempting to do so, we would draw heavily upon the recent works of some economists, regional scientists, and geographers.

Toward a definition of social justice

There are several directions from which one can attempt to define social justice. Richard B. Brandt, in his book, *Social Justice*, has treated the subject from many different angles. Modern economics springs from a search for a definition of economic justice. We are mostly interested in forming an idea about distributive justice. This consists primarily in the treatment of all people

1. According to the requirement of the greater good of a greater number, or the welfare of mankind, or the public interest.
2. According to a valuation of their socially useful services in terms of their scarcity in the essentially economic terms of supply and demand.

A theory of distributive justice should also take note of the following important elements:

1. The distributing procedure, that is, the principle of selection by means of which the distribution is to be arrived at.
2. The pattern of distribution to be arrived at.

The principle of utility is concerned with "the greatest good for the greatest number". The outcome of the distributive procedure or an economic game can be considered as equitable if it is in accordance with the individual preferences of the citizens of a country. Equity is supposed to have been achieved when society reaches the distribution of economic resources that generates the most agreement. But, how does society determine that two people are equally happy? Socially, we simply decide that individuals are economic equals under certain circumstances. Thus our specification might say that individuals are economic equals when they have the same quality of environment, same wealth, income, etc. In a similar manner we can perhaps specify socially an optimum distribution of economic resources. It might not, however, be possible to derive any optimum specification from an aggregation of private personal preferences. This could be the case, because the distribution of economic resources may itself be one of the factors in determining individual utility functions.

Economists have been trying to seek specifications of economic equity in the aggregation of individual preferences, or 'utility functions'. John Rawls in his recent and much discussed book, *A Theory of Justice*, has attempted to isolate several essential ingredients in the specification of economic equity. Some of these factors are worth considering in the context of what will be developed later in this Chapter.

Individuals have different levels of preferences. They have preferences about the rules of the economic system and the distribution of resources that it should generate. They also have preferences as to how to maximize their own utility under the prevailing economic system. Societies can, however, discuss what should constitute economic equity without worrying about individual differences in the efficiency with which people process economic goods. The social welfare function is the place where

society makes interpersonal comparisons. The individualistic social welfare function lets each person determine his own importance in social welfare. The individual societal preferences about the structure of economic system and its distribution of resources are continuously changing as preferences are molded by culture and progress of society; so economic equity is not in a static condition. Moreover, there can be no single distribution of economic resources that constitutes absolute equity, but there may be a distribution of economic resources that is more equitable than the one now in effect in some point in space. In other words, it is possible to consider different facets of equity and come to the conclusion that one particular distribution of economic resources is more reasonable, desirable, justifiable or equitable than another at some point in time and space.

To be concrete and provocative let me suggest a set of guidelines in mathematical terms for strong or weak social justice—a notion which has been derived mainly from the idea of economic equity. These are not my personal suggestions about the proper definitions of social justice, but are my interpretations of some of the recent works of scholars in the disciplines of regional science, peace science, and political science. Professors Walter Isard, Panagis Liossatos, Tord Höivik, to mention a few, have conducted studies about the distribution of resources and how distribution may be the dimension closest to daily human experience in terms of social justice.

Surveys of some of the major industry and population centers of the world show that per capita

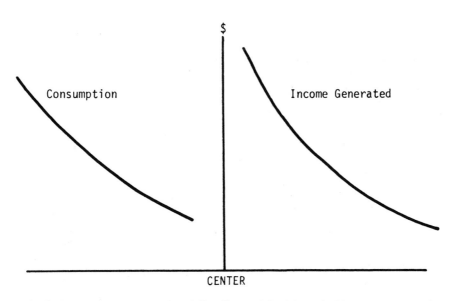

Fig. 1 Per capita consumption falls off parallel with capital income generated

income generated falls off rapidly from a peak at the center if one proceeds radially out from these centers. Per capita production and per capita use of capital and other productive resources also decrease as one moves away from the center.

In contrast to this the Twentieth Century planners notice that there is a new growth phenomenon called suburbanization. As a result of this, the high residential population is distributed at some distance away from the center. One can also notice considerable consumption by this population at this distant location away from the center. Can we, therefore, consider per capita consumption as falling off parallel with capital income generated (see Fig. 1)? The income generated and made available for consumption forms the key social justice variable and not the actual rate of consumption at a location.

For the purpose of analyzing the social justice variable, our central interest is a distribution over populations located in real physical space. This distribution can be easily worked out in terms of the usual (x, y) coordinate system.

A simple approach to analyzing the social justice condition would be to deal with a population density which is made uniform over a straight line coming out from an origin. The uniformity is achieved by a proper transformation of the (x, y) coordinates. Initially, any typical radial from the center is taken to represent an $\bar{x}$-axis. Then physical distances along this radial are stretched or contracted so as to obtain a uniform distribution of population along it. The resulting adjusted space is the x-axis.

Now let us define

$C_{(x,t)}$ = consumption per unit area, per unit time, at time t, at space point. The appropriate area is that which corresponds to a unit length along a radial and an appropriate length along the circumference.

$K_{(x,t)}$ = capital stock per unit length at time t at space point.

$R_{(x,t)}$ = index of pollution per unit length at time t at space point. Pollution variable R can be considered only in terms of real physical space, i.e., in terms of $\bar{x}$-axis. It may not be possible to show this meaningfully in the x-axis.

Now for any function, say, $G_{(x,t)}$, we can write

$$\overset{*}{G}_{(x,t)} = \frac{\delta G_{(x,t)}}{\delta x} \; ; \quad \overset{o}{G}_{(x,t)} = \frac{\delta G_{(x,t)}}{\delta t}$$

$$\overset{*o}{G}_{(x,t)} = \frac{\delta \overset{*}{G}_{(x,t)}}{\delta t} = \frac{\delta}{\delta t}\left(\frac{\delta G}{\delta x}\right)$$

According to what we have said in the preceding pages, strong social justice should suggest for any particular point of time t the same level of consumption, capital stock, and pollution at all locations x. Mathematically, the proper notation would be

$$\overset{*}{C}_{(x,t)}, \; \overset{*}{K}_{(x,t)}, \; \overset{*}{R}_{(x,t)} = 0 \quad \text{for all } t \text{ and } x \geqslant 0$$

That is, the slope along the x-axis at any point on the respective curve of any of these magnitudes is zero.

Since pollution is not desirable in the context of our present day environmental factors, we can consider decreasing the pollution index. As a consequence, the new definition of strong social justice takes the following form:

$$\overset{o}{C}_{(x,t)}, \; \overset{o}{K}_{(x,t)} > 0, \; \overset{o}{R}_{(x,t)} < 0 \quad \text{for all } t \text{ and } x \geqslant 0$$

In this case both capital and stock consumption increase with time at any location during the planning horizon, but pollution decreases.

Our discussion so far indicates that a case for strong social justice at any particular point in time and space implies, in broad terms, equality in the distribution of income, wealth, and resources. In the next section we shall incorporate this idea of equality with various other notions which together will help define social justice or injustice in more explicit terms.

Social justice and development

In the preceding pages an attempt has been made to define the criteria of social justice and the characteristics which unite them. It has been suggested that a more equitable distribution of wealth and income would be one of the needed criteria for promoting social justice. Even if income and its distribution should be the ultimate goal of social justice, the only practical way to equalize income distribution may be through improving the distribution of wealth and opportunity. The idea of improvement brings to our attention some notion of efficiency that needs to be considered in achieving social justice.

The considerations of equal distribution of income and efficient distribution of wealth and resources do not necessarily exhaust the issues of social justice. These issues must be properly analyzed and understood. Individuals in a society or a region desire equality in the distribution of goods, resources, income and so on. The psychological level of satisfaction attained along the dimension of equality by members of a society is indirectly determined by an efficient distributive mechanism which tells us how effective the mechanism has been in reaching a greater number of people. While we discuss equality and efficiency in the abstract, an operational point of view of social justice should tell us more about public involvement, i.e., public participation. Thus, in considering social justice valuing processes, we might ask: for a given value, how widely is it held?

Social justice is, in one sense, a tool for securing what is desired. So far in our discussion we have argued that individuals in a society desire equality, efficiency and to that list of criteria we should now add the condition under which private attitudes of individuals become public, or in other words, we

should add the condition of participation of all individuals.

The ideas of equality, efficiency and participation are highly interrelated. It is, however, useful to keep them separate because they may be goals in themselves. These goals are set by individuals in their mental images about a just society. Men have images of themselves and of society around them. These images create impact on human behavior. In the book, *The Image*, Kenneth Boulding has developed a theory of human behavior. According to him, human behavior consists essentially of setting in motion a course of events which is intended to carry the person into the most highly valued of his images of potential futures. The image that an individual builds of a just society may thus relate to a single criterion of equality or efficiency depending on the individual's mode of thinking at any given point in

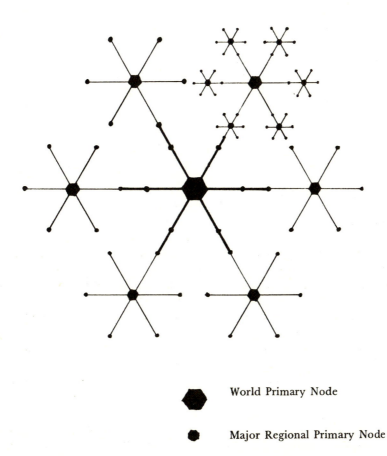

● World Primary Node

● Major Regional Primary Node

● Sub-regional Primary Node

· Local Community Nodes

Fig. 2 An organization of control points in a world hierarchy

time and space. The future does not, however, turn out as one expects, because the choice of a future does not necessarily guarantee it. There exists a set of functions relating the chosen future to the actual future. Let us say that $I_1, I_2,..., I_n$ is the set of images of the possible future, and $A_1, A_2,..., A_n$ is the set of actual futures. The choice of I_1 may not mean that one will get into the corresponding actual future A_1; it may mean, however, that for any I_1 that one selects, there is some A_j which corresponds to it. For many choices there is a high probability that A_j will, in fact, be the same A_1, but this is not necessarily true.

It can be easily understood that the difference between the chosen and the actual futures arises because the society is composed of interacting populations. Interaction forms an integral part of what we call social dynamics. Choices made by one group of individuals directly or indirectly interfere in another group's choices. As a result, one does not always get what one desires. In any case, the characteristics of various individuals' different choices, like equity, efficiency, or participation, in which the image of social justice plays an important part must now be analyzed separately and adequately if we are to examine the role which the image of social justice plays in the dynamics of space-time development. This analysis should be carried out in a spatial framework where the dynamic processes of society take place. Spatial frameworks can be constructed by theoretical models. Integrating some of the accepted and recognized basic principles of social sciences, we can build a spatial framework (ideal) as suggested by Wolpert, Isard, and others. Because of the interaction of these social science principles and some very restrictive assumptions, a network of world hierarchical spatial structure is conceivable. Before listing the basic principles of the social sciences, the following assumptions, which have been derived from the theoretical approaches in economics, regional science, and other social sciences, are given below.

1. An even distribution of population over a world surface, initially.
2. An even spread of all types of resources including human and technological know-how.
3. People of like taste, demands, motivations, and aspirations.
4. Transportation, communication, and migration possible in all directions at a constant cost per unit distance.

Now the social science principles which need to be integrated with these assumptions include the follow-

ing:

1. Scale economies lead to concentrations of different activities at different locations, and to trade and communication among these and other locations, *ceteris paribus*.
2. Agglomeration economies tend to intensify the concentration of activities at locations comparatively better in one strategic way or another, *ceteris paribus*.
3. Existence of transfer costs constrain the volume and intensity of trade in commodities, communications, and population migration, and thereby tend to foster the development of central places in many regions, *ceteris paribus*.
4. Uneven spatial distribution of resources leads to gains from trade, *ceteris paribus*.
5. Up to a point, and with other factors constant, the increase of participation by each member of a group of individuals in a decision-making process leads to a higher level of interaction, greater diffusion of knowledge, higher average productivity, *ceteris paribus*.
6. In order to base decisions regarding certain functions on a total set of information pertaining to all regions, and to reap scale economies in processing large masses of data, a highly centralized structure *re* such functions should exist, *ceteris paribus*.

Keeping these principles and assumptions in mind, we can construct many different types of spatial frameworks. However, we have chosen a hexagonal module to build a regional spatial structure. We take this structure as our world region. The structure is based on efficiency criteria, central place theories in economics, geography, and regional science. Figures 3, 4 and 5 show further details as the pattern of service and other activities are brought to one's notice. We have a simplifying uniformity assumption which makes possible the symmetrical structural-functional system portrayed in the figures. Figure 5 emphasizes the transportation and other flow phenomena among regions. The framework assures the planner, decision-maker, and policy-maker the conditions of equity, efficiency in the distribution of goods, resources, and services, and also indicates the possibility of direct participation of all individuals in the unified region. Formally the participation potential measure is given by the following expression:

$$P = \sum_{i=1}^{n} r_i \cdot {}_iV$$

where

$$_iV = G \sum_{j=1}^{n} \frac{w_j \cdot (M_j)^\beta}{d_{ij}^b}$$

P = total participation potential for a system of n nodes; $i,j = 1,...,n$

r_i = the percentage of decision making authority at node i

G = a constant

M_j = population at node j

β = an adjustment factor applied to M_j

w_j = weight to be applied to population at j

d_{ij} = distance between nodes i and j

b = an adjustment factor applied to d_{ij}

The above formulation merely indicates that the participation potential increases with decrease in the distance separating a population from points of interest. Referring to our figures, we can say that since there exists no barrier, there is no lack of communication; people are knowledgeable about

the current state of affairs, and they are likely to be participants in everything that goes on within the structural-functional system of a world region shown in the figures. Adequate socio-cultural interchanges take place within this framework. To be more precise, everybody can take the opportunity to come to a world library complex, to a world art center, to numerous other business, financial, and other government services. Furthermore, one should note that in the real world natural resources are unevenly distributed. Because of the existence of a hypothetical centralized regional structure as shown in the figures, it is possible that all people will share equitably in the consumption and use of these natural resources. This point, therefore, brings out the fact that equity and efficiency are also achievable in our hypothetical model structure. For the purpose

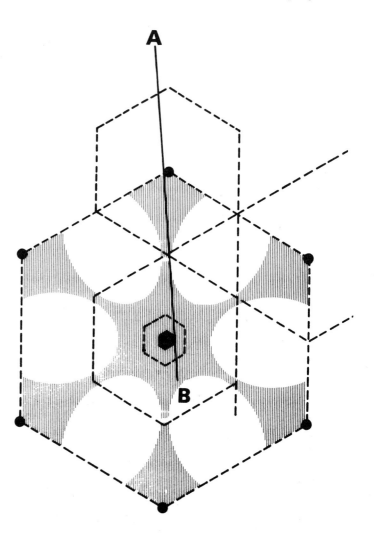

Fig. 3 A hypothetical spatial pattern of service areas

Fig. 5 A spatial pattern of transportation, communication, and other flows

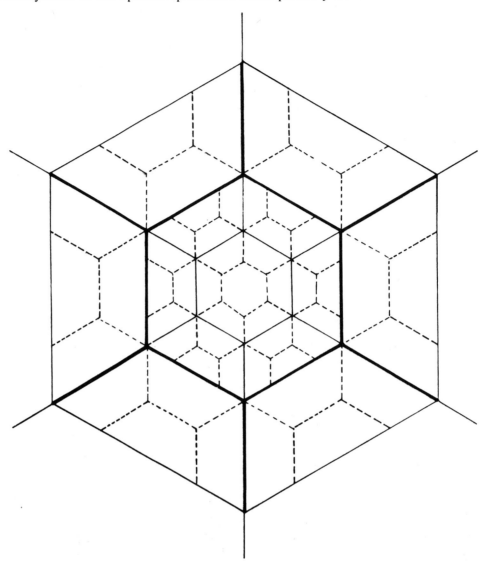

Fig. 4 Boundaries for four sizes (order) of service areas

of deriving or analyzing efficient distribution of scarce resources, we can use an interregional linear programming technique. This has received great attention in recent years. It is given by

Max $Z = cX$, subject to: $AX \leqslant R$ and $X \geqslant 0$
where

Z = Gross Product

X = a column vector of order Uv, listing the level of each of the v activities in each of the U regions of the world.

c = a row vector of order Uv, giving the income per unit level of each of the v activities of each of the U regions of the world.

A = a matrix of technical production coefficients or order $Us \times Uv$, where in general each coefficient indicates how much of one resource or commodity is required to produce or yield a unit of another commodity.

R = a column vector of order Us listing the constraints imposed upon the operation of the regional economy, in particular, those imposed by limited supplies of resources and intermediate commodities.

For the purpose of illustrating how the interregional linear program may be linked to the values and goals of a society, a figure has been reproduced here. See page 70.

On the basis of our very restrictive assumptions, given earlier in the Chapter, it has been possible for us to build a theoretical construct where the desirable elements of participation, equity, and efficiency in the management of services, in the distribution of resources are found. Social justice is, therefore, achievable in a situation like this. People might have different choices in their minds; and even if they have different choices regarding an ideal society where social justice according to their definition can prevail, our framework will probably satisfy all. So this is, in one sense, an optimum spatial development.

We should now relax our assumptions in order to achieve a bit of reality. Our world is not a single unified region politically, or socially, or for that matter, geographically. Let us, therefore, insert a barrier into our hypothetical world regional framework. Let this be represented by the line AB in the figures. This line cuts the region into two distinctly separate regions. There would now be an observable difference in the net benefits accrued from following an unaltered spatial structure and the net benefits realizable from the altered spatial structure. There are several types of measures of net benefits, the definitions of which require the conceptions of *input* and *output*. *Input* might refer to the "cost" of a course of action, where cost is being used in a very general sense which is not restricted to monetary considerations.

Output might be measured in terms of the economic resources which result from taking the course of action or the psychological or sociological characteristics of the resulting state. In short, output refers to the "return" or "pay off" resulting from a course of action. The type of measure of net benefits obtainable depends on whether the input and/or output are specified in the definition of relevant outcome. We might have a case where outputs are variable and inputs are specified. This is precisely the case in our particular illustration of the regional framework. Here alternative courses of action with a specified fixed input (namely, a political barrier) are evaluated relative to the amount of output they yield. This discussion of measuring net benefits could end here were it not for the fact that in most problem environments a course of action will yield different inputs and/or outputs on different trials. In other words, inputs and outputs vary, and this variation must be taken into account.

Keeping these relevant ideas in the back of our minds, we should now be able to understand that the difference of the two net benefits, obtainable from providing an input in any given situation, gives us a measure, called the *Opportunity Cost*. In the real world the computation of opportunity cost is very difficult, if not completely impossible. The difficulty arises because of the multidimensional character of the opportunity cost computational procedure and also because of our inability to specify and measure adequately the net benefits under some circumstances.

Benefit is a vague term which can mean monetary (in terms of income or wealth), material benefits (in terms of output per person) and/or physical well-being of individual members of an entire society. The measure might also include all geographical, social, occupational, cultural, religious returns in regard to rights and access to public services and developmental efforts. In other words, the term benefit in its broader context, implicitly assumes some measure of efficiency and equity in the distribution of activities, goods, and services. The notion is relevant for both the individual and the community —local, regional, and world.

Broadly speaking, we can say that a divided region reduces participation potential of all individuals on one side, via world authorities, in decision making on another side. But it also increases participation of individuals in local decision making. Under some circumstances this might prove beneficial. It is quite possible, however, that efficiency of government decision making in regard to overall planning and management of resource distribution would be reduced, because local individuals of a divided region might raise issues relating to the selection of criteria for efficiency and equity.

There are several ways in which the distribution of scarce resources can be achieved. The decision maker always faces a dual problem in determining which method assures efficiency and which method assures equity or which method assures both efficiency and equity. In this context, it would be interesting to review briefly the discussion made by Mancur Olson Jr. in his book, *The Logic of Collective Action*, and also in his article, 'The optimal allocation of jurisdictional responsibility: the principle of "Fiscal Equivalence".'

Let us take a bounded region as indicated in Figs 6a, b and c. Let us consider the distributional aspects of a scarce resource. The distribution can be made in many different ways. In order to make the best utilization of the resource, one can distribute

RESULTS → GOAL REFORMULATIONS → RERUNS, ETC.

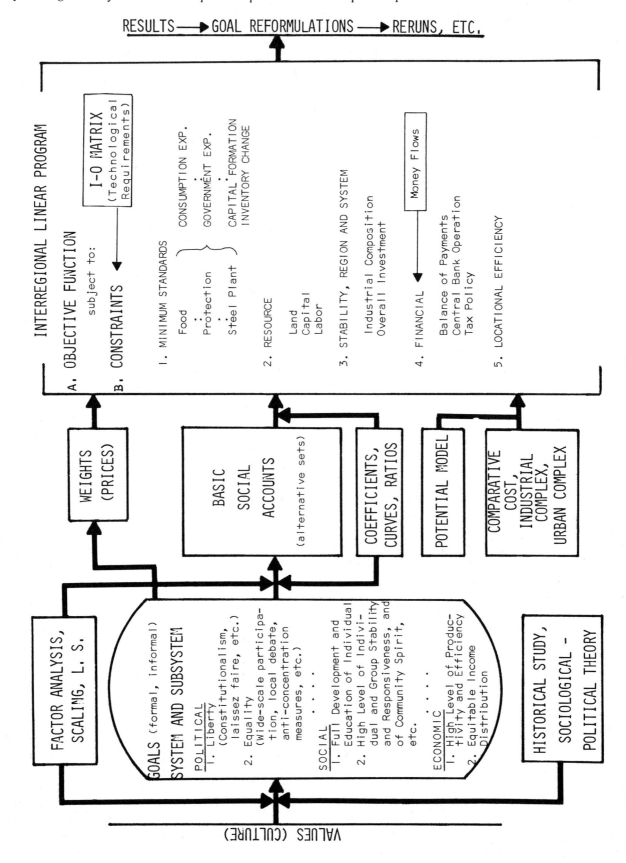

Figure 6a

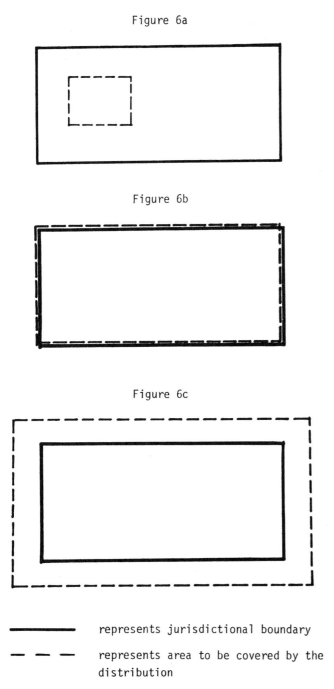

Figure 6b

Figure 6c

———————— represents jurisdictional boundary

— — — represents area to be covered by the distribution

Fig. 6 Different possible distributions of scarce resources over a defined boundary

this over a small area as shown in Fig. 6a. This does not, however, take care of all people's demand for the scarce resource. So because of the community's pressure the decision maker may be forced to give due consideration to equity aspect and thus he may choose a distribution that embraces the whole region.

Figure 6b explains the outcome. A problem with this kind of a distribution is that, in the strictest sense of the word, it is not equitable, nor is it efficient. Persons living in the peripheral areas of the region might not receive the same amount as others living in the central areas of the bounded region. This happens most often in water resource distribution. The decision maker's other alternative could be to extend the scope of distribution beyond the actual administrative boundary of the region—thus assuring equal distribution of the resource to at least all people within the region. This distribution definitely assures greater equity and efficiency. At the same time, this also raises another problem. Since the distribution extends beyond the boundary of the region, individuals within the region might raise political issues as to why the people of the outer areas should get any benefit at all; they do not pay the taxes and so on. In actuality the complexity remains in most cases unsolved. If one chooses to pursue a course which assures equity, one fails to provide a full measure of efficiency and vice versa. So there is a conflict between maximization of *equity* and maximization of *efficiency*. This happens because people in a society tend to emphasize and identify different values for obtaining social justice. This is where the image of perception problem comes to play a significant role.

The decision maker is concerned with establishing criteria for social justice for the entire population group. Even though an individual in his own mind may be committed to one particular form of optimization, a decision maker's efforts in establishing a suitable social justice for all would be characterized by a search for satisfaction taking many forms of optimizing behavior. It is required, therefore, that the decision maker choose a mechanism by which he can develop a compromise formula for the basic values of the society.

One way to arrrive at a suitable compromise decision regarding multiple goals in a society would be to choose a weighting mechanism. Different values in a society are given proper recognition according to changing standards of the society. So at any specific point in time the weights determine the trade offs between, say, equity and efficiency. Reiner and Freeman have shown interesting development of weighting models.

The weighting can be done explicitly. It could also be done implicitly, as when decision makers respond by depending upon their subjective evaluations of the relative importance of various factors which together help define social justice. Given the weights, it should in theory be possible to map the weights as a pay off function. The decision maker would respond to a mapping of the relative significance of two goals, equity (say "*a*") and efficiency (say "*b*"), which he sees as an indifference surface (see Fig. 7). In certain cases, this might be linear (Line L). It might also take the nonlinear form (Line N). This surface of the indifference curve enables the decision maker to compare alternate levels of attainment of each of several goals. The decision maker is supposed to be indifferent between goal levels attained at points L_1 and L_2 (similarly between points N_1 and N_2), and, since higher levels of social justice would be generally preferred to lower levels, he would prefer any point on curve N to any point on curve L. Moreover, the decision maker can gather enough

information on the cost of attainment of a given combination of goals. It might, therefore, be possible to identify optimum levels for the entire socio-economic system. Let C lines indicate the resources, e.g., capital (see Fig. 8). Line C_O is one of a set of relationships, shown as dashed lines, each of which expresses the input-output transformation from a given quantity of resources to goal attainment. Point P shows the optimal level of goal satisfaction achievable with C_O and line M is a curve which represents a decision maker's indifference to goal a and goal b combinations. Thus by using weights one can construct a macro objective function. Let the two goals be a and b, with a' and b' referring to some other standard established for these, and w_1 and w_2 as the prescribed weights. The aggregation of the

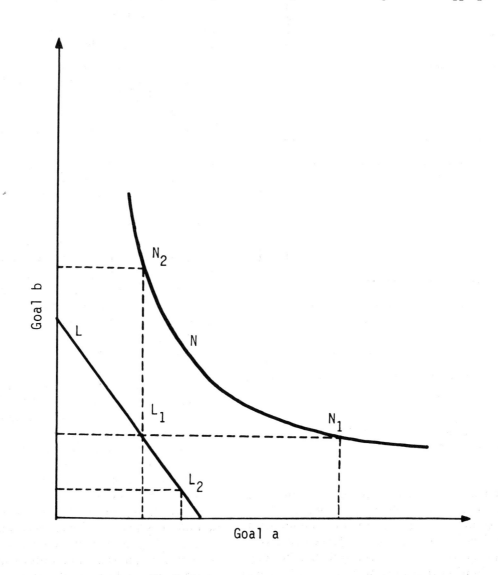

Fig. 7 Goal payoff function

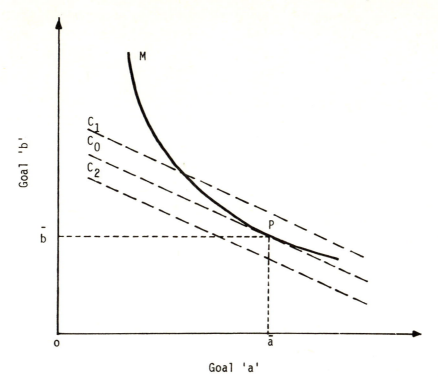

Fig. 8 Goal payoff function with constraint

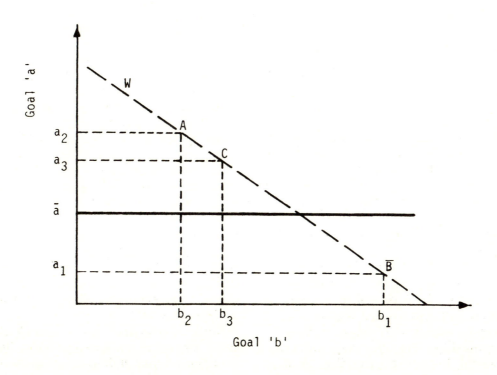

Fig. 9 Weighting model with threshold

joint value—our social justice index, say S, might, in a simple case, be described as

$$S = w_1 a + w_2 b$$

In another extension, it can be represented in the following way:

$$-S = w_1 |a'-a| + w_2 |b'-b|$$

In the above formulations, the combination of weighted terms has been taken as linear. The relation might as well take the following quadratic form:

$$-S = w_1 a^2 + w_2 b^2$$

or,

$$-S = w_1 (a'-a)^2 + w_2 (b'-b)^2$$

The weighting approach shows us that a low score along one measured dimension, say, efficiency, can be compensated by a high score in another dimension, say, equity. The skill with which one can detect differences, say in terms of social impact between the two aggregatively equivalent social justice situations, is a valuable one. This indicates the possibility of combining weighting models of social justice with impact models.

Alternate impacts can be considered by the use of weights. We can combine a weighting formulation with threshold concept. Thus in the following figure, Fig. 9, $\bar{a}$ is a social or political minimum established for attainment of goal a. A and C which represent two end states are acceptable and equivalent, but $\bar{B}$ is easily dropped out of consideration. The a_1 level of goal attainment associated with end state $\bar{B}$ is cleanly rejected because of political or social unacceptability criterion. It is less than $\bar{a}$.

The discussion on social justice index formulation has been important in the sense that the computational approach has shown the attribute of an aggregate. It is perhaps a subtle point, but an important one. It emphasizes A.K. Rogers' argument that social justice is a 'social concept', 'a concept of reason' which involves entering the list of rational discussion and being ready to generalize any reasons given. Generalization in this context implies that the decision making process must contain a drive toward social optimality. This drive may not always be wholly successful, but it is perhaps clear to us that we need to produce a much better human environment, even if it is somewhat short of being the

'best possible'. We will, therefore, concentrate hereafter on examining how Isard and Liossatos have attempted to develop a desirable (optimal) regional growth model with some considerable emphasis on its spatial aspects.

Before examining Isard-Liossatos' formulation, a few words need to be said about the theoretical construct that they develop. A model must be 'of' something, and hence a mathematical model is not a model but a form. Because of very simplistic assumptions, Isard-Liossatos' mathematical form does not correspond strictly to the real world phenomena. In their attempt to build a theoretical construct of problem situations, they show approximate representations of the real world. An 'exact' representation (even if it were possible) would lead to hopeless mathematical complexity. A simplified picture on the other hand, enables the researchers to avoid complexity.

One can also easily notice that for the purpose of attempting to establish some operational point of view, Isard-Liossatos' formulation sacrifices richness and completeness of the theoretical construct initially. They build the entire model sequentially. They observe the failures as they occur in the first simple formulation and use this information to decide, at the time of the failure, whether to insert new variables or to continue with the initial formulation. The methodological implication of this approach is as follows:

Situations in which very little information is available at the outset can nevertheless be approached in a systematic fashion, and may undergo continuous improvement as time goes on and more basic information becomes available.

Thus, in effect, Isard-Liossatos introduce a learning process in the use of sequential modelling technique. A last point is that economic policy is an art whose ideal often is to devise methods of intervention rather than to choose between old and well-known ones. In this context, it can be argued that the Isard-Liossatos attempt to use general economic theories for discussing the normative aspects of welfare distribution, i.e., the social justice, is a scientific one, because this consists of interaction between observation procedures and explicit theoretical construction.

Since the construct has been analyzed in great detail elsewhere, an overview would be given here. Some interesting findings and conclusions, which perhaps match our mode of thinking as discussed earlier in this Chapter, are mentioned here.

A simple space-time model

A continuous distribution of population in an isolated region has been considered at some point in space (x,t) and time $(0,0)$. The model has been examined in the framework of a large but finite unidirectional spatial dimension of the population spread $(0,B)$, and a time interval of 0 to t_1. Labor and land have been considered as free goods available in unlimited quantities in the hypothetical region. For simplicity and brevity only capital has been considered to be required for production of goods Y.

Taking production Y at any point of space-time as a nonlinear function of capital K, at that point of space-time, the following expressions are obtained:

$$Y_{(x,t)} = F[K_{(x,t)}] \ldots \tag{1}$$

with

$dF/dK > 0$ .... positive marginal product

$d^2F/dK^2 < 0$ .... diminishing marginal product for all $K > 0$.

Here,

$Y_{(x,t)}$ .... output per unit length, per unit time;

$K_{(x,t)}$ .... capital per unit length, at point $\underline{x}$, at time $\underline{t}$.

Output $Y_{(x,t)}$ at any point in space-time may be allocated to *consumption* $C_{(x,t)}$ at that point, investment $\partial K/\partial t \equiv \overset{o}{K}_{(x,t)}$ at that point, or net exports $\partial U/\partial x \equiv \overset{*}{U}_{(x,t)}$, where $U_{(x,t)}$ is the flow of goods through a point for use elsewhere for consumption, or investment, or both, per unit of time.

For any unit length dx,

$$\overset{*}{U}_{(x,t)} = (U \text{ at } x + dx) - (U \text{ at } x)$$

Net export may be either positive or negative, depending on whether the flow of goods is toward the origin or away from the origin. The first model, then, takes a simple DEMAND = SUPPLY formulation

DEMAND = Consumption + Investments + Exports

SUPPLY = Output + Imports

Therefore,

$$C_{(x,t)} + \overset{o}{K}_{(x,t)} + E_{(x,t)} = Y_{(x,t)} + I_{(x,t)}$$

At any point, the flow of goods involves transport cost, which in effect uses up part of production. σ has been chosen to represent transport rate in terms of product used per unit flow of goods with dimension of $1/\text{length}$. In actuality transport rate is a function of population density and distance. $\sigma U_{(x,t)}$ then represents transport cost of the flow U, at time t, which thus represents a demand for the single good produced. Accordingly the demand = supply equation for each space-time point is modified in the following way:

$$C_{(x,t)} + \overset{o}{K}_{(x,t)} + E_{(x,t)} + \sigma U_{(x,t)} = Y_{(x,t)} + I_{(x,t)}$$

$$C_{(x,t)} + \overset{o}{K}_{(x,t)} + E_{(x,t)} - I_{(x,t)} + \sigma U_{(x,t)} = Y_{(x,t)}$$

$$C_{(x,t)} + \overset{o}{K}_{(x,t)} + \overset{*}{U}_{(x,t)} + \sigma U_{(x,t)} = Y_{(x,t)}$$

or,

$$C_{(x,t)} = Y_{(x,t)} - \overset{o}{K}_{(x,t)} - \overset{*}{U}_{(x,t)} - \sigma U_{(x,t)}$$
$$= F[K_{(x,t)}] - \overset{o}{K}_{(x,t)} - \overset{*}{U}_{(x,t)} - \sigma U_{(x,t)}$$

Typically, the capital investment pattern varies from a central location, at which know-how and experience may accumulate, to a distant place from the central location. This happens because of mounting obstacles to transportation and communication. To reflect this phenomenon, $\overset{o}{K}_{(x,t)}$ in the above expression is replaced by $[1 + n(x)]\overset{o}{K}_{(x,t)}$. Here $n(x)$ is an increasing function of x and $n(0) = 0$. So the above demand = supply equation takes the form

$$C_{(x,t)} = F[K_{(x,t)}] - [1 + n(x)]\overset{o}{K}_{(x,t)} - \overset{*}{U}_{(x,t)} - \sigma U_{(x,t)}$$

The concepts of a Social Welfare Function

Even restricting Social Welfare Functions to their usual logical meaning, their social meaning remains ambiguous. As a matter of fact, there exist three thoroughly different concepts of such a Social Welfare Function. They are conveniently distinguished by the Kantian labels of Categorical, Pragmatical, and Technical.

1. *A categorical Social Welfare Function.* This aims at describing "society's preferences". This function is the object of Arrow's study, *Social Choices and Individual Values.*
2. *A pragmatic Social Welfare Function.* This describes social and ethical opinions of a rational individual who may be, for instance, the economist, a public official, etc. It is the object of

Bergson's and Samuelson's studies, among others.

3. *The technical Social Welfare Function.* There is a third concept of Social Welfare Function: the *Technical Social Welfare Function.* From this standpoint, this function is but one of the economists' computation and implementation tools. It may help him to specify an optimum which may generally be defined without it. The interest of this function is purely operational: it enables the economist to use maximization computation techniques, it may help in distinguishing the analysis of tastes and opinions from that of possibilities when this is meaningful. It is this Technical Social Welfare Function with which Isard-Liossatos play.

Let welfare $w_{(x,t)}$ at any space-time point (x,t) per unit of time and length be a function of consumption $C_{(x,t)}$ at that point. So

$$w_{(x,t)} = f[C_{(x,t)}]$$

where we assume,

1. positive marginal utility $\frac{\partial w}{\partial c} = fc > 0$

2. diminishing marginal utility $\frac{\partial^2 w}{\partial c^2} = fcc < 0$

   for all $C_{(x,t)} > 0$

An interesting variant of this formulation involves the application of different weights to welfare created at different space-time points. A weighting system which is a function of distance from the origin has been illustrated in the Isard-Liossatos model. Such a system indicates

$$w_{(x,t)} = [1 + q(x)]f[C_{(x,t)}]$$

The objective of the entire modelling effort has been to find that time pattern of investment which maximizes Social Welfare W over the space interval $x = 0$ to $x = B$ and over the planning period from $t = 0$ to $t = t_1$. Most generally, total welfare W is

$$W = \int_0^B \int_0^{t_1} w \, dx \, dt$$

The necessary conditions for maximizing W are given by the Euler-Lagrange equations. We will not, however, develop these equations here. (Interested readers might refer to Isard, Liossatos.) Instead, it should be adequate to mention here that with some assumed

boundary conditions the above maximization results can be and have been evaluated. The results of these evaluations have been examined against the criteria of Social Justice established earlier. The evaluations point out that in order to obtain Social Justice under realistic conditions it is necessary to introduce into the model structures new kinds of principles—for example, a consumption redistribution principle which operates through an allocation subprinciple. It might also be desirable to introduce the principle of taxation, a capital flow principle based upon Social Welfare pricing and the intensity of consumer needs reflected in such pricing.

Conclusion

This exploratory research paper addressed itself not so much to the large fabric of the ethical theory of social justice, as to the smaller, largely conceptual issues of equity, efficiency, and participation that link with the grand theories as threads holding the parts together.

An attempt has been made to explain the implications inherent in key concepts, to draw essential distinctions, to insist upon considerations in which the fulfillment of social justice requirements directly facilitates growth. The most important purpose of this Chapter has been to seek social justice properties which both stand a good chance to be considered as 'natural' and can be defined with precision.

There is a difference between the efforts made for developing methods of planning, and those devoted to developing methods of implementation. Planners, decision-makers, either consciously or unconsciously, plan without considering constraints on implementation in any serious and detailed manner. Yet it is implementation that determines the success of planning. The second important consideration, given in this Chapter, therefore, has been directed toward formulating a strategy for implementation of the ideas presented.

There are no simple short cuts to innovation in the science of regional systems modelling, but this Chapter merely explains that when research goals are directed toward understanding regional systems modelling activity, returns in the form of better policy performance can be expected to follow sooner or later. In this brief Chapter I have assumed away uncertainty, differences among regions in resource endowments and natural features, etc. Many of the basic dynamic forces of reality have also been ignored. However, it is my hope that this initial attempt at discovering some of the important ties will lead to the large amount of research which is needed in this field.

References

1. MAITRA, Amit K., 'Towards a science of regional systems', forthcoming *General Systems*, Vol. XVIII (1973).
2. WINGO, Lowden, 'The quality of life: toward a microeconomic definition', *Urban Studies*, 10, 3-18 (1973).
3. McNAMARA, Robert S., 'Can we win the fight against global poverty?', *War/Peace Report* (November/December 1972).
4. KEYFITZ, Nathan, 'Can inequality be cured?', *The Public Interest* (1973).
5. HÖIVIK, Tord, 'Social inequality—the main issues', *Journal of Peace Research*, 2 (1971).
6. ROGERS, A.K., *The Theory of Ethics*, The McMillan Company, New York (1922).
7. THUROW, Lester, 'Toward a definition of economic justice', *The Public Interest* (1973).
8. RAWLS, John, *A Theory of Justice*, Harvard University Press (1971).
9. RESCHER, Nicholas, *Distributive Justice*, Bobbs-Merrill, Indianapolis (1966).
10. FRANKENA, William K., 'The concept of social justice', *Social Justice* (edit. by Richard B. Brandt), Prentice Hall (1962).
11. VLASTOS, Gregory, 'Justice and equality', *Social Justice* (edit. by Richard B. Brandt), Prentice Hall (1962).
12. BOULDING, Kenneth E., 'Social justice in social dynamics', *Social Justice* (edit. by Richard B. Brandt), Prentice Hall (1962).
13. BOULDING, Kenneth E., *The Image*, University of Michigan Press (1956).
14. HANSEN, Bent, 'Development and social justice', *Economic Bulletin for Asia and the Far East*, Vol. XXII, No. 3, United Nations (December 1971).
15. ISARD, Walter and WOLPERT, J., 'Notes on social science principles for world law and order', *Journal of Peace Research*, 3-4 (1964).
16. ISARD, Walter, *Methods of Regional Analysis*, Cambridge, The M.I.T. Press (1960).
17. OLSON, Mancur, *The Logic of Collective Action*, Schocken Books, New York (1968).
18. OLSON, Mancur, 'The optimal allocation of jurisdictional responsibility: the principle of "Fiscal Equivalence" ', *The Analysis & Evaluation of Public Expenditure*, Vol. 1.
19. REINER, Thomas, 'A multiple goals framework for regional planning', *Regional Science Association Papers*, Vol. XXVI (1971).
20. FREEMAN, A.M., 'Project design and evaluation with multiple objectives', *Public Expenditures and Policy Analysis* (edit. by R.H. Haveman and J. Margolis), Markham, Chicago (1970).
21. ACKOFF, Russell L., *Scientific Method: Optimizing Applied Research Decisions*, John Wiley and Sons, Inc., New York (1962).
22. ISARD, Walter and LIOSSATOS, P., 'Social injustice and optimal space-time development', *Journal of Peace Science* 1(1) (1973).
23. KOLM, S.Ch., 'The optimal production of social justice', *Public Economics* (edit. by J. Margolis and H. Guitton), St. Martin's Press, New York (1969).

Operational niches in human ecosystems

EDGAR TASCHDJIAN
New York, USA

The word "niche" which originally meant a recess
for a statue or similar object, is derived from the
Latin words for nests and nestling, i.e., for a shelter
which an organism builds for its protection [1].
The ecological niche concept has undergone considerable evolution since it was first introduced into
biological terminology, when it denoted a kind of
microhabitat based on the average of a few selected
environmental variables [2, 3]. It was thought that
only one species could be maximally adapted to one
niche and that its members would therefore be in
competition with each other for the available food
[4]. This maximal adaptedness was thought to provide a "fit" which would mold the organism into
the contours of the niche. Whereas "fitness" refers
to a quality which may conceivably be improved to
any extent, as with the fitness of an athlete, the
"fit" of the species to its niche was thought of as
an adaptation to a limiting condition, as with the
accurate fit of a key to a lock [5, 6]. On this basis
Lotka and Volterra formulated the principle of competitive exclusion, which can be described as follows:

If two motile species, X and Z, live in the same
habitat and also live in the same "ecological niche",
i.e., exactly the same kind of life, the multiplication
of species X is described by the formula

$$x = Ke^{ft}$$

where x is the number of individuals of species X

at time t, e is the basis of the natural logarithms,
K is a constant standing for the number x at $t=0$,
and f is a constant determined by the "reproductive
potential" of the species.

Similarly, species Z multiplies according to the
equation

$$z = Le^{gt}$$

If the two species compete in the same universe,
the ratio of the numbers of the two species, x/z
can be represented by a variable y, so that

$$y = \frac{Ke^{ft}}{Le^{gt}}$$

Since K and L are both constants, they can be
replaced by another constant C. The same applies
to the constants f and g, which can be replaced by
another constant, say b, which brings us back to
the equation of exponential growth

$$y = Ce^{bt}$$

If b is positive, X is competitively superior and will
completely suppress and supplant Z, and if it is
negative, Z will multiply faster and exclude X from
the niche [7].

If the sampled area occupied by a species is not
isolated, its numbers will be influenced not only by
sexual or asexual reproduction, but also by emigra-

tion from and immigration to the area. The "reproductive potential" of the species has then to be substituted by a "recruiting potential" in which the factor f (or g) is replaced by $f + m_i - m_e$, where m_i represents immigration and m_e represents emigration. This situation can be studied more easily in organisms which undergo metamorphosis, where the transformation of the larval stage into the adult can be considered analogous to immigration into the adult population. In such a system Nicholson has shown that when there is selection for greater adult potency, there is deterioration in larval potency and that the recruitment of adult insects by pupation and emergence of imagoes may vary considerably due to internal readjustments which make the development and maintenance of both larval and adult potency compatible [9]. The niche thus becomes an open system, regulated in its population density not only by the balance between births and deaths, but also by the influx and outflow of migrants.

The next step in the evolution of the niche concept occurred when biologists began to realize that no single feature or quality of an organism determines the state of adaptation. What is adapted is not the wing length of a bird nor the leaf size of a plant, but the animal or the plant as a whole. One feature may compensate for another, e.g., drought resistance in plants may be achieved either by a larger root system or by a reduced transpiration surface; similarly, a prey may escape a predator either by a better running ability or by a better hiding ability [10]. The "spatial niche" had therefore to be replaced by a "functional niche" in which multidimensional relations determined the population density.

Furthermore, ecologists were soon driven to admit that the organism is not passively molded by the environment, that environmental factors not only select the organism, but that the organism also selects and molds the environment. The migration of birds from one climate to another or the invasion of new territories by a plant or a disease are examples of the selections of environments by organisms. The building of dams by a beaver colony or the changes in soil quality by ruminant herds are examples of environmental changes due to organisms. Thus, the niche resources which were assumed as given in the "potential niche concept" now became organism-directed, organism-ordered and organism-timed in the newer "operational niche concept" [11].

From this operational point of view, the niche refers to the profession of the organism in the eco-

logical business world rather than to its location in a specific habitat [12]. According to the potential niche concept, the presence of members of a species in a single niche causes their competition for its resources. But if the niche is defined operationally, then occupancy of the niche cannot be based on spatial criteria, but must be based on the operational criterion of competition. Whilst niche occupancy previously was the criterion for the existence of competition, now competition becomes the criterion for niche occupancy.

This evolution of the niche concept occurred in the realm of biological ecology, which did not include man. With the admission of man as an integral part of the ecosystem, the focus of interest shifted from the study of plant and animal populations and communities to the effect of human actions on natural resources. Now the point of view of the ecologist and conservationist began to conflict with that of the economist and it became gradually clear that ecological theory, by itself, was unable to provide reliable criteria for human action in the environment and that human norms and human priorities were required to decide, organize and implement our utilization of natural resources [13].

In this situation we may enquire into the applicability of the niche concept to the human ecosystem and ask what form of competition occurs in a niche occupied by human individuals rather than by plants or animals. Do all human individuals occupy a single niche and, if not, how are human niches to be defined? What is the role of culture and technology in niche formation and niche occupancy? What is the recruiting potential in a given niche and how do different niches communicate and interact in the human ecosystem? These are some of the problems which require elucidation and which we shall try to explore in the following paragraphs.

Since an operational niche is characterized by the presence of competing individuals functioning in a certain capacity, it is obvious that in human ecosystems there are as many such niches as there are job categories. Biologists are accustomed to think of all members of a species as occupying the same niche and of competing with each other on an equal footing. Actually, it can easily be shown that even in purely biological contexts all members of a species do not compete with each other. A male does not compete with a female, but only with other males; in a beehive, a queen bee does not compete with a worker or a drone, but only with other queen bees. Since an animal species is composed of many genetically different populations or "demes" which are usually not even roughly panmictic, adjacent demes differ in growth potential and are favored differently in interdemic selection [14]. Thus, the idea that all members of a species occupy the same niche is not even biologically valid.

In human ecosystems, the differentiation of functional roles is even more pronounced. A taxi-driver does not compete with an overland truck driver, but only with other taxi-drivers. The degree of competition within such an operational niche depends on the capacity of the niche and the number of potential occupants, in other words, on the number of job openings within one category and the number of applicants for these openings. It may be objected that taxi-drivers and truck-drivers do compete for food, gasoline or other commodities. But actually, such indirect competition depends on the money they earn in their respective jobs. If we were to admit such indirect competition as a criterion of niche occupancy, then, by the same token, a carnivore who eats grass transformed into the meat of a gazelle would be in competition with herbivores. Of course, in the last analysis, all organisms compete for energy, but if the niche concept were based on competition for energy, it would be so all-encompassing as to be completely meaningless.

The population density in an operational niche of a human ecosystem depends also on the recruitment of its members. In animal populations the recruitment takes place mainly through sexual reproduction; immigration and emigration play a less significant role. In human social systems, however, these two components overshadow in importance the purely biological reproduction. Only in very static societies does a farmer's son probably also become a farmer or a doctor's son a doctor. Even then, the recruitment into the operational niche is not due primarily to the process of generation but rather to the process of acculturation. In societies with social mobility, positive recruitment from the undifferentiated pool of the next generation as well as from other, already differentiated niches takes the place of sexual reproduction and immigration. The question then arises: What determines the frequency of this transformation? This question is analogous to one that we can ask when, in insect populations, we enquire about the probability that a larva will be transformed into an imago.

We can formulate this problem, on the basis of communication theory, as follows: Let us compare the operational niche to a communication channel with a variable channel capacity. If all the openings are filled, no inputs are processed, no information passes through the channel and input and output are in equilibrium. If some openings are unfilled, this information reaches the labor pool through a feedback loop and as a result input (i.e., applicants) passes from the sender (or pool) to the receiver (or niche population). But the frequency of these signals is subject to two disturbances: First, the difficulty of the necessary acculturation, which corresponds to the resistance or noise in the channel and, secondly, the frequency of "dropouts" which corresponds to the degree of equivocation in signal transmission. Only the transinformation measures successful recruitments. Fig. 1 illustrates this model. It can be seen that the set of signals in the feedback loop constitutes what the economist calls a "demand

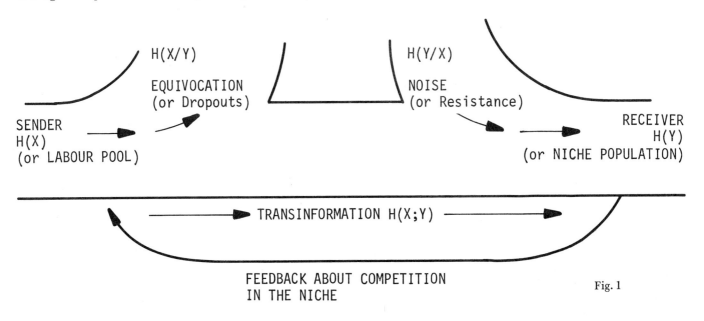

FEEDBACK ABOUT COMPETITION
IN THE NICHE

Fig. 1

function" and that the transinformation represents the corresponding supply.

It should be emphasized that the feedback about the attractiveness of the niche and the degree of competition within it takes place, itself, in a communication channel and that the information which passes through this feedback loop is also subject to entropy. This means that a prospective candidate must pay a certain price to obtain the information about the situation in the niche: He must spend time, money and energy to obtain the data which will allow him to compare different niches, even before he initiates the transformation process. This applies not only to recruitments from the as yet undifferentiated labor pool of the next generation, but also to recruitments from one niche to another [15]. Since both channels are subject to entropy and time lags, it follows that, although supply and demand are correlated, they are never in real equilibrium, but constitute a transient system in continual oscillation.

Next, let us consider shortly the role of culture and technology in the creation or abolition of operational niches in human ecosystems. In comparing different societies, from primitive to industrial ones, we can easily see that the more complex the culture, the greater is the number of diverse roles that can be played by its members. In a primitive hunting tribe there may be only three functions to be carried out: That of the hunter, that of the wife, and that of the medicine man. In an agricultural society there may also be some bartering of goods and some specialization in the manufacture of tools as well as in organizational functions such as village chieftain, priest or shepherd, but the majority of the individuals are still "pleomorphic" in that they are qualified to carry out more than one role alternatively. The more complex the technology and the more differentiated the organizational subsystems of the society, the greater is the number of functions to be performed and the number of operational niches to be filled. Every new invention creates one or more new niches and may also close out or restrict one or more others. What happens depends mainly on the time lags resulting from the inertia of the established institutions and vested interests to societal changes [16]. The importance of the time lags has been specially emphasized by Toffler [17].

In the past, the relations between supply and demand of labor has been studied by economists as one of the variables in the production process. The neoclassical theory of economics assumes that the supply curves of nonspecialized labor, like those of raw materials and intermediate goods, are positively sloped, that capital and labor can substitute for each other and that this substitution is elastic. The elasticity of substitution measures the relative responsiveness of the capital-labor ratio to given proportional changes in the marginal rate of substitution. However, this theory is unable to say anything about the short run supply of specialized labor. It assumes that in the long run specialized labor is also fully fluid, so that a master baker, given sufficient financial inducements, will become an apprentice candlestick maker [18].

The equations and graphs of the neoclassical theory were developed at first for a single product firm and they were all based on the assumption of linear cost and profit functions. But if a firm produces several commodities, each of them competes with all the others for the use of the available fixed factors of production. To account for this situation, economists developed the so-called Kuhn-Tucker theorems which permit the use of nonlinear functions and allow the substitution of inequalities and saddle points for equations, maxima and minima [19].

The neglect of the time factor in economic theory finds expression in several explicit and implicit assumptions: In the first place, the theory assumes that each transaction between two parties, say labor and management, is independent of previous transactions, so that the slate is always wiped clean when a new contract is to be reached. Actually, every new agreement depends as much upon measuring the improvement in position of the party from the preceding period as it does upon the market forces existing at the moment. Secondly, bargaining usually takes place under conditions of imperfect knowledge about market conditions, about the other party's preferences and about the level and elasticity of labor demand, so that market adjustments, even though they tend toward equilibrium, never reach it [20]. Thirdly, each party's calculation of the cost of disagreeing is largely expectational, since the anticipated future loss as the result of any course of action influences the choice strongly. Conversely, the cost of agreeing to the other party's offer results in a flow of income over time rather than in a lump sum [21].

It seems clear, in the light of the above considerations, that if we want to develop an adequate picture of the flow of competitive, specialized occupants in and out of the operational niches of a human ecosystem, we must abandon the idea that these flows are linear and that, therefore, the system as a whole is analogous to a Newtonian liquid in which all particles can occupy all positions with equal probability, so that displacements in one part will instantly and perfectly be transmitted to all other parts. Instead, we must realize that an ecosystem is a plastic system in which the fluxes are viscous and the fluid is non-Newtonian [22].

We have also seen that the system is in continual oscillation and that, even though it tends toward equilibrium, it never reaches it. We are dealing, therefore, with a perturbed system which is subject to stochastic influences from its past on its behavior in the present [23]. Speaking in the language of economics, this means that time lags, uncertainties and information costs influence the shifts in relative demands and supplies which cause frictional unemployment even when, theoretically, demand and supply are in perfect equilibrium [24].

Under these conditions, it seems that the place to look for a paradigm on which a useful theory can be based is in the field of colloid chemistry. When a pure Newtonian liquid is mixed with another, one can plot the volume fraction of the solute ϕ_1 as a function of the activity a_1, defined in such a way that in a pure solvent a_1 has the value of unity. This will give a straight linear curve (curve c in Fig. 2) because the number of sites (i.e., the niche capacity) for the solute molecules increases in proportion to the amount of solute added, with one site for every molecule added. In a Newtonian liquid the solute molecules can "elbow aside" the solvent molecules, so that the whole volume of solvent is accessible to them.

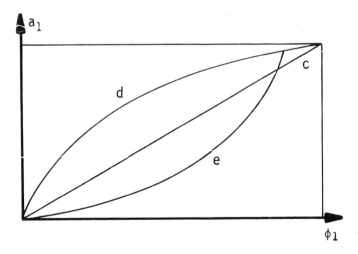

Fig. 2 Activity a_1 against volume fraction ϕ_1 of solvent sorbed in a high polymer

In a macromolecular gel, on the other hand, certain positions can be occupied with greater ease than others and as these sites are filled, the activity curve will flatten out (curve d). On the other hand, if the network of solute molecules undergoes rearrangement, the curve starts off with a slow slope, but then rises rapidly (curve e). Thus, the whole concept of a constant number of inert absorption sites loses its applicability in colloids, just as the concept of a potential niche lost its applicability in ecology.

The tendency of absorbing molecules to "stay put" which characterizes non-Newtonian liquids, will increase the probability of finding one molecule in a given position with respect to another. This probability is measured by B.H. Zimm's clustering function

$$G_{11} = (1/V)\iint [F_2(i,j) - 1]\, d(i)\, d(j)$$

where i and j are molecules of the solvent, V is the total volume and $F_2(i,j)$ is the distribution function defined by

$$(1/V^2) F_2(i,j)\, d(i)\, d(j)$$

which specifies the probability that the molecules i and j are each at the positions specified by the coordinates (i,j) in the range $d(i)$ and $d(j)$. The quantity $\phi G_{11}/v_1$, where v_1 is the molar volume of the solvent, is the mean number of solvent molecules in excess of expectation in the neighborhood of a given solvent molecule.

A clustering function of zero would mean that there exist no interactions at all between the molecules. If one molecule excludes one other from the volume it occupies, the clustering function is –1. If the first molecule occupies a special site and there are no other special sites available within the cube root of eight molecular diameters, the clustering function would be –8 [25].

In non-Newtonian liquids the apparent steady-state viscosity is not proportional to stress rate or pressure, but the relation is nonlinear. Under deformation, the elasticity of such a system is non-Hookean. This means that when the stress is small, the relations may approach linearity, but under higher stresses irreversible changes occur. Such structural modifications enormously alter the relative storage and dissipation of energy and markedly influence frictional resistance to translation of large particles while leaving the resistance to the movement of small particles relatively unchanged [26].

We can now link up this rheological approach to

the niche structure in an ecosystem with our previous approach which was based on communication theory. For Zimm's clustering function which measures a probability in excess of random expectation is obviously nothing but the information content of the distribution. While the description in terms of channel capacity and feedback loops corresponds to a microeconomic approach, the clustering function corresponds to a macroeconomic description of the system.

This rheological treatment may also be compared with one proposed by the famous economist Jan Tinbergen, who pictures the educational system of a country as an inverted fluvial system, in which the flow goes upstream from the large channel of primary to the smaller branches of higher education. This picture is very appropriate, for education obviously produces individuals which are more and more informed and whose existence is negentropic and improbable. Tinbergen treats the production of specialized labor as analogous to the production of capital goods, which means that the situation in a professional niche is determined both by its stock or inventory and by its flows in and out of the niche. If this analogy were completely valid, we should have to compute not only the time required for the production of a specialist—which may be as much as twenty years—but also the amortization rates for these human capital goods. But a recently graduated Ph.D. does not decrease in value with age, on the contrary he increases with experience. Consequently, these human "capital goods" would have to be assigned negative amortization rates. Obsolescence plays a role only as a result of changing technology in the reduction of the niche's capacity and in the consequent flow from one niche to another which may make retraining necessary [27].

In justification for the present non-ecological approach to human ecosystems, this writer, in a previous paper, has pointed out that ecologists can predict the composition of an isolated climax community in a constant environment, but that they cannot predict the time required to reach the steady climax state. Ecological predictions are therefore, unfortunately, untestable and unfalsifiable [28]. If ecology in general and human ecology in particular is to become more than a faith, if it is to become a theory able to provide us with reliable forecasts, ecologists will have to devote much more attention to the time dimension and to the inelasticities of ecological processes. Only if we shift our attention from equilibria to disequilibria, from reversibility to irreversibility, from fluidity to plasticity and from

linearity to nonlinearity can we hope to arrive at an adequate insight into the behavior of the complex man-nature ecosystem. It is hoped that the above considerations will promote such a change of perspective and that the viewpoints advocated may point in the direction of future ecological research.

References

1. KNIGHT, C.B., *Basic Concepts of Ecology*, p.171, The MacMillan Company, New York (1965).
2. PLATT, R.B. and GRIFFITH, J.F., *Environmental Measurement and Interpretation*, Preface p.VII and pp.4-5, Reinhold Publishing Corporation, New York (1964).
3. TASCHDJIAN, E., 'The evolution of ecological theory', *Systems in Society*, pp.57-69, Society for General Systems Research, Washington D.C. (1973).
4. DOBZHANSKY, Th., 'Concepts and problems of population genetics', Cold Spring Harbor Symposia on Quantitative Biology, Vo. XX, p.13 (1955).
5. NICHOLSON, A.J., 'Density governed reaction, the counterpart of selection in evolution', Cold Spring Harbor Symposia on Quantitative Biology, Vol. XX, pp.288-289 (1955).
6. NICHOLSON, A.J., 'Population dynamics in selection', *Evolution After Darwin* (edit. by S. Tax), Vol. I, p.503, The University of Chicago Press (1960).
7. HARDIN, G., 'The cybernetics of competition: A biologist's view of society', *The Subversive Science, Essays toward an Ecology of Man* (edit. by P. Shepard and D. McKinley), pp.282-284, Houghton Mifflin Company, Boston (1969).
8. WRIGHT, S., 'Ecology and selection', *Evolution after Darwin*, loc. cit., p.463.
9. NICHOLSON, A.J., 'Population dynamics in selection', loc. cit., p.509.
10. TASCHDJIAN, E., 'The evolution of ecological theory', loc. cit., p.59.
11. PLATT, R.B. and GRIFFITH, J.P., 'Environmental measurement and interpretation', loc. cit., p.5.
12. Ibid., pp.7-8.
13. TASCHDJIAN, E., 'The evolution of ecological theory', loc. cit.
14. WRIGHT, S., 'Genetics, ecology and selection', loc. cit., pp.462-467.
15. STIGLER, G.J., 'The economics of information', *The Journal of Political Economy* 69(3), 213-225 (June 1961).
16. QUIGLEY, C., 'History as a system', Paper pre-

sented at the Regional Conference of the Society for General Systems Research, College Park, Md., (2 September 1973).

17. TOFFLER, A., *Future Shock*, Bantam Books, Random House, Inc. (1970).

18. FERGUSON, C.E., *Microeconomic Theory*, Revised Edition, pp. 370, 373-374, 382, Richard D. Irwin Inc., Homewood, Ill. (1969).

19. FERGUSON, C.E., *The Neoclassical Theory of Production and Distribution*, pp. 202-204, Cambridge University Press (1969).

20. CARTTER, A.M. and MARSHALL, F.R., *Labor Economics: Wages, Employment and Trade Unionism*, p. 203, Richard D. Irwin, Inc., Homewood, Ill. (1957).

21. CARTTER, A.M., *Theory of Wages and Employment*, pp. 103, 111, 118-119, Richard D. Irwin, Inc., Homewood, Ill. (1959).

22. TASCHDJIAN, E., *Organic Communications*, pp. 87-88, Wm. C. Brown Book Company, Dubuque (1966).

23. TASCHDJIAN, E., 'A rheological approach to transient systems', *General Systems*, Vol. XV, pp. 35-45 (1970).

24. ALCHIAN, A.A. and ALLEN, W.R., Exchange and Production, Theory in Use, Wadsworth Publishing Company, Inc., Belmont, Calif., p. 491 (1969).

25. ZIMM, B.H., 'Concentrated macromolecular solutions', *Biophysical Science*, pp. 123-129, John Wiley & Sons, Inc., New York (1959).

26. FERRY, J.D., 'Rheology of macromolecular systems', *Biophysical Science*, loc. cit., pp. 130-135.

27. TINBERGEN, J., *Development Planning*, pp. 116-148, McGraw-Hill Book Company, New York/Toronto (1967).

28. TASCHDJIAN, E., 'The entropy of complex dynamic systems', *Behavioral Science* 19(2), (March 1974).

Evolution of computing as a community resource[*]

JOHN M. CARROLL and FANG-NING LIM
University of Western Ontario, London, Canada

What can computers do for people?

Our response to that challenge was that a computer could sort out the various human services society affords and put the person needing help in contact with someone able to help him.

In our city of ¼ million people, Information London was doing that already. This is a group of ladies who respond to phone calls and call upon published material and inter-personal contacts for answers. For a year and a half now we have been working with them.

The university made available $ 20,000 worth of free computer time. We are doing batch processing of files on their CDC 6400 and use their PDP-10/50 for on-line terminal access. Our Federal Department of Communications gave us $10,000. It went for supplies and salaries of part-time research assistants. I contributed two terminals: a CDC-700 visual display and a GE Terminet 300 hard-copy terminal—Control Data of Canada lent us another CDC-700 for a short time. Our terminals were linked to PDP-10 by telephone lines through acoustic couplers.

This Chapter discusses the problems of structuring information in community environment.

Two kinds of information must be handled: that which is to be given to users and that which describes the users' requests.

The two categories interact dynamically. A continuing analysis of requests guides the development of storage and retrieval strategies.

Over-all information structure

There are three data files:

(a) The Master file contains 5,000 short records, each consisting of name, address, phone number and classification code. The classification code specifies affiliation and what human service is furnished.

(b) Any number of ephemeral files linked to any unique code can be created. Each file can contain narrative information to any desired length.

(c) A scratch-pad file provides space for brief comments regarding organizations.

We have a relational file structure in which the code is a common link.

The master file is created and updated in the batch mode, but addresses and telephone numbers can be changed on-line.

[*] The research reported in this Chapter was supported in part by the Canadian Department of Communications, whose support is gratefully acknowledged.

Progress in Cybernetics and Systems Research, Volume 2

Batch mode is also used to produce listings of the file.

The individual print-outs are mailed to listed organizations when the master file is to be updated.

The directory listings can be produced in three formats:

1. By affiliation.
2. By service offered.
3. Alphabetically.

Directories in bound form are used by systems users not possessing terminal access. They provide alternative information resources where terminals exist.

There are six modes of operation implemented at terminals: search, display, create, release, change, and locate.

The alphabetic index is an inverted file. It consists of an entry table and 4,000 records. The entry table contains a list of the index terms obtained by a keyword-in-context permutation of the name field

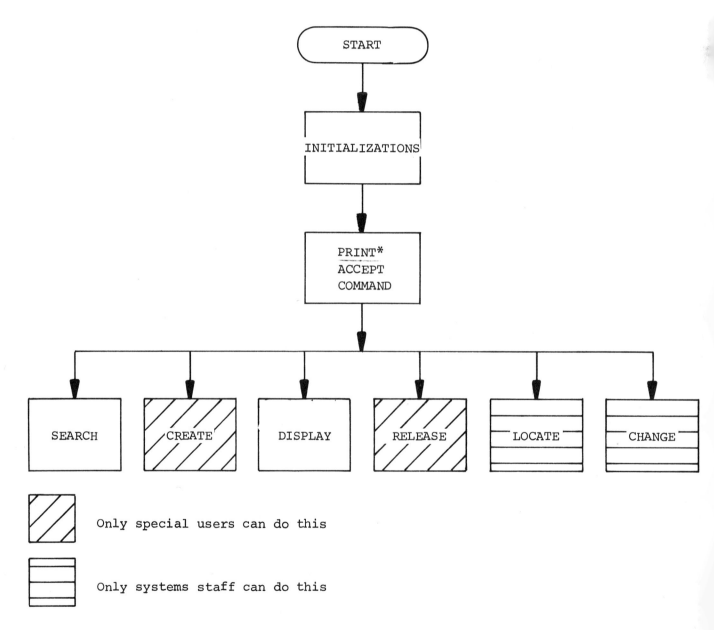

Fig. 1 What the user can get at his terminal

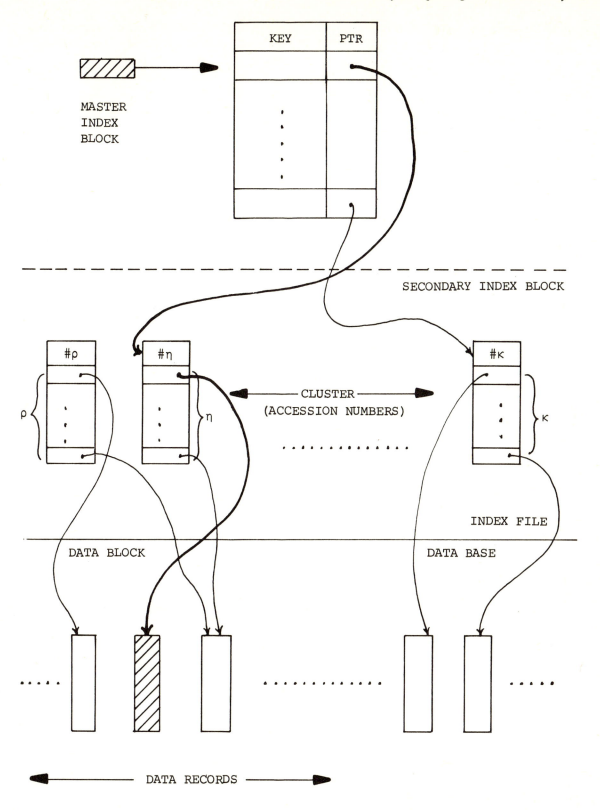

Fig. 2 Searching the Data Bank if you know any Part of the Name

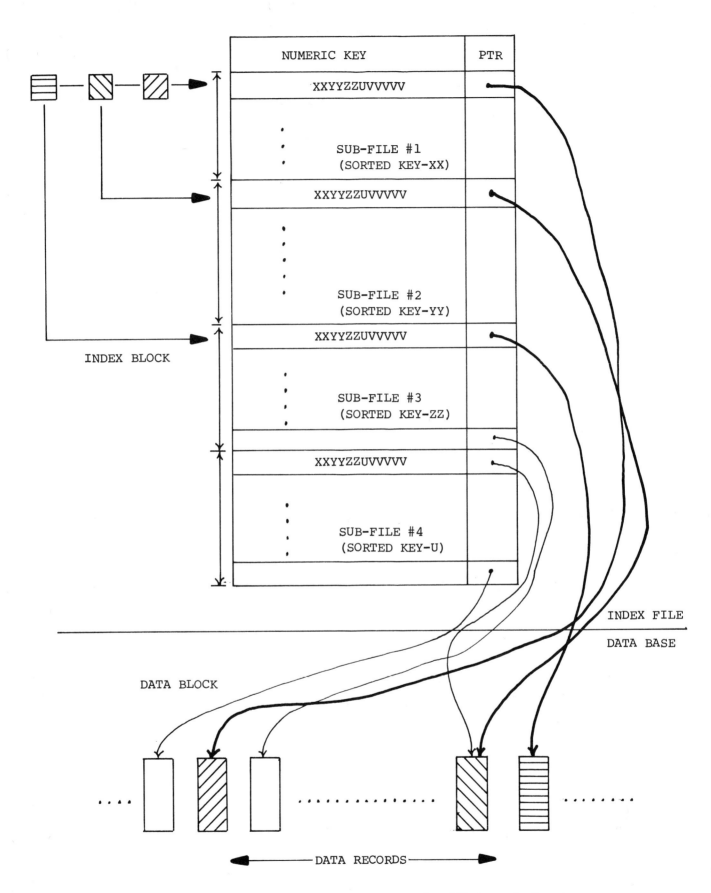

Fig. 3 Searching the Data Bank if you only know its Affiliation or its Function

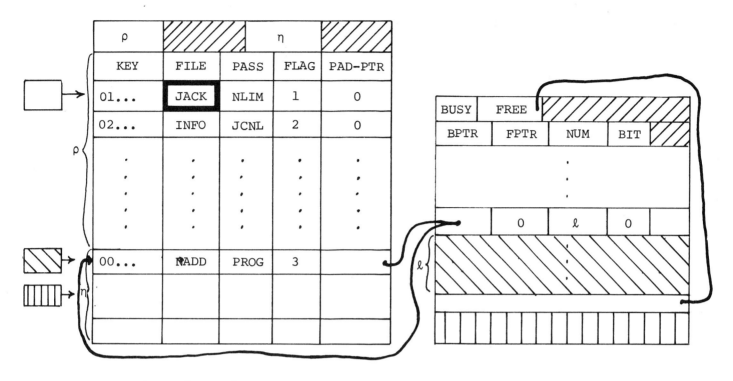

ρ			η	
KEY	FILE	PASS	FLAG	PAD-PTR
01...	JACK	NLIM	1	0
02...	INFO	JCNL	2	0
.	.	.	.	.
.	.	.	.	.
.	.	.	.	.
.	.	.	.	.
.	.	.	.	.
00...	RADD	PROG	3	

BUSY	FREE		
BPTR	FPTR	NUM	BIT
.			
.			
.			
	0	ℓ	0

ρ - number of entries sorted

η - number of entries unsorted

Fig. 4 Retrieving an Ephemeral File or a Scratch-Pad Notation   and Making a Notation

and a pointer to a record. Each record contains a header telling how many records satisfy that key and a list of pointers to master file records in which the key term appears in the name field (see Fig. 2). The alphabetic index entry table is addressed by binary search.

The numeric index is likewise an inverted file, but in four parts. Each part corresponds to a permutation of the code which brings the desired digit of the classification code into the indexing slot. Corresponding to each code is a pointer to the master file record (see Fig. 3).

Search logic permits any desired combination of the operators: AND, OR, NOT, AND-NOT, OR-NOT with alphabetic or numeric keys.

In searching the file, the user is given a report of the number of hits scored in response to his initial logical request. He is then afforded the opportunity to enhance the precision of his request by adding more terms to it.

Both the ephemeral and scratch-pad files are accessed by a key table (see Fig. 4). It is headed by a counter telling the number of keys sorted and the number of keys in an overflow table and contains codes of organizations for which either ephemeral or scratch-pad files exist.

Attached to each code is a file name if an ephemeral file exists; a password, status indicator and pointer if a scratch-pad notation exists.

The password corresponds to a password assigned to users who are privileged to create ephemeral or scratch-pad entries.

Ephemeral files can be lengthy. The ones describing tourist attractions contain descriptions, hours of accommodations, admission fees, and directions. These files are paged so that the user can look at each page heading and either have it displayed or skip to the next.

Success of the system as a community information medium depends ultimately upon each privileged user keeping his own ephemeral files up to date.

The ephemeral files realize a dynamic electronic bulletin board for the community at large.

The scratch-pad file, on the other hand, provides a convenient vehicle for entering brief comments regarding an organization offering some human service (see Fig. 4).

One use of the scratch-pad is to store information collected by the local Chamber of Commerce about the number of consumer complaints received about a business and the number of these complaints resolved to the consumer's satisfaction.

Analysis of user requests

The principal user of this system has been Information London. They handle about 1,500 queries a month.

Each query is categorized according to 24 characteristics which include the age, location, and economic status of the inquirer, the service required and the success or lack of success various agencies have had in satisfying his request.

The personnel at Information London record this information on mark-sense cards. Each month, these cards are processed by computer to produce a cross-tabulated report. Then such month's activity is added to a data-bank that can be addressed from terminals by an on-line inquiry program.

Our generalized cross-tabulation and on-line inquirer programs have had many applications.

We helped the Action League for Physically Handicapped Adults (ALPHA) analyze a survey of 900 handicapped persons. One result was to have signs placed on public washrooms showing whether the doorway would accommodate a wheelchair. Alpha is now campaigning to get lower steps on public buses, ramped entrances to public buildings, and bigger taxis to help handicapped persons get around. The statistics we helped them develop will play a significant role in this work. We found that 193 handicapped adults believed they could become self-supporting if such aids were available. This would represent a net annual saving to the province of half a million dollars in disability payments.

We helped a local artist classify some 2,000 examples of native rock paintings. From these studies, he was able to propose a tentative hypothesis regarding the age of the paintings, linking them with migrations of Canada's native peoples in the 17th to 19th centuries. These findings have stimulated interest in young native people in their cultural heritage.

We have developed easy-to-use program packages for tabulation, cross-tabulation, and on-line inquiry for citizens' groups who need to analyze surveys in preparing presentations on various subjects.

Future development of this system depends upon:
(*a*) Educating institutional users to make effective use of the dynamic file creation and updating facilities.
(*b*) Making the search and display facilities more accessible to citizen users regardless of their level of sophistication.

The second problem is basic to any plan aimed at making computing resources beneficial to citizens at large. One could visualize addressing the data bank by prestructured inquiry trees responsive to graphical input, or by text analysis of free-form inquiries, its ultimate solution will require a radical reconfiguration of terminal input/output mechanisms.

It is already evident that questions go quickly beyond the competence of local agencies and to be effective, any community information system must interface with the provincial and federal governments.

Furthermore, it is not sufficient to open channels of communication. They must be kept open. The more information we put into the system, the more users we attract; the more users we attract, the more information we need.

We ought to capture statistical information now published annually in the municipal guide book.

We ought to capture city council decisions as they are taken.

We need an inventory of housing, along with a collection of landlord-tenant complaints.

We need information on ownership, management, and employment of businesses.

CYBERNETICS OF COGNITION AND LEARNING

Ein Beitrag zu einer wortcodierten Sprachübertragung mit minimalem Datenfluß

J. KÜHLWETTER
Technische Hochschule, Darmstadt,
Bundesrepublik Deutschland

Um Sprache über bestehende postalische Telefonnetze mit möglichst geringem Datenfluß übertragen zu können, muß eine quellen- und kanalcodierte Sprachübertragung angewendet werden. Wie in [1] gezeigt wurde, kann mit einem Formantvocoder mit drei Formanten ein Datenfluß von 320 bit/s erreicht werden. Bei Verwendung eines Kanalvocoders mit 17 Synthese- und 9 Analysefiltern kann ein Datenfluß von 440 bit/s erreicht werden [2]. Bedeutend höher ist der Datenfluß von 4-12 kbit/s, den man mittels kurvenformcodierter Sprachübertragung erreichen kann [1, 3, 4]. Wie Tabelle 1 zeigt, ist der erforderliche Datenfluß von 320 bit/s des Formantvocoders mit drei Formanten für Sprachübertragungen mit vergleichbarer Telefonqualität am geringsten. Ist jedoch nur der gesprochene Text zu übertragen, so kann der dann erforderliche minimale Datenfluß nur mit einer wortcodierten Sprachübertragung erreicht werden (siehe Bild 1). Der dabei entstehende Datenfluß hängt von der Anzahl der Wörter des zugelassenen Wortvorrates und der Anzahl der in einer Sekunde gesprochenen Wörter ab. In Bild 1 sind die erreichbaren Datenraten in Abhäangigkeit der Sprechgeschwindigkeiten [5] für verschiedene Wortvorräte angegeben. Nach Küpfmüller [5], der sich in seinen Untersuchungen auf das von Kaeding

[6] 1898 in Berlin herausgegebene Werk "Häufigkeitswörterbuch der deutschen Sprach" bezog, besteht ein Wort im Mittel aus 5.53 Buchstaben und eine Silbe im Mittel aus 3.03 Buchstaben, wobei die Pause nicht mitgezählt wurde.

Wie nun eine sprecherunabhängige Worterkennung eines begrenzten Wortvorrates erfolgen kann, soll im folgenden beschrieben werden.

Sprecherunabhängige Worterkennung
Für eine sprecherunabhängige Worterkennung muß gefordert werden, daß die Worte deutlich mit normaler Sprechgeschwindigkeit und dialekt-frei gesprochen und außerdem kurze Pausen zwischen aufeinanderfolgenden Worten gemacht werden. Durch die Pausen können die Worte eindeutig eingegrenzt werden und dadurch auch die Wortdauer als Erkennungs-merkmal verwendet werden kann. Die Erkennung der aus Einzelzeichen (Buchstaben) aufgebauten geschriebenen Sprache erfolgt visuell. Die Worte sind hier durch Leerzeichen, die den Pausen in gesprochener Sprache (ohne Pausen der Plosivlaute) entsprechen, voneinander isoliert. Aus der Aufeinanderfolge der verschiedenen Einzelzeichen wird dann eine eindeutige Zuordnung zu dem entsprech-

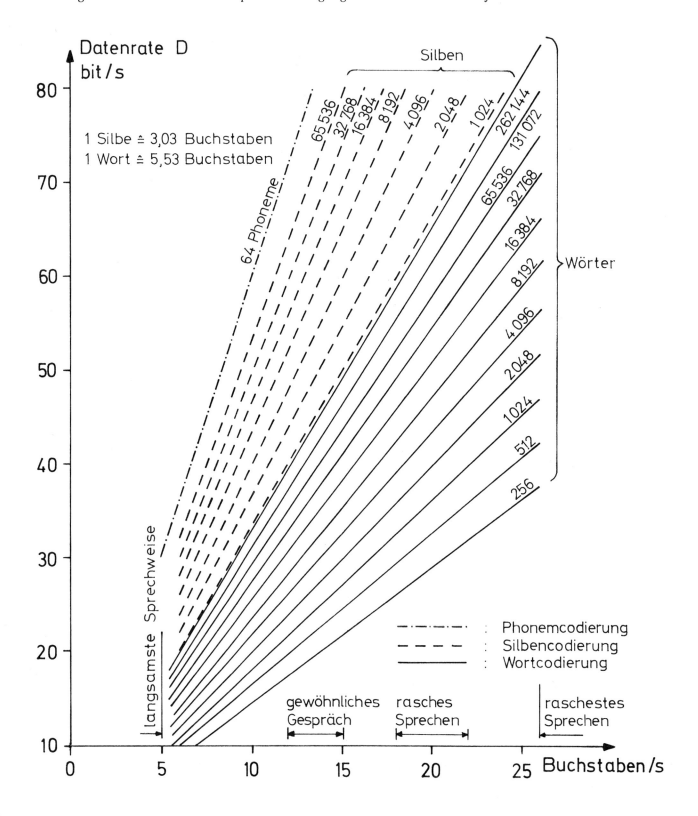

Bild 1 Datenrate D in Abhängigkeit von der in einer Sekunde gesprochenen Anzahl an Buchstaben und der gewählten Codierung des Sprachsignales

	erreichbare Datenrate	Qualität der synthetisierten Sprache
Formantvocoder 3 Formanten Grundperiodendauer	320 bit/s (240 bit/s) (80 bit/s)	Telefonqualität
Kanalvocoder 17 Synthesekanäle 9 Analysekanäle Grundperiodendauer	440 bit/s) (360 bit/s) (80 bit/s)	Telefonqualität
Kanalvocoder 13 Synthesefilter 7 Analysefilter Grundperiodendauer	360 bit/s) (280 bit/s) (80 bit/s)	Telefonqualität
Kurvenformcodierer 300 Hz bis 3.4 kHz S/N = 60 dB	12 kbit/s	Telefonqualität
Kurvenformcodierer 300 Hz bis 2.4 kHz S/N = 30 dB	6 kbit/s	100%-ige Wortverständlichkeit
Kurvenformcodierer 300 Hz bis 1.5 kHz S/N = 30 dB	3.75 kbit/s	95%-ige Wortverständlichkeit 100%-ige Satzverständlichkeit
Wortcodierung 262144 Wörter 4096 Wörter 1024 Wörter 256 Wörter	18 bis 90 12 bis 60 10 bis 50 8 bis 40 bit/s	100%-ige Wortverständlichkeit

Tabelle 1   Erreichbare Datenraten zur Übertragung des gesprochenen Textes

enden Wort, das in einem Speicher (Gedächtnis) bereitsteht, erfolgen. Auf ähnliche Weise soll eine automatische Worterkennung erfolgen. Hierbei müssen ebenfalls die Einzelzeichen (Phoneme) der Lautsprache erkannt und aus der Aufeinanderfolge der

Phoneme dann das entsprechende Wort aus einem Speicher abgerufen werden. Allerdings bereitet die Erkennung aller Phoneme noch sehr große Schwierigkeiten, so daß man sich zuerst auf die Erkennung der Phonemgruppen:

a) stimmhafte Plosive,
b) stimmlose Plosive,
c) stimmhafte Frikative,
d) stimmlose Frikative,
e) vokalähnliche Laute,
f) Vokale

beschränken kann. Eine weitere Unterteilung der erkannten Phonemgruppen, vor allem der Vokale und vokalähnlichen Laute in die einzelnen Phoneme gestattet dann schon die Erkennung eines kleineren Wortvorrates. Bevor nun die Kriterien zur Erkennung der Vokale und vokalähnlichen Laute angegeben werden, sollen zuerst noch einige Kriterien angegeben werden, die direkt aus dem Sprachsignal abgeleitet werden können und auf die hier nicht näher eingegangen wird. Diese Kriterien sind:

a) Die Dauer eines Wortes,
b) die Dauer der Phonemgruppen,
c) die Stimmhaft-stimmlos-Segmentierung des Wortes,
d) die Pause-Signal-Segmentierung des Wortes (Plosiv-Frikativ-Unterscheidung)
e) die Sprachmelodie,
f) die Variation des Maximalwertes des Zeitsignales je Grundperiode.

Dies sei an den beiden Tabellen 2 und 3 erläutert. Tabelle 2 zeigt eine Zusammenstellung von Worten, die nur einen Vokal enthalten (aus [6] entnommen). Tabelle 3 zeigt die dazugehörenden codierten Worte, wobei nur die Phonemgruppen angegeben sind.

Wie man aus Tabelle 3 ablesen kann, gibt es Überschneidungen von Worten, d.h. durch Unterteilung in die sechs Phonemgruppen (siehe Tabelle 3) ist keine eindeutige Trennung dieser Worte möglich. Hier müssen dann die Kriterien a) bis f) weiterhelfen.

Erkennungskriterien für Vokale und vokalähnliche Laute

Wie in [7, 8] gezeigt wurde, ist es möglich, aus den codierten Zahlenwerten, die aus den Amplituden und Frequenzen der ersten drei Maxima (Formanten) und drei Minima (Antiformanten) der grundperiodensynchronen Amplitudenspektren gebildet werden, die Vokale eindeutig zu erkennen. Es können die Frequenzverhältnisse (see page 98)

Tabelle 2   Wortliste mit 1 Vokal, nach KAEDING

1. Vokal

i	in	nie	sie	die	hin
	im	mir	wie	dir	hier
	ihm	mich	wir	bin	viel
	ihr	nicht	will	giebt	Schrift
	ihn	nichts	wird	bis	
	ins	mit	sind	dies	
	ich		sich	dich	
	ist		Sicht	Blick	
e	er	mehr	wenn	der	je
	erst	recht	sehr	den	her
	es	rechts	wer	dem	Herr
	et		selbst	denn	jetzt
			Welt	des	fest
			Weg	geht	stellt
			setz		steht
			setzt		
a	an	man	war	da	ja	kam
	am	mal	sagt	dann	fall	Tag
	all	nahm	was	dar	Zahl	trag
	als	Land	Satz	gar	Jahr	
	Art	mals		bald	Hand	
	ab	Mark		ganz	halb	
		nach		das	falls	
		maß		daß	hat	
		macht			zwar	
		Nacht			Stand	
		rat			Stadt	
ä		nächst			
		läßt			
u	um	nur		du	zu
	und	nun		durch	zum
	uns	muß		gut	zur
				grund	Schluß
ü					für
					führt

Tabelle 3   Codierte Wortliste

1. Vokal

i	—v	v—	F—	E—	f—v	
	—vf	v—v	F—v	E—v	fv—fe	
	—f	v—f	F—vE	E—Ee		
	—fe	v—fe	F—f	E—f		
		v—fef	F—fe	Ev—e		

e	—v	v—v	F—v	E—v	f—	
	—vfe	v—fe	F—vEfe	E—f	f—v	
	—f	v—fef	F—ve	E—e	f—vv	
	—e		F—E		f—fe	
			F—ef		f—ve	
			F—efe		f—e	

a	—v	v—v	F—v	E—	f—	e—v
	—vf	v—vE	F—Ee	E—v	f—v	e—E
	—ve	v—vf	F—f	E—vE	f—vE	ev—E
	—E	v—ve	F—ef	E—vf	f—Ef	
		v—f		E—f	f—e	
		v—fe			fF—v	
		v—e			fe—vE	
					fe—e	

ä		v—ffe				
		v—fe				

u	—v	v—v		E—	f—	
	—vE	v—f		E—vf	f—v	
	—vf			E—e	f—v	
				Ev—vE	fv—f	

ü					f—v	
					f—ve	

Codierung:
—   Vokal
v   vokalähnliche Laute
F   Frikativlaut, stimmhaft
E   Explosivlaut, stimmhaft
f   Frikativlaut, stimmlos
e   Explosivlaut, stimmlos

$$\frac{F2}{F1} \quad\Bigg| \quad \frac{F3}{F1} \quad\Bigg| \quad \frac{F2-F1}{F1} \quad\Bigg| \quad \frac{F3-F1}{F1} \quad\Bigg| \quad \frac{F3-F2}{F1} \quad\Bigg| \quad \frac{F3-F2}{F2} \quad\Bigg| \quad \frac{F3-F2}{F2-F1} \quad\Bigg| \quad \frac{F3-F1}{F2-F1} \quad\Bigg| \quad \frac{aF1}{F1} \quad\Bigg|$$

$$\frac{aF2-F2}{F1} \quad\Bigg| \quad \frac{aF2-aF1}{F1}$$

und die Amplitudenverhältnisse

$$\frac{A1}{A2} \quad\Bigg| \quad \frac{A1}{A3} \quad\Bigg| \quad \frac{A2}{A3} \quad\Bigg| \quad \frac{A1}{A2} : \frac{A2}{A3} \quad\Bigg| \quad \frac{A1}{A2} : \frac{A1}{A3} \quad\Bigg| \quad \frac{A1}{A3} - \left(\frac{A1}{A2} + \frac{A2}{A3}\right) \quad\Bigg| \quad \frac{A1}{aA1} \quad\Bigg| \quad \frac{A1}{aA2} \quad\Bigg| \quad \frac{aA1}{aA2}$$

gebildet werden.
Werden nur die aus den Frequenzen und Amplituden der ersten drei Formanten gebildeten und codierten Zahlenwerte verwendet, können die Vokale 2–4, 3–4, 7–8, 7–9, 7–10, 8–9, 8–10, 9–10 und 11–12 nicht voneinander getrennt werden. In Bild 2 sind die codierten Zahlenwerte der aus den Frequenzen der ersten drei Formanten gebildeten Verhältnisse angegeben [9,10]. Bild 3 zeigt die codierten Zahlenwerte der aus den Amplituden der ersten drei Formanten gebildeten Verhältnisse [9,10]. Durch Hinzunahme der Frequenzen und Amplituden der ersten drei Minima (Antiformanten) des grundperiodensynchronen Amplitudenspektrums und der daraus gebildeten Frequenz- und Amplitudenverhältnisse wird es dan möglich, die Vokale eindeutig zu erkennen [7,8]. In Bild 4 sind die Variationsbereiche der drei verwendeten Kriterien zur Erkennung der Vokale a-e-i-o-u in den Logatomen KAHL-DEEF-MIES-HOOG-SCHUL, die von zwei männlichen und einem weiblichen Sprecher aufgenommen wurden, angegeben. Bild 5 zeigt die codierten Zahlenwerte. Aus Bild 5 geht hervor, daß nun die Trennung der Vokale eindeutig und sprecherunabhängig ist. Bild 6 zeigt das decodierte Logatom MIES, Bild 7 das decodierte Logatom SCHUL. Aus den beiden Bildern 6 und 7 wird deutlich, daß die Vokale sehr gut erkannt werden, trotz der manchmal mangelhaften Grundperiodensegmentierung [11], die zu Fehldecodierungen führte. Mit den verwendeten drei Kriterien D1, D2 und D3 werden die vokalähnlichen Laute m als u und l als i erkannt. Wird nun noch der Maximalwert des Zeitsignales je Grundperiode als Erkennungskriterium verwendet, so sind auch die vokalähnlichen Laute zu erkennen. Um auch die Lautübergänge zu erkennen, müssen die Änderungen der ersten beiden Formantfrequenzen und der Grundfrequenz, sowie die Änderung des Maximalwertes des Zeitsignales aufeinanderfolgender Sprachgrundperioden bestimmt werden. Eine starke Änderung des Maximalwertes des Zeitsignales kennzeichnet den Übergang von einem Vokal zu einem stimmhaften

Laut (negative Änderung) bzw. von einem stimmhaften Laut zu einem Vokal (positive Änderung), wenn eine stimmhafte Kennzeichnung des betreffenden Sprachsignales vorliegt. Die Kennzeichnung stimmhaft-stimmlos und Pause-Signal kann nach [12,13] vorausgesetzt werden.

Vorschlag einer Worterkennung
Durch eine Stimmhaft-stimmlos-Segmentierung werden die Phoneme in die Phonemgruppen stimmlose Frikative und Plosive, sowie in stimmhafte Plosive und Frikative, Vokale und vokalähnliche Laute unterteilt. Die Plosive werden von den Frikativen durch eine Pause-Signal-Segmentierung getrennt, wenn die Plosivlaute nicht am Wortanfang stehen. Denn dann ist die Pause die gerade die Plosivlaute kennzeichnet, nicht mehr von der Pause, die aufeinanderfolgende Wörter trennt, zu unterscheiden.

Aus der Wortdauer, der Stimmhaft-stimmlos-Segmentierung, der Anzahl der Vokale und der Anzahl der Phoneme des betreffenden Wortes erfolgt eine Grobauswahl aus dem zur Verfügung stehenden Wortvorrat. Die endgültige Zuordnung des zu erkennenden Wortes erfolgt dann aus der Aufeinanderfolge der erkannten Phoneme bzw. Phonemgruppen.

Die ersten Hardware-Ansätze einer automatischen Spracherkennung wurden durch die Realisierung eines in Echtzeit arbeitenden Analysators verwirklicht. Dieser ermittelt grundperiodensynchrone Amplitudenspektren, die Frequenzen und Amplituden der ersten drei Maxima und Minima und einige der angegebenen codierten Frequenz- und Amplitudenverhältnisse. Außerdem werden die Änderungen der ersten beiden Formantfrequenzen und die Änderung des Maximalwertes des Zeitsignales je Grundperiode bestimmt. Bild 8 zeigt eine Fotografie des realisierten Analysators.

Bild 2 Codierte Frequenzverhältnisse

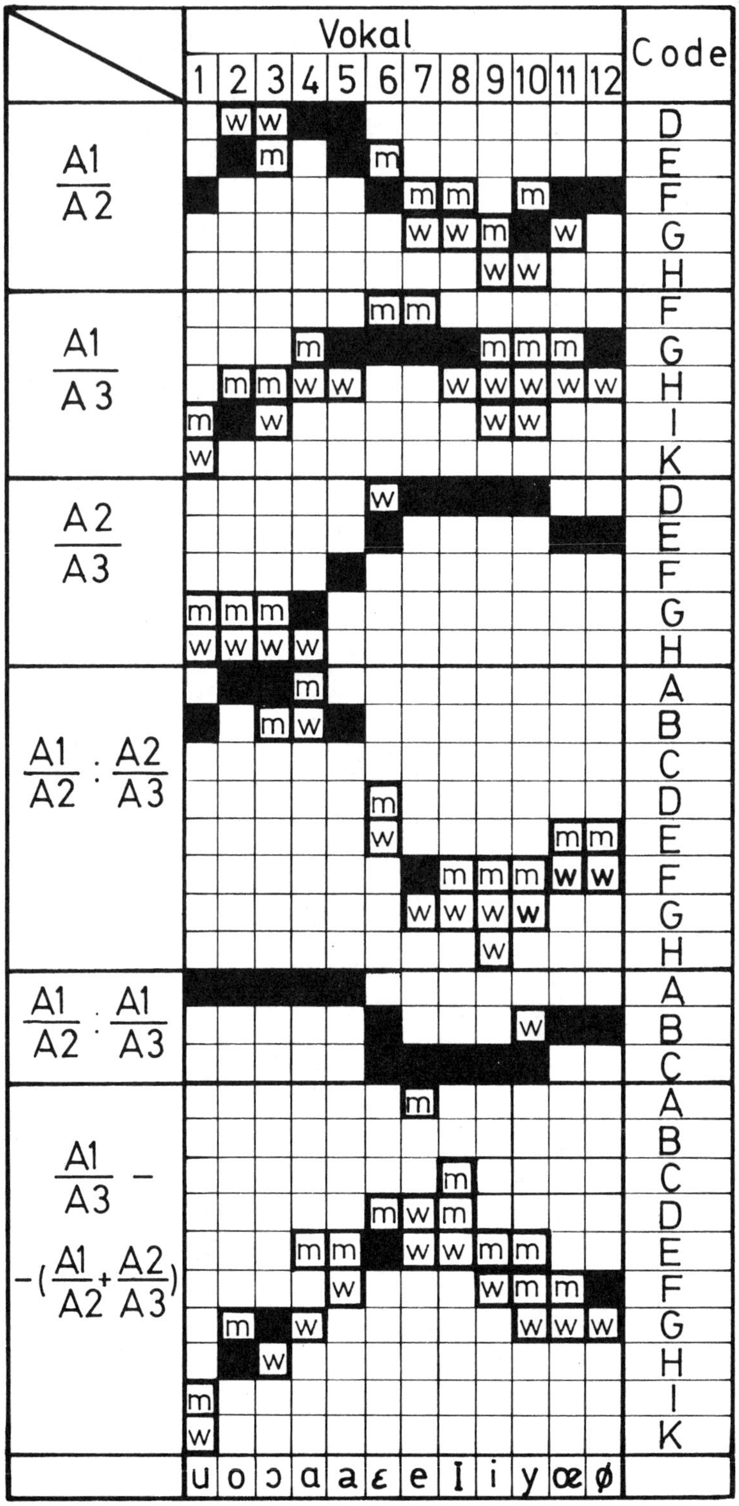

Bild 3 Codierte Amplitudenverhältnisse

Krit. Laut	D1	D2	D3
a	-4 ... -1	3 ... 7	3 ... 4
e	-1 ... 0	6 ... 10	6 ... 14
i	2 ... 6	4 ... 10	9 ... 13
o	-1 ... 1	0 ... 2	2
u	2 ... 5	0 ... 3	2 ... 3

$$D1 = K \cdot \log \frac{A1}{A2} \,, \quad D2 = K \cdot \log \frac{A2}{aA1} \,, \quad D3 = \frac{F2-F1}{F1}$$

Bild 4 Variationsbereich der drei verwendeten Erkennungs-kriterien D1, D2 und D3

	a	e	i	o	u	Schwelle	Code
D1	x	x	x			≤ 1	O
				x	x	> 1	L
D2			x	x		≤ 3	O
	x	x			x	> 3	L
D3	x			x	x	≤ 5	O
		x	x			> 5	L

Bild 5 Codierte Zahlenwerte der drei verwendeten Erkennungskriterien D1, D2 und D3

D1	D2	D3	D1	D2	D3	Decodiert	Phonem
3	1	4	L	0	0	U	
4	0	4	L	0	0	U	
4	1	4	L	0	0	U	m
3	1	4	L	0	0	U	
2	7	18	L	L	L	I	
>1	>3	>5	L	L	L	28 mal I	i
2	8	10	L	L	L	I	
1	7	11	0	L	L	E	
≤1	>3	>5	0	L	L	19 mal E	e
1	9	11	0	L	L	E	
2	5	9	L	L	L	I	
2	8	10	L	L	L	I	
4	2	9	L	0	L	Z	
4	5	10	L	L	L	I	s
4	3	10	L	0	L	Z	
1	9	26	0	L	L	E	
4	5	20	L	L	L	I	
Zahlenwerte			codierte Zahlenwerte				

Z: codefremde Kombination

Bild 6 Decodiertes Logatom MIES

D1	D2	D3	D1	D2	D3	Decodiert	Phonem
1	5	6	0	L	L	E	
3	2	4	L	0	0	U	
3	3	5	L	L	0	Z	∫
3	3	4	L	L	0	Z	
4	1	4	L	0	0	U	
1	3	5	L	0	0	2 mal U	
3	1	4	L	0	0	U	
2	3	4	L	L	0	Z	
3	1	4	L	0	0	U	
1	3	5	L	0	0	6 mal U	
3	2	2	L	0	0	U	
2	3	2	L	L	0	Z	
2	3	2	L	L	0	Z	u
3	2	2	L	0	0	U	
1	3	5	L	0	0	15 mal U	
2	2	3	L	0	0	U	
2	3	3	L	L	0	Z	
3	3	3	L	L	0	Z	
4	1	3	L	0	0	U	
1	3	5	L	0	0	4 mal U	
5	1	5	L	0	0	U	
4	5	15	L	L	L	I	
1	3	5	L	L	L	2 mal I	
3	7	11	L	L	L	I	l
3	2	11	L	0	L	Z	
3	6	11	L	L	L	I	
Zahlenwerte			codierte Zahlenwerte				

Z : codefremde Kombination

Bild 7 Decodiertes Logatom SCHUL

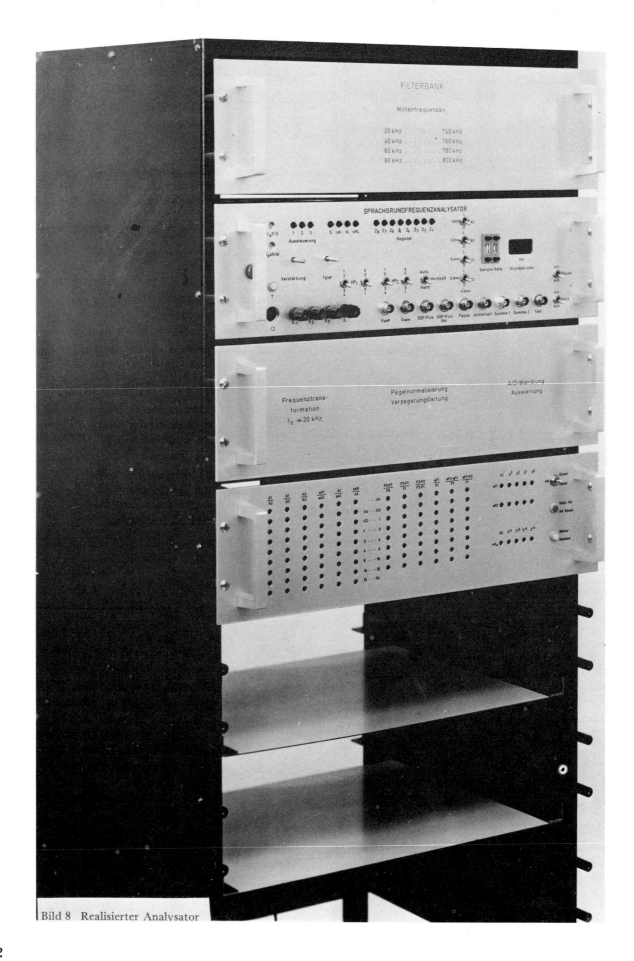

Bild 8 Realisierter Analysator

102

Ein Beitrag zu einer wortcodierten Sprachübertragung mit minimalem Datenflusz

Literaturverzeichnis

1. KÜHLWETTER, J., Prinzip und Anwendung eines adaptiven Differenz-Puls-Code-Modulations-Verfahrens mit 1 Bit je Abtastwert. Frequenz 27, H.12, S.330-334 (1973).
2. Übertragung von telefonbandbegrenzter Sprache mit einem Kanalvocoder bei einem Datenfluß von 440 bit/s. Frequenz 28, voraussichtlich in Heft 2 (1974).
3. PCM range greatly boosted with variable coding signals, *Electronic Design*, H.21,S.128 (1973).
4. BETTINGER, O. und WIECHERT, D., Digitale Sprachübertragung bei mobilen Funkdiensten. Nachrichtentechnische Fachberichte Band 42, Januar, PCM-Technik, S.126-135 (1972).
5. KÜPFMÜLLER, K., Die Entropie der deutschen Sprache. Fernmeldetechnische Zeitschrift 7, S.265-272 (1954).
6. KAEDING, F.W., Häufigkeitswörterbuch der deutschen Sprache. Selbstverlag des Herausgebers, Steglitz bei Berlin, 1897 (Auszug in Grundlagenstudien aus Kybernetik, 1963, Band 4, Verlag Schnelle, Quickborn bei Hamburg).
*7. KÜHLWETTER, J., Sprecherunabhängige Vokalerkennung. Forschungsbericht Nr.36 des Fachbereiches Nachrichtentechnik der TH Darmstadt, Fachgebiet Elektroakustik (April 1972).
*8. KÜHLWETTER, J., Erkennung von Vokalen und vokalähnlichen Lauten im Hinblick auf eine Worterkennung in Echtzeit. Forschungsbericht Nr.50 des Fachbereiches Nachrichtentechnik der TH Darmstadt, Fachgebiet Übertragungstechnik, (Februar 1973).
9. POLS, L.C.W., TROMP, H.R.C., und PLOMP, R., Frequency analysis of Dutch vowels from 50 male speakers. *Journal Acoustical Society of America* 53, H.4, S.1093-1101 (1973).
10. VAN NIEROP, D.J.P.J., POLS, L.C.W., und PLOMP, R., Frequency analysis of Dutch vowels from 25 female speakers, *Acustica* 29, Nr.2, S.110-118 (1973).
11. KÜHLWETTER, J., Sprachgrundfrequenzbestimmung mit dem Rechner. Angewandte Informatik 14, H.7, S.326-330 (1972).
12. ERB, H.-J., Eine Anordnung zur Erkennung der in einem Zeitsignal enthaltenen niedrigsten Frequenz. Frequenz 27, H.5, S.120-121 (1973).
*13. ERB, H.-J., Eine Anordnung zur Erkennung von Pausen in Sprach-signalen und zur Unterscheidung von stimmhaften und stimmlosen Lauten. Forschungsbericht Nr.51 des Fachbereiches Nachrichtentechnik der TH Darmstadt, Fachgebiet Übertragungstechnik, (Februar 1973).

*Forschungsberichte sind zu beziehen über: Technische Informationsbibliothek Hannover, Abt. Deutsche Forschungsberichte; 3 Hannover, Welfengarten 1B.

Abstract

Word-coded speech transmission with minimal data flow
J. Kühlwetter

Consideration is given to the use of source and canal-coded speech transmission in order to transmit speech over existing postal telephone systems with minimal data flow.

The level of data flow with various vocoders is discussed.

Description is given of the recognition of words of a limited range independent of the speaker and the conditions necessary to achieve this.

Limitation is made in the first instance to the following phonemic groups:
a) Voiced plosive
b) Voiceless plosive
c) Voiced fricative
d) Voiceless fricative
e) Vocalic sounds
Recognition criteria are given for vowels and vocalic sounds

Experimental results in the identification of translation schemes

P.L. DELLA VIGNA and **C. GHEZZI**
Istituto di Elettrotechnica ed Elettronica,
Politecnico di Milano, Italy

1. Introduction

A central problem in the automatic processing of programming languages is the formal specification of the transformations through which the input text which is read by the computer is transformed into a sequence of instructions in machine code.

Indeed, some phases of this process, namely the lexical and syntactic analysis, can be considered almost satisfactorily formally described but the most crucial point, actually the translation process, is not so well founded theoretically.

What really happens in the translation process is a sequence of *structural transformations*. The input program is firstly scanned and lexically processed and then transformed into a tree structure (parse-tree) by the syntactic processor; the parse-tree is then re-shaped by a sequence of transformations through which any possible redundant structure is removed, attributes are computed, common sub-expressions discovered (for optimization purposes), and so on [1, 2, 3].

It should be noted that the description above relies on the inherent structure of the translation process, even if in most compilers all these phases are inter-mixed quite inextricably.

Nevertheless, a formal description of these primitive transformations can be useful for characterizing without any ambiguity the exact result of a sequence of transformations.

Moreover, following the lesson of structured programming, we should expect each compiler to be modular and each module consisting in one basic transformation.

One transformation which seems suitable to perform the re-shaping of tree structures is the *syntax directed translation scheme (SDTS)* proposed by Lewis and Stearns [5].

SDTS-transformations will be formally described later on; here we only remind the reader that they re-shape a tree by deleting its terminals, introducing new terminals and permuting the descendents in each nonterminal node.

This Chapter is essentially concerned with SDTS-transformations. In particular we are interested in the identification of a SDTS which defines the translation between two context-free grammars, satisfying a suitable set of examples of translation between source and object strings.

The initial motivation of this work was to test SDTS in order to discover how suitable they are to describe nontrivial transformations.

Although the main concern here is still in the area of computer translation of languages, we feel that this work can have some implication in the area of mathematical linguistics [8]. SDTS-transformations

Progress in Cybernetics and Systems Research, Volume 2
Copyright © 1975 by Hemisphere Publishing Corporation

are closely related to transformational grammars and our program, if correctly driven by examples, can discover if two languages are *structurally similar*, that is parse-trees which correspond in the translation can be decomposed into subtrees of finite size with the same number of nonterminal descendents.

In the following Section 2, we will briefly resume the basic definitions which will be used extensively in the Chapter. After that, in Section 3, we will describe the problem in detail; in Section 4 we will describe the implementation and in Section 5 we will describe an example.

2. Some definitions

A *context-free grammar (C.F.G.)* [1] is a 4-tuple $G = (V_N, V_T, P, S)$, where V_N and V_T are two disjoint sets, respectively called *nonterminal* and *terminal alphabet*, $S \in V_N$ is the *axiom* and P is a finite set of productions $A \to \alpha$, where $A \in V_N$ and $\alpha \in (V_N \cup V_T)^*$.

In the sequel we will use the following convention:

- elements of V_N (*nonterminals*) represented by upper case letters;
- elements of V_T (*terminals*) represented by lower case letters at the beginning of the alphabet;
- strings of terminals by lower case letters at the end of the alphabet;
- strings of terminals and nonterminals by Greek letters.

Each production is assigned an identifier, which is an integer *index* and is characterized by its *order*, that is the number of the nonterminals appearing in its left part.

The relation $\xrightarrow[G]{1}$ is defined on $(V_N \cup V_T)^+$; it is

$\alpha A \beta \xrightarrow[G]{1} \alpha \gamma \beta$ if $A \to \gamma$ is in P.

A *derivative* is a sequence $\alpha_0, \alpha_1, ..., \alpha_N$ such that

$\alpha_0 \xrightarrow[G]{1} \alpha_1 ... \xrightarrow[G]{1} \alpha_N$; it is written $\alpha_0 \xrightarrow[G]{N} \alpha_N$.

The language defined by G is

$L(G) = \{x \mid x \in V_T^* \wedge S \xrightarrow[G]{*} x\}$.

In the sequel we will always implicitly refer to context-free languages and grammars.

A derivative can be immediately represented by means of a *derivation-tree (parse-tree)* as shown in Fig. 1.

In what follows we will be interested in the shape of trees, and so the terminal leaves can be ignored. The tree in Fig. 1 is thus transformed in the associated *labelled stencil-tree* (LST) shown in Fig. 2.

$$G_1 = (\{S\}, \{a,b\}, S, P_1) \qquad P_1 \begin{cases} S \to SaS \\ S \to b \end{cases}$$

$$S \xrightarrow[G]{1} SaS \xrightarrow[G]{1} SaSab \xrightarrow[G]{1} SaSaSab \xrightarrow[G]{1} baSaSab \xrightarrow[G]{1} babaSab \xrightarrow[G]{1} bababab$$

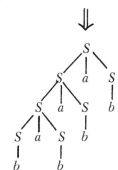

Fig. 1

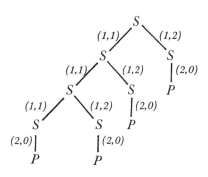

Fig. 2

The branches which leave a node of the LST are labelled by a couple of integers, the first representing the index of the production implied, the second, if positive, the position of the son in the right part, having numbered the nonterminals from the left; if the second integer is zero, the branch is terminal and the son is labelled F, such that $F \notin V_N \cup V_T$.

A *syntax-directed translation scheme (SDTS)* can be defined as a grammar with two right parts rather than just one; the second right part (the *transduction element*) is such that for each nonterminal in the first right part there is exactly one occurrence of the same nonterminal, while the terminals can belong to different alphabets.

According to the example shown in Fig. 3, the LST generated by G_2 shown in Fig. 4a is transformed by the SDTS into the LST shown in Fig. 4b.

In other words, the operations which a SDTS defines in each node of the source derivation-tree

are:
  a) Elimination of the terminal sons.
  b) Permutation of the nonterminal sons.
  c) Introduction of new terminal sons.

$G_2 = (\{S,A,B\},\ \{a,b\},\ P_2,\ S)$

Source productions	Transduction elements
1) $S \to aAB$	BAx
2) $A \to AbB$	$ByzA$
3) $B \to b$	z
4) $A \to a$	w

Fig. 3

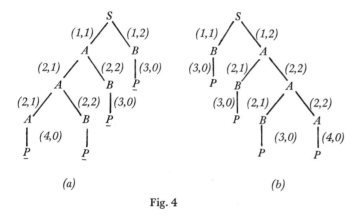

(a)   (b)

Fig. 4

It should be noted that a SDTS transforms the source context-free grammar (language) into an object context-free grammar (language). In the case shown in Fig. 3 the object context-free grammar is

$G_3 = (\{S,A,B\},\ \{x,y,z,w\},\ P_3,\ S)$

$$\left. \begin{array}{l} 1)\ S \to BAx \\ 2)\ A \to Byz \\ 3)\ B \to z \\ 4)\ A \to w \end{array} \right\} P_3$$

The definition given above imposes some very heavy constraints on two context-free grammars to be couplable in a SDTS; in fact the two grammars should derive identical LST's up to a possible permutation of branches in the nodes.

More formally, let $G_1 = (V_{N1},\ V_{T1},\ P_1,\ S_1)$ and $G_2 = (V_{N2},\ V_{T2},\ P_2,\ S_2)$. G_1 and G_2 can be coupled in a SDTS if:

  a) $V_{N1} = V_{N2}$;

  b) a function from P_1 onto P_2 exists which couples each production of G_1: $A \to \alpha_1$ with a production of G_2: $A \to \alpha_2$, where α_2 can be a transduction element associated to $A \to \alpha_1$.

A very useful way of describing SDTS's is a device, called *tree-transducer (TT)* [6, 7], which is essentially a finite state automaton relating in a deterministic fashion every LST of G_1 to a LST of G_2. For example, the translation implied by the SDTS of Fig. 3 is also described by the following TT (Fig. 5).

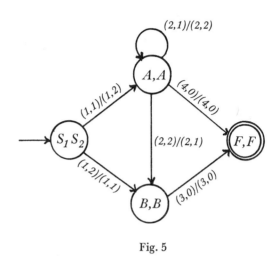

Fig. 5

Each state of a TT is labelled by a couple (X, Y), where $X \in V_{N1}$ and $Y \in V_{N2}$. Each transition of a TT is labelled by a couple α/β, where α and β represent the branches of two LST's which are coupled by the SDTS. Each branch leads to a state whose name is constituted by the couple of nonterminals to which the branches lead on the LST's.

3. Position of the problem

The definitions given in Section 2 imply that the translatability of two languages in a SDTS be fully dependent on the particular form of the grammars which derives them.

Nevertheless, if we are interested in the translation of $L_1 = L(G_1)$ into $L_2 = L(G_2)$ it would be convenient to modify G_1 and G_2 in order to obtain G_1' and G_2' such that $L_1 = L(G_1')$ and $L_2 \subseteq L(G_2')$, G_1' and G_2' can be coupled in a SDTS [6, 7]. The transformation of the original grammars we are interested in should change as little as possible the structure of sentences, that is, the associated trees.

In fact it is well-known that the grammar which derives a language, if appropriately chosen, is such that the structural description of sentences becomes closely related to their meaning. Thus we suppose that G_1' (G_2') have productions that correspond to derivatives of G_1 (G_2). We also suppose that these derivatives describe deterministically the LST's of G_1 (G_2), that is, each LST of G_1 (G_2) can be decomposed in only one way into subtrees corresponding to these derivatives.

The resulting translating device is thus a finite state machine whose transitions are a couple α/β, where α and β are derivatives of G_1 and G_2, respectively. The TT is such that each sentence generated by G_1 is translated into a sentence generated by G_2 in a deterministic way.

We are searching for a TT which satisfies a suitable set of examples of translations between source and object strings. The search will be performed for increasing length of the derivatives of G_1 and G_2. If k_1 and k_2 are the maximum length of the derivatives of G_1 and G_2 which can be considered in the search, we first assume $k_1 = k_2 = 1$ and, in the case of failure of the search, we change the couple (k_1, k_2) incrementally, according to a fixed law. The values of k_1 and k_2 for which the TT is found constitute a sort of complexity measure of the SDTS translatability of G_1 and G_2.

It should be noted that for each couple (k_1, k_2) the class of possible TT's is infinite, and to avoid this fact some reasonable constraint must be given. In this implementation the search will be limited to the class of TT's having no more than one state with a given label. Being the label of a state a couple of names of nonterminals of G_1 and G_2 respectively, this means that the TT's cannot have more than $m \times n + 1$ states, where m and n are the number of nonterminals of G_1 and G_2. This choice is reasonable because it can be shown that if a TT translating $L(G_1)$ into $L(G_2)$ exists, a suitable set of corresponding source-object strings can be found such that a TT is identifiable, having no more than $m \times n + 1$ states [6].

Of course, one possible philosophy of implementation is an enumeration of TT's until a device satisfying the set of examples is found, but this solution seems quite impracticable.

The strategy chosen here is such that the examples of translation are used by the algorithm while trying to construct the TT; moreover, new examples are asked by the algorithm only when no further construction can be made.

We do not intend to enter here into details concerning the formal description of the identification algorithm, which is given in [7]. Rather, its actual implement. on will be described in what follows.

4. The implementation

When dealing with a complex algorithm, as the one outlined above, an implementation is particularly suited to point out its feasibility and efficiency. Moreover, in this particular case, the use of the program is even more appealing as a source of new investigations. In fact the program has been designed according to the principles of structured programming [4], thus allowing easy expansions, modifications of strategies... with minor changes in the overall program.

The algorithm uses the source grammar G_1 to find how many examples are necessary to identify a TT. Moreover, the existence of an informant is postulated, able to give, when required, for each source string, the object string which is considered the translation.

Given $G_1 = (V_{N1}, V_{T1}, P_1, S_1)$ and $G_2 = (V_{N2}, V_{T2}, P_2, S_2)$, the TT translating $L(G_1)$ into $L(G_2)$ will be constructed, if it exists, through a sequence of configurations, each consisting of an incomplete TT, a list of transitions yet to be defined and a set of source-object strings. As at any step many following configurations are possible, the algorithm proceeds in a backtracking fashion, which is particularly efficient because very often the following configuration is immediately determined from the actual one. When this is not possible a secondary storage provides the following configuration.

More precisely a (h_1, h_2)-*configuration* is a triple (C, E, I), where C is an incomplete TT translating derivatives of G_1 (G_2) with maximum length h_1 (h_2), E is the associated set of examples (source-object LST's), and I is the set of incomplete transitions of C. C represents an incomplete TT which couples correctly initial subtrees of the given examples, while I contains the frontier of the incomplete TT, that is either input derivatives not yet coupled to an output derivative or whose pairing with an output derivative resulted in an incorrect choice.

A transition leaving from state q, coupling the input derivative of index m, with pairing of nonterminals defined by the permutation p is represented by (q, l, m, p).

A (h_1, h_2)-configuration is *initial* when the incomplete TT consists of a single state, labelled (S_1, S_2), I consists of all $((S_1, S_2), l_i, U, U)$, where U means that output and, consequently, permutation are undefined and l_i is the index of a production of G_1 whose left part is S_1.

In what follows we will describe the algorithm through stepwise refinements, focusing on those aspects whose different solutions correspond to different strategies which could be tested by experiments.

Another important aspect of the implementation is the strict connection between the stepwise definition of the algorithm and data structures. This means that data structures do not need to be defined *a priori*, but become more and more precisely detailed in connection with the refinements of the algorithm.

The over-all structure of the program is described by the following step 1, written in an ALGOL-like language; here and in the following a (?) will denote a point admitting different strategies which can sensibly affect the quality of the solution.

Step 1

```
begin comment
                  – TT is true when a TT is found,
                  – (h₁, h₂) is the actual complexity degree,
                  – a main loop searches a TT with maximum
                    admitted complexity degree (k₁, k₂),
                  – the law of increasing (h₁, h₂) is a point
                    to be experimented;
    TT = false;
    for (h₁, h₂) = (1, 1) step ( ? ) until (k₁, k₂) do
    begin comment
                  – SEC is a secondary storage holding
                    configurations;
        insert the initial (h₁, h₂)-configuration in SEC;
        while SEC is not empty do
        begin comment
                  – PICK is true if the incomplete
                    TT under consideration cannot
                    be further modified and there-
                    fore must be discarded;
            take a configuration from SEC;
            PICK = false;
        while PICK is false and TT is false do
            compute the following configuration ;
        if TT is true then stop;
        end;
    end;
end;
```

In the following step 2 we will detail the statement enclosed by [＿＿＿＿].

Step 2

```
begin
    if I is empty then TT = true else
    begin comment
                  – ex((A,B),l,E) is a function which gives the
                    elements of E which, used as input to the
```

incomplete TT, reach state (A,B) and such that the source tree leaves the state with a derivative indexed l,

– p is a permutation which pairs the non-terminals of the derivatives indexed l and m,

– $f_p(p)$ gives the successive permutation in a lexicographic order,

– $f_m(m,(A,B),l,E)$ gives an output derivative m' having the same order as l congruent with all the given examples and length $\leqslant h_2$,

m' is the successive to m in the order specified in Appendix A, case 1;

(take ?) an element $((A,B),l,m,p)$ of I;

if $ex((A,B),l,E)$ is empty then

find an input LST t and ask the informant its translation such that $E' = E\ U(t, t')$ defines $ex((A,B), l, E')$ not empty;

else

if $m = U$ and $f_m(m,(A,B),l,E) = U$ or $m \neq U$ and $p \neq U$ and $f_p(p) = U$ and $f_m(m,(A,B),l,E) = U$ then

begin comment

– $F(l)$ gives the set of all input derivatives up to a length h_1 which follow l in an order which is based on the grammar and is specified in Appendix A, case 2;

if $F(l) \neq U$ then

begin

insert in I the set $F(l)$;

consider the initial subtree LST_1 belonging both to an element of $F(l)$ and l. Consider the set S of transitions whose input derivative can be obtained by expansion of LST_1. Erase from I every element of S belonging to I; delete from the TT every element of S which is a transition of the TT, and consequently update the machine;

end

else

if $(A,B) = (S_1,S_2)$ then PICK = true else

begin

– comment no pairing of source-object derivatives leaving (A,B) is possible according to the set of examples which reach the state.

If more than one transition can enter (A,B), the incompatibility can be due to erroneous choices on each transition. Therefore it is necessary to reconsider as many configurations as the number of transitions entering *(A,B)*. To avoid parallel processing only one configuration is immediately considered, storing the others in SEC. The erasing of a transition usually implies the erasing of other transitions and consequently an updating of the TT (see Appendix A, case 3);

    insert in SEC as many configurations as the number of transitions entering *(A,B)*. Each configuration is obtained by erasing one transition and performing the necessary updating;

    end;

end

else

begin comment

    – a coupling of derivatives congruent with given examples has been found;

if *m = U* **then**

begin

    $m' = f_m(U,(A,B),l,E)$;

    p' = first permutation in the lexicographic order;

end

else

begin

    $m' = m$; $p' = f_p(p)$;

end;

compute the set Σ of states whose names are defined by *l, m', p'* and create the transitions from *(A,B)* to the elements of Σ. For every element $\sigma = (N,M)$ of Σ if it is not already in the incomplete TT then

begin

    create the state *(N,M)*;

    insert in *I* the set of elements (σ, l_i, U, U), where l_i is the index of a production of G_1 whose left part is *N*;

end

else

begin comment

    – new examples reach state *(N,M)* owing to the transition now created. It is necessary to test if all these examples are congruent with the incomplete TT so far identified;

for every transition where the congruence is not verified **do**

begin comment

    – all the transitions where the congruence is not verified must be cancelled and the

necessary updating performed;

    cancel the transition;

    insert the transition in *I*;

    update the incomplete TT;

    end;

    end;

    end;

    end;

end;

———

It should be noted that a number of stepwise refinements on the program can be designed without detailing the description of data structures. Access to data structures is performed by primitives such as:

"take an element from SET"

or

"insert *X* in SET"

These primitives imply that an element is inserted in or taken from SET according to the law by which SET is constructed (e.g., first-in-first-out or last-in-last-out law). This law is not necessarily known at the step which is presently developed, but can be delayed until further refinements can only be performed on a detailed structure.

Whenever this point is reached in the design, the programmer is forced to choose a particular data structure which is suitable to the previously defined primitives. If more data organizations can be appropriate, the best choice could be found only after a convenient experimentation.

For example, if we choose to detail the structure of SEC, we should remember that

a) SEC stores the configurations not yet examined to be taken into account in the backtracking phase. As our goal is to complete a TT as soon as possible, it is reasonable to resume the last inserted configuration, which is surely the most processed among the elements of SEC;

b) as it concerns memory space requirements, it is convenient to store SEC on an auxiliary storage (in our implementation a tape). The most efficient choice is thus to resume the last inserted configuration.

Both arguments *(a)* and *(b)* force a stack organization to be implemented for SEC.

As it concerns *I*, which stores the frontier transitions of the incomplete TT, different data organizations correspond to different strategies in attempting to complete the TT. Depending on a depth-first or breadth-first strategy in expanding the TT, I can be organized as a stack or as a queue, respectively. Besides these two opposite strategies, many alternative ways of organizing I could be devised if some heuristic information about the global nature of the TT is known. In the absence of information at all, a good way of dealing with I could be found by experiments.

5. Conclusion: an example

In this Section we will show by an example how the algorithm for determining the TT works, when it is fed with source and object grammars, an initial set of examples and the maximum complexity degrees k_1 and k_2.

$$G_1 = (\{S_1, A, B, D, F\}, \{a, b, c, f\}, P_1, S_1) \; ; \; k_1 = 2$$

$$G_2 = (\{S_2, G, H, L, K\}, \{g, h, k, x, y, z\}, P_2, S_2) \; ; \; k_2 = 2$$

P_1:	1) $S_1 \to AbB$	P_2:	1) $S_2 \to Gg$
	2) $A \to a$		2) $G \to HhL$
	3) $B \to cDc$		3) $H \to KKk$
	4) $D \to aE$		4) $L \to xyz$
	5) $E \to FF$		5) $K \to kK$
	6) $F \to fF$		6) $K \to k$
	7) $F \to f$		

In the initial set of examples only one pair of source-object trees exists:

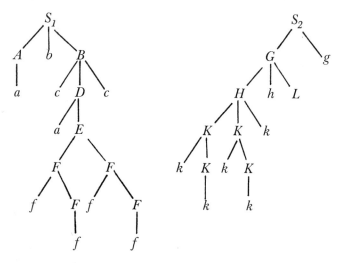

The algorithm of identification of the TT works as described by the following steps:

Step 1

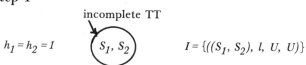

No possible coupling exists between the input derivative of index *1* and any output derivative of length *l*.

Step 2

$$h_1 = 1 \qquad h_2 = 2$$

The output derivative 7) $S_2 \Rightarrow Gg \Rightarrow HhLg$ can be coupled with the input derivative indexed *1*. If the first permutation between nonterminals is taken, the configuration becomes:

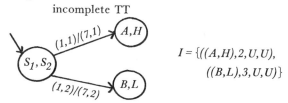

If we try to complete the transition leaving state *(A,H)*, no coupling is possible, neither for output derivatives up to a maximum length h_2, nor for input derivatives up to a maximum length h_1. Avoiding unnecessary details, we pass to the backtracking phase in which the coupling in state (S_1, S_2) is reconsidered.

Step 3

A new permutation of nonterminals between input derivative indexed *1* and output derivative indexed *7* is fixed:

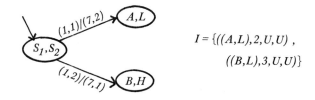

If we try to complete the transition leaving state *(A,L)*, a possible coupling is between derivatives *2* and *4*.

Step 4

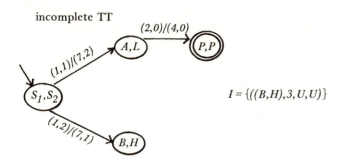

incomplete TT

$I = \{((B,H),3,U,U)\}$

If we try to complete the transition leaving state (B,H), no coupling is possible, neither for output derivatives up to a maximum length h_2, nor for input derivatives up to a maximum length h_1. Avoiding displaying unnecessary details, we pass to the backtracking phase reconsidering the coupling between derivatives 1 and 7 in (S_1,S_2). Note that this implies the elimination of what is derived from the coupling between 1 and 7.

Step 5

$h_1 = 2, \quad h_2 = 1$

The input derivative 8) $S_1 \Rightarrow AbB \Rightarrow abB$ can be coupled with the output derivative indexed 1. By imposing the first permutation we obtain:

incomplete TT

$I = \{((B,G),3,U,U)\}$

Step 6

$h_1 = 2, \quad h_2 = 2$

The output derivative 8) $G \Rightarrow HhL \Rightarrow Hhxyz$ can be coupled with the input derivative indexed 3.

incomplete TT

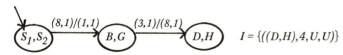

$I = \{((D,H),4,U,U)\}$

Step 7

The input derivative 9) $D \Rightarrow aE \Rightarrow aFF$ can be coupled

with the output derivative indexed 3.

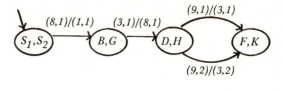

$I = \{((F,K),6,U,U),$
$((F,K),7,U,U)\}$

Step 8

Completing the transitions in I:

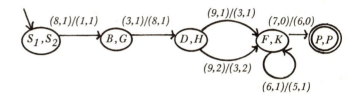

The TT is complete, and, consequently, I is empty.

Along this sequence of steps, only one example has been sufficient to define the complete TT. On the contrary, often, many examples are required to complete the TT, and this fact can generate an incompatibility between new examples and the incomplete TT already found. If, owing to different examples, an input subtree should be translated into different output subtrees, the incomplete TT must be changed deleting the transition which generates the incompatibility, and consequently updating the incomplete TT.

A computer program implementing the algorithm so far described has been written in ALGOL 60 for a Univac 1108 and various different strategies are presently under development.

APPENDIX A

Case 1

Let a and a' be a source and object derivative whose corresponding subtrees s and s' are shown in Fig. A1.

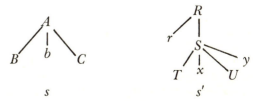

Fig. A1

Suppose that the coupling *(a,1)/(a',1)*, *(a,2)/(a',2)* defined in state *(A,R)* (Fig. A2) of the incomplete TT must be changed and that this implies that a new output derivative indexed *a''* must be searched. Also suppose that the current values of h_1 and h_2 are *2* and *4*, respectively.

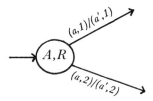

Fig. A2

Let *t* and *t'* be the only example of translation which, used as input to the TT, reaches state *(A,R)* As shown in Fig. A3.

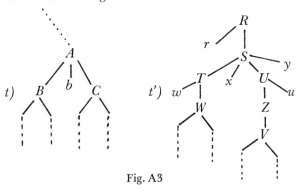

Fig. A3

Within the range $h_2 = 4$ the following subtrees of *t'* could be coupled to *s* (Fig. A4):

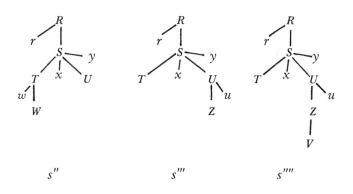

Fig. A4

It follows that an order must be superimposed so that each subtree is properly taken in its turn, and no subtree is considered more than once, which avoids loops in the algorithm.

The ordering algorithm is such that:
a) only the nonterminals at the lowest level are expandable;
b) among those, the leftmost nonterminal is expanded according to the example if the current value of the length of the subtree is $< h_2$. Otherwise the successive nonterminal at the previous level is expanded; if all single nonterminals have been expanded, couples of nonterminals are expanded, and so on.

In our case the derivative to be considered after *a'* is the one corresponding to *s''*.

Case 2

Given an input derivative indexed *1* more than one successive derivative exists. Indeed, the set of following derivatives is obtained by expanding the nonterminals according to all the alternatives described by the grammar. The expansion is performed according to the same rules shown in Case 1. It can be shown [6] that this algorithm implies that every source LST is translated into an object LST in a deterministic fashion, that is, only one possibility exists of decomposing the source LST's into subtrees according to the TT.

Case 3

As shown in Fig. A5 the elimination of the transition which connects *(A,B)* and *(C,D)* implies the elimination of the transitions from *(A,B)* to *(E,F)* and *(G,H)*. As a consequence the transitions leaving *(E,F)* and *(G,H)* must be eliminated.

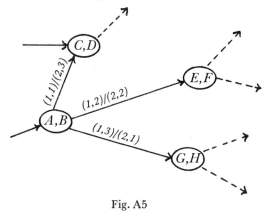

Fig. A5

References
1. AHO, A.V. and ULLMAN, J.D., *The Theory of Parsing, Translation and Compiling*, Vol. I, II, Prentice-Hall (1973).
2. McKEEMAN, W.M., 'Compiler construction', Ad-

vanced Course on Compiler Construction, Techn. Univ. of Munich (4-12 March 1974).

3. DELLA VIGNA, P.L., and GHEZZI, C., 'Teoria degli automi e dei linguaggi formali e progetto dei compilatori', *Rivista di Informatica*, 25-76 (1974).

4. DAHL, O.J., DIJKSTRA, E.W., and HOARE, C.A.R., *Structured Programming*, Academic Press, New York (1972).

5. LEWIS, P.M. and STEARNS, R.E., 'Syntax-directed transductions', *J.A.C.M.* 15, 465-488 (1968).

6. DELLA VIGNA, P.L. and GHEZZI, C., 'Are two context-free languages translatable in a syntax-directed translation scheme?', *Calcolo*, 1, 1-15 (1974).

7. CELENTANO, A., DELLA VIGNA, P.L., GHEZZI, C., and TISATO, F., 'Identification of syntax-directed translation schemes', International Computing Symposium 1973, North Holland Pub., 85-92 (1974).

8. KIMBALL, J., *The formal Theory of Grammar*, Prentice-Hall (1973).

System control—a case study of a statistical learning automaton

Dr D.W. RUSSELL and S.J. REES
Department of Electrical & Control Engineering,
Liverpool Polytechnic, Liverpool, UK

Introduction

The current trend in many of the advances in modern control theory is toward increasing mathematical sophistication and complexity. A complexity which is not alleviated by the tendency of real systems to be nonlinear and nonmathematical in nature. Furthermore, the difficulties of system analysis in such cases lead to obvious problems in the control application. With this in mind it is therefore proposed to discuss a learning controller which requires no *a priori* knowledge of the system as such, and hence circumvents the inherent problems of system analysis.

The underlying concept upon which is based the idea of being able to "learn" a control scheme may be described as follows:

In any system in which the development of the control scheme is resolved through a technique such as Pontriagin's Maximum Principle, Bellmans Dynamic Programming, etc., the net effect is to produce, what in two dimensions (variables) is known as a switching curve, in three as a switching surface, and in more, then a switching hypersurface. Thus any given control region will be divided into a number of fixed decision areas, separated by the switching boundary. Since in all practical systems the input is constrained to a maximum value, the problem of 'bounded input' arises. This implies that there is a region of controllability, outside which the controller is unlikely to be effective. Thus the task given to the learning controller is to attempt to determine the region of controllability, the respective switching curve, surface, etc., and hence provide the system with appropriate control inputs.

For the purpose of this case study an inverted pendulum is chosen as the system under consideration. This has a number of advantages:

1. It is a system which is easy to visualize.
2. It has been well covered from an analytical veiwpoint [1, 2, 3].
3. It is a mechanically unstable system, providing a continuously variable output and consequently, a good test for the controller.
4. It is well suited to bang-bang control, which will be the type of input to which the controller is restricted. The reason for such a restriction is twofold—firstly, for this type of system it is efficacious, and secondly, computation time is reduced as the switching boundaries can be easily represented by a sequence of zeros and ones.

1. System control

Figure 1 is an outline of the system under considera-

Progress in Cybernetics and Systems Research, Volume 2

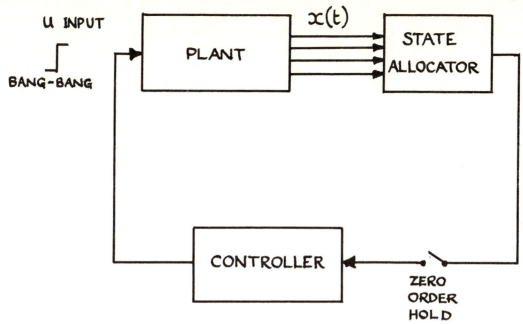

Fig. 1 General System description

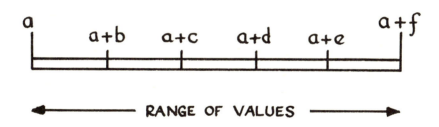

Fig. 2 To indicate subdivision of a variable range

tion. The process (or system) is obvious as that which is to be controlled; as is the controller as the means by which control signals are generated. The state allocator is the link between the system outputs that are measured and the controller. The principle is as follows:

2. State allocator

Each output variable has a range of values over which variations of different magnitude and criticality occur. Given a range for each variable as the maximum permissible excursion—it becomes possible to subdivide this into regions and subsequently identify the variable by an integer "state number" which indicates in which region the variable is currently residing (Fig. 2).

As a general empirical rule, the more critical the variable the more state divisions there ought to be. Consider for the moment that there are three variables, each of which has a range subdivided into five, then it can be seen that there are $5 \times 5 \times 5 = 125$ possible combinations or "states". Thus any set of output variables can, by this subdivision, be categorized into a discrete state, and if each subdivision is assigned a number, then by suitable arrangement of coefficients a unique "state" number may be generated. It is this "state" number which is transferred to the controller as the basis for the control decision.

3. Input "u" generation

As was stated earlier, the input is of the bang-bang form. For this reason the control input can very conveniently be represented by a zero or a one. From this point on the zero or one will be termed the "u-value", hence, the "state u-value" is the value of "u" in the condition described by the state number. The state number is a function of the output variables as defined in the previous section and may be any number between say one and one hundred and twenty five (for three variables subdivided into five). If there is associated with each state number an appropriate state u-value (zero or one) then the controller simply "looks up" the corresponding u-value to determine the control input. The allocation of the u-values is the problem to be discussed in this Chapter. The speed with which the control input is determined is limited only by the speed with which the controller can read the list of u-values.

4. Control run or game

Since this discussion centers on a type of learning controller, it is necessary to consider how to obtain the needed information from the system, on which to base decisions for determining u-values. The period (or periods) of information gathering we shall term either a "control run" or, because it is a convenient term used by Michie and Chambers [4] and in this context fashionable, a game. The object of the game is to prolong control as far as possible. (Run-time is considered the measure of success in the inverted pendulum system.) In other words, the longer the duration of the game, the more successful the controller has become.

The first game is begun with a pseudo-random sequence of u-values, in an attempt to obviate any biassing, which could cause the controller to require longer training periods before meaningful results are obtained. For initial conditions it is arranged that the system should be somewhere within the specified range for each variable—and in the case of the inverted pendulum, fairly close to the middle of the range, and certainly within the region of controllability. During the simulation for the proving of the algorithm, a second pseudo-random number sequence was used to generate the initial conditions.

Once the game has started, the system (as far as the controller is concerned) provides as output the process variables which are coded into state numbers (by the interface) for which the controller provides the appropriate control input. During the game the controller is fulfilling several other functions. These require a certain storage capability that is proportional to the total number of state options. For each state, the following information is recorded for a game started at zero time:
1. The times when that state is entered. Most states are entered on a number of different occasions, and every entry is recorded.
2. The number of separate occasions when that state is entered during a game.

The information acquisition is continued until such a time that one of the output variables goes outside its allocated range and causes a "fail" signal to be generated. This is the indication for the controller to stop allocating u-values and to enter the statistical updating or learning phase.

5. End-game sequence

At the end of a game the controller enters an algorithmic loop, which is designed to assess the control run just ended, and hence to amend the state u-value list as appropriate. The assessment is carried out, for each state, in the following way and closely follows the method of Michie and Chambers [4].

1. Each state will have associated with it a "zero life function", "one life function", "zero state entry function", and a "one state entry function". The combination of the respective functions into a "zero rating" and a "one rating" will, depending upon which is the greater, determine the u-value for that state in the next game sequence.

2. There is an over-all function, termed "merit" which is a weighted average of all the times of accumulated games. It is used in the evaluation of the zero and one ratings, and for a successful controller, should rise with an increasing number of games.

3. An algorithm to show the order of evaluation is shown in Fig. 3.

In this way, as the number of games increases, the controller learns to associate that u-value with any given state, which serves to prolong the game.

6. Results

The results that follow are those of digital simulation runs carried out on an ICL.1902 at Liverpool Poly-

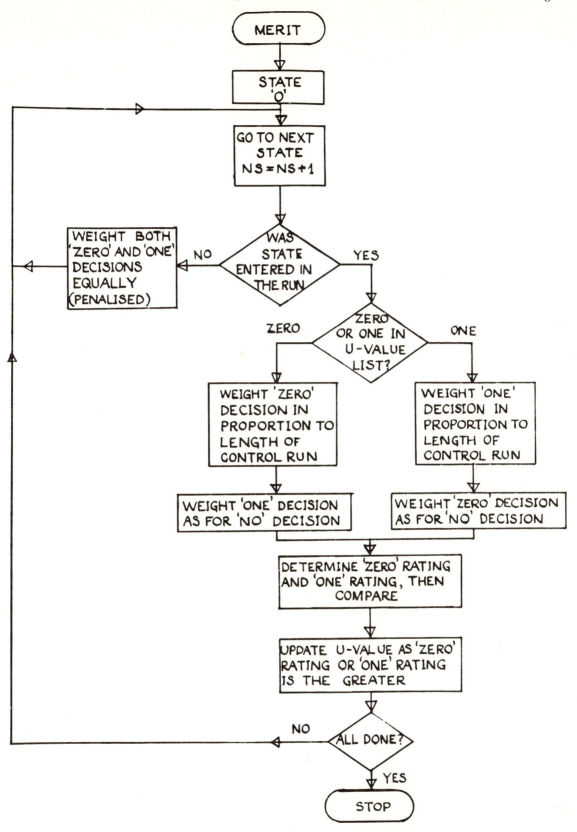

Fig. 3   Flow chart of learning algorithm

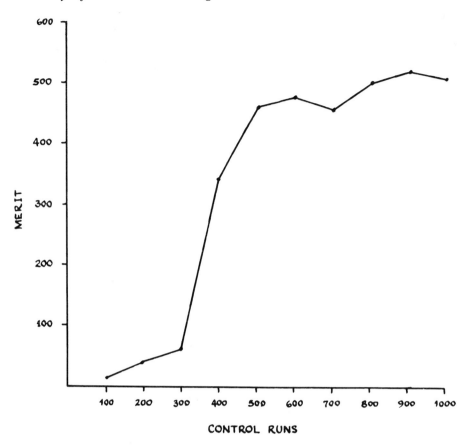

Fig. 4 Typical learning run

technic and on departmental PDP-8 computers. The simulation is being used in development work, before real-time system control is attempted.

A typical learning run is shown in Fig. 4. The state u-value sequence is shown in Fig. 5. For the run in question, the state number was obtained as a function of four variables. Trolley position (X), trolley velocity $(\dot{X})$, pendulum position (θ), and pendulum angular velocity $(\dot{\theta})$. It shows the u-value associated with each state entered during the learning period. If the state was never entered it is left blank, although a u-value from the initialization routine would be available. Clearly, many states, which are in effect well outside the region of controllability have never been entered. The example was chosen to demonstrate this. The state boundaries were as follows:

θ	-1	-0.1	-0.01	0.01	0.1	1	rad
$\dot{\theta}$		-0.5	-0.1	0.1	0.5		rad/sec
X	-1	-0.6	-0.2	0.2	0.6	1	m
$\dot{X}$		-0.5	-0.05	0.05	0.5		m/sec

A separate simulation of the system shows that with the trolley restoring force used for the run in question, the pendulum could not be recovered from an angle greater than 0.12 rad. Referring again to Fig. 5, those states which have developed a strong decision preference are shown underlined (these are the states in which much of a game will be spent). Some states accumulate a great deal of information without showing any particular preference either way. These states are shown encircled. The remaining states are those which are little visited and accordingly accrue little information.

7. Conclusions

Although the inverted pendulum was used for the discussion, and as the basis for obtaining results, this was merely a matter of convenience and in no way restricts the concept of the learning controller to this system. Indeed, the controller has no knowledge of the actual system and concerns itself only with the output variables. An extension to the idea of shielding the system from the controller is that

		θ1			θ2			θ3			θ4			θ5		
		θ̇1	θ̇2	θ̇3	θ̇1	θ̇2	θ̇3	θ̇1	θ̇2	θ̇3	θ̇1	θ̇2	θ̇3	θ̇1	θ̇2	θ̇3
X1	Ẋ1	1			0											
	Ẋ2	1														
	Ẋ3															
X2	Ẋ1	1			1	1	[1]	1	0	1	1	0	0			1
	Ẋ2	1	0		1	1	0	1	0	0		1	0			0
	Ẋ3	1	1		1	1	0	[0]	0	0		1	0			0
X3	Ẋ1	0			1	1	1	1	0		0	0	0		0	0
	Ẋ2	1	0		1	1	0	1	1	0	1	0	0		1	0
	Ẋ3	1	0		0	1	1	[1]	1	0	1	0	0			1
X4	Ẋ1				1			0			1	0	0		1	0
	Ẋ2	0			1	0		1	1		1	0	0			0
	Ẋ3	0	0		0	1	0	1	0	0	0	1	1			1
X5	Ẋ1															
	Ẋ2															
	Ẋ3				1	1		0	1							

Fig. 5 u-value Matrix

of normalizing the variables such that their real values do not need to be known by the state allocator interface.

From the results it may be seen that many of the strongly biassed states are adjacent to others with the same u-value. The next step is to remove these boundaries, but to add others where the state decision is split between zero and one. This, at the moment is carried out on an inspection basis, but the projection is to treat the boundaries themselves as variables in the sense of "able to be varied" and to obtain an optimal state boundary allocation in some heuristic way.

Bang-bang control was used primarily for simplicity and convenience. The problem of variational control has been posed and an approach along the lines of an input range with its own sectorization (possibly as a function of an output variable) considered; such an idea perhaps finding an application in, say, the so-called "fuel optimal problem". Multivariable input is another projection, though in all such cases the practical problem of information storage and management in real time rapidly begins to appear. However, the concept does have an advantage at present in that it can be based on microprocessor computing facilities.

The concept of "system control" is well defined in the paper as at no stage is the controller made aware of the actual reality it is controlling. The interface between the monitored variables and the controller simply produces a sequence of addresses from which a u-value is obtained by table look-up. In the course of a game the decision vector (u-vector) cannot be updated, and hence the control facility may be contained on a small random access memory chip. In order to update statistically the microprocessor "observes" the game, noting entry-times, etc. The learning algorithm is applied retrospectively with a view to producing a "trained u-vector" for actual control.

In the real physical system, over say one thousand games, an average run time for manual control of three seconds is usual, with peak performances of twelve seconds occasionally achieved. Estimated, corresponding times from the simulation are of the order of 500 sec and 1500 sec, respectively. The current project activity is that of enabling physical connection between the heuristic automaton and the mechanical plant.

Acknowledgements
Acknowledgements are made to the Science Research Council (B/72/2057), and to Professor D. Michie, University of Edinburgh.

References
1. EASTWOOD, E., 'Control theory and the engineer', *Proc. I.E.E.*, Vol. 115, pp. 203 ff.
2. HIGDON and CANNON, Jr., 'On the control of unstable multi-output mechanical systems', ASME No. 63-WA-148 (November 1963).
3. CANNON, R.H., Jr., *Dynamics of Physical Systems*, McGraw-Hill.
4. MICHIE and CHAMBERS, *Machine Intelligence 2 ...Boxes—an experiment in Adaptive Control*, Oliver and Boyd.

An application of concept formation techniques to the learning of a linear language

D.J.H. BROWN
Polytechnic of Central London,
London, UK

Introduction

This Chapter represents an approach to the study of simple linear language semantics. A model is proposed which has the necessary structure to build associations between patterns within a well-defined world and words used to describe those patterns.

The model is capable of discourse with external agents regarding the nature of the situation in which it finds itself. All communication is performed via a linear language. This discourse is made on a stimulus-response basis; the main difference between this and a pattern recognizer is the reference made to context: a given pattern may elicit a different word in different contexts.

Patterns are presented to the model, together with the context in which they occur and the word required as response when the model is in "learning" mode. The information is represented in the model as a hierarchical net of associations; context modes branch to word modes which in turn branch to concept modes. Each concept contains a description of the class of patterns from which it is formed.

When the model is in "discourse" mode it is presented with a context and a pattern and responds with the word or words which are associated with both. By making contexts previous contexts concatenated with agents' words a conversation in a highly stylized language can be undertaken.

A sample language

The language of Contract Bridge bidding has been selected to the initial test-bed for the model. Contexts are the histories of bids during an auction; words are bids and patterns are abstracted hands. As an example, let an abstracted hand be a vector of integers, which are the features of the pattern as shown below

pattern = (CP, DP, HP, SP, TP, CL, DL, HL, SL, D)

where CP, DP, HP, SP are the club, diamond, heart, and spade honor points calculated from the high cards according to the schema ace = 4, king = 3, queen = 2, jack = 1; TP is the total points being the sum of suit honor points plus 1 for each doubleton, 2 for each singleton, and 3 for each void; CL, DL,

Progress in Cybernetics and Systems Research, Volume 2

HL, SL are the lengths of the club, diamond, heart, and spade suits, respectively; and D is the distribution: 1 for balanced, 0 for unbalanced.

A word will be a string of two symbols, e.g.,

4C representing a bid of 4 clubs

A context will be a string of words separated by commas giving the previous bids, e.g.,

1D, NB, 2C, 2H, DB representing the auction:

Declarer	Opponent 1	Partner	Opponent 2
1 diamond double	No bid	2 clubs	2 hearts

Inductive learning of concepts

In general, patterns are vectors of any length of integral features[†]. The class description of a concept includes a vector of dimensions, where a dimension describes the range of values that patterns within its class can take. The range may be set redundant and a single limit set subsequently; this is explained in a later section.

The induction process

Let P_1 and P_2 be patterns and $f_1, f_2 \ldots$ features. Then

$$P_1 = (f_{11}, f_{12}, \ldots f_{1n})$$

$$P_2 = (f_{21}, f_{22}, \ldots f_{2n})$$

From these, a concept C may be formed

$$C = (d_1, d_2, \ldots d_n)$$

where

$$d_i = (\min(f_{1i}, f_{2i}), \max(f_{1i}, f_{2i}))$$

$$= (d_{i1}, d_{i2})$$

[†] The fact that features are integral means there must exist a mapping from the symbolic data in a pattern yielding values for which the usual arithmetic operations are consistent.

Suppose a new pattern $P_3 = (f_{31}, f_{32}, \ldots f_{3n})$ is presented as an instance of C. C is altered to give

$$C^1 = (d_1^1, d_2^1, \ldots, d_n^1)$$

where

$$d_i^1 = (\min(f_{3i}, d_{i1}), \max(f_{3i}, d_{i2}))$$

For example, let h1, h2, h3 be three hands and P_1, P_2, P_3 the patterns abstracted from them

hand	clubs	diamonds	hearts	spades
h1	A 6 4	J 9 8 3	K Q 10 4	A 6 2
h2	6 5 3	A K 2	Q J 9 5 4	Q 4
h3	J 9 5	A	K J 9 4 3 2	Q 7 5

Then

$$P_1 = (4, 1, 5, 4, 14, 3, 4, 4, 3, 1)$$

$$P_2 = (0, 7, 3, 2, 13, 3, 3, 5, 2, 1)$$

$$P_3 = (1, 4, 5, 2, 14, 3, 1, 6, 3, 0)$$

From P_1 and P_2 we derive

$$C = ((0,4), (1,7), (3,5), (2,4), (13,14), (3,3),$$
$$(3,4), (4,5), (2,3), (1,1))$$

and from C and P_3 we derive

$$C^1 = ((0,4), (1,7), (3,5), (2,4), (13,14), (3,3),$$
$$(1,4), (4,6), (2,3), (1,0))$$

Elimination of redundant information

The learning of a concept involves more than the basic induction process. In particular, irrelevant features must be discarded to promote efficient use of the concept. To achieve this, various heuristics are utilized:

H1: The more constrained a dimension is, the greater its relevance.
Let relevance = Mean/range; if relevance < 1 let that dimension be range redundant.

H2: If two dimensions are interdependent and one is found to be range redundant, let the other be also set range redundant.

Applying this to C^1 of the previous example, we have

dimension	mean	range	relevance
(0,4)	2	5	0.4
(1,7)	4	7	0.57
(3,5)	4	3	1.33
(2,4)	3	3	1
(13,14)	13.5	2	6.75
(3,3)	3	1	3
(1,4)	2.5	4	0.62
(4,6)	5	3	1.67
(2,3)	2.5	2	1.25
(1,0)	0.5	1	0.25

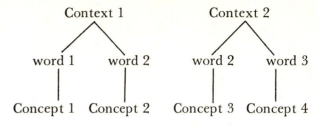

Fig. 1

Using H1, we obtain the revised concept

(*, *, (3,5), (2,4), (13,14), (3,3), *, (4,6), (2,3), *)

where * indicates a range redundant dimension.
Suppose the interdependencies are

CP & CL, DP & DL, HP & HL, SP & SL

their values in the concept so far are

CP *   (3,3) CL

DP *   *   DL

HP (3,5) (4,6) HL

SP (2,4) (2,3) SL

Using H2, we obtain

CP *   * CL

DP *   * DL

HP (3,5)   (4,6) HL

SP (2,4)   (2,3) SL

making the new concept

(*, *, (3,5), (2,4), (13,14), *, *, (4,6), (2,3), *)

Consolidation of knowledge
Although the meaning of a word in a language is dependent on the context in which it occurs, it is quite possible that its meaning will be the same in two different contexts.

Suppose the model's memory contains the associations given in Fig. 1. Here word 2 is associated with concept 2 when it occurs in context 1 and with concept 3 when it occurs in context 2. An example of this situation in English might be

Context 1: (word 2) "is a beautiful city"

Context 2: (word 2) "was a great leader"

where, e.g., Washington is word 2. Although the two appearances of word 2 are lexically identical, they have quite different meanings.

Now suppose word 2 appears in a new context, say: "Washington washed his face". This could be included in the net as shown in Fig. 2.

Now, the model will be able, by introspection, to notice that Concept 3 is identical to Concept 5 and that each is associated with word 2. Then the structure of the memory can be altered to that shown in Fig. 3, reflecting this comprehension.

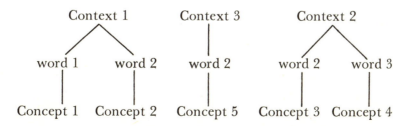

Fig. 2

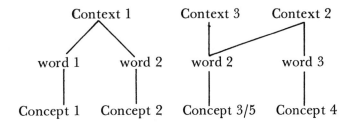

Fig. 3

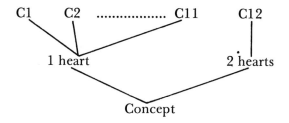

Fig. 5

An example from contract bridge bidding

Consider an opening bid of 'one heart': this may reasonably be made on the same hand, e.g.,

A42	clubs
K	diamonds
KQJ94	hearts
Q1052	spades
<u>Hand H</u>	

in any of the contexts

first in hand	: no previous bids
second in hand	: pass; 1 club; 1 diamond
third in hand	: (pass, 1 club); (pass, 1 diamond)
fourth in hand	: (1 club, pass, pass); (1 diamond, pass, pass); (pass, pass, 1 club); (pass, pass, 1 diamond)

Let these contexts be C1, C2, ..., C11. The structure for this knowledge is shown in Fig. 4, where concept includes the pattern for the hand H. However, this might elicit a different response in another context. For example, let C12 be (pass, 1 club, pass). In this case, a reasonable bid might be 2 hearts; giving the structure in Fig. 5.

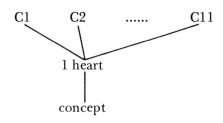

Fig. 4

A further point arises due to ambiguity. In English and Bridge bidding it is possible for a word to have more than one meaning within the same context. For example the question "If I told you that you have a beautiful body would you hold it against me?". The structure is given in Fig. 6.

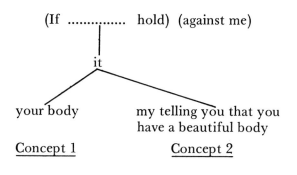

Fig. 6

In bridge bidding [according to Goren (1957)], an opening bid may be made provided the bidder has a rebid available, either a rebiddable suit or two biddable suits. Consider the case of opening 1 heart. This is feasible if opener has a hand describable by the concept:

$$C_1 = (*, *, (4,6), * (13,16), *, *, (5,6), *, *)$$

e.g., A,6,2 clubs; J,4,3 diamonds; K,J,9,4,3 hearts; A,2 spades,

or by the concept

$$C_2 = (*, (2,5), (2,5), *, (13,16), *, (4,6), (4,6), *, *)$$

e.g., J,9,4 clubs; A,K,5,3 diamonds; A,K,5,3 hearts; 10,8 spades.

The structure for this is given in Fig. 7.

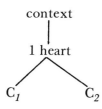

Fig. 7

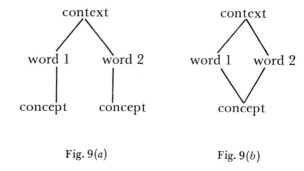

Fig. 9(a)   Fig. 9(b)

The concept of a hand on which one could bid 1 heart is thus disjunctive[‡] $(C_1 \cup C_2)$. It is not necessary to generate a new node, since all the associations necessary for the retrieval of the associated word are present. It should be noticed that the structure Fig. 8 does not give rise to a disjunctive concept (concept 1 $\cup$ concept 2) for word 1; in this situation they have quite different meanings.

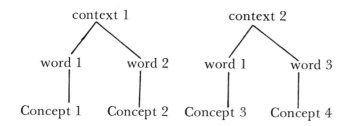

Fig. 8

Another situation is that in which, after some adaptation of concepts, two identical concepts are associated with different words within the same context. Unification of these transforms the structure of Fig. 9(a) to that of Fig. 9(b).

‡ Individual concepts are conjunctive, since they insist that all a pattern's features fall within the limits of the concept's dimensions.

Training philosophy

The objective of the trainer is threefold:

(a) To illustrate (by use of positive instances).

(b) To correct (by indicating that a given response is invalid).

(c) To provide counter-examples (by use of negative instances).

Objective (b) may be incorporated into (a) and (c), since a correction may comprise (i) an indication that the response made is incorrect, (ii) an indication of the correct response.

(i) is available under item (c), where the counter-example is the response previously made, and (ii) is available under item (a), where the positive instance is the correct response to the situation previously presented.

It can thus be seen that the model can be satisfactorily trained by the presentation of positive and negative instances.

The manner in which these instances are presented is critical for the learning performance.

The ability of the model to respond to questions asked of it enables the trainer to make his own assessment of the model's knowledge, without knowing it explicitly.

Positive focusing

When two dissimilar patterns are presented as instances of the same concept there are two possibilities:

(a) One or more dimensions of the concept are redundant.

(b) The concept is disjunctive.

In order to gain most information from this, both options must be pursued. The danger of adopting option (a) alone is that relevant dimensions might be ignored (when the concept is in fact disjunctive). The danger of adopting option (b) alone is that redundant dimensions might still be considered relevant (when the concept is in fact conjunctive).

125

Concepts are discarded when all of their dimensions are redundant due to over-generalization; compensation for this occurs automatically since every time a dimension is made redundant in one concept, another is created. Unification of concepts occurs when

(a) A concept is found to be a description of a subclass of another concept, and both have the same associations; in this case the concept which describes the subclass is preserved and the other deleted.

(b) Two concepts are found to have identical class descriptions but differing associations; in this case the concept formed will contain all the associations each of the two from which it was formed had had.

Negative focusing

Objectives (b) and (c) of the training philosophy are similar in that the trainer wishes to indicate to the model that a given association should not be made. To deal with a correction, the model must adapt a concept so that it no longer includes the given pattern in its class description. To deal with a counter-example, the model must perform a similar action on its memory, save that the concept might not exist. In this case, where no concept is attached to a word,[††] one must be created to the effect that:

"as far as I am aware, any pattern except this one (the negative instance) is a positive instance of this concept."

It is presumed that teaching concepts to humans by simply providing negative instances (without telling them what the correct response should have been) leads to considerable ambiguity which is reflected in the design of the model.

Conclusions

Current research into language emphasizes the requirement for a semantic theory, rather than a syntactic one. There seems a good case for arguing that methods used for pattern recognition should be

applicable, with some generalization to the learning of language. In this approach, problems of syntax are ignored in the initial phase of learning. At present, contexts are treated as single items, rather than higher order concepts. Additionally, associations are made directly between words and concepts, without intermediate semantic units. An extension of this theory might then be to include mechanisms for the recognition and assimilation of contexts, a problem which has many features in common with the learning of lower-order concepts. It thus seems likely that the model described would be best extended by generalization, rather than augmenting it with other, different learning mechanisms. An approach to providing intermediate concepts might be to consider the lower-order concepts as patterns themselves.

The use of a trainer is not obvious for these situations—after all, what is a "concept of a concept?"

References

BECKER, J., 'The modeling of simple analogic and inductive processes in a semantic memory system', Proceedings of the 1st International Joint Conference on Artificial Intelligence (1969).

CHARNIAK, E., 'Toward a model of children's story comprehension', M.I.T. Thesis (1972).

COLLINS, A. and QUILLIAN, M.R., 'Retrieval time from semantic memory', *Journal of Verbal Learning and Verbal Behavior* 8, 240-247 (1969).

CUNNINGHAM, M., *Intelligence: Its organization and Development*, Academic.

FEIGENBAUM, E., 'The simulation of verbal learning behaviour', Proceedings of the Western Joint Computer Conference (1961).

FEIGENBAUM, E. and SIMON, H., 'Performance of a reading task by an elementary perceiving and memorizing program', *Journal of Behavioural Science*, VIII, 3, 72-87.

GOREN, C., *Goren's Bridge Complete*, Barrie & Rockliff.

HOVLAND, and HUNT, E., 'The computer simulation of concept attainment', *Journal of Behavioural Science* 5 (1960).

HUNT, E., 'What kind of computer is man?', *Cognitive Psychology* 2, 57-98 (1971).

HUNT, E., *Concept Learning*, Wiley.

HUNT, E., MARIN and STONE, *Experiments in Induction*, Academic.

KOCHEN, M., 'Experimental study of hypothesis formation by computer', Proceedings of the London Symposium on Information Theory (1960).

---

†† The word itself might not be known, in which case it is created in the model with no associations with concepts to begin with.

KOCHEN, M., 'An experimental program for the selection of disjunctive hypotheses', Proceedings of the Western Joint Computer Conference (1961).

KOLERS, P.A. and EDEN, M. (eds.), *Recognizing Patterns: Studies in Living and Automatic Systems*, MIT Press (1968).

MEYER, D., 'On the representation and retrieval of stored information', *Cognitive Psychology* 1, 242-300 (1970).

MINSKY, M. (ed.), *Semantic Information Processing*, MIT Press.

NILSSON, N.J., *Learning Machines: Foundations of trainable pattern classifying systems*, McGraw Hill.

SIMON, H.A. and FEIGENBAUM, E., 'An information processing theory of some effects of similarity, familiarisation and meaningfulness in verbal learning', *Journal of Verbal Learning and Verbal Behaviour*, III, 5, 385-396 (1964).

TULVING, E. and DONALDSON, W. (eds.), *Organisation of Memory*, Academic.

WHR, L., *Pattern Recognition, Learning and Thought*, Prentice-Hall.

WATERMAN, D.A., 'Generalization Learning Heuristics', Thesis, Stanford University (1970).

WESTON, P.E., 'Cylinders: A relational data structure', Technical Report No. 18, Biological Computer Laboratory, University of Illinois (1970).

WINOGRAD, T., 'A program for understanding natural language', *Cognitive Psychology* 3 (1972).

WINSTON, P., 'Learning structural descriptions from examples', MIT Thesis (1970).

Modifiable automata and learning

M. DAL CIN
Institute of Information Sciences,
University of Tübingen, Germany

1. Introduction

By now, terms such as adaptation, modifiability, and learning belong to the biological as well as to the engineering sciences. They denote the plasticity of behavior shown by organisms and many artifacts like control systems [1], adaptive pattern-recognition devices [2], or failure tolerant computers [3]. Because of their universality these terms and similar concepts also form an essential part of the objectives of general systems theory.

This Chapter aims at the precise use of these concepts which emphasizes their role in automata-theoretic models of learning. Learning is considered as a goal-directed adaptive process of modifiable systems which is influenced by the system's environment or experience and which includes recognition as one of its major goals. Thus, when we speak about learning we think of a goal which has to be reached through the learning process. In general, this learning goal is an activity which one would not expect of the system prior to a learning phase. That is to say, a system that learns acquires a mode of behavior which cannot be realized merely by changing the system's state. This requirement rules out a number of already existing automata-theoretic learning models [4,5]. On the other hand, the proposed model encompasses the features of most discrete learning systems that have been put forward.

After defining modifiable automata (Section 2), i.e., automata which are able to change their transi-

tion structures (transition tables), learning goals and a performance measure will be introduced (Section 4). Illustrative examples are considered and some important results from tolerance geometry [6] are given (Section 3). In Section 5 the learning behavior of inert modifiable automata, i.e., automata which gradually transform their structures, is investigated.

Notation: Let X, Y be arbitrary sets, $S \subset X$ and $T \subset Y$. Any subset of $X \times X = X^{(2)}$ is a binary relation on X; it is a tolerance if it is symmetric and reflexive. Given binary relations ρ, $\sigma \subset X \times Y$, $x \in X$, $y \in Y$, and τ, χ, tolerances on X and Y, respectively, then:

(a) $\rho \cdot \sigma = \{(x,y) \mid \exists x' \in X \cap Y: (x,x') \in \rho, (x',y) \in \sigma\}$

is the relative product of ρ and σ (their sum $\rho + \sigma$ is simply $\rho \cup \sigma$).

(b) $\delta X = \rho^0 = \{(x,x) \mid x \in X\}$, $\rho^1 = \rho$, $\rho^n = \rho^{n-1} \cdot \rho$, $n > 1$.

(c) $\rho_* \tau = \delta Y + \rho^c \cdot \tau \cdot \rho$, $\rho^* \chi = \rho^0 + \rho \cdot \tau \cdot \rho^c$.

(d) $\rho^c = \{(y,x) \mid (x,y) \in \rho\}$, $\rho \backslash \sigma = \{(x,y) \in \rho \mid (x,y) \notin \sigma\}$, $\bar{\rho} = X \times Y \backslash \rho$.

(e) $S \cdot \rho = \{y \mid \exists x \in S, (x,y) \in \rho\}$, $x\rho = \{x\} \cdot \rho$, similarly for $\rho \cdot T$ and ρy.

If $\Delta \subset Z \times W \times X$ is a ternary relation then $\Delta \cdot \rho = \{(z,w,x) \mid \exists x' \in X: (z,w,x') \in \Delta, (x',y) \in \rho\}$. We denote by $/xx'...,y)$ the relation

Progress in Cybernetics and Systems Research, Volume 2
Copyright © 1975 by Hemisphere Publishing Corporation

$\{(x,y),(x',y),...\} \subset X \times Y$ and by $/x,yy'...)$ the relation $\{(x,y),(x,y'),...\} \subset X \times Y$; $\Delta = /z,xx'...)_w$ iff $\Delta = \{(z,w,x),(z,w,x'),...\}$; $pr_i : X_1 \times ... \times X_n \to X_i$ $(i=1,2,...,n)$ are projections, $sign(r) = +1$ if $r > 0$ and -1 otherwise, $r \in I\!R$ and $P(X)$ is the set of all subsets of X.

2. Modifiable automata

2.1 Configurations of modifiable automata

First we recall the concept of an automaton. Let X (Y) be a finite set of inputs (outputs), and Q a set of states of a complete automaton, A, operating sequentially on a discrete time scale. A is described by the quintuple $A = |X,Y,Q,\Delta,\omega|$ where $\Delta \subset Q \times X \times Q$ is the next state relation and $\omega \subset Q \times Y$ the output relation of A (Moore model). Now, a modifiable automaton MA is an automaton with time variant transition structure Δ. More precisely:

Let $A = |X,Y,Q,\Delta,\omega|$ be an automaton, $\Phi^A \subset P(Q^{(2)})$ a set of admissible binary relations on Q, such that $pr_1\phi = Q$ for all $\phi \in \Phi^A$. Then, the modifiable automaton MA is given by the relational structure

$$MA = |Q,\Delta,\omega,\Phi^A| .$$

At time t_n the performance of MA is that of the (finite or infinite, deterministic or nondeterministic) automaton $MA_n = |X,Y,Q,\Delta_n = \Delta_{n-1} \cdot \phi_n,\omega|$ for $n \geqslant 1$ and $MA_n = A$ for $n = 0$. The state relations $\phi_n \in \Phi^A$ are specified by the adaptation circuit AC of MA executing a map (Fig. 1)

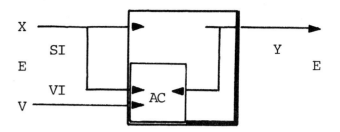

Fig. 1 Modifiable automaton; AC adaptation circuit, E environment, V valuation-, X input-, Y output-alphabet

$$AC : X \times V \times Y \times \Phi^A \to \Phi^A ,$$

where V is the set of values of inputs of MA. These inputs are selected by the environment of MA whose function comprises a specification of inputs $SI : I\!N \times Y \to X$ ($I\!N$ the set of time indices) and a valuation of inputs $VI : X \to V$. (Cf. Fig. 2. Dividing the system into blocks AC,Δ,Φ^A, etc., is arbitrary to a large extent.)

Automaton MA_n is called the configuration of MA at time t_n.

Remark: Selflearning by MA implies that $V = \phi$. In specific cases the adaptation circuit AC executes a learning (adaptation) algorithm. Most of the learning algorithms developed so far are concerned with the learning of system parameters. However, we contend that flexible transition structures are needed in complex, nonstationary environments. Tsypkin [7] gives the implementation of such algorithms, i.e., of

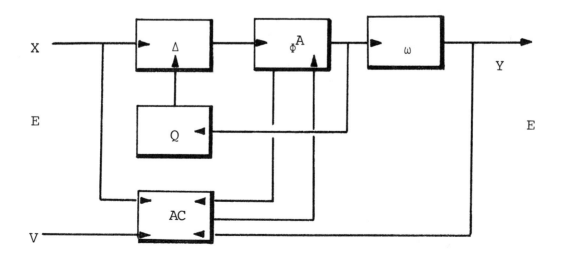

Fig. 2 Possible system configuration

the objects AC, VI and ϕ_n, by threshold elements, filters, etc., to a greater detail than is done in this Chapter. In order to implement AC or VI no information about Δ_n is needed and in many practical cases this information is also missing. The possible structural modifications of MA are determined by Φ^A and AC. (If $q \in pr_3 \Delta_n$ and $(q,q') \in \phi_n$ then AC determines instead of q a new next-state q' independently of Δ_n.) Modifiable automata are time-variant automata. The languages accepted by these automata have been characterized by Salomaa [8]. The learning automaton given by Tsypkin [7] can be viewed as a special, quite sophisticated, modifiable automaton.

2.2 Example

The area where modifiable automata may provide a useful mathematical model includes the assignment of physical objects or events to several pre-specified pattern categories (pattern classification). The adaptive threshold logic unit [9] is but the most elementary classifying system. (Just because of that it is mentioned here.)

The state of a threshold logic unit (TLU) is represented by a weight-vector $\underline{c} \in W$, where W is the ($r+1$ dimensional) weight-vector space. This state determines a hyperplane through the (r dimensional) pattern space X. If $Q = W$, Δ the identity relation on Q (independent of X) and $\Phi^A = \{\phi_c = Q \times \{\underline{c}\} \mid \underline{c} \in Q\}$ we have the adaptive TLU:

$$MTLU = |Q, \Delta, \omega = [\underline{c} \cdot (\underline{x}, 1)], \Phi^A |$$

which at each time instant acts as the automaton

$$MTLU_n = |X, Y = \{+1, -1\}, Q, \Delta_n = \phi_{\underline{c}_n}, \omega|$$

Relation $\phi_{\underline{c}_n}$ is selected by the AC-part of $MTLU$ which may execute an error correction procedure [2,9]. The choice of state $\underline{c}_n$ is induced by an external or internal valuation signal $v \in V = \{+1, -1\}$ (cf. Fig. 3). In particular, $MTLU_0$ is a threshold logic device. (Note that $MTLU_n$ is given as a Mealy-type automaton. It may be transformed into a Moore-type automaton by the standard procedure.) The weight-vector space W may be taken as the $r+1$ dimensional Euclidean space $\mathbb{R}^{r+1}$. However, W as well as the feature space X may be finite [2,3]. In this case, $MTLU$ is a finite automaton. If the pattern classes are linear separable the system reaches a terminal state in its learning procedure [2,9]. Generalizations to nonlinear and piecewise linear hyperplanes are conceivable [9] and TLU's have been composed to yield modifiable automata with richer structure and more discriminatory power.

It is not our intention to invent automata for specific learning tasks. Nevertheless, let us have a quick look at the mode of pattern classification executed by $MTLU$'s. Figure 4 shows typical hyperplanes (given by $\underline{c} \cdot (\underline{x}, 1) = 0$) separating pattern sets. In certain cases many hyperplanes and, hence, many

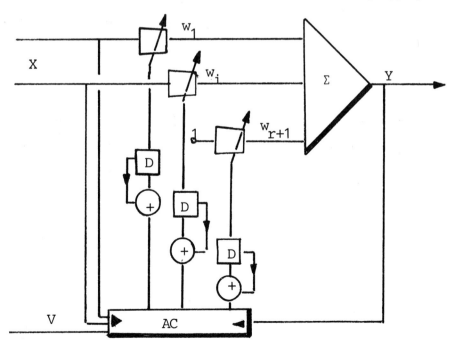

Fig. 3 MTLU, w_i adaptable weights, D delay unit, Σ summing device

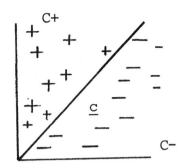 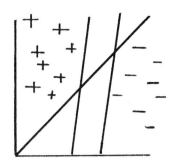 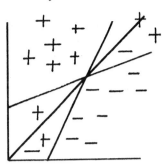

Fig. 4 Hyperplanes separating, or approximatively separating pattern sets

states of *MTLU* separate the two categories *C+* and *C−* equally well. In other cases they only approximately separate *C+* from *C−*. This observation suggests the introduction of a tolerance on *W* expressing the fact that differences, e.g., in the input-output behavior of a *MTLU* in two different states, are either inessential (tolerable) or essential.

Example: A tolerance τ_s, $s > 0$, on state space *W* may be given as

$$\tau_s = \{(\underline{c},\underline{c}') \mid \mid \{\underline{x} \mid \omega(\underline{c},\underline{x}) - \omega(\underline{c}',\underline{x}) = 0\} \mid < s\}.$$

That is, the number of differently interpreted patterns in state $\underline{c}$ and $\underline{c}'$ is less than *s* if $(\underline{c},\underline{c}') \in \tau_s$. Evidently, the tolerance τ_s depends, in general, on the pattern classes.

It is clear that the (abstract) notions of states and tolerances of a modifiable automaton are applicable to more complicated situations—even in pattern recognition. Compare Fig. 5, where relation τ_s is easily obtained despite the fact that the state $\underline{c}^*$ itself can hardly be given by an analytic expression.

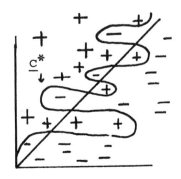

Fig. 5 A nonlinear decision surface

2.3 Learning in modifiable automata

In order to see whether or not a modifiable automaton acquires specific transition structures we have to define its goal of learning specifying a set Φ^L of binary relations on its state space. We then say:

MA reaches at time t_n the goal Φ^L under the action $E = (VI, SI)$ of its environment (teacher) if

$$\phi_{(n)} = \prod_{i=1}^{n} \phi_i \in \Phi^L$$ where the learning process $(\phi_1, \phi_2, \ldots)$ of *MA* is directed by its *AC*-part according to *E*.

Thus, $\Delta_* = \Delta \cdot \phi_*$, $\phi_* \in \Phi^L$, is one of the desired transition structures of *MA*. It may be one of a stochastic or, more general, nondeterministic automaton if the a priori information required about the learning goal is incompletely known. Obviously, *MA* reaches at any time the goal $P(Q^{(2)})$ under any *E*, and if it reaches Φ_i^L, $(i=1,2,\ldots,m)$ under *E* then also $\bigcap_{i=1}^{m} \Phi_i^L$. Certainly, if *MA* reaches its goal its performance should remain satisfactory from then on. The foregoing scheme brings out the features of many discrete learning systems in control theory and biology that have been put forward [1, 7].

Example: If $s_i = SI(i, y_i)$ $(i=0,1,2,\ldots,)$ is any training sequence, $VI(C\pm) = \pm 1$ and $\Phi^L = \{\phi_c \mid \underline{c}$ separates *C+* and *C−* linearly$\} \neq \phi$ then the *MTLU* reaches Φ^L under $E = (SI, VI)$ provided that *AC* implements one of the known error correction procedures [2, 9].

Of course, in order that *MA* is able to reach Φ^L, *E* has to be informative and Φ^L reachable. However, even if this is not the case, *MA* may, nevertheless, reach its goal approximately (cf. Fig. 5). Under such circumstances, it is important to introduce a tolerance τ on *Q* as a suitable performance measure. Thus, (Q, τ) will then be a tolerance space [6]. This measure characterizes the learning behavior of modifiable automata which gradually transform their function, are gracefully trainable or only approximately approach their goals.

We now recall a few elementary properties concerning tolerance spaces. For additional concepts and results about tolerance spaces we refer to Poston [6] and Dal Cin [10].

3. Tolerance geometry

The concept of tolerance space is due to Poincaré [11], Zeeman [12], and Poston [6]. These authors have different names for tolerance spaces, viz. physical continua, tolerance or fuzzy spaces, respectively. Arbib [13, 14] introduced these spaces into automata and control theory.

3.1 Tolerance spaces

A tolerance space (X,τ) (or loosely X) is a set X and a tolerance τ on it. If $(x,x') \in \tau$ we say x is within tolerance τ of x' and also write $x\tau x'$; $iX = X^{(2)}$ is the big tolerance and δX the little tolerance on X. If $f:(X,\tau) \to Y$ is a set theoretic map, $f_*\tau$ is the coinduced tolerance on Y. If $\iota:Y \subset X$ is an inclusion the induced tolerance $\iota^*\tau$ on Y is the subspace tolerance of Y and $(Y,\iota^*\tau)$ (or loosely (Y,τ) or Y) is a subspace of X. For instance, the tolerance neighborhood of $x \in X$ is the subspace $N(x) = (x\tau,\tau)$. The product of two tolerance spaces (X_α,τ_α), $\alpha = 1,2$, is given by $(X_1 \times X_2, \tau_1\tau_2 := \cap\, pr_\alpha^*\tau_\alpha)$.

Definition: Let $\rho,\chi \subset X_1 \times X_2$. We say ρ and χ are related by $\tau_2^{\tau_1}$ iff $\rho^c \cdot \tau_1 \cdot \chi \subset \tau_2$.

On a tolerance space (X,τ) is given a natural metric, the hop metric, $d: x^{(2)} \to I\!N \cup \{\infty\}$ defined as $d(x,x') = \min\{m \mid \exists$ a self-related map $\omega:(I\!N,\simeq) \to (X,\tau)$ s. t. $\omega(0) = x, \omega(m) = x'\}$ and $d(x,x') = \infty$ if there is no such ω ($\simeq = \{(m,n) \mid \|m-n\| \leqslant 1; m,n \in I\!N\}$). Given a subspace A of X, the interior of A is $\text{int} A = \{x \in A \mid d(x, X\backslash A) > 1\}$ where $d(x,A) := \min\{d(x,x') \mid x' \in A\}$ and the boundary of A is $\partial A := N(A)\backslash \text{int} A$ (with the corresponding subspace tolerances). For instance, let X be the pattern space of the *MTLU* and $A \subset (X,\tau)$ a nonvoid pattern class. Then the boundary index [15], b, of pattern A can be given as $b = |\partial A| / 2|A|$.

3.2 Tangent bundles

Definition: For a tolerance space (X,τ) the tangent bundle is the composite map (bundle projection)

$$t : TX \subset X^{(2)} \underset{pr_1}{\to} X$$

where $TX = (\tau,\tau\tau)$. We usually denote this tangent bundle by (TX,t) or TX. The tangent space T_xX to X at $x \in X$ is the tolerance space $T_xX = (tx,\tau\tau)$.

The set of all self-related maps $\hat{y}:(Z = \{0,1\}, iZ) \to (X,\tau)$ may be identified with TX where $y \in TX$ is identified with $\hat{y}$ iff $y = (\hat{y}(0), \hat{y}(1))$.

Remark: A tangent bundle on (X,τ) is a special example of a mixed contravariant-s- and covariant-r-tensor bundle on (X,τ). Hence, the following represents only a very small section of tolerance (fuzzy) geometry [6].

Definition: Let (X,τ) be a tolerance space with tangent bundle TX. A (geometric) vectorfield on X is a map $D:X \to TX$ satisfying $D \cdot t = \delta X$ where t is the bundle projection. A (real) scalar field ψ on X is a function $\psi:X \to I\!R$. Denote the set of scalar fields on X (with the ring structure of pointwise addition and multiplication) by $\underline{\Psi}X$ and the set of geometric vectorfields on X by $\underline{D}X$. For instance, D_0 is the trivial vectorfield on X, $D_0 : x \to (x,x), x \in X$.

Definition: Let $f:X \to X$ be a self-related map on X, $\psi \in \underline{\Psi}X$ a scalar field and $D \in \underline{D}X$ a vectorfield on X. The first difference Δf of f is the map $(f,f)|_{TX} : TX \to TX$. The difference $D\psi$ of ψ with respect to the (geometric) vectorfield D is a scalar field with $xD\psi = xD \cdot e_x \cdot \psi - x\psi$, $x \in X$, where e_x is the exponential map $e_x : T_xX \subset X^{(2)} \underset{pr_2}{\to} X$. Finally, the difference (covectorfield) $d\psi : TX \to I\!R$ of ψ is given by $yd\psi = -\hat{y}(0)\psi + \hat{y}(1)\psi$, $y \in TX$.

Lemma [6]: The operation D on $\underline{\Psi}X$ is linear and $D(\psi\,\overline{\psi}) = (D\psi)\overline{\psi} + \psi(D\overline{\psi}) + (D\psi)(D\overline{\psi})$; furthermore, $D\psi = D \cdot d\psi$ (proof easy).

4. Inert modifiable automata

We are now in a position to deal with modifiable automata whose structural transformations take place in small steps, i.e., are inert.

To be more specific, let $MA = |Q, \Delta, \omega, \Phi^A|$ be a modifiable automaton and τ a tolerance on Q. We call (MA,τ) a modifiable automaton with tolerance, and say MA has the property P if all its configurations have property P.

Definition: Modifiable automaton with tolerance (MA,τ) is said to be inert iff $\Phi^A = P(\tau)$.

In the following we wish to compare the performance of (MA,τ) in different configurations. To this end we define:

Definition: Two configurations, MA_i and MA_j, of MA are said to be interrelated by τ (or MA_j is a gradual modification of MA_i) iff their transition relations $\delta_x^{(i)}$ and $\delta_x^{(j)}$ are related by τ^τ for all $x \in X$ where $(q,\bar{q}) \in \delta_x^{(\alpha)}$ iff $(q,x,\bar{q}) \in \Delta_\alpha$. A self-interrelated configuration of MA is called a fuzzy-state (F–S) configuration. $MA_i \tau MA_{i+1}$ (interrelated by τ) implies that $\delta_w^{(i)} \tau^\tau \delta_w^{(i+1)}$ for all $w \in X^*$, where

$$\delta_w^{(\alpha)} = \delta_{x_1}^{(\alpha)} \cdot \delta_{x_2}^{(\alpha)} \cdot \ldots \cdot \delta_{x_n}^{(\alpha)},\ w = x_1 x_2 \ldots x_n,\ \text{and}$$

$\delta_\Lambda^{(\alpha)} = \delta Q, \Lambda \in X^*$ the empty input sequence.

Theorem [16]: The tolerances of MA which interrelate two configurations of MA form a distributive lattice (ordered by set inclusion).

The following straightforward results are presented without proofs. If A is a F–S configuration of an inert modifiable automaton MA then (MA,τ^n) is a modifiable F–S automaton for some $n \in IN$ with $1 \leqslant n \leqslant |Q|-1$ and the configurations of MA are interrelated by τ if τ is transitive. On the other hand, if τ is intransitive it follows that for some natural numbers ℓ_i the configurations of MA at t_i and t_{i+1} are interrelated by τ^{ℓ_i} $(i=0,1,2,\ldots)$. The smallest such numbers give us a measure of the extent to which the structures of MA are changing.

We will see that it is a quite strong requirement for configurations of MA to be interrelated. A somewhat weaker notion was introduced in [16], viz. ℓ-masked transition $(t-)$modifications. Suppose (MA,τ) is deterministic and inert. Relation $\phi \in P(Q)$ with $pr_1\phi = Q$ (t-modification of MA) is said to be ℓ-masked at time t_i if $\delta_w^{(i)c} \cdot \phi \cdot \delta_w^{(i,\phi)} \subset \tau^\ell$ for all $w \in X^*$, where $\Delta_{i,\phi} = \Delta_i \cdot \phi$.

If t-modification $\phi = \phi_i$ is 1-masked it is admissible and $\delta_w^{(i)c} \cdot \delta_w^{(i+1)} \subset \tau$ for all $w \in X^*$. However, this does not imply that $MA_i \tau MA_{i+1}$. On the other hand, $MA_i \tau MA_{i+1}$ implies that ϕ_i is 1-masked.

Theorem: Let MA be a deterministic modifiable automaton and $\omega_* \tau^\ell = \delta Y$ (Y output set of MA) for some natural number ℓ. Then MA_i and MA_{i+1} are equivalent automata and q and $q\phi_i$ equivalent states of MA_i if ϕ_i is $\bar{\ell}$-masked with $\bar{\ell} \leqslant \ell$. Hence, if MA_i is minimal no $\phi \in \Phi^A$, $\phi \not\subset \delta Q$, can be ℓ-masked at time t_i.

For a proof, [16] may be consulted where a decision algorithm is given which evaluates whether or not ϕ is ℓ-masked at t_i.

5. Learning in inert modifiable automata

5.1 Learning processes

Let us consider a finite deterministic modifiable automaton $MA = |Q,\Delta,\omega,\Phi^A|$. Suppose that we wish to determine a learning sequence for MA such that MA is gradually improving. That is to say, MA inertly modifies its transition structure according to an appropriate performance criterion. A useful criterion for the determination of a learning sequence is the following. Given a sequence $\psi^i \in \underline{\Psi}Q$, $i=1,2,\ldots$, we interpret $q\psi^i$, $q \in Q$, as the actual or the expected cost at time t_i in state q. Determine vectorfields D^i $(i=1,2,\ldots)$ on Q such that the expressions

$$C_Q^i \equiv \sum_{q \in Q} q D^i \psi^i$$

are minimal with respect to all $D \in \underline{D}Q$.

These vectorfields then give rise to the learning sequence $\phi_i = D^i \cdot e_q$ $(i=1,2,\ldots)$ of MA. It follows that $\phi_i \in P(\tau)$ and

$$C_Q^n(\Delta_n) \equiv \sum_{x \in X} \sum_{q \in Q} q c^n(\delta_x^{(n)}) \leqslant C_Q^n(\Delta_{n-1}) \qquad (*)$$

where $c^n(\phi) = \phi \cdot \psi^n - \psi^n \in \underline{\Psi}Q$, $\phi c Q^{(2)}$.

It is in this sense that MA is gradually adapting in order to minimize the cost of state transitions—in particular if the cost-functions are time-independent. To see this we use formula $c^i(\phi \cdot \phi_j) = \phi \cdot D^j \psi^i + c^i(\phi)$. Hence, $C_Q^n(\Delta_n) - C_Q^n(\Delta_{n-1}) = C_{pr_3\Delta_{n-1}}^n \leqslant 0$, since $qD^n \psi^n \leqslant qD_0 \psi^n = 0$ for all $q \in Q$. The AC-part of MA may accomplish the minimization of C_Q^i by searching algorithms à la Tsypkin [7]. (Details will be given in a forthcoming paper.)

Example (a): A frequently used cost function is the risk $R(\underline{c}) = \sum_{y \in Y} \sum_{x \in X} L[y,\omega(\underline{x},\underline{c})]P(\underline{x},y)$ of the classification in state $\underline{c}$ by $(MTLU,\tau_s)$. $L[y,\bar{y}] \in IR$ is the loss incurred when pattern $\underline{x}$ which actually should be classified as y is classified as $\bar{y}$, and $P(\underline{x},y)$ is the probability of the joint occurrence of $\underline{x}$ and y. It follows then from formula $(*)$ that the loss at t_n is equal or less than the loss at t_{n-1}; $R(\underline{c}_n) \leqslant R(\underline{c}_{n-1})$, if AC generates a learning sequence according to the above-mentioned performance criterion. Since $C_Q^n(\Delta_n) = C_Q^1(\phi_{\underline{c}_n}) =$

$= aR(\underline{c}_n) + b$, a, b independent of n. Moreover, at most s patterns are differently classified at t_n and t_{n-1} $(n=1,2,...)$.

Example (*b*): Consider modifiable automaton MA, with tolerance τ and MA_0 given by formula (1) and (2). As cost functions we choose the expectation values $E[SI(i,\omega(\cdot))]$ if MA interacts with a stochastic environment [17]. SI is again assumed to be time independent. We valuate input *1* as penalty and input *0* as reward. It follows that $q\psi$ is equal to the probability $SI(i,\omega(q))$ being *1*. Assume that this probability is known (Table 1). Relation ϕ_1 and MA_i are then given by the expressions (3) and (4-6), respectively, where $MA_{n>3} = MA_3$. For example, the probability that MA is rewarded after it received two inputs increases from *0,57* for MA_0 to *0,68* for MA_1 to $1-B\psi = 0,8$ for MA_3.

as the goal of learning. It follows:

Theorem: The configuration of MA at the moment MA reaches the goal Φ_*^L is a gradual modification of automaton $A^* = |X,Y,Q,\Delta_*,\omega|$. However, MA reaches Φ_*^L only if (A^*,τ^2) is a fuzzy-state automaton (i.e., self-related by τ^2).

Proof: (*a*) If $\phi_{(i)} \in \Phi_*^L$ then for all $x \in X$,

$\delta_x^{(i)c} \cdot \tau \cdot \delta_x^* \subset \phi_{(i)}^c \cdot \delta_x^c \cdot \tau \cdot \delta_x \cdot \phi_* \subset \phi_{(i)}^c \cdot \tau \cdot \phi_* \subset \tau$.

(*b*) If MA_i is interrelated with A^* then for all $x \in X$,

$\delta_x^* {}_* \tau^2 \subset \delta_x^{*c} \cdot \tau \cdot \delta_x^{(i)} \cdot \delta_x^{(i)c} \cdot \tau \cdot \delta_x^* \subset \tau^2$ since MA_i is complete, i.e., $\delta_x^{(i)} \cdot \delta_x^{(i)c} \supset \delta Q$.

Table 1

(1) $\Delta = /ABCE,D)_0 + /D,A)_0 + /A,B)_1 + /B,C)_1 + /C,D)_1 + /D,E)_1 + /E,A)_1$

   $Y = X = \{0,1\}$

   $\omega = /BCE,0) + /AD,1)$

(2) $\tau = Q + /B,E) + /E,BD)^. + /C,D) + /D,CE)$

(3) $\phi_1 = /A,A) + /BE,B) + /C,D) + /D,E)$

(4) $\Delta_1 = /ABCE,E)_0 + /D,A)_0 + /AD,B)_1 + /B,D)_1 + /C,E)_1 + /E,A)_1$

(5) $\Delta_2 = /ABCE,B)_0 + /D,A)_0 + /ACD,B)_1 + /B,E)_1 + /E,A)_1$

(6) $\Delta_3 = /ABCE,B)_0 + /D,A)_0 + /ABCD,B)_1 + /E,A)_1$

Q:	A	B	C	D	E
ψ:	3/5	1/5	1/2	2/5	3/10

5.2 Goal attainment

It has been stated that a system is adaptive if it reaches an (optimal) terminal state in its interaction with the environment. On the other hand, it may be said that learning occurs only if the system modifies its transition structure in order to improve its performance. (Apart from that, the connotations of "adaptive" are many.)

Let us assume, that MA has an initial F-S configuration and is truly modifiable. Moreover, let Δ_* be a transition structure which should be learned by MA. Since we are satisfied if the performance of MA is tolerable we may take $\Phi^L = \Phi_*^L \cup \{\phi_*\}$, $\Phi_*^L = \phi_*(\tau^T)$,

Remark: Given configuration $MA_j = |X,Y,Q,\Delta_i \cdot \phi_{i,j},\omega|$, $j > i$, where $\phi_{i,j} = \prod_{k=i+1}^{j} \phi_k$. Evidently, $MA_j = |X,Y,Q,\Delta_i \cdot \hat{\phi}_{i,j},\omega|$ where $\hat{\phi}_{i,j} = \phi_{i,j} \setminus (\overline{pr_3 \Delta_i \times Q})$, since $\Delta_i \cdot \phi_{i,j} = \Delta_i \cdot \hat{\phi}_{i,j}$. From now on we assume that the learning process is so normalized that $\phi_{i,i+1} = \hat{\phi}_{i,i+1}$. It follows then immediately that $\phi_{i,j} = \hat{\phi}_{i,j}$ $(j > i+1)$ and that ϕ_i is *1*-masked if $MA_i \tau MA_{i+1}$. Since $\sum_{x \in X} \delta_x^{(i)c} \cdot \delta_x^{(i)} \cdot \phi_i \subset \tau$ implies that $\phi_i \subset \tau$ and, hence, $\delta_w^{(i)c} \cdot \phi_i \cdot \delta_w^{(i+1)} \subset \delta_w^{(i)c} \cdot \tau \cdot \delta_w^{(i+1)} \subset \tau$ for all $w \in X^*$.

Assume now that the performance of *MA* is satisfactory at t_{i_0}, i.e., that of $A^* = |X, Y, Q, \Delta_* = \Delta \cdot \phi_*, \omega|$. How can we decide whether or not the performance of *MA* remains tolerable from then on? To this end we have to compute the following relation:

$$\gamma = \sum_{x \in X} [\delta_x^{*c} \cdot \overline{\sum_{\rho \in Rx} \rho}]$$

where $Rx = \delta_x^* \tau^\tau$.

Assertion: Modifiable automaton *MA* performs tolerably at time t_j $(j > i_0)$ if and only if

$$\phi_{i_0,j} \subset \tau \backslash \gamma \qquad (**)$$

This formula shows, for example, that *MA* inertly changes its structure at t_{i_0+1} if its performance remains tolerable.

Proof: Let $\rho_x = \sum_{\rho \in Rx} \rho$, $\Delta_* = \Delta_{i_0} = \Delta \cdot \phi_*$ and $\Delta_j = \Delta_* \cdot \phi_{i_0,j}$.

(a) If $\phi_{i_0,j} \subset \tau \backslash \gamma$ then

$\delta_x^{*c} \cdot \tau \cdot \delta_x^{(j)} \subset \delta_x^{*c} \cdot \tau \cdot \delta_x^* \cdot (\tau \backslash \gamma) \subset \delta_x^{*c} \cdot \tau \cdot \delta_x^* \cdot \overline{\gamma} \subset$

$\delta_x^{*c} \cdot \tau \cdot \rho_x \subset \tau$, for all $x \in X$, since $\delta_x^* \cdot \overline{\gamma} \subset \rho_x$. In order to see this let $q(\delta_x^* \cdot \overline{\gamma})q'$. It follows that there is a state $\overline{q} \in Q$ s.t. $q \delta_x^* \overline{q}$ and $(\overline{q}, q') \notin \delta_y^{*c} \cdot \overline{\rho}_y$ for all $y \in X$. Hence, (i) $q \delta_x^* \overline{q}$ and (ii) for all $\hat{q} \in Q$ and $y \in X$ with $\overline{q} \delta_y^{*c} \hat{q}$ it follows that $\hat{q} \rho_y q'$. Choose $q = \hat{q}$ and $x = y$. Hence, $q \rho_x q'$.

(b) Assume that MA_j is interrelated with A^*. It follows that $\delta_x^{*c} \cdot \delta_x^* \cdot \phi_{i_0,j} \subset \tau$. Hence

$\sum_{x \in X} (\delta_x^{*c} \cdot \delta_x^*) \cdot \phi_{i_0,j} \subset \tau$ and $\phi_{i_0,j} \subset \tau$, since $\bigcup_{x \in X} pr_2 \delta_x^* = pr_3 \Delta_* = pr_1 \phi_{i_0,j}$ (see Remark). Suppose that $\phi_{i_0,j} \not\subset \tau \backslash \gamma$ then $\phi_{i_0,j} \cap \tau \cap \gamma \neq \phi$. Hence, there are $x \in X$, $(q, \overline{q}) \in Q^{(2)}$ s.t. $q(\delta_x^{*c} \cdot \overline{\rho}_x \cap \phi_{i_0,j})\overline{q}$. Hence, there are $x \in X$, $\hat{q} \in Q$ s.t. $\hat{q} \delta_x^* q$ and $\hat{q} \overline{\rho}_x \overline{q}$. Therefore $\hat{q}(\delta_x^* \cdot \phi_{i_0,j})\overline{q}$ and $(\hat{q}, \overline{q}) \notin \rho_x$. It follows that $\delta_x^{(j)} \not\subset \rho_x$; This contradicts the assumption $\delta_x^{(j)} \in Rx$.

The advantage of formula $(**)$ is that it is now easy to find out at what time *MA* performs satisfactorily —if γ is computed once for all.

Example: Let A^* and τ be given by the expressions (7) and (8) where $X = \{0,1\}$. (ω is arbitrary.)

(7) $\Delta_* = /ABD,A)_0 + /C,B)_0 + /ABD,C)_1 + /C,B)_1$

(8) $\tau = \delta Q + /A,BC) + /BC,A)$.

It follows that

$\rho_0 = /Q,A) + /Q,B) + /BD,C)$

$\rho_1 = /Q,A) + /BD,C)$ where $/Q,X) = /ABCD,X)$.

Furthermore,

$\gamma = /A,CD) + /B,BCD) + /C,BCD)$

$\overline{\gamma} = /Q,A) + /D,Q) + /A,B)$ and

$\tau \backslash \gamma = /ABC,A) + /A,B) + /D,D)$.

(These relations are easily computed representing them by Boolean matrices.) Thus, the only performances of *MA* which are tolerable are those of $A_i^* = |X, Y, Q, \Delta_* \cdot \phi^{(i)}, \omega|$, $i = 0,1,2,3$, where $\phi^{(0)} = \delta Q$, $\phi^{(1)} = /A,B) + /BC,A)$, $\phi^{(2)} = /A,A) + /BC,A)$ and $\phi^{(3)} = \tau \backslash \gamma$.

6. Conclusion

Special branches of systems theory have by now achieved a high level of sophistication and much effort toward the unification of these branches is being made [13, 14]. Modifiable, time-variant, and topological [18] automata are comparatively new contributions to this effort. Their theory is still in a state of development. However, our approach has already led us to formulations and questions which provide guidelines and goals for a promising program of research. Compared with "classical" automata theory, the greater relevance to certain aspects of artificial intelligence such as our ideas of the brain and the construction of such "machines" motivates this research.

Acknowledgement

The author wishes to express his gratitude to Professor W. Güttinger for his interest in this work. He also thanks Drs E. Pfaffelhuber and M. Conrad for fruitful comments.

References

1. FU, K.S., 'Learning control systems—review and outlook', *IEEE Trans. AC*, 210-221 (April 1970).
2. MINSKY, M. and PAPERT, S., *Perceptrons*, MIT Press (1969).
3. PIERCE, W.H., *Fault-tolerant Computer Design*, Academic Press N.Y. (1965).
4. MENZEL, W., *Theorie der Lernsysteme*, Springer, Berlin (1970).
5. GAINES, B.G., 'Axioms for adaptive behavior', *Int. J. Man-Machine Studies* 4, 169-199 (1972).
6. POSTON, T., 'Fuzzy Geometry', Doct. Thesis, Univ. of Warwick (1971).
7. TSYPKIN, Ya.Z., *Adaptation and Learning in Automatic Systems*, Academic Press N.Y. (1971).
8. SALOMAA, A., 'On finite automata with time-variant structure', *Inform. a: Control* 13, 85-98 (1968).
9. NILSSON, N., *Learning Machines*, McGraw-Hill, N.Y. (1965).
10. DAL CIN, M., 'Fault tolerance and stability of fuzzy-state automata', Lect. Notes on Computer Science Vol. 2, 36-44, Springer, Berlin (1973).
11. POINCARÉ, H., *The Value of Science*, Dover Edition (1958).
12. ZEEMAN, E.C., 'The topology of the brain and visual perception', *The Topology of 3-Manifolds* (edit. by M.K. Fort), 240-256, Prentice Hall, Englewood Cliffs (1961).
13. ARBIB, M.A., 'Automata theory and control theory—a rapprochement', *Automatica* 3, 161-189, Pergamon Press, London (1966).
14. KALMAN, R.E., FALB, P.L., and ARBIB, M.A., *Topics in Mathematical System Theory*, McGraw-Hill, N.Y. (1969).
15. ARKADJEW, A.G. and BRAWERMAN, E.M., *Zeichenerkennung und Maschinelles Lernen*, Oldenbourg, München (1966).
16. DAL CIN, M., 'Modification-tolerance of fuzzy-state automata', *Int. Journal of Computer and Information Sciences* 4, 63-80 (1975).
17. TSELTIN, M.L., *Automata Theory and Modeling of Biological Systems*, Academic Press N.Y. (1973).
18. BRAUER, W., Zu den Grundlagen einer Theorie topologischer sequentieller Systeme und Automaten, GMD Bonn, Bericht 31 (1970).

On the role of general system theory in the cognitive process

T. GERGELY and I. NÉMETI
Hungarian Academy of Sciences,
Budapest, Hungary

The cognitive process of an open goal-seeking system can be analyzed in terms of its interaction with its environment. From the point of view of the system, this interaction means the appearance of problem situations. Some of these problem situations become actual problems to be solved by the system and others do not. Therefore the cognitive process can be analyzed in terms of the functioning of a complex problem-solving system, i.e., the cognitive process is a complicated problem-solving process which anticipates the sequential solution of problems that require various kinds of problem-solving systems. The purpose of the present study is to describe the various problem types and to analyze the requirements of their individual adequate problem-solving systems.

The role that the General Systems Theory (GST) plays in the working of the individual solving systems will be analyzed here.

1. Problem-solving

The functioning of an open, goal-seeking system can be analyzed in terms of its interaction with its environment. The environment of a system is here understood to be a universe that, being a logical system, can be regarded as a set of statements. The environment therefore acts on the system via statements. Depending on the corpus of knowledge embodied in the system, a statement may be comprehensible or incomprehensible. Statements of the latter kind are what we call problems.[†] Some statements represent marginal cases; that is, although they are not understood by the system, they are potentially comprehensible to it. These we can call actualizable problems. The development of the system is related precisely to these: if it draws on this potentiality of problem-solving which results in understanding such a statement, then its corpus of knowledge will be extended, while its *level of knowledge*, which separates the comrehensible from the incomprehensible, will be raised, and thereby newer problems will be brought into a position where they are potentially capable of being solved.

[†] Strictly speaking, problems are not, of course, statements but only aggregates of objects and predicates of which a part are not understood by the system; nevertheless, for brevity they will be referred to as statements.

The knowledge of a system concerning its universe appears in the form of statements formulated in a language. This language can be regarded as a sub-algebra of the σ-algebra defined on the universe. It represents both the potential for deductive extension of knowledge and at the same time sets limits on this process. The elements of the algebra are concepts, which can be either objects or predicates, depending on their role in the language.

The primary knowledge of the system can be regarded as those partitions, defined on the universe, for which the system possesses some methods of analysis that can be employed in deciding what class of a partition some given element of the universe belongs to. Partitions can be regarded as properties, while classes are the values assumed by some given property of an object or predicate. (The expression *variable* may be used as a synonym for *property*.) Let P be the set of partitions constituting the primary knowledge. We can define on this P, in the usual manner‡, a partial ordering, denoted "$\geqslant$". Since for every pair of elements there exist a greatest lower bound and a least higher bound, the set P can be used to generate a lattice F, the elements of which give the definable (secondary) properties, i.e., those properties that can be established deductively from the primary knowledge relating to the universe. The minimum element of the lattice F gives the most detailed breakdown of the universe of which the system is capable on the basis of its primary knowledge P.

The language in which the knowledge of the system is expressible is the σ-algebra generated by the classes of partition P. The resolving power of the language (or its level of detail) is likewise given by the minimum element of the lattice F. This means that the *smallest* (or finest) concepts that we are able to define—or produce and differentiate deductively—are classes of the minimum elements of lattice F. The actual linguistic level of detail used in a description determines the level of description.

Selection of an *adequate level of description* is of fundamental importance in formulating (or reformulating) a problem. If the level is not deep enough, the problem will be insoluble because the required distinctions cannot be made. On the other hand, if

the descriptional level happens to be too deep, the problem will not be solved *efficiently*, for the process of solution will demand more effort than is necessary, due to our involvement in unnecessary detail. The level of description of a language can be regarded as a partition that is defined by the lowest classes* of the language, thus this level is identical with the minimum element of the lattice of properties. It follows that the partial ordering can also be defined in terms of the levels of description.

We therefore think of a language of good resolving power as one that displays a low level of description and small minimal concepts. The attempt to minimalize divergence from some original objective (solution of a problem complete description of a problem, etc.) and at the same time maximalize the descriptional level is what we shall term the *minimax principle*. A level selected in this way is called an adequate level of description.

More precisely, we can introduce the idea of two cost functions at the descriptional level: the cost functions of expenditure and of divergence from an objective. The first function results in greater costs the lower the *level of description* (descriptional complexity, processing time, etc., are augmented as the level is reduced). The second function grows with increasing deviation from the goal, and—above a certain level—this divergence (e.g., the quality of the solution) increases as the level is raised. The level of description is said to be adequate when the sum of both cost functions is minimum.

In accordance with the preceding, a problem is some new message of the environment that contains incomplete information. In other words, when we have *problem statements* comprising hitherto unknown concepts (objects or predicates), or variables of unknown value, the problem will only be actualizable provided at least some of the objects of the statement bear sufficiently closely on the current corpus of knowledge for the system to be potentially able to identify the problem.

The problem-solving process will be examined here by breaking it down into three main stages: those of *problem identification, problem formulation* (or reformulation) and *solution seeking*. Problem identification takes place when a system notices (recognizes) a message of the environment which is incom-

---

‡ If p_1 and p_2 are two partitions, then the statement $p_1 \geqslant p_2$ denotes that each class of p_2 is included in some class of p_1.

* The cardinality of a concept means the number of elements of the universe that pertain to it.

prehenisble, or only partially comprehensible, to it. The process of recognition is started as a result of those parts of partially comprehensible messages which can be identified; therefore, generally speaking, only partially comprehensible messages can be identified. An example is Mendeleev's periodic system, which realized the problem of the missing elements. The information pointing to the existence of missing elements had already existed before Mendeleev, but until the information had been organized in tabular form nobody else realized this.

The aim of problem formulation is to produce a description of a problem on the basis of which *a*) the problem can be solved, and *b*) it is capable of being solved with the minimum effort and cost. During problem formulation we look for the most suitable language satisfying these conditions, and then for the most suitable description that can be produced in the language chosen. The product of this optimalization—the most suitable language—will be, as we say, *adequate*. Some of the criteria of adequacy have already been discussed above (see descriptional level, etc.).

The three stages are performed in the sequence listed and stand in heuristic relation to each other. This means that when the ith stage is executed it may be realized that the result of the step $j < i$ was incorrect. In such a case the jth step has to be repeated and, of course, all steps $k > j$. The success of the jth step therefore predetermines the success of all steps $k > j$; that is, if j is repeated all steps $k > j$ must be repeated too. For instance, if it turns out that a problem has been erroneously diagnosed, then it is necessary to repeat not only the problem-identifying step but the descriptional step as well. Problem identification is manifestly an exceedingly important stage, as it is the one that starts the entire problem-solving process. Indeed, at a social level it can be very valuable even in cases when the problem identifier is unable to solve the problem himself. For instance, it was Cantor who first hit upon the decision problem of the continuum hypothesis, but the problem was not actually solved until much later by Cohen. Similarly, Mendeleev did chemistry a great service by drawing attention to the problem of the missing elements, even though he himself did not discover them.

An important distinction must be made at this point between problems that can be located purely deductively and problems which require inductive steps. Deductive—in contrast to inductive—recognition of a problem calls for only trivial extensions of primary knowledge P (partition). (An extension of

P is trivial, if it does not result in some extension of F.) The deductively identified problem is thus a problem only if the σ-algebra of a system has not generated from the elements of P those elements which are needed for a complete understanding of the statement in question.

Thus there is a qualitative difference between elevating the level of knowledge of a system deductively and doing this inductively; an inductive solution quite clearly raises the level of knowledge sharply (thereby opening up an infinite vista of new, deductive problem solutions).

Inductive problem identification is an exceptionally valuable activity, though one that is proportionately difficult and demanding in insight. The principal value of interdisciplinary theories is precisely their ability to help in locating problems of this sort. The problems thrown up within a fully developed theory (this will be defined later as T level) can generally be identified without the extension of P (that is, in a deductive way). It is this which makes the development of interdisciplinary theories so difficult, so demanding in intuition, and at the same time so extremely important.

As a result of the interdisciplinary character of systems theory, special attention will be devoted here to problems which can be specified in an inductive way only.

2. Phases of cognition of the universe

Let us examine the process by which a system gains cognizance of a part of the universe; we shall call this the process of theory construction. The process can be divided into four phases, given by the letters O, S, D and T.[†] Each phase has a structure characteristic of the known part of the universe and of the structure of the knowledge it accumulates on this part.

Let us take these structures in order (note that each of the levels presupposes the presence of lower-level structures):

1. *Partitional structures (O)*. At this level the system can distinguish only between objects, the predicates of the language used serving for the partitioning of these objects (e.g., "the dog is not an anthropoid, but a mammal").

2. *Structures of static relation (S)*. At this level the system uncovers relations between objects which are stable in time; these are reflected by

[†] These are the phases introduced by Piaget [1].

the predicates. The known part of the universe begins to cohere from scattered, unrelated parts into an integral whole.

3. *Structures of dynamic relation (D)*. The description is expanded with predicates which describe relations changing in time. In other words, the measure of truth associated with the description becomes time-dependent.

4. *Complete structures (T)*. This is the level at which the description is raised to the status of a theory (a unified whole). The known part of the universe hereby becomes a *system*: that part of the universe the aspect of which has taken the form of a theory, now constitutes a structural and functional unit (a structure whose individual units contribute to the functioning of the system with a differentiated activity in functional harmony with the whole). This implies that the system is structurally and functionally adequate to its environment.

The degree of intuition required to identify problems stemming from any part of the universe depends on which of the four levels a system has reached in its cognition of that particular area. Thus hardly any intuition is needed for the recognition of problems deriving from the T level; whereas on the S level, extreme insight is necessary, etc.

In the course of problem-solving it is necessary to retrace the successive passage through the steps $\{O,S,D,T\}$, but now exclusively in relation to the specific area of the problem. The traversing (or construction) of this $\{O,S,D,T\}$ quartet is a heuristic process in which the success of any one step depends on the previous step. Thus it may come to light during step D that the O structure was erroneously elaborated by the person solving the problem. In such cases step O and then step S must be recapitulated, and only after this can attention be turned again to the structure D.

Provided the theory needed for the solution of a problem (the aspect of that part of the universe from which the problem arose) stands at the T level, it is easy to build up the relevant $\{O,S,D,T\}$ quartet; but if the theory is, for instance, only at the S level, then analogous D, T structures *adequate* to the solution of the problem must be sought among other theories.

1. The behavioral aspect of a description, which takes into account the system's reactions to different external influences and/or internal states, is analyzed at the level of its operational mode.‡ In the operational mode we can distinguish a number of components, each one of them complicated in its own right [2, 3].

The components of the operational mode are selected in such a way that only those moments of the solution process most important from the behavioral standpoint and which, at the same time reflect the solution dynamics with adequate fidelity (completeness), are considered. The individual components can therefore be equally simple or complex operations.

2. The level of the structural aspect must permit the functioning of the system as described above. The system is therefore described structurally by an operational system the action of whose elements assures the functioning of the whole system on this level [3].

This task demands increasingly more intuition the further the knowledge required for solving the problem becomes removed from the T level (and in the case of low O- or S-level knowledge this solution is very seldom successful). It is to surmount this difficulty that we need systems theory.

The systems theory (ST) as is well-known is a set of many theories between which connections and interactions are possible. The most abstract part of ST is the General Systems Theory (GST). The interpretations of GST are the Special Systems Theories (SST). The SST's are theories oriented to the individual types of systems (biological, technical, etc.). This two-level classification (GST and SST) is, however, only a rough approximation of the real situation.

As the GST is steadily developing, newer and more abstract levels appear (in the case of inductive extension a whole new theory may be generated), new SST's are thrown up as new interpretations of the GST; meanwhile the articulation of the ST grows more refined, and new levels appear between GST and its SST's.

3. Structural and functional analysis of the problem-solving system

In the analysis of the problem-solving system we start from the following considerations:

---

‡ An operational mode is a set of operations which permit the identification of objects and predicates for the problem-solving system and the specification of their properties, on the basis of which, and in relation to which, different logical transformations are made possible.

Any SST can be partitioned into Analytical Aspects (AA) and—independently—into Analytical Levels (AL). These two kinds of partitioning are orthogonal to each other and their joint application is a basic step in using an SST.

An AA is grounded either on a theory or a subtheory. Such a base may be provided by an abstract theory, or part of a theory.

This theory or subtheory is called the base of the aspect (BA).

The AA's differ from each other in the way they examine the given type of systems, and consequently, what kind of apparatus they utilize. For instance, there are information theoretical, automata theoretical, control theoretical, and energetical aspects.

We illustrate the role of AA in the formation of an interdisciplinary theory.

Consider a family of theories $T_1, T_2, ..., T_n$ dealing with different system types.

If we want to base an interdisciplinary theory on this family of theories, we must form a theory $\hat{T} = T_1 \cup T_2 \cup ... \cup T_n$; then, by the extension of this in an inductive way, we can create a further theory T' the interpretations of which are the theories $T_1, T_2, ..., T_n$. The latter correspond to $SST_1, SST_2, ..., SST_n$ and T' corresponds to the GST. It is first of all necessary to choose the AA. To do this we shall need to utilize some new subtheories (which are independent of T), such as information theory, automata theory, etc. If the information theory, for instance, is represented by $\hat{T}_{inf}$, the information theoretical aspect will have the form $\hat{T} \cap T_{inf}$. The AA obtained are then broken down to the level of the theories $T_1, T_2, ..., T_n$ and used to form the classification needed for the abstraction.

The AL's differ from each other in the detail of the analysis of the given system type; that is, how small those subsystems are that are analyzed functionally only, and how large those that are analyzed both functionally and structurally.

For example, on the highest AL we are restricted to the study of the relations between the system and its environment, the system being regarded as a single undifferentiated unit or a *black box*. On the second level the system may be broken down to its immediate component parts, that is, the system is analyzed as the family of its immediate subsystems. On lower levels the system is seen in a more and more detailed analysis progressing to an apparently arbitrary degree of refinement, to whatever number of levels of abstractions we wish. The selected AL can be said to be adequate to a task (or problem), the problem to be solved with the minimum effort (i.e., without having to go into unnecessary detail).

Let us investigate the application of a theory *(T)* to find the adequate AL for a problem *(p)*, which will be a statement of a language.

We introduce the following notation:

$$T \overset{\sim}{\underset{<=>}{\ni}} p \quad \overset{def}{\underset{<=>}{}} \quad (\exists T' \subseteq T) \ (T' \overset{\sim}{\to} T'' \ \& \ p \in T'')$$

where $\overset{\sim}{\to}$ is the symbol of homomorphism.

If $T \overset{\sim}{\ni} p$, then we say that problem p is *embeddable* in theory T. Let T be a subalgebra of the σ algebra of some universe J, and let $p \in J$. T'' is now a subalgebra of T. To solve p we must look for the minimal *subalgebra (T'')* of T in which p can still be solved ($p \in T''$); this T'' is called the *level* of the theory adequate to problem p. It is easy to see that this level will not be "homogeneous"; that is, the classes of the minimal partition of the selected subalgebra σ will not be of equal cardinality. The minimal partition of an algebra σ is taken to mean the *infimum* (or greatest lower bound) of the partitions generating the algebra.

If the theory T'' which is adequate to the problem necessitates decisions which cannot be made within the theory T, then the problem can be solved by the theory T only after this has been extended. Let k be the most detailed partition formed by theory T on the universe (i.e., k is the greatest lower bound of the partitions generating T) and let k'' be one of the partitions generating T''. It follows that the decisions of T'' can be generated in T provided $k'' \geqslant k$. In other words, T must be extended to such an algebra σ of the universe J as has a subalgebra adequate to p.

Naturally we can speak of the adequacy of the AL only if the aspect selected is appropriate. Selection of the adequate level and its aspect is inseparable from the process of problem-solving (optimalization). In its course the level and the aspect are modified alternately, until both of them are suitable for the given purpose. Thus the GST provides a logical frame for the hypothetical extension of low-level theories to the T level; for instance, the search for hypothetical D, T structures for an S-level theory.

Accordingly, systems theory plays a fundamental role in the development of *non-T-level theories* and in the identification and formulation of problems which cannot be solved by purely deductive means. Moreover, application of systems theory *ipso facto* results in its own further development, both through extension with a new SST or AA and

141

through refinement of the GST as a logical frame. The GST can thus considerably assist the problem-solving system in its attempts to add to its knowledge about the universe.

4. Components of the problem-solving system

4.1 The system can be broken down structurally into three components:
1. Thesaurus:
   (Knowledge, theories, hypotheses, etc. formed about the universe.)
2. Collection of subsystems:
   Problem-identifying subsystems
   Problem-formulating subsystems
   Solution-seeking subsystems.
3. Coordinator:
   (Does not necessarily exist) coordinates the functioning of the subsystems.

The interrelationship of the problem-solving subsystems is shown in Fig. 1. (N.B. The order presented there is not intended to represent the time sequence of the operations.)

4.2 Components of the subsystems
Each subsystem can be reduced in turn to the following components:
1. Thesaurus: (The subsystem has the system thesaurus, or at least a part of it, at its disposal.)
2. Set of operators: These are the smallest structural units the operation of which gives a functional unit. The functioning of a problem-solving system can, in fact, be reduced to the functioning of program-coordinated operators. In selecting the operators an effort

has been made to ensure that the level be adequate; that is, the previously introduced minimax principle was held in view. As a result, the level of the breakdown is not uniform throughout: some of the operators obtained perform only small, partial tasks, others undertake very complex ones. More detailed breakdown of the latter would not have brought us any nearer to our present objective.
3. Program Ω: This selects which operator should work and when, as well as the degree of effectuation at which it should operate. (One and the same operator can be effectuated or activated at various levels and in different modes.)

4.3 Operators of the problem-identifying subsystem
O_1: Semantic analysis of statements received from the environment for identification of the objects and predicates. This operator utilizes the thesaurus containing the known part of the general grammar of the environment.
O_2: Analysis of statements to identify the relations. This operator identifies those combinations of predicates and objects that actually occur in a given case (i.e., the partial statements), utilizing the same thesaurus as operator O_1.
O_3: Partition of the given statements (objects and predicates) into known and unknown concepts.
O_4: Creation of a hypothetical statement structure: in other words, hypothetical exposure of the relation between the known and unknown. If that part of the universe from which a statement derives constitutes a T-level theory, then this operator can function

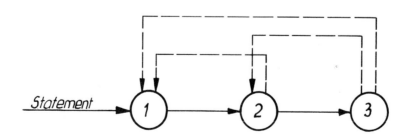

Fig. 1 Interrelationship of subsystems within the problem-solving system. 1—problem-identifying subsystem, 2—problem-formulating subsystem, 3—solution-seeking subsystem

in a deductive way. The functioning of O_4 requires a very high degree of intuition, if knowledge about the part of the universe in question is only organized by, say, an S-level theory. The situation is eased if a suitable interdisciplinary theory exists with the aid of which the S-level theory can be extended hypothetically to the T-level. One of the most essential functions of systems theory is to serve as such an interdisciplinary theory. Examples of such functioning of systems theory in a significant part of the universe are provided by the recent stages in the history of non-T-level sciences, such as biology, sociology, psychology, etc.

O_5: This is the hypothesis generator. Its functioning results in whatever hypothetical extension of existing theories and the existing thesaurus of concepts is needed to permit the interpretation of a statement as a problem. An extension of a theory can be called hypothetical when it does not extend the core of the theory (shrinking extension). A hypothesis is, in fact, a means of specifying a problem. As with the preceding operator, in cases when the insight available to a system is insufficient to allow functioning of this operator, systems theory may provide a useful means of sur-

mounting difficulties. It is fair to say that the hypothesis generator is the most essential operator of the problem-identifying sybsystem, since its success determines the success of the problem-identification step as a whole. In the case of problems locatable only in an inductive way, the lower the level of the theory the more intuition is needed for the operation of the hypothesis generator.

O_6: Analysis of the hypothetical statement-structure on the basis of the hypothesis. Depending on the result of the analysis, either a new statement-structure or a new hypothesis is generated, or we go on to the next step, which is the execution of operator O_7.

O_7: Specification of the problem concealed in the hypothesis in terms of the language of the statement. This operator applies the thesaurus containing the general grammar of the universe.

O_8: Formation of the problem.

O_9: Test operator. This operator checks the result of all the operators after their execution and also the over-all product (the formulated problem) of the whole problem-identifying subsystem. The latter is accomplished by comparing the formulated problem with the original statement. If the result of the

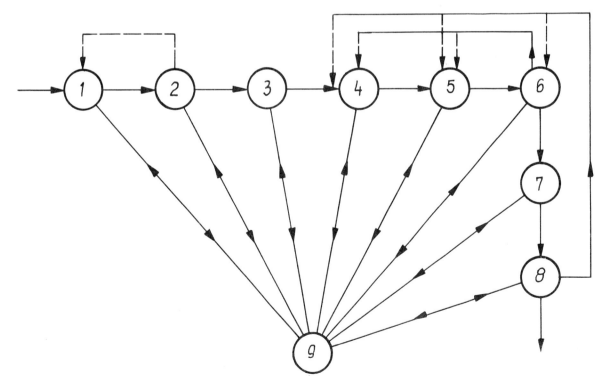

Fig. 2 Interrelationship of operators in the problem-identifying subsystem

check is not satisfactory, then we must return to the hypothesis-generating step O_5 or to operator O_6. If the result is satisfactory, then the formulated problem will represent the output of the subsystem.

The interrelationship of the operators in the problem-identifying subsystem is shown schematically in Fig. 2, and a graphic representation of its operation can be seen in Fig. 3. (Operators are denoted with arrows with the arrowheads pointing to the product of the operator's action.)

4.4 Operators of the problem-formulating subsystem

This subsystem receives as input an identified problem formulated in terms of the language of the universe. The output is the problem adequately formulated from the point of view of the descriptional level, the analytical level, and other aspects.

O_1: Semantic analysis of the problem utilizing the thesaurus of the grammar to identify objects, predicates and relations. This operator corresponds to operators O_1 and O_2 of the problem-identifying subsystem.

O_2: Specification of the problem structure using the thesaurus of concepts and theories; that is, partition of the problem into known and unknown concepts and the clarification of the relationship between the two. This operator corresponds to operators O_3 and O_4 of the problem-identifying subsystem.

O_3: Generation of an embedding theory. This operator seeks to find a theory T_B which includes a subtheory $T_b{}^*$ analogous to theory T in which the problem can be formulated. The statement that T_B is an embedding theory for a problem p is denoted by the relation $T_B \overset{\approx}{\supset} p$.

Definition of the embedding theory:

$$T_B \overset{\approx}{\supset} p \iff (\exists T_b \subseteq T_B)\ (\exists T_b \overset{\approx}{\rightarrow} T)\ (p \in T)$$

The operator works in the following way.

First a search is conducted in the thesaurus of theories for a theory which satisfies the condition $T_B \overset{\approx}{\supset} p$. If there is no such theory, then the operation produces some epitheory which is suitable for embedding p. In this case, T_B is given by extension of some set of theories $\{T_1, ..., T_n\}$. In deductive extension less, and in the case of induction more, intuition is needed (in deductive cases the rules of inference provide a frame for the search). The operator complies with the minimax principle by minimalizing either the complexity of the extension or the level of intuition that is required. (For example, if a problem can be solved by deductive extension, then this course will be selected and the cardinality of the set $\{T_1, ..., T_n\}$ will be minimalized etc.) The operator minimalizes the complexity of the theory T_B (the cardinality of the axiomatic system and of the rules of inference) and maximalizes the descriptional level of the language E_B (the language of T_B). The latter means that an interpretation of the theory $T_1 \cup T_2 \cup ... T_n$ will be sought which achieves a maximal level of description while still satisfying the condition $T_B \overset{\approx}{\supset} p$.

In applying *systems theory* itself, selection of a set $\{T_1, ..., T_n\}$ corresponds to selection of the necessary SST's and AA's. Achievement of the necessary interpretation of these may result in an extension of the set of SST's or AA's. The search for the interpretation giving an adequate descriptional level involves selection of the adequate AL.

This operator corresponds to operator O_5 of the problem-identifying subsystem, i.e., it also relies to a considerable extent on the hypotheses generator. Owing to the way in which the hypothesis generator is used, systems theory again plays an important role here, as discussed in the Section on $\{O,S,D,T\}$.

O_4: Comparative analysis of embedding theory T_B and problem p. The operator checks whether the descriptional level of theory T_B is adequate to the problem in accordance with the minimax principle.

O_5: Search for the embedded theory $T_b \subset T_B$. The operator looks for the smallest subtheory still analogous to the problem, or the subtheory with an analog still fully describing the problem. More precisely, it holds for the sought theory T_b that:

$$T_B \supseteq T_b \overset{\approx}{\supset} p \ \&\ (\forall T' \subseteq T_B)(T' \overset{\approx}{\supset} p \Rightarrow T_b \subseteq T')$$

---

*T' is a subtheory of the theory T if it is both a subset of T and a theory, i.e., if $T' < T$ and T' is closed under the rules of inference. The language E' of the subtheory is the minimum subset of the language of T (E) which is still able to express T'.

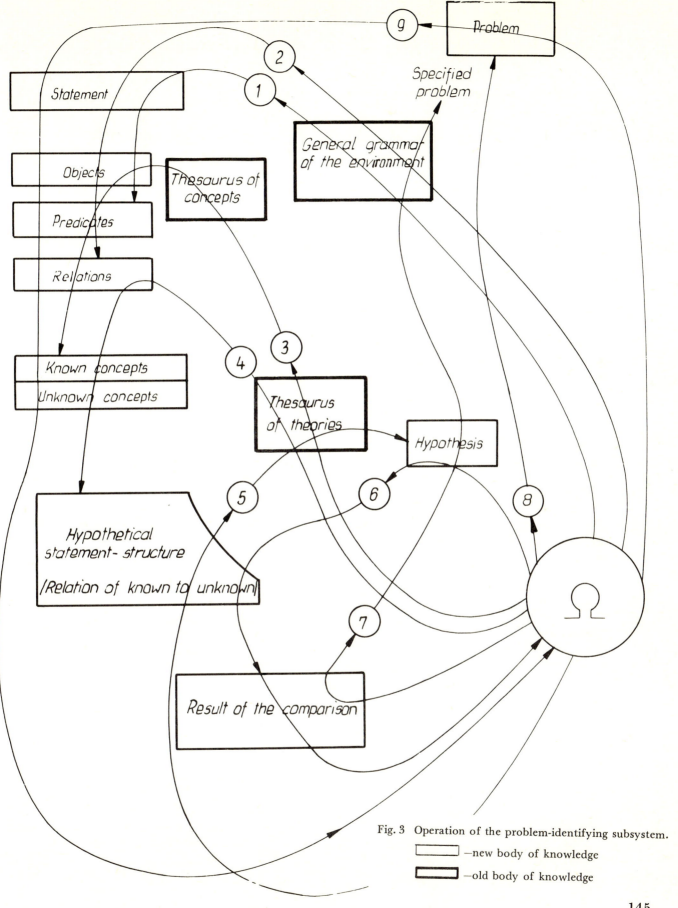

Fig. 3 Operation of the problem-identifying subsystem.

☐ —new body of knowledge

■ —old body of knowledge

Statement

Objects

Predicates

Relations

Known concepts

Unknown concepts

Thesaurus of concepts

General grammar of the environment

Specified problem

Problem

Thesaurus of theories

Hypothesis

Hypothetical statement-structure
/Relation of known to unknown/

Result of the comparison

Ω

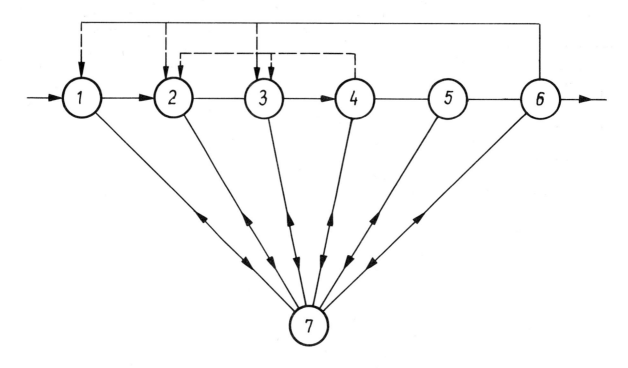

Fig. 4   Interrelationship of operators in the problem-formulating subsystem

Application of the minimax principle in this manner yields an analogous theory adequate to the problem, and provided operators O_4 and O_5 function satisfactorily, the descriptional level of language E_B of the embedded theory will also be adequate.

O_6: Application of the embedded theory to the specific problem via the interpretation $T_b \rightarrow T$.

O_7: Formulation of the problem. This operator brings the problem into the final and—with respect to the grammar of embedded theory— correct form. (Strictly speaking, both here and in the case of O_5 we should have spoken of T and not T_b; however, the adequacy of T depends on the adequacy of T_b.)

O_8: Test operator, identical in function with the test operator of the problem-identifying subsystem.

The interrelationship of the operators in the problem-formulating subsystem is illustrated in Fig. 4, and their functions in Fig. 5.

4.5 *Operators of the solution-seeking subsystem*

O_1: Semantic analysis of the problem.

O_2: Operator creating the problem structure.

O_3: Looks for a hypothetical analogous problem structure, if necessary by extending the thesaurus of theories.

O_4: Analysis of the problem structure on the basis of the analogous structure. Depending on the result of the analysis, either O_2 or O_3 may have to be repeated; otherwise the analysis proceeds further.

O_5: Operator transforming the constructed problem structure. Reformulation of the problem in the light of the comparison.

O_6: Selection of the solution heuristics. The product is again a hypothesis: the operator conceives a plan of solution using the appropriate thesauruses containing the solution methods and heuristics applied before.

O_7: Application of the solution heuristics. The product is a detailed plan of solution of the problem which is constructed by the operator by the choice of specific operations and algorithms from the solution heuristics.

O_8: Performance of the solution heuristics. This operator gives the result of the problem-solving process.

O_9: Test operator. Its function is identical to that of the test operators introduced earlier.

146

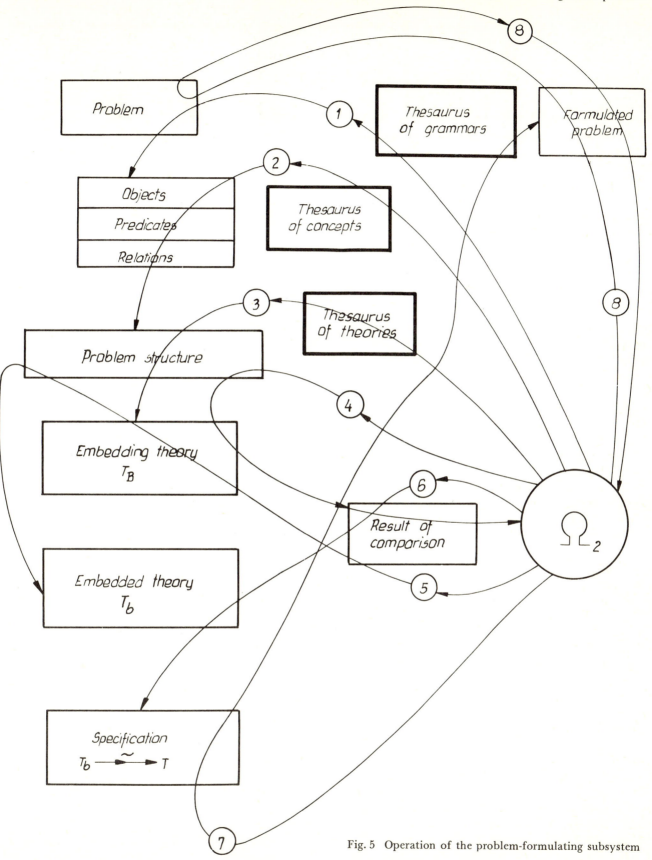

Fig. 5 Operation of the problem-formulating subsystem

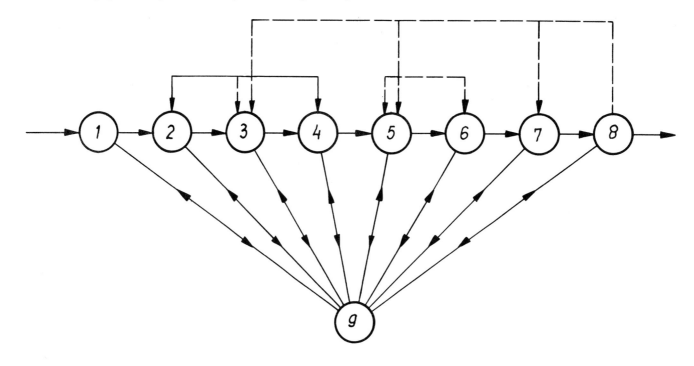

Fig. 6 Interrelationship of operators in the problem-solving subsystem

If no solution is found, then the procedure must be traced back to the problem-formulating subsystem. The interrelations of the operators in the problem-solving subsystem are shown in Fig. 6, and their functions in Fig. 7.

5. Conclusions

1. Systems theory, by virtue of its interdisciplinary character, offers a scheme for the indispensible process of elevating our low-level theories to the level of quasi-completeness and it must by now be evident from the foregoing just how important it is in the processes of problem identification and formulation in science at its present state of development. Naturally, when it comes to tackling the actual solution of particular problems we need to elaborate theoretical structures much more specific than those provided by systems theory, both to obtain adequate solutions and to create the conditions for developing and extending low-level theories.

2. In addition, systems theory is an invaluable tool to use in the erection of the interdisciplinary platform we need in constructing quasi-*T*-level theories adequate to our specific problems—and for this reason its logical foundations merit very close

scrutiny, with particular regard to its future development. It has been demonstrated that the development of the GST and the SST's obey the same logical laws as the construction of an epitheory.

3. It should also be noted that this approach holds some promise of being able to clarify the logico-dialectical grounds of theoretical evolution. The structure of a theory must obviously be adequate to the structure of the universe, for it is only in this way that its adequate functioning can be assured as our understanding of the universe expands. By adequate functioning of a theory we mean, of course, its capacity to accommodate extensions in knowledge about the universe. In other words, provided a theory is structurally adequate or sound vis-à-vis the universe, then newer theories invoked to describe our ever growing store of knowledge must stand in recursive relation to it. (Lower-level theories can be embedded in theories situated at higher levels of the spiral.) An approach of this kind also makes feasible the elaboration of a methodology of applying systems theory.

References

1. PIAGET, J., et autres, *L'enseignement des mathématiques*, Neuchatel et Paris, Delachaux et

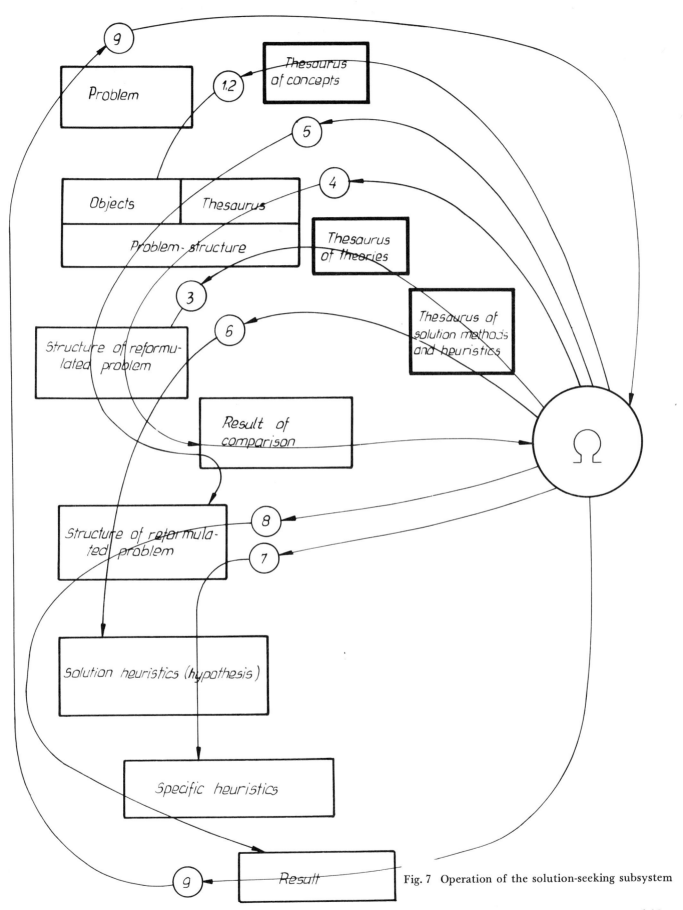

Fig. 7 Operation of the solution-seeking subsystem

149

Niestlé, 11-34 (1955).

2. GERGEI, T. and MASHBITS, E.I., A model for the solution of educational problems, Questions for Psychology (In Russian: 'Ob odnoi modeli resheniya uchebnykh zadach', Voprosy Psikholo-gii) (1972).

3. GERGELY, T. and POKROVS'KYI, Ye.O., 'A semantic information model as a basis for an efficient teaching automaton', *Soviet Automatic Control* 15(1), (1970).

Matroids and heuristically guided search in problem solving[*]

F. MAFFIOLI
Istituto di Elettrotecnica ed Elettronica,
Politecnico di Milano, Italy

1. Foreword

Problem solving has been an area of strong research activity in recent years both in relation to artificial intelligence and to combinatorial optimization. The final task would be to obtain a computer program capable of (i) representing a large class of (large-scale) problems arising from reality (ii) searching for optimal or suboptimal solutions to a given problem by efficient methods.

An intermediate step which strongly suggests itself is to analyze the given problem in order to choose the best suited approach to its solution. In this work matroids theory is proposed as a tool for approaching this intermediate step in a wide class of (non-numerical) problems.

In the next Section a few elementary notions of matroids theory will be reviewed.

Section 3 will be devoted to a brief introduction to the complexity of problems and their classification as 1, 2, and 3 matroid problems. In Section 4 a heuristically guided search will be reformulated for three matroid intersection problems.

Dynamic weighting will be considered in this context and the problem of lower bounds will be analyzed in Section 5.

Progress in Cybernetics and Systems Research, Volume 2
Copyright © 1975 by Hemisphere Publishing Corporation

2. Matroids [1, 2]

A matroid $M = (E, \mathscr{I})$ is a structure in which E is a finite set of elements and $\mathscr{I}$ is a nonempty family of subsets I of E satisfying the following axioms:

A.1) If $I \in \mathscr{I}$ and $I' \subseteq I$, then $I' \in \mathscr{I}$.
A.2) If I and $I' \in \mathscr{I}$ and $|I| = |I'| + 1$ then
$\exists\ e \in I - I'$ such that $I' + e \in \mathscr{I}$.[†]

The members of $\mathscr{I}$ are called independent sets, a set which is not in $\mathscr{I}$ is called dependent.

A minimal dependent set is called a circuit. A maximal independent set is called a basis of the matroid.

Let A be an arbitrary subset of E. The rank of A, $r(A)$ is the cardinality of a maximal independent subset $I \subseteq A$. All such maximal subsets have the same cardinality. The span of A, denoted by $sp(A)$, is the unique maximal superset of A having the same rank.

[*]Partially supported by The Centro di Telecomunicazioni Spaziali of C.N.R. by the Politecnico di Milano.

[†] $|I|$ indicates the cardinality of set I. $I + e$ and $I - e$ are shorthand notation for $I \cup \{e\}$ and $I - \{e\}$, respectively.

We shall assume in the following that a Subroutine for Testing of Independence (STI) of a given subset I of E is available.

Given any subset A of E, the construction of the $sp(A)$ or the test for A being a circuit are easily derived subroutines once the STI is available.

As an example, let E be the set of arcs of a given graph G and $\mathcal{I}$ be the family of subsets of arcs which contain no cycles (i.e., trees or forests of G). Then $M = (E, \mathcal{I})$ is a matroid, called the graphic matroid of G. Any spanning tree of G is a basis of its graphic matroid.

Let $P = \{p_i \,; i=1,...,m\}$ be a partition of a set E into m blocks. Let $d_1, d_2,...,d_m$ be given nonnegative integers. Let $\mathcal{I}$ be the family of all subsets I of E such that

$$|I \cap p_i| \leqslant d_i, \qquad (i=1,2,...,m)$$

Then $M = (E, \mathcal{I})$ is a partition matroid (ordinarily $d_1 = d_2 = ... = d_m = 1$).

Let $M_1 = (E, \mathcal{I}_1)$ and $M_2 = (E, \mathcal{I}_2)$ be two given matroids defined over the same set of elements E. A subset $I \in \mathcal{I}_1 \cap \mathcal{I}_2$ is said to be an intersection of M_1 and M_2.

Let G be a bipartite graph in which each arc extends between a node in a set S and a node in a set T. A matching in G is a subset of its arcs no two of which meet at the same vertex. Let M_1 be a partition matroid which has as its independence sets all subsets of arcs, no two of which meet at the same node of S, and M_2 be another similar partition matroid with respect to T. Every matching of G is an intersection of M_1 and M_2 and vice versa.

Consider now a directed graph G, its graphic matroid M_1 (for which the orientation of arcs of G is irrelevant) and two partition matroids, M_2 and M_3, the first having as its independent sets all subsets of arcs no two of which are directed *into* the same node and the second having as its independent sets all subsets of arcs no two of which are directed *out* of the same node. The problem of finding a maximum weight independent set of arcs which is an intersection of M_1, M_2, and M_3 is equivalent to the travelling salesman problem since it amounts to finding a maximum weight spanning simple path of G [3,4].

3. Complexity of algorithms [5]

A fundamental parameter in evaluating the complexity of algorithms is the computing time. This may be quite different from one implementation to

another, but it depends in any case on the number of elementary computational steps the algorithm requires. Upper (and lower) bounds to this number are therefore of paramount importance in evaluating the efficiency of a certain method with respect to others.

In [5] Karp classified problems into two main classes: "easy" problems and "hard" problems.

A problem is "easy" if the number of computational steps is upper bounded by a polynomial function in the size of the problem, while a problem is classified in the "hard" list if this upper bounding function is growing exponentially (or even faster).

Lawler has shown that, provided the testing for independence is an easy problem, then one matroid and two matroid intersection problems are also easy, while three matroid intersection problems are hard.

There is also strong evidence (although not yet a proof) that efficient (i.e., polynomially bounded) algorithms for any one of the hard problems will never be found.

Nevertheless, two matroid intersection problems are not the most general matroid problem which can be solved in polynomial time (provided the test for independence is itself an easy problem). A more general class is constituted by the matroid parity problems, which may be formulated as follows.

Let $M = (E, \mathcal{I})$ be a matroid whose elements are arranged in pairs, i.e., each element e has a uniquely specified mate $\bar{e}$. A parity set $A \subseteq E$ is a set such that for each element e, $e \in A$ iff $\bar{e}$ also $\in A$. Find an optimal independent parity set in M. Matroid intersection problems may be shown to be a particular case of matroid parity problems. These may naturally be generalized to k-parity problems, but for $k \geqslant 3$ they belong to the hard list.

The following fundamental theorem due to Lawler [8] constitutes one of the pieces of evidence that polynomial bounded algorithms for three matroid intersection problems will never be found.

Theorem 1: There exists a polynomial bounded algorithm for the 3 matroid intersection problem iff there exists a polynomial bounded algorithm for the k-parity problem *for all* $k \geqslant 3$.

This theorem has two consequences: first, that one is almost certain that a polynomial bounded algorithm for the 3 matroid intersection problem will never be found since otherwise an infinite and infinitely complex class of problems would also be in the easy class; secondly, that one is eager to solve 3 matroid intersection problems any way due to their paramount importance.

What will be done in the following is in fact to generalize to 3 matroid intersection problems one of the most powerful (although nonpolynomial bounded) methods presently known.

4. Heuristically guided search for 3 matroid intersections

Let $M_k = (E, \mathscr{T}_k)$, $k = 1, 2, 3$ be three matroids of the same rank n and $w : E \to I\!R^+$ be a weighting function. Let there exist a polynomial bounded algorithm for the testing of independence of any $I \subseteq E$ in each one of the M_k. It is then possible to construct a polynomial bounded algorithm for solving the two matroid intersection problem involving, say, M_1 and M_2 [2]. Let this be called the basic algorithm (BA). The three matroid intersection problem is considered here as the problem of finding a minimum weight independent set of maximum cardinality belonging to $\bigcap\limits_{k=1,2,3} \mathscr{T}_k$.

Let $D = (V, T)$ be a digraph of vertices $v_i \in V$ and links $(v_i, v_j) \in T$. Each vertex v_i of D is defined as follows.

$$v_i = \{ I : I \in \bigcap\limits_{k=1,2,3} \mathscr{T}_k \text{ and } sp_3(I) = A_i \}$$

where

$$sp_j(I) = \{ e : I + e \notin \bigcap\limits_{k=1}^{j} \mathscr{T}_k \}, \quad j = 1, 2, 3$$

and $A_i \subseteq E$.

We shall write shortly $v_i = (A_i)$. There will, of course, be a "void" vertex $v_a = (\phi)$ and a "complete" vertex $v_z = (E)$.

The links of D will be defined by the following successor generating rule. For each $e_j \in E - A_i$ there exists a link (v_i, v_j) where $A_j = sp_3(A_i + e_j)$. The length of link (v_i, v_j) is $t_{ij} = w(e_j)$.

From the above definitions it follows that a shortest directed path between vertex v_a and v_z in D corresponds to a solution of the three matroid intersection problem. Among the many references about the shortest path problem we will mainly refer to [11]. The distance d_{ij} from vertex v_i to vertex v_j $(i \neq j)$ is defined as:

i) The length of a shortest directed path from v_i to v_j if such a path exists;

ii) $d_{ij} = \infty$, otherwise. When $i = j$, $d_{ij} = 0$.

Starting from the vertices adjacent to v_a a parameter p_j is defined for every vertex v_j. Then V is partitioned with respect to p_j into three classes.

(a) Closed vertices, for which $p_j = d_{aj} = d_j$.

(b) Open vertices, for which $p_j \geqslant d_j$.

(c) Blank vertices, for which p_j is unknown.

Let there be an estimate q_j of the cost of a shortest path from v_j to the complete vertex v_z, such that

$$q_j \leqslant d_{jz} \tag{1}$$

and

$$q_j \leqslant d_{jk} + q_k \tag{2}$$

We assume that this estimate can be obtained analyzing each problem domain.

The algorithm proceeds as follows.

Step 1. Close the open vertex v_j for which the total estimate $f_j = p_j + q_j$ is minimum.

Step 2. If $v_j = v_z$ stop.

Step 3. Expand v_j, i.e., take into consideration all the vertices which can be reached from v_j with one link. Let v_k be any one of them. If v_k is open,

$$p_k = \min \{ p_k, p_j + t_{jk} \},$$

if v_k is blank,

$$p_k = p_j + t_{jk}$$

and v_k is adjoined to the open list. Go to step 1.

The efficiency of the heuristically guided search is heavily dependent upon how close q_j is to d_{jz}. The problem of finding such an estimate will be the subject of the next Section

A more flexible algorithm can be implemented using as total estimate not $f_j = p_j + q_j$, but rather

$$f_j = (1 - \gamma_j) p_j + \gamma_j q_j$$

where $0 \leqslant \gamma_j < 1$. For $\gamma_j = \frac{1}{2}$ one obtains the regular heuristically guided search. For all values of γ_j in the interval $[0, \frac{1}{2}]$ one is assured of finding the optimum, while this is no more the case when $\gamma_j \in (\frac{1}{2}, 1)$. However, in this case the search may be speeded up considerably leading to heuristic rather than heuristically guided procedures. The concept of dynamic weighting [10] can also be implemented to try to avoid what Pohl calls computational catastrophes. In this last case γ_j is given by a formula of the following kind:

$$\gamma_j = \frac{(1+a)n + (1-a)|I_j|}{2(n + |I_j|)}$$

where n is the rank of E and $0 \leqslant a < 1$. The search modifies from depth-first-like at the beginning to breadth-first-like at the end becoming a lot more efficient although not guaranteed to find the optimum.

5. Estimates and lower bounds

Let $v_i = (A_i)$ be a vertex of D and $\bar{A}_i = E - A_i$. Let $M_{ki} = (\bar{A}_i, \mathscr{T}_k)$, $k=1,2,3$, be three reduced matroids. We shall assume as q_i the weight of a minimum weight independent set of maximum cardinality of the intersection of M_{1i} and M_{2i}.

Property 1:

$$q_i \leqslant d_{iz} \tag{3}$$

Since d_{iz} is the shortest directed path in D from v_i to v_z, it is a solution to the three matroid intersection problem involving the M_{ki}'s, which has to be greater than or equal to the solution of the two matroid intersection problem involving only M_{1i} and M_{2i}.

Now let $v_j = (A_j)$ be such that there exists a path of D connecting v_i and v_j. Then $A_i \subset A_j$ and we may define a nonvoid subset X of E such that

$$X \cup \bar{A}_j = \bar{A}_i$$

and

$$X \cap \bar{A}_j = \phi$$

Let $M_k^o = (X, \mathscr{T}_k)$, $k=1,2,3$.

Property 2: q_i as defined by (3) obeys the consistency assumption (2).

Proof: Let x be the weight of the solution to the two matroid intersection problem involving M_1^o and M_2^o. Then

$$q_i \leqslant x + q_j \tag{4}$$

In fact, assume $x = w(I^o)$, $q_i = w(I_i)$ and $q_j = w(I_j)$. Since by hypothesis $I^o \cap I_j = \phi$

$$\bar{I} = I^o + I_j$$

is such that

$$w(\bar{I}) = w(I^o) + w(I_j)$$

Moreover $\bar{I}$ belongs to the intersection of M_{1i} and M_{2i} so that $q_i \leqslant w(\bar{I})$ and (4) follows. From the definition of d_{ij} it turns out that d_{ij} is the weight of an independent set of maximum cardinality belonging to the intersection of the three matroids M_k^o ($k=1,2,3$). Therefore, $x \leqslant d_{ij}$ and (2) follows from (4).

To obtain more sophisticated and effective estimates, we need now to assume a certain structure of the weighting functions which can be defined on E.

Let

$$\pi : E \to \mathbb{R}^+$$

be a weighting function such that all maximal independent sets belonging to the intersection of the three given matroids are modified by the same amount when we weight them in the following way:

$$w'(I) = \sum_{\forall e \in I} [w(e) + \pi(e)] \tag{5}$$

That is if both I_1 and I_2 belong to $\bigcap_{i=1,2,3} \mathscr{T}_i$ and have maximum cardinality,

$$w'(I_1) = w'(I_2) + K$$

where K does not depend upon I_1 and I_2.

Let this hypothesis not hold if I_1 and I_2 are constrained to belong only to $\mathscr{T}_1 \cap \mathscr{T}_2$. It is then possible to define q_j as

$$q_j = \min_{I} \max_{\pi} w'(I) \tag{6}$$

where the minimization is performed over all the I's belonging to the intersection of M_{1i} and M_{2i}.
To find $\max_{\pi} w'(I)$ an ascent-relaxation method of the kind developed in [4,9] could be used. Properties 1 and 2 may be shown to hold also for (6). Formal proofs of these as well as the previous versions of properties 1 and 2 require a rather cumbersome notation [12], despite their intuitive evidence and are therefore omitted here for the sake of brevity.

6. Conclusions

Matroid theory has been shown to constitute a general frame for the analysis of the complexity of a problem. When such analysis shows that a given problem is (polynomial) complete the method of heuristically guided search is suggested for finding a solution either optimal or suboptimal. Further research would be needed to realize this approach in a practical problem solver, mainly in order to solve automatically the important step of matroid complexity evaluation of a given problem.

7. Acknowledgement

The author is pleased to acknowledge the help of his friend P.M. Camerini in discussing and correcting this work.

References

1. WHITHEY, H., 'On the abstract properties of linear dependence', *Amer. J. Math.* **57**, 509-533 (1935).
2. LAWLER, E.L., 'Matroid Intersection Algorithms', Memo No. ERL-M333 Electronic Research Lab., U. of California at Berkeley (1971).
3. BELLMORE, M. and NEMHAUSER, G., 'The travelling salesman problem. A survey', *Ops. Res.* **16**, 538 (1968).
4. CAMERINI, P.M., FRATTA, L., and MAFFIOLI, F., 'A heuristically guided algorithm for the travelling salesman problem', *J. of the Institution of Computer Sciences* **4**, 31-35 (1973).
5. KARP, R., 'Reducibility among combinatorial problems', *Symp. on Complexity of Computations*, Miller & Thatcher (editors), Plenum Press, 85-103 (1972).
6. EDMONDS, J., 'Matroids and the greedy algorithm', *Math. Programm.* **1**, 127-136 (1971).
7. LAWLER, E.L., 'Matroid with parity conditions: a new class of combinatorial optimization problems', Memo No. ERL-M334, Electronics Res. Lab., U. of California at Berkeley (1971).
8. LAWLER, E.L., 'Polynomial bounded and (apparently) non-polynomial bounded matroid computations', Memo No. ERL-M332, Electronics Res. Lab., U. of California at Berkeley (1972).
9. HELD, M. and KARP, R., 'The travelling salesman problem and minimum spanning trees: part II', *Math. Programm.* **1**, 6-25 (1971).
10. POHL, Ira, 'The avoidance of (relative) catastrophe, heuristic competence, genuine dynamic weighting and computational issues in heuristic problem solving', III I.J.C.I.A., Proc., Stanford, California (August 1973).
11. HART, P., NILSSON, N.J., and RAPHAEL, B., 'A formal basis of the heuristic determination of minimum cost paths', *IEEE Trans. SSC*, Vol. 4, No. 2, 100 (1968).
12. CAMERINI, P.M. and MAFFIOLI, F., 'Heuristically guided search for three matroid intersection', Int. Rep. 74-8 LCE-IEE Politecnico di Milano (1974).

An outline of teleogenic systems theory

A. LOCKER* and N.A. COULTER, Jr**
*Institute for Biology,
Austrian Research Center, Vienna, Austria
**UNC Medical School, North Carolina, USA

1. Introduction

Systems that pursue goals are well-known. But where do the goals come from? In engineering control systems, they are provided by the designer or operator of the system. Systems that generate their own goals are also possible; indeed, living organisms have this capability. Such systems are called Teleogenic Systems (Coulter [1]).

In this Chapter some foundations for a theory about such systems are presented. These stand in relation to the description and prescription of a system, which, in the case of the Teleogenic System (TES) must merge together in order to enable the system to formulate (i.e., to generate) goals for itself. Since this generation of goals requires a capability analogous to man's it will be necessary to assume an entity having a brain-like character, lying in the system. In case Teleogenic Systems Theory (TSTh) were to aim at implementing a system that entirely and effectively simulates man, it must be admitted that such an endeavor can never succeed. However, the process of goal generation can be imitated provided it is theoretically sufficiently understood.

The Chapter begins by delineating the problem of a system's description and prescription and then continues by considering the process of goal generation. After having briefly mentioned some preliminary computer simulation experiments and proposals

for a mathematical approach, possible applications of a TSTh are sketchily outlined.

2. Some aspects of system description and prescription

For a system it is necessary to distinguish between the *un*concerned observer and the concerned observer. The former is confronted with a system for whose existence he is not responsible, so that he only describes it according to the means at his disposal. He possibly may infer from his description what the knowledge of the concerned observer has been. The latter is identical with the designer.

The unconcerned observer (briefly called now: observer), the system and the designer, taken together, form a *Cognitive Domain* (C.D.). The languages which are used by the designer and the observer, respectively, are of importance. The designer uses a language which, if obeyed, leads to the achievements of certain goals; it is therefore called *Prescription*-Language (P). In it goals must be formulated. On the other side of the Cognitive Domain, the observer, because he has no full knowledge about the goals prescribed, uses a language, called *Description*-Language (D); usually $D \subseteq P$. With respect to language it seems justifiable to ascribe also to the system the capability to "speak"; it

Progress in Cybernetics and Systems Research, Volume 2

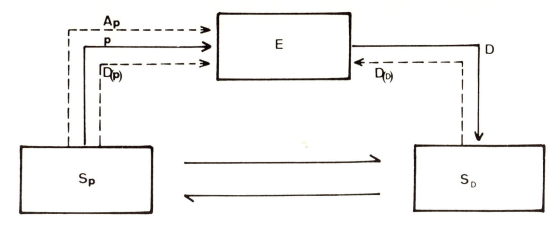

Fig. 1 An outline of the Cognitive Domain. S_P: Prescribing subject (= designer), S_D: Describing subject (= observer), P: prescription language, D: Description language, E: System, D(P): Metalanguage description of prescription, D(D): Metalanguage description of description, A_P: Action prescribed (for the system's design)

expresses its own activity by means of an *Execution*-Language (E). The C.D. is schematically outlined in Fig. 1 [2].

A description can be classified, according to contents and context, which it embraces or in which it is embedded, as *local* and/or *global*. By means of the application of *constraints*, the observer is able to form a hierarchy of levels that reaches from the local up to the global description [3]. The constraints cannot be arbitrarily set, but only according to the requirements of reality. Local and global description can, in general, be distinguished by mutual exclusion of stringency and vagueness [4].

It is impossible to speak of a system in a purely formal respect. Thus, for a system's description the language must be used in its full respect, that is, its *intentional* nature: i.e., its directedness toward reality. Here, the relation between the notions "formal" and "real" can be regarded as indicative for the role the languages D and P must play.

In this respect we quote Rosen [5] who has clearly pointed out that a multitude of *real* models (i.e., realizations) can be built from one *formal* model previously conceived. All of these models realize a certain aspect of the original model. On the other hand, we can easily understand, that a *real* constellation of facts (i.e., a system) can be described by a variety of *formal* models.

It is easy to show that the interplay between the notions of "formal" and "real" reflects itself in a corresponding interplay between P- and D-languages, respectively. Prescription starts with a concept and ends up in the moment of its full realization, where

it passes into execution. Description in turn proceeds from the really existing system, and ends up with a formal entity, i.e., the description itself. In order to transform a prescription, which exists only as a formal concept, into a really existing system, it is necessary that the designer act upon his prescription by means of effects he exerts onto the environment in order to force some building blocks existing there into the prescribed relations such that the prescribed system comes about. To enable actions of this kind the prescription, as a concept for a process, must be "embodied" into the designer's own design system, which acts as a processor for the description (Pask [6]). An action must also be carried out by the observer in order to obtain the description of the system. Action, therefore, is not a feature of the system alone but of the whole Cognitive Domain. Let us consider the action of the designer, once more:

1. In the case of the *Teleonomic System*, which has been so designed as to follow one (or several) goals that do not change, the action of the designer has been accomplished when the system works, so that he can retreat from his work without endangering the execution of the latter.

2. In the case of the *Teleozetic System* [2], to which has been ascribed an ensemble of goals, out of which the system may choose, according to the requirements, i.e., environmental situations, with which it is confronted, the action of the designer must certainly be of higher complexity, but eventually he could equally well be allowed to retreat and to let the system work independently of him.

3. In the case of the *Teleogenic System* (TES), however, the action of the designer cannot come to an end, since the system must *always* successfully cope with new situations. It generates new goals just at the moment when it can manage no more within the framework of its momentary faculties. Then, action is perpetual and designer and system must be continuously linked.

3. Goal generation in general

Goals can be preliminarily defined as follows: with a given mechanism, the goal can be considered an input representing a *future state* of the system, toward which the output tends. With a "semantic system" given in addition, a goal signal may be produced as its output, which serves as the input to the

feedback control system (Fig. 2). The semantic system must be endowed with the capability of *mapping*, not the *actual* states of the controlled quantity, but a domain of *potential* states. It must also be endowed with a decision-making power, i.e., a power of selecting one of these states as a goal and of committing the control system to the pursuit of that goal, by transmitting a goal signal to the feedback control system. Thus, in the semantic system, the goal is a signal, representing a potential state of a control system's output; in the control system, the goal signal is the *input* signal which drives the control system until the goal, corresponding to this input, is achieved [7].

There have been given more sophisticated definitions of goals, e.g., in combinatory logics [8] and in representations of problems in computer languages [9], which indicate quite generally the fact that con-

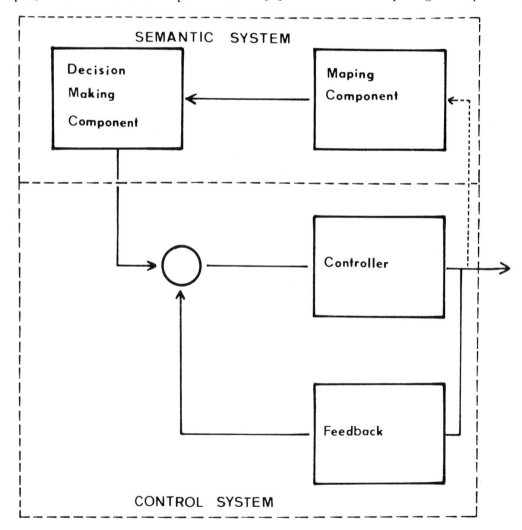

Fig. 2 Description of the connection of the goal generating semantic system with the executing control system

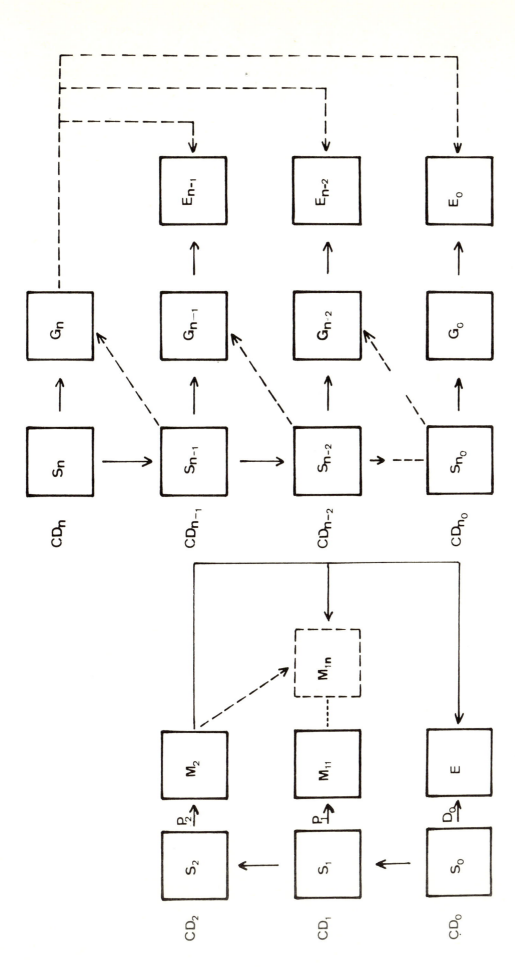

Fig. 3A Structuralization of the Cognitive Domain by means of model building in the D-Domain

Fig. 3B Structuralization of the P-Domain by means of global goal setting (G_n) and by comparing with G_n the increasingly specified local goals (G_{n-1}, etc.), each of them being connected with a system (E) conceptually designed according to the pertinent goal

cepts are goal-directed procedures [10].

Of much higher difficulty than the problem of goal definition is the problem of goal generation. To gain some understanding of what is going on (in the human mind) when a process of generation is conceived, let us consider a problem intimately linked with it, viz. that of the origin of life. In a recent symposium, dealing with "Biogenesis–Evolution–Homeostasis, Rosen [11] has convincingly pointed out that for building up a theory of the origin of life two different concepts should be envisaged:

1. *Transformation Theory*, that tries to understand the evolution of organic forms through the motion of representative points in phase space, sometimes thought of being optimized according to a cost functional. Here, all characters are represented by coordinates of the state space and therefore are already known a priori.

2. *Emergence Theory*, which assumes that with random occurrence of certain compounds and with favorable conditions, a new form that exhibits the character of a living organism, may suddenly "emerge". However, it is not easy to grasp how the state variables that are necessary for a description of any higher complexity, could effectively be generated when the description itself remains at the lowest, viz., the molecular level.

It appears that both theories have justifications of their own and it is necessary, therefore, to show how they could be reconciled. By referring to the Cognitive Domain, we must admit that both "transformation" (i.e., transition) and "emergence" cannot belong to the same semantic level. Indeed, we must assert, that a process, which at the *one* level can be understood as transition, can be described at *another* level as emergence, relevant conditions being presupposed. For describing a process as transition, both states, during which the transition occurs, must be known or, in principle, be recognizable; in the process of "emergence", the initial state of any alleged process remains beyond recognizability, such that the freely pending result appears as something new.

The Cognitive Domain, therefore, has to be considered as structured into hierarchically ordered levels (Fig. 3A). Let us assume that at the lowest level of the C.D., the subject (S_0) registers some features of the system E and composes a preliminary description D(E) of the system. In the attempt to provide this description with a general character, the model M_1 is designed by the observer, who, during this process of model design, places himself into the next higher level (S_1). In order to compare the model with the original description D(E), new models must be designed being so universal as to allow not only for comparisons between the model M_1 with the original description, but also between the models themselves. Since this process will be repeated, more and more structure of the C.D. will be formed. Finally, however, there is the possibility that a model is found (i.e., *designed*) which is so perfectly adjusted to E that it delivers more *details* and *generalities*, as well, than the original description D(E) ever did. Thus, this *surplus* is the apparent *novelty*, which appears at the lowest level of the C.D., as "emergence", in case this process of its structuralization remains unconscious [12].

It should be emphasized here that even this extremely schematic outline of the process of cognition, which goes hand in hand with a structuralization of the C.D., shows an intimate interplay between description and prescription already at the description side of the C.D. Here, built up over a description, the *determinacy* increased, the higher the subject (i.e., the observer) mounted its levels. It is to be proposed that the build-up of the prescription side of the Cognitive Domain is an opposite one: here the *global* goal is indeterminate at the large [10] and the *local* goals are achieved by means of more and more restricting concretizations.

Thus, as Fig. 3B tries to indicate, in descending from the global goal set, the local goals "arise", i.e., become specified, due to a process, being quite similar to the "emergence" of novelty in the D-domain (i.e., the description side), with opposite direction only. Whereas in the D-domain the eventual model encompasses the original insufficient description, in the P-domain (i.e., the prescription side of the Cognitive Domain) every local goal adds some specification to the indeterminacy, by which the global goal was characterized, and thus transcends the latter in an extensional way.

4. On goal generation within the system

Up to now the generation of goals in the P-domain has been assumed to be similar to the generation of novelty in the D-domain. However, such a consideration remains inappropriate with regard to a TES as long as it does not sufficiently take into consideration the necessity that here, in the TES, goal generation must take place *within* the system itself. Thus, the three portions of the Cognitive Domain, viz., designer, system and observer, must fuse in the TES. Therefore, in the ultimate respect, a TES must be

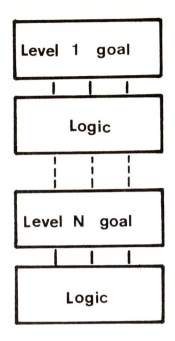

Fig. 4 Outline of the hierarchy of goals with pertinent logical levels (after [13])

endowed with a capability analogous to human consciousness. In terms of this analogy a special embodiment in the form of a "brain" is required [12].

This "brain" must be:

1. An *Organizational Center*, recording internal and external conditions and situations and coping with these (thus, substituting the P- and D-portions, respectively, of the Cognitive Domain).

2. An *Internal Model* of the system, thus being $D'(D \cup E \cup P)$. The Organizational Center expresses the ability of the system to *act*, whereas the Internal Model expresses the ability to *"contemplate"*. Since both kinds of activity are of a *self-referencing* nature, the entity comprising the two (formally) may with some reluctance, of course, be called *Self-like Entity* (SLE).

Then, if such an SLE for a TES can be assumed, the system's total organization cannot be considered as objective only, like that seen by an outside observer. There are aspects of the system's structure that must reveal an increasingly subjective character. We may distinguish, therefore, between:

1. The *Performance Structure*, which is deeply physically embodied, i.e., recognizable as matter and energy.

2. The *Communication Structure*, mediating the origin, distribution and processing of information.

3. The *Intent Structure*, denoting the relationships between the goals superimposed upon the two kinds of structure mentioned; it includes the basis for decision procedures by means of which goals are selected. The general scheme after Warfield [13] shows logic levels alternating with goals whereby AND- as well as IOR- and EOR-elements are included (Fig. 4).

4. The *Generative Structure*, being a kind of structure that elicits new structure and, what means the same, the structure which arises due to the generating of new goals, in response to situations, such as needs, threats or potentials, detected by the SLE.

The SLE has to simultaneously exhibit the character of being free, i.e., of possessing spontaneity, and of being bound, i.e., of being objectively determined. This double character, exactly reflecting the "brain's" double internal organization (v. above), can be described also as a conflict or tension between autonomy and heteronomy, between self-determinism [14] and extraneous (objective) determinism. This conflict can be overcome in a unique way, only, viz. through *action*.

This action refers to:

1. *Time*. An anticipation of the future situation is needed, in order to direct action.

2. *Modality*. Concomitantly with such an anticipation, the possibility (to act) subjectively precedes the actuality (to act). Through the carrying out of action, the existing possibility becomes the more restricted, the more it finally reaches reality, which then objectively precedes. Otherwise phrased: as far as a C.D. can be separated from a system, it must be said that in its P-domain possibility is prevailing and in its D-domain actuality is prevailing. Only in the system itself actuality coincides with possibility. When transferred into the SLE this identity of actuality and potentiality means that the SLE's "consciousness" is able to anticipate the system's total history.

3. *Intentionality.*† The connection between goals and action is not conceivable as a fixed geometric

---

† For touching upon reality the action must be divided into a fraction which is explicitly directed toward objective reality, be the latter the system itself (as a "body") or the environment or both. The part of the SLE that is concerned with this kind of action may be called the "I" [24]. The other fraction of action, which always accompanies the first, touches upon subjective reality; the corresponding part of SLE may be called the "Self". Principally, of course, action must always be built up by both fractions.

relationship, but as a continuous cyclic, evolving process. Thus, for example, prior to its realization, an action must be prescribed and its result anticipated; its realization must be noticed and this record forms the basis for a new concept of action, which, in turn, takes cognizance of the former concept plus the corresponding action, etc. What is said about action, can be equally said about goals since the latter are specifications of the directions for action.

The following distinctions are useful:

1. We have to distinguish between (*a*) the *conceived* goal, that is purely formal as long as it remains within the concept of the design, and which corresponds to the *concept* of action for building a system, and (*b*) the *realized* goal, which, also remaining within the concept of the design, instead corresponds to the accomplished, constructed *system.*

2. In between the conceived and the realized goal "exists" the *actual* goal, i.e., a kind of goal, of which it is thought that it has already left the purely formal sphere of the conceived goals—since processes are going on to realize it—but has not yet attained its realization.

If we consider now goal generation proper—by admitting that what was said in the preceding paragraph was nothing but the illustration of a correspondence between "emergence" of novelty and specifications of goals—we have to state the following: goal generation consists in the transition of a potential goal into an actual goal. The actual goal is connected with (and enables) the construction of the system and, therefore, a part of the prescription for a particular system. By means of the action of the system's construction the actual goal is transferred into the realized goal.

The spaces of the actual and of the potential goals, as well, can be considered as connected. From a certain point of view, the set of actual goals can be considered a subset of the set of potential goals; from another point of view, with a suitable generation capability at hand, goals can be generated into an (apparently) unstructured space and thus become potential and real, as well. Both views do not contradict one with the other, but rather are exact reflections of the double (or dual) nature of cognition, which is not only *discovering*, but also and before all *contriving*. Indeed, this fact marks the very distinction between a teleogenic system and a teleozetic, i.e., goal seeking system. For the TES the most characteristic feature is not a search procedure among pre-assigned goals (even a set of them), but rather the generation of the goal space.

On the local level alone goals cannot sufficiently be conceived, if the frame within which they have to be generated has not yet been laid out previously. When we consider the *duality* existing between the P- and D-sides of the Cognition Domain, and the duality existing between potentiality and actuality, then it appears that also a duality between local and global goals must be assumed. If the setting or generating of local goals would not have been guided by the setting or generating of global goals, the former would arise more or less randomly only and chaotically spread out (therefore, any optimization principle could assume the role of a global goal). We contend that the last mentioned duality is very strict that a so-called *"pleromorphic mapping"* (from Greek: *pleres*, replenished) could be postulated [15]. It formulates the fact that the expansion (or spanning out) of the space of *local* goals (being tantamount with goal generation in the sense outlined above) is balanced (or held together) by the concomitant contraction of the space of *global* goals (being equally well tantamount with the goal generation). This will formally be outlined in more detail in the next Chapter.

It has been argued also that teleogenesis is intrinsically linked with the *origin* of the system [15]; in particular, the existence of a global goal set by the TES would on the whole already generate this very same system. This problem touches upon paradoxes similar to, but obviously still more profound than those arising in automata theory if self-replication is formally treated [15, 16, 17]. It shall not concern us any further. Also the problem of the design of a TES, as treated elsewhere [18], will not be dealt with here.

5. A sketchy description of the TESS-1 computer simulation

Since TSTh aims at eventually implementing a system that generates its own goals (or, at least, simulates such a process), it is necessary to ponder on its build-up (Fig. 5) [19]. The system's joint intent- and generative structure is given by the ensemble of the Director, the Forecaster and the Evaluator. The whole system, except the environmental field, is called Teleoid. In the environmental field appear some objects which are endowed with both a program of motion and contingent movements having the feature that *if* a particular relationship between the object and the teleoid occurs, the object will *change* its motion. The teleoid reacts by assigning particular *worth values* to the object according to

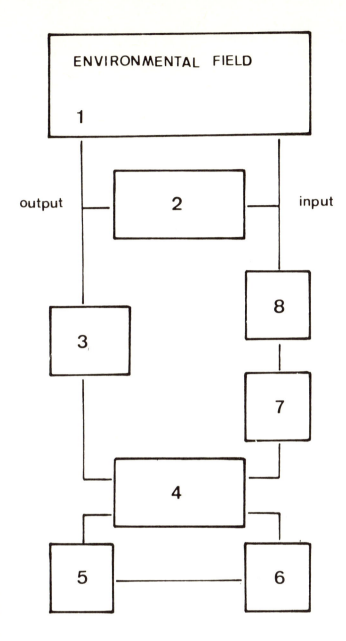

ENVIRONMENTAL FIELD

1

output   2   input

8

3

7

4

5   6

Fig. 5 Display of the TESS-1 simulation basis, also called Teleoid. 1: Objects in the environmental field, 2: Metabolic process, 3: Apperceptive manifold, 4: Director, 5: Forecaster, 6: Evaluator, 7: Executive, 8: Output servos. Further description in [14].

the motion of the object toward the system. This means that during the period during which the object moves it is analyzed and identified as belonging to one of the teleoid's own concepts (categories). The teleoid selects specified goals from its goal repertoire, forecasts the probable outcome for each specific goal and assigns a worth value to that out-

come. It then decides whether or not to adopt one of these specific goals, by comparing it with a decision threshold. If no specific goal equals or exceeds the decision threshold, the teleoid initiates a *probe*, i.e., a predetermined movement toward the object's movement to sense the latter's contingent movement. The teleoid switches between *Action Mode*, i.e., an action after having adopted a specific goal, and a *Search Mode*, i.e., an exploration of the object's movement.

During each new period (of such a switch) the teleoid ascends the hierarchy of goals, e.g., instead of selecting *specific* goals, it goes through a decision procedure for selecting a *sequence* of specific goals (called *generic* goal). Also the Action Mode differs at a second run, in that it becomes, e.g., an Action Policy, comprising a variety of actions, i.e., movements toward the objects, etc.

There happens a historical development of the teleoid, in that by means of the sequence of encounters with the objects the system itself learns.

Further simulations are under progress [19], but it must be acknowledged that up to now they do not yet deal with goal generation in the proper sense since the goals are designed by the *outside* designer of the simulation model and since the system only *selects* among them.

6. Some preliminary mathematical descriptions suitable for a TES

Apart from a specific formal approach to goal generation that will be dealt with in the next Chapter, some other possibilities for a mathematical description of typical characters of a TES comprise the following:

1. Having found it necessary to postulate an SLE, which is in itself an internal observer and prescriber, as well, we can mathematically express this character by borrowing a result from the theory of multivariable systems, viz. the theory of *controllability* and *observability*. It can be shown [14] that under certain conditions a multivariable system may include state variables that are, in a technical sense, unobservable. By this is meant that while these state variables may be responsive to system inputs or to other state variables, they have no effect on the output variables of the system. It can equally well be assumed, that state variables exist that remain uninfluenced by the input, thus representing *uncontrollable* or *self-determined* components.

2. As the TES belongs to a class of systems which may be described as *anticipatory*, then the simplest

form of such a system is one describable by differential-difference equations of advanced type [20, 12].

3. For the mathematical description of the free historical development of teleogenic systems, the theory of *hereditary processes* (after Volterra, recently Jones [21]) may be used [14], provided certain additional features are included. The state vector of a teleoid depends not only on the input and output conditions, but also on the past history of the teleoid. Since (according to the TESS-1 model) the *states* are not appraised continuously but only at the conclusion of each encounter, a differential-difference equation with constant (but not necessarily equal) time lags may be used.

7. Outlook for application of TSTh and conclusion

It is tentatively thought of applying TSTh even in its presently immature state to the study of disturbed language in schizophrenia, i.e., speech analysis. Further possible applications lend themselves for the individual cognitive development in the child [22, 14], possibly for Artificial Intelligence also and for the theory of evolution [23].

There is no doubt that TSTh, in its present stage, is nothing but a preliminary approach. But possibly the considerations made and also the future research pursuing the paths already envisioned, may lead to a more consistent image of a system whose capabilities exceed those of a simple goal seeking and, thus, constitute a system high in the hierarchy of complexity.

Literature

1. COULTER, N.A.Jr., 'Towards a theory of teleogenic control systems', *Gen. Systems* 13, 85-89 (1968).
2. LOCKER, A. and COULTER, N.A.Jr., 'Towards a theory of teleogenic systems I: A new look at the description and prescription of systems', in preparation for *Behav. Sc.*
3. PATTEE, H.H., 'Physical conditions for primitive functional hierarchies', *Hierarchical Structures* (edit. by L.L. Whyte, A.G. Wilson, and D. Wilson), Amer. Elsevier, pp. 161-177 (1969).
4. KALMAN, R.E., 'Remarks on mathematical brain models', *Biogenesis—Evolution—Homeostasis* (edit. by A. Locker), pp. 173-179, Springer-Verl., Berlin (1973).
5. ROSEN, R., 'Biological and physical realizations of abstract metabolic models', *Quantitative Biology of Metabolism (2nd Int. Symp.)* (edit. by A. Locker, F. Krüger, and O. Kinne), Helgoländer Wiss. Meeresunters 14, 25-31 (1966).
6. PASK, G., 'A fresh look at cognition and the individual', *Int. J. Man-Machine Stud.* 4, 211-216 (1972).
7. LOCKER, A. and COULTER, N.A.Jr., 'Towards a theory of teleogenic systems II: The problem of the origin of systems as related to goals', in preparation for *Behav. Science.*
8. BARALT-TORRIJOS, J., 'A programmatic interpretation of combinatory logics', Thesis, Georgia Institute of Technology, pp. 56 (1973).
9. AMAREL, S., 'Representation of problems and goal-directed procedures in computers', *ASC-Comm.* 1(2), 9-36 (1969).
10. PASK, G., 'The cybernetics of behaviour and cognition; extending the meaning of "Goal"', *Progress of Cybernetics* (edit. by J. Rose), Vol. 1, pp. 15-44 (1970).
11. ROSEN, R., 'On the generation of metabolic novelties in evolution', *Biogenesis—Evolution—Homeostasis* (edit. by A. Locker), pp. 113-123, Springer-Verl., Berlin (1973).
12. LOCKER, A. and COULTER, N.A.Jr., 'Towards a theory of teleogenic systems III: On the description and self-description of teleogenic systems', in preparation for *Behav. Sc.*
13. WARFIELD, J.N., 'Intent structures', *IEEE-Transact. SMC* 3(2), 133-140 (1973).
14. COULTER, N.A.Jr., and LOCKER, A., 'Towards a theory of teleogenic systems IV: On self-determinism and control of teleogenic systems', in preparation for *Behav. Sc.*
15. LOCKER, A. and COULTER, N.A.Jr., 'The origin of systems and the emergence of goals (On the possibility of teleogenic systems), Int. Cybern. ASC-IEEE-Conf., Washington, D.C. (October 1972), in press.
16. LÖFGREN, L., 'An axiomatic explanation of complete self-reproduction', *Bull. Math. Biophys.* 30, 415-425 (1968).
17. NEUMANN, J. von, *Theory of Self-reproducing Automata*, Univ. of Illinois Press, Urbana (1966).
18. LOCKER, A. and COULTER, N.A.Jr., 'Towards the design for a teleogenic system', Paper presented at the 5th Ann. Southeastern Symp. System Theory, Raleigh, N.C. (March 1973).
19. COULTER, N.A.Jr. and PAVLOV, I., 'Towards a theory of teleogenic systems VI: TESS-1 and 2 systems as possible simulations of teleogenic systems', in preparation for *Behav. Sc.*
20. BELLMAN, R. and COOKE, K.L., *Differential-Difference Equations*, Academic Press, New York

(1963).

21. JONES, G.S., 'Hereditary structure in differential equations', *Math. Systems Th.* **1**(3), 263-278 (1967).

22. BRUNER, J.S., OLVER, R.R., and GREENFIELD, P.M., *Studies in Cognitive Growth*, John Wiley & Sons, New York (1966).

23. LOCKER, A., COULTER, N.A.Jr., and MAGO, G.A., 'L'origine, le développement et la croissance des systèmes téléogénétiques comme paradigme des Processus Evolutifs Biologiques', *Revue de Biomath.* (Paris), in press.

24. FISCHER, R., 'A cartography of the ecstatic and meditative states', *Science* **174**, 897-904 (1971).

Toward a mathematical model of goal generation

G.A. MAGO* and A. LOCKER**
*University of North Carolina,
Chapel Hill, North Carolina, USA
**Institute for Biology,
Austrian Research Center, Vienna, Austria

Introduction

Pask [1] has recently stated that a purely formal theory that might lead to a causal explanation of goal setting seems almost certainly unattainable. He adds, however, that this prediction should not discourage workers in the field from trying to explain or illuminate certain aspects of the problem by formal means.

This Chapter is part of such an attempt; it assumes some finite representation of goals, and concentrates on the generative aspects of goal setting. In an attempt to find a mathematical description of a process that can be *interpreted* as goal generation we can resort to several procedures and try to apply them to our problem. Therefore, we shall proceed according to the following build-up of the Chapter.

After a preliminary presentation of how goals are assumed to be related, we will assume that they exist in a goal space and hence try to describe this space. A definition for grammars to generate the diagrams of the goal structures will follow. There is the possibility of mapping the diagrams back onto string languages. To emphasize that the Hasse-diagram represents the skeleton of a process by which goals are achieved one after another, there is also the pos-

sibility of expressing them as Petri nets. Insofar as in the goal generation several processes may concur (according to the "principle of redundancy of potential command") the application of Petri nets lends itself as a respectable way of expressing concurrency; here also a brief comparison with the much-talked-about AND/OR graphs of A.I. research is done. Finally, the formal procedures will be interpreted in the light of the foregoing Chapter.

There, it has been said that goal generation has intrinsically to do with the passage from the "potential" to the "actual" and that in the ultimate respect we have to carry out a kind of mapping, called "pleromorphic mapping". It was meant by this term that the one:one mapping or the many:one mapping have to be supplemented by a one:many mapping and it was argued that such a kind of procedure possibly takes sufficiently into account that the local (specified) goals are directed by the global (unspecified) goal.

This can be expressed in one but superficial way, using the concept of function as $f : A \to P(A)$, where $P(A)$ is the power set of A, the codomain (range) of the original (pleromorphic) mapping. f has the

Progress in Cybernetics and Systems Research, Volume 2

property of $x \in f(x)$ for every $x \in A$. If the image of $X \subseteq A$ is defined as

$$f(X) = \{y \mid y \in f(x) \text{ for some } x \in X\}$$

then f has the property $X \subseteq f(X)$ for every $X \subseteq A$.

Thus, the power set contains all the possible subsets of goals that can ever be attained by different mapping procedures. The condition mentioned above expresses the fact that by starting this particular mapping procedure and thus arriving at a distinct special goal it is possible to regain the original goal by mapping the ultimate into the first. This mapping is schematically depicted in Fig. 1.

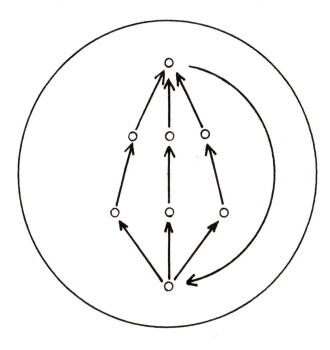

Fig. 1 Illustration of mapping(s) within the power set of mapping

Goal space and its structure

For the purposes of this Chapter goals are considered abstract entities that are characterized by their interrelations only and not analyzed any further. It is hoped that this is the right level of abstraction on which a useful discussion can be based. The situation appears to be similar to mathematical logic, where all propositions are treated as abstract entities that can be true or false, but the full semantic content of these propositions is never analyzed. Of course, many important aspects of goal setting cannot be treated on this level (self-reference, etc.) but

we shall not pursue this point any further here.

We begin with the definition of the goal space, which should contain all possible goals, i.e., the potential and actual goals, as well. At this stage of the work, for the sake of simplicity, all goals are considered well defined and clearly distinguishable, one from the other. Thus, more or less vaguely defined goals, whose existence might impose an additional structure on the goal space, are not considered.

During the activity, i.e., evolution of the system, at any moment, some of these goals are assumed to be achieved already, thus constituting the past achievements, whereas others are to be achieved in the future. Accordingly the following relation can be defined on the goal space (G):

> For any $a,b \in G$,
> $a \leqslant b$, if b can be achieved only by first achieving a.

Obviously, this relation is reflexive, antisymmetric and transitive; hence we can conclude that G is a *partially ordered set*. This fact in turn justifies our calling G a space, since every partially ordered set can easily be made to correspond to a topological —in fact a T_0—space.

We assume in addition that G has a *least* element, representing the coming into existence of the system, and a *greatest* element, representing the ultimate goal of the system. If $a \leqslant b$, i.e., achievement of b implies that a and b had been achieved, hence *combination* of the original goals should be considered as distinct possible goals. But the resulting expansion of the goal space must not be confused with the true generation of goals, which appears (at a certain level of the Cognitive Domain, cf. preceding Chapter) as a creation "from nothing".

Thus, we can extend $(G,\leqslant)$, i.e., the partial order denotations, given by the set and the order relation, to $(G',\leqslant')$, whereby $G' \subseteq P(G)-P(G)$ standing for the power set of G and $\leqslant'$ is defined as follows:
1. If $a \leqslant b$, $(a,b \in G)$, then $a' \leqslant' b'$, $(a',b' \in G')$, where
   $a' = \{x \mid x \leqslant a; a \in G\}$
   $b' = \{y \mid y \leqslant b; b \in G\}$.
2. If $a \nleqslant b$, $(a,b \in G)$, then $a' \vee b'$ is to be added to $(G',\leqslant')$, and if in addition $a \leqslant c$, and $b \leqslant c$ $(a,b,c \in G)$, then $a' \vee b' \leqslant' c'$ and c' becomes $a' \cup b' \cup c'$.
3. As the least element ϕ has to be added to $(G',\leqslant')$ (examples are given in Fig. 2).

Obviously, the expanded goal-space G' is a *lattice*, reflecting the original partial order.

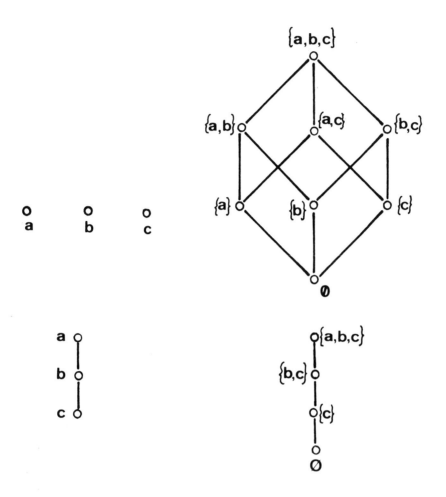

Fig. 2 Examples of goal space expansion from *(G, ≤)* to *(G', ≤')*

Some formal means for goal generation

One may ponder on the nature of the expansion of the goal space just outlined and call in question the justification of the term. Surely, the delineation made up to now is still lacking any hint at a formal procedure by which the expansion described could be brought about. Therefore, it seems appropriate to designate the process of expansion together with the formal tools responsible for it as goal generation.

Here it is necessary to focus interest on grammars that are able to (formally) generate the diagrams mentioned above. There exist grammars that allow for generating Hasse diagrams of finite partially ordered sets. These grammars are spcial cases of the so-called plex-grammars [2] and can be represented (*inter alia*) by a six-tuple

$$G = \langle N, T, P, S, Q, q_0 \rangle$$

where N is a finite non-empty set of diagrams, called the non-terminal vocabulary;

T is a finite non-empty set of diagrams, called the terminal vocabulary. N and T are disjoint sets (i.e., $N \cap T = \phi$; ϕ: empty set);

P is a finite set of productions or replacement rules (see later);

$S \in N$ is the initial diagram;

Q is a finite set of symbols called identifiers (whereby $Q \cap (N \cup T) = \phi$);

$q_0 \in Q$ is the null identifier.

Before entering into more detail by using such rewriting systems (i.e., grammars), we shall briefly

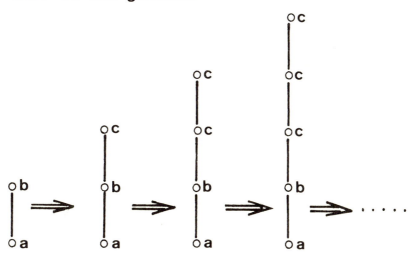

Fig. 3 Generation of new diagrams according to the rules → and ⇒

discuss the nature of the operation made possible through application of the grammar. It is determined by the role of the identifiers (i.e., the elements of Q) in that they refer to the attaching points and thus strictly restrict the production to the *local* operation. However, it can be safely stated, that locality is of great advantage in understanding or implementing the process; its main advantage is to avoid vagueness. If we start, as, for example, depicted in Fig. 3, with a certain initial diagram and a relation, contained in P, then new diagrams can be generated.

But the following comment is necessary: since there is a finite number of productions only, the diagrams that can be generated are by necessity *limited*. That means, whatever primitives, i.e., production rules, we choose, it is impossible to generate, for example, arbitrarily large distribution lattices, since the distributive lattices are *globally regular*.

As soon as useful restrictions on the form of productions are found, characterization of the languages generated by such restricted classes of grammars can be attempted. Here, however, we are more interested in possible forms of the rewriting rules, and in their

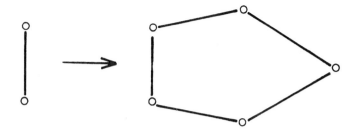

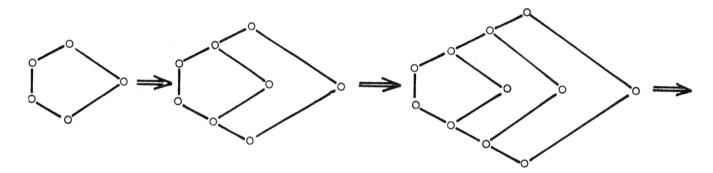

Fig. 4 Some ways to define the form of possible mechanisms

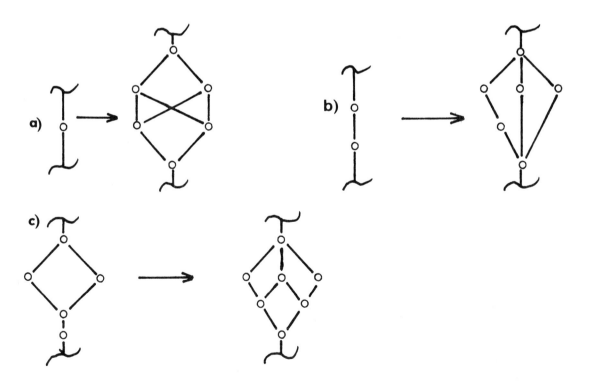

Fig. 5 Three possibilities of form expansion within larger diagrams (indicated by the irregular lines) which remain the same before and after rewriting

interpretations. Figure 4 shows that there are many ways to define the form of possible productions. In Fig. 5 examples are given to show three possibilities: (*a*) the elements are created "from nothing" (for elements read: goals); (*b*) subgoals are defined by refinement, i.e., going into more detail; (*c*) the whole "strategy" of achieving a goal (i.e., a node in the lattice) is changed—what, for instance, could be interpreted as abandoning certain goals.

The sets of diagrams defined above can be made to *correspond to* certain *string languages*. The basis for this is the Szpilrajn-theorem [3]:

Theorem: For every partially ordered set $(X, \leqslant)$ there exists a totally ordered set Y and a bijection (i.e., a one:one mapping) such that for all $x, x' \in X$

$$x \leqslant x' \to \sigma(x) \leqslant \sigma(x')$$

What can be visualized by Fig. 6 can also be an example of a quotient formation as a method for constructing new forms. We shall try to show in the Section devoted to interpretation what this mapping back could mean with respect to our problem.

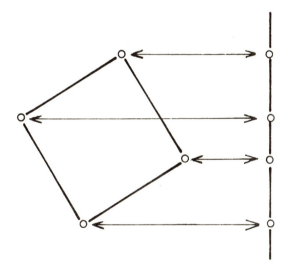

Fig. 6 Mapping back of diagrams to string languages

The process of goal generation

To emphasize that the Hasse diagram (of goals) is based on the order in which the goals can be achieved, it can be restated as a *Petri net*. This brings the benefit of taking into consideration also the concurrency between several lines of pursuit

that sometimes (as Pask [1] has so lucidly pointed out) determine the process of goal generation. The rules of transformation introduced in Petri nets are such that they allow both for concurrency and conflict as well. In a Petri net conditions are represented by circles, called *places*, and events are represented by vertical bars called *transitions*. Processes are defined as follows:

means: every occurrence of event e ends one holding of condition c.

means: every occurrence of event e begins one holding of condition c.

In the Petri net to represent a holding of condition, a token is placed in the circle.

Formally, a Petri net is described as a triple $P = (W, U, C)$, where

$W = \{w_1, w_2, ..., w_n\}$ is a finite set of transitions (corresponding to events),

$U = \{u_1, u_2, ..., u_m\}$ is a finite set of places (corresponding to conditions), and C (the control) has for its basic component a set of directed arcs (edges) $A = \{a_1, ..., a_p\}$ which connect elements of W to elements of U, and vice versa. If $a_i = (u_j, w_k)$, then u_j is an input place to transition w_k and the set of input places to w_k is defined as:

$$I_k = \{u_j \mid u_j, w_k \in A\};$$

similarly

$$O_k = \{u_j \mid w_k, u_j \in A\}$$

By means of the tokens the places can either be made full [i.e., containing one or more token(s)] or empty (i.e. without a token). The holding of condition directs the occurrence of event (i.e., the firing of transition). In order to go ahead (or "fire") a transition must have all its input places full. The firing of w_k removes one token from each member of I_k and places one token in each member of O_k. At a time the distribution of tokens marks the state of the system, which is changed by transitions. Figure 7 (taken from Baer [4]) gives an example of a Petri net in a given state.

The Petri net can be used to demonstrate the very process of goal generation by means of simulation. The following steps must then be carried out [4]:

1. Define the initial conditions, i.e., the set of places $U_0 \subseteq U$, which initially have tokens (i.e., the initial state).
2. Define a new system state, with a current state given, by choosing any of the transitions which

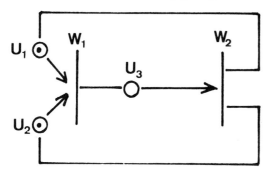

Fig. 7   Example of a Petri net in a given state

are able to fire and let them fire.

3. Stop if no more firing can occur, or after some finite number of firings (thus satisfying the achievement of a certain goal).

The simulation itself can be represented by an *acyclic directed graph G(W,U)*, where W and U are the sets of vertices and arcs, respectively, with the proviso that vertices can be linked with more than one arc. Such graphs are called occurrence graphs (Holt [5]). Petri nets are suited to simulate situations where two transitions are in conflict, if they share a common input place and the two transitions are enabled. For example, in Fig. 8 (after [4]), w_1 and w_2 share the input place u_1. When a token is placed in u_1 there occurs an infinite number of different simulations depending on which of w_1 and w_2 is fired, since both are eligible.

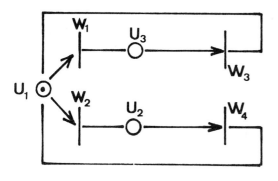

Fig. 8   Example of a conflict in a Petri net

By using marked graphs, i.e., Petri nets having the restriction that neither input nor output places can be shared by transitions [6], concurrent conditions can be studied (e.g., u_1 and u_2 in the Petri net

of Fig. 7, which is also a marked graph) whereas conflicting situations are avoided. Another subset (with transitions having only one input and one output place which can be shared) corresponds to state machine graphs (Fig. 8).

Since Petri nets, being on the same level of abstraction as the previously described Hasse diagrams, express control/interconnections, and can treat concurrency situations, and since there is the possibility of making them equivalent to a.d. graphs, that become bilogic if the vertices w_i are associated ordered pairs of logical equations ($*,+$), such that they can express AND-input/output logic, otherwise Exclusive-OR (EOR)-input/output logic, our diagrams obviously also relate to the so-called *AND/OR graphs* of Artificial Intelligence Research. An example is the following (Fig. 9), where B, C, and D are subproblems (goals) of A and the graph has the meaning that A can be solved either by solving *B and C or* by solving D (Nilson [7]). Up to now, our diagrams cannot express *alternatives*, as AND/OR graphs can. In juxtaposing the two kinds of representation we find the following Table.

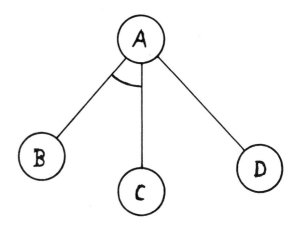

Fig. 9   Example of an AND/OR graph

Our representations	AND/OR graphs
1. Cannot express alternatives immediately	Can express alternatives
2. Dynamic	Static
3. Conceptual tool (alternatives can be expressed by re-writing the goal space according to some algorithm, see above)	Practical tool

Interpretation

In trying to interpret the description made we have to correlate it with our foregoing discussion of goal generation (cf. the first Chapter). There, the main problems could be circumscribed as:

1. The distinction between a potential (i.e., ideally pre-existing) and an actual (i.e., realized) goal; the latter being recognized by a definite change in the system's state.
2. The connection of the global goal with local goals; the latter being directly "convertible" in local causal mechanisms.
3. The connection of goal generation, principally of the global goal, with the system's origin.

Our present formal attempts can, of course, only preliminarily deal with items 1) and 2). It must be conceded, in addition, that the interpretation offered is strongly arbitrary and probably will require major modifications in the course of our future work.

The statement made in the introduction to this Chapter, viz. that the goals are mutually interconnected (i.e., by starting with an initial goal and arriving at a distinct ultimate goal it is possible to map back the ultimate into the first) should now be formulated in a somewhat more stringent way. If it can be *postulated* that any generation of the local goal always coincides with the generation of the global goal, then

1. The global and the local sphere (or level) have to be clearly distinguished, and
2. there is an opposite arrangement of the order of achieved goals at the two levels. According to the so-called *"pleromorphic mapping"*, it can be assumed that the mapping carried out at one level is exactly balanced by the mapping at the other.

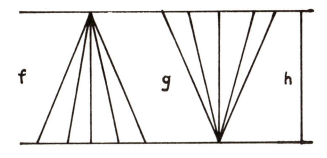

Fig. 10 Illustration of "pleromorphic mapping"

What Fig. 10 *schematically* depicts means, e.g., that the union of the two sets (at the level *n–1*) exactly equals the union of the mapped sets (at the level *n*):

$A \cup B = A' \cup B'$, where

$A = \{a_1,...,a_n\}$; $B = \{b\}$; $A' = \{a'\}$; $B' = \{b'_1,...,b'_n\}$,

and $f:A \to A'$; $g:B \to B'$, then

$$f(a) \text{ o } g(b) : \Rightarrow h(c); \quad hh^{-1} = 1$$

such that the resulting mapping *(h)* is a bijection.

In order to distinguish, by definition, between *(a)* the purely formal range of goals, out of which goals, in the process of generation, must be realized (i.e., actualized), and *(b)* the range where this actualization directly occurs (i.e., the permanent transform of the "potential" into the "actual"), and *(c)* the tool, by means of which the process as such is enabled, we could tentatively equate

a) the formal range of goals with the string languages exhibiting complete order wherein the coherence of words is guaranteed,

b) the "transform" range with the Hasse diagrams, and

c) the process tool with the grammar, in particular with the plex grammar.

This setting equal of goal generation with forms and procedures, respectively, would clearly delimit the relational versus the operative side of the problem.

Although it be granted that the coordination suggested is highly arbitrary it none the less appears to offer two advantages. First, it allows, via the interpretation, for an application to the conceptual framework TSTh is using, especially with vistas of possible implementations of the formal means into a computer simulation. Secondly, it agrees with a kind of ontology, that takes account of being *and* becoming, or of contriving *and* discovering.

With respect to the inverse arrangement of local and global goals it may be postulated that the mapping of the (partially ordered) Hasse diagram into the (completely ordered) string (compare Fig. 6) must be done according to a *dual homomorphism*. Thus, when partially ordered sets X and Y are connected by the mapping h, then the latter reverses the order between the elements. Therefore, if $a,b \in X$, $a \leqslant b$ in X, then $h(b) \leqslant h(a)$ in Y.

Then, the first local goal would correspond to the last (i.e., the absolutely ultimate) global goal. This fact could be understood as the necessity that any setting (or generating) of goals must be permanently guided by the awareness of the ultimate goal. Inasmuch as the purely formal goals cannot exist in an independent Platonic range of ideas, but rather must

Toward a mathematical model of goal generation

be conceived by the designer, we are possibly not going astray in assuming that the dual homomorphism mentioned is an endomorphism.

References

1. PASK, G., 'The meaning of cybernetics in the behavioural sciences (The cybernetics of behaviour and cognition; Extending the meaning of goal)', *Progress of Cybernetics* (edit. by J. Rose), Vol. 1, pp. 15-44 (1970).
2. FEDER, J., 'Plex languages', *Inform. Sciences* 3, 225-241 (1971).
3. SZPILRAJN, E., 'Sur l'extension de l'ordre partiel', *Fund. Math.* 16, 386-389 (1930).
4. BAER, J.L., 'A survey of some theoretical aspects of multiprocessing', *Computing Surveys* 5(1), 31-80 (1973).
5. HOLT, A.W., Information System Theory Project, Final Report Inf. Syst. Theory Project, Contr. A.F., No. 30,602-4211, Applied Data Research Inc. (1968).
6. HOLT, A.W. and COMMONER, F., Project MAC Conference, ACM Conference Record (1970).
7. NILSON, N., *Problem-Solving Methods in Artificial Intelligence*, McGraw Hill, New York (1971).

A mathematical proof of Gestalt

PHILIP JAMES OWEN
University of Illinois, Urbana, USA

As I reconsider the title, "A mathematical proof of Gestalt", I confess that it probably promises much more than I am prepared to deliver. This Chapter will be neither a thorough going discussion of the issues of Gestalt psychology, nor a complex or intricate mathematical demonstration. Rather, I shall make an effort to comment briefly that the structure of hierarchical information functions, as I have written about them before [1], provides a logical system which supports a typically Gestalt view of brain-like functions. What I propose to do, then, is the following:

First, to clarify the terms in which Gestalt argument is characteristically presented.

Second, to recast these terms in a mathematical structure.

Finally, to reinterpret Gestalt principles according to their mathematical characteristics.

The structure of Gestalt argument

The origin or development of organization in brain-like processes has historically been the major issue by which Gestalt theory is advanced. The Gestalt psychologist concludes that there are primary factors of organization which are not subject to learning. As they are normally presented, however, the arguments in favor of Gestalt thinking do not provide a structure in which the notions of Gestalt may be verified. Nevertheless, to proceed, let us clarify what is meant by organization and learning by briefly considering the arguments regarding the explanations of two kinds of brain-like processing: the perception of pattern and the conception of a logical structure.

The Gestalt position regarding perception was clearly set forth years ago by Wolfgang Köhler in his recently republished *Gestalt Psychology* [2]. A fundamental thesis in our interest claims that sensory organization is a "characteristic achievement of the nervous system", and not a property of environments themselves. In vision, for example, light waves are the only communication between objects around us and our eyes. The point is that the organization of the environment is lost in the means of communication. Köhler explains as follows:

"...waves of light, I repeat, do not as such contain the slightest indication of the fact that some are reflected by parts of one physical object and others by objects in its environment. Each element of a physical surface reflects light independently; and in this respect two elements of the surface of an object, such as, for instance, a sheep, are no more related to each other than one of them is to a surface element in the animal's environment." [3]

The problem, then, in explaining perception is one of explaining how the organization of the environment is reconstructed from unstructured communication channels like light waves.

Without ever having solved the problem of explaining perception, psychological theorists have divided over the characteristics which the process may be

Progress in Cybernetics and Systems Research, Volume 2

presumed to possess; that is, the Gestalt theorist denies the more behavioral or empirical view that such perceptual organizing capacities are learned. Without denying the impact which previous experiences may have on the meaning we give to objects, Köhler states his position as follows:

"...there is a large step to the statement that papers, pencils, and so forth, would not be segregated units without that previously acquired knowledge. How is it proved that before I acquired this knowledge the visual field contained no such units? When I see a green object, I can immediately tell the name of the color. I also know that green is used as a signal on streets and as a symbol of hope. But from this I do not conclude that the green color as such can be derived from such knowledge. Rather, I know that as an independently existent sensory fact, it has acquired secondary meanings, and I am quite willing to recognize the advantages which these acquired meanings have in practical life. In exactly the same fashion, Gestalt Psychology holds, sensory units have acquired names, have become richly symbolic, and are now known to have certain practical uses, while nevertheless they have existed as units before any of these further facts were added." [4]

This argument, as I understand it, is weakly stated; that is, in the absence of any explanation as to how a brain might learn to organize perceptual units from smaller pieces, I must conclude that the perceptual units pre-exist.

Before any more is said of this argument, let us consider a similar situation regarding the conception of logical structure, as advanced by linguists like Noam Chomsky. The phenomenon to be explained is the obvious circumstance that children acquire in a relatively short time a complex facility with at least one natural language. The logical structure which is concomitantly exhibited is, of course, the grammar of the language. In Gestalt fashion, Chomsky reaches the conclusion that the fundamental units of a grammar are an achievement of the nervous system, and not a property of language environments. It is clear, for example, that grammatical considerations are applied in the production and/or interpretation of sentences which the speaker-hearer has never confronted before. Grammar, then, exists apart from any particular instance of language. At the same time, a grammar is not subject to being induced from particular examples of a language. The noun-verb relation, for example, exists at an abstract level which is completely separate from instances of a language and the process by which one might dis-

cover such relations has not been formulated. To summarize, in Chomsky's words:

"The structure of particular languages may very well be largely determined by factors over which the individual has no conscious control and concerning which society may have little choice or freedom. On the basis of the best information now available, it seems reasonable to suppose that a child cannot help constructing a particular sort of transformational grammar to account for the data presented to him, any more than he can control his perception of solid objects or his attention to line and angle. Thus it may well be that the general features of language structure reflect not so much the course of one's experience, but rather the general character of one's capacity to acquire knowledge—in the traditional sense, one's innate ideas and innate principles." [5]

Chomsky's argument, like Köhler's, is weakly stated, in that I am asked to accept his conclusion on the grounds that no proof exists for its apparent logical alternatives. The structure of these arguments, therefore, rather than setting forth the necessary and sufficient conditions for Gestalt, specifies the conditions under which Gestalt thinking may be denied. Consequently, the Gestalt view of brain-like processing is not more verifiable than the alternatives which it seeks to discredit. In any case, however, the arguments presented by Köhler and Chomsky do clarify what is meant by organization and learning. Organization consists of units in an environment which have relation to other units in one level and which consist of smaller parts or are parts of larger wholes at different levels. Color and other basic "sensory units" are examples of the former, and noun-verb relations in specific instances of language are examples of the latter. Learning is an addition to the organization of an environment by a process of creating unitary distinctions among the elements in an environment according to some known or delineable principle or rule of induction. We may say, then, that the arguments do, at least, specify the terms in which a proof might be constructed.

A mathematical structure for self-organization

According to the arguments presented by Köhler and Chomsky, verification of any explanation of brain-like processing depends on our being able to demonstrate a principle, process, or rule by which organization of a brain-like process can increase. Such principles by which organization can increase may be available from the explanation of self-organization which is supplied by the structure of hierarchical information functions [6]. This explanation is derived from the issues as presented in a 1960 paper by Heinz von Foerster, "On self-organizing systems and their environments" [7].

The basic principle of self-organization is established by way of an example, only part of which is reviewed here. Consider a closed box containing small cubes which float under friction as provided by filling the box with tiny glass pebbles. The cubes are constructed such that each of the sides is magnetized perpendicular to its surface and "characterized by opposite polarity of the two pairs of those three sides which join in two opposite corners" [8]. If no particular order is used in filling the box, no particular structure should be apparent among the cubes. Now, if the box is fed "cheap undirected energy" simply by shaking it, von Foerster claims, "an incredibly ordered structure will emerge, which, I fancy, may pass the grade to be displayed in an

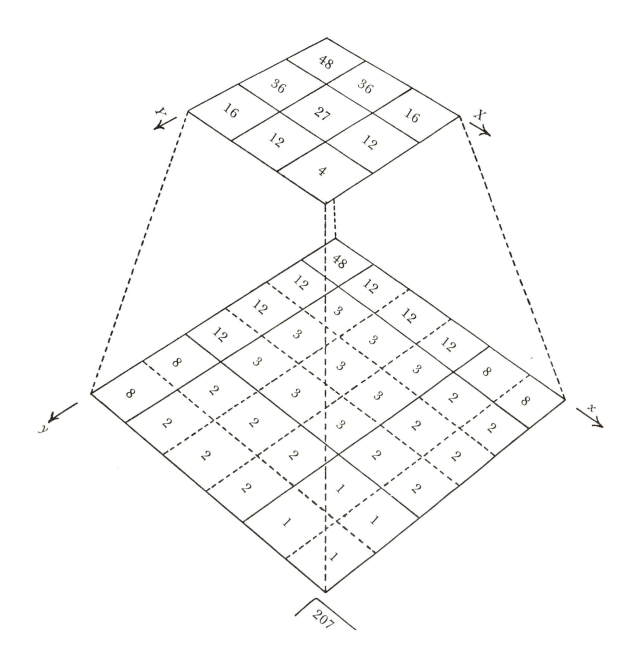

Diagram 1

A mathematical proof of Gestalt

exhibition of surrealistic art" [9]. Since no order is fed to the system, von Foerster has called this phenomenon order-from-noise.

Although the impact of von Foerster's illustration is certainly clear enough, the dispositions of the variables which contribute to the increase of order are difficult to trace. A more general and more formal analysis of these same issues is possible, however, with hierarchical information structures. First, we must be quite clear as to the nature of the noise which von Foerster speaks of. When he says that undirected energy is fed into the box, it is apparent that von Foerster means by this omnidirected energy. The point of shaking the box is to create energy in all directions so as to maximise the randomness with which a new distribution takes place. Turning now to hierarchical information structures,[†] a reference Diagram 1 will show that randomness has been introduced into this system by the partition of the within-class matrices of the lower level of generalization. The undifferentiated cell (x_2, y_2), for example, is differentiated into a 3×3 within-class matrix, in which each cell = 3. It would seem apparent that no order is introduced into the system by the clear randomness of the within-class matrix. Using as the measure of order, as von Foerster does, Shannon's concept of redundancy,

$$R = 1 - \frac{H}{H_{max}}$$

it may be shown that none of the within class matrices of Diagram 1 contain any internal order of their own. Their internal redundancies are zero in every case.

The redundancy of the system is not, however, unaffected by hierarchical differentiation. The class matrix, as a non-hierarchical structure, exhibits the following order as measured by redundancy:

$$R_{X,Y} = 1 - \frac{H(X,Y)}{H_{max}(X,Y)}$$

$$= 1 - \frac{2.9073}{3.1699} = 1 - 0.9172$$

$$= 0.0828$$

[†]An Appendix is supplied at the end of this Chapter which explains the notations used here, and which provides the mathematical proofs from which hierarchical information functions are constructed.

In measuring the redundancy of the hierarchical system, either of two expressions may be used:

$$R_{X,Y;x,y} = 1 - \frac{H(X,Y;x,y)}{H_{max}(X,Y;x,y)} \qquad \text{(A)}$$

or

$$R_{X,Y;x,y} = 1 - \frac{H(X,Y) + H_{X,Y}(x,y)}{H_{max}(X,Y;x,y)} \qquad \text{(B)}$$

For (A),

$$R_{X,Y;x,y} = 1 - \frac{4.3650}{5.1699} = 1 - 0.8443$$

$$= 0.1557$$

For (B),

$$R_{X,Y;x,y} = 1 - \frac{(2.9073 + 1.4579)}{5.1699} = 1 - 0.8444$$

$$= 0.1556$$

These measures clearly show, contrary to the initial appearances, that the addition of randomness to the class matrix system by means of differentiation within class has actually increased the order in the structure. Organization has increased by a method which is itself completely disorganizing; that is, the disaggregation of an entity into statistically unrelated parts. Yet, order is created from this noise.

It is important to emphasize that the increase in organization as illustrated is the result solely of the hierarchical differentiation, and not the product of any within-class order. It should be added, however, that such within-class redundancy would serve to increase the organization of the system still further. Consider in Diagram 2 the alterations of the within-class matrices (x_2, y_2) and (x_3, y_3), such that diagonal cells are differentiated from nondiagonal cells. Clearly, the organization of the class matrix is unchanged, but the total uncertainty associated with the within-class matrices is reduced. For (x_2, y_2), the change is the difference of

$$\frac{27}{207}(9)\left(-\frac{3}{27} \log \frac{3}{27}\right) \text{ from } \frac{27}{207}(3)\left(-\frac{9}{27} \log \frac{9}{27}\right)$$

or *0.2068*.

For (x_3, y_3), the change is the difference of

$$\frac{4}{207}(4)\left(-\frac{1}{4} \log \frac{1}{4}\right) \text{ from } \frac{4}{207}(2)\left(-\frac{2}{4} \log \frac{2}{4}\right)$$

or *0.0193*. The within-class differentiation results in a loss of total within-class uncertainty $H_{X,Y}(x,y)$ from 1.4579 (Diagram 1) to 1.2318 (Diagram 2). This loss is $H_{X,Y}(x,y)$ increases the redundancy $R_{X,Y}(x,y)$ as follows:

$$\left[1-\left(\frac{2.9073+1.2318}{5.1699}\right)\right]-\left[1-\left(\frac{2.9073+1.4579}{5.1699}\right)\right]$$

or   *0.1993*   –   *0.1557*

that is, a gain of redundancy by *0.0436*. It should be noted that increases in redundancy of this second type do not depend on hierarchical structures. The change in organization occurs at only one level. Care must be used, then, to differentiate order-from-noise and this second type of order, which perhaps may be called (after Erwin Schrödinger) order-from-disorder.

The information functions created by hierarchical ensembles do not, in themselves, specify the kinds

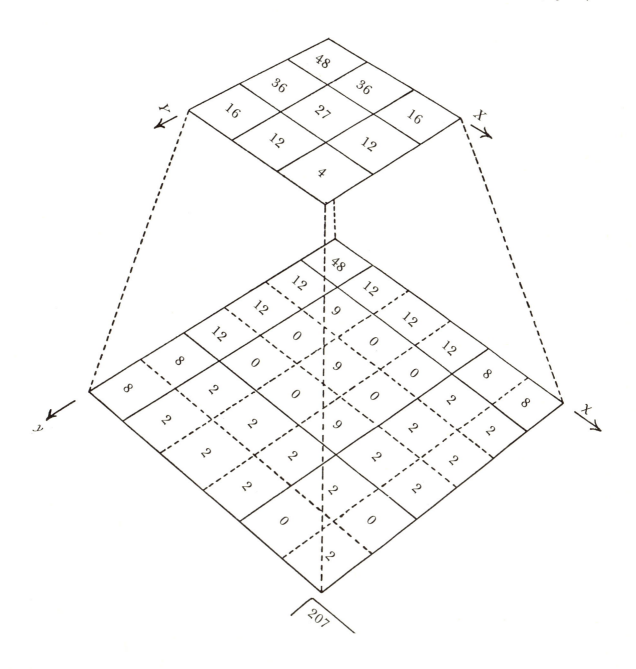

Diagram 2

of processes, but rather the forms of the processes, which might produce order-from-noise or order-from-disorder. The specification of specific organizing mechanisms is, however, the goal of Gestalt theory. In the final part of this Chapter, then, we shall consider some of the ways in which the theory hierarchical structures may help to clarify a framework in which the goals of Gestalt theory can be verified.

A formal interpretation of Gestalt

The hierarchical explanation of self-organization, as outlined above, provides a formal structure in which to consider the issues of the Gestalt argument. The class matrix-element matrix relation may be used to unambiguously specify the relations of organization implied by Köhler and Chomsky. If we accept the idea that the matrices represent a partition or the segregations of a field in the environment, then the cells of the matrices may be used to reflect the relations among the units in an environment. Furthermore, if units are seen as made up of parts, then the class matrix represents the units and the element matrix, the parts. On the other hand, if units are seen as parts of larger wholes, then the element matrix represents the units and the class matrix, the larger wholes. Within class matrices, which have no counterpart in an environment, may be thought of as reflecting the amount of perceptual, cognitive, or logical structure which is required to derive any particular hierarchical partition of an environment [10]. Specified in this way, then, hierarchical information functions seem clearly to reflect the kind of organization which is required by ideas such as sensory segregation of environments into circumscribed wholes or the relation of concepts like noun and verb to collections of words at lower levels of conception and to grammatical structures like phrases at higher levels.

It might be worth noting, here, that no special claims in behalf of Gestalt theory are presumed in the correspondence of the formal theory of hierarchical structure and the Gestalt view of environmental organization. Empirical explanations of brain-like organizing processes seem to be equally hierarchical in their structure. The Gestalt-empirical argument is essentially over the origin of or the process of organization, not its form.

The strong implication which may be derived from the hierarchical explanation of self-organization is a denial—in principle—of the empirical explanations regarding the acquisition of organization. The basic empirical position that sensory and cognitive entities are formed through experience with their elements in an environment can only be interpreted in the formal sense to mean that class matrix relations are formed from the parts of an environment as specified by element matrix relations. The explanation of self-organization makes it absolutely clear, however, that increases in organization are dependent on processes of hierarchicalization which proceed from class relations to element relations and not from the converse. Such conclusion is simple to verify formally. Increases in the organization of hierarchical systems are verified by increases in the redundancy of the system, as given from the forms

$$R_{X,Y;x,y} = 1 - \frac{H(X,Y;x,y)}{H_{max}(X,Y;x,y)} \qquad (A)$$

or

$$= 1 - \frac{H(X,Y) + H_{X,Y}(x,y)}{H_{max}(X,Y;x,y)} \qquad (B)$$

The numerator of (A), $H(X,Y;x,y)$, is the information function which is derived from the element matrix relations. The numerator of (B), $H(X,Y) + H_{X,Y}(x,y)$ represents the information functions defined for, respectively, class matrix relations and the total of all within-class matrix relations. Since the numerators of (A) and (B) are quantitatively equivalent, a change in the processing of an environment from an elemental level to a higher class level (with the concomitant within-class cognitive processes) does not alter the organization of the environment as measured by R. In principle, then, as established by the formal logical system of hierarchical information structures, it is not possible to increase the sensory or logical organization of an environment by grouping or generalizing its previously known elements.

The weak implication which derives from the hierarchical explanation of self-organization is the affirmation of Gestalt principles. From the formal viewpoint, the necessary and sufficient condition for increases in the organization of an environment is a hierarchicalization of the information structures in which the environment is organized by a process which proceeds from class relations to element relations. The issue of this Chapter is, of course, whether or not these formal conditions have anything to do with Gestalt principles. However, since the necessary and sufficient conditions of Gestalt processes have not been established, we cannot in principle proceed to verify any further conclusions. What we can do, then, seems to be as follows: Let us make an effort to determine what the character of self-organizing hierarchicalization in a brain-like process would be, and, finally, decide whether or not we are willing to call such characteristics Gestalts.

The formal structures of self-organization may be of some additional help. We know that the increases in self-organizing processes accrue to within-class relations which have no environmental counterpart. Furthermore, it is obvious that these within-class relations must be created in the process of moving from class relations to element relations. Apparently, it is possible for this creation to assume two forms: one is the random process described by order from noise, the other is the nonrandom form of order from disorder. In either case, however, the basic principle which operates is that a unitary or class structure is broken up into parts subject to two constraints: one, that the parts are segregated wholes or are mutually exclusive, and two, that the parts do not transcend the boundaries of the unit from which they are derived. Said a different way, increases in the organization of an environment are the result of our making additional nondeterministic segregations within a pre-established structure of the environment. At this point, it seems fair to repeat the conclusion which was promised: the structure of hierarchical information functions provides a logical system which supports a typically Gestalt view of brain-like functions.

Notes and references

1. OWEN, Philip James, 'Another information theory of grammar', *Advances in Cybernetics and Systems Research*, Vol. I (edit. by F. Pichler and R. Trappl, pp 194-210, Transcripta Books, London (1973).
2. KÖHLER, Wolfgang, *Gestalt Psychology*, Liveright Publishing Corporation, New York (1970).
3. KÖHLER, p. 161.
4. KÖHLER, p. 139.
5. CHOMSKY, Noam, *Aspects of the Theory of Syntax*, p. 59, The M.I.T. Press, Cambridge (1965).
6. The following is taken from Philip James Owen, "The contribution of hierarchical information structures to cybernetic ontology", 1972 International Symposium, American Society for Cybernetics, Washington, D.C., (March 13-14, 1972); to be published by Spartan Books, Washington, D.C., in the ASC's 5th International Symposium.
7. VON FOERSTER, Heinz, 'On self-organizing systems and their environments', *Self-Organizing Systems—1962* (edit. by M.C. Yovits, George T. Jacobi, and Gordon D. Goldstein), pp. 31-50, Spartan Books, Washington, D.C.
8. VON FOERSTER, p. 45.
9. VON FOERSTER, p. 45.
10. For a more complete development, see Owen, Note 6.

APPENDIX

The following formal analysis is taken from 'A hierarchical information analysis of the order of words', presented by Philip James Owen at the 1972 International Conference on Cybernetics and Society, 9-12 October 1972, Washington, D.C.

Hierarchical information structures

The conditions which are necessary for the construction of a hierarchical probability space may be found in the experiment based on a set of urns, each of which contains a set of numbered balls. We may assign to each urn a value represented by a random process, such as the throwing of dice or the spinning of a roulette wheel, etc. We may assign to each ball its face value represented by the random process of selecting a ball blindfolded from a well-stirred urn. Clearly, the sense in which the term elementary outcomes might be used is obscured by such experimental conditions. Rather, it might be suggested that the outcomes fall into three important categories:

(1)   1. The specification of a particular urn (μ_κ) from the set of urns (M).
     2. The specification of a particular ball from an urn $(\omega_{\kappa\ell})$ from the set of balls (Ω_κ).
     3. The specification of a particular kind of compound outcome, the hierarchical outcome, by the selection of one outcome $(\mu_\kappa, \omega_{\kappa\ell})$ from each of the hierarchical levels (M) and (Ω).

The traditional concept of the *sample space* is similarly obscured by the experimental conditions. Again, however, we may appeal to hierarchical organization as a means of unambiguously specifying three collections which make up the sample space. Since the urns and numbered balls form a class-element relation, we may specify a finite discrete hierarchical sample space as a collection of subspaces as follows:

(2) 1. *Class space*: the collection of all outcomes (μ_κ). This space consists of n points where $\kappa = 1-n$.

2. *Within-class spaces*: the set of n collections of all outcomes $(\omega_{\kappa\ell})$. Since the number of balls need not be the same in each urn, each collection of outcomes $(\omega_{\kappa\ell})$ consists of m points, where $\ell = \kappa 1 - \kappa m$ and m is specified for each κ.

3. *Element space*: the collection of all outcomes $(\mu_\kappa, \omega_{\kappa\ell})$. This space consists of $\sum_{\kappa=1}^{n} \kappa\ell$ points where $\ell = \kappa 1 - \kappa m$ which is given by the hierarchical summation $\sum_{\kappa=1}^{n} \sum_{\ell=\kappa 1} \kappa m$. This hierarchical summation is, of course, equal to the total number of balls in all urns.

Clearly the concept of the family of events associated with sample spaces must be modified in order to account for hierarchical organization on the one hand, while on the other maintaining the traditional requirement that if A belongs to the family and B belongs to the family, then $A \cup B$, $A \cap B$, and $A\theta B$ also belong to the family. It will in fact be apparent that a total of $n+2$ distinct families of events must be defined in order to account for all sets of possible outcomes from the hierarchical sample space. One such family may be defined on the class space (M), such that it contains all possible sets of outcomes (μ_κ), including (M) and its complement the empty set (ϕ). A second family may be similarly defined on the element space (M,Ω), such that it contains all the sets of $(\mu_\kappa, \omega_{\kappa\ell})$, including (M,Ω) and (ϕ). Finally a set of n families may be defined, one for each of the n within-class spaces (Ω_κ), such that each family contains all sets of outcomes (ω_κ), including (Ω_κ) and (ϕ).

A set function P may be defined for each of the family of events such that the following traditional axioms are not violated; that is [1]:

(3) 1. $P(\Omega) = 1$

2. $0 \leqslant P(E) \leqslant 1$

3. $P(\cup E_i) = P(E_1) + P(E_2) + ... +,$

provided $E_1, E_2, ...$ are pairwise disjoint.

For the family of events defined on the class space,

(4) $P(M) = P(\mu_1, \mu_2, ..., \mu_n) = \sum_{\kappa=1}^{n} P_\kappa = 1$

Similarly for the element family of events

(5) $P(M,\Omega) = P(\mu_1, \omega_{11}; \mu_1, \omega_{12}; ...; \mu_{11}, \omega_{1m};$

$...;$

$\mu_n, \omega_{n1}; \mu_{n2}; ...; \mu_n, \omega_{nm})$

$= \sum_{\kappa=1}^{n} \sum_{\ell=\kappa 1}^{\kappa m} p_{\kappa, \kappa\ell} = 1$

A set of n set functions P may be defined for the n within-class families such that

(6) $P(\Omega_\kappa) = P(\omega_{\kappa 1}, \omega_{\kappa 2}, ..., \omega_{\kappa m}) = \sum_{\ell=\kappa}^{\kappa m} p_{\kappa\ell} = 1$

In keeping with traditional practice, it should be assumed that probabilities are determined as the proportion of the possible set of conditions which lead to the event.

We are now in a position to describe a hierarchical probability space as a triple (Ω, S, P), which should be interpreted as follows:

(7) 1. $\Omega = \begin{cases} M = \text{the class sample space} \\ M,\Omega = \text{the element sample space} \\ \Omega_\kappa = \text{the } n \text{ within-class sample spaces} \end{cases}$

2. $S = \begin{cases} S^M = \text{family of events associated with } M \\ S^{M,\Omega} = \text{family of events associated with } M,\Omega \\ S^{\Omega_\kappa} = n \text{ families of events associated with } \Omega_\kappa \end{cases}$

3. $P = \begin{cases} P^M = \text{set function associated with } S^M \\ P^{M,\Omega} = \text{set of function associated with } S^{M,\Omega} \\ P^{\Omega_\kappa} = n \text{ set functions associated with } S^{\Omega_\kappa} \end{cases}$

From a hierarchical probability space it is a straightforward task to construct a hierarchical ensemble for information functions. The hierarchical class-element relation may be expressed by a structure in which the cells of a transition matrix become themselves matrices. Consider the two-level analysis defined in two dimensions as represented by the pyramidal structure of Diagram 3. The Diagram is intended to show that each cell of the upper matrix has been partitioned into a submatrix, which forms a part of the total matrix of the lower level. For clarity let us specify the following definitions:

(8) 1. The upper level matrix is the *class matrix*.

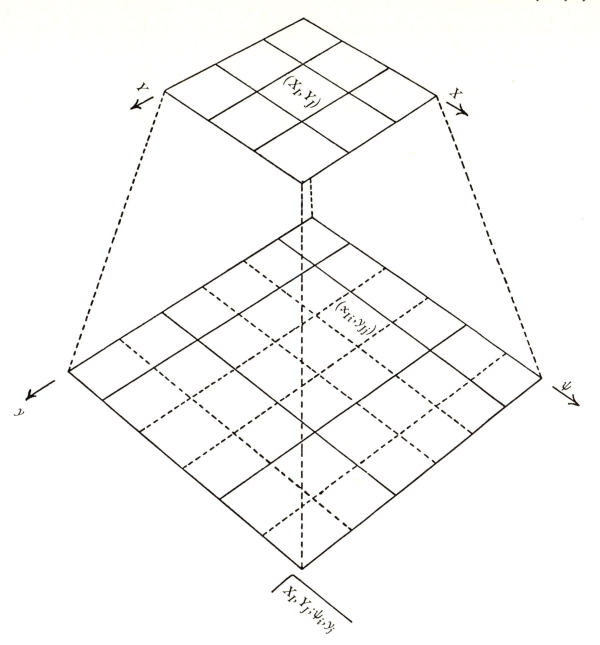

Diagram 3

2. Any cell of the class matrix is given by

(X_I, Y_J) $I = 1-N$
        $J = 1-M$

3. The partition of each cell of the class matrix is a *within-class matrix*.
4. Any cell of a *within-class matrix* is given by

(X_{Ii}, Y_{Jj}) where I and J are given by (X_I, Y_J)

$i = I_{(1-n)}$
$j = J_{(1-m)}$

n and m may be different for each I,J.

5. The lower level matrix is the *element matrix*.

A mathematical proof of Gestalt

6. Any cell of the element matrix is given by

$$(X_I, Y_J; x_{Ii}, y_{Jj}).$$

The subscript format, $_{Ii}$ and $_{Jj}$, is designed to indicate the identification of the entity is dependent on two levels of analysis, as well as the two dimensions X, Y. With such a structure, these definitions will allow for a meaningful description of a hierarchical ensemble for information functions. Since the element matrix is formed from within class partitions of the class matrix, it will hold by definition that

$$(9) \quad \sum_{Ii} \sum_{Jj} (x_{Ii}, y_{Jj}) = (X_I, Y_J)$$

It will also hold, therefore, that

$$(10) \quad \sum_{IJ} \sum_{\substack{\Sigma \Sigma \\ Ii\ Jj}} (x_{Ii}, y_{Jj}) = \sum_{IJ} \sum (X_I, Y_J)$$

The notation $\sum_{IJ} \sum_{\substack{\Sigma \Sigma \\ Ii\ Jj}}$ is introduced to designate hierarchical summation; that is, the quantities must be summed in accordance with the hierarchical relations indicated. These hierarchical subscripts are admittedly clumsy; but since it is important to clearly differentiate hierarchical levels from linear dimensions, they will for the present be retained.

The assignment of probability measures to the classifications of the elements in the hierarchical ensemble is relatively straightforward. Clearly, the probability associated with the event (X_I, Y_J), $p(I,J)$, may be expressed as follows:

$$(11) \quad p(I,J) = \frac{(X_I, Y_J)}{\sum\sum_{IJ}(X_I, Y_J)} \quad \sum_{IJ} \sum (I,J) = 1$$

The uncertainty associated with the class matrix is thus given by

$$(12) \quad H(X,Y) = -\sum_{IJ}\sum p(I,J) \log p(I,J)$$

The event (x_{Ii}, y_{Jj}) may be associated with a set of within-class events $\sum_{Ii}\sum_{Jj}(x_{Ii}, y_{Jj})$, for any (X_I, Y_J). Accordingly, the within-class probability $p(Ii,Jj)$ may be given by

$$(13) \quad p(Ii,Jj) = \frac{(x_{Ii}, y_{Jj})}{\sum_{Ii}\sum_{Jj}(x_{Ii}, y_{Jj})}, \quad \text{for any } (X_I, Y_J),$$
where
$$\sum_{Ii}\sum_{Jj} p(Ii,Jj) = 1$$

With regard to the ensemble, the probability of a within-class event is clearly conditioned on the event (X_I, Y_J), and thus may be expressed

$$(14) \quad p_{I,J}(x_{Ii}, y_{Jj}) = p(I,J)\frac{(x_{Ii}, y_{Jj})}{\sum_{Ii}\sum_{Jj}(x_{Ii}, y_{Jj})}$$

The uncertainty associated with any within-class matrix is, therefore, given by

$$(15) \quad H_{X_I, Y_J}(x_I, y_J) = -p(I,J)\sum_{Ii}\sum_{Jj} p(Ii,Jj) \log p(Ii,Jj)$$

The total uncertainty associated with all within-class matrices is

$$(16) \quad H_{X,Y}(x,y) = -\sum_{IJ}\sum p(I,J)\sum_{Ii}\sum_{Jj} p(Ii,Jj) \log p(Ii,Jj)$$

The event $(X_I, Y_J; x_{Ii}, y_{Jj})$ is the joint occurrence of the two mutually dependent elements of the ensemble. The joint probability associated with any such event is given by

$$(17) \quad p(I,J;Ii,Jj) = \frac{(X_I, Y_J; x_{Ii}, y_{Jj})}{\sum_{IJ}\sum \sum_{Ii}\sum_{Jj}(X_I, Y_J; x_{Ii}, y_{Jj})}$$

where $\sum_{IJ}\sum \sum_{Ii}\sum_{Jj} p(I,J;Ii,Jj) = 1$

The uncertainty to be associated with the element matrix is therefore

$$(18) \quad H(X,Y;x,y) = -\sum_{IJ}\sum \sum_{Ii}\sum_{Jj} p(I,J;Ii,Jj) \log p(I,J;Ii,Jj)$$

Equations (12), (16), and (18) are related, as might be expected, by the following:

$$(19) \quad H(X,Y;x,y) = H(X,Y) + H_{X,Y}(x,y)$$

This relationship can be shown by expanding (18) such that

(18.1) $H(X,Y;x,y)$

$$= -\sum_I \sum_J \sum_{Ii} \sum_{Jj} p(I,J;Ii,Jj)[\log p(I,J) + \log p(Ii,Jj)]$$

(12.1) $= -\sum_I \sum_J p(I,J) \log p(I,J) \sum_{Ii} \sum_{Jj} p(Ii,Jj)$

(16.1) $-\sum_I \sum_J p(I,J) \sum_{Ii} \sum_{Jj} p(Ii,Jj) \log p(Ii,Jj)$

Line (4.1) is equivalent to Eq. (12) since $\sum_{Ii} \sum_{Jj} p(Ii,Jj)$ is always 1 for any X_I, Y_J. Line (16.1) is identical to Eq. (16) as it is.

Interacting with a work of art

STROUD CORNOCK
Leicester Polytechnic,
Leicester, UK

Preamble

This paper is written with a broad group of people in mind: the users of art, and hence those intimately involved in the life of a particular culture. For this reason it has been thought advisable to avoid jargon and to explain those systems concepts which appear, while nothing is said of the work of specific artists. To achieve a brevity consistent with clarity, inessential observations have been set together with the references at the end of the Chapter.

Introduction

Our experience would suggest that, for the majority, art is a passive business. But it is my feeling that the arts can best be understood by looking at relevant interactions taking place at various levels.

Level One	The individual
Level Two	The small group
Level Three	A culture
Level Four	Cross-cultural interactions

My concern is with Level One, looking first at a simple model of an art system, and going on to look in turn at problems of cognition, communication, learning and arousal, before drawing some conclusions.

System

It is essential to this argument to regard the basic

artistic interaction as taking place within an art *system*.

A system will, for present purposes, be regarded as a number of components which relate together as a whole, and it is important to emphasize here that what we are concerned with is the behavior of that whole; what is also of defining importance is that we cannot add to nor take from the whole without significantly affecting its behavior. In this case the system will comprise an artefact, and a person in communion with it.

Though the word 'communion' has been used, Fig. 1 shows a link between the two components so drawn as to imply that the artefact has an effect upon the user, while the user has no reciprocal effect upon it. Hence the term 'annunciation' would seem to be more appropriate than 'communion'. But this is only true at a material level; the communion occurs entirely at a symbolic level (in the overwhelming majority of cases—see note [14]). Which means that it will be necessary to attempt a model of the psychological, or to be more accurate, the cognitive processes involved.

Cognition

By cognition I mean that operation which, when performed in the mind, represents our ability to distinguish some 'thing' against the background of experience, whether that 'thing' be concrete, or

Progress in Cybernetics and Systems Research, Volume 2

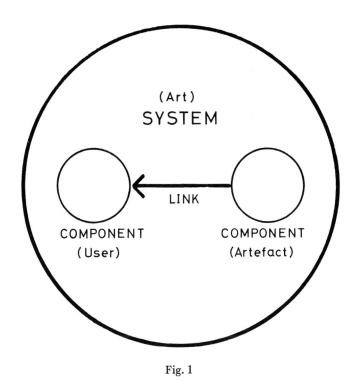

Fig. 1

abstract, or imaginary. (This notion of a 'thing' is illuminated in an interesting paper [1] in which some relevant root definitions are set out: 'thing'—object of thought; 'real'—thing-like; 'exist'—to stand out from.) Cognition is associated with but distinct from perception, in that all information from the environment—visual, audible, tactile and olfactory—has to be acted upon *before* it will yield up the 'things' of which our experience is composed. The association is between our 'things' (objects of thought) on the one hand, and available sensory impressions (stimuli) on the other. Thus one's consciousness of a 'thing', whether 'it' be Probability Theory or an Umbrella, is associated with a certain number of sensory impressions or stimuli drawn from a set [2].

This simple model suggests that we arm our senses with advance information as to what sensory sets to expect of the physical and psychological environment. When actual encounters are made (with, for example, a gallery, a picture frame, a painting, and a brush-stroke) they will be so to say approved as they fall into the appropriate sets; leaving *un*expected phenomena to be examined in a different fashion.

Unexpected encounters will be of two main kinds. The first is an encounter with a familiar sensory or psychological experience, but out of the context in which it would normally be associated with the appropriate 'thing': in this case the relevant set of

associated stimuli will have to be extended. (An example would be the phenomenon of *street* theatre.) The second class of encounter with the unexpected will include entirely novel experiences: this does present something of a challenge to the simple approach being made here, but it does not seem possible to disassociate the interaction fundamental to any art system from the act of learning.

Communication

So far this description has followed a flow of information from a material artefact to a person; that person normally encounters the work in such circumstances (perhaps an art gallery) as lead him to anticipate—to look for, the appropriate associative sets [3]. The particular sensory information received from the artefact may or may not be associated, and therefore be recognized as some 'thing'; that 'thing' might, in one instance, be recognized as a reference on the part of the artist to something in the real world, and in another instance what is recognized may be a formal convention of Modern Art. (A visual pun which condenses these meanings into one painting is reproduced in Fig. 2.)

Once some 'things' have been established in the consciousness of the person encountering the artefact, he is engaged in a symbol manipulation exercise. It is at this symbolic level that learning will take place—not as an import of meaning from the artefact, but strictly as a generative act on the part of the person who is manipulating the symbols that have been established.

Implicit in what has been said is the idea that, although art is the product of a special kind of communication, tangential to the normal learning process, it is nevertheless untrue to describe the process as 'learning what the artist has to say'.

The artist presents us with a number of indications as to where we should direct our attention (the frame, the proscenium arch and the pedestal are among the more familiar). Within that framework he presents us with more clues as to what boundaries demarcate *his* understanding of the 'things' that he has isolated against *his* conceptual and sensational background.

Learning

In speaking of human communication Dr Colin Cherry suggested that: "...it is customary to speak of signals as 'conveying information', as though information were a kind of commodity. But signals

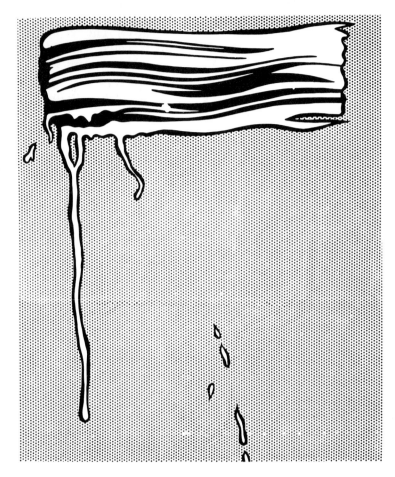

Lichtenstein. *Yellow Brush Stroke I*, 1965. Oil and magna on canvas, 68×48″. Collection: Fred Mueller. Leo Castelli Gallery, New York.

Fig. 2

do not convey information as railways trucks carry coal. Rather we should say: signals have an information content by virtue of their *potential for making selections*. Signals operate upon the alternatives forming the recipient's doubt; they give the power to discriminate amongst or select from, these alternatives." [4]

This encourages us to look more closely at what goes on when a person encounters an art work, and to ask what happens as he becomes a component in the art system described above?

In order to simplify matters we can assume that he has already received various signals from the artefact, and that he has effectively recognized all of the 'things' that he could anticipate: so far

nothing new has been learned by him. At this stage a sense of meaning (or more than one) has to be generated out of the symbols available. It is not easy to discuss how this may be achieved without separating out some aspects of the user (aspects of the 'user' component of the art system described), among which some interactions can be said to take place.

The relevant aspects seem obvious:

The artefact.
The meaning to be, as we say, 'got out of the artefact'
The individual user himself.

These three essential elements happily correspond

188

with the elements forming a triadic relationship in any learning situation (Fig. 3). Cherry says of this triad that "A sign cannot be said simply to signify something, but only to signify something to somebody. The user is essentially involved." [5]

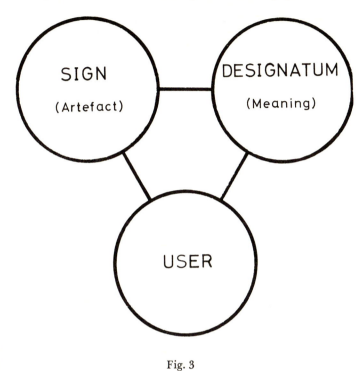

Fig. 3

Between the three symbolic entities in Fig. 3 the crucial interaction takes place, one analogous to that to which Charles Peirce refers when he suggests that we can argue with ourselves, and that such searchings have the nature of a dialogue, expressed in signs, just as though we were holding an internal conversation [6]. However, it is necessary to observe that there are almost certainly signs and symbols that are particular to the arts, and, even more important, that the syntactic relations standing between them may differ significantly from the language which Peirce may have had in mind. Now we can consider a person looking at a work of art using a combination of the representations in Figs 1 and 3. Figure 4 summarizes these representations, and refers to the context in which such encounters are made. Note that the 'environment' of a system includes whatever clearly affects or is affected by the system, and no more.

Arousal

It is to the eternal discredit of the industrial cul-

tures that they have purged our society of passion. Our politicians, industrialists, and military leaders unashamedly parade their disdain for cultural values [7]. Dullness and homogeneity are the order of the day, and in such circumstances it has become unreasonable to associate the use of art with arousal, or the cultural life with passion [8]. Yet is is essential for any useful model of the artistic process to cope with the living, warm-blooded animal condition of art, and not merely with the faint shadow of the European fine art tradition that haunts the museums to which we have relegated it.

It has for example been shown that we are not structurally endowed with spatial perception and orientation, but that these are skills, and skills which can only be learned actively; what happens is that the brain requires that there be a systematic relationship between actions which we initiate, and consequent effects felt as the real world impinges on us. Merely to be shown is not enough. [9]

In learning to deal with things around us which behave, what has been demonstrated is that we do not simply observe and record, but again that we actively form hypotheses, and that we go out and test them. This applies as much to babies as to scientists, and it is interesting to note that studies have shown this behavior to persist in situations which offer the subject no prospect of reward. [10]

Beyond these rather technical points about the interactive nature of learning processes there is evidence to support our observation that ability to understand is proportional to level of interest. Emotional arousal, even conflict, is essential if we are to make our contribution, as users, to the artistic process. [11]

Conclusions

Two conclusions are offered. The first is perhaps justified by the observations made above, while the other is more in the nature of a plea for the systems approach to problems of art and culture.

The purpose of these notes has been to present art appreciation as a creative act of participation, and to refute the notion that anything is *given* to those who 'use' the arts. Since, though signals can be transmitted from artist to audience, meaning cannot, the user is seen to be as much artist as the artist himself. *If he is not, the system does not work.*

What remains is to offer a note on the choice of the system as a paradigm.

We live in an era of mechanization, when the

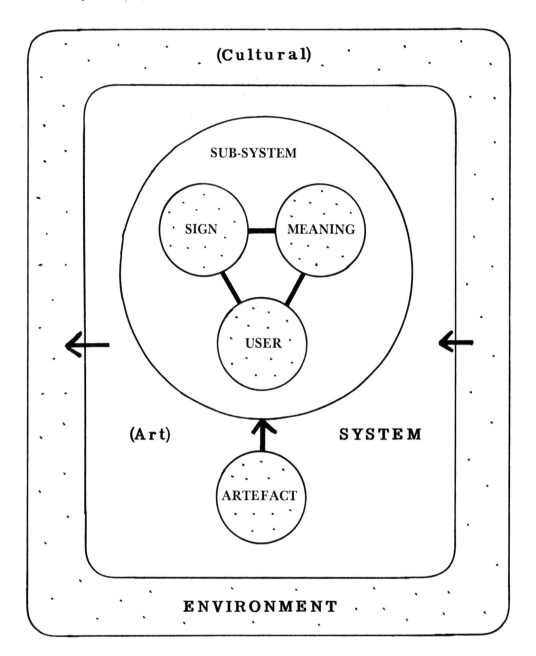

Fig. 4

artist and those who sympathize with him see his cause as one of opposition to all that mechanization represents to our culture: coldness, conformity, sterility. Unfortunately the concept of organization is often associated with this mechanical millieu. Yet we all now enjoy common insight on the breath-taking achievements of nature and human intellect, and understand the crucial role of organization in achieving them. So that, whether we consider the structure of an ameba, or the structure of ourselves as organisms able to join in that consideration (as a result of scanning these patches of ink), we are bound to acknowledge not only the degree of organization in either case, but the remarkably sensitive balance in which those organisms hold themselves. When we proceed to the relationship

190

touched on in the appreciation of a work of art it becomes apparent that a very high order of organizational complexity is involved. [12]

That complexity is concentrated as individual senses of meaning build up, through shared experience, into a defining sensibility (such as 'the Baroque'), and hence into interaction with other cultural factors—politics, religion, economic circumstances, and so on, until alien cultures meet.

System theory is the science of organization. In helping us to concentrate our attention on dynamic relationships rather than upon individual qualities, the systems approach offers a valuable adjunct both to analysis and to plain common sense. [13]

Notes and references

1. WALTER, R.I. and WALTER, N.I.McN., 'The equivocal principle in systems thinking', *General Systems Yearbook*, Vol. XVI, pp. 3-5, Society for General Systems Research, Washington (1971).
2. If we designate cognitive entities 'R', and sensory stimuli 'S', then R_i will be associated with a selection from the set S_i1, S_i2, S_{in}. Some proviso is made concerning a threshold above which an association will be effected.
3. CHERRY, Colin, *On Human Communication*, p. 273, 4.2, M.I.T., USA (1957).
4. Ibid., p. 169.
5. Ibid., p. 264.
6. Ibid., p. 263.
7. This is to judge by deeds, not words. Cf. any of the many studies on Renaissance patronage by each of these classes.
8. This is to reject utterly the universal acceptance of the idea that the arts are leisure activities, to be treated as a luxury.
9. HELD, Richard, 'Plasticity in sensory-motor systems', *Scientific American* **213**(5), 84 (1965).
10. BOWER, T.G.R., *Learning in Infancy*, Freeman, London (1974). The behaviorist, B.F. Skinner, remarked during a brief conversation at the Royal Society in 1971 that art is simply a form of reinforcement, sought by those who have previously received aesthetic pleasure from the arts.
11. BERLYNE, D.E., *Conflict, Arousal and Curiosity*, McGraw-Hill, New York (1960).
12. LANGLEY, L.L., *Homeostasis*, Van Norstrand Reinhold, New York (1965). This is a breathtaking account of the automatic regulatory systems in the human body, based on the work of Claude Bernard in the 19th Century, and the more recent studies of Walter Cannon.
13. BERTALANFFY, Ludvig von, *General System Theory*, Allen Lane, London (1971). The man who created our understanding of the general properties of systems, drew attention to the special properties of 'open' systems, and to whom non-scientists like myself owe a great debt for his consistent adherence to the principle that systems approaches should be expressed in non-technical terms *before* they are justified by recourse to elaborate and disciplined languages.
14. CORNOCK, Stroud, 'The role of the artist in a post-industrial culture—a systems approach', *Advances in Cybernetics and Systems Research*, Vol. II, pp. 418-420, especially the 'reciprocal artwork', Transcripta Books, London (1973).

The Systems Research Group of the Leicester Polytechnic welcomes the opportunity to provide further reference to, or to learn of, work in this field.

SYSTEMS EDUCATION

A systems view of organizing education

BELA H. BANATHY
*Far West Laboratory for Educational
    Research and Development,
Berkely, California, USA*

During the last two decades we have learned to understand that our increasingly more complex technological, environmental, economic, and social problems cannot be solved with the thinking and tools of single, analytically-oriented disciplines. Thus has emerged systems science which offers a new way of thinking, a new approach to disciplined inquiry. Systems science cuts across the various fields of investigation and has the capability to attack highly complex and large-scale problems. It has evolved models—constructed of general systems concepts and principles—which are applicable to more than one of the traditional domains of knowledge. The integration of systems concepts and principles into our thinking leads us to acquire the systems view. Systems view, then, can be applied to the analysis, design, development, and management of systems and to the solution of systems problems.

Education is a system of great complexity. Systems thinking applied to education has led us to develop conceptual models and strategies by which we can approach education comprehensively and develop new understandings as to what education is about and how it can be better organized and improved.

In this Chapter the organization of education is examined, and a systems way of looking at or thinking about the organization of education is developed.

There are a variety of configurations in which systems concepts and principles—applicable to social systems, such as education—can be considered and organized.[1] I have selected a particular configuration that appeared to be most relevant to the organization of schooling.[2] I have displayed the selected concepts and principles in the form of a set of operations that I have found useful in examining schooling as a special system. The set includes the following operations:

1. Clarify the systems levels that constitute the systems hierarchy of formalized education.
2. Designate the primary system level.
3. Identify the systems that operate at the various levels.
4. Clarify the key systems entity around which the various systems are built.

---

[1] An education-focused organization of systems concepts and principles—different from the one developed here—was presented in BANATHY, B.H., *A Systems View of Education, A Systems Models Approach*, Fearon Publishers, Belmont, California (1973).

[2] A self-imposed limitation is that I discuss the selected topic mainly from the point of view of organization of systems properties.

Progress in Cybernetics and Systems Research, Volume 2

5. Reveal the purposes of these systems, and specify their
6. Input, and 7. Output.
8. Designate the decider at the various system levels.
9. Display the relationships among the various systems.
10. Define the degree to which the systems are closed or open.

Let us explore these ten operations and see how they might help us to better understand schooling.

1. The *systems hierarchy* in education is a structure constituted of three (systems) levels. The *institutional level*, created by the society, interfaces and interacts with the society, and organizes the instructional level. The *instructional level* attends to the function of education (and other functions defined at the institutional level) and it deals with the learner at the *learning experience level*. The learning experience level has recently come to the fore; a full partner in the systems hierarchy of education. (We should note that these levels may have and often do have a hierarchical structure of their own.)

2. The designation of the *primary (systems) level* is probably the least understood aspect of schooling, even though it is probably the most crucial decision one can make in organizing education. Depending upon which one of the three levels is selected as the primary level, several distinctively different organizational models of schooling may emerge.

3. At each level a *system* (or a system complex) *exists* and can be identified. The school system operates at the institutional level, and the instructional system at the instructional level. At the learning experience level we have begun to recognize recently the notion of "learner systems" as separate and viable entities.

4. Systems thinking leads us to clarify the key *systems entity* around which each of these systems is built and operates. The teacher, information, goals, resources, instructional objectives and the like are often designated as interchangeable key entities of the various systems. Such lack of being specific has led to confusion and has hindered adequate analysis (and solution) of educational problems.

The three systems are to be further defined—and understood—by the specification of (5) their *purpose*, (6) their *input*, and (7) their *output*. Here systems thinking has helped us again to understand the relationship between purpose, input, and output. It has made it clear, for example, that we cannot designate "learning attained" as output at the institutional or instructional level but only at the learner systems

level. It has also legitimized the goals of the individual learner as a viable input of the instructional system.

8. The designation of *systems control* and *decision-making authority* at the various system levels is another salient point of clarification. As the three contrasting models will be described in this Chapter, three decision-making configurations will emerge and accentuate the differences among the three models of organizing schooling.

9. The nature of *relationships* among the various systems that comprise the systems complex of schooling is determined by the designation of the primary (systems) level and by the qualification of those relationships, such as subordinate, centralized, or egalitarian.

10. The degree of *open-* or *closed-ness* of schooling is another critical systems dimension. The traditional thrust in education has been toward closing and isolating schooling from its environment. This tendency has become a major source of discontent, dissatisfaction, and loss of support. It is rather unfortunate that the early systems approach movement in education has borrowed "closed systems models" from systems engineering and the physical sciences, resulting in a "systematic approach" to education overlooking the basically open systems nature of education, the uniqueness of the various environments in which schooling operates and, most importantly, neglecting the uniqueness of the individual learner.

Depending upon the selection of one of the three levels as the primary systems level and upon the choices made relevant to the other operations described above, I have found three distinctively different operational models of schooling emerging. A display and discussion of the three models and an understanding of their contrasting features will help us to see the *learner system* in proper perspective.

The organization of education: alternative models
Three models are introduced in Figs 1, 2, and 3.[3] They have been constructed in view of the ten operations presented above. (The numbers placed in parentheses, e.g., (2), refer to the ten operations.)

[3] An adaptation from BANATHY, B.H., 'A systems view of selecting educational resources', *Educational Media Yearbook, 1974* (edit. by T. Brown), R. Bowker, New York (1974) (in press).

Model A: The institutional level is the primary level. This model represents formalized education in societal contexts where educational authority is highly centralized, e.g., where there is a national system of education or—in the case of local control—educational/curriculum decisions are made at the top level of the local hierarchy. Fig.1

The Institution as the *Primary Level* (2)

Levels in the hierarchy (1)	The *System* operating at that level (3)	*Purpose* of the system(s) (4)	*Key entity* around which the system is built (7)	Primary *decision-maker* in the system (8)	System *Input* (5)	System *Output* (6)
Institutional level (National or local)	The School System as an institution	To enculturate and educate children and youth	National, societal (cultural) goals	The educational authority (president of the board, superintendent, minister of education, etc.)	Societal needs, values, financial resources available to education and constraints that limit education	Educational goals, organizational schemes, budgets, specifications of educational programs, standards, methods, materials, policies, etc.
Instructional level	Instructional systems	To provide instruction in line with the defined institutional purpose	The (prescribed) curriculum	Department chairman, principal, etc.	The output of the institutional level plus staff facilities and students	Specification of instructional experiences; organization of teachers, staff, students; instructional arrangements; scheduling; etc.
Educational experience level	Class(es) of students	To attend classes, to respond	Instruction	Teacher	The output of the instructional level and the instructional materials, aids, lesson plans, tests, etc.	Student passing courses, earning grades, diplomas, etc.

Relationships (9). If the primary level is the institutional level then the system operating at *other* levels will respond to it and are subordinated to the institution as indicated by the arrows (⇩).

The model described above implies a rather *closed educational system* (10) in which decisions are being made far removed from the learner and external influences are regulated by the top decision maker(s). An educational institution represented by this model would operationalize a *uniform* curriculum and educational experience.

Model B: The instructional level as the primary level. The most typical application of this model can be found in those contexts of formal education where a so-called instructional system approach has been used. College and university teaching manifest a more traditional representation of this model.

Fig. 2

The Instructional Level as the *Primary Level* (2)

Levels in the hierarchy (1)	The *System* operating at that level (3)	*Purpose* of the system(s) (4)	*Key entity* around which the system is built (7)	Primary *decision-maker* in the system (8)	System *Input* (5)	System *Output* (6)
Institutional level	School System	To provide facilities and resources in support of the instructional system	Needs, requirements of the instructional system	School resources, manager policy maker	Societal needs, and values, resources requirements of the instructional system, financial resources available, etc.	Over-all educational goals, allocation of resources in support of instruction, and policies regulating the use of resources.
Instructional level	Instructional Systems	To provide instruction to students	Instructional objectives	Instructional Systems Manager (Principal, Department Chairman, etc.) (Primary decision maker)	The output of the institutional level, aims/instructional design, staff, facilities, students	Instructional objectives, instructional arrangement
Educational experience level	Classes (groups) of	To be educated, to learn to perform on instructional objectives	Instruction	Teacher	The output of the instructional level and implementation plans geared to specific instructional environments.	Students who can perform on instructional objectives

Relationships (9). The instructional system governs the systems complex. This is an interacting relationship between the institutional and instructional levels, and the learning experience level is subordinated to the instructional level.

The model described above implies a system which is *more open* (10) than that described in Fig. 1. The system is somewhat open to external influences. Primary educational decisions are made at the middle level, closer to the learner. Consequently, within a specific educational institution, a variation of instructional systems and educational experiences may be operationalized. Any given instructional system, however, is rather closed.

Model C: **The educational experience level is the primary level.** Some of the earlier experimental programs and some of what is happening today in innovative programs attempt to move formal education toward the operationalization of this model.

Fig. 3

The Educational Experience is the *Primary Level* (2)

Levels in the hierarchy (1)	The *System* operating at that level (3)	*Purpose* of the system(s) (4)	*Key entity* around which the system is built (7)	Primary *decision-maker* in the system (8)	System *Input* (5)	System *Output* (6)
Institutional level	School System	To provide facilities and resources in support of the instructional/learning resources system	The requirements of the instructional/learning system	School resources manager and policy maker	Societal needs, values and requirements of the instructional/learning resources system. Financial resources (constraints), etc.	Over-all goals, allocations of resources available to the instructional/learning systems and policies regulating the use of those resources, etc.
Instructional level	(Instructional) Learning Resources System	Provide (information about) resources and arrangements by which to facilitate learning	Learner(s) needs, objectives	Manager(s) of the instructional/learning resources system	The output of the instructional level, information about learner's systems, learner's requirements staff, etc.	Information about the over-all curriculum framework, instructional/training resources and arrangements, and organized readily available resources
Educational experience level	The learners' systems	To become educated to master learning tasks	Learning	Learner(s)	The output of the instructional level, learners' needs/objectives, and specific plans for making use of the instructional/learning resources	Learning tasks mastered, progress toward becoming educated

Relationship (9). If the educational experience level is the primary level then the systems complex is built around and responds to the learner's system(s). The systems are interactive. The governing direction, however, flows from the learning experience level.

The model described above projects a *rather open educational system* (10). Decisions relevant to the educational experiences are made primarily by the learner. Within an educational institution there are as many organized learner systems as learners. Furthermore, the boundaries of the learners system are (often) extended beyond those of the school.

199

We would probably seldom find a perfect match between any one of the models and a specific on-going educational operation. Most of what exists in the real world is probably a mixture of what the three models represent. Whichever model is operationalized in a given situation depends upon several factors, including

° The socio-political configuration of the particular society. (More open, democratic, and progressive societies will tend to move toward Model C; more closed, autocratic, and traditional societies have schools that are more like Model A.)
° The unitary versus pluralistic nature of the society. (A pluralistic society will not be likely to support a uniformed system of schooling such as the one represented by Model A—see Fig. 1.)
° The value system of the society. (In societies where the uniqueness and freedom of the individual is valued, the trend will be probably toward Model C—Fig. 3.)
° The prevailing conception of learning and the learner. (If individual differences are recognized and the learner is judged to be capable of making his or her own decisions in learning, Model A will be probably rejected.)

A discussion of the models can be developed around several thrusts of inquiry. A few are suggested here.

One can speculate that the three models mark three different stages of the evolution of education.

Model A represents "traditional" education; that is, education in societies or communities with long-standing, uniformed, and stable values and cultures, or societies that might be labeled as pre-technological.

Model B appears to be the efficiency-oriented educational model of the modern technological society.

Model C appears to be a representation of an emerging educational model of the post-technological era characterized by an increasing concern for humanism, the uniqueness of the individual, and non-material values.

The models do not necessarily project a continuum in time. Education in a given society might shift from Model A to Model C. Furthermore, if we take a historical perspective, we can discover manifestations of Model C as far back as the Classical Greek or the Renaissance periods.

The organization of education: structure vs. function

The models just discussed enable us to take a com-prehensive view of education. At a more detailed level of analysis, we shall next consider specific educational *functions* and *structures* and their relationship.

The two critical aspects of a system *per se* are its function and organizational scheme or structure. To determine a system's function, one asks: For what is the system made? To determine its structure, one asks: Of what is the system made? These two inquiries lead us to create different systems abstractions or models.[4] There is, however, an intricate and complex relationship between those two ways of viewing systems. That relationship indicates the essence of our present examination.

Traditionally, scholars have analyzed systems essentially in structural terms. In fact, information about specific structures, from atoms to societies and galaxies, comprises the bulk of our scientific knowledge.[5] Recently, however, we have become quite "function conscious", for two reasons. An historical analysis of systems has led us to realize that structure often "takes over" and functions tend to be lost. Furthermore, as we have become increasingly more active in creating new synthetic entities, our primary concern has become the building of systems that can perform specific functions, thus, the crucial relationship of structure and function. How can desired functions be attended to by a system consisting of a defined set of structured pieces? How can various desired functions coexist in the same structure? These are some of the questions that we pursue these days, and these questions will guide our present examination of functions versus structures.

Functions of education

These are the major functions that education may address:

[4]BANATHY, B.H., 'Structural model and process model', *A Systems View of Education*, Fearon Publishers, Belmont, California (1973).

[5]ROSEN, Robert, 'On the design of stable and reliable institutions', *International Journal of General Systems*, Vol. 1, No. 1 (1974).

° The custodial function (taking care of students while they are in school).
° Inculcating values and mores inherent in the culture, developing understanding of the world in which the individual lives.
° Transmitting information and knowledge (developing knowledge and understanding of humanities, arts, and sciences).
° Developing effective communication skills.
° Developing cognitive skills and sharpening analytic skills.
° Developing occupational competence.
° Developing problem-solving skills and other life skills/habits.
° Developing facility in making independent value judgments and independent decisions.
° Developing understanding of the relationship of the individual and the environment.
° Developing social interaction.
° Facilitating an individual's unique self-development.

(The functions of certification/selection can be added to the list above.)

Based on their orientation and/or requirements, different societies and communities assign different order of priorities to these functions; the order within one society varies over time. Most importantly, differences in the order of priorities imply different structures or organizational schemes of education.

The prevailing classroom-based structure and its organizational scheme of education were most appropriate for responding to the mass-instructional, assembly-line thrust of the *early 20th century industrial society* and its "melting-pot" orientation. That educational approach emphasized the top half of the functions on the continuum (see above). Those may be labeled as the more traditional functions of education characteristic of an educational system that can be represented by our Model A organizational scheme (Fig. 1). More specifically, priority functions included custodial function; the key functions of enculturation (namely transmission of information/knowledge and inculcation of values and mores); development of cognitive skills; and, to some extent, vocational skills. Obviously, the classroom-based structure has proved to be less than adequate for developing life skills, social skills, problem-solving skills, and decision-making skills; it also basically counteracts the emphasis on individual self-development.

The post-World War II emergence of *the technological society* in this country and others had created a new order of priorities of educational functions.

Next to information/knowledge acquisition, skill development became a high priority, possibly of a priority parallel to those of cognitive, occupational, and life skills. To accommodate such a new order of priorities, variations in the classroom-based structure have been necessitated, including new arrangements, based on a media-oriented educational technology and aiming at supporting instructional and training systems. This technology-oriented educational thrust, exemplified by our Model B organizational scheme (Fig. 2), has experienced, and is now experiencing, increasing difficulty in attending to cultural pluralism, thrust for individualization, diversification of life-styles, facilitation of independent value judgment and decision-making.

Th post-technological era—if we may use this term to refer to the period now emerging—appears to extend its priorities of functions into the facilitation of the unique self-development of the individual through life-long learning; the development of social skills in addition to the development of cognitive, occupational, avocational, leisure and life skills. The context of this emerging model of education (Model C, Fig. 3) is a pluralistic society with a wide range of life-styles, and operating based on highly diversified value systems. The shift in functions resulted in a search for new structures and organizational schemes.

In searching for such new organization or structure, and to compensate for the limitations of the classroom-based or technology-oriented organizational schemes of education, some new structures recently have emerged under various labels, such as the open school and alternative school. However, they appear to have problems of their own that are similar to those of the organizational arrangements they have aimed to replace. They may attend rather well to some of the functions (such as self-development, social skills, life-skills); however, they often fall short in providing for other functions such as, for example, information/knowledge transmission and cognitive skills. To sum it up, the problem appears to be the difficulty that formalized education has in coping with a large set of educational functions and the dynamics of changing functions.

Systems thinking helps us to cope with this problem. It leads us to understand that functions should dictate structure and, thus, *different* educational *functions* such as skill development, enculturation, custodial care, socialization, and development of self may imply *different structures* or different modes of organizing education. Therefore, a solution of the problem of functions vs. structure in educa-

201

tion may be found in (a) defining the various educational functions to be attended to and, (b) developing structures that fit them and organizing arrangements that have the capability of providing for those functions. Thus, rather than having *one* structure and *one* organizational arrangement such as the classroom-based scheme, or an alternative to it, we need to think in terms of a *set of arrangements organized into a complex of complementary struc-*

tures.

It is beyond the scope of this study to explore and evolve these arrangements and their structure. It can be said, however, that a basic requirement that those arrangements and structures have to meet is dynamism—the capability of adapting to new, evolving, and shifting functions—and, that they have a capacity for continuous self-renewal and improvement.

A systems approach to the training of systems analysts

O.J. HANSON
The City University of London, UK

Introduction

The range and importance of the functions of modern central government are enormous—some indication of the scope is given in A.H. Jones' paper [1] in setting the scene for local government—and naturally this leads to very complex systems problems that require solutions. As a contribution toward finding these solutions, the Graduate Business Centre of the City University has cooperated with the Civil Service College over a number of years.

A series of basic systems analysis courses was run for the Civil Service College in 1970-72, in parallel with similar courses run by the College itself. The results of these courses were satisfactory, in that students felt they had learnt useful new techniques and attitudes, while a pass rate of over 95% was achieved in the externally controlled National Computing Centre Basic Certificate in Systems Analysis examinations, as against a national pass rate of 83%. At the end of this series the Systems group in the Graduate Business Centre was asked to develop a more advanced program of Systems Analysis training. Negotiations between the Civil Service College, the Central Computer Agency (which is responsible for the training and selection of computer personnel in the Civil Service) and the Graduate Business Centre led to agreement on an outline syllabus and

a set of training aims and objectives. It was decided that the course should be one academic year in duration, and should lead to the award of a Diploma. The level was intended to be similar to that of a taught M.Sc. course, but as many potential students did not have first degrees, it was not possible to award a Masters degree. It has subsequently proved that entrants without first degrees but with suitable practical experience are at least as able as many post-graduate Management students (see under *Student selection*). The development and teaching of the Diploma have been carried out on lines guided by systems considerations, and it is this process that is described in this Chapter.

Philosophy

The difficulties in applying systems techniques in Universities as a whole have been described by G. Dohmen [2]. As a comment on the difficulties Dohmen outlines, it may be that the way to control the complex set of interacting and sometimes conflicting aims, methods and intended results to be found in a University is to rely on devolution, rather than central control. The task of the administrator may be defined as that of allocating resources, monitoring and assessing results, rather than

Progress in Cybernetics and Systems Research, Volume 2

attempting to control the actual operation of the various groups making up the whole. The Graduate Business Centre of the City University is divided into a number of Subject Groups, and these are the basic operational unit. The Systems Group in the Graduate Business Centre has the advantage that it is small, and composed of people who agree on aims and methods, and hence it avoided many of the potential problems Dohmen mentions. The influence of Civil Service requirements was also helpful; one cannot retreat into an ivory tower when insistent and knowledgeable customers are waiting for results.

It was decided that the Diploma should prepare students for immediate employment as systems analysts in responsible roles on completion of the course. A secondary aim was to provide them with the background for ultimate administrative responsibility. In order to decide whether these objectives were being met, a feedback system was necessary. The many complex short-term loop systems used during the course are given later: however, only study of the progress of students over a number of years after they complete the Diploma can provide the necessary feedback to assess the practical achievements of the course. The advantage of having a large body of students from the Civil Service is that control groups are easily selected, and that the careers of Diploma holders can be followed far more readily than those of students returning to many diverse occupations. Despite this, the Civil Service offers experience in many different fields, and we can expect to be able to compare the performance of ex-students working under widely differing conditions. As this is inevitably a long-term exercise, I hope to report on it further at the appropriate time.

In order to achieve the over-all aims set out above, a number of prerequisites were identified. (These correspond to the 'components' and 'functions' discussed by Banathy [3], just as the 'aims' above are equivalent to his 'goals'; in many ways this Chapter describes a concrete example of the general principles he put forward.) These were

1. Potential students must already have adequate experience in data processing, preferably as programmers.
2. New members of staff must have considerable experience of commercial work as systems analysts; while scientific data processing presents its own fascinating systems problems, these were not felt to be appropriate for a course of this nature.
3. The Diploma should provide as much practice

in genuine Systems work as possible. The only difference between the case studies used during the course and systems tasks in the field is the opportunity to have solutions discussed and analyzed in depth.
4. Maximum feedback should be provided in every part of the course, whether technical, academic, or personal.

Course development

The syllabus for the Diploma was agreed in discussions with the Civil Service, and passed by the Senate of the University. The syllabus was in four parts:

i) *Fundamental Concepts*: basic computing; operational research techniques; computer applications. (The intention here is to ensure that all students have a common basic foundation on which to build systems skills.)

ii) *Data Processing*: file organization and handling; program design and specification; procedure oriented languages; real time and on-line systems; documentation; applications.

iii) *Design and Implementation of Information Systems*: the organization and structure of businesses; problem definition; system design; implementation; project control; user problems.

iv) *Human communications in systems development*: interviewing techniques; presentations; training; investigations; report preparation; human problems in computer applications.

This provided the bare bones of the Diploma. While many specialists were available in the University to teach specific topics in this syllabus, it was clear that each main division shown above required development in an integrated fashion, to ensure a course without overlap and without omissions. Thus each part was allocated to one staff member, and the system adopted was as follows:

a) Total times for each part of the syllabus were allocated.

b) Lecture topics were prepared separately, but all of the Systems Group were sent details.

c) Weekly meetings were held to resolve overlaps, shortage or excess of lecture time, and to clear up other outstanding problems.

d) A timetable was evolved, to check that all the lectures were properly placed, and particularly that necessary basic work was covered before it was used.

e) Case-study titles, content and position in the course were determined in relation to lecture

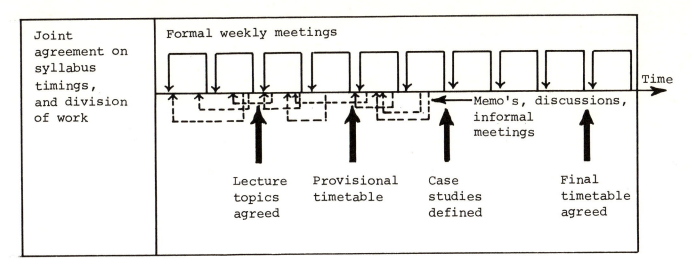

Fig. 1 Timetable development

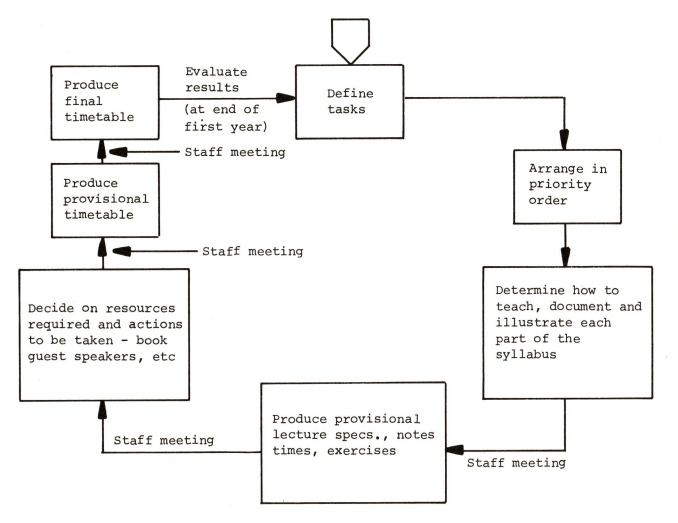

Fig. 2 Staff development work

content. (These case studies cover the whole spectrum of systems work. Topics are given below.)

f) Those subjects that are best covered by outside experts were identified, and the responsibility for contacting such people was allocated amongst the various members of the staff.

g) A final timetable taking all the above into account was prepared and circulated.

This process is illustrated in Fig. 1, and the functions of each individual member of staff in this exercise are shown in Fig. 2. It will be seen that Fig. 2 is similar to the 'seven steps of a training manager's job' given by Gane [4], with the exception that feedback at the end of the loop was provided by other members of staff.

Student selection

The students, despite coming from a relatively controlled environment, presented a number of unusual selection problems.

First of all, candidates had widely differing educational backgrounds. Some of the more experienced had only taken GCE 'O' Level examinations. Others had passed GCE 'A' Level in a number of subjects. (This examination is roughly equivalent to 'Abitur' in standard. Specialist subjects are studied to a higher level, but normally only three subjects are taken.) Finally, a number already had University degrees, or had started reading for a degree and given up during the course. This meant that previous academic attainments were unlikely to be a useful guide.

Secondly, candidates varied markedly in age. The range was from 21 to 36, and this implied a probable difference in the time since the candidate had studied full time. Only those concerned with education will appreciate what problems full-time academic work can pose for the older student. (We were, of course, aware that such a person may benefit from a maturer outlook and richer experience. But how to quantify these conflicting factors?)

Thirdly, candidates had very different practical backgrounds. Most were programmers—some scientific, some commercial—while others had operating and hardware design experience.

Faced with this heterogeneous group of candidates, it was decided to rely largely on the well-tried but hardly quantifiable technique of interviewing. Each candidate was examined to reveal their understanding in the following areas: Numeracy, data processing awareness, the inter-relationship of computing

Table 1

ATGSB SCORE (x)	$(x-\bar{x})^2$	COMMENT
451	9900.25	ACCEPTED
458	8556.25	ACCEPTED†
462	7832.25	REJECTED
487	4032.25	REJECTED
509	1722.25	ACCEPTED
516	1190.25	REJECTED
516	1190.25	ACCEPTED
549	2.25	REJECTED
552	2.25	ACCEPTED
560	90.25	ACCEPTED
567	272.25	ACCEPTED
570	380.25	REJECTED
574	552.25	ACCEPTED
578	756.25	ACCEPTED
588	1406.25	ACCEPTED
596	2070.25	ACCEPTED
603	2756.25	ACCEPTED‡
610	3540.25	ACCEPTED
621	4970.25	ACCEPTED
643	8556.25	ACCEPTED‡

$$\bar{x}=550.5 \quad \Sigma(x-\bar{x})^2 =59779$$
$$\sigma=54.67$$

The official Princeton figures for 262,295 candidates tested between August 1970 and July 1973 give $\bar{x}_1=463$; $\sigma_1=106$.

Adopting the null hypothesis that the above group of 20 students is part of this distribution, we obtain

$$\bar{x}-\bar{x}_1 = 87.5$$

$$\text{Variance }(\bar{x}-\bar{x}_1)= \frac{\sigma^2}{n} + \frac{\sigma_1^2}{n} = \frac{11236}{262295} + \frac{2989}{20} = 149.5$$

The standard error of the difference is
$$\{\text{variance }(\bar{x}-\bar{x}_1)\}^{1/2} = 12.23$$

Hence the two means are separated by 87.5/12.23 = 7.16 times the standard error of the difference. This great a separation is very unlikely to occur by chance.

---

† Dropped out after the start of the course.
‡ Did not take up places due to prior promotion.

and human activities, general interests and concerns. The Civil Service had interviewed 38 candidates, of whom 20 were thought good enough to apply to the University. These 20 were ranked as a result of the interviews with systems staff, and the top 15 were offered places.

Interviewing, as has been stated above, is difficult to quantify, and results are dependent on interviewer as well as interviewee. Hence we looked for other possible selection tests. A systems analyst requires both verbal and quantitative ability, and it seemed possible that the Admission Test for Graduate Study in Business (often called the 'Princeton' test), which covers these two areas, might be appropriate. All candidates were required to take the ATGSB, but in the first year it was agreed not to use the results as a basis for selection. A histogram of the over-all results for candidates who were selected and rejected on the basis of interviews is given in Fig. 3.

The most interesting thing coming out of these results is that the group of 20, taken as a whole, are clearly above the average of the ATGSB candidates in the last four years. An analysis of the results shows there is less than one chance in 10,000 that such a difference could arise by chance—for details see Table 1. This implies that the Diploma students despite their very differing academic standards and ages, are of consistently high ability as measured by ATGSB. Of course, this group was already a selection, as 18 other candidates had not been passed by Civil Service interviewers, while others still had not been approved by their Heads of Department, and thus had not come into the reckoning. In addition a number of Universities use the ATGSB only for candidates with poor or as yet not determined qualifications—this is done by the Graduate Business Centre of the City University, for instance—and the average results may reflect this use of the test.

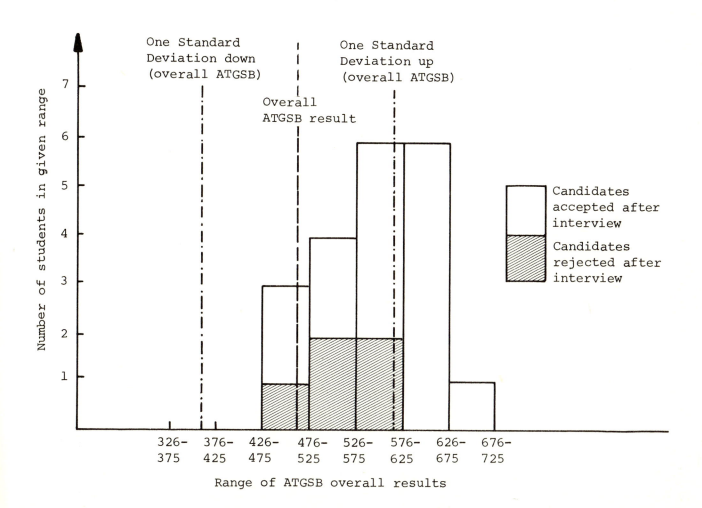

Fig. 3 Histogram of over-all ATGSB results for 20 Diploma candidates

However, I believe that the mature student may well be at an advantage in the ATGSB, and figures produced for an internal report on the test by the Senior Tutor of the Graduate Business Centre [5] appear to bear this out. A publication of the ATGSB Research and Development Committee, however, quotes administrators in the USA as saying that the test itself may be a barrier to the older student [6]. This might reflect some difference between British and American conditions, and we shall be studying the performance of future students in the ATGSB, the Diploma and their subsequent careers with great interest. A report by T.W. Harrell on the selection, course performance and later business careers of MBA graduates covers much this same area for business studies [7].

Course structure

1. Timetable

There are twelve hours of lectures per week, and these are divided into three separate one hour sessions on every morning except Wednesday. On Wednesday mornings each student has two subject tutorials. These are nominally one hour, but usually each last about one and a quarter to one and a half hours, and the timetable allows for this. Case studies and interviewing practice are held on three afternoons a week, leaving Wednesday and Friday afternoons free for private study.

2. Feedback sessions

The first of these is the subject tutorial. As the syllabus is divided into four parts, a student will have a tutorial in each area of the syllabus every two weeks. Essays or examples are set for each tutorial, and every student's work is analyzed and discussed during the tutorial. This in itself makes staff members aware of their student's grasp of the subject, but any other query can also be raised during a tutorial. This means that a student should not lose touch with any part of the syllabus for more than two weeks before a member of staff is alerted and corrective action taken.

The second form of feedback is at meetings of staff and students, to discuss course progress and identify any over-all problems that have occurred. At least one of these has been held each term, and students can request further meetings at any time. They have in fact requested one additional meeting, as a result of student worries about work-load during the first term of the course.

The personal equivalent of this is individual interviews, held with each student by at least two senior members of staff (separately) once a term. At these meetings the student's progress is assessed, both from the student and staff points of view, and problems in individual lecture series can be identified. The purpose of having two separate interviews is that the student may have difficulties with the lectures his interviewer gives, and might be inhibited from commenting if this were due to the lecturer's

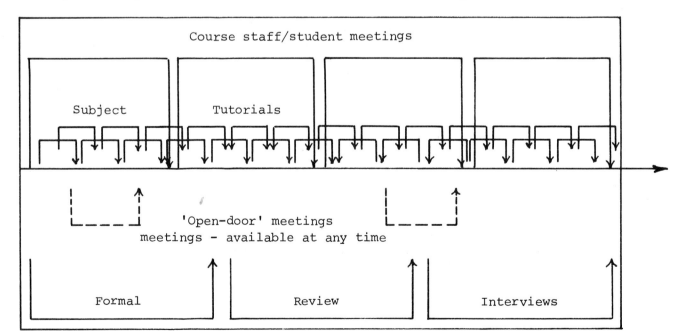

Fig. 4*a* Course feedback arrangements

personality or style of lecturing. The comments arising from these interviews are treated very seriously by staff; sources of comments are not given, but lecturers are expected to take action on criticisms. All members of staff operate on the 'open door' principle that they are available to students at any time (given reasonable notice).

Finally, each member of staff has a 'personal' tutorial group of up to five students. The intention here is to create a channel by which personal problems that may arise, and prejudice the students performance during the course, can be allowed for and, hopefully, put right. Obviously some students may not find it easy to establish rapport with their allocated personal tutor, and in this case it is open to them to change. However, members of staff have been enthusiastic about the system and their obvious wish to get to know their students, expressed in such ways as attendance at student parties, arrangement of tutorial group and individual lunches has been well rewarded. This is in no sense a 'moral tutorial' system. Students are older than is usual in Britain, many are married and some are older than their tutors. It is purely a further feedback loop, so that the real reasons for student actions can be recognized and appropriate action taken. The full series of interrelated loops is shown in Fig. 4.*a*.

3. *Lectures*

The course relies heavily on lectures, as these take up twelve hours per week. However, they are deliberately kept as informal as possible, and constant student participation is aimed at; a quiescent student group is regarded as a danger signal. All the usual techniques—blackboard, flip charts, felt board, magnetic board and overhead projector— are used, with occasional films. Where students have special knowledge of a subject, as often happens with an experienced student group, they are given an opportunity to prepare and deliver a talk on it. This aspect of student-student interaction is constantly encouraged, as no teaching group could afford to ignore the hundred or more man-years of data processing experience available in the class.

4. *Case studies*

The cases used are taken from actual business situations—mainly those experienced by staff personally—and reflect the whole spectrum of systems analytical work. They range from a document assimilation exercise, through fact finding, feasibility studies, systems definition exercises, design of data handling, batch and on-line systems to the design of an inte-

grated system, development of a systems project and the techniques used in assessing the success of an implemented system in meeting its objectives. The relationship of these phases in the analysis of a system is very well covered by J.E. Bingham and G.W.P. Davies [8]. In carrying out the case-studies, students are required to work singly on some occasions, and in pairs or groups on others. The results are sometimes written reports, sometimes group discussions, and often oral presentations. With the need for interviews in fact-finding for the case-studies, this adds up to a very full training in communicating techniques, and the emphasis on this aspect of systems analysis is more typical of computer manufacturers training methods than a conventional academic course. Presentations are sometimes held in the City University Television Studio, in order to record the exercise on Video-tape. Assessments of individual and group performances are then made and discussed with the students before the play-back of the presentation. We have found that a student who may feel he has been hard done-by before a play-back session will almost always agree with his assessment when he has had a chance to see his own performance. This is shown in Fig. 4*b*.

5. *Interviewing training*

Although students get a number of opportunities to practise interviewing techniques during case-studies, these techniques are so crucial to an analyst that a separate program of training is provided (see also [9]). All of these are held in the Television Studio, because of the feedback possibilities this provides; at first this can be inhibiting to some of the students, but they are encouraged to get to know the equipment and conditions as well as possible, and to use the studio privately in addition to scheduled work, in order to minimize this problem.

A series of interviews takes the student through simulations of the establishment of contact at all levels of staff, from the shop floor to senior management, through fact finding and problem handling to very testing human situations where the analyst is either not welcome, in a false position or highly feared. The interview and assessment are handled as for presentations—see Fig. 4*b*. Where appropriate, outside interviewees are used (as for example senior managers from industry) and they are able to play their own 'part' in the exercise. In other cases staff fulfil this function, but again in most cases they play roles from their own industrial experience, in order to have the sort of background knowledge that such a person would possess.

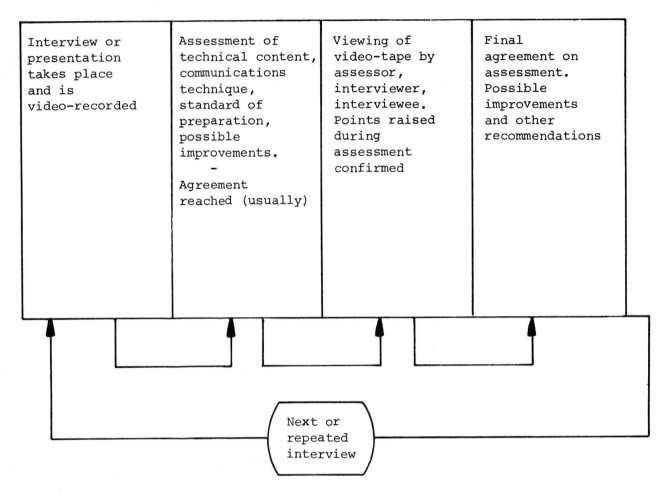

Fig. 4b Interview and presentation assessment

As an exercise to demonstrate to the students that staff genuinely had skill in this field, the students arranged a series of interviews with briefs for staff, who acted on this occasion as interviewers. Such an exercise can be fraught with danger, as malicious handling of the situation by students could cause very bad feeling. However, we have found it very successful; this is a tribute to the mature and responsible attitude of the students, and in that light has helped establish mutual confidence and respect between staff and students.

6. *Personal*
The opportunities for feedback of personal problems have already been discussed. However, an unexpected result of running a one year course for Civil Servants should be mentioned. During some years of holding six week courses, students were notably punctual, and tended to keep the tidy, sober-suited and moder-

ate appearance and attitudes of the career Civil Servant. Despite encouragement to use the University facilities, and to regard themselves as full members of the University, students seldom did so. If a class member was late or absent it was due to personal problems, illness or unavoidable hold-ups in public transport, rather than to laziness or inebriation.

The Diploma course has been quite different, True, for some time students did not begin to alter, but after an 'incubation' period casual dress, longer hair and a change in attitude became apparent. This was followed by persistent lateness and occasional absenteeism—although it must be made clear that only a handful of students were guilty of this. As the course continued, a further change has become noticeable. Now, with the end in sight, questions on future career prospects are raised, promotion boards are visited and newly cropped hair appears. With our sights firmly fixed on the goals, methods and

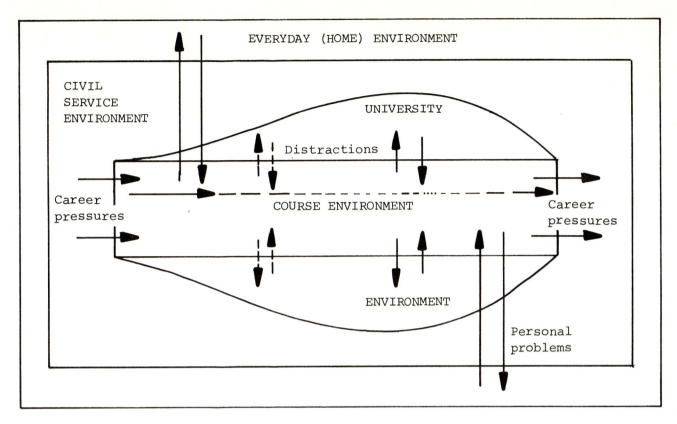

Fig. 5 The various influences acting on the student
NOTE: Broken lines indicate weaker influences. The shape of the University Environment is intended
to indicate its relative effect on the students during different times in the progress of the Diploma course

problems of the course itself, we had omitted to allow for the effect of the over-all student environment (see Fig. 5). Only the lateness and absence caused any difficulty, and it is clear that, if a responsible way round this cannot be found, sanctions of some sort will have to be invoked.

Assessment of student success
As is only reasonable in a Diploma that is so strongly biased toward Human Communications, course work in this field makes up 25% of the final student assessment. Human skills have been assessed as being 60% of an analysts job [10], but to award so high a proportion of marks for this would leave results open to very strong subjective influences, and in any case not all systems work is so highly human skills oriented. However, a student who passed the Diploma examination with flying colors, but did poorly in this area, would be advised to concentrate on the *Systems*, rather than the *Human*, aspects of systems analysis. The final examination, carrying

75% of the marks, is based on the four parts of the syllabus—one of which is Human Communications in Systems Development—in roughly equal parts.

Conclusion
As will be seen from the foregoing, the planning and structure of the City University Diploma in Systems Analysis is exceedingly feedback-oriented. The real success of the Diploma course can only be measured by the results of its students in their own environment. We are confident that students will be better communicators, and will have learnt useful new techniques; only time will tell if their work justifies their new ability to 'sell' themselves and their ideas. A very heavy price (in terms of staff time) has to be paid for the course structure decided on, and we shall wish to be sure this use of time produces a proportionally useful course. Planning has certainly not ignored the student; if anything, the program could be accused of an almost hypochondriac concern with students' views, reactions and progress.

We make no apology for this, as we wish by our own example to teach students a vital lesson in systems analysis, by showing them and their problems the same genuine concern that a successful systems analyst must show for his customer and the customer's difficulties.

References

1. JONES, A.H., 'The development of professional expertise in management information systems design for local government in the United Kingdom', Proc. 1973 International Conference on Cybernetics and Society, Boston, Mass., p. 389 (1973).
2. DOHMEN, G., 'Der Gegensatz Zwischen Zweckrationaler Systemplanung und Traditioneller Lehrfreiheit + Demokratischer Selbstbestimmung im Hochschulbereich', Proc. 1972 European Meeting on Cybernetics and Systems Research, Vol. II, p. 154 (1972).
3. BANATHY, B.H., 'General system theory and education', Proc. 1972 European Meeting on Cybernetics and Systems Research, Vol. II, p. 393 (1972).
4. GANE, Christopher, *Managing the Training Function Using Instructional Technology and Systems Concepts*, George Allen and Unwin Ltd.
5. VAUGHAN, G.D., 'Level of scores in the Princeton test', Paper to the Board of Studies in Management Studies, City University, 23 Goswell Road, London EC 1M 2BB (5 December 1973).
6. CASSERLY, Patricia L. and CAMPBELL, Joel T., ATGSB Research and Development Committee Brief No. 9, P. 18.
7. HARRELL, Thomas W., ATGSB Research and Development Committee Brief No. 1.
8. BINGHAM, John E. and DAVIES, Garth W.P., *A Handbook of Systems Analysis*, Macmillan.
9. As above, pp. 44-51.
10. As above, p. 43.

Introduction to systems analysis in science courses*

Professor LUIS BOJÓRQUEZ
*Universidad Nacional
Autónoma de México, México*

A. Introduction

In the last few years systems analysis has proved to be a most adequate tool for studying and solving problems on almost all kinds of complex structures and processes such as those involving organisms, behavioral and sociological phenomena, elaborated physical and chemical systems, and the like. The power of this relatively novel approach lies fundamentally in the treatment of scientific objects as simplified conceptual devices—so-called *boxes*, being sources, channels, or receptors of information in the form of an input-output relationship in which an operation derived from the properties (internal states) of the box is effected on the input to produce the output. They can be regulated or controlled systems. No matter what the system really is (a molecule, a bird, an urban group) it can be represented as described above, customarily as a block diagram, with greater or lesser physicomathematical sophistication, but as a first approximation of a given problem involving systems, the mere construction of its corresponding block diagram with identification of variables, its magnitudes and dimensions, conveys more information than that obtained with common descriptions.

It can be said that theories of systems (including black box theory, cybernetics, information theory,

game theory, and so on) are strategies designed for working with problems of *organization*, or more explicitly, of dynamical interaction of organized entities, including their environment. One basic problem, for example, is to determine stability properties, as is done in control theory (DiStefano *et al.* [1], Milhorn [2]). Another extraordinarily useful research activity derived from theories of systems is the design of both theoretical and experimental models.

These well-known facts have been reviewed here to emphasize why systems theories have been most fruitful when applied to such different fields as education (Couffignal *et al.* [3], Rezik [4]), ecology (Patten [5]), and management (Churchman [6]). In this context it is not difficult to see the importance of learning the fundamentals of systems analysis in school (and the earlier this knowledge is acquired the better) in order to prepare students for

*The main part of this Chapter was submitted for discussion to the International Conference on Education of Teachers for Integrated Science, ICSU-UNESCO, University of Maryland, April 3-13, 1973.

Progress in Cybernetics and Systems Research, Volume 2

the needs of our increasingly complex technological world. However, it must be pointed out that there is a great lack of literature about how to teach systems analysis, and also the little attention paid to the interesting pedagogical possibilities offered by systems theories when they are applied to show how science is structured in a methodological sense.

In this Chapter is described the way in which students of science courses have been introduced to the basic concepts of systems theories by means of simple laboratory experiments in which the importance of black box is specially stressed. A sample is also presented of the kind of media used in order to stimulate and develop in students a "systemic attitude" to the operations of scientific methods, from the theoretical as well as from the practical points of view. The level involved has been very elemental, as the detailed examples will show later. Also, it must be noted that the experiences with this approach are very recent, scarce and irregular: this method has been used since 1970 in courses of Animal Physiology, and Biophysics (university level; biologist's curriculum; age of students: 20-22), in courses of Experimental Biology and Experimental Method (university level; biologist's and physicist's curricula; age of students: 18-20), and in courses of Elemental Biology, and General Science for candidates to Montessori Teacher status (in this case, the ages and previous knowledge of students have been more diverse, but the level of the courses

has been maintained closer to the way they would be used with children). In spite of these shortcomings, the author is convinced that the systems approach has been shown to be fruitful and can be extended to different levels of science teaching, especially to integrated, or unified, science courses.

B. The game of black boxes
The following activities are examples of those designed to reach the objectives implicitly outlined above. They must be carried out in the laboratory. The class can be organized into squads (two or three members each) which select one, and only one, of the black boxes presented to them. A suggested duration of the session is from two to two-and-a-half hours (including discussion). The game consists of deducing what is inside each black box (i.e., system) observed.

B.1 Material
One active animal (rat, mouse, cockroach, earthworm, are most adequate) in an appropriate cage with food and water. One full wave rectifier circuit (device to convert alternating current to direct current) enclosed in a chassis with outputs where indicated in Fig. 1. One logic switching circuit (Fig. 2) en-

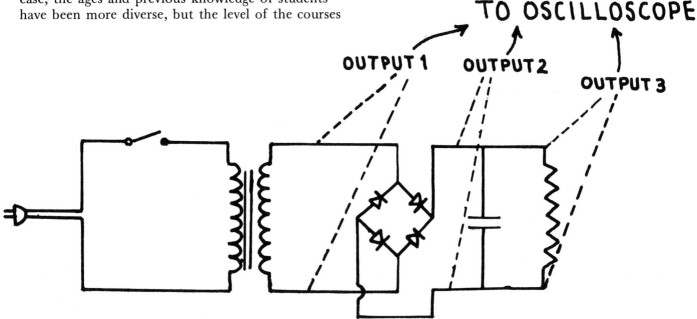

Fig. 1 Rectifier circuit. Components are enclosed within a box (chassis). Students have access to the circuit only at the outputs 1, 2, and 3.

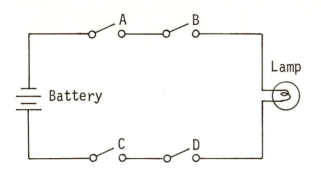

Fig. 2 Switching circuit used as a black box. Students must deduce the connections shown here by manipulating external switches and observing the states (on, off) of the lamp.

closed in a chassis and showing four switches (single pole) and one lamp (output). One black painted vessel, or covered with black paper, containing water and calcium carbonate (marble chips), stoppered with a two-hole rubber stopper; in one of the holes is attached one thistle tube extended below the surface of the water; in the other is attached a short glass L-tube connected by means of a rubber tube to a collector tube inverted inside a container of water. HCl 0.1N, 200 cm^3. Oscilloscope (minimum sensitivity approximately 100 V/division. One hand lens. One chronometer (or wrist watch with second-hand). One pipette (5 to 10 cm^3).

B.2 Rules of the game
Students shall observe, count, touch, measure, or anything else not trivial in order to know the properties of the system with which they work. The animals must be manipulated with care and gentleness. It will be clear that an oscilloscope is to be used with the rectifier circuit. For the switching circuit it is sufficient to move the switches and observe the lamp. The chemical system is obvious and needs no further explanation.

This part must be no longer than one hour. Once the squads have worked with the systems the teacher starts the discussion, focusing it firstly by means of questions (written on the blackboard, for example), and then analyzing the answers with a convincing set of operational principles, such as those suggested in B.4. The theoretical background can be initially acquired by reading the elementary treatments given by Ashby (*op. cit.*), Raisbeck [7], and Quastler [8], and consulting directly the great authors through the diverse readings which have appeared, such as those edited by Singh [9], Emery [10], and Beishon and Peters [11].

B.3 Questions for students
How do you define the inside of each box? What did you do (inputs) in order to know the inside of the box? What results (outputs) did you get? Why did you select those sets of inputs and outputs? What are your conclusions about the inside of each box?

B.4 Guide to discussion (for teachers)
It is very important to get precise information of any system studied, but first it is necessary to state precisely what one is looking for (to make this statement clear is the intention of the first question of the previous paragraph). Nobody engaged in real practice of scientific research asks how does a rat's brain function, or *why* is there a reaction going on inside a test tube. Scientists make *operational questions*, for example: What is the relationship between increment of temperature and reaction rate (expressed in millimols of product/min) of the reaction $H_2 + I_2 \rightarrow 2HI$? What is the dependence of the extent of experimental cerebral lesions (grams of tissue removed) on the number of errors made during the 'solution' of a given maze by laboratory rats?

At this time it is pertinent to invite the students to represent systems by squares (or points, or circles) and inputs and outputs by arrows. It must be clearly explained that what is to be considered as a system in a particular situation is entirely arbitrary, and so is the extension of the system (the entire circuit, including a meter and the a.c. source, or only the rectifier section, for example).

The advantages and disadvantages of enclosing a very large system conceptually in a box must be discussed. An exceedingly large system, an ecological community, for example, will not permit a knowledge of the individuals, but will reflect the behavior of a group of species coexisting in a certain environment. This is not trivial, as some hypothetical situations can show, as when a zoologist studying the emigration of wild geese attempts to explain the phenomenon completely by invoking only the synaptical processes taking place inside the brains of individuals.

Next comes the discussion about the selection of inputs and outputs, and the quantifying of the variables involved. This is an easy task in the case of physical and chemical systems, but it is very difficult when we are considering behavioral responses because frequently the system is the entire individual, and because of this fact it is very difficult to separate one behavioral action from others (Calhoun [12]). It is very likely that the students could adequately design their observations in such a way that they can overcome those difficulties; however, the teacher must be prepared to point out the behavioral studies that can be appropriately made by students at this level.

The rectifier circuit provides an opportunity to explore in detail different parts (subsystems) of a system. Obviously in this case, the more familiar the students are with elementary a.c. circuits the easier the solution, but the important thing is that previous information makes the black box less black; it is a system partially known, a "gray box" (Negrete [13]). On the other side, the switching circuit (a system with discrete states) offers a very interesting situation: the behavior of a black box cannot be specified by just one possible configuration (Fig. 3) but by many (Which one is to be selected? Tell the students about Occam's razor). Discussion of this relevant point must be conducted in such a way that students comprehend that this situation is related intimately with the existence of alternative hypotheses to explain a phenomenon, a situation not uncommon in science.

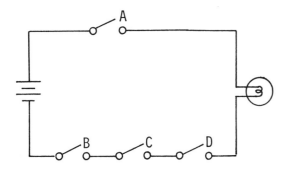

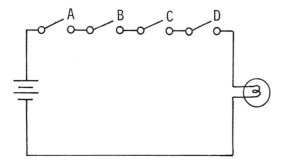

Fig. 3 Two possible switching circuits whose behavior (A.B.C.D. → ON) is indistinguishable for the circuit shown in Fig. 2

Finally, the chemical system probably will be more easy to understand (the input is known and it will not be very difficult to show that the output is CO_2, so inside the box surely there is a carbonate), but in this case the interesting thing is to see if students try to obtain a simple quantitative relationship, v.gr. reaction rate versus quantity of HCl added. But this can become slow or invalid if the volume of hydrochloric acid is large, or the quantity of the other reactant (carbonate) is much reduced; also the measurement of gas produced must be carefully made.

Other "systemic experiments" used with good results by us are: fatigue of human muscles; model of beans and board to simulate population growth— as described by Bojórquez and Galván [14]—recodification of learning using an Edwards' maze (Edwards [15]); electromechanical automata; and so on.

C. Systems analysis and scientific methods

Now all the previous results and concepts obtained and developed in various sessions of practical work and discussions must be combined in a discussion in order to identify a set of elementary operations of experimental methods based on black-box concepts, and to establish a coherent picture of the scientist's work. The next guidelines indicate and develop the main themes to be discussed.

C.1 Working hypothesis

In any experimental situation it is necessary to specify what is to be measured, what actions will be executed upon the system and, mostly, what the investigator wants to know about the system. By means of systems analysis it is possible to state clearly the condition given by the experimental design. The working hypothesis in the form "if ..., then ..." can be reduced to stating after the word *if* the inputs to the system, and after the word *then* the expected outputs. The specifications of the system are equivalent to stating the box and its environment (including the investigator and its instrumental equipment).

Although it seems that scientific study in most instances can be conceived as an analytical strategy to know what is inside a black box, there exist two other alternatives, but they are less frequent: *a*) to know what *was* the input, given the internal states and output; and *b*) to predict what will be the output, given certain input and the internal states (Grodins [16]).

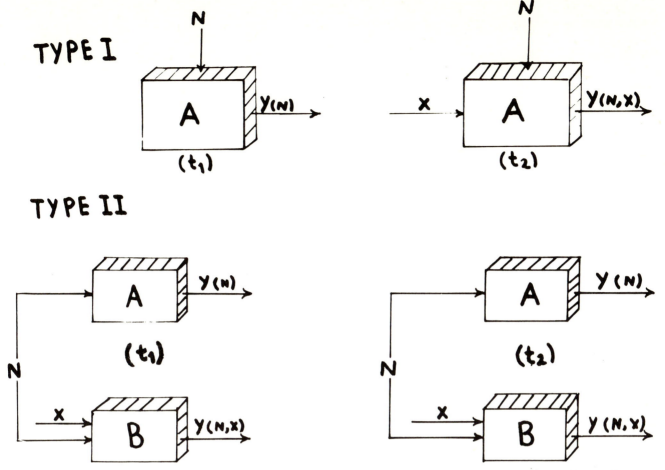

TYPE I

TYPE II

Fig. 4 Two general types of experimental control. In type I the system is compared with itself, first (time t_1) observing its output when it has received noise (N) from the environment as an input, and second (time t_2) observing the output generated when the inputs are the noise and the selected controlled experimental variables (X). In type II two very similar systems (two individuals of a biological species, for example) are observed simultaneously, in the same environment which generates N, and their outputs are compared for two different times.

C.2 Experimental design: controls

Scientists normally work with systems whose inputs are known and ideally they can control all of them, with the possibility of varying one input in a specified pattern. They sometimes take considerable pains to ensure that no other relevant variables can be considered as parameters, but this situation is very difficult to obtain. The old solution can be represented with boxes and arrows. In Fig. 4 are illustrated two kinds of experimental control devised by scientists to overcome the difficulty posed by extraneous environmental and/or internal variables that can give contributions to the output.

Scientists look continuously for outputs uncontaminated by *noise* (this concept is used in class with some liberality; the student is asked to be cautious because its meaning is well specified in Information Theory). Very frequently the kind of systems studied, and practical and economical factors (time, cost, etc.) make it impossible to eliminate noise, and the work of extracting information difficult.

C.3 Protocols and graphical representation

The properties of the system can be deduced from the relationship of inputs and outputs. The procedure consists in elaborating a list or table which contains the succession in time of different states (vector input-output) of the system. This table, known as *protocol* is essential to the student's report or scientist's notes. Careful analysis of protocol searching for regularities reveals basic characteristics of a system. It can happen that its behavior be determined, or probabilistic; this distinction is extremely important (Ashby [17]).

Very often a system produces quantifiable responses so that it can be represented graphically, but very often also, one desires an analytic expression (an equation) to describe more briefly the behavior

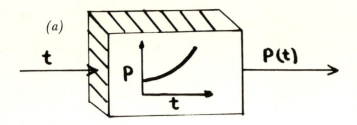

(a)

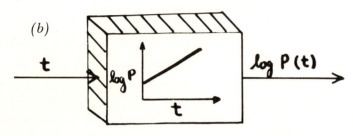

(b)

Fig. 5 Population growth and representative graphics for a very simple case. Assuming an exponential function $P(t) = P_0 e^{kt}$, valid for a certain interval of time t, recording of output, as indicated in (b) is a method for calculating parameter k.

of the system and make reasonable predictions (extrapolations). These mechanisms are shown with a very simple example in Fig. 5. Note that a box can "contain" a graph or an equation representing the content of the black box. It must be discussed that of course this is not the unique content, but for the ends of a particular observation there is no more to look for.

C.4 Statistical analysis and modeling

Again, these very important aspects of scientific inquiry can be presented in a simple, but essentially correct block diagram (see Figs 6 and 7).

In our courses the pupils are continuously encouraged to develop simple theoretical and/or physical models; some of them employ their time in the design and construction of apparatus for school research projects. These activities are motivated to a great extent by previous work, and as we believe, by a greater confidence in their knowledge and skills obtained through the familiarity with the point of view of systems analysis. The students of biology and physics can easily understand what each other is talking about when they discuss problems on design and analysis of models; this has been one of the most promising results we have obtained, and

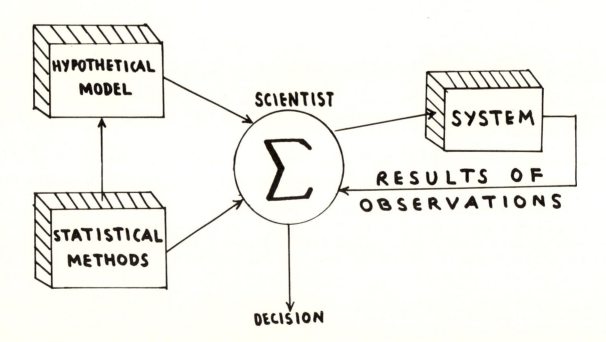

Fig. 6 Block diagram illustrating the role played by statistics as a source of theoretical models, and the scientist as a comparator between the results predicted by the model and actual results obtained when the real system is observed under given conditions

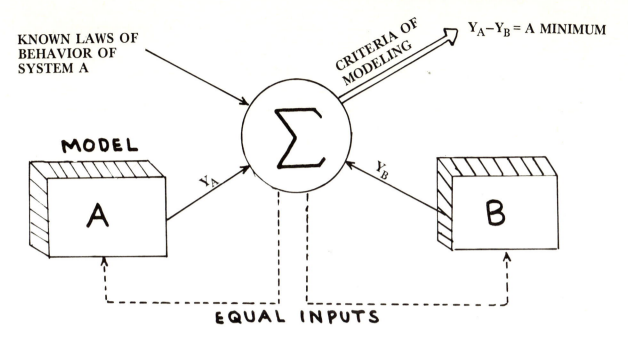

Fig. 7 Modeling can be stated as a comparison between outputs of a prototype system (model) and a real system. To select the best model a scientist takes some laws as a theoretical basis or frame of reference. System A is more effective as a model of B if the differences between its outputs and those of B are below a given maximum.

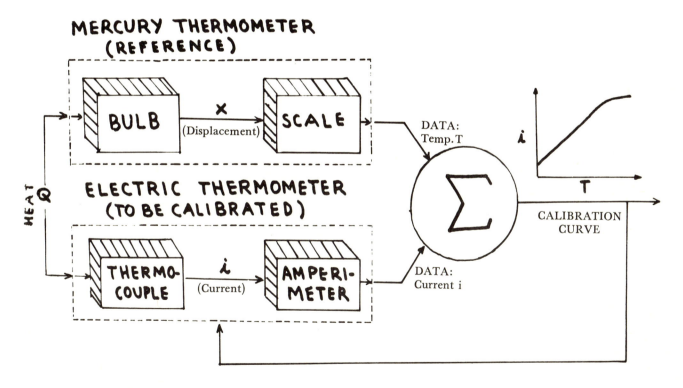

Fig. 8 Calibration of an electric thermometer as an example of determination of unknown characteristics of designed systems. The role played by the observer as a comparator is shown, as well as its relevant output in this context: a calibration curve.

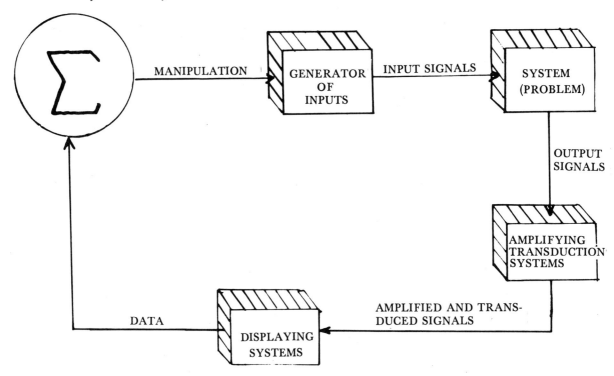

Fig. 9 Elemental relations between the observer and the most common systems involved in a modern ordinary experiment. Actually the interactions are much more elaborate including complex feedback circuits between the investigator, apparatus, and problem (system) studied.

this can be a starting point for integrating introductory courses on scientific themes at a university level.

A final comment

Is anything gained using the systems analysis approach?

Perhaps systems analysis, at this level, does not introduce anything new, but much clearer ideas can be gained about the general logical background and the framework of relationship of any well defined experiment. Our students in general have been able to develop greater precision in handling data, and they take more conciously the role played by themselves in the experimental situation, as we have been able to judge by the results obtained in personal interviews, examinations, and above all, their performance in the laboratory. The better understanding of what exactly the problem system is, its boundaries and environment, which are the variables, parameters and relations between measuring, detection, amplifying, and displaying signals systems (Figs 8 and 9), and how the researcher is related to

some of them, and finally, the clearer comprehension of the logical structure of the actions involved, all of these results are more surely attained. At least particularly we can answer yes to the opening question.

The systems analysis approach can be usefully applied in teaching science to children because of its generality and flexibility to be adopted to most situations, including the most elemental. We think this concept should be equal in importance to the concept of set of modern mathematics, and must be taught accordingly.

The systems approach could be the best solution to integrate science courses in a set of coherent principles that show the unity of science through its methods, and at the same time, that may develop the critical attitude, *l'esprit scientifique*, that must be the fundamental goal of all the science courses.

References

1. DiSTEFANO III, J.J., STUBERUD, A.R., and WILLIAMS, I.J., *Theory and Problems of Feedback and Control*, Schaum Publishing Co., New

York (1967).

2. MILHORN, H.T., *The Application of Control Theory to Physiological Systems*, W.B. Saunders, Co., Philadelphia (1966).

3. COUFFIGNAL, L. *et al.*, *La Cibernética en la Enseñanza*, Edit. Grijalbo, México (1968).

4. RAZIK, T., 'Systems Approach to Teacher Training and Curriculum Development: The Case of Developing Countries', UNESCO: International Institute for Educational Planning, Paris (1972).

5. PATTEN, B.C. (editor), *Systems Analysis and Simulation in Ecology, Vol. I*, Academic Press, New York (1971).

6. CHURCHMAN, C.W., *The Systems Approach*, Delacorte Press, New York (1968).

7. RAISBECK, G., *Information Theory. An Introduction for Scientists and Engineers*, M.I.T. Press, Boston (1964).

8. QUASTLER, H., 'Systems Analysis', *Theoretical and Mathematical Biology* (edit. by T.H. Waterman and H.J. Morowitz), Cap. VII, Blaisdell, New York (1965).

9. SINGH, J., *Great Ideas in Information Theory, Language and Cybernetics*, Dover, New York

10. EMERY, F.E. (editor), *Systems Thinking. Selected Readings*, Penguin Books Ltd., Harmondsworth, Middlesex (1969).

11. BEISHON, J. and PETERS, G. (editors), *Systems Behavior*, The Open University Press, London (1972).

12. CALHOUN, W.H., 'The observation and comparison of behavior', *Animal Behavior in Laboratory and Field* (edit. by A.W. Stokes), W.H. Freeman & Co., San Francisco (1968).

13. NEGRETE, J., 'The Role of Simulation in Biology and Medicine (Mimeographical notes)', Technische Universität, Berlin (1968).

14. BOJÓRQUEZ, L. and GALVÁN, S., 'Cómo Crecen las Poblaciones?', *Biología (Mex.)* 3(2), 163-166 (1973).

15. EDWARDS, E., *Information Transmission*, Chapman and Hall, London (1969).

16. GRODINS, F.S., *Introduction to Biological Control Systems*, Columbia University Press, New York (1963).

17. ASHBY, W.R., *An Introduction to Cybernetics*, John Wiley & Sons, New York (1965).

(1966).

CYBERNETICS IN ORGANIZATION AND MANAGEMENT
(Macro-aspects)

The scientific library – a cybernetic system

JOSEF MAYERHÖFER
Österreichische Nationalbibliothek,
Vienna, Austria

1. The scientific library as an information store

Scientific activity is nearly always based on the achievements of other scientists. Since nobody is able to know all the earlier scientific results by heart, stores of knowledge must necessarily exist, which contain the scientific literature to date by means of: books, articles in periodicals, reports, etc., that is, in the way of documents. Institutions which collect these documents, store them, and make them accessible, are called libraries. In this definition those documentation centers which actually own these documents are included.

Before we start a systematic consideration of the institution "library" we have to face an objection against the very existence of libraries. It is due to the theory of information. During the last few years the idea of information has won an overwhelming significance. In its modern form the old dream of Francis Bacon "knowledge is power" is not only a credo but also an expression of actual fact. The sciences of information, informatics and related fields have flourished. Free exchange of information is considered both a cultural and a political aim. In the end you can almost draw the conclusion: "all is information".

Technically applied information has been found to be stored easily in single elements, the so-called "bits". The great success of electronic data processing especially depends on the possibility of working up the single element of information. Referring to this, people deduced that not only can any information be split up into information elements, but also every piece of information eventually to be taken from a document can be recorded, stored and recalled equally. However, one has to consider an important difference: There are scientific facts which can be recorded in space and time and other data values, e.g., events observed, physical or chemical constants, statistical data, etc. To these, cases of law or medicine or other case work belong as well. Here we have the wide field of data documentation. The single data can be formatted principally, they can be scheduled in tables, etc.

It would be a total misjudgement of scientific activity, however, to believe that results of science principally are recorded in schedules or have to be formatted. The overwhelming majority of scientific production, i.e., monographies, articles in periodicals, reports, etc., actually contains information, but it cannot be foreseen which kind of information a potential reader would possibly deduce or take from these documents. The one reader will be interested in concrete results and hard facts, the other one in questions of methodology, a third one in problems of presentation and style, the fourth reader has in mind to study the personality of the author in comparison to other publications of the latter. It seems hopeless to anticipate all these questions by formatting the contents of the publication. Full text storing in an electronic medium will not change anything either. The complete dissolution of a book into "information elements" is a mere utopia.

It is of special importance to remember this fact, because just recently writers in the theory of information have tried to consider the difference between formatted information and all the information contained in a document a "trifle". Since nothing can be done with a document, people only work at data documentation. It has neither been proved theoretically nor demonstrated by the example of a single book, that its content of information can be totally dissolved into data.

It is the same with formatted information. If information is given formatted one can never be sure of having exhausted all the content of information. For decades, schedules of atom weight—arranged in one dimension—had been in existence, before Lothar Meyer and Mendeleev recognized that a matrix arrangement of these data—the so-called Periodic System of Elements—provided much additional information; an arrangement that finally led to the atomic theory of Niels Bohr. Besides, formatted information offers no final dissolution into ultimate elements of information.

Therefore, it is not sufficient to restrict ourselves to mere information elements in theoretical consideration; one must on the contrary have a look at the documents and their stores, the libraries. Here genuine libraries as information stores are to be understood and not the "library of the future", as it has been presented by both the science fiction and the World Exhibition of Seattle fifteen years ago. With the help of a computer-stored encyclopedia many questions and their combinations should be answered in no time. But scientific interest is not restricted to questions of a quiz "Ask me a question". A scientific book is no imperfect product of the human mind to be dissolved into data principally; on the contrary, the data taken from a book offer very imperfect aspects of a totality. A true storage of scientific results can only be achieved by physically storing the documents.

2. Contribution to systems analysis of scientific libraries up till now

Though the library belongs to the oldest institutions of mankind, it has just recently become a subject of scientific research. This is due to the fact that a library is a very complex framework which can be studied—if at all—only from an interdisciplinary point of view. But ten years ago in the international field neither the fundamental attitude nor the scientific methods, like operations research or systems analysis, were developed sufficiently for this purpose. On the one hand, the impact was due to the attempt to improve the management of libraries (it was caused by the shortage of personnel), on the other hand it can be attributed to the projects of introducing electronic data processing into libraries.

Austria was one of the first countries in which research work referring to the industrial management of libraries was done. In cooperation with an institute for industrial engineering of the Technical University of Vienna in the summer term of 1964, the first studies were done at the Austrian National Library. On the occasion of the planning of an extension of Austrian university libraries, the first concrete cybernetic problem arose in 1965: If a library should receive more funds for books, should it get additional staff as well, and how many persons?

In 1966 the Austrian Institute for Library Research was founded, which soon detected a decisive weakness in the management of large libraries: While the average working time spent for processing a book takes two hours only, the time in which the book is "in process" takes many weeks or even months. As far as we know, these circumstances are similar in all countries.

In the meantime several schools of learning have developed in different countries, which try to solve the problems of libraries with the support of modern remedies. Above all, I want to cite the University of Lancaster, Purdue University, etc. In Western Germany attempts have been made to apply the black box method to libraries.

In an article in "Zentralblatt für Bibliothekswesen 1970", for the first time a library is compared to a control system. Indeed, the manifold functions of a library are condensed into one diagram. The control is nearly exclusively orientated to the fulfilment of plans and not to the cooperation with readers. Therefore we present in this Chapter a fundamentally new kind of presentation of a scientific library's problems.

3. The scientific library—a cybernetic system

We have termed the library a store of physical documents. The documents are available to the public, i.e., they can be used but not purchased or acquired by any means. At best, one can get a copy but the original must remain in the library.

From the point of view of a systems analysis, a

library in the first place is a lending institution, otherwise almost unknown to the public. It is of no importance whether there is a lending out or whether the document has to be used in the building itself (reading room). You can buy electric current, you can rent a seat in a transportation system, but—with the possible exception of a medical installation—you cannot borrow transportable public goods except books. Sociologically, it is a very interesting fact, because it is based upon the idea that knowledge is a general public property.

The ideal organization of a library is the open shelf system. The documents are physically stored and freely available to the public, but on two conditions: 1) a strict display with which the reader has to familiarize himself; 2) the reader must be willing to look for the documents himself. Scientific libraries generally have only a part of their stock displayed on open shelves. In order to help the reader to consult books that cannot be fetched from open shelves a new device has been put in between: the library catalog. We will speak on of it later on.

Controlled conditions 1

Library vs. reader

Controlled conditions	Actual values	Set values	Correcting values	Supply values	Disturbance qualities
Book stock	"	plan readers' wishes	order	budget	out of print price increase
Seats offered	"	plan readers' wishes	building	budget	crowding in of readers
Hours of opening	"	plan readers' wishes	alteration shifting	personnel	sociological facts
Open access	"	plan readers' wishes	measures	budget personnel	theft
Time of raising books	"	minimum	organizing and technical measures	budget personnel	illness of personnel
Loan period	"	maximum	regulation	considerations	paying regard to others
Waiting period	"	minimum	regulation	considerations	paying regard to others
Processing time	"	minimum	organizing measures	systems analysis	irregular supply by book dealers
Detailed subject classification documentation	"	plan readers' wishes	order regulation	budget personnel	changing interest
Reference journals	"	plan readers' wishes	order	budget	stoppage new publications

Fig. 1 The scientific library—a cybernetic system. Controlled conditions 1

Naturally there are information desks (offices) in every library, which can be addressed, but they are not main departments, only additional offices. Thus the preliminary statement of the systems analysis is not 'institution for the conveyance of information', but 'lending institution for documents'. The information must be taken from the documents by the readers themselves.

Let us consider the management of the lending institution "library". The immediate result is a control system as follows:

The library is the control object; part of the staff is the controller: the director, the medium and the lower staff, i.e., the management as a whole. Now we get to the schedule shown in Fig. 1.

Some remarks are necessary:

a) The library when considered as a cybernetic system differs fundamentally from the static conception that was formerly used in library literature. The library, however, is *not* an institution which, after having been established, is to perform its functions in a monotonous way. As a matter of fact in a library, which is based on a certain structure, a continuous adjustment is not only possible but even necessary. The dynamic factor must not be overlooked.

b) A controller from the cybernetic point of view, i.e., the management as a whole, has two functions: receptor and effector.

In its function as a receptor it not only knows all planned set values but also continually has to get information about actual values and changes of set values. This proves the importance of an internal management information system (MIS). An important part of it will be the subject of the last section of this Chapter, the catalog. Another part of this MIS is statistics. Having been used in librarianship for many years already it often has its end only in itself. Library statistics always wait for "getting evaluated", but then they lag behind for months or even years and have little actuality. In order to offer the controller a necessary basis for action, current information should take place quickly. The appearance of a dependable internal MIS in a library in detail should be the topic of serious research. It is obvious that the statistical library values will have to be defined again in order to get more immediate evidence.

User-research doesn't end in itself, either, but it adds to the cybernetic aspect of a library, since it informs about known and unknown readers' needs.

The receptor's counterpart in a control system is the effector. The library management and the leading staff must not only be informed about actual values, but have to have the possibility of interfering with events and changing the correcting values. Possibilities of budget and personnel are to be considered. In many places the hierarchic organization of a library complicates intervention, especially when the responsibilities are delegated. Therefore, the organization of a library has to be reconsidered from the cybernetic point of view.

c) In the above schedule of Fig. 1 controlled conditions of a library are quoted as far as they are of any importance to the user. But there are other controlled conditions, that are important to the aims of a library as an institution. They contain the responsibility toward the supporter of the library. They mainly refer to costs and effectiveness. (See the schedule of Fig. 2.)

By means of these two schedules the idea of a scientific library as a cybernetic system seems to have been fundamentally proved.

4. The library catalog and its cybernetic function

Now I should like to speak about a partial problem, which—as far as I know—has not yet been treated in the literature: the library catalog as seen from the position of systems analysis and cybernetics. In previous parts of this Chapter we considered the objects of a library—the documents—as physical entities, corresponding to mental entities. It is their speciality that they all—or nearly all of them—are different from each other, that their number is very great, and that they must be traced individually. Here we have a problem of quantity. It is not a statistical one as it is with the number of seats for the readers, but it is a problem of availability of an individual book in a large number of books. Finally, the readers are individuals, too; the library has to think of them as well, but they have not to be looked for, as they simply exist.

In order to bring about a better understanding of the catalog we must begin far back. The most important means of organization when dealing with a great number of individuals is the naming. This was a religious ceremony or at least a public rite at all times. Today ships are still baptized in a public ceremony as well. Often the knowledge of the name is a strictly hidden magic secret: in a German fairy-tale a magician possesses his might only as long as nobody knows his name.

With the growing number of human beings getting in touch with one another the simple Christian name was not sufficient any longer. Additional names and

Controlled conditions 2

Library vs. supporter

Controlled conditions	Actual values	Set values	Correcting values	Supply values	Disturbance qualities
Costs: purchasing a book	"	minimum	cheaper acquisition exchange?	knowledge of the market	purchase from abroad
Costs: processing of a book	"	minimum	organizing and technical measures	analysis of management	staff difficulties
Costs: binding of a book	"	minimum	external services? own workshops?	industrial and economical knowledge	staff difficulties
Costs: reading-room attendance	"	minimum	organizing and technical measures	analysis of management	staff difficulties
Costs: books on loan	"	minimum	organizing and technical measures	analysis of management	staff difficulties
Costs: inter-library loan	"	minimum	organizing and technical measures	analysis of management	fees? replacement by photo-prints, etc.
Rate of utilization	"	maximum	public relations propaganda	services of the library	number of students change of readers' wishes, excessive charge
Effectiveness	"	maximum	motivation instruction of staff organization	systems analysis of the library	illness of staff discontinuation of funds

Fig. 2 The scientific library—a cybernetic system. Controlled conditions 2

house names were invented and used. At the beginning of modern times the surname was invented which made man's name twofold. But this was not sufficient either for clear identification. Additional data are the birthday, the names of the parents, one's profession, the status (married or single, etc.), address, and so on. All this information can be recorded in a personal identification card. These details do not convey a logical definition, e.g., by genus proximum and differentia specifica but an enumeration of ontological characteristics of an individual being.

Nowadays people try to condense all the different personal characteristics into a personal number. Thus nothing is changed principally as the personal number must necessarily be translated into the usual characteristics.

The principle of naming persons can be transmitted to the marking of commodities. In a catalog of commodities one can find the name of the producer, the name of the product, also the weight, dimensions, price, date of delivery, etc. There are abbreviations of the commodities' numbers as well, which can be seen in a catalog of an export firm.

From the time of a book's publication to the time when a user or a library buys the book, it is a commodity. As mentioned above, a book is characterized in short by the name of the author and by its title. It is not uninteresting to point to the fact that, historically seen, the title page was invented even after the invention of bookprinting had taken place. Before that time, the books were characterized by a more or less free description of the contents. As the art of printing became known more and more it was soon necessary to compare books quickly, which was guaranteed by a title page—in fact a sort of labeling.

The "bibliographic description" of a book mainly consists of the author's name and the title (a relation often compared to that of father and son). Additional characteristics are the publisher, the printer (who both have the material responsibility for the product), and the place of publication, the year, the number of pages, etc.

These characteristics are valid for each book of an edition, they denote the specific notion. Scientific quotation must contain at least the most important items of them. The library accepts them and adds indications specific to the library: the call number, additional elements of the subject catalog, because the title of the book has lost its original function; today it is only considered an element of "formal" cataloging as opposed to subject cataloging. For means of documentation you can establish a document profile (recherche profile).

Similar to the personal numbers, there are the standard book numbers. An international standard book number was invented recently (ISBN). There is also a "finger-print method" in existence which deliberately introduces elements for characterizing a book. Both methods are able to reduce the numbers of letters that are necessary for the complete description of a book from 300 or 500 down to 10. ISBN is not only apt for cataloging but it is considered an element of bibliographical description, too.

After having discussed these fundamental conditions from the point of view of systems theory, we can now distinguish two functions of a catalog:

1. It is an information system for the reader which helps him to find a certain document.
2. It is a means of decision for the library whether a book has to be purchased or not.

Let us regard these two functions in detail.

Every reader who uses a library catalog for the first time is astonished at the bulk of information contained in it. This information is mostly of no special interest for him. The supplements of the bibliographical data especially—the Christian names of the authors, the names of publishers, etc.—are very little appreciated as they hinder his work but do not in the least attract him.

These data are very important for the librarian, however, because their use grants a precise order so that a book can be looked for quickly and exactly. On the other hand, this exact order helps the librarian to decide whether a book has to be purchased; therefore, a direct consultation of the books in their stacks is not necessary. The idea is a strict avoidance of duplicates, since the funds of a library are always restricted.

For the library the catalog is part of a MIS, by which the purchasing of books with consideration of funds available can be controlled. The catalog helps to achieve a true cybernetic function. This leads us to the following reflection.

Must a catalog necessarily be identical for the reader as well as for the librarian? Or do other forms of catalog exist, forms that meet the wishes of the one or the other?

In this connection the short title catalog must be mentioned. It is sometimes used in libraries and for bibliographical work. It only contains the author, the title and the year of publication (there are even examples without the year).

With conventional production, two different catalogs are impractical. If it takes additional work to omit some elements of information, two catalogs make no sense. The invention of the unit card as a consequence of card reproduction was time-saving. However, if a computer print is used, the short title catalog brings significant advantages; it is not bulky but does not diminish the information value for the reader. In the documentation of articles in periodicals the subject aspect is more underlined, too, while other elements are omitted, e.g., the place of publication and the publisher.

Data in bibliographies, library catalogs and documentation work can be formatted. They constitute auxiliary information systems about documents and all the information contained in them, therefore they constitute as a matter of fact an information system of second order. Library information not only covers data information but also bibliographical and catalog data. But one should not forget that the scientifically relevant data cannot even be traced in the best catalogs but only in the documents themselves. For their storage, scientific libraries have been established.

Research libraries in an information system

LAURENZ STREBL
Federal Ministry of Science and Research,
Vienna, Austria

1. Human society as a learning system

1.1 The importance of science. The learning society (Die "Bildungsgesellschaft")

Science as a methodical way of consideration penetrates all fields of the society of today; its share reaches from popular education to the creation of comprehensive models and conceptions in interdisciplinary research and is always supported by a multitude of scientific results. This was made possible by the "universality and precision of research methods" as Karl Jaspers says [1].

The increase of knowledge in the formal similarity of biological and technical systems—comparable to an organic process of growth—consists of the reception, processing and discarding of useless material. The process of both systems consists of intake—digestion—assimilation—utilization. [2] During this process the function of memory is very important [3], since every evolution depends on secured and fixed knowledge.

The rôle of the library is expressed by the words of Schopenhauer, "Libraries are the paper memory of mankind" [4]. This is one of several points of view with respect to the position of the library in society.

The more training and consciousness of the tradi-

tions found, the better the strategies, the know-how and the sense of scientific research developed in a human society, the better will be its capacity and efficiency.

1.2 Knowledge as a factor of productivity

Some analyses are based not only on material factors of production (such as capital, industry, treasures of the soil, traffic, and so on) but also on immeasurable values like training, quality of work, and investments in intellectual capital [5]. Also in this connection must be considered the cultural, artistic and literary capital of a country.

The notion of a "system" as a logically ordered whole may render useful service for the elucidation of structures and the appraisal of the importance and influence of the single functions within a system [6]. Different subsystems can be imagined—the output of the one is the input of the other system—all in relation to the whole. Human society can be considered as a learning, and therefore as a developing and selfstructuring system. In this system there exists a subsystem, the necessary information system. By making use of the stored information of the past, of the guaranteed and fixed know-

Progress in Cybernetics and Systems Research, Volume 2

ledge, new information is given to the steering part of this theoretical model of human society. The library plays an important and manifold rôle in this system [7]. Society as a communication network needs some supporting capacities, e.g., the ability to write and to read [8].

Based on the theories of political economy by Adam Smith and Friedrich List, F. Machlup understands knowledge "as a product, a function of resource allocation". Parts of his concept of "production of knowledge" are for him "disclosure, dissemination, transmission and communication" [9]. The process of innovation makes the connection between science and economy. The results of research are converted into products, which are sold under economic aspects [10].

1.3 The basis of the research process

Positive evolution of a society depends on existing energy resources, the structure of the society and on information processing. This contribution has the intention of stressing the part played in this process by libraries and institutions of documentation and information.

Scientific documentation of literature, in cooperation between libraries and institutions of documentation and information, can be considered in differentiated degrees (natural sciences or humanities) as basic to every research process, on the same level as laboratories, experimental stations, and so on. The use to which documentation and information are put determines the success of scientific work.

2. The research library

2.1 Fundamental functions. Documentation and information

The complex phenomenon *library* may be seen from different points of view: for the cultural sciences the library is the institution of preservation, the trustee of the cultural heritage as far as it has found its results in printed or handwritten form.

The social sciences see in the library the sociocultural place of transformation. The "environment" of the library comprehends its social and legal structures.

The main functions of the library—storage, retrieval, dissemination—show the library as an information system, which stores data, processes them and yields them to the user. The library can be described and organized on management principles [11]. The cybernetic model of human society as a learning

system with an information system previously mentioned gives the library the special function of a data bank. The catalogs of research libraries or regional central catalogs play the part of data bases [12,13], but research libraries play also the part of a documentation system and of an information store and retrieval [14,15].

The Research Library

Data Bank	Information System
Books, Periodicals Reference works	Marketing of the library Classified arrangement Open access library
Catalogs Accessions register Bibliographies Special bibliographies	Reference activities Information on books Assistance to readers in using the library Library guides Training of users
Documentations Abstract journals Progress reviews	
Magnetic tapes	Automatic information retrieval Selected dissemination of information
Union catalogs	National and international loan

2.2 Types of library

Not only the main functions of a research library but also its belonging to a special type of library contribute to its inner structure.

Of the manifold tasks of a National Library there should be mentioned the storage of the national book production—a function which is of great importance also from the international point of view, because thus one may be certain to find a place, where the whole library production of the country —even that to be obtained with difficulty or not on sale—is kept. The output of this task are the national bibliographies, often with a supplement containing a bibliographic description of literature published abroad [16].

The system of university libraries is being reformed from a system of libraries existing side by side in an uncoordinated way into a cooperating and coordinated library network. In Central Europe there has been an uncoordinated side-by-side growth of university libraries and institute libraries since the beginning of the century. Nowadays the aim is to profit from the advantages of a more effective library system with a central administration, combined with a user service that is nearer to the research process [17].

The scientific research library for one or more disciplines is used by a smaller group of readers. In this framework the possibility of documentation, which can be used by the searcher, is given more easily.

3. The research information system

3.1 Systems of libraries. Library networks
There are many kinds of classification of possible informations systems (e.g., management information system, planning information system). The research information system [18] is described here, which has the task of supporting the research process. Not only in this system, but also in the others, the research library can and will have to play an important part. The material prerequisites are its catalogs. The electronic data processing brings new forms and possibilities [19, 14]. But also the open access in systematically ordered libraries is an offering of the services of the library.

But no single library has the possibility to answer every question and to fulfil every demand. A library network with a graduated and differentiated scope of duties will certainly raise the effectiveness of libraries.

Since the beginning of the century a systematic mutual interaid of libraries has been known: the regional and international loan service, efforts for creation of central and union catalogs, the acquisition of special scientific literature by some research libraries. These efforts resulted in the creation of library systems. The evolution is different, it seems important not to create extensive networks, but to begin with particular systems: accessing or processing or using. These systems are connected with one another. Financially seen, the creation of systems is not an economizing of means, but it brings better results for the users. The question of optimizing arises: if the system becomes too large, it is difficult to control and carry out; if it is too small, the advantages of a system would be given up.

3.2 Bibliographies, reference works
With the growth of book production the importance of bibliographical resources has increased. Bibliographies are only representatives of further information. Computer-based information services (e.g., MEDLARS, Chemical Abstracts, and so on) bring

new possibilities of bibliographic help to the scientists [20]. But the target is only attainable with cooperation between documentation and libraries. The library helps to get the book or article.

3.3 Clearing houses, sources of information
Library directories and guides to documentation and information sources are important, as they give a survey of the possibilities to retrieve the literature in different fields of research. To promote the documentation on sources of information is a real promotion of research.

4. Realizations and projects

4.1 Common enterprises of libraries, especially in Austria
The technology of modern communications (e.g., telewriter) and electronic data processing offer new possibilities for cooperation among libraries. The advantage lies in the economical centralized services. The uncoordinated side-by-side growth of library institutions called for new planning, in order to make better use of the existing facilities. Among the best known and recent examples of projects are: LIBRIS in Sweden, PICA in the Netherlands, and various projects in the Bundesrepublik Deutschland [21].

Starting from the recognition of the necessity of having central institutions, there began in the twenties and thirties of this century a series of common enterprises, in which federal libraries and libraries of other institutions in Austria took part.

4.1 Common enterprises of Austrian libraries
Some enterprises, tested over many years, give hope of a further successful completion and a continued development of the library system in Austria in connection with international library organisations.

The following common enterprises are carried out by the Austrian National Library in Vienna:
- The Foreign Accessions Catalog of Austrian Libraries ("Zuwachskatalog österreichischer Bibliotheken").
- The Union Catalog of New Foreign Periodicals and Series in Austrian Libraries ("Zentralkatalog neuer ausländischer Zeitschriften und Serien"), with some 450 participating libraries in Austria.
- Austrian and international loan.
- The International Exchange Service ("Internationale Austauschstelle").
- The Printing of Catalog Cards of the Austrian

Book Production in connection with the Austrian Bibliography ("Österreichische Zetteldrucke").
- Training courses for librarians [22].

Some common enterprises exist in the universities and between libraries in the capitals of the Bundesländer (e.g., Zentralkatalog der wissenschaftlichen Bibliotheken des Landes Oberösterreich, Zeitschriften-Zentralkatalog für Steiermark, Tiroler Zeitschriften-Zentralkatalog, and so on) [23].

4.2 Library planning, concepts, models

Under the pressure of the changes taking place in the world of learning, and in order to intensify the output of work and to enable a better planning and coordination of projects, the Council of Research Libraries attached to the Federal Ministry of Science and Research took the initiative to have worked out a "Plan for the improvement of the Austrian libraries" by Josef Mayerhöfer in 1965.

In 1971 a board was created with the purpose of being a forum, where library specialists would have the possibility of exchanging their experience and of making suggestions for improvements. This board is the "Study commission for library reform". At present the commission is working out a proposal for a reform of the library system including the improvement of the scientific documentation and information system [24].

A "Planning Centre for the Scientific Libraries" located at the Austrian National Library will form the basis of all planning activities. Its purpose will be to find out the present shortcomings, because only an exact recognition of the present shortcomings can be the basis for reform, and further to formulate new ideas.

4.3 Concept for electronic data processing in the Austrian scientific libraries

The use of modern data processing and modern communication technology, the available magnetic tapes with bibliographies offer a new dimension to library work. One of the first results of the considerations of the mentioned study commission has been a "Basic concept for electronic data processing in the Austrian research libraries" in 1972. The principal purpose of this concept is to establish a network of Austrian libraries with a coordinated acquisition, cataloging, and editing of catalogs on the basis of the manifold use of a common comprehensive data processing machine [25]. One of the presuppositions for a computer-based library network is the creation of a format for the acquisition and

storing not only of bibliographical data, but also of data relating to individual libraries, such as the code numbers of certain libraries [26].

4.4 Training of users, exploration of habits in research work

In considerations on developing information storage and retrieval systems, the user of the libraries may not remain in the background. The introduction to using the library should take the form of an introduction to reading a scientific discipline. Therefore, user research needs as well subject knowledge as methodological knowledge of the various scientific disciplines. The using of libraries varies: a historian has a different relation to the library from that of a natural scientist. The different techniques of scientific working bring different information needs and ask for a classification of users.

4.5 Professional information and training of librarians in Austria

Information is not to be underrated in the process of planning. An important function is fulfilled by the Austrian journal BIBLOS (editor's office: Austrian National Library) containing scientific essays and current news concerning all fields of librarianship. The possibility for discussion of library problems is also given in its pages.

It is important for the librarian to be open to all fields of science and to be in contact with the user. The effectiveness of the existing library capacities is greatly augmented by talks between scientists in all fields, information mediators, system analyzers in their connecting and coordinating function, and the librarians.

The modernization of the training of librarians is important; only a well trained librarian is able to maintain a functioning library system. The necessity of having efficient libraries as an important support for the development of science and research is generally recognized. Alongside the increase of the importance of libraries in the social system, grows also the responsibility of the librarians in accomplishing their task of collecting and making available the literary products.

References

1. JASPERS, Karl, *Ursprung und Ziel der Geschichte*, p. 334, Zürich (1949).
2. WEISS, Paul A., 'Knowledge, a growth process', *The Growth of Knowledge. Reading on Organization and Retrieval of Information* (edit. by Man-

fred Kochen), pp. 209-212, New York, London (1967).

3. SCHMITT, Otto H., 'Biologically structured microfields and stochastic memory models', *The Growth of Knowledge. Readings on Organization and Retrieval of Information* (edit. by Manfred Kochen), p. 216-222, New York, London (1967).

4. SCHOPENHAUER, Arthur, *Parerga und Paralipomena*, Bd. 2, p. 515, Wiesbaden (1947).

5. MILLENDORFER, Hans und GASPARI, Christof, 'Immaterielle und materielle Faktoren der Entwicklung. Ansätze zu einer allgemeinen Produktionsfunktion', *Zeitschrift für Nationalökonomie*, Jg. 31, pp. 81-120, Wien, New York (1971).

6. KLIR, George J., (editor), *Trends in General Systems Theory*, New York, etc. (1972).

7. ROESSLER, Dietrich, 'Systemtheorie und Anwendungsmöglichkeiten der Systemanalyse im Bibliothekswesen', *Verband der Bibliotheken des Landes Nordrhein-Westfahlen*, Köln. NF 22, Nr. 2, pp. 184-192 (1972).

8. MILLENDORFER, Hans und GASPARI, Christof, *Entwicklung als gesellschaftlicher Lernprozess. Ein ökonometrischer Rahmen für sozialwissenschaftliche Untersuchungen*, Wien (1970).

9. MACHLUP, Fritz, *The Production and Distribution of Knowledge in the United States* (especially pp. 5-7), Princeton, New Jersey (1962).

10. MEYER-UHLENRIED, Karl-Heinrich, 'Notwendigkeit und Möglichkeiten integrierter Informations- und Dokumentationssysteme', *Dokumentation und Information*, Hrsg. von Ernst Lutterbeck, Frankfurt/M, pp. 43-60 (1971).

11. MAYERHÖFER, Josef, 'Betriebswirtschaftliche Untersuchungen in österreichischen Bibliotheken. Aus der Tätigkeit des Österreichischen Institutes für Bibliotheksforschung, Wien', *Zentralblatt für Bibliothekswesen*, Leipzig, Jg. 82, H. 3, pp. 129-140 (1968).

12. HEYDRICH, Jürgen und WELK, Alexander, 'Zentralkataloge als Datenbanken', *Bibliotheksarbeit heute. Beiträge zur Theorie und Praxis*, Festschrift für Werner Krieg, Hrsg. von G. Lohse und G. Pflug, pp. 142-157, Frankfurt/M. (1973). (Zeitschrift für Bibliothekswesen und Bibliographie. Sonderheft 16.)

13. LUTZ, Theo und KLIMESCH, Herbert, *Die Datenbank im Informationssystem*, München, Wien (1971).

14. *Interface. Library Automation with Special Reference to Computing Activity* (edit. by C.K. Balmforth and N.S.M. Cox), Cambridge, Mass. (1971).

15. KAEGBEIN, Paul, 'Bibliotheken als spezielle Informationssysteme', *Zeitschrift für Bibliothekswesen und Bibliographie*, Jg. 20, H. 6, pp. 425-442, Frankfurt/M. (1973).

16. FIEDLER, Rudolf, 'Über Wesen und Sinn der Nationalbibliotheken', *Festschrift für Ernst Kolb*, Innsbruck (1971). (Veröffentlichungen der Universität Innsbruck. 69.) pp. 91-103.

17. *Vom Strukturwandel deutscher Hochschulbibliotheken*, Hrsg. von W. Haenisch und Cl. Köttelwesch, Frankfurt/M. (1973). (Zeitschrift für Bibliothekswesen und Bibliographie, Sonderheft 14.)

18. KUNZ, Werner und RITTEL, Horst, *Die Informationswissenschaften*, München, Wien, pp. 44-45 (1972).

19. HAYES, Robert M. and BECKER, Joseph, *Handbook of Data Processing for Libraries*, New York, etc. (1970).

20. URAY, Heinrich, 'Dokumentation mit dem Computer als Ausweg aus der Informationskrise?', *Biblos*, Wien, Jg. 22, H. 1, S. 2-17 (1973).

21. *Das Informationsbankensystem*. Vorschläge für die Planung und den Aufbau eines allgemeinen arbeitsteiligen Informationsbankensystemes für die Bundesrepublik Deutschland, Vol. 1-3, Bonn (1971).

22. *World Guide to Library Schools and Training Courses in Documentation*, Paris, UNESCO, (Austria, see p. 22) (1972).

23. *Handbuch österreichischer Bibliotheken*, Bd. 1, Bibliotheksverzeichnis, Hrsg. von der Vereinigung Österreichischer Bibliothekare, Wien (1971). (Biblos-Schriften. 62.)

24. ZESSNER-SPITZENBERG, Josef, 'Der Arbeitskreis für Bibliotheksreform beim Bundesministerium für Wissenschaft und Forschung', *Biblos*, Wien, Jg. 21, H. 3, pp. 183-197 (1972).

25. *Grundkonzept für ein österreichisches Bibliotheksnetz auf EDV-Basis*, Wien, Bundesministerium für Wissenschaft und Forschung (1972).

26. STOCK, Karl F., 'Plans for an over-all automated network for Austrian scientific libraries', *UNESCO Bulletin for Libraries*, Paris, Vol. 27, No. 5, pp. 265-277 (1973).

Das politische System der Gesellschaft

J.J. HAGEN
Universität Salzburg, Austria

1.

Gesellschaftliche Gesamtanalysen müssen nicht notwendig den Nachteil abstrakter Theorie besitzen, wenngleich diese Gefahr sozusagen permanent ist. Diese Gefahr läßt sich zum einen durch die Angabe der Konkretisierungsbedingungen weitgehend bannen, zum anderen muß sie der forschungslogischen Notwendigkeit wegen in Kauf genommen werden, praktische Fragen auf allen Stufen vom Besonderen zum Allgemeinen einer wissenschaftlichen Behadlung zuzuführen. Die Gefahr besteht ja auch nicht darin, gegen empiristische Beschränkungen des positiven Wissenschaftsbegriffs zu verstoßen, sondern die materielle Einheit und den allseitigen Zusammenhang nur noch in übereinstimmenden oder analogen Strukturen zu sehen, die historisch und gesellschaftlich bereinigt sind. Die soziologische oder politologische Verwendung kybernetischer Denkfiguren und Modelle muß darum Raum lassen für den Einsatz realer Bedingungen, die das Gesamtsystem konkret festlegen. Aber die Gefahr des Reduktionismus und der unzulässigen, weil ideologischen Beschränkung auf Strukturen besteht auch in der mechanistischen Darstellung des Verhältnisses von Struktur und Funktion. Die im gesellschaftlichen System bestehenden und gesetzmäßig wirkenden Zusammenhänge sind prinzipiell von der Art, daß sie nur in menschlichen Handlungen sich realisieren. Damit ist nicht nur der dynamische Charakter des Systems bezeichnet, sondern die zentrale Bedeutung vermittelnder Größen oder intervenierender Variablen. Die Tatsache, daß gesellschaftliche Gesetzmäßigkeiten sich nicht automatisch, sondern nur durch das Handeln wirklicher Menschen durchsetzen, ist vom historischen und dialektischen Materialismus philosophisch und grundsätzlich formuliert worden. Es liegt nun nahe, diesen Grundsatz des dialektischen Determinismus [1] systemtheoretisch nachzuformulieren und weiterzuentwickeln.

Der theoretische Einwand des Mechanismus ist dahingehend zu präzisieren, daß es der soziologischen Systemtheorie nicht gelungen ist, die Eigenart sozialer Systeme und damit die Abgrenzung gegenüber anderen Systemen herauszuarbeiten [2]. Es geht konkret um die Charakterisierung der aktiven Elemente und der Verfahrensweisen, mittels deren sie gegebene Strukturbedingungen in Handlungen transformieren. Dabei muß jedoch die Entwicklungsfähigkeit und Entwicklungsbedingtheit dieser Transformationsweise Berücksichtigung finden. Bekanntlich können objektive Situationen unbewußt, sozusagen hinter dem Rücken der betroffenen Subjekte sich durchsetzen und dann spontane Handlungsfolgen äußern, andererseits können sie aber auch nach einem bewußten und rationalen Kalkül zu Handlungsanweisungen verarbeitet werden. Daraus ergibt sich theoretisch die Forderung, makrosoziologische und systemtheoretische Aussagen im Hinblick auf die Handlungsstruktur der gesellschaftlichen Elemente zu modifizieren oder, anders ausgedrückt, die Träger der Funktionen, in denen sich gesellschaftliche Strukturen verwirklichen, in die Analyse miteinzubeziehen. Dies bedeutet, das gesellschaftliche System

Progress in Cybernetics and Systems Research, Volume 2
Copyright © 1975 by Hemisphere Publishing Corporation

als *Entscheidungssystem* aufzufassen. Dafür lassen sich Ansätze der entwickelten und organisatorisch erweiterten Entscheidungstheorie benutzen, die nicht mehr nur eine ökonomische und betriebswirtschaftliche Anwendung erlaubt, sondern als offene und nicht vollständig formalisierte Theorie allgemeinen Charakter besitzt [3]. Die Auffassung der Gesellschaft als Entscheidungssystem ist mehr als eine bloß terminologische Variation; sie impliziert eine Reihe von relevanten Folgerungen. Sie bedeutet zunächst eine Vielzahl von Aktoren, die in einem vertikal und horizontal gegliederten Verhältnis zueinander stehen. Die Überwindung spontaner und naturwüchsiger Gesellschaftsstrukturen erlaubt es, diese Gliederung selbst als Organisationsaufgabe und damit als spezielle Entscheidungsklasse aufzufassen. Auf diese Weise fließt im übrigen auf allen Ebenen das theoretische mit dem praktischen Interesse zusammen. Die Behandlung der Gesellschaft als Entscheidungssystem ist auch insofern gerechtfertigt, als die Interdependenz zwischen den Entscheidungsträgern auf eine spezifische Weise hergestellt wird. Im Gegensatz zu maschinellen Regelkreisen existiert hier kein Automatismus, der die Berücksichtigung übergeordneter Entscheidungen als Führungsgröße garantiert. Diese Interdependenz kann ebenfalls nur mit dem differenzierenden Begriffsapparat der Entscheidungstheorie erläutert werden. Es handelt sich um die Frage, wie fremde Entscheidungen zu Prämissen eigener Entscheidungen gemacht werden. Herkömmlicherweise wird diese Problem als *Legitimation* thematisiert. Gesellschaft als Entscheidungssystem heißt darüber hinaus prinzipielle Anerkennung der Rationalisierbarkeit gesellschaftlich relevanten Handelns, d.h. planmäßiger und umfassender Einsatz wissenschaftlicher Verfahren zur Objektivierung und Optimierung der Entscheidungen auf allen Ebenen, einschließlich der Möglichkeit einer wissenschaftlichen Politik. Vor allem aber enthält dieses Konzept eine Konkretisierung des dialektisch-deterministischen Grundsatzes. Die Analyse des Entscheidungsverhaltens, die in eine gesamtgesellschaftliche Theorie eingebracht werden soll, muß die wesentlichen Determinanten des Handlungstyps Entscheidung herausarbeiten und ihr gegenseitiges Verhältnis klären.

2.

Die elementare Bedeutung der Entscheidung für eine Systemtheorie der Gesellschaft als Entscheidungssystem erfordert ein näheres Eingehen auf die Elemente des Entscheidungsmodells, die zugleich den determinierten Charakter ausdrücken. Es handelt

sich dabei um Umwelt (Daten), Alternativen, Wertsystem, Entscheidungsregeln, Algorithmen und Programme bzw. Heuristiken und vor allem den Aktor (Entscheidungsträger). Die Abbildung der Umwelt und der verschiedenen Zustände, die sie unter der operativen Einwirkung des Aktors oder von sich aus annimmt, nennt man mit Gäfgen [4] das "technologische" Modell, das, auf gesellschaftliche, also interagierende Umwelten übertragen, "soziologisches" Modell genannt werden müßte. Anhand dieses technologischen bzw. soziologischen Modells der Umwelt kalkuliert der Aktor die Menge der zulässigen, d.h. der möglichen Alternativen. Aus dieser Menge muß mittels einer vollständigen und schwach transitiven Ordnung aller Alternativen, also durch eine Bewertung über den gesamten Alternativenraum, die optimale Alternative ausgewählt werden. Für die gewiß zahlreicheren Fälle, in denen der Alternativenraum nur unvollständig oder nur der Wahrscheinlichkeitsverteilung nach bekannt ist, wurden sogenannte Entscheidungsregeln entwickelt, die auch eine rationale Entscheidung unter Unsicherheit und unter Risiko erlauben sollen. Daß diese Modelle des Entscheidungsverhaltens unrealistisch sind, weil sie die Informationsverarbeitungskapazität der Entscheidungsträger bei weitem übersteigen, kann inzwischen als unbestritten gelten. Erweiterungen der Entscheidungstheorie in kognitiver und informationsverarbeitender Richtung sind aus dieser Einsicht zu erklären. Vor allem unter dem Einfluß von *Simon* [5] wurde der Schwerpunkt der Entscheidungstheorie immer mehr auf die Formulierung der Entscheidungsprämissen, der Problemdefinition, der Restriktionen auf der einen Seite und der Programme und Heuristiken auf der anderen Seite verlegt. Nicht mehr der Ansatz eines vollständigen Algorithmus figuriert hier als Problemlösung, sondern die inkrementale, heuristisch angeleitete und vom inneren Modell der Außenwelt gesteuerte Reduktion des Lösungsaufwands. Im Zentrum des Interesses steht die Frage, wie sich beschränkte Informationsverarbeitungskapazität und Komplexität von Problemen vereinbaren lassen. Es darf nicht verschwiegen werden, daß die weitere Entwicklung der Entscheidungstheorie, wie sie hier skizziert wurde, zunehmend psychologistische und behavioristische Züge annimmt, die sie für eine Explikation des Determinismusprinzips unbrauchbar machen.

Ausschlaggebend für eine geselschaftliche Verwertung des Entscheidungsbegriffs ist jedoch seine Eignung, Kriterien zur Unterscheidung der verschiedenen Aufgaben im gesellschaftlichen Gesamtprozeß anzugeben. Ein Entscheidungsbegriff, der Gesetzgebung,

Leitungstätigkeit und Konsumentenverhalten in einem Term und unterschiedslos vereinigt, wäre schlechte Abstraktion. Der elementare Charakter der Entscheidung besteht lediglich in der Homomorphie gesellschaftlicher Strukturen mit denen des kognitiven Systems. Der dialektische Zusammenhang von Gesetz, Gesellschaft und Handlung ist im Entscheidungsbegriff abstrakt ausgedrückt als Einheit deskirptiver, präskriptiver und appraisiver Elemente. Umwelt und objektive Gesetzmäßigkeiten konstituieren ein Möglichkeitsfeld, in dem der jeweilige Aktor seine Interessen optimiert. Um welche Möglichkeiten es sich handelt und welche Interessen befriedigt werden sollen, muß offen bleiben. Das ergäbe sich aus der gesellschaftlichen Charakterisierung der Entscheidungsstelle und ihrer Aufgaben. Denn die Prämissen, gleichgültig ob deskirptiver oder normativer Natur, können nicht schlicht als gegeben angenommen werden, sondern müssen systematisch abgeleitet werden. Auf diese Weise verweisen Entscheidungstheorie und gesellschaftliche Systemtheorie gegenseitig aufeinander.

3.

Daß die Eigenschaften der elementaren Einheiten das gesellschaftliche Entscheidungssystem strukturieren, bedeutet nicht, daß die Einheiten sich notwendig und automatisch zum System zusammensetzen. Vielmehr handelt es sich um eine Organisationsaufgabe, deren Bewältigung vom historischen Stand der Entscheidungsrationalität abhängt. Dieser Entwicklungsbedingtheit von Entscheidungsrationalität und Systemorganisation entspricht es, daß jeweils nur ein Teil der Kopplungen zwischen den Entscheidungseinheiten offiziell und formal organisiert ist, während der andere Teil einen naturwüchsigen und unorganisierten Zustand besitzt. Die nichtorganisierten Kopplungen funktionieren über soziologisch beschreibbare Mechanismen, wie Interaktion, Rollenerwartungen, soziale Kontrolle usw., sowie im Zeichen der warenproduzierenden bürgerlichen Gesellschaft über relativ autonome ökonomische Mechanismen, insbesondere die Warenzirkulation auf dem Markt. Diese naturwüchsigen Mechanismen besitzen nach allen Erfahrungen eine typische Instabilität und treiben die interagierenden und konkurrierenden Aktoren zu latenten oder offenen Kooperationen, aber stets beschränkt auf Teilsektoren, sodaß die soziologischen und ökonomischen Mechanismen nur auf eine andere Ebene verschoben werden. Konzentrationsbewegungen des Kapitals schränken zwar den Kreis der Aktoren ein, führen aber nicht automatisch zu rationalen Produkt-

ions- und Investitionsentscheidungen auf gesamtgesellschaftlicher Ebene. Dieser für die kapitalistische Gesellschaft charakteristische Dualismus von offiziellen und inoffiziellen, formalen und informellen, privaten und staatlichen, ökonomischen und politischen Entscheidungen legt es eigentlich nahe, nicht die Gesellschaft als Entscheidungssystem aufzufassen, sondern das Entscheidungssystem als Teilsystem der bürgerlichen Gesellschaft zu bezeichnen. Dem allgemeinen Sprachgebrauch entsprechend kann dieses isolierte Teilsystem als das politische System der Gesellschaft bezeichnet werden. Der hier benützte systemtheoretische Ansatz besitzt allerdings, wie auch die klassische Entscheidungstheorie, normativen Charakter: aus dem Entscheidungspotential, aus dem Anwachsen der Produktivkräfte werden die Organisationsformen des gesellschaftlichen Gesamtprozesses abgeleitet. Die deskriptive Aussagekraft, die davon nur analytisch zu trennen ist, bezieht sich auf die jeweiligen objektiven Prämissen praktischer Organisation, insbesondere auf die gegebenen gesellschaftlichen Verhältnisse. Die Berechtigung, strukturelle Aussagen auch gegen den gesellschaftlichen Schein zu formulieren, ergibt sich sowohl aus der formalen Gültigkeit kybernetischer Gesetze wie aus dem praktischen Anspruch von Wissenschaft als Produktivkraft.

4.

Die Bildung und die Organisation des gesellschaftlichen Entscheidungssystems ist abhängig von der Notwendigkeit, komplexe Probleme, die aus der gegenständlichen Praxis hervorgehen, zu bewältigen. Die Mittel der isolierten Entscheidung sind Faktorisation und Stufung, Umwandlung von Komplexität in sequentielle Verfahren, Reduktion von Informationen und nicht zuletzt Beschränkungen der subjektiven Rationalität. Die Aufgabe, Probleme mit beschränkter Rationalität, in einem vertretbaren Zeitaufwand und einer stochastisch bestimmten Treffsicherheit zu lösen, ist speziell Aufgabe heuristischer Entscheidungsverfahren [6]. Der Kern dieser verfahren liegt in der Problemdefinition, in der operationale und nicht-operationale, wohl-definierte und schlecht-definierte Teile vorkommen. Die Schließung dieser offenen Beschränkungen [7] und die Richtung des Suchprozesses werden von Appraisoren oder Sollwerten gesteuert, en denen jeder Schritt im Wege der Rückkopplung gemessen und bewertet wird. Dieses Strukturmuster kehrt im organisierten und gesellschaftlichen Entscheidungssystem wieder, wo Beschränkungen an Kapazität, Rationalität und Komplexität vermindert werden können. Der Entscheidungsprozeß kann ganz generell als Vorgang zunehmender Selektion vom Allgemeinen zum Besonderen beschrieben werden, wobei die allgemeinsten Schritte Vorentscheidungen für die nachgeordneten darstellen. Dementsprechend sind die allgemeinsten Entscheidungen, d.h. die Entscheidungen mit der größten Lösungsextension, zugleich am wenigsten operational und benutzen die am schlechtesten definierten Kriterien. In der Entscheidungsorganisation mit ihrer Vielzahl von interdependenten Aktoren werden die einzelnen Entscheidungsschritte ausdifferenziert und auf kommunikativem Wege verbunden. Daraus ergibt sich logisch zwingend eine hierarchische Struktur des Entscheidungssystems. Die Aufgabe der Formulierung von Sollwerten, ihre Algorithmisierung zu operationalen Handlungsanweisungen und schließlich deren Realisierung bedingen im gesellschaftlichen Entscheidungssystem die Bildung getrennter Entscheidungsebenen, die herkömmlich als politische, administrative und operative Ebene bezeichnet werden. Damit ist das Entscheidungssystem strukturell charakterisiert, also ohne Rücksichtnahme auf die speziellen und historisch bedingten Verfahren und Institutionen. So ist z.B. die administrative Ebene nur durch ihr Verhältnis zu den anderen Entscheidungsebenen sowie als spezielle Entscheidungsklasse charakterisiert, es wird jedoch nicht, wie im bürgerlichen Gesetzesstaat, nach Verwaltung und Rechtsprechung unterschieden. Diese Trennung ist im übrigen auch nicht funktional zu rechtfertigen, sondern lediglich historisch als ideologisches Phänomen zu erklären. Sie dient, wie der kapitalistische Staat als Ganzes, der Verschleierung des Klassencharakters der Gesellschaft.

5.

Die Entscheidungen, die alle übrigen Ebenen präjudizieren, also die im entscheidungstheoretischen Sinn politischen Entscheidungen, beanspruchen naturgemäß das Hauptinteresse. Diese vorrangige Behandlung der eigentlich politischen Entscheidung ist auch aus anderen Gründen gerechtfertigt. Auch im Zeichen des PPBS und der allgemeinen politikwissenschaftlichen Planungsdiskussion [8] werden politische Entscheidungen, wenn nicht überhaupt als Störfaktoren, so doch dezisionistisch begriffen. Dieser pejorative Begriff des Politischen bedeutet entscheidungstheoretisch die Eliminierung des Wertsystems oder, anders ausgedrückt, er impliziert die These, daß Rationalität und Wissenschaftlichkeit sich im Entscheidungssystem ausschließlich auf das technologi-

sche Instrumentarium des Aktors beziehen. Nachdem politische Entscheidungen nach ihrer systematischen Stellung in der hierarchischen Gliederung die Formulierung von Sollwerten bezwecken, erlaubt diese These keine systematische Ableitung der normativen Prämissen in gesellschaftlichen Entscheidungen. Angenommene oder, genauer gesagt, gesetzte Zielkriterien sind zwar im Modell als Variable mit der administrativen und operativen Ebene durch Rückkopplungen verbunden, aber die daraus abgeleiteten Erfahrungen der politischen Instanzen führen, abgesehen von minimalen Spielräumen, nicht zu neuen Zielfunktionen, sondern lediglich zur Wahl neuer Technologien. Tatsächlich können Zielfunktionen kybernetisch nicht abgeleitet werden, weil die Rückkopplungen negativen, d.h. stabilitätserhaltenden Charakter haben. Im Regelkreisschema werden gegebene Zielkriterien stets vorausgesetzt, die im Sinne der Effektivität der dadurch ausgewählten Maßnahmen auch die Rückkopplung steuern. Daraus ergibt sich der zwingende Schluß, daß auch politische Entscheidungen als echte Entscheidungen aufzufassen sind, also nicht nur als prinzipiell nicht rationalisierbare Metaentscheidungen für andere, administrative und operative Prozesse. Es hat ganz den Anschein, als müßte gesellschaftliche Systemtheorie als Strukturwissenschaft hier an ihre Grenzen stoßen. Aber das trifft nur dann zu, wenn man gesellschaftliche Strukturen unter Ausschluß der materiellen Bedingungen definiert. Wenn dagegen die Struktur der Gesellschaft mit ihren Produktions- und Reproduktionsformen gleichgesetzt wird, lassen sich auch die Zielfunktionen des Entscheidungssystems ableiten. Allerdings muß dann die konvergenztheoretische Perspektive aufgegeben werden, die vom historisch bestimmten Charakter der Gesellschaft abstrahiert.

6.

Die Ableitung politischer Zielfunktionen muß im Kapitalismus mit dem nur sektoral organisierten und im übrigen inoffiziellen Charakter der Gesellschaft rechnen. Trotzdem kann insoweit von einem kapitalistischen System gesprochen werden, als der als Staat institutionalisierte politische Bereich Funktionen des nicht-staatlichen Bereichs erfüllt. Diese Funktionen, die in Entscheidungen konkretisiert werden, erscheinen mehrfach vermittelt im politischen Wertsystem auf: einmal durch die Klassenverhältnisse, zum andern durch den optisch getrennten Staat und die besondere Kategorie von Menschen, die die "öffentliche Gewalt" verkörpern. Die kapitalistische Warenproduktion reproduziert durch ihren Grundwiderspruch

—gesellschaftliche Produktion und private Aneignung —zugleich die gesellschaftlichen Klassen, solange die konstitutiven Voraussetzungen gegeben sind. Die allgemeinen Funktionen des Staates bestehen danach in der Aufrechterhaltung der Reproduktionsbedingungen der kapitalistischen Gesellschaft, nämlich der "freien" Lohnarbeit und des Privateigentums an Produktionsmitteln. Die allgemeinen Funktionen der Aufrechterhaltung der kapitalistischen Reproduktionsbedingungen spiegeln sich in den ausdifferenzierten Gebieten staatlicher Kompetenzen in verschiedenen politischen Formen wieder. Das vielschichtige Problem der Vermittlung ökonomisch bestimmter gesellschaftlicher Verhältnisse in Inhalt und Form politischer Entscheidungen ist Thema der politischen Theorie und der politischen Soziologie, in der der Machtprozeß, die Bildung politischer Eliten, ihre Legitimation usw. analysiert werden. Die systemtheoretische Betrachtungsweise bietet den Vorteil, von diesem Personalismus abstrahieren und das Wesentliche im Zusammenhang von Produktion, gesellschaftlichen Verhältnissen und Politik herausarbeiten zu können. Die strukturelle Bedeutung der Produktion ergibt sich im kapitalistischen System gerade aus ihrer relativen Autonomie. Aber dieser automatisierte Prozeß verfügt über keine ausreichenden kompensatorischen Rückkopplungen, die über eine beliebig lang gewählte Zeitstrecke selbsttätig Störungen abfangen und Stabilität garantieren könnten. Diese Störungen sind größtenteils endogener und systemimmanenter Natur. Sie ergeben sich aus der Schwierigkeit, Aktoren als aktive Elemente in einen ökonomischen Automatismus zu integrieren, der ihren spezifischen Eigenschaften als unmittelbare Produzenten widerspricht. Für die Koppelung von Lohnarbeit und Kapital existiert keine krisensichere Regelungsautomatik, die ein störungsfreies Funktionieren auf ökonomischer Ebene garantiert. Der ökonomisch gesteuerte Prozeß von Produktion und Reproduktion verlangt darum nach einem außerökonomischen marginalen Mechanismus, der spezielle Bestandssicherungs- und Stabilitätserhaltungsaufgaben wahrnimmt [9]. Die allgemein mit Aufrechterhaltung der Reproduktionsbedingungen umschriebene Funktion staatlicher Politik bedeutet somit Abfangen von Störungen und Bewältigung von Krisen im kapitalistischen System.

Da diese ökonomisch bestimmten Funktionen sich im politischen Entscheidungsprozeß nicht automatisch durchsetzen, bedarf der systemtheoretische Ansatz einer entscheidungstheoretischen Ergänzung. Dabei müssen ebenfalls spezielle Formen der Vermittlung wie Pressure Groups, Parteien, Parlament-

arismus sowie normative Verfahren und konstitutionelle Eigenarten außer Betracht bleiben. Die strukturierende Wirkung des ökonomischen Prozesses ist entscheidungstheoretisch als eine Menge von Restriktionen zu erfassen, denen zugelassene Entscheidungsvarianten zu genügen haben. Wegen des in hohem Maße schlecht-definierten Charakters der restringierenden Zielfunktionen besitzen die politischen Instanzen in der Regel einen mehr oder minder großen Interpretationsspielraum, der entsprechend der personellen Repräsentation und den taktischen Erfordernissen der Tagespolitik ausgefüllt wird. Der oft betonte opportunistische Charakter bürgerlicher Parteien hat in diesem Verhältnis von gegebener Zielfunktion und taktisch variabler Interpretation seinen Grund. Die Prämissen der politischen Entscheidung, die sich aus der objektiven Situation ableiten, sind hierarchisch strukturiert und besitzen die allgemeinen Zielfunktionen als Patriarchen. Die Determiniertheit politischer Entscheidungen stellt sich somit als komplexes multistabiles System dar, in dem die ökonomischen Strukturen nur im Wege einer Reihe von relative autonomen Prozessen politische Funktionen hervorbringen.

7.

Eine systemtheoretische und entscheidungstheoretisch verfeinerte Konzeption der Gesellschaft, die von den Produktionsverhältnissen als deren Strukturen ausgeht, besitzt einen normativen und praktischen Sinn. Denn in dieser Darstellung können die Appraisoren und Präskriptoren, die zusammen mit den technologischen Informationen die Entscheidungsprämissen bilden, nicht eliminiert werden. Unter kapitalistischen Verhältnissen aber sind die ökonomischen Strukturen, obwohl sie die gesellschaftliche Organisation determinieren, nicht als Entscheidungsaufgabe zugelassen; sie bestimmen damit nicht nur die Grenzen des Entscheidungssystems, sondern auch der möglichen Entscheidungsrationalität. Dagegen ist das Entscheidungssystem des demokratischen Zentralismus [10] so strukturiert, daß der ökonomische Bereich seinem vollen Umfang nach Gegenstand bewußter Entscheidung und Organisation wird. Es besitzt damit ein ungleich höheres Maß an Rationalität. Während bei beibehaltener Autonomie der Warenproduktion ökonomische Kriterien nur auf unkontrollierte Weise in den politischen Entscheidungsprozeß einfließen, können sie hier im Wege eines wissenschaftlichen Verfahrens in politische Handlungsanweisungen transformiert werden. Damit wird eine rationale Entscheidung auch auf politischer Ebene möglich.

Fußnoten

1. HÖRZ, H., 'Der dialektische Determinismus in Natur und Gesellschaft', Berlin/DDR (1971).
2. Vgl. MEURER, B., 'Kritische Bemerkungen zur Systemtheorie. Das Beispiel Niklas Luhmann', in: Das Argument, Jg.15, H.11/12 (1973).
3. Vgl. HIRSCH, W., 'Entscheidungsprozesse', Bd.I: 'Verhaltenswissenschaftliche Ansätze der Entscheidungstheorie', Wiesbaden (1970).
4. GÄFGEN, G., 'Theorie der wirtschaftlichen Entscheidung. Untersuchungen zur Logik und ökonomischen Bedeutung des rationalen Handelns', Tübingen (1968).
5. SIMON, H.A., 'Models of Man', New York—London (1957).
6. Vgl. KLEIN, H.K., 'Heuristische Entscheidungsmodelle. Neue Techniken des Programmierens und Entscheidens für das Management', Wiesbaden (1971).
7. REITMAN, W.R., 'Heuristic Decision Procedures, Open Constraints and the Structure of Ill-Defined Problems', in: 'Human Judgements and Optimality' (Edit. by M.W. Shelly and G.L. Bryan), New York—London—Sydney (1964).
8. Vgl. NASCHOLD, F./VÄTH, W. (Hrsg.), 'Politische Planungssysteme', Opladen (1973).
9. Vgl. NARR, W.-D./NASCHOLD, F., 'Theorie der Demokratie', Einführung in die moderne politische Theorie, Bd.III, Stuttgart (1971).
10. Vgl. KLAUS, G., 'Kybernetik und Gesellschaft', Berlin/DDR (1973).

Abstract

The political system of society
J.J. Hagen

The Chapter studies the problems of collective social analysis with discussion of the use of models together with advantages and disadvantages.

Formulation and development is made in systematic theory of the basis of dialectic determinism.

The authors develop the concept of society as a decisive system and the implications of this: agents in vertical and horizontal relation to one another.

Included is discussion of the elements of decision (decisive system, environment—data, alternatives, algorithms, the decision maker, etc.). The 'technological' model and the 'sociological model' are described.

Feedback mechanism between mezzoeconomic structure and micro- and macroeconomic interests

Professor ŽIVKO K. KOSTIĆ
University of Belgrade, Yugoslavia

Mezzoeconomic structure

Every organizational system of people and material resources with an economic goal is a specific economic structure, the mezzoeconomy, bounded by its specific goals from the macroeconomy (social economy) and from the microeconomy (economy of individuals) which are integrated in the mezzoeconomy or are outside it [1].

The mezzoeconomy, by its functioning within its macroeconomic environment, influences the state of the macro- and microeconomies and causes changes in them, being subject itself to influences of the macro- and microeconomies which manifest themselves in changes of the state of the mezzoeconomy.

The complex of states and changes of states in the macro-, mezzo-, and microeconomies and their mutual effects make up the global social economy.

All these effects have their repercussions in the mezzoeconomic structure.

The mezzoeconomic structure, as an organizational system, is made up of its subsystems: the human (the working collectivity of the enterprise), the material and the financial subsystems. In the first, three further subsystems are acting: the executive function, the function of management, and the function of administration [2]. In the second, the following ones are differentiated: the technical-technological subsystem (working resources, equipment, and technological proceedings), the subsystem of material supplies (raw materials, parts, commodities in stock). The third consists of: the allocated financial resources, expenses and income. (See Scheme 1.)

All these subsystems, by their functioning in the mezzoeconomic structure, make it possible for the mezzoeconomy, as an organizational system, to perform its function in the process of social reproduction, thereby providing for the macro- and microeconomic interests and simultaneously realizing its own mezzoeconomic interests. Each disturbance in the functioning of any subsystem gives as a consequence a certain degree of disorganization in the mezzoeconomic system, entropy of that system and reduction of the economic quality of the results of functioning of the mezzoeconomy in the process of social reproduction, that is reduction of the economic quality of the exit from the system. Such a result of functioning of the mezzoeconomy affects the macro- and microeconomic interests, this being reversibly reflected both in the mezzoeconomy and

Progress in Cybernetics and Systems Research, Volume 2

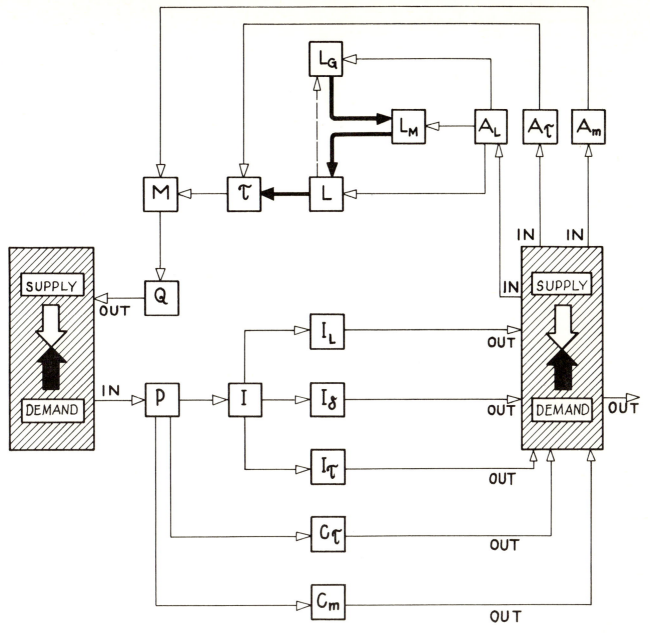

Scheme 1 Mezzoeconomic structure.
L—work, working collectivity; L_E—executive functions; L_G—executive subsystem; L_M—managers; τ—technical and technological subsystem; M—materials; Q—quantity and quality of products; P—prices; I—income; I_L—personal income; I_δ—contributions to society from the income; I_τ—accumulation; C_T—amortization expenses; C_M—expenses of material; A—resources engaged for reproduction

its structure [3].

Macroeconomic interests in the mezzoeconomy
The basic goal of the macroeconomy as an economic system appears in the final analysis as the satisfaction of social and individual needs, this being provided by the functioning of the mezzoeconomy in the process of social reproduction and the physical product as the result of such functioning.

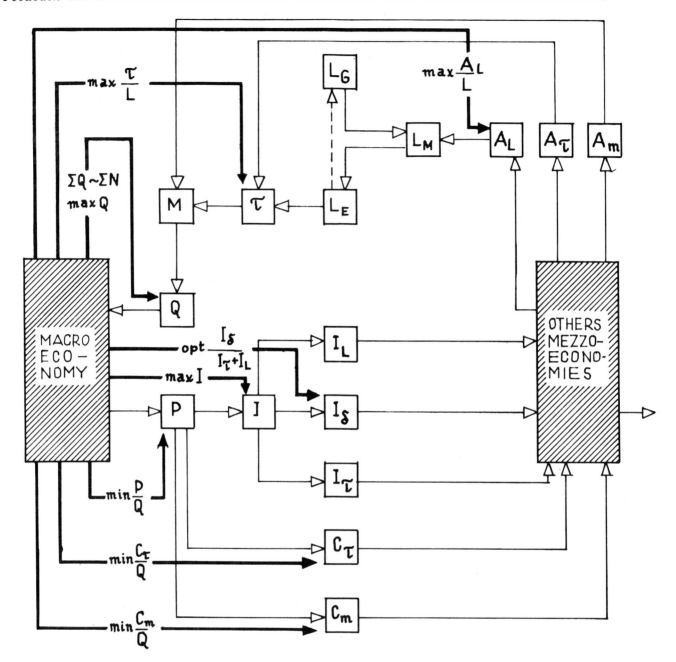

Scheme 2 Macroeconomic interests in the mezzoeconomy

A series of macroeconomic interests in the mezzo-economy and mezzoeconomic effects in the macro-economy ensue from this basic purpose of the macroeconomy and the basic relation of the macro- and mezzoeconomy (see Scheme 2):

1. Complexity of actual social needs *(N)*, namely the needs of common social consumption *(N$_\delta$)* and individual consumption *(NL)*, requires from the mezzoeconomy a corresponding production of a corresponding assortment of products *(ΣQ)*. A higher degree of congruity of the assortment of products and the social needs provides for a more adequate satisfaction of the macroeconomic interests, on the one hand, and for a higher degree of the economic quality of mezzoeconomic results, on the other hand, since it makes a higher selling price of the product *(P)* and a larger mass of income of the enterprise *(I)* possible.

2. The macroeconomy, taking into account the development of society and the growth of needs, is interested in the satisfaction also of future social needs, which thing mezzoeconomies realize through the development of their capacities and through the research and development work in the field of technique and technology (τ). The consequences in the mezzoeconomy are an increased production, changes in the structure of the product in the sense that the value of invested technical-material factors $(V_{M\tau})$ increases in relation to the value of supplied work (V_L), resulting in a reduced cost price per product unit $(\Sigma C/\Sigma Q)$ and an increase of the total mass of income.

3. Such a tendency of the dynamics of relations between the production volume and the prices is of essential interest for the macroeconomy and for the mezzoeconomy. The macroeconomy has the interest of satisfying the social needs in the mass and of constantly increasing the living standard of individuals as members of the society, and the mezzoeconomy in such dynamics of relations finds its interest in the reduction of overhead expenses per product unit and in the increase of income resulting therefrom.

4. The condition for the realization of this tendency is the constant introduction of new techniques and technology. In this activity, too, the macro- and mezzoeconomy find their interest equally, as well as all those mezzoeconomies which do not introduce the concrete new technique, provided that they are not in a competing line. The reduction of cost price in any phase on the vertical line of economic connections is in the interest of all linked mezzoeconomies.

5. Hence results the interest of the macroeconomy for the provision of accumulation (I) in the mezzoeconomies with the purpose of introducing new techniques wherein the interests of the macro- and mezzoeconomy also coincide.

6. Drawing on the income for the purpose of accumulation is conditioned by the total policy of income distribution. When distributing the income it has realized, the mezzoeconomy is faced with demands and pressures from society, which wants a part of the income (I) for its functioning. On this question, from the point of view of short-term policy, the interests of society and the mezzoeconomy are at variance, whilst from the point of view of long-term policy they can coincide, but not necessarily so. The degree of pressure from social demands against the income realized in the enterprise is reflected in the mezzoeconomy, in its functioning and its economic result, and through that in the macro-

economy. Hence macro-, mezzo-, and microeconomic optima are necessarily required in the relations of income distribution $(I = I_\tau + I_\delta + I_L)$.

7. The economic quality of the mezzoeconomic results (E_{per}), expressed by the degree of satisfaction of the principle of productivity (P), economic efficiency (E), and profitability (R) is equally in the interest of the macro- and mezzoeconomy. The economic result of the functioning of the mezzoeconomy in the process of social reproduction, in market conditions, as a rule consists in part of the new value which, in the form of income, has flowed, in the primary distribution, from some mezzoeconomies to others. The macroeconomy is indifferent to the concrete cases of such overflowing, but it is interested that the overflowing in principle takes place as a result of a higher level of business running, because it appears as the incentive for the uplifting of the level of organization and thereby of the economic quality of the results of all the mezzoeconomies.

Microeconomic interests in the mezzoeconomy

The microeconomies interested in the mezzoeconomy and in its economic result are the microeconomies in the mezzoeconomy, integrated in it, where they appear as its subsystems, and the microeconomies outside it.

The basis of the interest of the microeconomies in the economic level of the mezzoeconomy is to be found in the fact that through the functioning of the mezzoeconomy in the process of social reproduction the satisfaction of the requirements for life of people is made possible.

From this main interest a series of interests derived therefrom and mutual effects between micro- and mezzoeconomies result (see Scheme 3):

1. The specific quality of the mezzoeconomy, created through the integration of the microeconomies in it, is reflected in its higher economic potential in relation to the sum of potentials of the isolated microeconomies, which is a characteristic of any organizational system. Consequently, the motives for integration do not lie only in the interests of the microeconomies which have integrated, but also in the interests of the mezzo- and macroeconomy. Hence there is unity of interests between the mezzoeconomy and the microeconomies integrated in it, this acting as a centripetal force in the mezzoeconomic system.

2. Nevertheless, the interests of associated microeconomies are not covered entirely by the interests

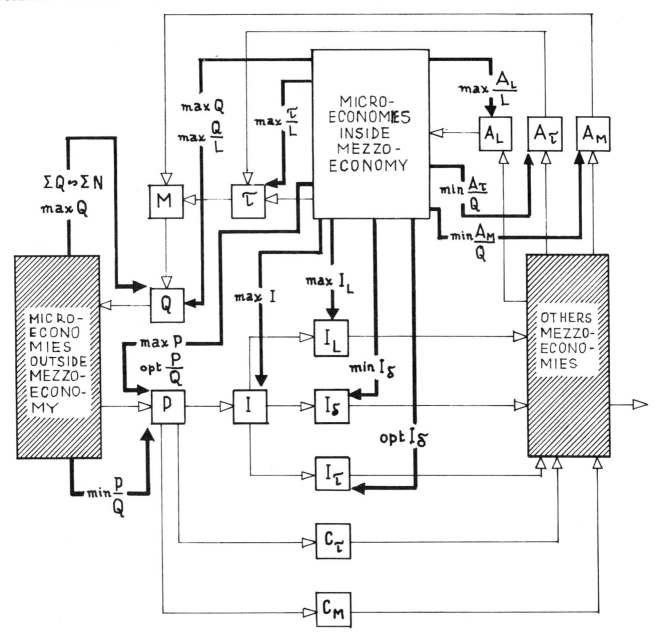

Scheme 3 Microeconomic interests in the mezzoeconomy

of the mezzoeconomy, whilst the mezzoeconomic interests go beyond the microeconomic interests. Hence, besides unity there are also interest conflicts between the mezzo- and microeconomies, which in the mezzoeconomic system act as a centrifugal force which endangers the integrity of the system. This integrity can be saved through the establishment of unity of the opposite interests.

3. As the interests of the microeconomies, integrated in the mezzoeconomy are satisfied through the results being achieved by the mezzoeconomy, the same limits are set to their satisfaction if the mezzoeconomy is to subsist and develop. In each mezzoeconomy it is necessary to establish an equilibrium of forces which act centrifugally and centripetally. The problem of this equilibrium is the key problem

of the distribution of the results achieved in the mezzoeconomy, and the problem of distribution is the essential problem of the organization of society, the problem of social conflicts of our time.

4. Hence, notwithstanding the tendency of the workers to achieve maximally possible earnings (I_L) in the enterpise as the mezzoeconomic structure, micro-, mezzo-, and macroeconomic interests are maximally satisfied only by optimum proportions of all the three basic funds (I_L, I_δ, I_τ) in the distribution of the total mass of income (I). And these proportions are conditioned by the economic principles which regulate the functioning of all the three economic structures.

5. The microeconomies outside of the mezzoeconomy are interested in the lowest possible prices of the products contrary to the microeconomies within the mezzoeconomy which are interested in the realization of the highest possible selling price of their own products.

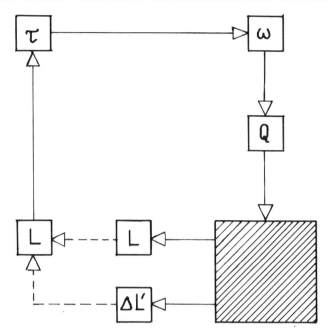

Scheme 4 Feedback of human, technical and organizational factors in the process of social reproduction.

L—necessary work invested for the realization of the process of work in the reproduction cycle; τ—technical outfit of work;i ω—level of organization; Q—product; $\Delta L'$—surplus of work deriving from the first cycle of reproduction

The feedback of the macro-, mezzo-, and microeconomic interests as a dynamic factor of mezzoeconomic structure

The complex of identical and contrary interests in the mezzoeconomic structure is regulated by business policy and organizational measures.

In order to provide equilibrium of interests and development of the mezzoeconomy, the organization and business policy must be harmonized with the principles of constitution and functioning of organizational systems and the economic principles of their business running.

The feedback mechanism of the respective identical and contrary interests is built on the economic basis of the development of the mezzoeconomy, which is made up by the organization of the working process, from which the surplus of work results, whose distribution in the expanded social reproduction has the increase of the organic component of capital as a consequence (see Scheme 4).

The sense of association of the microeconomies in the mezzoeconomy is found in the causal connection between the degree of technical division of labour and the share of the surplus of labor in the new value. The division of labor has an increase of productivity as a consequence, and the effect of this increase in the mezzoeconomic result is an increase of the surplus of labor. This effect is the stimulating factor of the dynamics of the mezzoeconomy. The uplifting of the degree of division of labor as a higher level of organization is a process which begins

in one enterprise and is accomplished by taking up the majority of enterprises. Then the productivity of the average producer is raised to a higher level, owing to which fact the economic effect of the formerly realized higher level of organization disappears, and so does its dynamizing effect in the mezzoeconomy. Nevertheless, the enterprise passes soon from this static state into a new dynamic one, if through the distribution of the surplus of work accumulated in the dynamic period it secures new investments, new technique with a higher degree of creativeness, a higher level of organization with a higher degree of technical and social division of labor (see Scheme 5).

The circle of mutual effects between the human and technical factors is thereby closed. The quantity and quality of the mezzoeconomic result according to the scheme shown grows spirally.

In the exhibited mechanism of feedback, the economic demands and economic sizes which are built into that mechanism by measures of organization and business policy act as dynamizing factors [5]:

1. In the orientation of its own activity any mezzoeconomy, if it wishes the harmonization of

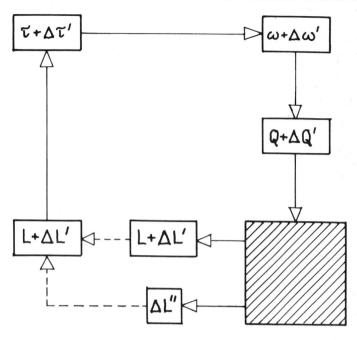

Scheme 5 Effects of feedback of human, technical, and organizational factors in the mezzoeconomic structure

its interests with those of the macroeconomy, the dynamics of its own system and the elimination of entropy, must strive through its production to contribute to the maximal possible social production and maximal possible congruity of the structure of the produced varieties and the social requirements

$$\max \sum_{i=1}^{n} Q_i \backsim \sum_{i=1}^{n} N_i$$

2. The entries necessary for the realization of the above defined purpose (Y) must aim at their possible minimum per unit of the exit from the system (X). The exits appear in the form of products (Q), value of products (V), and achieved income (I), while the entries into the system appear as work accomplished (L), cost price (C), and total average engaged financial resources circulating in the process of reproduction (A). The economic efficiency of the business running of the mezzoeconomy (E) is the function of the stated sizes

$$E = f\left(\frac{Q}{L}, \frac{V}{C}, \frac{I}{A}\right)$$

The economic goal of the business running of the mezzoeconomy is to obtain the maximal possible economic efficiency (max E), namely in the dynamics of reproduction, from the point of view of the development of the mezzoeconomy, to obtain the maximal coefficient of positive change in the economic efficiency of the mezzoeconomy (max K_e), in the new cycle of reproduction (n) as compared with the basic cycle (o)

$$K_e = \frac{\Delta E}{E_o}$$

where

$$\Delta E = \frac{Q_o}{Y_o}\left(\frac{1+K_q}{1+K_y} - 1\right)$$

wherein K_q is the coefficient of the increase of production in the nth cycle in relation to the basic cycle, wherefrom results

$$K_e = \frac{1+K_q}{1+K_y} - 1$$

3. If K_e is to tend to a maximum, the rate of technical equipping must also tend to the maximum (max K), where it is measured by the ratio between the investments which are the function of technical factors (τ) and the investments which are the function of organizational, human, factors (ω)

$$K_\tau = \frac{Y_{f(\tau)}}{Y_{f(\omega)}}$$

4. The organizational measures directed at the maximization K_τ make it possible to achieve in the mezzoeconomy in the nth period positive shiftings in the relations between the total (V), the transferred $(V_{M\tau})$ and the new value (V_L) per unit of product, which are expressed as

$$\left|\frac{V_{M\tau}}{Q}\right|_n < \left|\frac{V_{M\tau}}{Q}\right|_o$$

$$\left|\frac{V_L}{Q}\right|_n < \left|\frac{V_M}{Q}\right|_o$$

$$\left|\frac{V_{M\tau}}{V_L}\right|_n > \left|\frac{V_{M\tau}}{V_L}\right|_o$$

5. These positive moves lead to possible maximization of income (max I) in whose distribution the

optimum relations between the fund of earnings (I_L), the fund of the social seizure of income (I_δ), and the funds of accumulation for the complex reproduction (I_τ) are to be found. Since the respective coefficients, which regulate the relations of these funds and the total mass of income $(K_{IL}, K_{I\delta}, I_{I\tau})$, are sizes which limit one another

$$K_{IL} + K_{I\delta} + K_{I\tau} = 1$$

their optimal sizes have to be fixed $(\text{opt}\, K_{IL}, \text{opt}\, K_{I\delta}, \text{opt}\, K_{I\tau})$ which will have a stimulating effect on the integrated microeconomies and will make it possible to achieve the maximal total business success of the mezzoeconomy $(\max E_{per})$ [6].

6. The model of the business success of the mezzoeconomy (E_{per}) by which the degree of satisfaction of the principles of productivity (P), economic efficiency (E), and profitability (R) is expressed

$$E_{per} = (P \cdot E \cdot R)^{1/3}$$

contains all the necessary parameters in which the effects of the organizational measures aiming at the harmonization of macro-, mezzo-, and microeconomic interests are expressed

$$E_{per} = \left(R_o\, \frac{1}{1+L_{Lk}} \cdot \frac{1}{L+C_{ck}} \cdot \frac{1+K_i}{1+K_\beta} \right)^{1/3}$$

where R_o is the profitability in the basic period $R_o = I/A$ with the premise that $I = C$; A is the average sum of engaged capital $A = \sum_{i=1}^{n} a_i \cdot t_i / T_\tau$ in the technological phase of the cycle of reproduction T_τ; β is the coefficient of the engagement of capital $\beta = A/C$; $L_{Lk} = [(1+K_L)/(1+K_q)] - 1$; $C_{ck} = [(1+K_c)/(1+K_q)] - 1$; $K = [(1+K_a)/(1+K_q)] - 1$.

The metaeconomic factors of the dynamics of mezzoeconomic structure

The feedback mechanism between macro-, mezzo-, and microeconomic interests does not include also the automatism of that mechanism. Constant decisions are required from the administrative subsystem in the mezzoeconomy, through which decisions, in the sense of business policy and respective organizational measures, the economic processes are guided in the direction of the goals laid down. The goals are defined in such a way that in the field of identi-

cal macro-, mezzo-, and microeconomic interests the realization of corresponding economic maxima is aimed at, whilst in the field of conflicting interests the tendency is to find out corresponding economic optima.

The definition of these economic sizes and their insertion as criteria of economic efficiency of the functioning of the mezzoeconomy and criteria of economic quality of the results of that functioning, that is the economic quality of the exit from the system, requires constant analytic follow-up and regulative acting by the administrative subsystem which with its decisions has to influence the processes in order to put their economic effects back into the boundaries set, in case they surpass the boundaries of toleration [7].

Nevertheless, these administrative decisions are complicated by the fact that the factors of dynamics and the factors of the entropy of the mezzoeconomic system are not to be found only in the sphere of economic processes.

The mezzoeconomic structure in contemporary society is no longer only a subsystem of the macroeconomy, but also a subsystem of the total social structure.

On the other hand, the working collectivity of the contemporary enterprise no longer represents only integrated microeconomies, but also associated human personalities whose behavior is not determined by their economic interests only. Although any behavior has its economic effects, the economic effects and economic goals are not sufficient to explain the social character of individual acts.

Individual reactions cannot be separated from their social surroundings, from the social structure and its institutions, and the social structures are subject to the dialectical dynamics of society wherein, with the transition from one system to another, the laws of the economy of the enterprise also change [8].

The role which the mezzoeconomy as an organizational system receives in society is becoming more and more important, because the mezzoeconomic structure is growing to become a society in miniature, is becoming a subsystem of the aggregate social structure, which fact commits the administrative subsystem in it to much more complex and responsible decisions, which will also include the extraeconomic factors of the development of the mezzoeconomy and the more so regulate the mutual reversible relations of macro-, mezzo-, and microeconomic interests.

Notes to the text

1. See the paper at the European Meeting on Cybernetics and Systems Research, Vienna (1972): Prof. Dr. Ž.K. Kostić, 'La mésoéconomie comme soussystème de la structure macroéconomique et les critériums de son fonctionnement et de son développement (Mezzoeconomics as a subsystem of macroeconomic structure and criteria of its functioning and development)', *Advances in Cybernetics and Systems Research*, Vol. II, Transcripta Books, London (1973).

2. In the Yugoslav social system that is self-administration.

3. On the functioning of the mezzoeconomic structure, more details are in Prof.Dr. Živko K. Kostić, *Osnovi teorije mezoekonomije (Foundations of the theory of mezzoeconomy)*, pp. 280, published by Savremena administracija, Beograd (1974).

4. See Prof.Dr. Stevan Kukoleča, *Osnovi teorije organizacionih sistema (Foundations of the theory of organizational systems)*, pp. 233, published by PFV 'Oeconomica', Beograd (1972).

5. The economic sizes relevant for mezzoeconomy, the study of which is the subject of all the works in the field of enterprise economy and cost theory, are treated in an original way by Prof.Dr. Stevan Kukoleča, 'Ekonomika preduzeća (Enterprise economy)', published by 'Savremena administracija', Beograd (1974), Volume I, 8th edition, pp. 703, Volume II, 3rd edition, pp. 381.

6. The theoretical explanation of the models of total business success of enterprises has been given by Prof.Dr. Stevan Kukoleča in his book *Merenje poslovnog uspeha (Measurement of business success)*, 2nd edition, pp. 303, published by 'Savremena administracija', Beograd (1974).

7. On the organizational function of the administrative subsystems more details are in Prof.Dr. Živko K. Kostić, *Osnovi organizacije preduzeća (Foundations of the organization of enterprises)*, 12th edition, pp. 455, published by 'Savremena administracija', Beograd (1974).

8. In Yugoslavia the position of the working man in social reproduction is regulated and guaranteed by the Constitution, which proclaims that the foundation of the socialist self-administrative relations is the social-economic position of the working man in social reproduction which provides for him to work with means that are social property, to decide immediately and with equal right with the other people in associated work, to realize his personal, moral and material interest, to take advantage of the results of his work and of the acquisitions of general material and social progress. Following such a position, the workers, associating their work, form the basic organization of associated work in which they secure their microeconomic interests and through which, with an appropriate social mechanism, they act on the macroeconomy and the social structure in general, since in the basic organization of associated work the social-economic position of the working man as the foundation of socialist self-administrative relations is manifested.

Stabilization of a fluctuating simple macroeconomic model

CARL-LOUIS SANDBLOM
The University of Birmingham, UK

1. The Phillips model

In two now famous articles, A.W. Phillips [1, 2] studied the effects of feedback control policies on a simple macroeconomic model. His results were discouraging as regards the practical applicability of such feedback controls, indicating that the timing of the control was crucial. With a given lag structure of the system and the control and with given system parameters, a well established system was shown to be very sensitive to changes in the lag parameters and lag structures and could easily become unstable.

Phillips' stabilized model is extremely simple with only four equations. The first one relates aggregate production $P(t)$ to aggregate demand $D(t)$ via an exponentially distributed lag.

$$\dot{P}(t) = a(D(t) - P(t)) \tag{1}$$

Aggregate demand $D(t)$ is given by the following equation:

$$D(t) = (1-l)P(t) + D^o(t) + D_{ap}(t) \tag{2}$$

where l is the "marginal leakage" out of the system, and $D^o(t)$ is a step function defined by

$$D^o(t) = \begin{cases} 0, & t \leq 0 \\ -1, & t > 0 \end{cases}$$

and $D_{ap}(t)$ is government "actual policy" demand, used as a stabilization instrument in an effort to counter-balance the effect from $D^o(t)$, a sudden and permanent drop in demand. $D_{ap}(t)$ follows $D_{pp}(t)$ with an exponential lag

$$\dot{D}_{ap}(t) = b(D_{pp}(t) - D_{ap}(t)) \tag{3}$$

where $D_{pp}(t)$ is government "potential policy" demand, which is the intended stabilization feedback control at time t. Equation (3) represents the delay between deciding on a policy and obtaining the effects of it.

The system (1)-(3) is then closed by applying the alternative feedback controls

$$D_{pp}(t) = -f_p P(t) \tag{4'}$$

$$D_{pp}(t) = -f_p P(t) - f_i \int_0^t P(s)\,ds \tag{4''}$$

Progress in Cybernetics and Systems Research, Volume 2
Copyright © 1975 by Hemisphere Publishing Corporation

$$D_{pp}(t) = -f_p P(t) - f_i \int_0^t P(s)\,ds - f_d \dot{P}(t) \qquad (4''')$$

known as *P-*, *PI-* and *PID*-controls, respectively, and where each one, in turn, is a generalization of the previous one.

For given system parameters a, l and b (all positive), Phillips then applies the control policies (4')-(4''') using various different values for the control parameters f_p, f_i and f_d to steer the system toward the desired state $P(t) \equiv 0, \forall\, t$. The conclusion is that the best stabilization is achieved by the *PID*-control, i.e., a feedback policy with positive f_p, f_i and f_d parameters, but that the values of the parameters had to be chosen carefully, as the f_i and f_d elements of the control have a tendency to make the system unstable.

Using elementary stability theory, one can easily establish the following necessary and sufficient conditions for stability, assuming $a, b, l > 0$ and $f_p, f_i, f_d \geqslant 0$ (Sandblom [3])

$$(l + f_p)(al + b + ab f_d) > f_i$$

2. Fixed time lag control of the Phillips model

Instead of using the exponentially distributed control lag of the previous section, we shall now operate with a simple lagged feedback *P*-control

$$D_{ap}(t) = -f_p P(t - \lambda) \qquad (5')$$

where $\lambda \geqslant 0$ is the time lag constant. We shall also investigate the system behavior when the control has an error term

$$D_{ap}(t) = -f_p P(t - \lambda) + \epsilon(t) \qquad (5'')$$

where for each $t \geqslant 0$ the random variable $\epsilon(t)$ has zero mean, i.e., $E(\epsilon(t)) = 0$, and variance σ^2, i.e., $E(\epsilon^2(t)) = \sigma^2$.

Our model, then, is the system (1), (2), (5'') [as (5') can be regarded as a special case of (5'') with $\epsilon(t) \equiv 0$, we need only consider the latter variant]. From (1), (2) and (5'') we obtain

$$\dot{P}(t) = a(D^o(t) - f_p P(t - \lambda) - lP(t) + \epsilon(t)) \qquad (6)$$

We shall assume $P(t) \equiv 0$ for $-\lambda \leqslant t \leqslant 0$, and, as before,

$$D^o(t) = \begin{cases} 0, & t \leqslant 0 \\ -1, & t > 0 \end{cases}$$

For $\lambda = 0$ and $\epsilon(t) \equiv 0$ we can solve (6) to get, for $t > 0$

$$P(t) = -\frac{1}{l + f_p}(1 - e^{-a(l + f_p)t}) \qquad (7)$$

For $\lambda > 0$ and $\epsilon(t) \equiv 0$, (6) is a differential-difference equation, and although one can prove that a unique solution $P(t)$ exists, it cannot be written in a simple closed form (Bellman and Cooke [4]).

To enable an evaluation of how the system performs for different parameter values, an objective function $J(t)$ has to be defined. We take $J(t)$ to be the ratio between $R(t)$, the stabilization revenue, and $C(t)$, the stabilization cost, defined as follows:

$$R(t) = \int_0^t \min(0, P(s))\,ds - \int_0^t P^o(s)\,ds \qquad (8)$$

$$C(t) = -\int_0^t f_p P(s - \lambda)\,ds \qquad (9)$$

where $P^o(t)$ is the path of the unstabilized system (i.e., with $f_p = 0$).

$-\int_0^t P^o(s)\,ds$ measures the loss over the period $(0, t)$ of the unstabilized system; similarly $-\int_0^t \min(0, P(s))\,ds$ measures the loss of the system over the period $(0, t)$, but neglecting inflationary situations [i.e., when $P(s) > 0$].

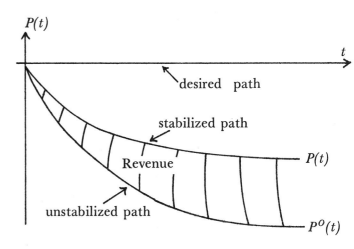

Thus we have

$$J(t) = \frac{R(t)}{C(t)} = \frac{\int_0^t \min(0, P(s))\,ds - \int_0^t P^o(s)\,ds}{-\int_0^t f_p P(s-\lambda)\,ds} \quad (10)$$

$J(t)$ can be interpreted as the return on one resource unit spent in the stabilization policy. According to (6), for a stable solution in the non-stochastic case we get $P(\infty) = -1/(l+f_p)$, from which we get

$$\lim_{t \to +\infty} J(t) = \frac{-\dfrac{1}{l+f_p} + \dfrac{1}{l}}{f_p \dfrac{1}{l+f_p}} = \frac{1}{l} \quad (11)$$

which is independent of f_p. $J(t)$ can be regarded as an average over time of a dynamic multiplier (see, e.g., Evans [5]). We shall attempt to find f_p such that $J(t)$ is maximized.

For $\lambda = 0$ and $\epsilon(t) \equiv 0$ we get the following expression for $J(t)$:

$$J(t) = -\frac{1}{f_p} + \frac{(l+f_p)^2}{f_p l^2} \frac{a l t + e^{-alt} - 1}{a(l+f_p)t + e^{-a(l+f_p)t} - 1} \quad (12)$$

From this expression we see that $J(t)$ is an increasing function of t, $\lim_{t \to +0} J(t) = 0$ and $\lim_{t \to +\infty} J(t) = 1/l$ [the last result was already obtained in (11) above].

For fixed t, we can regard $J(t)$ as a function of f_p and obtain, again for $\lambda = 0$ and $\epsilon(t) \equiv 0$

$$\lim_{f_p \to +0} J(t) = \frac{2}{l} + at - \frac{a^2 l t^2}{alt + e^{-alt} - 1}$$

We are interested in the value of $J(1)$, the return after one year. Assuming that our model describes a recession, the magnitude of which the stabilization is aimed at reducing, the choice of a one year stabilization period is natural, as empirical evidence indicates that the duration of recessions in practice is about one year (Evans [5, p. 418]).

Our model was solved on a C D 3600 computer, using a second order Taylor expansion of $P(t)$ as expressed by Eq. (6) with a step length of $1/40$; the time unit is one year. The parameters a and l were given the values 4 and $1/4$, respectively (as in Phillip's 1954 model [1]). The results for different values of f_p and λ are given below. No figure is given for the case $(f_p, \lambda) = (2, 0.5)$, which produced explosive oscillations.

Table 1   Values for $J(1)$ with $\sigma = 0$

$\lambda =$	0	0.05	0.1	0.2	0.5	
$f_p = 0.25$	1.07	1.11	1.04	0.91	0.45	
0.5	1.17	1.20	1.14	1.03	0.59	solutions below this
1	1.26	1.27	1.24	1.16	0.62	line are
2	1.34	1.36	1.35	1.41	—	oscillatory

The return figures $J(1)$ from Table 1 show the remarkable feature that for a given policy strength f_p, the best return is obtained not for a zero lag λ but for a small positive value of λ [although, of course, the larger the λ the smaller $\min_{0 \leqslant t \leqslant 1} P(t)$].

This is true also if we include the oscillatory cases, except for $(f_p, \lambda) = (2, 0.2)$. As was expected, for a given lag λ, $J(1)$ increases with f_p.

We have so far only considered the non-stochastic case and proceed to the situation where $\sigma > 0$. At each integration step in our solution of the model, $\epsilon(t)$ has been an independent observation of an approximately normally distributed random variable. The step length being $1/40$ of a year, this means that the disturbances have occurred roughly every nine days. See Appendix for details on how $\epsilon(t)$ was generated. Tables 2 and 3 below show the $J(1)$-values for $\epsilon(t) \in N(0, 0.05)$ and $\epsilon(t) \in N(0, 0.2)$, respectively.

Table 2   Values for $J(1)$ with $\sigma = 0.05$

$\lambda =$	0	0.05	0.1	0.2	0.5
$f_p = 0.25$	1.10	1.15	0.92	0.87	0.36
0.5	1.17	1.20	1.12	1.08	0.64
1	1.33	1.27	1.24	1.20	0.62
2	1.34	1.38	1.37	1.43	—

Table 3   Values for $J(1)$ with $\sigma = 0.2$

$\lambda =$	0	0.05	0.1	0.2	0.5
$f_p = 0.25$	1.10	1.38	0.50	0.78	1.00
0.5	1.17	1.28	1.00	1.21	0.91
1	1.53	1.31	1.21	1.29	0.70
2	1.29	1.41	1.42	1.47	—

Apart from the $\lambda = 0.5$ cases, which are less stable than the others, Tables 2 and 3 show very much the same behavior as Table 1, indicating that our objective function is not very sensitive to the impact of shocks in our model. Whether this is a desirable property or not can be discussed (e.g., see Barrett *et al.* [6]).

An investigation of our objective function values after four years [i.e., $J(4)$] reveals an even less error-dependent situation.

Our conclusion for optimizing the stabilization policy is that if the lag λ is given, f_p should be chosen as large as possible. If λ belongs to the set of parameters under the control of the policy-maker, the first step would be to try to obtain a λ-value of about 0.05 or 0.1.

If the policy-maker puts the additional constraint on his stabilization, that only minor policy-generated oscillations ("over-shoots" and "under-shoots") are acceptable, our material indicates that this requirement is satisfied (but only just) if $f_p \lambda \leqslant 0.2$.

The following six graphs show the path of $P(t)$ for a few combinations of f_p, λ and σ.

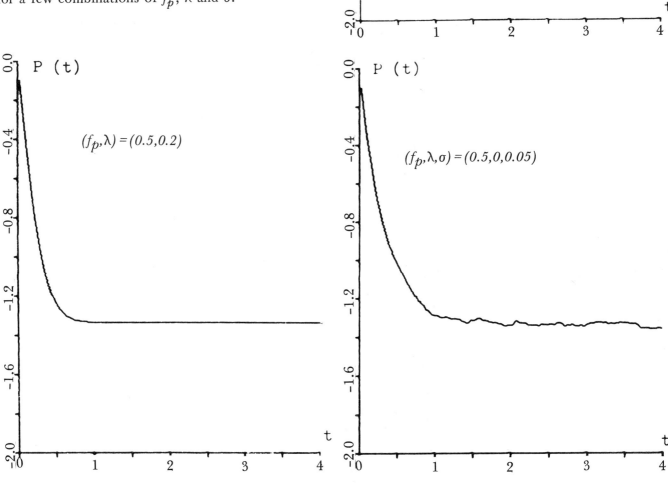

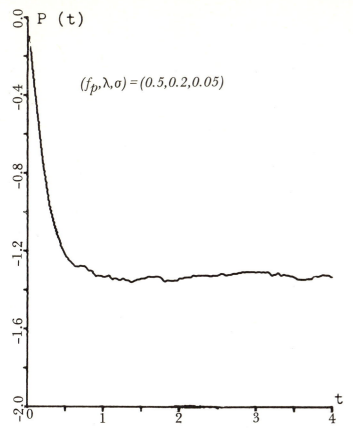

$(f_p, \lambda, \sigma) = (0.5, 0.2, 0.05)$

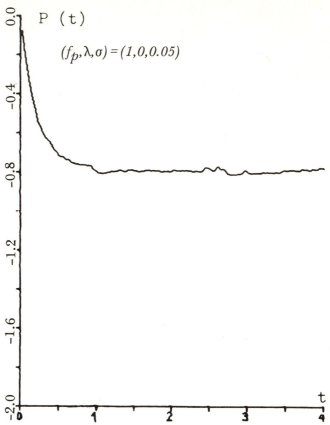

$(f_p, \lambda, \sigma) = (1, 0, 0.05)$

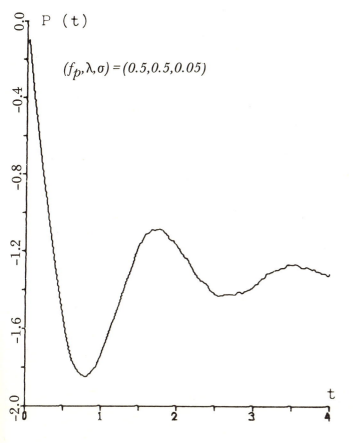

$(f_p, \lambda, \sigma) = (0.5, 0.5, 0.05)$

3. Goodwin's model

The Phillips model we have used so far is adequate for analyzing the recession part of a cycle, but cannot explain the self-oscillatory behavior which is observed in the real world. This, however, is possible with the Goodwin model (Goodwin [7]), which we briefly outline in its simplest form.

Consider a closed economy with national income $Y(t)$, consumption $C(t)$ and net investment $I(t)$

$$Y(t) = C(t) + I(t) \qquad (13)$$

$$C(t) = c_1 Y(t) + c_0 \qquad (14)$$

where $c_0 < 0$ and c_1, $0 < c_1 < 1$, are constant parameters. From (13) and (14) we obtain

$$Y(t) = \frac{1}{1-c_1} I(t) + \frac{c_0}{1-c_1} \qquad (15)$$

Furthermore, the desired capital stock $\xi(t)$ is proportional to $Y(t)$

$$\xi(t) = k Y(t) , \qquad (k \text{ constant}) \qquad (16)$$

255

The discrepancy between the desired capital stock $\xi(t)$ and the actual capital stock $K(t)$ determines net investment $I(t) = \dot{K}(t)$

$$I(t) = \begin{cases} I' > 0 & \text{if } \xi(t) \geqslant K(t) \\ I'' < 0 & \text{if } \xi(t) < K(t) \end{cases} \qquad (17)$$

It is easy to show that the model (13), (14), (16) and (17) is periodic with period

$$T = \frac{k}{1-c_1}\left(2 - \frac{I'}{I''} - \frac{I''}{I'}\right) \qquad \text{(Sandblom [3])}$$

and with the $Y(t)$-path as follows (cf. Goodwin [7, p. 5]):

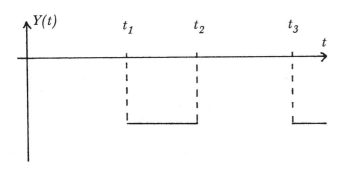

4. Stabilization of a generalized Goodwin type model

To obtain a more realistic $Y(t)$ behavior than in Section 3 [where $Y(t)$ was piecewise constant] Goodwin [7] discussed various generalizations of (17). We shall use yet another generalization, which is as follows:

$$\bar{I}(t) = \begin{cases} I' > 0 & \text{if } \xi(t) \geqslant K(t) \\ I'' < 0 & \text{if } \xi(t) < K(t) \end{cases} \qquad (18)$$

where $\bar{I}(t)$ is desired investment at time t and $\xi(t) = k\,Y(t)$ as before. Furthermore, $\bar{I}(t)$ is related to real investment $I(t)$ according to

$$I(t) = \bar{I}(t) + \beta e^{-\alpha t} \qquad (19)$$

where β and $\alpha > 0$ are constants. Each time $\bar{I}(t)$ switches, according to (18), β switches in such a way that $I(t)$ is a continuous function of time. We see that (19) implies that $\dot{I}(t) = \alpha(\bar{I}(t) - I(t))$, i.e., $I(t)$ follows $\bar{I}(t)$ with an exponential lag.

Our model consists of the equations (13), (14),

(18) and (19). $t = 0$ is assumed to be the end of a boom, $Y(0) = 0$ and $\bar{I}(t)$ switches from I' to I''. $Y(t)$ will then look like the following:

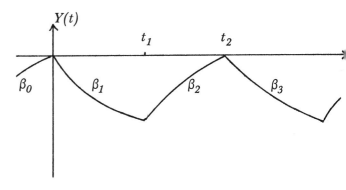

(cf. Goodwin [7, p. 14, Fig. 7]).

When simulated on a computer, this model produces periodic cycles, and we have stabilized it by adding government demand $G(t)$ to the right-hand side of Eq. (13)

$$Y(t) = C(t) + I(t) + G(t) \qquad (13')$$

where

$$G(t) = -f_p \min(0, Y(t-\lambda)) + \epsilon(t) \qquad (20)$$

(20) represents the same type of control as (5'') in Section 2 above, apart from the safeguard mechanism preventing any adverse policy during inflationary periods. The disturbance term $\epsilon(t)$ has been generated in the same way as in Section 2. Although our model could easily be further generalized according to Goodwin [7] or Thalberg [8], e.g., to obtain rounded instead of sharp corners of the $Y(t)$-trajectory, such further generalizations have not been thought worthwhile in the present context.

The model has been simulated on a Univac 1108 computer for $t = 0$ to $t = 16$, the time unit still being one year, and using an integration step length of 1/40.

Initial values have been constant boom up until $t = 0$:

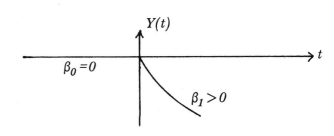

and the parameters were given the following values: $c_1 = 0.6$, $c_0 = -0.3$, $\alpha = 2$, $I' = 0.3$, $I'' = -0.5$, $k = 0.2$. With this set of parameter values, the unstabilized case $(f_p, \lambda) = (0,0)$ had a cycle period of 4.1 years and somewhat longer booms than recessions, in accordance with empirical data (see, e.g., Evans [5]). The following pages show the path of $Y(t)$ for different combinations of f_p, λ and σ.

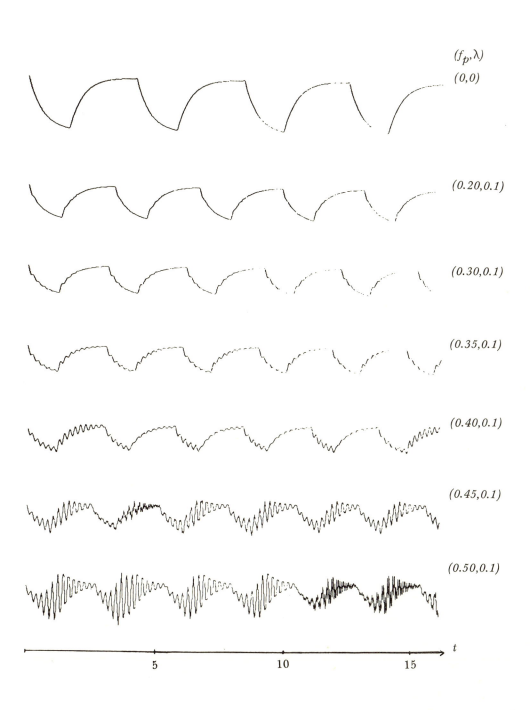

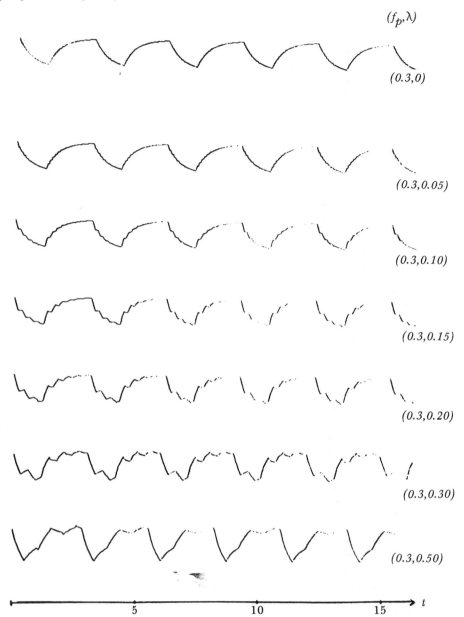

(f_p, λ)

$(0.3, 0)$

$(0.3, 0.05)$

$(0.3, 0.10)$

$(0.3, 0.15)$

$(0.3, 0.20)$

$(0.3, 0.30)$

$(0.3, 0.50)$

5. Analysis of the Goodwin type model simulations

Although our model, having a "floor" and a "ceiling", cannot explode like our Phillips model in Section 2 above, it is still possible, for $f_p > 0.4$, to obtain high-frequency "bang-bang" solutions. We see this if we combine (13'), (14) and (20) and use $c_1 = 0.6$

$$Y(t) = -\frac{f_p}{0.4} \min(0, Y(t-\lambda)) + \frac{I(t) + c_0 + \epsilon(t)}{0.4}$$

As in Section 2, we then introduce the objective function J for our system. But instead of looking at the return after one year, J has been calculated

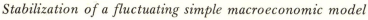

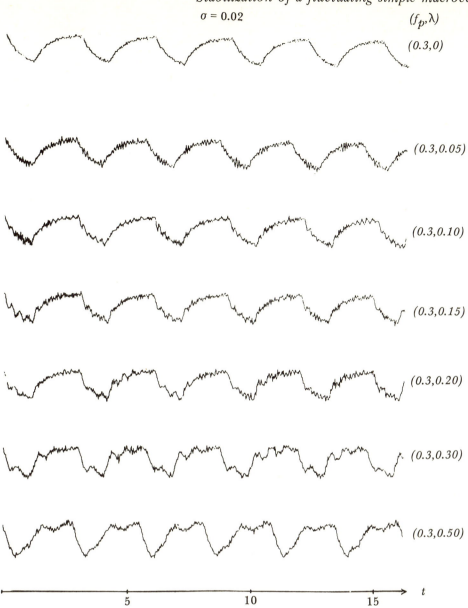

for completed cycles only. The advantage with this approach is that the return J now becomes time-independent. Table 4 gives values of J for the non-stochastic case.

Table 4   Values for J with $\sigma = 0$

$\lambda =$	0	0.025	0.05	0.1	0.2	0.5
$f_p = 0.2$	2.50	2.50	2.50	2.50	2.50	2.48
0.3	2.49	2.49	2.49	2.48	2.48	2.42
0.4	2.50	2.50	2.49	2.50	2.44	2.37

The three values in the lower right corner are smaller than the others. This was expected, as a long lag and strong policy (large λ and f_p) will cause inflation during the booms. The resulting positive $Y(t)$-values reduce some of the stabilization revenue but not the cost. The ratio, which is our return, will therefore be lower, although the difference is only about 5%, according to Table 4. If we disregard these three cases, the remaining values of Table 4 are all between 2.48 and 2.50. This constancy of the return J for different combinations of f_p and λ disqualifies J as an instrument for selecting between

259

$\sigma = 0.05$

(f_p, λ)

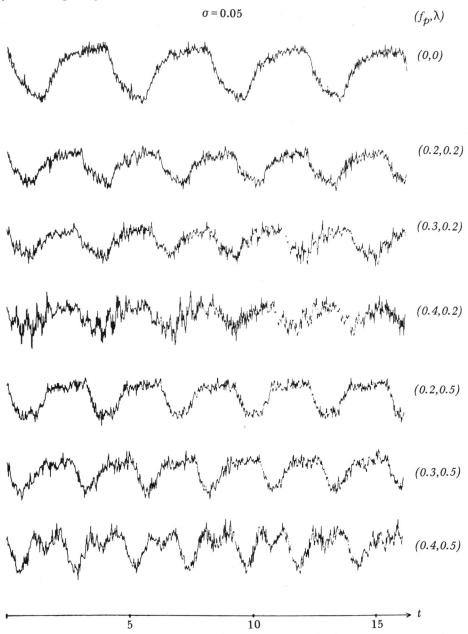

(0,0)

(0.2,0.2)

(0.3,0.2)

(0.4,0.2)

(0.2,0.5)

(0.3,0.5)

(0.4,0.5)

alternative policies. The same conclusion is valid for the stochastic case as shown by Table 5.

Table 5   Values for J with $\sigma = 0.05$

$\lambda =$	0.05	0.1	0.2	0.5
$f_p = 0.2$	2.49	2.43	2.47	2.56
0.3	2.38	2.40	2.49	2.33
0.4	2.46	2.35	2.34	2.22

As the disturbances now create inflation even for small λ and f_p, we are not surprised to find generally lower J-values than in the nonstochastic case.

Instead of using the return J we shall now see if Y_{min} can serve as a stabilization performance indicator. In the unstabilized nonstochastic case we have $Y_{min} = -1.91$.

From Table 6 we conclude that with the aim of minimizing $|Y_{min}|$, we should, for a given λ choose f_p as large as possible or, for a given f_p choose λ as

Table 6   Values for Y_{min} with $\sigma = 0$

$\lambda =$	0	0.025	0.05	0.1	0.2	0.5
$f_p = 0.2$	−1.21	−1.21	−1.22	−1.22	−1.23	−1.25
0.3	−1.02	−1.03	−1.03	−1.04	−1.07	−1.29
0.4	−0.87	−0.86	−0.91	−0.98	−1.11	−1.26

small as possible. If we do not accept high-frequency oscillations in our model, our results for the non-stochastic case indicate that the strongest f_p policy for given λ is

$\lambda = 0.025$, $f_p = 0.4$ $\lambda = 0.2$, $f_p = 0.3$

$\lambda = 0.1$, $f_p = 0.35$ $\lambda = 0.5$, $f_p < 0.2$

6. Conclusions

In this Chapter we have studied the effects of lagged feedback controls for the stabilization of two very simple macro-economic models. Although the results obtained may be of a very limited applicability to our present problems of actual economic policy making, it seems obvious that such studies are necessary for building the foundation on which will be based the policy making of tomorrow's world. Yet the literature on this subject is surprisingly small, perhaps due to the discouraging results obtained some twenty years ago by A.W. Phillips [1, 2]. It is only recently that the question of stabilizing and controlling economies has attracted the attention of more than a few scientists. Some examples are G.C. Chow [9], J.K. Sengupta [10], D.A. Livesey [11], B. Thalberg [12, 13], Pindyck [14], and Young *et al.* [15]. The IFAC/IFORS Conference "Dynamic Modelling and Control of National Economies" in July 1973 will probably have a major impact on the amount of research being undertaken in this field in the near future.

Another factor which may have discouraged research in the control of economic systems is the size to which many models have been allowed to grow in later years. It takes a brave man to attempt controlling an econometric model with hundreds of variables and equations, and it has been slightly out of fashion to deal with small models. But this trend has now reversed and a big model is no longer considered a priori and necessarily better than a small one. This tendency toward economic models of moderate or even small size will most certainly promote the development of cybernetic and control

engineering approaches to economic problems.

Appendix
Our problem is to obtain an approximately normally distributed random variable when at our disposal we only have random numbers between 0 and 1. In other words, we have available independent observations of a rectangularly distributed $\eta \in R(0,1)$. Now, $E(\eta) = 1/2$, $V(\eta) = 1/12$.
We form

$$\sigma \frac{\sum\limits_{i=1}^{16} \eta_i - 8}{4\sqrt{\frac{1}{12}}} = \sigma \frac{\sqrt{3}}{2}\left(\sum\limits_{i=1}^{16}\eta_i - 8\right)$$

where $\eta_i \in R(0,1)$ are independent. Using the central limit theorem of probability theory (see, e.g., Rao [16, p. 107]) we obtain

$$\sigma \frac{\sqrt{3}}{2}\left(\sum\limits_{i=1}^{16}\eta_i - 8\right) \sim N(0,\sigma)$$

Thus we obtain an observation of an approximately $N(0,\sigma)$ random variable by observing η 16 times, adding the results, subtracting 8 and multiplying by $\sigma(\sqrt{3}/2)$.

References
1. PHILLIPS, A.W., 'Stabilization policy in a closed economy', *The Economic Journal*, 290-323 (1954).
2. PHILLIPS, A.W., 'Stabilization policy and the time form of lagged responses', *The Economic Journal*, 265-277 (1957).
3. SANDBLOM, C.L., 'Om reglerteknik och konjunkturstabilisering (On control theory and economic stabilization, in Swedish)', Nationalekonomiska Institutionen, Lunds Universitet (1970).
4. BELLMAN, R. and COOKE, K.L., *Differential-Difference Equations*, New York (1963).
5. EVANS, M.K., *Macroeconomic Activity*, New York (1969).
6. BARRETT, J.F., COALES, J.F., LEDWICH, M.A., NOUGHTON, J.J., and YOUNG, P.C., 'Macroeconomic modelling: a critical appraisal', Paper presented at the IFAC/IFORS Conference "Dynamic Modelling and Control of National Economies", University of Warwick, Great Britain (July 1973).

7. GOODWIN, R.M., 'The nonlinear accelerator and the persistence of business cycles', *Econometrica* **19**, 1-17 (1951).

8. THALBERG, B., *A Trade Cycle Analysis*, Lund, Sweden (1966).

9. CHOW, G.C., 'Optimal stochastic control of linear economic systems', *Journal of Money, Credit and Banking* **2**, 291-302 (1970).

10. SENGUPTA, J.K., 'Optimal stabilization policy with a quadratic criterion function', *Review of Economic Studies* **37**, 127-146 (1970).

11. LIVESEY, D.A., 'Optimizing short term policy', *The Economic Journal* **81**, 525-546 (1971).

12. THALBERG, B., 'Stabilization policy and the nonlinear theory of the trade cycle', *The Swedish Journal of Economics*, 294-310 (1971).

13. THALBERG, B., 'A note on Phillips' elementary conclusions on the problems of stabilization policy', *The Swedish Journal of Economics*, 385-408 (1971).

14. PINDYCK, R.S., 'Optimal policies for economic stabilization,' *Econometrica* **41**, 529-560 (1973).

15. YOUNG, P.C., NOUGHTON, J., NEETHLING, C., and SHELLSWELL, S., 'Macro-economic Modelling: A Case Study', Technical Report No. 48, Department of Engineering (Control Division), University of Cambridge, Great Britain (1973).

16. RAO, C.R., *Linear Statistical Inference and its Applications*, New York (1965).

Organizations for v. against creativity. A challenge for interdisciplinary and systems approach

ALBERT HAJNAL
Institute of Economic Planning,
Budapest, Hungary

Art starts where Nature finished
—PARACELSUS

"We are all great poets, but only the greatest poets know it." Paul Whitman wrote this in the Preface to *Leaves of Grass*. Whitman's formula is doubtlessly a metaphorical one. But recent researches on creativity allow us to interpret it in a more general way: we all are creative potentially, but only the most creative men know it.

The image of the 'creative man' is a specific one: the self-discovering man's image about himself. We don't know when it emerged first, and it would be difficult to gather all its variations imagined by people of different eras. Nevertheless, it may be stated, that this image is a sort of symbolic representation of such a man who potentially exists and may be developed. This image was not merely the creation of the imagination. It was moulded on living patterns, on such men whose lives and works provided the patterns. The last two to three centuries reinforced the credit of this image through a great many living patterns of a new type. The latter have stimulated the increased interest of more and

more scientific researchers in creativity.

At present we are in possession of a two-faced certainty about human creativity. We have indisputably discovered that creativity existed and formed one of the basic features of man. But we have also realized that the nature of creativity has been and still is incompletely understood. So he who revived and embodied this image in himself did it rather instinctively than consciously, moreover, he was helped in it by fortunate coincidences as well. Apart from all these there are many empirical evidences for showing that when creativity is inhibited or atrophied, there is something basically unhealthy in it. Consequently, the belief or even conviction in many of us seems to be very plausible, that if we understand the nature of creativity scientifically, this potential ability can be far more purposefully and effectively evoked in many more people than before. Thus he who revived, embodied the creative man in himself realized himself too and became healthier and more integrated than those who have

Progress in Cybernetics and Systems Research, Volume 2

not done so.

Everybody is a member of some kind of community or organization or even of more than one. Many results of research call our attention to the fact that such organizations may help as well as inhibit the development of creativity, or if it already exists, the manifestation of it. One may be helped or inhibited by his family in childhood and later on by the school, by the organizations in which he works, by the subculture which surrounds him or still more generally by the organizational-social 'climate' in which he lives. Many are convinced, and their conviction is perhaps a bit extreme but not without any foundation, that this climate is mostly responsible for the undeveloped or atrophied creativity, and that the interactional schemes of an organizational subculture are the most determining features herein.

The most important consequence of man's manifested creativity is that he creates some kind of original work or opus. This opus is the creative man's product. His product may be manifold: a material object (machine, building, technical equipment, etc.), a mental image (having informational nature), or a brought up child. We may observe that when speaking of creative man we always think of man as an individual, both in the case of abilities and of products. But we have to become aware of the obvious fact that the number of such products that cannot be created by a single individual rapidly increases in our present age. Such works are already extremely complex and can be realized within the frames of highly organized institutions only. Although examples of this organizational creativity may be found back in the past, no examples for such complex opuses and so highly organized institutions existing in our days can be met. Perhaps there is enough evidence and experience to state that beside individual creativity there exists organizational or communal creativity, too. But, of course, the nature of the organizational version is much less understood than that of the individual version.

There are many common features in the two kinds of creativity, and it is also obvious that organizational creativity cannot exist without individual creativity. Furthermore, it can also be experienced that although each member of an organization is creative as an individual, the organization may still be noncreative. Or, taking the other extreme, although there is only one single member in an organization in whom creativity has been unfolded, under special conditions he can create together with the other members of the community such an original and complex opus that he could not do by himself. There are many

experiences of the same and similar nautre. But we have only very little scientifically satisfactory knowledge about organizational creativity. Even speaking of it requires us to use characteristics of individual creativity as metaphors. We must do so even if the creative organization or community has brought about such an important opus as a civilization, a subculture in which material objects, products of art (folklore) are equally to be found. But it seems that the organizational-communal creativity has its own specific characteristics deviating from the individual version.

Based on the fact that the organizational-communal creativity really exists, it is an obvious belief or—to put it more boldly—conviction that the scientific examination and understanding of its nature results in at least as much benefit as the research of the individual creativity. Using the characteristics of the individual creativity as metaphors, the 'creative organization or community' can also be looked at as an image. It is the image the organization has of itself as to what it can become. It is therefore essential to emphasize it because a community, a subculture, may exist without manifested creativity as well which means that its state has been preserved, it does not develop any more. But it is exactly our age that indicates how creativity—even if existing spontaneously—provides the basic condition of development. The conscious version is of course more promising. Scientific research makes us sensitive to the undiscovered organizational versions of creativity, we can better understand ourselves as a planetary culture and, besides many other facts, the organization can supply a more favorable frame for the individual, i.e., the number of promoting organizational effects can be increased while the inhibiting ones can be restricted.

Up till now the researchers of creativity have dealt mainly with individual creativity. They identified the features of the creative individual at least in a phenomenological descriptive manner. What is striking is that mostly psychologists are to be found among the researchers. But it is even more striking that only a few interdisciplinary approaches were made. And it is simply astonishing that the knowledge about the creativity of organizations appears as a by-product of the research work of sociologists, organization researchers and pragmatically oriented management scientists. Upon preliminary considerations we came to the idea that a new and promising way of research may be obtained if *the individual and organizational creativity be examined in their interrelation.* We assumed that interpreting one field in the frame of reference of the other will make the understanding of both of them easier. The two frames make us at the same time sensitive to characteristics which have not been consciously observed and identified yet. We restricted our investigations to the seemingly most relevant features. We wanted to find out whether, by connecting the two frames, some hidden features would reveal themselves. But we had yet another motive. The nature of the individual and organizational creativity is presumably so very complex that this fact alone means a challenge for an interdisciplinary system-approach in the investigations. During our work we reinterpreted already-documented research results and tried to reveal undiscovered features in them.

According to the above-described approach we set forth our considerations in the following way. First we interpret some basic phenomenological features of individual and organizational creativity. We examine the typical organizational forms established in our days and investigate the possibilities of the individual and organizational creativity in them and the limiting factors endangering their manifestation. Finally we propose—so to speak from a bird's-eye view—some new ways for the interdisciplinary investigation of creativity. In conclusion, we venture on some inferences, too.

Outlines of a typology for some phenomenological features

One of the most ancient references to the nature of creativity is to be found in the Egyptian Book of the Dead written several thousand years ago. "If I gain mastery over my heart, I gain mastery over my two hands, I gain mastery over my legs, I have the power to do whatsoever" (*The Book of the Dead*). At first sight it seems perhaps forced to connect this magic text with creativity. But if we think of what the contemporary researchers of creativity have also recognized, i.e., that this ability is not only of logical-rational character but man's entire being, including his emotions activated in it, then this ancient text will point to an important experience of creativity.

Since then we have formulated it more precisely and clearly: the creative man creates two works. One of them is the *outer opus*, its basic characteristics being originality. The other, which could be called the *inner opus* is the ability with which the outer opus was created without having existed prior to this, merely the possibility at its most (Progoff, 1967).

The two works are necessarily connected with one another and the creative ability. This interpretation has a lot of implications. For instance, that he who wants to create an opus has to transform himself, too. Another implication is, that with an unenriched ability we only repeat the outer opus at best. In the course of our investigations we have found that the joined inner opus/outer opus concept is very fortunate, for it has an extremely great organizing power.

Further on we shall use an abbreviation for the two joint works: OIO (Outer and Inner Opus). When we use it in the sense and context of 'OIO concept' we refer to the above-described phenomenological implications, too.

It can be understood without longer argumentation that the OIO-concept can refer not only to the individual but to organizational creativity as well. The difference between the two can be made explicit through the following notation:

individual creativity: IND—OIO
organizational creativity: ORG—OIO

In the first approach the creative ability of the organization can be interpreted as the mass of the abilities created in the collaborating individuals which become active upon special conditions, and where the members create jointly an opus which could not be created nonjointly.

According to the nature of the outer opus we can identify two groups of creativity. One of them is the *discovering*, the other the *idea-embodying* creativity. Let us denote them DC and EC. They can be interpreted as follows:

DC—The creative man gets in touch with an already existing but uncontrollable phenomenon and although he does not make any alterations to it, his relation to it changes basically; for instance, he has understood its behavior, or formulated an earlier not known principle of it. But the discovering creativity is characteristic of Columbus or of the arctic explorers, too.

EC—Within the scope of the phenomena he can exert influence on, the creative man creates something not existing earlier. The specific products of the different cultures, the technical equipments of our day are of this nature.

It is important to differentiate between these two types, although we find them rarely in the literature about creativity. The importance of the difference lies mainly in the nature of inner opus joined to the outer opus. It is the inner opus of DC of which Pasteur stated: "The great discoveries meet only those who are adequately prepared to receive them."

We think that both DC and EC can be recognized within the frames of individual and organizational creativity. The groups collaborating in basic researches or the organizations establishing new technical equipments are good examples for their representation.

We can also state that DC generally precedes EC. In the history of the modern natural sciences and technical culture a lot of examples may be encountered for the case where two centuries had to pass until the results of a scientific discovery could be used for producing a technical device. This sequential relation of DC and EC is expressed in the recently so often-applied concept of 'innovation'. In this specific relation of DC and EC the maturing process of knowledge can be recognized. The generally applied term for this maturing process is the 'innovational transfer'. The process is essentially a particular continuum, along which—depending on the nature of the outer opus—several characteristic phases can be identified. These phases are, however, arbitrary for they do not make the subtle transitions explicit. But they have pragmatic use if we distinguish the following I_i *(i = 0,1,2,3,4)* degrees along the process of the *innovatively maturing knowledge*:

I_0 man is in the pre-discovery state, his behavior is accidental;

I_1 one can identify a phenomenon, he describes it repeatedly;

I_2 he recognizes regularities, cause and effect relations, in a certain phenomenon and on the basis of these he can conclude to its past and future states; knowledge has thus matured to law, principle;

I_3 in the knowledge of the regularities, law and principle, man can exert influence on the phenomenon concerned in a predetermined manner so that it will come into the required condition;

I_4 knowledge has matured to a degree where, through its application, man can embody original ideas.

If we combine these degrees with the DC and EC versions of creativity, obvious analogies may be seen. DC joins mainly I_1 and I_2, while EC will be connected to I_3 and I_4. The I_0 degree can be interpreted as the starting point of the process.

The phenomenological features set forth provide an already rich and relatively well organized typology to our further investigations. This typology allows a great number of hidden implications, too. Thus, for example, in the I_1–I_2 degrees man can be merely *responsively creative* and changes his relation to the understood but uncontrollable phenomena.

In this phase the inner opus has also adjusted itself to this responsive creativity. In the I_3–I_4 phases the scope of creativity becomes wider and man can already be *initiatively creative* in the circle of uncontrollable phenomena. The I_i series is quite general and can be applied both to the individual and organizational creativity as well.

Further implications arise if we apply the I_i series as a typological organizer not only to the outer but to the inner opus as well. Namely, nothing excludes the possibility of creating *the inner opus necessary to the outer opus on the basis of the knowledge matured through the innovational transfer stages*. The astronauts offer a quite recent example of this. Their creativity can be claimed to contain manifold DC and EC components; in a three-man crew of a spaceship, specific representatives of the IND—OIO and the ORG—OIO may be observed; finally, it is obvious, too, that in their case a lot of innovational transfer joins their particular ability which enables them to make this unique venture, both in the individual and the organizational frame, furthermore according to the inner and outer opus alike. But the mutations of this typology can be recognized in other human roles and in other organizational forms, too.

We are consciously aware of the fact that this outlined typology and its components are a mere sketch, insensible to the multitude of subtle inner details. We also emphasize that they represent a small fraction of the aspects only based on empirical evidences. The fact that they still proved to be applicable is due to their *high degree of relevance*. In our samples we demonstrated that, through their cross-classificational combinations, such versions could be generated which correspond to real life versions. The variety of the typology could be enriched with further phenomenological features, of which the research results obtained world-wide could represent an immense stock. We have chosen only some of the most important ones.

Plan and planning in the creative process

New versions of individual and organizational creativity had appeared when we consciously discovered that by conceiving in our imagination the opus and the order of operation, on the basis of which the former is established, our creative undertakings can be rendered safer and more effective. This imaginary form of the opus and the implementation—in other words the *opus plan* and the *action plan*—is the symbolic representation of the product and the operations, and of information-like character. These images order the activity of the implementer and make explicit that the creative man creates his opus purposefully and according to program.

This aspect of creativity had previously been less emphasized. Due to its representing new features and its decisive role, particularly in the organizational creativity, it has, nevertheless, to be dealt with. Although from a different viewpoint, Guilford's and Hallman's researches touch upon these features (Guilford [1], Hallman [2]). Their results may be favorably reinterpreted for our approach and reinforce, from a different angle, that assumption of ours that plans play a distinguished role in creativity.

All this implies the question and the objection whether indeed creativity is planned, purposeful and according to a program. A great deal of evidence and the development trend of our present civilization induces us to give a positive answer. Moreover, it has to be asserted that creativity has always been planned—even when we were not aware of it. The creative man embarks upon things with a high degree of uncertainty and gets imaginatively prepared during his activity to gradually eliminating his uncertainty. In its embodied form the opus is already clear-cut and definite.

What are the most outstanding features of planned creativity? The characteristics bearing significance with respect to the following are summed up below.

It is expedient to mark off two stages of the planned work process. One of them is the preparatory *intellectual, imaginary stage* (INT–STAGE), the other one the *embodying stage* (EMB–STAGE). At the beginning of the INT–STAGE the product and the order of operation possesses an extremely simplified imaginary (symbolic or iconic) representation: the objective and the strategy. *The creator is a specific variety generator* that puts forth the goal and strategy forms in minute detail, i.e., as goal plans and program plans. During the EMB–STAGE these plans will become reference bases with which the creator compares reality. This means that the goal plan and program plan act as reference bases for the two negative feedback loops of the creator. Features of this kind may equally be recognized in the DC and EC versions, although for the latter we have more conscious experiences. Apart from their common features, divergent specific characteristics show up naturally, too.

If during the INT–STAGE only the goal and the strategy are imagined and they are representations of very little variety of the goal and the operations and this is immediately followed by the EMB–

STAGE, much more tentative attempts are needed than when detailed plans are prepared. For DC, the goal and the program may evidently be conjectured only and following from its nature it can thus be less planned. More and more signs are, however, indicating that even in DC a many-sided purposefulness may be applied (Ouinn-Cavanaugh [3]).

Guilford pointed out that among the goals of the intellect a particular building sequence asserts itself; the goals can be units, classes, relations, systems, etc. (Guilford [1]). He who can conceive a system has creative abilities capable of a more complex opus than those who merely identify the existence of certain things. In the Bourbaki-Piaget model there are numerous similar features as well, in which the system types formed according to the arche-structures are the key concepts (Piaget [4]). Of these it follows obviously that if during the INT–STAGE the variety of the plans is increased the plan is essentially conceived in system form.

Can the planned creativity be interpreted according to the full OIO concept? It is perhaps unusual to speak of plans of the inner opus, but nothing speaks against it in principle. Numerous examples of past, characteristic versions may be cited. The plans of the inner opus were mainly cultural or subcultural patterns. Individuals had only seldom created an individual inner opus plan shaped to their own personality and if so, they had only seldom embodied it. (The BUTTON FOUNDER in Ibsen's play wants to cast Peer Gynt in the big foundry because he had failed to be he himself.)

One additional important feature of the creative work needs to be mentioned. The creator uses in its opus, i.e., the product, some kind of raw material. If the character of his product is information, his raw material must be just the same. A researcher orders the information gathered about some kind of phenomenon and elaborates it so that its product can be formulated in the form of laws. With respect to the inner opus, the interpretation can be given that the creator transfers some former stage of his to another one displaying new abilities as well. Or yet, in another case, the organization transforms itself from a less developed into a more developed stage. This transforming process is often very long, for the final product may be reached from the initial stage or raw material through a series of many intermediate products. These have to be represented in the goal plans and program plans as well.

On the basis of these, a simple model concept is suggested joining the features enumerated so far. Figure 1 gives a graphic representation of this model.

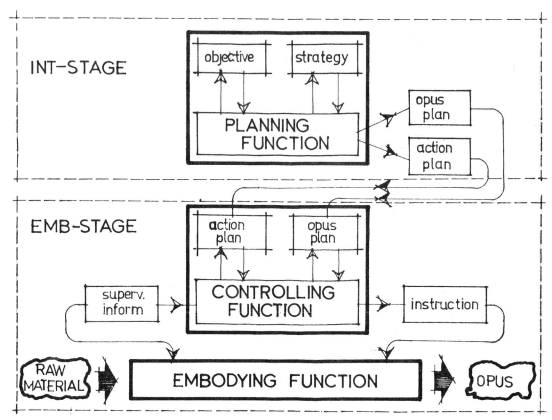

Fig. 1

It may be absolutely generally interpreted, i.e., for the inner and outer opus, the individual and organizational creativity just the same as for the DC and EC cases. If we consider furthermore the OIO concept, the creator could be depicted as model by *joining two such models, one adjusted to the outer and yet another to the inner opus.* This possibility is not put forth here, merely alluded to. What we emphasize, however, is that when we speak of planned creativity, two such joined models can always be thought of, the ordering model of which is provided by Fig. 1. Although the model is a rough simplification, it still represents the basic features together with their correlations. It is not necessarily the creator's model because real life examples may be encountered even if the products do not satisfy the criteria of creativity. Such is the case when an industrial enterprise purchases the documentation and manufacturing process (know-what, know-how) of certain products. Figure 1 is accordingly the model of a planned production system. With respect to the inner opus some kind of creativity can, of course, be spoken of, even in such a case, because the organization must create within itself the abilities of manufacturing the new product.

The draft model gives an impulse to refine the interpretation of creativity. As a criterion of creativity we have so far demanded the originality of the opus. Experience has shown us that a product can be arrived at in different ways. When someone elaborates a new procedure to produce an already existing product, the opus is not an original one but the method is. The version can also be met that by means of a known procedure products previously not manufactured are produced. Consequently, *the 'what' and the 'how' can be original independently of each other*. The OIO concept of creativity may thus be enriched with new aspects functioning at the same time as a novel typological organizer.

The creativity in organizational frames

Many of us often evoke with nostalgia the fortunate past ages when, even two to three centuries ago, a single individual could be in one person a discoverer, researcher and systematically producing engineer. He carried through the whole process of innovation in his own person, recognized some kind of natural principle, and conceived a sort of idea to be embodied and realized in the light of the new law. His mind, body and emotions called into life this individual version of creativity as an integrated unit. Since those days, and above all in the last few decades, the variety of the division of labor has increased as if explosion-like. As a consequence of this the ability components of the creative personality have also become disintegrated. It is not only the DC and EC-like creativity that has become separated. Within DC itself the researchers interlink through a long chain of division of labor, and the same applies to EC as well. The variety of roles has been multiplied with respect to planned creativity in the same way; an ever-increasing number of people draw plans in the INT–STAGE, whereas the EMB–STAGE has become extremely differentiated according to the criteria of the assembly system. It is not difficult to notice, either, that some people are preparing goal plans exclusively, while others make program plans. These phenomena are in close connection with the most recently established organizational forms and the nature of organizational creativity at the same time. The most important features are briefly discussed below.

Several processes are attached to the organizational creativity. Along these, coherent role chains have emerged due to the division of labor. We have selected three such aspects of the process, one of them being *the process of innovational transfer*. The latter is a process at the near end of which the basic researchers can be found, while at the far end are the makers of the embodied ideas. The basic researchers themselves can be either curiosity-oriented or mission-oriented. The curiosity-oriented researcher represents the DC in its purest form. The opus of the mission-oriented researchers is already organized by their knowledge of the idea of the product made at the termination of the innovational process; thus DC and EC are intermingled in them. In the phase between the two extremes a long series of basic, applied and development researchers are in connection with each other. This series can be understood as the spectrum of creative functions along the continuum of the innovational transfer. The spectrum also disposes of some subtle indicators worth mentioning. The approach to the process of innovational transfer may be two-fold. On the one hand, can be investigated how many joining possibilities of one single discovered natural principle to products may exist; let us call it *principle-oriented transfer*. On the other hand, we can explore how many principles have to be known to one single type of product matured through all the I_i stages; it can be denoted the *product-oriented transfer*. An intrinsic feature of the principle-oriented transfer is the analogical thinking as expressed organizator. An intrinsic feature of the product-oriented transfer lies in that the idea antecedently nonexisting but to be embodied—i.e., the imaginary representation of the product—is the determining organizator, or more exactly, the process of the idea's genesis. We can thus identify that in the one DC, in the other EC is dominating. Apart from these two aspects of the transfer a striking feature of the innovational processes is the duration of the period between the two extremities. As another indicator, may serve the geographical route of the process, i.e., the number of countries and organizations it passes through. It is obvious that the longer the duration or the route, the more disintegrated the creativity components become.

From the processes in connection with creativity there is another one that can be interpreted as the chain of 'raw material—intermediate product—final product' (production verticum). Our presumption is that along the whole product chain the knowledge is matured up to the I_4 stage. In our days the product chain contains more and more elements, and gets longer and longer. Every verticum can be defined with a two-fold approach, one of them being the *raw-material oriented* image, a diverging branch, while the other is the *product-oriented* image, a converging branch. It also disposes of duration and geographical route aspects. An obvious feature of this process is its joining special competences and creating thus from the EC versions different spectra of the creative functions. Creative functions may be attached to every single element of the product chain.

The third group of the processes is dominated by *aspects of the planned creativity*. They have, above all, an INT–STAGE and an EMB–STAGE component. The division of labor has nowadays such a great variety of forms that the set of creative people in the first approach divides into two subsets. One subset restricts creativity to the intellectual-imaginary preparation, the other to the embodying opus. In the spirit of the master model of Fig. 1 there is yet another function, the 'operative control of implementation'. It seems as if this did not require creativity at all. If the EMB–STAGE is determined to such an extent that it runs in open-loop control, there is actually no need for creativity, but for deterministic automatisms or mechanism. In the closed-loop control some version of creativity may the more be needed the less the simple stabilizing controller is appropriate and the more superior, for example, ultrastable controllers are necessary. After all, the planned creativity allows for a differentiation according to three components and the division of labor: the versions of *planning creativity, controlling creativity, and implementing-embodying creativity.* Although this differentiation of the division of labor could be derived from the master model, we can identify its real life equivalents without difficulty. Moreover, it is reality that calls our attention to the further division of labor within the operative controlling function, too; a great number of people spend their lives by supervising within the closed-loop control whether the embodying function is realized according to the plan or not, while a similarly great number of people give instructions in the same area. This image is, however, very rough yet. Along the INT—STAGE and EMB—STAGE we encounter different versions of the division of labor depending on the complexity of the ready product. Taking samples only from the simplest articles of consumption through to the more complex machines of industrial plants, complexity is gradually increasing and experience shows that the variety of the division of labor is growing in the same sequential order within both stages. The scope of the planned products is enlarged in our time by such complex phenomena as the national economy. The complexity of a product increases further if not only the national economy is planned, but the whole society of a country. It is already an almost hopeless undertaking to get a precise image of what kind of versions of the division of labor have come into existence along the INT—STAGE interpreted within the frame of the national economy or during the EMB—STAGE within the operative control function. And it can only be conjectured how many variations of the division of labor will arise, if the planned economic development changes over to planned social development (Báger-Hajnal [5]).

According to the processes linked with creativity, we could identify in different organizational frames three big sets of the spectrum of the creative functions. Apart from those there are, however, other organizational specialities disintegrating the creative components of personality just the same. We will examine some of these.

It belongs to the nature of every social organization that it comprises many levels of managerial hierarchy and the nonmanagers on the lowest level. The more detailed the goal plans and program plans that exist, the more predetermined the labor on the lowest level will become. As in present-day organizations a system of the division of labor has come into being in which the greatest degree of freedom to choose may be found on the senior managerial level

and, in parallel, when approaching the lowest levels the degree of freedom to choose diminishes, a further spectrum of the related creative functions may be gained: i.e., the possibility of creativity is gradually decreasing further down until it practically disappears at the lowest level. Herein we can also define that the creativity of a senior manager is primarily of planning character mixed with controlling creativity, while going down the scale the planning component diminishes and the emphasis on the controlling component gets stronger.

The relationship between mass production and creativity is an often cited phenomenon. Obviously, the bigger the number of products and the longer they are produced, the more this fact inhibits creativity in the whole organization.

It is also well-known that while some organizations function appropriately through many years following their establishment if they produce invariable products, others often change both their products and their technology. With respect to creativity this fact implies that the faster an organization changes, the more possibilities of creativity its members have; the least chances are given in the steady-state organizations (Ansoff-Brandenburg [6], Beer [7], 1972).

What kind of image can be gained of the organizations if analyzed upon both the inner and the outer opus? As far as I know there have not been any investigations of this nature so that we can form an image indirectly only and from conclusions drawn from our previous analyses. A great variety of such considerations is imaginable; accordingly, we indicate here some of the most important aspects as a kind of sampling. The two OIO variations may be joined with the spectra set forth previously on the basis of the 3 processes. Resulting from the spectrum according to innovation the inner opus of a man who is attached to the initial phase of the innovation process, that man's whole life will be of a totally different nature than that of someone who spends his life in a factory. The division of labor according to the INT—STAGE and EMB—STAGE strongly diversifies the inner opus, too, for he who has made plans throughout life (some product plans, others program plans) will apparently create a diverse inner opus compared to the person who merely has experience in implementing plans made by others. If we look upon the ORG—OIO frame, considerable features may also be interpreted. On an organizational level the inner opus is the organization itself. From the results of research into organizations we know well that totally different organizational forms are needed in research institutes from those needed in mass production plants. These differences have so far been phenomenologically registered. It would be, however, very fruitful if the various organizations were studied with respect to creativity as well, or even if the results of the organization research were reinterpreted.

If we consider organizations differentiated according to the INT–STAGE and EMB–STAGE, the various versions of the planning organizations are rapidly growing in connection with the ever-widening sphere of large complex works. A particularly large number of organizational forms have emerged since not only national economic, but larger regional plans are established. And if the economic planning changes over to social planning, new planning organizations will probably be needed. In such large and complex frames, new qualitative factors appear as well, the nature and outcome of which are not known yet, and accordingly, the planning organizations cannot adjust themselves to them. The operative control function is carried out in such large systems by separate independent organizations executing, for instance, control merely in the whole negative feedback loop for a long time, which results in a particular attitude of the organization and its inner opus, respectively. Being examples only, these still suggest that a regular and systematical analysis of the organizations in the sense of the IND–OIO and ORG–OIO concepts would be profitable.

There is one additional interesting aspect of the organizations closely connected with various components of creativity, namely, that each organization has a formal and an informal aspect. A great many researches have examined directly or indirectly, whether or not the interaction of the formal and informal aspects exerts an influence on creativity (Argyris 1963, McGregor [8], McPherson [9]). We can observe that if members regard the formal organization as inappropriate, they commence establishing small informal organizations within the organization itself. In organizations of this kind the interpersonal relations are predominantly coalition-like, both among individuals and larger groups. If the formal organization proves appropriate, the members join much rather in institution form. In the former the competitive relation is dominating among the members, while in the latter cooperative relation is pertaining. But the motivation of the individuals differs in the two cases. From various observations it can be concluded that if the formal and informal organizational aspects do not fit in well with one another, both the individual and the organizational creativity is disturbed; as in such organizations the inner opus

would be restricted to the informal aspects only and would hardly be manifested in formal aspects. Thus it can be claimed—and it is suggested by a lot of evidence—that the joining of the concept of the formal and informal organization with the OIO concept of creativity is desirable both in the frame of IND–OIO and of ORG–OIO.

Summarizing the basic concepts and propositions
Our ideas about creativity expounded so far have been descriptive approaches to a guessed but more complex architecture of a theoretical framework. This frame can be of formal character, too. In the foregoing the concepts were dealt with which were based on empirical evidence and belonged to the basic concepts of the creativity concept. It has been indicated, too, how the image gained about a subject area can be enriched if we operate with joint concepts as well and even the outlines of some kind of typology could be drafted. For testing whether the real life equivalents can be discovered, we combine some concepts as samples. With this set of concepts and their proposed relations it can now be demonstrated more precisely, what is the nature of the challenge of this subject area like to the systems and interdisciplinary approach as well as the possible advantages of such an undertaking. Before speaking of this challenge, we briefly sum up the topics discussed hereto.

One of our basic propositions was that creativity had two reference frames:
– individual creativity (IND),
– communal-organizational creativity (ORG).
This statement is reinforced by empirical evidence. Numerous things indicate how organically the individual and the organizational creativity are joined in our culture. Thinking in these two reference frames and their interrelationships we propose the following basic concepts and their joint combinations:
1. OIO–CONCEPT. Creator has two works: the outer and inner opus, which are necessarily joined together. Variations of this concept:
   – IND–OIO
   – ORG–OIO.
2. DC and EC. There are two orientations, each in the sense of OIO:
   – DC: discovering creativity, toward unknown existing phenomena.
   – EC: embodying creativity, toward yet non-existing phenomena.
3. I_i $(i=0,1,2,3,4)$. Innovational transfer stages in the process of maturing new knowledge.

4. In the process of innovation DC and EC are joined together, and the pattern of their interrelations alters according to the I_i stages.

5. Creator uses plans in the sense of OIO, especially
   - goal or product plans
   - program or action plans.

6. INT–STAGE and EMB–STAGE. The two successive phases of the creative process:
   - INT–STAGE: intellectual, imaginary preparing or planning stage,
   - EMB–STAGE: embodying stage.

   During the EMB–STAGE the program and product plans are two kinds of reference bases for the control of embodiment.

7. Criteria for creativity. Both the opus and the program of how to embody it are original, independently and/or together.

8. Both DC and EC need plans and control for implementations.

9. Both IND–OIO and ORG–OIO need plans and control for implementation.

10. In the personality of the creator DC and EC, the ability to plan, to embody and to control harmoniously co-exist in the sense of OIO.

These concepts and propositions contain several implications. They can be made explicit if individual concepts are developed more differentiated for both the IND–OIO and the ORG–OIO frames alike. On a sampling basis we have investigated such a one, too, interpreting it for phenomenological characteristics primarily. The most important conclusions of our considerations were the following:

a) In our days, organizational creativity is ordered by three processes, being new themselves and having effectuated changes in creativity as well. These are:
   - the innovational transfer,
   - the series of raw material—intermediate product—and final product,
   - the successive phases of the INT–STAGE and EMB–STAGE.

   All three have the effect of separating the unity of subabilities realized in a creative personality into a wide and varied spectrum of subfunctions along the different processes. This spectrum is at the same time the pattern of the chain of the division of labor.

b) The innovational transfer separates according to DC and EC. On the one end of the process there are predominantly DC, at the opposite end EC representatives to be met.

c) Along the process of the INT–STAGE and EMB–STAGE the unity of the creative ability will be separated into three subfunctions, i.e., into planning, controlling and embodying functions.

d) The series of product chains further differentiates the previous two spectra primarily according to scientific and practical competences.

e) As the three processes separated the components of creativity in a division of labor-like manner, in connection with this the inner opus has become altered, too, in the sense of OIO. Can it be that resulting from this attitude castes have emerged? The castes of the discoverers, idea-embodying persons, planners, controllers and implementers. With respect to inclination persons can enter these castes who have built up an appropriate personality for themselves. It may be expected, and what is more have been already experienced, that differences among the attitude-castes may get distorted into conflicts. The interrelations of their representatives are becoming gradually competitive both in the frames of intraorganizational and interorganizational relations, although in the personality system they have integrated into creative abilities through cooperative relations. The discoverer, for instance, is anxious about the freedom and openness of his mind and is very reluctant to submit himself to limitations that every idea generates if we want to implement it; it is a very important source of conflict between the representatives of DC and EC. Or the implementing individual accuses the planners of having lost their feeling for reality and of planning things that cannot be implemented; this becomes extremely acute if the organizational product is large and complex, just as in the case of a larger region of a country. The role of the controllers has become even more peculiar who merely signal danger when the implementing persons deviate from the plans—although very often alterations are the very conditions of the substantial embodiment of the original idea. These castes have already appeared in interorganizational groupings as well.

f) The disturbed OIO aspects of creativity bring about inner tension, and, moreover, competition among the formal and informal organizational patterns. The game triggered in such a form ends usually with the victory of the informal patterns that again exert a disorganizing effect on the organizations.

These insights are also known from direct empirical experience. Our contribution is merely that we have connected them with the aspects of the individual and organizational creativity and have ordered them —not very rigorously—according to the typology generated from them.

Example for further implications

The above-described conceptual framework contains many other implications, too. As a sample we have chosen a group that is plausible in our opinion even without being proved. It can be asked: what kind of excessively strengthened and disproportioned inclinations may be caused by the fact that the aspects of creativity have become to specific organizational roles? First of all, let us examine the DC and EC attitudes and subsequently the planner, controller and implementer attitudes.

DC attitude: principle- or law-oriented; inclines to think in an analytical way; inclines to study unknown but existing phenomena; prefers to theoretize experiences.

EC attitude: thinks and acts in a frame of such ideas that don't exist but that can be embodied; prefers to think in terms of already well-known principles or laws or in an analogic way; inclines to think in a synthesizing way; prefers practice.

Planner attitude: inclines to think in the frames of the future; spends a longer part of his life in an imaginary rather than the real world; weakly cultivated sensitivity toward reality.

Controller attitude: inclines to think in the frames of the present; disproportionate sensitivity toward the danger of deviation from plans; certain rigidity in judging the deviation from plans (or norms, which are also plans in a sense).

Implementer attitude: inclines to think in the frames of the present; expects to get ideas from others.

These specific features may, of course, be disputed but in my estimate they display heuristic value.

Some conclusions

Our present-day organizational culture affects with manifold compelling force both individual and organizational creativity, and differentiates the concrete individual and organizational OIO forms. Due to its separating effect, some components of the potential creativity will be strong, others uncultivated. And the consequences are disorganizing for the organizational culture.

It would be a mistake, however, to see dangers merely from the viewpoint where the relation of the individual and organizational creativity may still be looked upon in a more explicit form. In our present-day organizational culture there are advantageous features as well, for they have made our life richer and more varied and rendered a higher degree of freedom both in individual and social frames. More precisely, these advantageous features derive from the fact that the innovational transfer, the vertical product chain and the processes of the planned production have shaped the components of creativity to organizational roles, following the division of labor.

The tendency of changes seems to have become consolidated for a long time. What makes us draw this conclusion? In the spirit of our frameowrk we can explain the main symptoms of this tendency in the following way:

OPUS. The extent and complexity of purposefully created works (in the sense of outer opus) is steadily increasing. Even half a century ago, merely buildings, equipments, factories were created in a planned way. Nowadays we already plan the economic development of a whole country. Moreover, aggregate associations of several countries exist, the members of which coordinate the development of their economies. In the case of the economy, the opus is the surplus added to the previous economic state during a given plan period. At the same time the precursors of the new features of the near future have already appeared: the economic frame changes over to a social frame, and economic planning to the planning of society.

INNOVATION. The scientific knowledge necessary to works has excessively accrued. Vast intricate chains of the innovational processes taken in the sense of I_i (innovatively matured knowledge) have come into being. It is true, that we have brought this to consciousness with respect to the outer opus only. But there seems to be demand to conscious innovation regarding the inner opus as well, both in the frames of individuals and organizations.

COMPETENCE. The variety of competences rooted in scientific knowledge and of skills based on spontaneous social, subcultural, individual, etc., experiences is going to increase for a long time to come. One of the reasons lies obviously in the fact that individual abilities can only be unfolded within biological limits. The more complex the products of our civilization become, the greater the variety of competences and skills which must be activated in order to have such an opus embodied. Thus it can be expected that these products will require new organizational forms, for the limits of the individual can be cleared away within organizational frames exclusively, through highly organized cooperation. These tendencies are evidently only those that are in direct relation with the proposed framework. Several things have not been touched upon, such as the educational system, the extreme differences in development, the consequences resulting from the social-political systems. In them tendencies may be predicted having some kind of connection with creativity. Despite all these, the limited frame could still be chosen because it covers—in my belief—part of the most relevant concepts.

How should these endowments and their tendencies be judged from the point of view of individual and organizational creativity? The following main insights come up.

The above-mentioned three subject areas are full of peculiar inner contradictions. Their inherent source of danger is at the same time a specific form of development. And it could hardly be defined whether the conscious or the spontaneous variations include more possibilities of tension. This mutually interactive relation of the individual and organizational creativity is naturally not the one and only strained phenomenon of present-day civilization. What distinguishes it from the others is that these aspects of human creativity are responsible to a great extent for other contradictions as well. Human creativity has namely a high position along the cause and effect chains with conflict output. At the same time we also know that the activating sources of development are tensions of exactly such a nature. It would not be favorable, however, if the contradictions became too excessive. Thus a civilization could come into existence in which only some would be creative, while others would participate in the development of the civilization with atrophied personality. We are not far from A. Huxley's *Brave New World* either. Our technological systems show many similar aspects even nowadays. But other problematic phenomenon areas are also prevailing. For instance, the situation of the rich and the poor which futurologists have referred to recently as the "Matthew syndrome": 'For unto every one that hath shall be given and he shall have abundance: but from him that hath not shall be taken away even that which he hath'. It is extremely difficult to recognize the detrimental extremes in connection

with creativity when the nature of its individual and organizational versions is very incompletely known yet. No doubt, that in the interest of scientifically conscious understanding research has started all over the world. Hereto the danger pertains that we might investigate irrelevant aspects, and subsequently our conclusions may also mislead. Just to take the example when we do not adequately reveal the complexity of the phenomenon. The present Chapter desires to show up two such aspects that cannot be left out of consideration without the danger of oversimplification if we want to get a grasp of the nature of creativity. These are:

a) there exists individual and organizational creativity,

b) the creative individual just as the organization has two joined works: the outer and inner opus, i.e., IND—OIO, ORG—OIO.

These two basic aspects of the subject area present a challenge to interdisciplinary and systems approach researchers right away. Systems researchers might be particularly interested in

– such a system that creates an outer product for the sake of enriching its inner abilities,

– such a system, the elements of which are of *limited* creativity in the sense of OIO and that bypasses this limit just by getting organized into a more complex system; this more complex system is itself creative in the sense of OIO and manifests itself under such conditions that its elements not only preserve their creativity within their own limits, but develop as well.

By understanding the nature of such systems, the subject area of innovation may considerably be expanded. The subject of innovation can be not only the outer opus but the inner opus as well, moreover, in a specific form: the IND—OIO and the ORG—OIO separately and jointly.

To end with, let us look into some thoughts and a draft of how the interdisciplinary and systems approach may be interpreted in this subject area.

A challenge for interdisciplinary and systems approach

In recent years a vast scope of knowledge has accumulated with direct or indirect relation to the nature of human—individual and organizational—creativity. A heavy burden hangs over this knowledge in that it has not been adequately formulated with the *complex* nature of creativity. It embraces partial aspects of creativity without incorporating them into some kind of integrated theoretical construction. At the moment we have sufficient empirical and experimental knowledge at hand that an integrated theoretical construction could be attempted in the near future by the researchers concerned. *This Chapter has tried to demonstrate those empirical evidences that urge on commencing researches in this field.* The evidences introduced suggest the necessity of enlarging the reference frame surrounding the subject of research, i.e., human creativity or even more precisely the creative man as phenomenon. We have used such a possible frame variant in our Chapter, i.e., individual and organizational creativity and some of their relevant relationships. It has provided simultaneously an ordering frame to reasoning. The larger frames obviously increase the complexity of the research tasks. But on the other hand, they call attention to so far neglected but relevant aspects of the subject area.

A more complex subject area and research tasks, as well as the need for integrating elements of knowledge, call forth the necessity for new research strategies, too. In the spirit of one of these strategies we have to formulate the question: *which principles and laws and what kind of interrelations of theirs are responsible for the permanent existence, modification, creation and cessation of the creative man and creative organization as specific phenomena* (entities). Due to the complexity of the subject area, this question can be economically answered through interdisciplinary researches only.

It is well-known that every *interdisciplinary research generates severe problems: disciplinary aspects have to be integrated.* In the present development stage of sciences the systems approach proved to be one of the most economical possibilities for organizing above all integration, preserving at the same time the attitudinal sensitivity and ordering force of the disciplines. Consequently, we can assert with conviction that the creative man and the creative organization provoke interdisciplinary research teams and systems researchers to better understand the complexity of their nature, too.

What other, so far little regarded possibilities present themselves to the interdisciplinary and systems approach? In our study we have ordered our considerations around such relevant phenomenological aspects whose ordering force proved to be sufficiently large.

Based on the chosen concepts, we derived the group of questions as well that were formulated at the end of the preceding section. The concept of the joined inner and outer opus (OIO) largely contributed to our being able to word in a relatively

clear-cut form the questions interesting mainly systems researchers. The OIO concept proved to be such a heuristic *ordering concept* in both the IND—OIO and the ORG—OIO versions that it deserves being made explicit. Numerous disciplines lend their results to a better understanding of this aspect of creativity, e.g., cybernetics offers the theory of self-organizing systems and learning systems. McGregor's X—Y concept deserves attention, although it is not duly appreciated. Important possibilities are latent in Bertalanffy's open system theory. These are merely examples. It would be worth while systematically disclosing all promising interdisciplinary knowledge. OIO, a characteristic of creativity that was brought to consciousness several thousand years ago, contains enough organizing force for encouraging further research. Because of its ancientness, this concept may function as an ordering principle for not only interdisciplinary but intercultural or cross-cultural investigation, too. Although, upon superficial consideration merely, it seems that some greater cultures did not appreciate the *priority-relations of the inner and outer opus* in an equal manner. On the scale of values of the Western civilization the outer opus has much greater importance than the inner opus. In some ancient cultures the inner opus was esteemed more highly—and the outer opus was, at best, the verbally handed-down experience of the inner opus. In our days, the nature and relation of the inner and outer opus seem to be reorganized again, for which the rapidly developing organizational culture is primarily responsible. These considerations suggest that it is worth while paying greater attention to the unfolded intrinsic possibilities of the OIO concept. Even if compared with these thoughts, the great value of I. Progoff's above-mentioned study is retained, namely, that it grasped man's knowledge about himself in the process of selfdiscovery so simply and crystallized.

The discovering and embodying creativity—DC and EC—interpreted together as innovation provide a very relevant aspect of both individual and organizational creativity. Their phenomenological aspects having already been identified, we indicate that their manifestation is almost exclusively dominated by spontaneous features. In the social changes, political construction and economic development of the Western civilization they represent a highly significant factor. Or perhaps an effect, a consequence? Or is it merely a symptom? Turning again to examples to illustrate the possibilities of interdisciplinary approaches, this subject area promisingly attracts the scope of knowledge of organization theory in addition to the scope of knowledge of psychology, social psychology, and sociology. The researches looking back upon a relatively insignificant past that deal with the general and specific nature of the theories as well as the techniques of theory generation are also promising. Here the semiotics, this very little-used discipline can be suggested, too, that may assist us in better understanding the nature of the intellectual-imaginary map of reality as well as that of the communication of this image. This subject area possesses several pedagogical implications, for every fundamental discovery reorganizes the knowledge to be taught to the on-coming generation. In our days, at the time of accelerated changes, this brings forth the appearance of different social strata purely as a result of the present population groups having totally different knowledge from their 10 years older precursors (the great majority does not keep pace with the latest information). In our study we have pointed out from many angles that, although both the OIO concept and innovation are important aspects of creativity on their own, the integrated concept of the two might have a much greater ordering force than either of them separately. Such an ordering concept of integrated nature would make us more susceiptible to the still hidden details of the nature of creativity.

The role of plan and planning in the manifestation of the creative ability seems to be far more significant than estimated up till now. With respect to this, a specific line of development may be observed. In the sphere of the creative organizations it was first realized how excessively accelerated the creation of an opus becomes if both the opus and the order of embodying operations, the program is planned. Once upon a time, long series of tentative trials, deadlock and centuries were needed to create a significant common opus. It is the more astonishing how seldom we apply these experiences in planning to personal life. As far as the interdisciplinary researches are concerned, many more disciplines offer their results in this subject area than in the foregoing. Planning as problem solving, planning as information processing, planning as series of choice and decision, are concepts which have found their way into our everyday life. In the literature on creativity there are few traces of them (Newell-Shaw-Simon [10], Simon [11]). The process aspects referred to in this study as IND—STAGE — EMB—STAGE as well as the three subfunctions of creativity attached to the process (planner, controller, implementer functions) offer so far untouched research areas. We do not yet understand the nature of the process that com-

mences with clearly formulating the goal, i.e., the highly simplified imagery representative of the final product; continues with developing the image of the goal into greater and greater detail; and terminates with the embodiment of the imagined goal. In an analytical form and manner the program joins to the starting point and at the other end the operational order of the opus to the embodying stage. This specific genesis, that could be called *idea genesis* is followed through much more instinctively than consciously. This subject area on its own can insert the principles of cybernetics into a new interpretation frame (e.g., what kind of control-constructions ensure the stability of the idea and the program along the process; what kind of adaptive functions operate during the planning stage), just the same as our knowledge about thinking, our image about the coordination between the emotional and rational subsystems of the personality, etc. As before, we have to mention the possibility of building into a formal theoretical construction—in an integrated manner—the concepts of the OIO, the innovation and that of planning made explicit. This means that all of them will be reinterpreted in terms of the others. The thus matured concepts are more adequate to the nature of creativity than without them.

The above thoughts do not represent a research program but personal and very random-like reflections to a challenge coming from the subject area. I presumed that they might evoke thoughts or provoke discussions.

In my country, Hungary, an old joke is very often cited as a parable. A drunken man leans against a big advertizing pillar. He slowly gropes round it for the third time, when he desperately cries: 'Help! I am walled in!''— We all have such a pillar: our unknown personality. He who discovers his own creativity, also realizes that he isn't walled in.

References
1. GUILFORD, J.P., 'A revised structure of intellect', Rep. Psychol. Lab. No. 19, Los Angeles, University of Southern California (1957).
2. HALLMAN, R.J., 'The necessary and sufficient conditions of creativity', *Creativity: its educational implications* (Edit. by Gowan, Demos, and Torrance), Wiley, New York (1967).
3. OUINN, J.B. and CAVANAUGH, R.M., 'Fundamental research can be planned', *Harvard Business Review*, No. 1 (1964).
4. PIAGET, J., 'L'enseignement des mathematique', Delachaux et Nieste, Neuchatel et Paris (1955).

5. BÁGER, G. and HAJNAL, A., 'Organizational aspects of social planning', Paper read at the Second European Meeting on Cybernetics and Systems Research and included as a Chapter in this book, p. 24 (1975).

6. ANSOFF, H.I. and BRANDENBURG, R.G., 'A language for organization design', (Edit. by E. Jantsch) *Perspective of Planning*, OECD, Paris (1969).

7. BEER, S., 'Aborting corporate planning', *Perspectives of Planning* (Edit. by E. Jantsch), OECD, Paris (1969).

8. McGREGOR, D., *The Human Side of Enterprise*, McGraw Hill, New York (1960).

9. McPHERSON, J.H., 'Assessing the relationship between the industrial climate and the creative process', *Climate for Creativity* (Edit. by C.W. Taylor), Pergamon Press, New York (1973).

10. NEWELL, A., SHAW, J.C., and SIMON, H.A., 'The process of creative thinking', *Contemporary Approaches to Creative Thinking* (Edit. by Gruber, Terrel and Wetheimer), Atherton, New York (1962).

11. SIMON, H.A., 'Understanding creativity', *Creativity: its educational implications* (Edit. by Gowan, Demos and Torrance), Wiley, New York (1967).

12. ARGYRIS, Ch., 'Interpersonal competence, organizational milieu and innovation', *Research Management*, No. 2 (1966).

13. TAYLOR, C.W., 'Can organizations be creative too?', *Climate for Creativity* (Edit. by C.W. Taylor), Pergamon Press, New York (1973).

277

The development of systems thinking by systems practice–a methodology from an action research program

Professor P.B. CHECKLAND
University of Lancaster, UK

Introduction

The systems outlook, and work done within the broad boundaries of the systems movement, is based on a proposition which is accepted, at least implicitly, by all systems thinkers. The proposition is that *system* is the name of a general model or paradigm which can usefully be employed to understand, explain or engineer aspects of the real world. The systems thinker carries in his head 'a systems map of the universe' (Checkland [1]), and uses the system concept to interpret perceived connectivities.

The strength of the systems paradigm, as well as its weakness, derives from its generality. Political action, the ecology of a swamp, music, and project management, can all be viewed 'in systems terms' and this gives strength to the paradigm, yielding the possibility of insights in one area being transferred to another. But at the same time there is in any concept of such generality a virtually limitless possibility for content-free speculation; there will be a temptation, rarely resisted, to pursue abstractions; there will be a great reluctance, encouraged by the generality of the concept *system*, to frame conjectures which can be *tested*.

In this context the present work set out to develop a set of systems concepts which could be used in real-world problem situations. Its parsimonious guiding principle was that only concepts *used* in actual problems would be incorporated into the findings, and that the outcome should be a *methodology* for using systems ideas to find a structure in, and hence solve, real-world problems of a 'soft' or ill-structured kind.

The work has consisted of an action research program in which client-sponsored systems studies were tackled by the author and his colleagues; and it was part of a Masters program at the University of Lancaster: postgraduate students of average age 27 or 28 had the opportunity to work on the studies, which were managed by members of staff or by consultants employed by a University-owned Company, ISCOL Limited, set up in association with the Department of Systems Engineering.

Intellectually, the starting position was the set of systems methodologies which derive essentially from concepts relevant to the engineering of 'hard' systems: Hitch [2], Hall [3], Chestnut [4], and Jenkins [5]. As it was found difficult to use these methodologies in 'soft' systems, so experience-based modifications were introduced which were then subsequently tested in further systems studies.

The work has been described in detail elsewhere (Checkland [6]). The purpose here is to discuss some general aspects of it and to suggest the way in which it can be used to assimilate systems thinking from many different sources.

1. Problem-solving

The work has been concerned with seeking to engineer improvements in 'human activity systems' (Checkland [1]), that is to say, with *problem solving*. But 'problem' is here conceived in a very general sense. Problem solving is taken to be the usual mode of activity for human beings: a 'problem' is taken to be

> any perceived mismatch between what is seen to exist, and a normative view of what might exist in the same situation.

Thus the manager of a plant making synthetic fibres does not have to be ankle deep in waste before he accepts that he has 'a problem'. He has a problem, in my sense, if his total management system (structure, procedures, expectations, measures of performance, etc.) could be conceived as being better than they are. Note that he does not have to have a notion of what form the 'improvement' might take —that will emerge from the study—only that improvement is conceivable.

What is needed from the program, then, is a methodology based on systems ideas for problem solving in real-world situations. What is the status of 'methodology'? I take a methodology to be intermediate in status between a philosophy (using that word in a general, rather than a professional sense), and a technique or method. A philosophy will be a broad, nonspecific guideline for action: it might be a *philosophy*, in this sense, that political action should aim at a redistribution of wealth in society, or that environment protection should have priority over industrial expansion. At the other extreme a *technique* is a precise, specific program of action which will produce a standard result: if you learn the appropriate technique and execute it adequately you can, with certainty, solve a pair of simultaneous equations or serve a tennis ball so that it swerves in mid-air.

A methodology will lack the precision of a technique but will be a firmer guide to action than a philosophy. Where a technique tells you 'how', and a philosophy tells you 'what', a methodology will

contain elements of both 'what' and 'how'. In this sense, the action research program sought a methodology for using systems concepts having the following four characteristics:

1. It should be capable of being *used* in actual problem situations.
2. It should be *not vague*, in the sense that it should provide a greater spur to action than a general philosophy.
3. It should be *not precise*, like a technique, but should allow insights which precision might exclude.
4. It should enable any of the developments in 'systems science' to be used if appropriate to a particular situation.

2. The methodology

For brevity the methodology is here expressed in the form of a diagram. It represents a chronological sequence, and is to be 'read' from 1 to 7. Only brief notes on the individual phases will be given here.

1. It is assumed that we start with a relatively unstructured problem situation. Its boundaries will be uncertain, and may or may not coincide with organizational boundaries. Some of the actors in the situation will be obvious, others will emerge later.

What we can be certain of is that a concerned person is aware of—is perhaps part of—a situation in which unspecified 'improvement' is thought to be possible. Statements of 'the problem' have included the following in different studies which were part of the action research program:

"Make a systems study of distribution."

"Enable us to answer questions of the kind: What resources should we have in five years time."

"How should conflicting demands on the uplands of Northern England be reconciled?"

"Examine and improve information flow for management decision taking."

"Make me plan." (This from the managing director of a small firm.)

All these problem statements indicate an area of concern but remain usefully vague.

2. Now it is necessary to see the problem situation in a more structured way, but without commitment to any particular solution, or even a particular kind of solution.

It has been found useful to use three guidelines at this stage, asking specifically, separately, and in turn

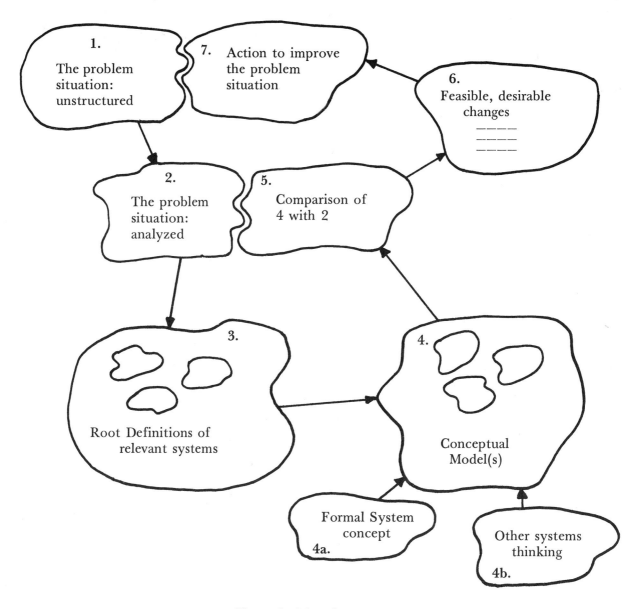

The methodology in summary

What are the elements of structure in the situation?

What are the elements of process?

What is the relation between structure and process, what is the 'climate' of the situation?

'Structure' is taken to include the slow-to-change elements, 'process' the constantly-changing ones. The relationship between the two is an important core characteristic of the situation. For example, in the aircraft industry we observed a chaotic mismatch of structure and process in one organization, while the climate was one of hectic improvization aimed at making the enterprise succeed, thanks to an enthusiastic dedication on the part of middle managers to the technology, to the concept of flight. You would look in vain for a similar dedication to chemistry in the chemical industry, but the aircraft manufacturer was in fact ill-served by the determination of its middle management to make unworkable procedures work.

The end point of this stage in the analysis should be a picture of the problem situation, one as rich as can be assembled in the time available.

3. The next stage is a crux in the methodology. It is now necessary to *choose a way to view the problem situation* given the picture from (2) of this Section and the definitions of 'the problem' as it appears to various interested actors in the situation. The crucial selection is done by naming 'relevant systems', relevant that is to achieving some kind of improvement. These systems will be human activity systems, and might or might not coincide with existing organizational groupings—departments, sections, projects or business areas; on the whole it is probably better if they do not coincide with existing groupings, in the interests of radical thinking.

In a study based in the Research Department of a chemical company, the company's innovation system was chosen as the relevant one. Part of the Research Department was a part of this system, and this led to useful insight into the Research problems.

Having selected a relevant system, or several relevant ones, it is now necessary to formulate and discuss 'Root Definitions' which express a view of the *essential nature* of the relevant systems. Root Definitions express the chosen way of viewing the problem situation, and the aim in formulating them, to quote the earlier paper (1972) is "a penetrating definition, derived from the richness of the analysis, which is revealing to those involved in the day-to-day workings of the systems concerned."

As an example of a Root Definition which provided useful insights in an organizational study, I quote that formulated by my colleagues T.R. Barnett, J. Gilbert and F. Schwarz in a systems study of the charity organization Oxfam:

A transfer system for transferring information concerning the needs of the 'third world' to the richer world in such a way as to involve the richer world in helping the poorer world by
  1. Stimulating public and governmental concern for the problems of the 'third world'.
  2. Raising and providing funds for aid for specific projects.

4. With the formulation of Root Definitions, systems thinking proper now begins. The fourth stage is to make conceptual models of systems which meet all the requirements of the Definitions, including their implications. Many kinds of model or combinations of models are feasible, of course, but it has been found that the most generally useful is a con-

ceptual model of the relevant human activity system described by the Definition, compiled by working out the *minimum necessary sequence of activities* needed for the system to 'be itself'. Possible structures may then be postulated and systems which serve activity systems—especially information systems —can be added (Checkland and Griffin [7]).

It is at this stage that simulation models, including for example, systems dynamics models, may be useful, a point discussed below, but it must be realized that true validation of conceptual models built to meet a given Root Definition is not possible. We can ensure that they are coherent, logical, not missing some vital component or subsystem, but since they are not representations of any existing system there is no question of validation by reference to real-world observation. Their purpose is not to illustrate 'what is', certainly not to demonstrate 'what should be'; it is *to structure a comparison* in the next phase (5) between the existing situation and a systemic view built on the basis of the Root Definition(s).

In order partially to 'validate' the conceptual models, at least as adequate models of human activity systems, it has been found useful to compile a generalized model of such a system based on Jenkins' "summary of properties of systems" [5] and Churchman's "Anatomy of System Teleology [8]. The basic components include purpose, measure of performance, connectivity, subsystems, wider systems, environments, resources, decision-taking process and guarantee of continuity.

5. 'Comparison' is the next stage. The picture of the problem situation developed in phase (2) is now formally compared with the systems constructs from stages (3) and (4). This is the point at which the real situation is confronted with the systems view which has been abstracted from it. The purpose is to articulate a debate about possible changes which people concerned with the problem situation can agree are likely to bring about improvement.

If the systems models are closely similar to what already exists, it may be necessary to go back and formulate more radical Root Definitions. If on the other hand there is an unbridgeable gap between systems models and the reality, it may be necessary to formulate a more constrained Definition. Either way, the aim is to define potential changes to be implemented.

In one rather frustrating study, a quality control system was the subject of a Root Definition which chose to view it as a balancing system, one which aimed to achieve a balance between the cost of achieving a certain quality and the cost of lost sales if that quality were not achieved. At the comparison stage the client accepted this analysis as useful, but because of various prevailing attitudes chose to concentrate implementation solely on one subsystem of the conceptualized system, namely that dealing with customer complaints.

The comparison stage must, of course, be carried out with people who are currently within the problem situation. Experience has shown that it is best done consciously in a formal manner, and four ways of doing it have been tested in a number of studies. These include general discussion leading to isolation of differences on flip charts; definition, from the systems models, of specific questions which are then asked of the real situation; reconstruction of a historical sequence of events and comparison with what would have happened according to the conceptual models; and formulation of the existing situation in a model of the same form as the systems models, so that direct comparison by 'model overlay' is possible.

6. This stage consists of defining changes which are agreed to be both *desirable*, as improvements, and *feasible*, given the power and resources needed for implementation, and the attitudes which exist in the problem situation, including the readiness to accept change.

The changes themselves may be structural, procedural or attitudinal, or a mixture of some or all of these.

7. Finally, as a result of the work done in the 'systems loop' of phases (2)-(5) we may return to the problem situation itself and make the desirable, feasible changes. How to do this may be obvious, or, if it is not, the implementation may itself be subject to the methodology, with 'the problem situation' becoming 'the need to bring about an agreed change', The methodology has been used both to decide what to do and to decide how to do it.

3. Further development of the methodology

It is of course not possible to 'prove' a methodology. If it is regarded as a hypothesis put forward tentatively to see if it can survive severe tests, in the proper spirit of scientific investigation (Popper [9]) then we cannot know whether a 'failure' is due to the methodology itself or to incompetence in using it, just as we cannot know that 'success' would not have occurred in any case, in spite of the methodology. The point is that a methodology for problem solving cannot be tested in this way. It can be tested only in relation to, and as part of a decision to confront, a problem situation. The question to be asked is: Was the problem situation improved? And we shall be able to develop confidence in a problem-solving methodology only gradually as real problems are solved, and as it is accepted by concerned people that problem situations have been improved. (The situation is analogous to the problem of the irrefutability of philosophical theories (Popper [10]).)

For this reason we should be harsh with any problem solving methodologies which are merely postulated, which have not been tested against actual problems. We should reject them as worthless, for there is no meaning in a problem-solving methodology unless actual problems have been solved by using it.

Similarly we can never regard a methodology as finally established. Rather we should allow our confidence in it cautiously to grow as experience of its use is assimilated, and allowed to dictate its further development.

In the case of the systems-based methodology described here, it was developed in nine client-sponsored systems studies in 1969, 1970, and 1971, and tested and refined in more than 20 studies since then. Referring back to the characteristics sought in this methodology, as listed in Section 1, the first three—capable of actually being used, not too vague, not too precise—have been met to a reasonable degree. It remains to discuss the fourth, the capability to absorb 'systems science'.

During phases (1) and (2) of Section 2, when problem-situation analysis is the goal, all the developments within systems science, and within the whole range of management science are available to those making the systems study, and may be used as a means of developing a rich appreciation of the situation. In order to obtain a 'feel' for the structures and processes involved it may well be fruitful to construct systems dynamics models, to simulate operational systems, to make cash flow models, to analyze regulative mechanisms by making use of the concepts and laws of cybernetics. The important point is that the status of such efforts must be that they are only a means to achieving the desired end, namely a rich appreciation of the situation. (It is the tragedy of management science that it has become technique-oriented rather than problem-oriented.)

But it is at the stage of constructing systems models in phase (4) that the methodology provides potentially the most fruitful means of using any or all of the systems science.

In the 20-odd studies which have developed this approach so far, the parsimonious principle of taking in only those concepts which could be *used* has led to a concentration on conceptualizing human activity systems via a sequence of verbs denoting the minimum necessary activities. The models thus constructed have then been checked against the general model of any human activity system which I have called 'a formal system'. This is the rock bottom procedure. But it is at this stage that any other systems thinking which the individual finds insightful can be utilized: the conceptual models can, if desired, be transformed into the language of systems dynamics, or checked against the fundamental ideas of control engineering. If the systems thinker responds to the Tavistock concept of the task system which is inseparably both a social system and a technical system (Emery and Trist [11]) or to the analogy between an organization and the central nervous system (Beer [12]) then the conceptual models in phase (4) may be examined for 'validity' in these terms. Any such concepts may be used, and in a purposive way to engineer the final concept which is carried back to the real-world situation for the comparison stage (phase 5).

Personally, the systems thinking which I have found most insightful, both in the analysis of phase (2) and the conceptualization of phase (4), is the concept developed by Vickers of an 'appreciative system', namely "the interconnected set of largely tacit standards of judgement by which we both order and value our experience" (Vickers [13]). This concept, as Vickers has developed it (Vickers [14] and 1968) accords closely with my own experience of the *texture* of human activity systems, and I have found it useful to examine systems constructs in these terms, asking how 'appreciative systems' do, or could, operate in the systems I have chosen to abstract as a means of structuring the problem.

The further development of the methodology will probably involve a more coherent, a more formal use of 'other systems thinking' of this kind, always remembering that while requiring more precision than a generalized 'philosophy', we must avoid the rigidities inherent in 'technique'.

Acknowledgement

I am very grateful to all the students, colleagues and managers with whom I have struggled in carrying out the systems studies which are the source of this methodology.

References

1. CHECKLAND, P.B., 'A systems map of the universe', *J. Sys. Eng.* 2(2), (1971).
2. HITCH, C., *An Appreciation of Systems Analysis*, Rand Corporation (1955).
3. HALL, A.D., *A Methodology for Systems Engineering*, Van Nostrand (1962).
4. CHESTNUT, H., *Systems Engineering Methods*, Wiley (1967).
5. JENKINS, G.M., 'The systems approach', *J. Sys. Eng.* 1(1), (1969).
6. CHECKLAND, P.B., 'Towards a systems-based methodology for real-world problem solving', *J. Sys. Eng.* 3(2), (1972).
7. CHECKLAND, P.B. and GRIFFIN, R., 'Management information systems: a systems view', *J. Sys. Eng.* 1(2), (1970).
8. CHURCHMAN, C.W., *The Design of Inquiring Systems*, Basic Books (1971).
9. POPPER, K.R., *The Logic of Scientific Discovery* 1934, published in English, Hutchinson (1959).
10. POPPER, K.R., 'Conjectures and refutations', *The Problem of the Irrefutability of Philosophical Theories*, Chapter 8, Section 2, Routledge and Kegan Paul (1963).
11. EMERY, F.E. and TRIST, E.L., 'Socio-technical systems', *Management Science, Models and Techniques* (edit. by Churchman and Verhulst), Vol. 2, Pergamon (1960).
12. BEER, S., *Brain of the Firm*, Allen Lane, The Penguin Press (1972).
13. VICKERS, G., *Making Institutions Work*, Associated Business Programmes (1973).
14. VICKERS, G., *The Art of Judgement, Part 1*, Chapman and Hall (1965).
15. VICKERS, G., *Value Systems and Social Progress, Part III*, Tavistock (1971) (also Basic Books and Penguin Books).

A systems approach to personnel assignment

Dr J.J. CONN
Manpower Analysis, Ontario, Canada

Personnel management is a matter of critical concern in any large, labor-intensive organization. This is particularly true in peace-time, for a volunteer military force which depends upon popular public acceptance for manpower and financial resources. In the absence of wartime pressures, it is essential that an organization, such as the Canadian Defence Department, demonstrate proven effectiveness in the management of financial, material and personnel resources.

To this end, each of the functional divisions will likely apply modern scientific techniques to their resource management problems, and develop information systems for financial management, logistics management and personnel management. Each system will generate demands for improved, and larger, data processing facilities. This situation will culminate in a decision to integrate all of these functional Management Information Systems (MIS) into an over-all Departmental Management Information System, utilizing one or more of the largest data processing systems available. As might be expected, the integration of these smaller systems will lead to a consolidation of the technical and specialist resources into a strong central organization which has an appearance of efficiency and effectiveness.

Unless there is a thorough understanding of the concepts involved in the design and development of an Information System, an inherent danger will exist that an over-all MIS will divert vital resources from the functional systems, which were the original raison d'être of the system. Critical considerations of responsiveness, timeliness, accuracy and flexibility, which were the keys to success in the functional systems, may have to be compromised in the name of over-all efficiency. A smooth-running, production-oriented MIS, generating voluminous reports on schedule, may be quite efficient, as measured by any number of current criteria, such as cycle time, figures of merit, core utilization, etc. However, it may not be apparent that the system is not meeting the real needs of the decision makers for whom it was developed.

This Chapter will outline a concept of development of an Information System in support of personnel management activities. In particular, the Personnel Posting Support System, as developed by the Directorate of Manpower Analysis, will be used to illustrate the problems encountered in system design, development, implementation and evaluation, particularly in relation to its place in an over-all departmental MIS.

Progress in Cybernetics and Systems Research, Volume 2
Copyright © 1975 by Hemisphere Publishing Corporation

Basic Information Subsystems

Historically, the justification for the use of computers in many organizations has been the automation of routine clerical operations. From these beginnings, an Information System is a natural outgrowth. In order to control this growth, it is essential to understand the fundamental divisions of MIS activities and their implications on the MIS design.

There appear to be three basic divisions: namely, transaction processing, reporting and control, and decision support. *Transaction Processing* are those activities which are initiated by a transaction, and form the backbone of most MIS, i.e., payroll, credit card sales, inventory stock control, etc. In general these activities are highly structured and rigidly formatted. *The Reporting and Control* activities represent more refined processing in response to routine or special requests. The generation of weekly/monthly production reports, inventory statistics and personnel statistics are some examples of such activities. These output are semi-structured in nature, with format and content under discretionary control by management. The transaction processing system and the reporting/control system form the bulk of current Management Information Systems, especially at the operational level in an organization. To date, many books and papers have been written on the design and evaluation of Information Systems, but unfortunately they appear to confine themselves largely to only these two system components.

The third division, *Decision Support*, has been touched upon in the literature in the past few years. The activities associated with Decision Support are generally initiated by a need to take action. This system produces the required information, in the detail and format needed by the manager, upon which the manager can base his decision. It is this system, the Decision Support System (DSS), which is of concern in this Chapter.

Decision Support Systems

Much effort has been directed in recent years to the use of computers to aid decision-making. It is evident that much more than mere data processing is involved. The spectrum of computer involvement goes from the computer itself making the decision to merely providing reduced data.

The man/machine decision-making process demands that considerable attention be paid to the problem of sharing the various aspects of the decision problem between the man and the machine. In the design of decision support systems, a basic objective must be to establish measures of effectiveness for the man/machine system and to seek an optimal division between humans and machines with respect to these measures.

A management decision is essentially a human act which blends information, analysis and experience. The DSS supports the decision-making process by producing information, reducing data and analyzing possible alternatives. Initially this support is completely unstructured and highly interactive, with extensive user involvement. When some of the decision-making activities become routine, that portion of the Decision Support System can be incorporated within the Reporting and Control System.

The skills required for the design and development of a Decision Support System are quite different from those required for a transaction processing or Report/Control System. The designers must have knowledge of data processing, quantitative models, group and individual behavior, organizational behavior and detailed knowledge of the decision processes. There must be greater involvement by the decision-maker himself, whether he be from top or middle management or from the operational levels of the organization. This user involvement is necessary for the system analyst to understand the decision problems and current solution practices. Often a problem-oriented approach to defining the decision problems reveals unforseen problems, which require completely different solution approaches. Frequently, managers gain insights into their own problems by trying to explain them to someone else.

Personnel Management System

Consider now the Personnel Management Information System (PMIS), which has been developed and implemented by the Canadian Forces and operating on an IBM 370/Model 155 computer. The PMIS maintains a comprehensive record of personnel occurrences for all officers and men in the Canadian Forces and provides a wide variety of reports to meet the needs of commanders, personnel managers and functional authorities at all levels.

The over-all system is supported by a personnel data base containing essential data concerning each person's career status, qualifications, personal and family data and other data of historical significance. The contents of each data record are constantly being updated as changes occur in career status and personal circumstances.

Another database provides information on each individual establishment position in the Forces, identifying their specific requirements, their current status, and projected status.

Utilizing these databases, the Personnel Management Information System is able to satisfy the requirements of those transaction processing and report/control activities which have been identified to date. By most measures of effectiveness the system is operating satisfactorily. The number of transactions per month, i.e., updates, is increasing, the routine reports are prepared on schedule and in the required volume, and special requests are processed with a response time satisfactory to the user. There are undoubtedly many other equipment-oriented measures which would gladden the hearts of data-processing managers.

However, some disturbing questions could be asked. Are the increasing transactions true changes or largely error corrections? Should there be new, more relevant data items added to the database and obsolete data items removed? Are the routine reports relevant and are they meeting the needs of the individual user? How many special requests are never made at all because the system could not respond quickly enough to provide information for a critical decision?

These are the types of questions which must be answered when designing a personnel decision support system. The Directorate of Manpower Analysis has designed a Personnel Posting Support System to assist decision-making by the personnel managers. These managers have the responsibility for all matters pertaining to the career employment, posting and appointment of personnel and for controlling the allocation of personnel resources to meet the demands of the Forces.

One of the major tasks of the personnel manager is that of posting personnel from one position to another position, often in some other location in Canada. There are numerous reasons for the initiation of a posting; included are promotion, retirement, resignation, or death of a position incumbent, for broadening experience and additional training, and to spread the hardship postings in remote areas among a greater number of personnel. Whatever the reasons, roughly 25-30% of the Forces are involved in a posting each year. Each posting decision involves many critical factors: should the individual be replaced, what are his prospects for promotion, what about his family's schooling, are there medical problems, are there language restrictions, does he have necessary special qualifications, has he recently had a hardship posting? These are but a few of the factors which must be considered for each proposed move.

In the past, the posting process has been a manual process, conducted in a serial fashion. When a demand was raised for a position to be filled, the manager would check his manual personnel records to identify a number of possible candidates and to choose the most suitable one. A replacement would now have to be found for this individual, and the process iterated until a position was found which could be left empty. This is referred to as posting turbulence. Essentially the personnel system has been a reactive system, responding to a variety of stimuli. While many of the stimuli can be foreseen and predicted, the interactions of the personnel policies and requirements place the complete solution beyond the manual capabilities of the managers.

The decision-making processes involved in this posting and career system were analyzed by the operational research staff. Critical and dominant interrelationships among the system elements were identified, quantified where possible, and were given explicit consideration when the decision support system, the Personnel Posting Support System, was designed.

Personnel Posting Support System
This Personnel Posting Support System (PPSS) has the basic aim of providing the personnel manager with a computerized tool to assist him in his posting activities. It was designed
  a) To relieve the manager of much of the routine workload of file searching, sorting, matching, etc.
  b) To store and retrieve previous decisions.
  c) To store, evaluate and report information that is not yet part of the PMIS system.
  d) To allow maximum ready intervention and adjustment by the managers at intermediate stages.
  e) To reduce the posting turbulence of the manual system.
  f) To provide a rational and consistent forecasting mechanism.
  g) To provide the managers with personnel information relevant to the posting function.
  h) To provide a means to achieving financial savings in total moving costs while safeguarding the rights of individuals and service requirements

The PPSS is essentially a 4-step system as outlined in Fig. 1.
The first two steps of the system do not represent any major breakthrough. They merely result from a computer search through the personnel data records

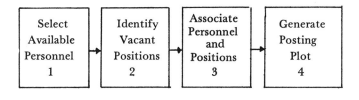

Fig. 1

and the establishment data records. All personnel and establishment positions which match certain selection criteria are listed for further consideration by the appropriate personnel managers. Such processing is routine and can be performed quarterly or monthly as the managers prefer.

What is not so routine are the criteria for selection. The listings are a forecast of personnel and positions which will be available over any stated period of time—currently the forecast covers the next nine months to one year. The selection criteria have been tailored to the individual manager's general, and particular, criteria of availability. Factors such as the length of time an individual has been in his current position, whether he has or will be promoted, educational requirements of his dependents, just to name a few, can all be considered in the availability of a person. For positions, the current or projected status must be considered. Is it empty now or will it be empty in the near future, when the incumbent retires or is promoted? If the incumbent is considered available, the position may be available.

The key element to be remembered here is that the data processing system is reacting to the demands of the user. Each personnel manager now has lists of personnel and positions which are and/or will be available in the foreseeable future. He may exercise his judgement and experience to add or delete people or positions as he sees fit.

The third step of the system is a systematic attempt to match the personnel and positions. Each available individual is considered for each available position. Their suitability is determined by their professional qualifications and personal requirements and by the requirements of the positions and the unit facilities where the position is located. The present system considers a person as "suitable" for a position if he successfully matches all checks. If he fails to match even one check he is considered "not suitable". In this manner a "suitability" matrix can be generated. For this early system, it is not possible to assign a degree of suitability for each match. Each man is either suitable or unsuitable. However, an important factor of moving costs can be assigned to each match. This will be a function of the number of dependents, weight of furniture and effects and the distance moved.

When he is found to be suitable for a position, an estimate is made of the dollar cost involved in moving the man, his furniture and effects, and his dependents from his current location to the position under consideration. Whenever he is found to be unsuitable, the dollar moving cost is set arbitrarily high—about 20 thousand dollars. In this manner a cost matrix is generated, the elements of which are the estimated moving costs.

The checks are imbedded in the system as either hard or soft checks. Hard checks are those which are considered in every run, whereas the soft checks are those checks which may be considered at the discretion of the individual manager, for any or all personnel or positions.

The final step in the system processes the cost matrix in order to assign each person to a position so that the *total moving cost is a minimum*. The output report that is passed to the personnel manager consists of several parts

a) Summary of general and specific parameters which were considered in the BLOCK 3 step.

b) A listing of all positions for which each individual was found suitable, including the estimated moving cost.

c) The listing of the recommended postings, showing the positions from which and to which the man is posted, and the name and current location of his replacement, if any.

d) The listing of personnel who were considered for a posting but were not posted at that time.

e) The listing of all positions which were left empty.

f) The listing of all positions for which there were no suitable personnel and all personnel who were unsuitable for any of the positions.

g) The *total* moving cost estimate and the average cost of the recommended postings.

It is at this point that the personnel manager can apply his service experience and personal knowledge of the individuals. This posting plot now serves as the basic solution to the posting problem. The manager applies his subjective judgement to the recommended postings to take account of the many factors which the computer has not been able to consider. He can accept or reject them as he sees fit. He can bring some of the other personnel into the plot. He can indicate some of the empty positions which he wishes to have filled. He may now wish for some of the personnel to be considered for positions at a higher rank, since they are about to be promoted. He may over-ride the recommended plot and post a man to some other position. He may restrict some men to specific functional units, such as only air bases and headquarters units. He may relax or tighten some other constraints such as position language requirements or trade specialty qualifications requirements.

The manager informs the system operator of his tentative decisions and a new posting plot is generated, with the revised constraints being considered. The new plot is the one which minimizes total moving cost under the revised constraints. This process can be repeated several times until the manager is satisfied that all relevant factors have been taken into account. At this point the postings may be accepted and promulgated.

Problems of design and implementation

The lengthy description of the Personnel Posting Support System was necessary to provide an insight into the intimate involvement by the decision maker in the identification of the decision solution processes. The initial concept was developed over 10 years ago, even before the integration of the Canadian Forces. The design of the PPSS was not begun in earnest until the PMIS personnel and establishment databases were developed.

The PPSS was designed and developed as an R&D project, outside of the PMIS framework, by an operational research team working in the Personnel branch. The PPSS database has the PMIS personnel and establishment data bases as its core, but includes additional data items not yet part of the automated personnel information system. The personnel managers were consulted every step of the way and their suggestions regarding format and relevant content of reports were generally incorporated into the system with minimum delay. This rapid feedback was largely instrumental in building user confidence in the system. The development has been completed and the PPSS is in limited production for approximately 40 per cent of the men. It now remains for the PPSS to be incorporated within the PMIS framework.

The main problem of implementation of the PPSS within the PMIS framework has been a conceptual problem. The individual information systems, which were developed to cater to the logistics, financial

and personnel functions, had reached the stage of development where consolidation of facilities and resources became inevitable. A large computer facility was purchased, followed by a second one. Data processing personnel, programmers and analysts, were integrated into a central organization, under the financial management division. This central group was considered to form the main body of expertise as system creators or developers, and their conception of their role was to develop the best, most perfectly functioning MIS possible.

While this conception is essential as an ideal goal, it contains the seeds of dissention. In order to evaluate progress toward the goal of perfection, measures of effectiveness were developed. Since the system was almost entirely oriented toward transaction processing and reporting/control functions, the measures were data processing-oriented. Increasing emphasis on improving efficiency of computer operations tended to discourage speculative processing to test new ideas. The lack of intimate contact with the user groups resulted in the gradual deterioration of the ability of the MIS product to meet the information needs of the user. The MIS does make a strong effort to improve its product but the bureaucratic machinery of change cannot react rapidly. Fortunately, efforts are now being made to institute important changes in the management of data processing resources. Instead of adapting the user groups to MIS technology, senior management have recognized the vital need to find ways to make the MIS technology serve the user groups.

The renewed emphasis on user involvement will greatly ease the problems of incorporation of the PPSS within the PMIS framework. Technical problems will remain, but will be resolved in time. The financial implications of incorporation within the PMIS framework are not inconsiderable. From a data-processing point of view it is an added computer workload and added programming expense. The programs are probably not as efficient as the processers might wish them to be and some of the reports may appear to duplicate reports which are already being produced. It also does not fit neatly into the data-processing-oriented pattern of operations. To be fully implemented, additional data items would have to be introduced into the database and the data collection/update procedures developed. Thus incorporation of the PPSS into the PMIS will result in additional costs in data processing resources and personnel. There will even be some additional user personnel required for the system.

To counterbalance the cost figures there must be

some benefits, hopefully in quantitative terms. One major benefit is the projected reduction of the average moving cost by several hundred dollars. In total, a reduction in total moving costs of several million dollars per year is estimated. This results from the reduction of the average cost of a posting as well as the savings associated with the elimination of unnecessary postings. Other immediate benefits which cannot be quantified are *a*) better management of personnel resources, *b*) better utilization of personnel manager resources, and *c*) reorientation of the information system to a more user-oriented configuration.

Further benefits would accrue if a modified PPSS were to be used in a policy-capturing mode. By varying one parameter at a time, the marginal cost of various policy changes could be examined, insofar as they affect posting costs. Language policies and training policies can be tested and costed prior to their implementation.

It is a fact of life that the decision-maker has to make many decisions under pressure. Not knowing what decisions will be required prevents the Information System from being prepared ahead of time. However, the management of the Information System must recognize that the requirement exists to respond rapidly to solve decision-makers' problems.

Conclusions

To date, the development of Information Systems has been largely an equipment- or data-processing-oriented activity. Cost benefit analyses rely mainly on technical measures of effectiveness which seldom reflect the utility of the system to the users. Unless new, more relevant measures of effectiveness are developed by a systems approach, it will be an extremely difficult task to reconcile the apparently conflicting requirements of an Information System and a Decision Support System in order to develop an effective Management System, whether it be for the logistic, financial or personnel management function.

Considerations in the design of man–machine systems

F. INCE
The Scientific & Technical Research Council of Turkey

Introduction

In spite of technological developments in the last couple of decades that may be described as revolutionary, especially in computers (both hardware and software) and in control theory, man still remains an integral and indispensable part in the control of many systems, due to his unique abilities that cannot be duplicated by machines, at least not yet. However, those technological developments call for a re-examination of the roles and functions of men and machines in man-machine systems.

It is a well known principle in the design of man-machine systems that machines should be made to fit man's characteristics. What may be called the static aspect of this rule has drawn considerable attention in human factors and ergonomics studies. It includes the physical appearance, dimensions, sizes, shapes, relative locations and types of displays, controls, and other objects in the total work space. There has been considerably less work done on the dynamic aspect which includes the mathematical relationships in the controls, displays and the variables of the system under control. It is this dynamic aspect that gets to be critical with the increasing complexity of man-machine systems.

Whether it is the design of control or display dynamics, the studies have been done mostly with specific situations, and have not offered a general systematic approach. One notable exception is the study by Birmingham and Taylor [1] in which they analyzed the human characteristics in manual control. It was concluded that the human operator is not a very good differentiator and integrator, therefore his role in manual control should be mostly one of amplification, and involve little in the way of differentiation and integration. Birmingham and Taylor introduced the concepts of aiding, quickening and unburdening as means toward this goal.

Modeling studies to understand human control behavior have remained at that level and not progressed to general systematic methods for the design of control and display dynamics. They have used complex mathematics at times, with little regard to practical real world situations.

The major part of modeling studies has come from investigators with control systems background, and therefore has reflected their mathematical tools and means. Until the late fifties and early sixties, frequency domain analysis was the more common method of analysis. This gave rise to human transfer functions which give an average functional relationship between man's input and output. From a practical point of view this approach had several drawbacks. First, the transfer function was dependent on the dynamics of the controlled system.

Progress in Cybernetics and Systems Research, Volume 2

Second, it did not directly give performance measurements, such as RMS error or mean time on target, that are used by actual system developers and testers. Third, it gets too involved as the order of the system exceeds three or four with multiple inputs and outputs. Fourth, there are "guidelines" for good designs, but there are no quantitative criteria of optimality.

The development of modern control theory, among other things has brought forth definitions of optimality and optimal control. By employing a model based on modern control theory, the human operator's behavior in controlling complex higher order manual control systems can be analyzed and predicted. Such a model has been proposed and evaluated to predict human performance in manned vehicle control, as well as to determine display requirements in such tasks [2,3]. The cited references give detailed information about the model. However, the main points will be briefly summarized.

The optimal control model of the human operator assumes that, subject to his inherent limitations, a properly motivated, and trained human operator behaves optimally in some sense. Optimality implies the minimization of a cost functional which is a subjectively weighted combination of system errors and expended controls. The inherent limitations are represented in a lumped fashion by a delayed, noisy observation and a noisy output. Also the fact that human operators in general make smooth rather than abrupt control movements, is represented by an error weighting on the rate of control movement. The remarkable fact is that the parameters which represent the inherent limitations remain relatively invariant with respect to changes in the dynamics of the controlled system. Without going into further details it is stated that given the system dynamics, the model parameters and the subjective error weightings, the model can yield much information about the system performance.

In addition to serving its obvious purpose, the model implies another piece of important information. Although the model is not claimed to be a resemblance of what goes on inside the human operator, it points out that the net contribution of the human operator to the over-all system performance is one of deterioration as compared to a control purely by a machine, because of man's inherent physiological limitations. But yet the human operator is the decision maker as to how the system is going to behave. All value judgements and the expression of desired performance originate from him. Therefore, a new design of the man-machine system

is called for, that reconsiders the roles and functions of man and machine.

The task
The word task may have different meanings in different situations. Functionally speaking, the task of controlling a machine may be divided into four subtasks or task phases. Although functionally distinct, the task phases are generally intermingled, overlapping and simultaneous, and therefore may or may not be separable in time.

1. Determination of target performance, that is the ideal, desired values of the variables of interest. Target performance is not merely a satisfactory performance. In real situations, actual system performance will rarely match target performance. There will almost always be some deviation, however slight, because of outside disturbances, limitations and other unexpected happenings. For example, for a certain part of a flight path, this task phase may set target performance as 25,000 ft altitude, 90° heading angle, 560 mph airspeed, zero bank, zero side force, etc. At any one instant the actual values may be 25,100 ft, 89°, 557 mph, 3°, and 0.01 g, respectively.

2. Determination of the control strategy. This task phase involves both value judgements and mathematical operations. First, there are the relative costs and values of the variables of interest. These include the costs on the deviation of the state variables from their desired values, costs and values on time, costs on fuel and other expendables, etc. To give a simple example again from the case of an airplane, one might want to pay 3% more on fuel to reach destination in 2% less time or vice versa. This is a value judgement that is usually affected by factors outside of the system. After the determination of the relative costs and values in a combined form, there comes the usually complex mathematical process of formulating how to treat the observations (task phase 3) in view of the performance costs and values. This is a problem that has been extensively, but by no means completely studied in literature, under the various headings of optimization, linear programming, nonlinear programming, dynamic programming, etc.

3. Determination of the state of the system. This task phase involves mainly observations and very likely some mathematical operations on the observed variables. Observation occurs either directly from the physical source or indirectly by means of displays. The mathematical operations on observed variables may be necessitated in multivariable systems with only some of the variables directly obtainable. Assuming observability, the other variables may be computed.

4. Determination of the control variables. This task phase involves the mathematical operation of applying the control strategy to the observed state of the system and the target performance. It may vary from simple linear multiplication by a constant, to quite complex mathematical operations.

The four task phases may be mathematically represented in this way. Let x represent the target or desired state as determined by task phase (1). The control strategy H is determined task phase (2). Task phase (3) determines y the current state of the variables of interest. Task phase (4) applies the control strategy H to x and y to generate the control variable u. That is,

$$u = H\{x, y\}$$

In the context of manual control all the task phases are essentially performed by the human operator. However, it is not claimed that the human operator works that way in his mind, at least not consciously. But the net effect may be analyzed as such.

Task phases (1) and (2) may be preset and remain constant, or they may change continuously or discretely during the course of control. On the contrary, task phases (3) and (4) have to be exercised during the whole course of control, although they may be exercised intermittently.

Conventional manual control systems

Traditionally, the dynamics of the system to be controlled has been accepted as a fixed, given part of the whole man-machine system. Some improvements have been made for the purpose of making the operator's task more manageable, such as stability augmentation in high performance aircraft. However, a systematic effort to make the task as manageable as possible, has been generally lacking. The four task phases remain primarily the operator's responsibility.

Given the system dynamics, the operator observes the output, and directly manipulates or controls u, the control input. Increased system complexity, as in high performance air, water and space vehicles,

can make the control task of the human operator a very difficult one, because in order to control the output, the operator has to work through the complex system dynamics rather than on the output itself.

For example, in the longitudinal dynamics of a light airplane the operator controls the elevator position and the power of the engines, whereas the desirable variables are vertical speed, altitude, and airspeed. The operator's controls change thrust, pitch rate, pitch, angle of attack, drag, and other quantities which in turn combine dynamically to give the desired output. Similarly for the lateral dynamics of an airplane, the pilot controls aileron and rudder positions, whereas his real interest lies in controlling bank angle and direction of heading.

With the conventional control system, the operator has total control over the system. He has to correct for outside disturbances, as well as generate the control to match the system output with desired output. Because he has to exercise continuous control, he has less time left for other necessary tasks (communication, navigation, monitoring, etc.) than if he were partly relieved of the control task. Increased task complexity is also expected to result in increased training time and a decreased safety factor.

The performance control system

The basic assertion of Birmingham and Taylor [1] published 20 years ago has not changed. Man still is a poor integrator and differentiator, but yet he remains to be an indispensible part of many systems due to his flexibility, general intelligence, and other capabilities that cannot be substituted by machines. What has changed is the development of computer technology, systems and control theory since that time. Unburdening and quickening now appear to be somewhat obsolete methods for the compensation of man's shortcomings in manual control.

Going back to the four task phases, it is seen that task phase number one involves a decision making as to the purpose of the system. This is a function belonging solely to the human operator and should remain so. On the other hand, task phase number four consists only of mathematical operations and is best done by machines. Task phases two and three include value judgements, observations and mathematical operations which can be divided between men and machines. In general, value judgements and some of the observations should originate from men. Other observations, including more demanding measurements, and mathematical operations again should be in the machine domain.

What evolves may be called a performance control system after Roscoe and Kraus [4]. By putting an interface between the operator and the machine it is possible not only to unburden the human operator but also to increase system performance considerably without necessarily losing any control authority of the human operator over the machine. Without going into details which can be found elsewhere [5,6], the workings of the interface will be briefly explained.

The interface accepts as inputs from the human operator values that are determined by him, such as desired states, costs and values of the variables of interest, and other subjective data. It performs the necessary mathematical operations on these and other machine derived data, and generates the control variables to drive the system. In other words, the operator tells the interface how he would like the system to behave, and the interface does the work of driving the system as close to the desired state as possible. The two actions are continuously ongoing and simultaneous. Therefore the interface is not a preprogrammed controller in the ordinary sense. It may be called an instantaneously programmable controller. It also has or should have adaptive capabilities.

With the PCS system the operator has direct control over the variables of interest. He does not have to worry about how to move his control wheels, levers or knobs to control those variables. He has less mental work, and more time to do other tasks. The design of a PCS system brings up new problems in the designs of controls and the determination of the extent of control authority between the operator and the interface. For a discussion of the latter problem see [7].

Application of the performance control principle to airplane dynamics

Flying an airplane is a collection of an indefinite number of complex tasks: cruise at different speeds and altitudes, landings, takeoffs, ascents, descents under various conditions, and a multitude of maneuvers. Additional necessary tasks of communication, navigation, planning and monitoring place a heavy work load on the crew, which may be one to three persons. Autopilots have existed for some time now, but they are designed to control the airplane for unpressed uncritical steady state conditions, and are not of much help in the more difficult tasks of landings, takeoffs or maneuvering in congested terminal areas.

A complete evaluation of a performance control system as applied to airplane control, involves an extensive set of experiments. As a first experiment in a series being conducted at the Aviation Research Laboratory of the University of Illinois, performances of pilots were compared between PCS and the conventional systems in an area navigation task [4], in a Singer Link GAT-2 flight simulator. The GAT-2 simulates a general aviation light twin-engine airplane, but not any one particular make or model. With the PCS system fore-aft and right-left movements of the yoke corresponded to desired or commanded vertical speed and bank angle, respectively. Conventionally, these yoke movements control elevator and aileron positions. Since lift compensation in turns, slips, and skids are automatically provided, there was no need for rudders.

An analytical evaluation of the task of straight and level flight in the GAT-2 was also performed both for the PCS and the conventional systems, using the optimal control model of the human operator. Although there was no fine tuning of model parameters for a best fit to data, both the mathematically predicted and experimental results showed dramatically improved performance with the PCS.

Mathematical predictions were calculated for different outside disturbance and visual loading conditions. An improvement index defined as percentage of improvement from the conventional to the PCS system showed improvements from 34% to 92% for heading angle errors with an average of 55%. The average improvement index in the experiment was 73%.

An even greater improvement was obtained in longitudinal dynamics. Model predicted altitude tracking improvements for the various disturbance and visual loading conditions changed between 161% and 282% with an average of 218%. The experimental conditions yielded an average improvement index of over 400% surpassing all predicted figures.

In addition to the improvements in standard flight error measurements, there were also a marked reduction in blunder type errors and an increased rate of processing a side task. The latter shows that there is also the benefits of more time left to the pilot to do other tasks. All the experimental results show a high degree of statistical reliability.

Further experiments both in the air and in simulators incorporating various other tasks should provide other interesting and valuable data.

Conclusion

Prompted by developments in machine capabilities and control theory, a reinvestigation of the task of manual control leads to a new principle for the design of man-machine systems. Implementation of the proposed principle to the pilot-airplane system shows that much benefit is to be gained: This view is supported both experimentally and by modeling predictions.

The principle is applicable to systems whose dynamics can be accurately described by mathematical equations that are solvable in at least real time. These include airplanes, ships, space vehicles, and many industrial systems. The concept may be extended to nonelectromechanical systems such as ecological and biological systems, which can be accurately and reliably modeled.

What has been presented is not claimed to be an all new novel idea. Elements have already been practised such as in fly-by-wire systems. However, it is believed that those have been results of necessity rather than an analysis of the role of men and machines and therefore have not presented a general unified, systematic approach to the design of man-machine systems.

The design of the interface is not a straightforward matter. It brings up questions and areas of research not only in hardware and software but also equally importantly, in the human factors aspects. Aside from the design of controls and displays, a thorough analysis of the tasks in each individual case is necessary for the determination of the extent of control authority between the operator(s) and the machine.

References

1. BIRMINGHAM, H.P. and TAYLOR, F.V., 'A design philosophy for man-machine control systems', *Proceedings of the IRE*, 42, 1748-1758 (1954).
2. KLEINMAN, D.L., BARON, S., and LEVISON, W.H., 'A control theoretic approach to manned-vehicle systems analysis', *IEEE Transactions on Automatic Control*, AC-16, 824-833 (1971).
3. KLEINMAN, D.L. and BARON, S., 'A control theoretic model for piloted approach to landing', *Automatica*, 9, 339-347 (1973).
4. ROSCOE, S.N. and KRAUS, E.F., 'Pilotage error and residual attention: the evaluation of a performance control system in airborne area navigation', University of Illinois, Aviation Research Laboratory Savoy, Ill. ARL-73-3/AFOSR-73-1/FAA-73-1 (March 1973).
5. INCE, F., 'Application of modern control theory to the design of man-machine systems', Savoy, Ill. University of Illinois, Aviation Research Laboratory ARL-73-17/AFOSR-73-11 (August 1973).
6. BRYSON, A.E.Jr. and HO, Y.-C., *Applied Optimal Control*, Waltham, Massachusets, Blaisdell (1969).
7. BERGMAN, C.A., SIVIER, K.R., and ROSCOE, S.N., 'Control authority with a flight performance controller', Savoy, Ill. University of Illinois, Aviation Research Laboratory, ARL-73-23/AFOSR-73-14 (October 1973).
8. KALMAN, R.E., FALB, P.L., and ARBIB, M.A., *Topics in Mathematical System Theory*, New York, McGraw Hill (1969).

Systems analysis of scientific research and development

Dr VINCE GROLMUSZ and **GYÖRGY DARVAS**
Institute for Science Organization,
Hungarian Academy of Sciences, Budapest, Hungary

Introduction

In the present stage of development of the sciences, when the integration of the different branches of science is more and more characteristic and the problems needing research become more and more complex and complicated, the significance and role of systems research is growing fast.

The objective base of the relatively rapid development of systems research is that the systems approach as an independent discipline—although it is at the beginning of its development—is growing dynamically and gives more and more possibilities for its theoretical and practical applicability in the most diverse fields.

Now, systems research is going on in two parallel directions. On the one hand, we are studying the *general principles of systems theory*, the determinants and inherency of it as an independent discipline, and on the other hand, we are carrying out *conscious systems analysis based upon the examination of concrete systems*. The spontaneous systems approach applied necessarily in science-methodology could be met in several fields of science long before the exact systems approach had appeared, but since the appearance of the exact systems approach we can speak about the *conscious utilization of the systems approach.*

The present parallelism in systems approach arises from the fact that practice brings up more and more such problems. Their solution requires urgent research based upon scientific systems approach which will yield indicators for particular systems. The development of the systems approach as a science therefore demands a permanent dynamic relation and feedback between its two directions, i.e., between the general systems approach and the experience of its application.

According to the ideas mentioned above, our Chapter falls into two parts:

- In the first part we discuss some of those problems of general systems theory which are—from the point of view of practical use—of primary significance.
- In the second part we attempt to make concrete the general systems theory in a specific sphere of activity—on research and development—and to draw some significant conclusions.

PART I

1. General criterions and modeling of systems

1.1 General criterions of systems

The question: "What is a system?", has been one of the main questions of the systems approach since the first works of Bertalanffy and his followers in this field. One can ask whether now, when systems science has a past of some decades, can such a fundamental question be the subject of a scientific dissertation? The fact that several different definitions of "systems" can be found in the special literature reflects the fact that this problem hasn't yet been satisfactorily solved. Without increasing the number of the existing systems definitions, we should like to approach the question by examining those aspects which can form a basis for answering it.

Let us first examine the question: What can be the criterions of a system? The criterions of all systems can be divided into two groups: *general and specific systems criterions*. As general criterions of a system, we mean those which are common and characteristic of all systems. These criterions are discussed in the first part of our Chapter. The specific criterions of the system characterize and distinguish certain types and groups of the systems or the individual systems. We give an example of the definition of these in the second part of the Chapter.

Examining the general criterions of the systems, let us take first the following trivial ones:

(A′) Each system is a set of its elements.
(B′) Each system as a whole is itself an element of other systems.
(C′) Each element is itself a system of other elements.

Let us see whether the (A′), (B′), and (C′) criterions are sufficient to characterize a general system. The deficiency of this three-criterion characterization is that it allows the frequent mistake of mixing the idea of the system with that of the mathematic set. No one system can be interpreted only as a set of its elements, it becomes a system only by a certain *relation* of its elements. This fact must be embodied also in the definition of the general systems criterions. Therefore we can say,

(D′) In each system the elements are interrelated with each other. These relations can be bilateral or multilateral, and can even play the role of conveyor between all the elements of the system.

Let us now examine these four criterions in detail. We have operated with two fundamental conceptions: the *element* and the *relation*. What can be elements of a system and what can form interrelations in a system? Shall we say that in a wider sense each material formation can be an element of a system. The formations of consciousness are also included, because these are of material origin as well. The interrelations between the objects can be of perfectly abstract, incorporeal nature and material exchange conveyances alike. Obviously, the same phenomena may appear in one aspect as an element of a system and in another aspect as the relation of elements of another system. For example, a given language acts as a connecting link in the system of people living in the given linguistic area (in that society), but in another type of system, in that branch of the linguistic science where the system of languages spoken by mankind is studied, it appears as an element of this system. Considering that nowadays scientific investigation has enlarged to a material reality, on the whole we can speak about the objects of science, instead of the elements of a system. Through the previous example we could illustrate that the same object can appear in the role of both an element and a relation. Moreover, in different relations the very same object can be an element of different systems. For this reason, to each system belongs an *aspect of examination* (or that system of aspects!), on the basis of which we are able to select the objects forming the very system. ($\underline{E}'$) In this way, for instance, the special sciences have separated. The flying bird and the launched rocket can be objects of the same moving system for the physicist, but in the system of examination of an ornithologist the latter has no sense.

We shall state that each system is a set of its objects, which can be of whatever formation of the material world we take, and which are connected by some common aspect (aspects). But to be correct we have to say more about the aspects of examination of a given system. Namely, when we select the set of elements of a system we want to examine and the relations connecting its elements from the whole of the material world, we arbitrarily pick it out of the complex system of objects of the material world at the same time. In each concrete examination the aspect of examination given in advance lends a distinguished role to the selected set, which is dealt with in the examination as an individual closed unit, picked out of the unit of the material world. On the one hand, we distinguish objects, which are regarded as belonging to the given set according to the given aspect of examination; on the other hand, we distinguish relations, which from the aspect of examination are regarded as significant in the set. But meanwhile we must never leave out of consideration that, from another aspect, the objects belonging to the set can be connected with other objects, not belonging to this set, and similarly that from other aspects of examination there can be found other relations between the objects of the same set. The endlessness and inexhaustibleness of the material world makes us sure that there will always be objects out of the system, selected from any aspects. Moreover, the selected system itself—as a whole—may appear as an element of broader systems. Similarly the system itself and its objects can be divided into further subsystems and elements and further systems may be immanently included. These individual systems selected from another aspect may appear as single elements of the system studied by us. For example, the Sun and its planets are elements of the Solar system, but at the same time the Solar system itself is an element of the broader Galaxy. On the other hand, the planets belonging to the Solar system and their satellites form an individual system from another aspect of examination. Similarly each celestial body and the set of the molecules forming it is a system in dynamic equilibrium. The molecules of the system are also systems of atoms and these can be divided into further elementary particles, which—on their own level of examination—can also be regarded as individual systems. Even the Earth, as one of the elements of the Solar system, has such living systems, which can be ignored during the examination of the Solar system, but which, in the examination of the Earth on another level of study, can appear as systems of a new type.

Regarding the matter as it is elaborated in the dialectical materialism, the material objects are in permanent change and dynamical interaction. Accordingly, the material systems show permanent change as well, and consequently their closed unity is relative. At the same time we have to emphasize that the material objects and the material systems are relatively independent during the permanent change. Each concrete material system strives to reflect this relative independence. The dialectical unity of these two circumstances can really only be explained by a coherent systems approach. This is expressed when we say that *each system*—as a definite complex of objects selected from a certain aspect and having relations according to this selection—*is in permanent interaction with its external and internal environment.*

Correctly this means the following. Referring to the external environment, the system is, on the one hand, *a*) itself an element of broader systems, and on the other hand, *b*) its objects have not only interrelations with each other, but are connected with other objects outside the system as well. These are called the *external relations* of the system and its objects. Referring to the internal environment, *a*) the objects of the system can themselves be divided into further parts as well, and besides their interrelations with each other, they are connected —although in another way—with these parts too; further, *b*) these building elements of the objects can also form systems having connections with the studied system. These are called the *internal relations* of the system and its objects. Regarding both the external and the internal relations, it can be stated that each object of the system and the system as a whole, which from another aspect can be regarded as an object as well, has such relations. Here we have to emphasize that by external, and respectively internal relations, we mean not only structural, respectively spatial division, but a qualitative, functional and other division in the widest sense alike.

No doubt, the above-mentioned approach to the examination of systems is strongly ontologic. But we must not leave out of consideration the fact that we always approach the single objects or the material systems, or the material world, as an ontologic totality to get newer knowledge, on the one hand, and that—on the other hand—our present-day knowledge about them is the result of cognitive processes as well. Therefore, the strict division and counterposing of the ontologic and gnosiologic aspects in the examination of general systems does not seem to be effective.

To briefly sum up the foregoing: After selecting the given aspect of examination the (material and conscious) *objects of the material world* have been divided into two groups depending on whether they belong to the set of the system being studied or to the complementary set. We have selected those *relations of the objects* which were regarded as significant from the given aspect of examination. These can be divided into three groups: interrelations of the elements of the system, and their external [(*a*) and (*b*)] and internal [(*a*) and (*b*)] relations. Apart from them there are innumerable other relations between the objects but these are not explicitly specific for the set of objects belonging to the system, so there is no reason to group them in this way. In consequence of the above-mentioned idea of relativity, these divisions are never to be explained strictly;

neither the objects nor the relations build closed sets, particularly not in the case of strongly dynamic systems.

As the general criterions for describing systems, we can correctly set out the following:

(A) Each system is a set of material or conscious *objects*.
(B) Each system and its objects are connected with their external environment, they have *external relations*.
(C) Each system and its objects are connected with their internal environment, they have *internal relations*.
(D) The objects of each system have bilateral and multilateral interrelations (interactions) with each other characteristic of the system.
(E) To each system belong those *aspects* which determine the set of objects belonging to the system and the relations characteristic of the system.

1.2 Systems modeling
It is necessary to say something about systems modeling. From a certain point of view, each model is a simplified, uncomplicated reflection of the many-colored reality, the totality of the material world. In making a model in science, we always pick out those features of the phenomenon or object to be modeled, which are significant and characteristic from a certain aspect, while the less significant features therein are neglected. We have seen a similar problem while examining the general criterions of systems, and this can be found more so in the examination of specific characteristics of concrete systems. As a matter of fact, the demand for modeling often comes up in practical systems analysis.

We may state that in the history of sciences there has hardly been any science which has had a greater demand for the model science (model theory) than systems research.

Systems modeling has been a great problem for mathematicians. For examination of concrete systems we generally can find the most adequate mathematical structure. But on the general level we have no adequate basis.

For modeling of the system-conception outlined in the first part of the Chapter, the most adequate means is a graph in which the objects are represented by the points of the graph and the interrelations between them by the edges of the graph.

Usually, this is the best known model in systems

research, although its deficiencies already appear on the most general level. It makes possible representation of only the interrelations between the objects of the system, but the possibility for representing the external, respectively internal, relations is limited; it is limited to adequately representing the relations between the objects of the system if different relations from different aspects are permitted between them; it is limited to representing the intensity of relations, and the possibility of representing many-dimensional systems is also limited. The greatest disadvantage of the model is that it is appropriate only for representing bilateral interrelations—we cannot use it for representing multilateral relations, which are so much a characteristic of the systems approach. Yet the systems approach may contribute to the scientific results mainly by analyzing these relations. Such multilateral relation is conveyed, e.g., by the electromagnetic or gravitational field in dead matter, by the biosphere in animate nature, or by social consciousness in society. None of the examples mentioned here can be connected to definite elements of the given systems, but only to the whole of the system.

Science has attempted to remove these difficulties of modeling with graphs by using different algebraic structures. Such an attempt was seen, for example, in quantum mechanics at the end of the thirties and in the lattice representation of the Hilbert space of physical states in the sixties. But the present algebraic structures did not prove to be adequate for general systems modeling. In this respect a further elaboration of the general theory of algebraic structures may greatly stimulate general systems modeling and general systems science.

PART II

2. Research and development as a system

2.1 Justification of a systems approach to R and D
Research and Development—similarly to any other activity—can be studied and defined generally from many aspects. So far, in studying R and D the *activity aspect* has been dominant.

From the activity aspect, R and D can be characterized as a separated (specialized) branch of activity of social division of labor. We may identify
  – the *goal*: observation and cognition of the phenomena of the objective world; exploration of internal relations and laws of natural, social and consciousness phenomena; elaboration of

concrete methods, technologies; production of new materials or constructions on the basis of the new scientific knowledge gained in the above-mentioned way; solution of other practical problems by scientific approach and methods;

- the *method*: theoretical or experimental methods of scientific regularity (in conradistinction to routine tests, discoveries by chance and simple endeavors);

- the *result*: new scientific knowledge, new concrete method, technology, process, material, construction, etc., the complex of which—in definite situations—may become new productive forces, respectively social forces which are able to give impulse to scientific-technological progress.

Thereby the R and D activity has been defined mainly from an activity aspect. This was enough to separate the R and D activity from other ones and to emphasize the significance and distinguished role of scientific work in the life of society.

Parallel with the relatively hasty growth of the volume of R and D activity, the effective organization and management of this enlarged sphere of activity has become more and more urgent all over the world. But efficient organization and management claim deep knowledge of motives, material-personal-organizational elements and their structures, interrelationships, mechanisms, laws, etc., with regard to the R and D activity. From this claim has grown up a new discipline, the "science of science", the goal of which is just such a study of developmental processes and their laws in sciences, that is, the study of the R and D activity itself.

As a rule, each new science—in the first stage of its development—attempts to disintegrate the object of its examination into parts and to concentrate its attention on these. Nor can the "science of science" avoid this rule. New research branches have arisen: the philosophy of science, sociology of science, psychology of science, economics of science, development of science, prognostics of science, etc. Although these trends together have developed and enlarged our knowledge about the sphere of science, they have not made it possible to examine the sphere of R and D as a totality in such a way which could have met the demands of an effective organization and management. This problem has necessitated here the enforcement of the *systems theoretical aspect*.

The concept of "system" can be interpreted in many ways. General systems theory limits the domain of explanation to certain criterions. But these criterions are still too general to be suitable for concrete analysis. The demand for making the

systems-criterions concrete, results from this fact.

According to general systems theory, a "system" is generally a complex of different elements being in interaction. Starting from this fact we have to make further restrictions.

As the R and D as a totality—according to our a priori supposition, which is confirmed by our experiences until now—can be a system only of goal-oriented, functional, developing and relatively homogeneous elements, the criterions of such a special system must be defined as follows:

1. This system contains elements oriented to an identical special goal.
2. Within the functional processes of the elements belonging to this system appear identical laws.
3. The common resultant of the real development of elements belonging to this system is reflected by the progress of the whole system, and the developmental possibilities of each element are determined by the objective developmental possibilities of the whole system.
4. Each element belonging to this system gets impulses of an identical nature from its external environment and the reaction of each element to these impulses is generally similar.

The purpose of these strict restrictions is to help in the reasonable outlining of the given system (the reasonable drawing of its lines) and the reasonable definition suitable for efficient organization and management. (Apparently, other special criterions are to be defined for systems of other types and for other goals.)

How are these special criterions interpretable for the system of R and D? The R and D—in its totality —as a system:

1. Includes organizations and activities aiming at a characteristically identical goal; this identical goal is generally: a conscious, organized and methodical striving for something new.

2. In the life, progress and permanent activity process of R and D organizations we can see more or less equally characteristic laws (e.g., deepening of cognition of objective reality, increasing the scientific division of labor and strengthening the scientific cooperation at the same time, simultaneous spreading of specialization and integration, the self-development of the organization, etc.).

3. The common resultant of the real progress of R and D organizations and activities is reflected in the development of the whole of the R and D; and respectively: the developmental possibilities of the R and D organizations and activities are basically determined by the developmental possibilities of the

whole system of R and D; this refers to the mutual, necessary and functional relation of the individual elements and the whole system.

4. Each R and D organization and activity gets impulses of identical nature from its external environment (generally demands for R and D results and products) and the reaction of each organization and activity to these impulses is generally similar (they produce and give R and D results).

In our judgement all these give sufficient reason *to consider research and development as a totality as a special system and to manage this as such a system.*

2.2 The features of R and D as a system

The R and D system—as it has been mentioned previously—is a special system, which in many respects differs from other ones of similar type.

Which features are characteristic of this special system? The most characteristic features of R and D as a system can be summarized in the following eight points:

1. It is a material system consisting of people, their means and organizations and of the products of this special activity (A).
2. It is a complicated system, as the number of its elements in most countries of the world is rather big and the interrelations of the elements are of many kinds.
3. It is an active system, as its elements have interrelations during moving and changing of state (D) and it is a reasonably active system at the same time, because its activity aims at definite purposes.
4. It is a dynamically progressing, adaptive system, because it is generally able to adjust its purpose performance and its method of activity to the environmental conditions, and it is able to self-create, self-develop too, as it is able to change its organizational and functional structure.
5. It is a system producing innovational transfer effect, as in its basic process the known scientific results transfer to activity and new creations.
6. It is a system producing information, as the output of its basic process is mainly information, namely generally new information (about the nature of phenomena of the objective world, about its coherency and laws and about the practical usefulness of all these).
7. It is a complex system, as each of its elements (e.g., the R and D organizations, the activity process and its elements, the available resources,

management inside the organizations, etc.) also can be explained as systems in themselves (C).

8. It is an open system, because—despite its relative autonomy—it enters into more and more closed and varied relations, dependence and interrelationship with the external environment (i.e., political, economic, cultural systems, and so on), so we shall say that—assuming a system-hierarchy—it is an integral part or element of broader systems (B).

Of course, we have not exhausted the characterization of this special system in this way; our purpose was only to show those most characteristic features, which have been considered the most significant ones. *These, together with the other existing features, build specifics of the concrete system of R and D.*

2.3 The functional system's model of R and D

Regarding the effective organization and management of the R and D activity, such a summary of the whole complex of R and D is necessary which gives the possibility to explore the interrelationships of elements and to represent the whole complex mechanism of the activity process in R and D. This can be achieved by an adequate functional system's model.

Constructing a *functional system's model*—examining from a cybernetical aspect—we suppose such a system in which a process runs over, and in this process the system makes conscious transformation in the cause of definite purposes. We don't particularly need to prove that the system of R and D is suitable, or moreover that it is especially suitable for constructing such functional system's model(s). These models can also be varied depending upon what concrete demands are to be satisfied by constructing them. In the following we draw up such a functional system's model, which first of all wants to determine and suitably illustrate the main elements of the system of the R and D, their historical-logical order, the dual role of the external environment and the place of research management in the system.

These purposes—in our opinion—are mostly satisfied by a functional system's model of R and D, the main elements of which—in historical-logical order—are the following:

1. The existing concrete system of R and D, which gives—by its demands for R and D results—permanent impulses, forces and means to this system (in the case of demands, e.g., concerning the purposes, directions, etc., of the base activity or by

concrete definition of the problems arising in practice and demanding scientific solution); this environment also can be explained as a system or systems (e.g., economic system, educational system, etc.).

2. The managing subsystem of the system of R and D in itself can be named research management system, too. Its main elements are the following:

2.1 the system of purposes and means of science policy (here given purpose can be a device to get some higher purpose, respectively a given device can be the purpose of some other devices being on a lower level of hierarchy);

2.2 the system of research prognoses, programs, plans, which contains the whole process of their elaboration and the output of this process: the prognoses of different type and period, programs and plans, which may cover each significant element and relation of the system of R and D and the development of the whole of this system (including the other elements of the system of research management);

2.3 the system of different regulators, which includes the whole knowledge and technology of application (perhaps art) and the whole order of application of the possible and necessary direct and indirect regulators (especially economic regulators, e.g., income taxes, duties, state credits, etc.);

2.4 the system of the systems of R and D and their interrelations, which includes regularity of foundation, activity, reorganization and dissolution of these organizations, the existing concrete structure of them, the rights of the managing bodies, the system of interrelations of the managed and the managing organizations and that of the organizations cooperating with each other or changing activity with each other.

3. The complex of (mental and material) resources available to the functioning of the system of R and D and that of the set of (scientific and other) information.

4. The directed basic process running over the system of R and D, that is, the R and D activity itself. For special purposes those usual activities of the R and D institutions can be ranged here—e.g., scientific services, experimental production—which organically supplement the base process, or strictly become mixed with it or are some by-products of the process. It is the base of the existence of the system of R and D. This base process can be classified in many ways (e.g., according to the origin of

demands, the topics, the stages before the applicability—e.g., basic research, applied research, development—according to the just existing structure of the studied sciences, etc.), but each phase-process (that is, each R and D process started for supplying some given demand) has such common features—from the aspect of the functional system's model—as the following:

4.1 acceptance of demands of the external environment and translation of these into an adequate scientific technical language, that is, the scientific explanation of the problem being studied;

4.2 separating of the acquirements suitable for solving the given problem from the available scientific and other knowledge, fixing and realization of the concrete R and D activities on the base of the separation (if the problem has already been solved, this last phase can be left);

4.3 outputting the new information in connection with the given problem into the external environment and paying regard to the form of this information.

5. The external environment accepting the products of the system of R and D, which—by the real or potential utilization or neglect, or respectively direct refusal of these products—may react on the system of R and D or may output impulses fed back (e.g., the utilization of the new information requires scientific solving of new problems, the success reached is the basis for realizing demands considered to be unrealizable previously, etc.).

It appears from these facts that this model differs in many respects from similar previously known models. There are significant differences, e.g., that

– this is a model elaborated not on a micro- but macrolevel, and

– the external environment appears not in one, but in two roles representing the fact that here the environment really has two, perhaps very different states and behaviors. But by this division of the environment into two parts, it is perhaps better to emphasize that *not only have other systems an environmental function to the given system of R and D, but the given R and D system has such a function to other systems as well.*

From the developmental aspect, the functional model of the system of R and D practically may indicate homocentric (spiral), respectively helical self-development—in perfect accordance with experiences—in which

- starting from a supposed basic situation, the external environment gives impulses of a definite number to the system of R and D, the managing subsystem draws up a scientifico political strategy to solve these (impulses), the division of tasks, forces and means is carried out, the necessary new organizations and the interrelationships among them are organized, the suitable stimulators are worked up, the necessary R and D activity is performed and its products are given to the external environment (to the customer);

- the supplied demand creates new demands and the external environment gives more impulses to the system of R and D as previously (including the delivering of supplementary forces and means as well); the system of R and D reacts in a similar way and while it develops itself, the system of R and D transfers more and more new information to the external environment, and so on...

In such a dynamic course of development the external environment itself is permanently developing too and in the cause of the undisturbed self-development of the given system, each element is almost forced into being permanently adapting. This is especially important in the research management system, because a possible inflexibility or severity of this system may greatly slow down the progressive self-development of the whole system, or it may —without reason—deform the structure of progress in the cause of development, both on a national and international level.

In our opinion such or similar functional models of the system of R and D greatly promote the really effective organization and management, in so far as application in practice of concrete systems analysis and the utilizing of the experiences gained follows

the elaboration of these models.

Such systems analysis affords the opportunity—by confronting the model with the already existing practice—for exploring such functional problems of the concrete national system of R and D which—without systems approach—could have been discovered only by chance. The great practical importance of this special mode of approach results just from this fact.

It is enough to refer here only to the fact that the functional system's model drawn up previously has been successfully applied in Hungary to making the system of research planning at macrolevel and to exploring its functional problems that need solving.

Conclusions

In the first and the second part of this Chapter we have expounded that:

- on the one hand, the general systems approach must be developed with regard to practical adaptability on a larger scale; and
- on the other hand, in the special application of the general systems theory such special system theories must be elaborated which are valuable contributions to the general systems theory as well.

From this respect, it would be effective—by adequate international collaboration and cooperation—to define those spheres which first of all demand the elaboration of a special systems approach. On international scientific forums, symposiums ought to be organized first of all on these priorities and on elaborating recommendations.

In this way, systems theory itself as a discipline can be developed by a systems approach as well.

Epistemology, systems theory and the model of shells

VOLKER D. VESPER
Freie Universität Berlin, West Berlin, Germany

The reductionism-holism issue is a central problem in the epistemological justification of Systems Theory. Jacques Monod [1, p. 100 f.], for example, as a leading author in biological research rejects very definitely any holistic approach; in contrast to this opinion, the systems approach seems to be fruitful in practical research (cf., e.g., von Bertalanffy [2], *passim*; Vesper [3]). There exist sophisticated epistemological essays on this subject, e.g., by Ernest Nagel [4, p. 232 f.], who gains the surprising result that the question whether the whole is more than the sum of its parts, depends on the meaning of the words "whole" and "sum". Considering the fruitfulness of some branches in epistemological thinking, Ludwig von Bertalanffy [5, p. 8], who can be regarded as the originator of Systems Theory, has stated that positivism and philosophy of science is a "singularly sterile movement". This implies the question whether or not epistemology is sterile in general. I do not completely agree to this thesis. Epistemology may be useful in so far as it helps us to find a strategy in practical research which is better than trial and error; however, it must not be exaggerated. The critical point in my opinion is that a theory must have predictive power. It does not matter if there is any epistemological justification or not. Regarding the reductionism-holism issue, I do consequently agree to the pragmatic solution of

Herbert A. Simon [6, pp. 63-64] who regards the properties of the whole as a nontrivial result of the interaction of its parts. Thus, holistic thinking is no metaphysical nonsense but thinking which does not forget the patterns, which many classical sciences are missing still today.

These sciences deal with single problems or aspects and not with real phenomena. The German "Betriebswirtschaftslehre" (business administration and managerial economics), for example, deals traditionally with the economic problem of the firm and not with the firm as a whole. Predictions, however, concern the behavior of a whole phenomenon and cannot be ascertained via a partial analysis. This point seems to be the main reason for the present frustration in the economic and social sciences, which are talking about so-called "interdisciplinary research" as early Ptolemaic astronomy about its epicycles—and apparently with the same poor results.

I shall now propose a classification of sciences which shows the following properties:

1. It classifies according to real phenomena and not according to aspects.
2. It integrates mathematics, Systems Theory, heuristic and natural sciences into a homogeneous scheme.

In common with Bertrand Russel [7, pp. 138 and 145], I have the opinion that the real world consists

Progress in Cybernetics and Systems Research, Volume 2

of material which possesses a certain structure, i.e., a position or behavior in space and time. Now it is possible to make progressive abstractions from the material component of the reality: A total abstraction from the material delivers mathematics. In this view, mathematics would not be purely formal but the structural essence of the reality. The well-known mathematician Gottlob Frege (cf. Waismann [8, pp. 212 ff.] supported this opinion which, however, did not succeed in mathematics. On one less abstract level below mathematics we would have to classify General Systems Theory (GST), which deals with real systems but in a very abstract manner. The next less abstract, i.e., more concrete, level consists of a science which I shall call *Special Systems Theory* (SST) and which deals with general features of open self-organizing systems. Further we find on the same level theoretical physics, which concerns general features of the nonliving world. The lowest, most concrete level, shows below the SST-sector the arts, social sciences and biology. Below the sector of theoretical physics it shows the special natural sciences. This most concrete level of sciences follows applied technologies. Since some levels are divided into sectors, it has to be emphasized that this division is not a sharp one; there are transition zones: a biologist, e.g., needs some parts of chemistry, etc.

As can be seen, the more abstract level includes all sciences of the lower, less abstract level. If we see this like an onion (according to a proposition of Daniel Verney [9, p. 71], in a comment on my model), then we have an abstract structural center and more and more concrete shells which finally touch the reality via technologies. In the previous scheme, I made a distinction between an abstract GST which, according to its aims, includes nearly all sciences, and an SST which deals with open, self-organizing systems. This distinction seems necessary since GST is more or less a pure terminology with no specific predictive power. SST, however, possesses predictive power as will be explained below. For this reason, I prefer to waive GST in my classification subsequently. It is a terminological approach which may have some heuristic function, but not a science.

The above-designed "onion of sciences" is a very general application of my *Model of Shells*, which concerns the internal structure of open, self-organizing systems, and which thus will be the basic model of SST. Since the system of sciences itself is a symbolic system, it is open and self-organizing and consequently subject to SST. I explained the complete Model of Shells at the Seventh International Congress on Cybernetics, Namur, Belgium, in 1973. Basic ideas have been published formerly (Vesper [10]). On its major points I shall give a short summary.

Open, self-organizing systems have in common an abstract informational code, e.g., the genetic code in living beings, or statutes and goal structures in human organizations. This code, called the *Central Code* (CC), effects direct interferences in the environment via a hierarchy of processes. The levels of this hierarchy of processes may be regarded as shells which afford the sensitive CC graduated protection against the hostile environment. The central shell, very rich in energy, is the subtle milieu in which the code can flourish; the outer shells transform the regulating commands of the CC into more and more concrete processes. The utmost shell finally interferes directly with the environment. Thus each outer shell can be regarded as an artificial environment of the next inner shell. Consequently, a construction is obtained which consists of artificial environments following one another; these environments grow increasingly abstract and more and more rich in energy toward the center. The shells allow the code to survive within the "noise" of the hostile outer environment. Thus the CC regulates the behavior of the whole system. This model permits the understanding of structural adaptations in the construction of the system. This structural adaptation is a characteristic feature and cannot be explained by the Cybernetic feedback approach because Cybernetic regulation presupposes a fixed structure, according to von Bertalanffy (cf. [2, p. 149 f.]).

The features of these shells reveal a great regularity in the realm of SST. To confirm this, I shall continue with the design of a standard system which will be applied to concrete systems below.

This standard system has central shells for data-processing organs and outer shells with organs for material processes—if it is not a symbolic system, of course. The data-shells consist of the CC and shells which are processing behavioral commands of the CC and which sometimes produce predictions on the environment. The material shells follow with productive or metabolic organs and finally with input-output organs which are interacting with the system-specific environment.

In a special case, one organ has to be added within the data-shells: It is an organ for the variation of the CC. Applied to reality, this means organs for genetic interaction within a species or *political organs within a social system*. It can be supposed that CC-variation organs are a characteristic feature of species and will not be found in individuals. Stafford Beer [11, p. 163] regards a business firm as a species which confirms this opinion. In biological systems, e.g., plants, we have to consider that the flower of a plant is an organ of the species, it formulates and varies the genetic pool, i.e., the CC of the species, via acceleration of the exchange of genetic information. For the individual plant, however, the flower brings no advantages; on the contrary, it grows much better if the bud of the flower is removed (cf. Zimmermann [12, p. 146]). Consequently, the existence of CC-variation organs seems to be a criterion as to whether we speak of an individual or a species. According to this, beehives are individuals because a single insect cannot participate in the variation of the genetic information—except during the swarming time.

Now we shall try to apply the standard system to real systems in general. Some examples may suffice, however:

Central Code: constitutions in states, statutes in business firms, genetic pool in species, genetic code in individuals, general laws in sciences as an example of a symbolic system

data-shells: government in states, board of directors with its staff in firms, mitosis in species, brains in individuals, special laws in sciences.

It is easy to complete this list with respect to the material shells. Finally, however, I want only to mention the *system-specific environment* in the sense of the "fertile soil" the system is growing in:

Human individuals (citizens), business firms and foreign governments for states; human brains for firms (generally called "markets"); individual genetic code for species; nature for individuals; human brains for symbolic systems.

This intuitive synopsis makes no claim for logic rigor, of course.

The importance of this model for economics and social sciences can only be understood, if regulation and control among these systems has been analyzed.

In the Figure to this Chapter you can see typical self-organizing systems and their regulating relations. The cone within each system symbolizes the CC, the first surrounding circle indicates the data-shells, the next circle the material shells, and the joint arrows indicate the interference of the system with its specific environment, the serpentine circle. Since via this interference a partial modification of this environment takes place, it can be stated that the system regulates those other systems which are the elements of its specific environment. This regulation is symbolized by connecting streams. Of course,

this is a simplified drawing which shows the main streams only.

Generally, it has to be stressed that there is no closed feedback-loop but an open, autonomously regulated chain. The autonomous sources of this regulation are natural selection, and social and cultural trends, which cause a social and cultural selection. Biological evolution is a unidirectional process and thus a function of time (cf. Eigen [13], Monod [1, p. 154]). Similarly social and cultural evolutions are a function of time also. No individual can lastingly influence these trends, because they depend on the amount of information which is common knowledge of a whole people. Inventors or scientists or politicians become only famous when the time is ripe for their ideas. Thus the autonomously regulating source is time itself. Each level in this chain undergoes from the top to the bottom regulating system-interferences, which are of increasing complexity as a function of time, since self-organizing systems increase their complexity in the course of evolution (cf., e.g., von Förster [14]).

It is obvious that the Cybernetic feedback approach is not sufficient to explain this regulation: Apart from the lack of a fixed structure, mentioned above, there is no homeostasis but evolution. In contrast to the Cybernetic homeostasis, I have proposed speaking of "teleostasis" in this case (Vesper [15]). All feedback loops which can be observed *within* the systems, are *secondary effects*, which Ludwig von Bertalanffy (cf., e.g., [2, p. 213]) has called "progressive mechanization".

Does this model, i.e., SST, have predictive power? I think it allows predictions in a similar way to the "periodic law" in chemistry. It delivers general laws on evolution, regulation, organizational construction, and—as published earlier (Vesper [15])—on typical kinds of growth as a function of the energetic content of the environment.

Since, in social science and economics we cannot experiment on our research-objects in test-tubes, such general laws, transferable from one type of system to another one, are in my opinion the only chance to overcome the present scientific stagnation in the social and economic sciences. This can clearly be seen in the use of new, fashionable terminologies for old things, and in the catchword "interdiscipline" which very often means that "too many cooks spoil the broth". We need, in contrast, however, theories which actually enable predictions to be made in order to cope with the tremendous social and economic problems of today and the near future; and we need these theories very soon.

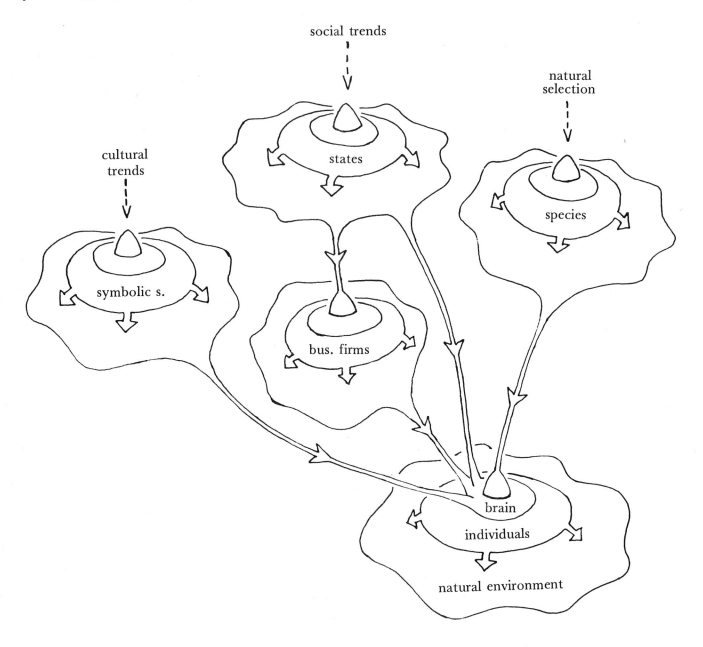

Figure The realm of self-organizing systems

References

1. MONOD, J., *Zufall und Notwendigkeit*, München (1971).
2. VON BERTALANFFY, L., *General Systems Theory*, New York (1969).
3. VESPER, V.D., Internationaler Kybernetik- und Systemforschungskongreß 1972, *Zeitschrift für Betriebswirtschaft* (November 1972).
4. NAGEL, E., Über die Aussage: 'Das Ganze ist mehr als die Summe seiner Teile', *Logik der Sozialwissenschaften*, (edit. by E. Topitsch), Köln, Berlin (1965).
5. VON BERTALANFFY, L., 'General Systems Theory—A Critical Review', *General Systems* (1962).

6. SIMON, H.A., 'The Architecture of Complexity', *General Systems* (1965).
7. RUSSEL, B., *Das ABC der Relativitätstheorie*, Reinbek (1972). ['The ABC of Relativity', London (1969)].
8. WAISMANN, F., Einführung in das mathematische Denken, München (1970) [Wien (1936).].
9. VERNEY, D., Aperçus sur le 7ème Congrès International de Cybernétique—Namur—1973, In: *Cahiers SYSTEMA* (January 1974).
10. VESPER, V.D., 'Beyond the goals—the existence-function of the firm', *Advances in Cybernetics and Systems Research* (edit. by F. de P. Hanika and N. Rozsenich), Vol. II, pp. 21-27, Transcripta Books, London (1973a).
11. BEER, S., *Kybernetik und Management*, Frankfurt/M. (1967).
12. ZIMMERMANN, W., *Geschichte der Pflanzen*, Stuttgart (1969).
13. EIGEN, M., 'Selforganization of matter and the evolution of biological macromolecules', *Die Naturwissenschaften*, pp. 465 ff. (October 1971).
14. FOERSTER, H.v., 'On self-organizing systems and their environments', *Self-organizing Systems* (edit. by M.C. Yovits and S. Cameron), New York, London, Oxford, Paris (1960).
15. VESPER, V.D., 'On the internal structure of open systems—a model of shells', Paper read at the VIIe Congrès International de Cybernétique, Namur, Belgium (10-15 September 1973b).

Systems methodology–its nature, structure and applications. Some remarks

Dr W.W. GASPARSKI
Institute of Organization, Management, and Control of
the Polish Academy of Sciences and Ministry of Science,
Warsaw, Poland

The concept of system

In the systems literature there are lots of definitions of the term "system" and it is not difficult to notice that the majority of them have been built apragmatically. The addition of a new apragmatic definition of "system" would be an increase of chaos rather than a uniformization of the systems movement terminology. It seems to be more efficient to consider the "system" pragmatically, because in the world there are not "systems", the "systems" are created by us. "To be a 'system' means to be treated as such by a systems-oriented scientist, researcher, investigator, planner, designer, etc.

If it is, we can formulate the following statements:

i. To consider an object as a system means the selection of things (called elements of the system) as conveyors of qualities (attributes) to the given relation or as conveyors of relations to the given qualities (attributes). (Ujumov [1], Gasparski [2].)

ii. Relations/qualities given are the structure. The structure given in the form of information constitutes the system *in abstracto*. The structure given in the energo-material form makes the system *in concreto*. (Gasparski [2].)

The concept of methodology

Consulting dictionaries we discover, at least, two definitions of the term "methodology". According to the first one, "methodology" means a generally described procedure, or a set of basic rules, of a scientific (or almost scientific, i.e., designing, planning, etc.) activity. "Methodology" is understood there as a method rather, or as an ill-defined technique, of you wish.

The second definition of "methodology" is: a science or study of methods, especially in an academic subject. In that meaning the "methodology" is a scientific discipline, whose domain is methods, procedures, techniques and rules of their utilization in different circumstances.

The well-known Polish logician and methodologist Ajdukiewicz described a framework for the methodology of science, treated as a discipline, of course (Ajdukiewicz [3]). According to his description there are two kinds of partition in the discipline:

a) the methodology is divided into general methodology of science and detailed methodologies of scientific disciplines;

b) the methodology is divided into pragmatic methodology and apragmatic methodology,

Progress in Cybernetics and Systems Research, Volume 2

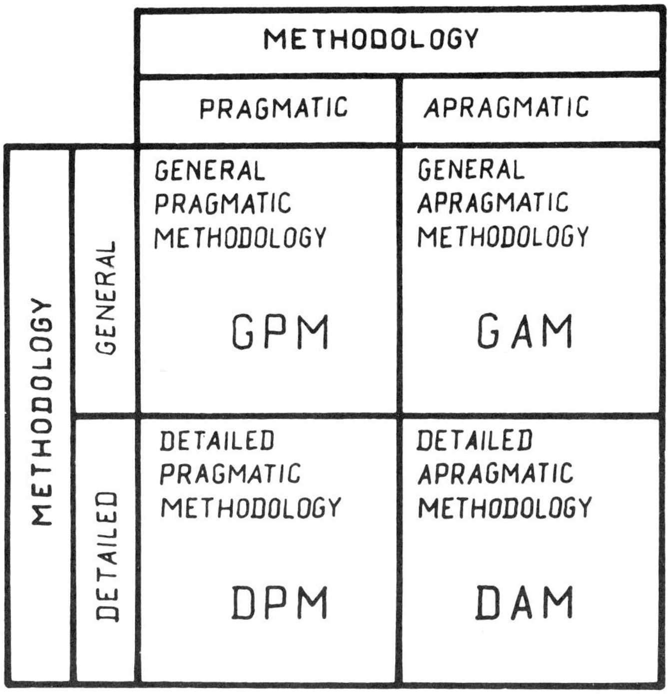

METHODOLOGY		
	PRAGMATIC	APRAGMATIC
GENERAL	GENERAL PRAGMATIC METHODOLOGY GPM	GENERAL APRAGMATIC METHODOLOGY GAM
DETAILED	DETAILED PRAGMATIC METHODOLOGY DPM	DETAILED APRAGMATIC METHODOLOGY DAM

Fig. 1a

Fig. 1a.

General methodology deals with the concepts of such kinds of scientific activity that are common to all scientific disciplines. They are: the concept of inference, the concepts of induction and deduction, the concept of definition, and many others.

Detailed methodologies deal with concepts of such kinds of scientific activity that are characteristic for different scientific disciplines or types of disciplines; e.g., the concepts of observation, experiment, measurement, hypothesis, and testing are typical for natural and social sciences, but do not exist in formal sciences like mathematics.

All methodologies—general and detailed—are broken down into a pragmatic and an apragmatic part. Pragmatic methodology, from the Greek word $\pi\rho\alpha\gamma\mu\alpha$ = action, deals with the activity of scientists as such. There are three tasks of that methodology:

1. to distinguish types of scientific actions, analyze and define them;
2. to describe scientific procedures;
3. to identify tasks, to the fulfilment of which scientists, consciously or unconsciously, aim, and to codify principles of correct proceedings in scientific activity based thereupon.

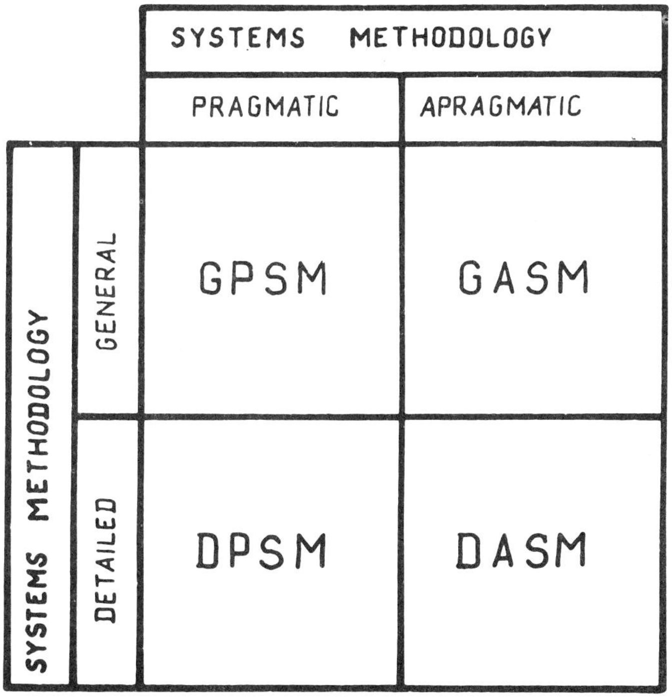

Apragmatic methodology deals with the results of scientific activity realized or even potentially realizable.

We propose to treat Ajdukiewicz's concept of methodology as a base for systems methodology studies.

The concept of systems methodology and the concept of studying it

The concept of systems methodology comprises the two following meanings: (*a*) a systems-approached methodology characterized above as a discipline, (*b*) a detailed methodology of a certain discipline or type of discipline (type of scientific or almost scientific activity).

According to the first meaning and Ajdukiewicz's description of methodology, the systems methodology includes: on the one hand, the general and the detailed systems methodologies, and, on the other hand, the pragmatic and the apragmatic systems methodologies, Fig. 1b.

As far as the second meaning of the systems methodology is concerned, there is no doubt that it is first of all the detailed methodology of such types of discipline that are called prospective, i.e., practical or applied sciences and engineering.

SYSTEMS METHODOLOGY		
	PRAGMATIC	APRAGMATIC
GENERAL	GPSM	GASM
DETAILED	DPSM	DASM

Fig. 1b

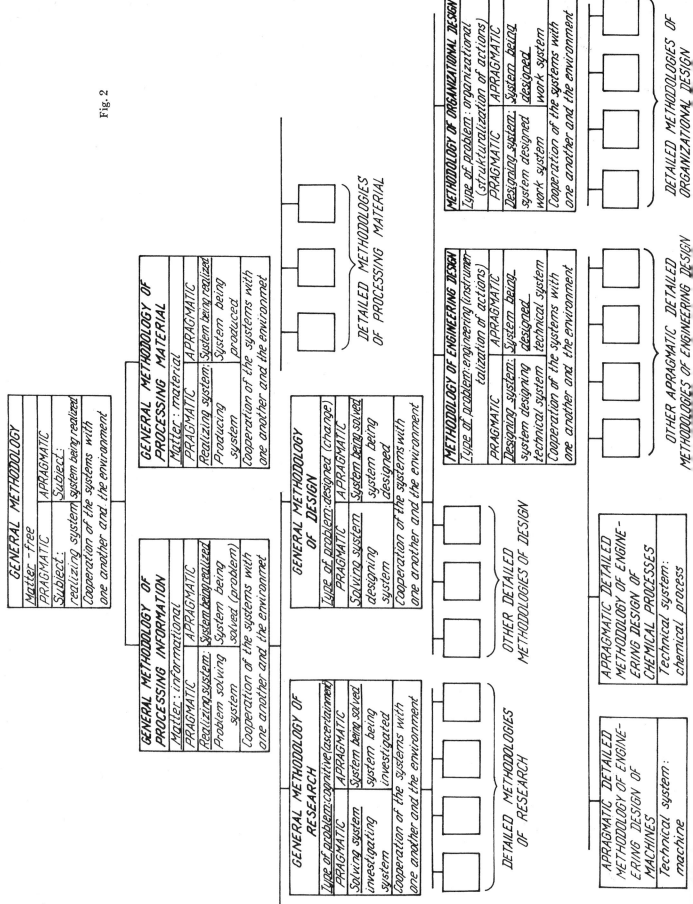

Fig. 2

310

Is it possible to identify systems methodology now? This means: is it possible to describe types of actions, which are characteristic for that methodology, to define its procedures and point out its tasks, to the fulfilment of which scientists and engineers aim? The general answer to that question is that it has not been possible to formulate it up till now; there are only a very few particular cases and subquestions of them, which could be answered approximately. It is also impossible to define the normative systems methodology.

Systems methodology, as with every methodology, or, more generally, every discipline, comprises the description of a certain domain. The methodology domain is, as was stated above, the scientific activity. What is the domain of systems methodology, therefore? It is such a kind of scientific and almost scientific activity as is realized by "systems-oriented" scientists, engineers, etc., i.e., operators or agents, whose methodological attitude and/or approach is named as a systems one by themselves, the other members of the "systems-oriented community" having no doubt that it really is. By studying, and only by studying, such an operationally defined area is the only way to the adequate reconstruction of the procedures caused by the active agent's (Kotarbinski [4]) attitude and/or approach. The final result of the systems methodological studies should be the systems methodology as a discipline, i.e., as a scientific system. The structure of the methodological knowledge is shown in Fig. 2. The methodological studies proposed are praxiological studies because of their subject: methods of actions; in that case the actions consist in processing information, particularly scientific (research or investigative), and designing actions. The studies ought to be developed from both systems-oriented and non-systems-oriented positions, Fig. 3. It is because of systems paradoxes (Sadowski [5]), wherefrom one of them, called the systems methodological paradox, told us that adequate knowledge about real systems is possible to perform only on the basis of systems-methodology research, but such methodology should be only constructed as a result of adequate knowledge of the real systems. The paradoxes of systems thinking should be overcome by way of the iteration process of studying: the systems, the studying of systems, the systems again, the studying of systems once more, etc.

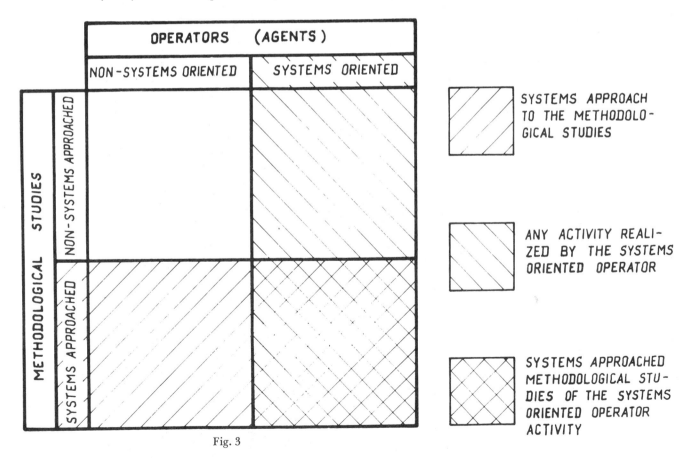

Fig. 3

311

Let us consider the preliminary results of the example of the (above-described) application of methodological studies.

The example: design methodology

Designing is understood here as the informational preparation of action, aimed at a change of reality, based on cognition and consistent with a recognized social criterion of evaluation. Designing consists of solving a problem, the latter being a formal presentation of need (standard) in a language of the designing system. The result of designing is a model (standard) of an object and/or process. The model acts as a practical recommendation and has the form of an operational definition of an object, that is, its project (design).

On the basis of the project, preparatory actions, consisting of realization (static and dynamic) of an object are undertaken. These preparatory actions lead to the construction of an object, i.e., a functioning product, being realized, which—utilized in a basic action—enables its realization, thereby constituting the satisfaction of the need. The process of satisfaction of the need, starting from its generation and ending in the utilization of the system being designed, has a quasi-cyclic character, shown schem-

atically in Figs 4-19 (Gasparski [6,7]).

The model of the problem situation of the design methodology studies covers two subsystems (Fig. 20); subsystem A—the investigated activity, which is design in this case, and subsystem S—the remaining social activity. The two subsystems are linked by the following relations: substantive (R?)—the needs of subsystem S to be met by subsystem A (in this case: needs from which the design problems stem); substantive (R.)—the meeting of the needs of subsystem S by subsystem A (in this case: solutions of the design problems); control (R!)—steering of the subsystem A by subsystem S (in this case: the science and economic policy in relation to design activity). In decomposing the model, particularly subsystem A (in this case: the design), we can distinguish the following components (Figs 8 and 9): designers, equipment used by them, the flow of information from the design problem to its solution and relations between the designed and designing subsystems—the methods of designing.

The last-named—methods of designing—are the main subject of design methodological studies, and the others—elements of the problem situation described above—are the subject of auxiliary studies because those elements are the parts of the design methods, or, more generally, the design activity environment.

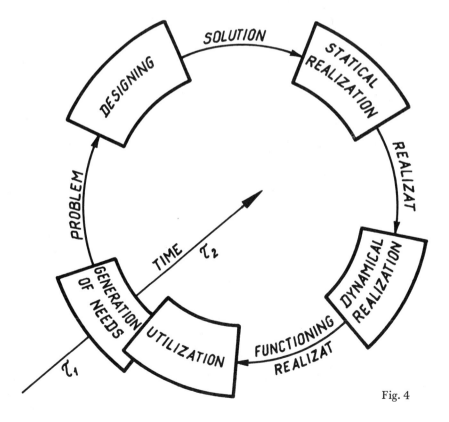

Fig. 4

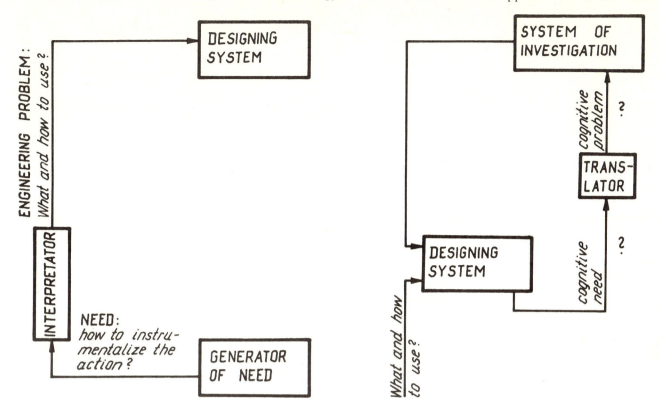

Fig. 5   Fig. 6

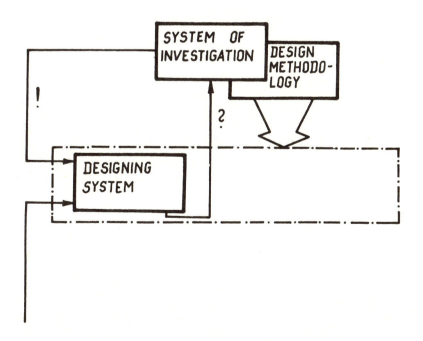

Fig. 7

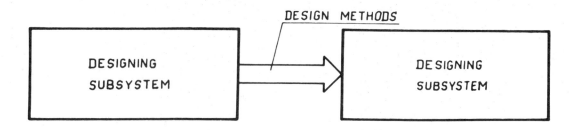

Fig. 8

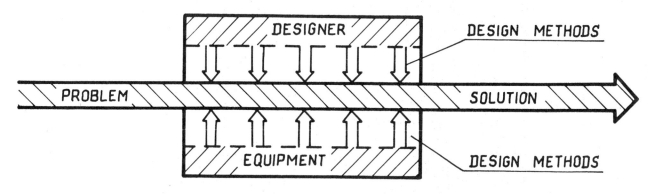

Fig. 9

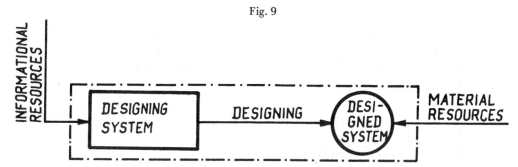

Fig. 10

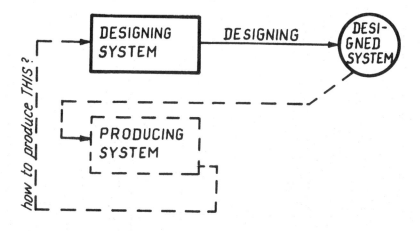

Fig. 11

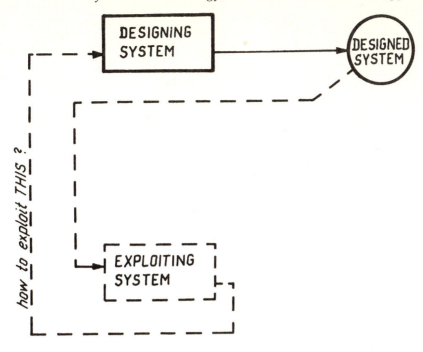

Fig. 12

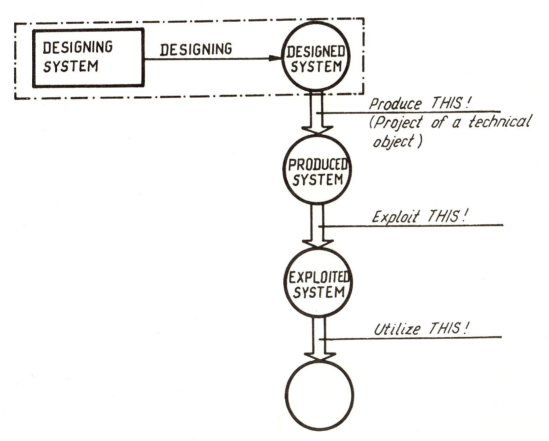

Fig. 13

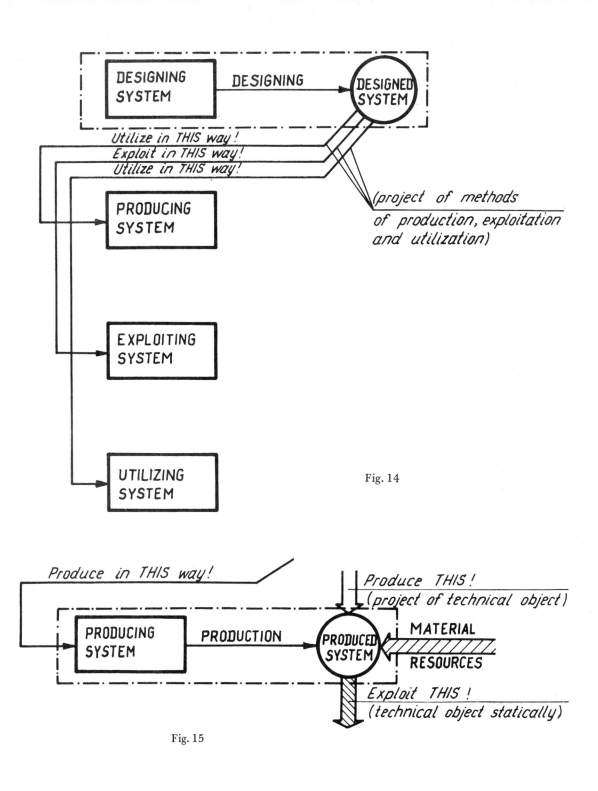

Fig. 14

Fig. 15

Fig. 16

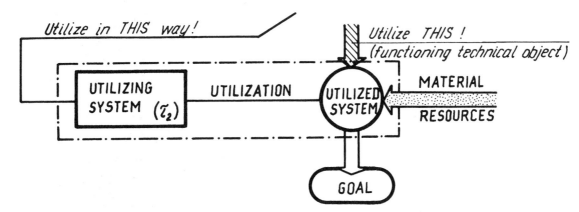

Fig. 17

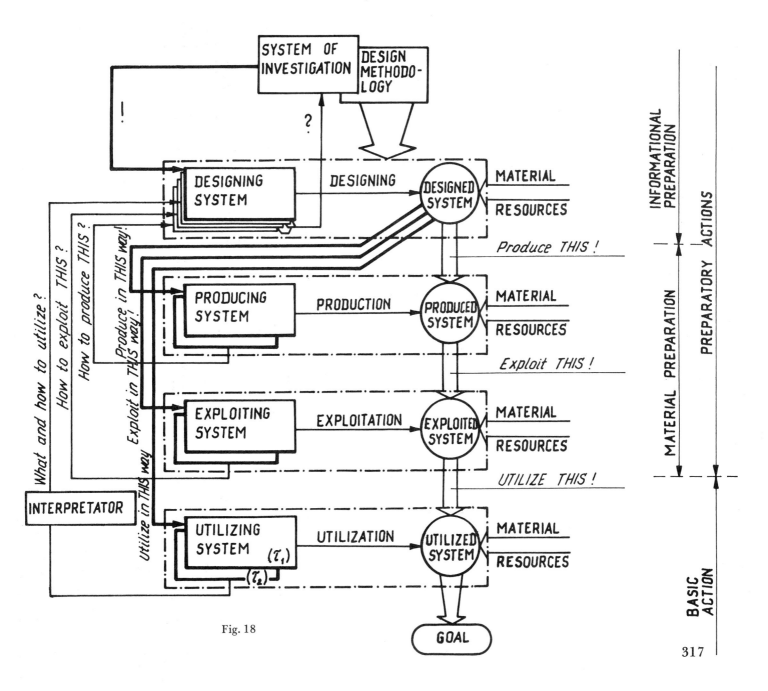

Fig. 18

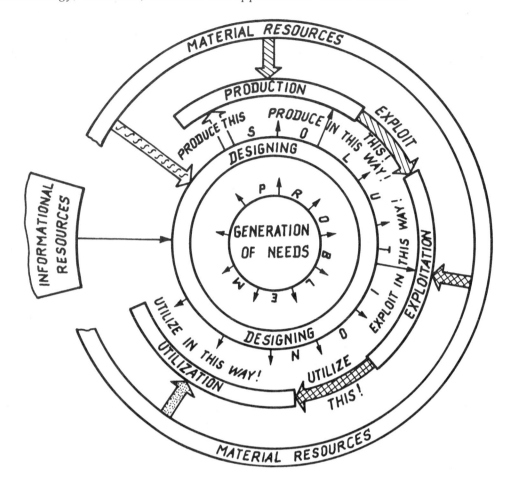

Fig. 19

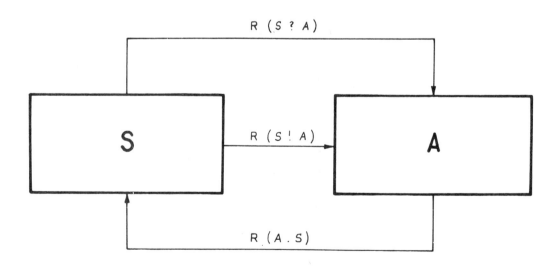

Fig. 20

General methodology: laws, rules, approaches or attitudes?

There are a few methodological directions in science aiming at the very similar domain of purposes. They are cybernetics, general systems theory and praxiology (or general methodology, as it is called as well). It is rather difficult to explain the similarities and differences between them. This is because neither cybernetics, nor general systems theory, nor praxiology are theories in the strong meaning of that term. They are rather collective or general names of the scientific directions and one can find well defined theories only inside each of those directions. All the directions create a common scientific movement, in the same way that all the colors create the rainbow. And I am in agreement with P.K. McPherson when he calls that movement 'systems movement' (McPherson [8]), the more so since T. Kotarbinski, the founder of Polish praxiology, had noticed belongingness of praxiology to the theory of events, which is nearly the same as the general theory of systems (Kotarbinski [4]).

Let us try to compare praxiological and systems approaches, which seems to be more reasonable than looking for similarities and differences between general systems theory and general theory of efficient actions, as praxiology used to be called. There are different levels of generality, then it would be done rather with the theory of events than with the praxiology.

Although many years have passed since the theories mentioned above were designed, they are still *in statu nascendi* theories. Being the programs, in practice the theories first of all suggest some approaches not creating at that time closed theoretical systems, i.e., laws or rules.

Taking into consideration the differences between systems and praxiological approaches the *genetic* difference should be pointed out. The systems approach arose basically from the observation of the special kind of activity where the cognition of reality is the final objective. However, praxiological approach derives from the observation of practical activities. Praxiology announced in itself that all activities are understood as a subject of its description, but the program postulating the praxiological approach concerns, with some exceptions, the activities, which change the reality.

The second difference, the *subject* difference, results from a different level of generality. The systems approach is oriented first of all on an object called the system, e.g., the system of actions, whereas the praxiological approach is oriented mainly on the subject of actions.

The third difference, so called the *basic attribute* difference, consists in that the holistic treatment of any object is specific for the systems approach, whereas the praxiological approach is the efficiency of the treatment. That difference is easily understood when we compare the meanings of the adjectives "systemic" (or "systems") and "praxiological" (or "praxiologic"); the first means "holistic treated", but the second "efficient" or "effective". After all, the praxiological approach cannot be understood as a resignation of the wholeness, and the systems approach as a resignation of the effectiveness. For the praxiological approach the wholeness is the derivation from the actions considered as efficacious, and for the systems approach the effectiveness is the derivation from the holistic consideration of phenomena.

For both approaches, the way to achieve the final, optimal in given conditions, solution (goal) is similar: efficacious and synthetic considerations of phenomena.

It is easy to find out that the systems and praxiological approaches are close to one another, and the differences between them, apart from the genetic, are not the *sensu stricto* differences, but only differences of shades.

The similarity of systems and praxiological approaches and other methodological directions inside the systems movement is the result of the integrative tendency specific for contemporary processing information activities, especially for science and engineering. It is the sign of searching for the methodological tool, making possible the overcoming of informational barriers between different scientific disciplines as well as between science and technology and both of them and practice. (Gasparski and Lewicka [9].)

The Epilogue

When George J. Klir in 1970 asked about the relation between cybernetics and general systems theory by formulating a few questions, he wrote, "...I shall try to find unique and reasonable answers to some of these questions. However, the reader should be aware of my warning. The answers must not be considered as true or false but rather as reasonable or unreasonable." (Klir [10]).

I would like to look at my Chapter as a continuation of the presentation, in the form of an essay on the relation between modern scientific directions. Throughout, the subject of the comparison has been the praxiological and systems approaches. It has been done in the methodological environment because of the methodological faces of both approaches, and I think that their future development would be by dint of methodological studies in the real world.

As far as systems methodology as a discipline is concerned, there were not statements in the Chapter as to "what it is", but a description of the proposed way of "how to look for the answers to that question". Was the way reasonable or not? The reader may kindly wish to judge.

References

1. UJUMOV, A.I., 'Sistemy i sistemnyje issledovanja (Systems and systems research)', *Problemy Metodologii Sistemnovo Issledovanja (Problems of the Systems Research Methodology)* (In Russian), Mysl, Moscow (1970).
2. GASPARSKI, W.W., 'On systems research methodology' (In Russian), Proceedings of the XIIIth International Congress of the History of Science, Moscow (1971).
3. AJDUKIEWICZ, K., *Logika pragmatyczna (The Pragmatic Logic)* (In Polish), PWN, Warszawa (1965).
4. KOTARBINSKI, T., *Praxiology. An Introduction to the Science of Efficient Action*, Pergamon Press (1965).
5. SADOVSKY, V.N., 'Paradoxes of systems thinking', *Advances in Cybernetics and Systems Research*, Vol. I (edit. by F. Pichler and R. Trappl), Transcripta Books, London (1972).
6. GASPARSKI, W.W. (ed.), *Metadologia projektowania inzynierskiego (Engineering Design Methodology)* (In Polish), PWN, Warszawa (1973c).
7. GASPARSKI, W.W., 'Design in the System of Actions', Proceedings of the IIIrd Tchechoslovak Systems Engineering Conference, Marienbad (1974).
8. McPHERSON, P.K., *A Perspective on Systems Science and Systems Philosophy*, The City University, London (1973).
9. GASPARSKI, W.W. and LEWICKA, A., 'Probelmatyka badań systemowych. Próba charakterystyki (Problems of Systems Research. A tentative systematization)', (In Polish), *Prakseologia* 2(46), Warszawa (1973).
10. KLIR, G.J., 'On the relation between cybernetics and general systems theory', *Progress in Cybernetics* (edit. by J. Rose), pp. 155-165, Gordon and Breach, New York (1970).
11. GASPARSKI, W.W., 'Design activity as a subject of studies, Design methodology', *Theorie a Metoda*, Vol. V/2, Prague (1973a).
12. GASPARSKI, W.W., 'The design activity as a subject of studying—the design methodology', Proceedings of DRS/DMG Design Activity International Conference, London (1973b).

CYBERNETICS IN ORGANIZATION AND MANAGEMENT
(Micro-aspects)

Some fundamentals of general system theory and their application to business systems

G.J. McCAUL
McCaul Associates (Pty) Limited,
Johannesburg, South Africa

We shall begin with a brief inquiry into the nature of systems. Bertalanffy has defined systems as "Sets of Elements standing in interaction". It may be thought that this definition is rather vague and all-inclusive. It is intended that it is so. We have another definition which may be a little bit more clear, as follows: "A System is a Set or assembly of things connected, associated or interdependent, so as to form a complex unity". However when we go further into the concept of Systems we find that we must admit they do not exist simply as static, unchanging phenomena. One cannot go too deeply into the matter here, but it can be shown that systems are inextricably associated with change and because change takes place through time only, we have to examine systems as dynamic phenomena. We therefore feel that one can say "a system is something which is a dynamic combination of sets of things in an ordered relationship, such that it can repetitively change these sets of things into different combinations of themselves".

The basic system

The fact that a system is a single entity must lead to the concept immediately that it is separate from the surroundings in which it exists. Anything must exist in space. We therefore find that a system is something, an entity, which exists somewhere in space. The space is one, two or three dimensional. We think in the first place of a business being carried on in three-dimensional space, such as a building. If we take the open space of our surroundings, we can use a number of iconic graphic symbols to illustrate the concepts of systems. We will use only a two-dimensional concept together with another concept of time, which adds another dimension. We show here open space. Into this space one can place a graphic representation of a system by enclosing an area within boundaries, Fig. 1. Inside these boundaries the system exists as a set of elements in interaction. However, the systems are dynamic in that

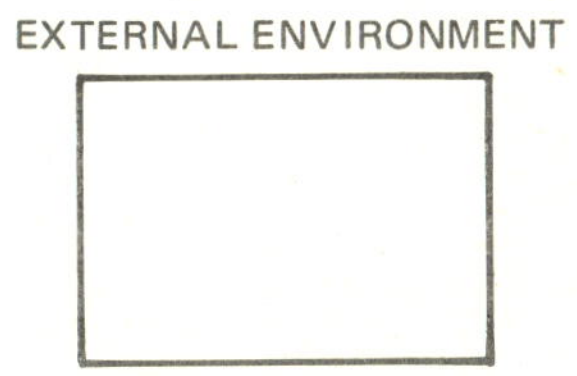
EXTERNAL ENVIRONMENT

Fig. 1

Progress in Cybernetics and Systems Research, Volume 2

Fig. 2

Fig. 3

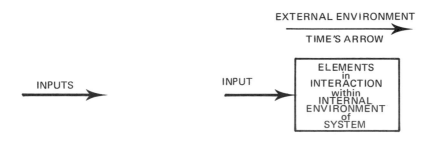

Fig. 4

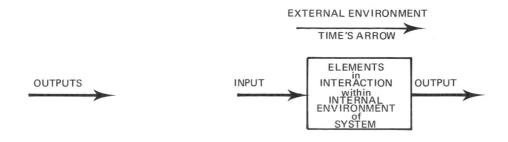

Fig. 5

they also exist in Time. Thus Time becomes a fourth dimension of the system. Unless we think of a system existing and moving in Time, we probably cannot conceive of it at all. We therefore add an indication of Time in the form of an arrow, which we can call "Time's Arrow". See Fig. 2.

Time, as we see, is outside the boundary of the system, but it is not an input to the system. We can say that the system exists in Time as well as in Space.

Every system is enclosed in some actual or abstract boundary, which separates it from the general external space. Within this boundary the interaction of elements takes place. See Fig. 3.

The elements within the system must have come from somewhere. The source of the elements would appear then to be, in the first place, the external environment. Those things which go into the system, we can therefore call inputs. These inputs are the things which interact with one another. We show these inputs by placing an arrow outside the system but with its head pointing into the system. This indicates that the inputs come from the external environment and go into the system. See Fig. 4.

The interaction of the elements within the system will lead to some change in them. The changed form of the elements will come out of the system and return to the external environment, in the form of an output. Graphically we indicate this output by placing an arrow opposite the input, but with the head of the arrow pointing outwards. See Fig. 5.

We see now that the input symbol and the output symbol are exactly the same. There is a very sound reason for this. Systems are interdependent as well as being intradependent. The output from one system becomes the input to another system. Man is an example of the system which has an output in the form of energy which he uses primarily to bring himself the various inputs he needs to keep himself going as a system. His outputs therefore become changed into the things he needs, through the whole series of activities which take place in the economic world with the ultimate objective of providing himself with the inputs which he needs. These inputs go towards supplying him with the energy to do just this. Thus, we see the system in the simplest form as being enclosed within its own boundaries, having an input from the external environment which consists of many different elements. These elements interact within the system and produce an output, which returns to the external environment.

The dynamic system and its control system

Systems of all sorts seem to come into being and to die. Whether they relate to the millions of years of the life of a galaxy or the short period of life of a rocket or a hydrogen bomb, this cycle seems to take place. Some systems, like the human system, can continue to exist through this time cycle at a comparatively even level of activity. This activity can be primarily defined as an input-output relationship which maintains a 'steady state'. W.B. Cannon calls this situation Homeostasis. Homeostasis would appear to be the condition which exists when a system continuously seeks a state of equilibrium. One cannot go too deeply into this aspect now so one should accept this particular phenomenon. The state of equilibrium is never reached because apparently many factors in the external environment tend to disturb the equilibrium state of a system. Nevertheless, the continuous seeking of equilibrium has been called a "Steady State" condition.

The "Steady State" or condition of Homeostasis, seems to be achieved by a peculiar phenomenon which is termed Negative Feedback. Negative Feedback is a regulatory or control mechanism in which a measurement of the output from a system is fed back to influence the input, after having had its polarity reversed. It controls then the input by decreasing it if the output increases or increasing it if the output decreases. This implies the setting of some kind of level or state, in which the system deems it desirable to function. A very good example is that of the human body, which seems to have found it desirable to exist at a rate of combustion indicated by the fact that its temperature is maintained at a temperature of 98.4° F. The concept of feedback control, is shown graphically in our system in the simplest form, by the reverse arrow (Fig. 6). This we see connects the output to the input. We must always remember that this control acts with a negative or reversed polarity in relation to the output.

Negative feedback control as a system

We have shown the negative feedback control in a comparatively simple form. It is however more complicated than it appears here. It is believed that it exists in a manner which we will now describe by again using iconic symbols to show graphically the basic concept of negative feedback control.

Control is a word which has been derived from two French words. The one is "contre", meaning 'against' and the other is "rôle" meaning 'a part'.

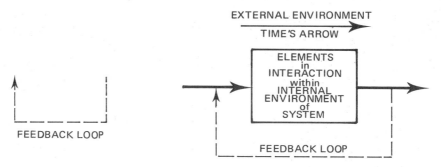

Fig. 6

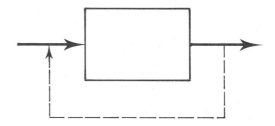

Fig. 7

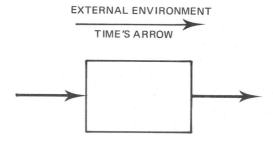

Fig. 8

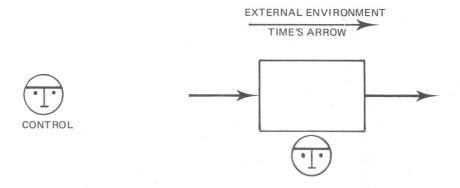

Fig. 9

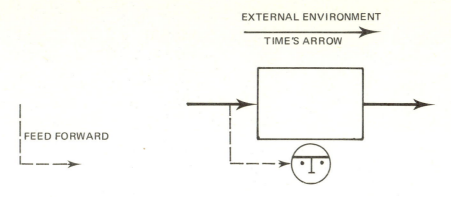

Fig. 10

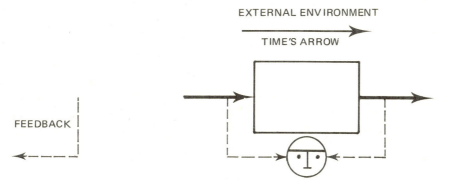

Fig. 11

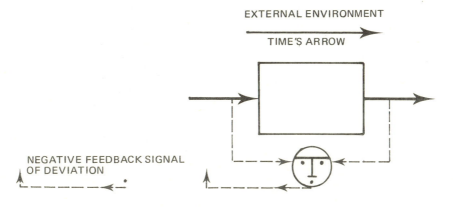

Fig. 12

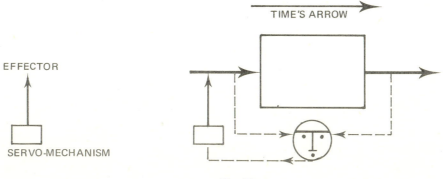

Fig. 13

Control therefore means 'a part' which is played 'against' something. We find that the same word appears in German when we use the word 'Gegen-probe' to illustrate this concept. The idea of something being placed against another thing implies that there must be two things. We therefore find that one aspect is expressed by an indication of the level of achievement which any dynamic system seems continuously to seek. Against this level of achievement, we can set up the actual achievement. When these two things are compared, they will show agreement or deviation. The deviation may be positive or negative in that the outputs may be above or below the desired level. The polarity of this deviation is reversed and must then be used to activate some force which will alter the levels of inputs until the desired equilibrium is achieved. The dynamics of a system, however, as we have said, indicate that this state of equilibrium is seldom reached.

We shall start now with our formal iconic symbol for a system under feedback (Fig. 7).

We therefore show these aspects in the following way. In the first place we take away our simplified symbol for the negative feedback control loop (Fig. 8).

In its place we shall put in the following iconic symbols. We need a special subsystem to exercise control. We use a symbol here which is intended to convey two aspects. In the first place, we use an accounting convention and show a T form of account. The two dots represent entries to either side of the account. When compared they show deviation. This is a balance on the account. In other words, we place one value against the other interpreting the concept of "contre-rôle". The iconic symbol we use does have another meaning. It represents the head of an individual. In this case the two dots represent a form of receptor mechanism viz, the eyes. Communications are received by receptor mechanisms in the control system to sense what goes on in the outside world so that the comparison for control purposes can be made. The deviation then becomes a further communication, to what we shall see, is an effector mechanism. See Fig. 9.

We must now consider the implications of communication and information. From the input side, we have information which represents some kind of measure or standard which is a function of the inputs, in relation to the desired output levels. This has been given various names, but an accepted term can be "Feed Forward" in contradistinction to 'Feedback', the one that then follows, Fig. 10.

From the output side, we have the reverse, in that we now show the 'Feedback' (see Fig. 11).

As will be seen, these two aspects are brought into apposition with one another through the receptors in the control mechanism. The receptors receive this information through the established communication channels. The symbol for control shows how these two information data aspects of 'Feed Forward' and 'Feedback' are placed in conjunction with one another.

The comparison of the two aspects against one another is shown by the deviation. This will lead to the communication of information as an input signal of reversed polarity to some mechanism which, a system in itself, must be the effector to apply the necessary force, as a function of the deviation, to alter the relationship of the inputs. See Fig. 12.

This mechanism is usually called a 'Servo-mechanism'. The signal to the effector comes as a communication as it were, from the mouth of the symbolic representation of the head of the person (Fig. 13).

This Servo-mechanism can exist in many forms. We have the mechanical servo-mechanisms which can alter the inputs of systems using greater or lesser applications of force to do it. A typical example is the force required to regulate the input to a hydro-electric system where it must open and close the input of water against the pressure of the millions of tons of water behind a dam wall. Another very simple form, but of a totally different sort, is the spiritual force required in a business, where the exercise of managerial authority brings about change in the behavior of the individuals to ensure that the inputs are organized to reach the desired levels of output. The force of the servo-mechanism is thus applied to the input side to change the inputs to achieve the desired level of output. We must not forget that the whole of the system is acting in Time.

The total system

We now see the system as a complete entity in which there are actually three subsystems. We have the system enclosed within its boundary where the interaction of elements takes place. We have the control system where the level which is actually achieved is compared with the desired level of activity. From this we have the feedback signal which is reversed in polarity and fed to the third system, the servo-mechanism, in order to regulate the inputs

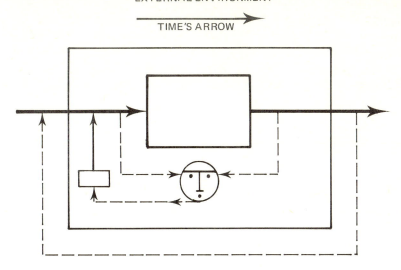

Fig. 14

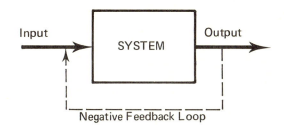

Fig. 15

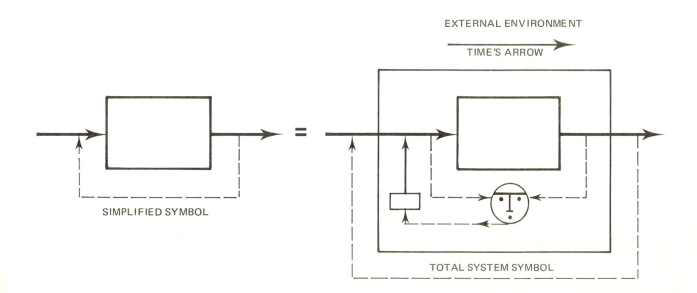

Fig. 16

to achieve the desired steady state relationship to the output. We can regard these three subsystems as being parts of a system in itself. We can therefore place around them a further boundary which then includes them all inside another larger system. It is most important to appreciate the implications of the communication and information flow indicated by the dotted lines. Without these aspects there can be no control. See Fig. 14.

We shall now remove the complicated control system and its servo-mechanism system and 'Time's Arrow', and leave the simplified version of the system with the feedback loop. It is significant that the Control System and the servo-mechanism system exist outside the system which they control. They must however exist within the larger system. Fig. 15.

We can of course apply to the external part of this larger system another complete control system which brings then the inputs from the external environment again into a steady state relationship with the outputs. This process of systems within systems goes on throughout the universe in which we exist.

The system comprises its inputs, its outputs and the negative feedback loop. The arrows of input-output indicate, at the same time, the flow of the system through Time. The effect of negative feedback is not to correct the inputs relative to the particular measured output. It always corrects the inputs for some future output because the whole system moves continuously in time. We will now always express the Total System by this simplified symbol (see Fig. 16).

The application of these concepts to the business system

It can be shown that any Business system also has inputs and outputs. The inputs consist of the efforts of human beings combined with many of the output products from other systems which are run by human beings, as well as outputs from systems of nature. We find that the tendency is to describe the inputs to systems in economic terms as being land, labour and capital. In addition the classical approach says that land is material and labor is all effort of human beings. The complicated diversified economy in which we live is characterized by an intricate division of labor which was identified by Adam Smith. However, in our terminology, we find that, whether we call it materials, labor, overheads, capital, land, or any other name, all these things are inputs to a subsystem in the economic system which we

can describe as the business system. They are used to produce some kind of output. The outputs are many and varied. They may be in the form of services or in the form of material goods. A simple example of a service is the power which is supplied by a power station, while a material output would be steel produced by a steel works. These outputs can be inputs to other business systems.

We can show a business system as having inputs and outputs in the same way as our general concept of systems. However, it becomes necessary to show some more detail because the business system has a certain number of peculiarities which, in the first place, seem only to refer to business systems. However, analysis has shown that it refers to all systems. We do not have sufficient time to show how this comes about, but will refer these concepts only to business systems. We find that the inputs in a business system are described in generic terms by the accounting names given to the different kinds of inputs. We use the general terms, materials, labor, and expenses. We speak also of capital. Materials are described as raw materials or consumable materials. Labor is described as labor paid in the form of wages or as salaries. Expenses consist of a vast number of different Kinds of Costs for services which all have their origin from other systems in the external environment.

The interaction of these input elements seems reasonably clear when we analyze it. The output from a business system is something which came from the inputs. In most cases of manufacturing businesses we can identify the outputs with the inputs from which they come. If we put a piece of steel rod as a material input into a business system which makes bolts and nuts, we can identify the outputs with the steel bar inputs. Many examples can be cited where this relationship is reasonably clear. However, the change in the material inputs has been brought about by some agency, within the system. This agency is a combination of some of the other inputs to the system. We find machines and the people who operate them, and the time of the management whose efforts are combined in bringing a manufacturing process into a 'steady state'. We have the same kind of thing in a commercial operation where people's efforts are combined to bring about a trading operation. These combined inputs together form some process activity which expresses itself as an entity. This is the agency which brings about change in the material input. We can show these aspects again simply in a graphical form. Here we have our system boundary with the inputs from the external environment (Fig. 17).

We see that the inputs group themselves into services, which combine to provide a single entity, viz., the process or agency. This output from the activity of combining, is one of the inputs to a process of bringing about change. The other input is the material input. The output from the process becomes then the output product from the main system. As we can see in each case, we add the negative feedback link to show that each one of these systems and subsystems is under control and thus seeks to achieve a steady state. If this is not the case in a business system for *any* reason whatsoever, it becomes bankrupt.

The systems described here can be multiplied considerably within the system. We have shown a single process. They can be combinations of processes. Here we show again a system which has inputs which form subsystems which link with one another. The output product of the one becomes the input product of the other and so the material moves

through a series of processes producing ultimately the output product which goes to the external environment. We can have another combination where these Systems branch into more than one flow line. In each case we have added the negative feedback loop (Fig. 18).

One can describe all of these particular combinations of activities as activity centers. A combination of activities forms the characteristic technology of a particular kind of business. The inputs to these various activities however, are common to all systems in the National Economic Activity. They consist of those things which we have already described as being kinds of costs. They are mainly people and the outputs coming from other individual economic systems in the form of machines, raw materials and services. Each of the activities shown here is made up of the complete concept of systems that we have initially described. If they are to function as systems in a steady state, they must necessarily have the inputs and the outputs together with the feed-

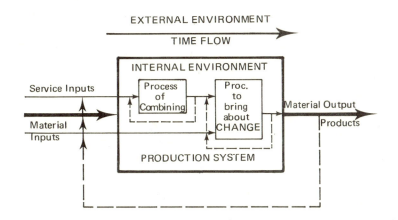

Fig. 17

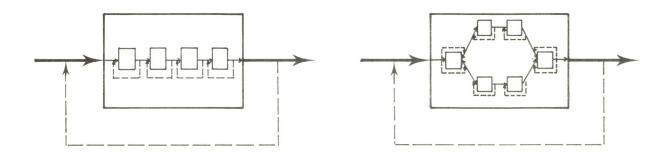

Fig. 18

back loop for control that we have shown in our introduction. (See Annexure 1, Diagram 1.)

Furthermore, each activity in itself consists of the combination of services which forms the agency or process which expresses itself as an entity. This entity is applied to the material input and produces the output product. In the multi-activity systems we show here, the output products from each of these subsystems form the inputs to the next activity in the chain. It is only when the output product of the last system moves out into the external environment again that we can say the cycle is complete, relative to a particular system. (See Annexure 1, Diagram 2).

It is clear that the business system is a very complicated combination of systems and subsystems within itself. One is inevitably reminded of the groups which exist in nature. The various types and kinds of systems are evident around us. In the world of business and economics the various firms or entities each consist of a combination of such systems. Each business entity is itself, a system among many others of similar kinds in the national economic system. Some systems of government can be regarded as systems of control, whereas others are systems which carry out activities leading to other output products. When we combine all of these business systems together with the government agencies and the agencies of local authority we can conceive of the total economic system of the nation. When we add to these, systems made up of the individual family units, together with the other non-profit institutions like the Church, which are characteristic of our social order, we find that they all combine together with the business systems to form the concept of the social economy of a particular nation.

The business system is a complex combination of interlocking systems

The Business system in itself can also be shown to be a number of similar kinds of activities which center around the distinctive activity of the technology of the business. (See Annexure 2, Diagram 1.) Here we have the national economic system in which a business entity exists. If we look inside the business entity we find that it consists in itself of two different systems. First we have the undertaking. The undertaking has received money from the external environment which is turned into input factors in order to carry on the business. The undertaking expects to produce a reward for the money employ-

ed in the form of dividends. Within the undertaking we find the economic activity. The economic activity concerns itself with producing goods from the inputs which are comprised of services and materials. Within the economic activity, we find the process activity which, as already described, is characteristic of the distinctive kind of technology of the individual business. The process activity produces a particular kind of output from the material inputs. This kind of output is characteristic and unique to the particular business entity.

We have shown how, even within the boundaries of the process activity, there are still a number of subsystems which are causing the elements of the inputs to interact and to produce some kind of output. We can give many examples of the distinctive combinations of technologies which produce their own unique output products. One has only to think of the difference between the operation of a railway, the operation of a steel mill or the operation of a supermarket. Even the activity of the professional man, the doctor or the lawyer, can be classified as the specific process activity contained in the inside heart of each individual economic activity. As we move back from a single isolated concept of the process activity, we can see how the different forms of control are exercised through the accounting technologies.

The process activity is controlled by the manufacturing account. The economic activity is controlled by the trading account. The undertaking is controlled by the profit and loss account. The economic entity is controlled by the appropriation account, which indicates the dividends it puts back into the external environment. The whole is shown in its static form of equilibrium by the balance sheet. And so we have taken the fundamental concepts of General System Theory and have shown briefly how it can be interpreted in its application to the individual business economy or economic entity which in itself exists within the national economy of any group or nation. The concepts have been used to build computer programs which produce models of businesses in their total form as shown here. These programs, can undoubtedly be applied to extending the models and to build them up to show for the national economy, the dynamic position of the steady state. Hitherto, models of national economies show only the balance accounting concepts of the balance sheet.

An understanding of the basic dynamics of general systems in which a clear distinction is made between the dynamic equilibrium of the steady state and the

NATIONAL ECONOMIC SYSTEM

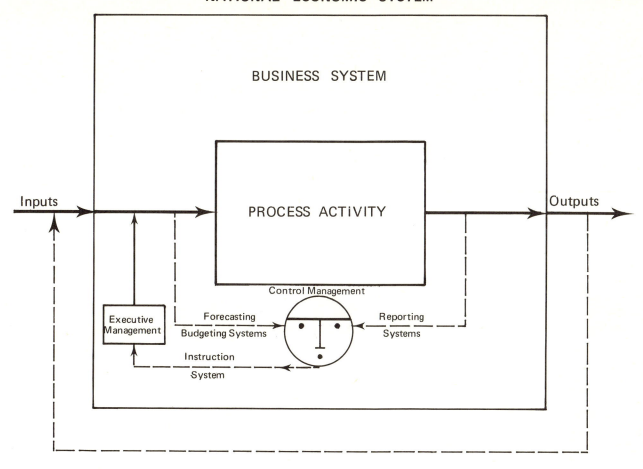

Diagram 1

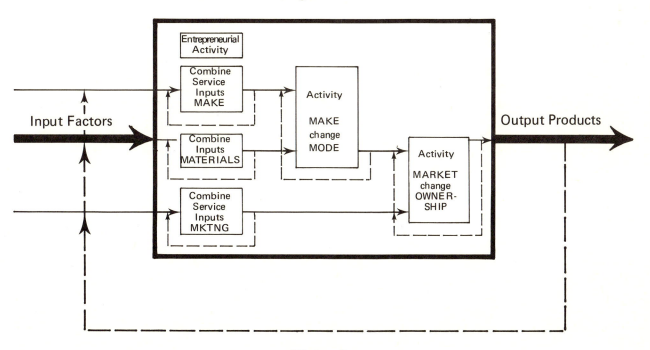

Diagram 2

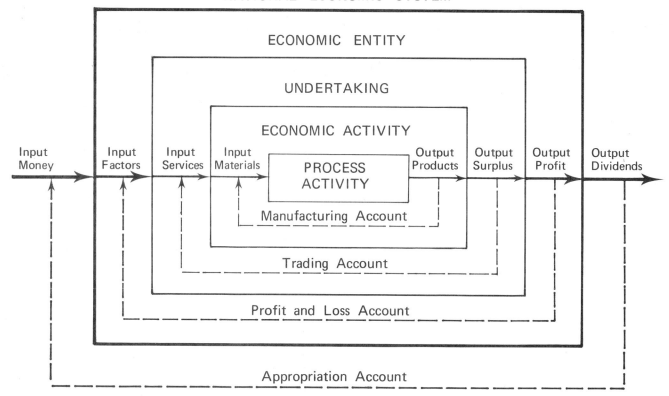

NATIONAL ECONOMIC SYSTEM

ECONOMIC ENTITY

UNDERTAKING

ECONOMIC ACTIVITY

PROCESS ACTIVITY

Input Money | Input Factors | Input Services | Input Materials | Output Products | Output Surplus | Output Profit | Output Dividends

Manufacturing Account

Trading Account

Profit and Loss Account

Appropriation Account

Diagram 1

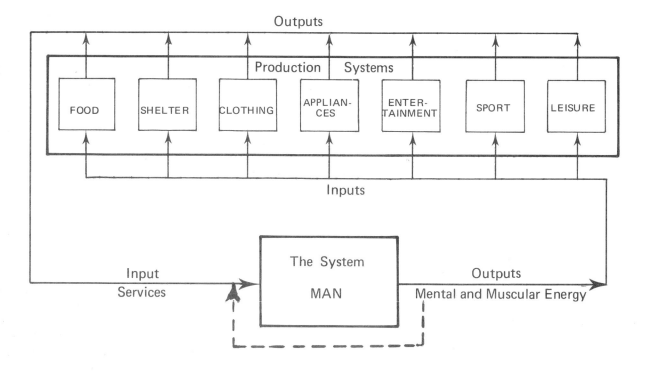

Outputs

Production Systems

FOOD | SHELTER | CLOTHING | APPLIANCES | ENTERTAINMENT | SPORT | LEISURE

Inputs

Input Services

The System MAN

Outputs Mental and Muscular Energy

Diagram 2

static equilibrium which is revealed by the so-called 'Moment-aufnahme' of the balance sheet. It is our conviction that a clear understanding of the dynamic 'steady state' concept of systems can be applied to economics of the business systems and the national economic system to bring about an understanding of the interplay of inputs and outputs. From this concept we should be able to find solutions to the economic problems of inflation and of the relationship between the reward paid to human beings in the form of wages and salaries and the prices they must pay for the output products of the system for which they are the principal inputs. These payments for wages and salaries will thus determine to a large measure the prices they must pay when they use the outputs from these man-created systems as inputs to their own human living systems. (See Annexure 2, Diagram 2.) When they form inputs to these human systems, they become subsequently the outputs of mental and muscular action which are fed into the business systems in the form of the personnel employed. There is probably a long way to go in bringing about an understanding of these concepts on the part of the mass of people. However, it must ultimately come, if we are able to achieve that state of steady dynamic equilibrium which enables the living organism of our form of civilization to survive through time.

Bibliography

1. GUTENBERG, Erich, *Economie de l'Entreprise, La Production Sirey*, Paris, 1st Edition (1951).
2. GEORGESCU - Roegen, N., *The Entropy Law and the Economic Process*, Havard University Press, Boston, 1st Edition (1971).
3. MUMFORD, Lewis, *Techniques and Civilization*, George Routeledge & Sons Limited, London (1951).
4. VON BERTALANFFY, Ludwig, *General System Theory*, Braziller, New York (1968).
5. FISHER, Roland, Consulting Editor, Interdisciplinary Perspectives of Time, Annals of the New York Academy of Sciences, New York (1967).
6. GUTENBERG, Erich, *Grundlagen der Betriebswirtschaftslehre*. Die Produktion, Springer-Verlag, Heidelberg-New York (1970).
7. BRILLOUIN, Leon, *Science and Information Theory*, Second Edition, Academic Press Inc., New York (1960).
8. SCHRÖDINGER, *What is Life? and Mind and Matter*, University Press, Cambridge (1967).
9. BAYLISS, L.E., *Living Control Systems*, The English Universities Press Limited, London (1966)
10. YANOVSKY, M., *Anatomy of Social Accounting Systems*, Chapman and Hall Limited, London (1965).
11. CANNON, W.B., *Wisdom of the Body*, W.W. Norton and Co., Inc., New York (1939).

Management decisions in the political subsystem of the firm

WOLFGANG DOROW
Freie Universität, Berlin, Germany

I. Systems Theory and Management Science

The publications of the last few years on the subject of Management and Organization of the firm gave the impression that Systems Theory has gained a continuously increasing importance. Their various conceptions appear to offer suitable perceptions about the structure and functioning of Management Subsystems.

Narr distinguishes between three conceptions of Systems Theory:

1. General Systems Theory.
2. Cybernetic Systems Theory.
3. Structural-Functional Theory.

The functional conception is strongly connected with the cybernetic conception, too, and is of fundamental importance for the analysis of social systems.

Systems Theory cannot, as yet, be regarded as a closed scientific conception. But it already shows the way to new perspectives of research and questions for the social sciences, especially for Management Science.

The various conceptions of Systems Theory have one subject in common, namely, the question of systems behavior and systems relations.

Systems Theory which as a scientific method is intensively discussed within the German "Betriebswirtschaftslehre", will finally be judged on whether or not, with this method, explanations about the behavior of firms as systems and their subsystems can be made.

This is also valid for the systemtheoretical Management Science which will explain the decision processes of the managers in the different subsystems of the firm.

This is, however, at the moment a very distant goal of the systemtheoretical Management Science, the preliminary steps of which should be seen in a terminological determination of relevant management subsystems.

Systems Theory fulfills an important heuristic function for Management Science: the research of the interactions between the system elements is stressed, thereby making it possible to describe effective relations between the elements of management subsystems. In addition, the variables of the subsystems must be recognized.

Moreover, Systems Theory helps to develop models which will serve to organize goal-orientated subsystems.

Progress in Cybernetics and Systems Research, Volume 2

Systems Theory makes it possible to see into the logical and analytical connections of the behavior-interactions of system elements. If Systems Theory is applied to management analysis, it necessitates the connection of its logical and analytical categories with the empirical facts of the viewed problem.

Systems Theory can thereby to a great extent be considered as a theory of interaction of variables. For the development of a management science it will be regarded as a systematical research method. It furnishes a general frame of reference for the description and explanation of management actions and their interdependences. If the specific decision processes of the management are defined as systems variables of the different management subsystems, it will result in a connection of Behavioral Decision Theory and Systems Theory.

Systems Theory and Cybernetics thereby offer new bases for better analysis and organization of decision structures and processes in the firm. This will result in advantages of the metadisciplinary conceptions of Systems Theory over classical management analysis.

But it is difficult in Management Science to fulfill the following methodical conditions:

1. The Management Systems must be clearly determined from their surrounding systems (identification of the boundaries of the system).
2. The goals of the systems must be identified.

For the description and explanation of management systems with the help of systemtheoretical and cybernetical models, both conditions are, to a great extent, unsolved problems. There are missing clear empirical indicators for the boundaries and the goals to be achieved for a social system which is neither structurally and functionally fixed nor has concrete physical boundaries, as, for example, organisms.

II. Problems of determining subsystems of the firm

A system is generally defined as a unit of structured elements. These elements have different qualities and are connected by relations. The whole of these elements makes a structure. As regards the type of elements which form a system, generally no restriction exists. Therefore each relation of elements can be interpreted as a system.

Each system can again be seen as an element of another system. This system which has a fewer number of elements, can be described as a subsystem. That system which comprises additional elements is called supersystem or higher-order system. The definitions supersystem and subsystem describe a formal relation of the systems.

For the definition of systems we require data on the elements of interest, their qualities, and relations.

Boulding, Beer, Grochla, and others, have developed criteria for describing systems, on which I cannot enlarge here.

It depends on the specific aspects as to which elements or subsystems of the firm are considered. Thus the determination of management subsystems is regarded as a problem of definition, the solving of which must however fulfill the aim of the research.

Thus, the firm is defined—depending on the question—as a man-man system, man-machine system or machine-machine system.

Katz and Kahn differentiate five groups of subsystems of the firm, based on functional aspects:
1. Production or technical Subsystems.
2. Supportive Subsystems.
3. Maintenance Subsystems.
4. Adaptive Subsystems.
5. Managerial Subsystems.

Bleicher names three subsystems of the firm:
1. Operation System.
2. Innovation System.
3. Policy System.

In the following I would like to discuss the purpose and behavior of the political subsystem.

However, prior to discussing the political subsystem of the firm, I will discuss Easton's model of the political system of a society.

III. Easton's Model of the Political Subsystem

Based on the structure-functional and cybernetical Systems Theory, Easton has developed a model of the Political System, which has gained a great deal of attention. The Political Subsystem represents a specific behavior system of the complete system of a society. The Political System is defined by the interactions of its members who allocate authoritative values for the society. "The authoritative allocation of values", which are binding for the society, so defines Easton the specific aspect of the Political. The political aspect has two criteria:

a) The *relevance* of the decisions of the political system (intensity of the decisions).
b) The *range* of the decisions in the society, influencing the entire societal system (extension of the decisions).

According to Easton, the political decisions influence, in view of their intensity and extension, the actions of the society.

However, political decisions, that is, the allocation

of values, are not clearly fixed and can be manifold: statements, performances for the members of the society, goals, acts, and so on. These political decisions represent the output of the political system.

This is described by Easton as a functional model (see Fig. 1). The model comprises the following variables:

1. Input variables.
2. Transformation variables.
3. Output variables.

The input variables include wants, demands, and support, which are addressed by the intra-societal and extra-societal supersystem to the political system.

The wants, for example, represent motivations, ideologies, interests, the public opinion of the members of the society, and can be regarded as a background to the demands and supports. According to Easton, support means all the contributions by the governed class to the political system.

A certain amount of support is necessary for the survival of the political system. If the demands constantly exceed the support, the survival of the political system is endangered. In addition, the political system needs a certain amount of substantive and procedural consensus, that is, about the political goals and about the rules of the political decision process.

The demands brought forward by the intra- and extra-societal system formulate the decisions expected from the political system. The demands as information input are converted to categories of output within the political system.

Easton describes different variants of the transformation of demands into outputs. The demands, for example, can either be drowned, accepted without

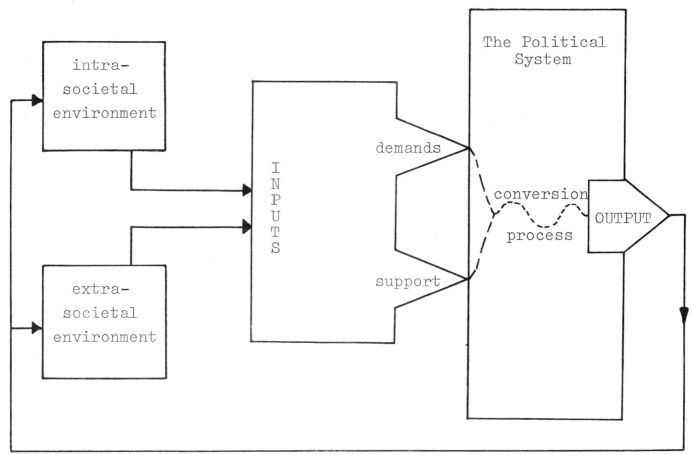

feedback loop

(See EASTON, D., *A Systems Analysis of Political Life*, New York-London-Sydney, 1965, p. 30)

Fig. 1

any discussion, reduced, selected or amalgamated in the political system.

The output represents the performance of the political system, namely, the making and execution of decisions for a society. As already mentioned, the output can comprise all possible decisions.

As a further variable of the output aspect, Easton quotes acceptance: the decisions made by the political system must be accepted by the members of the society, that is, they must agree to the decisions.

Finally, there exists a feedback relation between output and input of the model, for the quality of the output determines the quality and intensity of the input, for example, the extent of support which the political system receives from the members of the society. By means of the feedback mechanism the political system can also control developments in the society, correct its own decisions, make adaptations and effect changes.

IV. Critical notes on the Easton Model

1. Easton's model is based on a relatively schematic and formal definition of the different elements of the political system.

   Although the conversion process of the demands and of the support in outputs is of central importance for the determination and description of the political decision process, in the Easton model this process remains to a great extent unanalyzed.

   Thus the model remains a "black box".

2. Also, the variables do not clearly constitute the political system, as they can also be understood as components of other subsystems of a society, especially of the firm.

   If, for example, one tries to construct an economical subsystem of the firm, then also here the allocation of values appears as an output variable of the system.

3. If one further refers to Easton's criteria of the Political—intensity and extension of the decisions of the political system—so politics obviously means the solution of basic problems of a society, the setting of general goals and generally acknowledged values.

This definition of the Political corresponds to the American Business Policy and the German classical "Betriebswirtschaftspolitik". These conceptions define the political decisions of the management as the setting of long-range, general goals of the firm. Thereby the political aspect is shortened.

The definition of the political aspect of the firm —*setting of long-ranging, general goals*—does not

cover the proper character of political decision processes. Since the Easton model does not analyze the specific problems of the political decision process, no proper difference is made between political and nonpolitical decision processes.

V. The decision process of management in the political subsystem of the firm

It would be leading too far, to go intensively into the politicological literature for the determination of the Political.

Max Weber defines Politics as the process of exercising power, that is, to make sure that one's goals are attained even against the resistance of others.

Narr understands by Politics not the setting of goals but ensuring that goals are reached.

Political action is thereby understood as a specific action or a specific decision process, which will safeguard the realization of one's own goals against colliding goals of others by means of power. These specific decision processes represent processes of influence on the ranges of action of colliding individuals or groups.

The general purpose of a political decision process is the safeguarding of an endangered goal.

The political decision process is a choice of an action to safeguard own goals against colliding goals of others.

The important question which has been left open by Easton therefore is:

How does the decision process for the safeguarding of goals function?

Transferred to the business firm and its management, this means that the management decisions in the political subsystem are directed to safeguarding the attainment of economic goals which the management has set in the other subsystems of the firm, or which have been delegated to the management for realization.

Political decision processes of management result from situations of conflict [A/B]. Situations of conflict arise, if the actions of the managers [A] collide with those of other participants of the firm [B]. Political decision processes are not only initiated through existing conflicts but also through colliding behavior which may be expected. (Refer to Fig. 2.)

The political decision process in the firm therefore is defined by Dlugos as a "process of determining colliding ranges of action which should safeguard the realization of own or delegated goals against

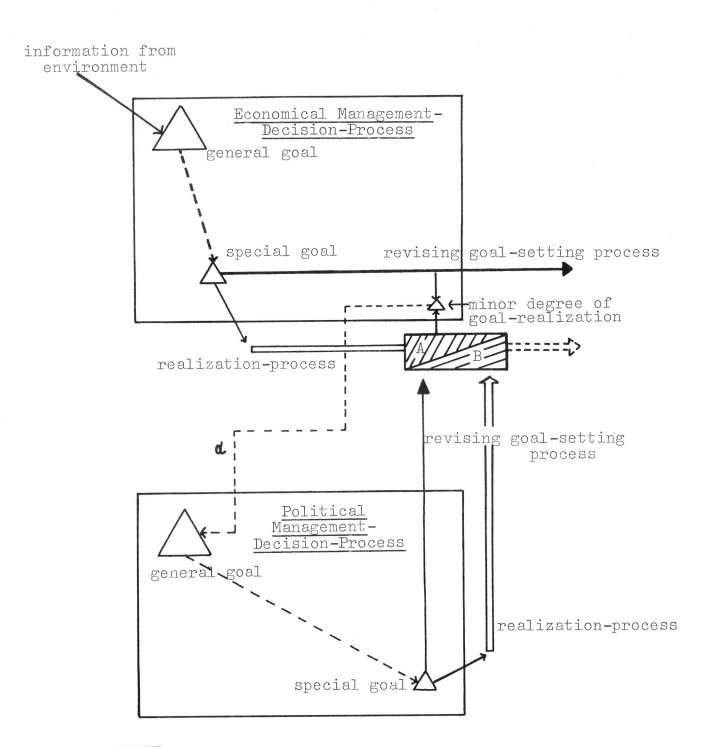

information from environment

Economical Management-
Decision-Process

general goal

special goal   revising goal-setting process

minor degree of
goal-realization

realization-process

A   B

revising goal-setting
process

α

Political
Management-
Decision-Process

general goal

realization-process

special goal

A / B : colliding range of action

α : information about colliding range of action

(See the complete model offered by DLUGOS, G., 'Untermehmungspolitik als
betriebswirtschaftlich-politologische Teildisziplin', in: *Unternehmungsführung*,
edit. by J. Wild, Berlin, 1974, p. 61)

Fig. 2 A simplified model of economical and political management-decision-processes

340

colliding, opposing goals".

On the basis of this definition, Dlugos has analyzed the structure of political decision processes of the business firm and its implications, to which I am going to refer briefly.

Information [α] to the effect that management goals are jeopardized because of the colliding behavior of other participants of the firm [B] represents the input variables of the political subsystem of the firm. This information will motivate the managers [A] to initiate a political decision process. As a result of this decision process, they will choose a specific determination action to safeguard their endangered goals.

This determination action [ε] represents the output variable of the political subsystem of the firm and will be the input variable of the goal system of opposing actors. The group of opposing actors may be regarded as the group which demands a revision of the economical goals of the managers. For example, the employees demand a maintenace of the present standards of performance, whereas the managers try to increase the work productivity. The political decision process consists of transforming the input variables, which give information about the conflicts in the firm, into output variables, which are actions to overcome the conflict [ε].

I will now discuss some of the problems of this management decision process in the political subsystem.

The general goal of the political management decision process is the safeguarding of endangered economic goals against actual or expected opposing behavior. It comprises general ideas on possible actions of determination of the colliding individuals or groups.

The basic problems of these actions of influence are broadly discussed in the literature under the aspect of power exercising. The processes of exercising influence are based on different sources of power. French and Raven differentiate the following bases of power: reward power, coercive power, legitimate power, referent power, and expert power.

The sources of influence, which are available to the managers, can be differentiated into a formal and a personal aspect. Formal power sources are given to them by their competence in the firm, whereas the personal power sources lie in their personality and their abilities.

The following alternatives of political decision processes are regarded as basic forms of determining colliding ranges of action:

a) Communicative determining: Order
Persuasion
Manipulation
Bargaining
Rewarding

b) Determining the surroundings of the colliding range of action: Organization
Contracts
Lock-out
Giving notice

The communicative determination influences the goal-setting process of the opponent actor, whereas the other basic action of determining directly influences the colliding realization process.

A further problem of the political decision process is the choice of one of these alternatives. The preferable alternative points out the specific goal of the political decision process, for example, a certain action of manipulation. In order to choose the specific goal, the consequences of the alternatives for each political criterion have to be determined.

From the aspect of maximum safeguarding of the endangered management goal, one of the political alternatives will be chosen as an action of determination.

The determining action as output of the political subsystem can, for example, be the decision to offer a wage increase of 10%, to give notice, or to transfer the person, etc., in order to overcome the conflict of, for example, inferior work productivity.

The output of the political system is therefore not the overcoming of the goal conflict between management and opposing actors, but an action to overcome the conflict, that is, a specific action of determination. The purpose of this action is to have the opponent actor revise his colliding goal.

If, however, the management's actions of determining fail and if the political subsystem keeps receiving input information about the conflict, then the management can

1. Revise its own political decision process and choose a different determining action, or
2. Revise its own endangered goal, which had originally to be safeguarded, and adapt its own goal to that of the opponent actor.

In this way there is a feedback relation between output and input of the political subsystem.

Finally, it should be mentioned that the management itself can be influenced by the opposing actors. Such bilateral relations consist, however, of more complicated structures of political decision processes, which could not be discussed here.

References

ACKOFF, Russell L., 'Towards a system of systems concepts', *Systems Behaviour* (Edit. by John Beishon and Geoff Peters), pp. 83-90, London (1972).

BEER, Stafford, *Kybernetik und Management*, Frankfurt, Main (1962).

BLEICHER, Knut, 'Die Entwicklung eines systemorientierten Organisations- und Führungsmodells der Unternehmung', *Zeitschrift für Organisation*, Vol. 1-4 (1970).

BOULDING, Kenneth E., 'General systems theory—the skeleton of science', *Management Science* 2(3), 197-208 (1955/56).

DLUGOS, Günter, 'Analytische Wissenschaftstheorie als Regulativ betriebswirtschaftlicher Forschung', *Wissenschaftstheorie und Betriebswirtschaftslehre* (Edit. by G. Dlugos, G. Eberlein, and H. Steinmann), pp. 21-53, Düsseldorf (1972).

DLUGOS, Günter, 'Unternehmungspolitik als betriebswirtschaftlichpolitologische Teildisziplin', *Unternehmungsführung. Festschrift für Erich Kosiol* (Edit. by J. Wild), pp. 39-73, Berlin (1974).

EASTON, David, *A Systems Analysis of Political Life*, New York (1965).

EASTON, David, *The Political System. An Inquiry into the State of Political Science*, 2nd Ed., New York (1971).

FRENCH, John R.P. and RAVEN, Bertram, 'The bases of social power', *Studies in Social Power* (Edit. by D. Cartwright), pp. 150-167, Ann Arbor (1959).

GROCHLA, Erwin, 'Systemtheorie und Organisationstheorie', *Zeitschrift für Betriebswirtschaft* 1, pp. 1-16 (1970).

KATZ, Daniel and KAHN, Robert L., *The Social Psychology of Organizations*, New York (1967).

LASSWELL, Harold D. and KAPLAN, Abraham, *Power and Society. A Framework for Political Inquiry*, New Haven (1950).

MARCH, James and SIMON, Herbert A., *Organizations*, New York, London, Sydney (1958).

NARR, Wolf-Dieter, *Theoriebegriffe und Systemtheorie*, Stuttgart (1969).

ULRICH, Hans, 'Der systemorientierte Ansatz in der Betriebswirtschaftslehre', *Wissenschaftsprogramm und Ausbildungsziele der Betriebswirtschaftslehre*, pp. 43-60, Berlin (1971).

The practical application of cybernetics and systems research methodology

D.J. BAMBER
Beecham Pharmaceuticals, Brentford, UK

Introduction

General systems theory identifies the existence of isomorphisms within various fields. The management of a firm is concerned with the achievement of objectives for survival and growth, some of which are defined, and some of which are undefined. The author is a manager responsible for systems development within a relatively large international company, and his work is therefore subject to the goals and the objectives of the firm.

The Chapter is therefore concerned with identifying the value of General Systems Theory and other related general theories to the management of the firm. It also seeks to provide a feedback to research teams at universities, identifying areas where further conceptual thinking about systems will be of value.

Definitions

There are substantial variations in the usage of terms such as cybernetics and systems research, as also of terms for other management sciences, including systems engineering, operational research, and systems analysis.

For example, cybernetics is used by some to refer only to self-regulatory feedback control mechanisms. Within a firm this might refer to a simulation model embedded in an automatic communication or information system. Others [1] use the term Management Cybernetics to apply to any method of planning, decision taking or problem solving which takes account of the dynamic and adaptive nature of the system. In the latter case, parts of the cybernetic system will be behavioral, not mechanistic.

The variations in meaning and usage of terms such as systems engineering, systems analysis and operational research are even greater but their usage can in fact overlap with the usage of the terms cybernetics and systems research.

Such variations in terminology are often misleading and counter-productive to someone attempting to implement theory. This is particularly so where research articles or papers expound on the development of cybernetic models or on the identification of isomorphisms between biological systems and management systems, without identifying the objectives of the systems modeled or compared.

It would seem valuable therefore to explore applications of cybernetics or systems research to the management of the firm through a series of steps, outlining at each stage our understanding of the theory, and of the objectives for application of the theory.

Definition of the systems approach

The systems approach to problem-solving in the firm is identified by the following simple classification regardless of the terms used by those expounding or implementing theory (such as Systems Dynamics, Systems Engineering, Management Cybernetics, Operations Research or simply Systems Analysis).

1. The problem (and the approach to the solution) is concerned with the total system, considered as a dynamic open system in exchange with the environment.
2. The systems approach is that outlook which in a problem confronting situation seeks not to be reductionist.
3. The system under investigation is complex and to a large extent self-regulatory.
4. The solution proposed will take the form of either a policy decision to change the structure of the system, for example, a change to the organization or the introduction of a new feedback control mechanism of some kind to allow a more effective achievement of the objectives of the organization.

The objective of applying the systems approach to the management of the firm is to establish improvements in the firm's ability to survive and to grow in the long term. That the improvements implemented as a result of this total systems approach will in most cases be substantially different from and more effective than the results of improvements diagnosed and installed within the individual subsystems of the firm will be fully accepted by all those reading this book. This was also particularly well presented at the 1972 European Meeting of Cybernetics and Systems Research in Vesper's paper on the existence-function of the firm [2].

All of the examples cited in this present Chapter have these features in common, that improved systems are adopted which

a) Are not identified with single subsystems in the firm.
b) Are directed at providing the firm with the means of communication and control which will prolong survival and encourage growth.

Behavioral theories of the firm

Practical value of behavioral theories
The practical value of behavioral theories of the firm is confined at present to aiding clear diagnosis of organizational problems and of clarifying the objectives and goals of the organization.

There are two basic types of theory: those which are usually expressed in terms of conceptual or qualitative relationships, and those which are expressed in terms of mathematical relationships. Mathematical theories are helpful as a means of exploring the validity of conceptual relationships as for instance presented in W.B. Horsmann's paper at the 1972 E.M.C.S.R.—"Biological specialization and the communication system of the firm" [3]. However, no mathematical theories of systems can at the present time be applied to practical problem-solving in the firm or help in the design or restructuring of a business organization (see Professor G. Jenkins [4]).

Action research
The approach used by the Systems Development Function at Beecham Pharmaceuticals is based on the extremely simple but practical conceptual model, which Jenkins and Checkland at Lancaster University describe as "Action Research". Figure 1 shows Jenkins' simple diagram representing the interaction between theory and practice in Action Research. In

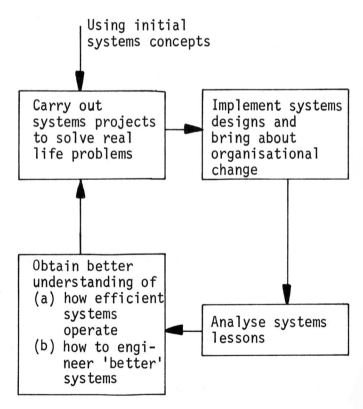

Fig. 1 Interaction between theory and practice in action research

a sense, this is at present the sum total of theory which can be *directly* applied to problem-solving or organizational development in the firm [5]. Jenkins also sets down features defining the system which is capable of being designed [6].

A similar kind of practical approach has been applied by Professor R.W. Revans with substantial success to the education of Managers from Stichting Industrie–Universiteit, Brussels.

General systems theory

It is therefore the conceptual content of General Systems Theory first presented by Bertalanffy [7] which has practical value by helping to increase understanding of the firm and how it functions. The concept of the open system [7] and the concept of the existence-function (Vesper [3]) have value in helping identify some of the qualitative parameters which define the organization of the firm. Much of the literature since Bertalanffy's paper has concentrated on the development of mathematical theories and definitions of relationships. On the one hand is an immensely valuable conceptual theory, on the other hand research workers seek to develop mathematical theories often before practical Action Research has established the necessary fund of empirical knowledge on systems and organizations required to give such theories practical value. Particularly because of the importance of the human relations parameters involved, it is unlikely that mathematical theories of organizations can be constructed or applied which will help with the design of improved systems until an adaptive learning program of Action Research has taken place extending over a number of years ahead.

Further concepts in systems thinking applied to the firm

The objectives of the firm

Some of the most valuable aspects of System thinking have been derived from the isomorphisms which have been sought between biological systems and the system of the firm. But there are important differences between organisms and social organizations such as the firm, which do not appear always to be recognized. An organism is self-organizing and by its nature its goal is substantially that of survival. The firm is self-organizing up to a point, and does seek to survive. But the firm is not a fully evolved organism. It must also be self-transforming to seek goals and objectives which are continuously set for

it above survival [8]. These higher goals may be referred to loosely as objectives for 'growth' (but not simply growth in turnover and profitability).

Breakthrough decision taking

Direct action to achieve the higher goals of the organization is required of the hierarchy of managers within the firm.

Vesper [2] refers to the goals or more accurately the behavioral commands within the firm not being the property of single persons but being a property of the system itself; that is, they result from a common interest of a section or majority within the firm. However, the formulation and restructuring of Vesper's Central Code must be effected by a hierarchy of managers within the firm and this continuous restructuring of the firm's goals is central both to the long-term survival and growth of the firm.

Direct actions must be taken to:

a) Add to or delete from the organization.

b) Add to or delete from the systems and procedures in the firm.

c) Add to or delete from the specific goals of the business (products, markets, etc.).

The importance of direct managerial action and decision taking on the success of the firm seems largely ignored in work on cybernetics or systems research. It is necessary to refer to literature on Management Conferences for reference to the theory of managerial breakthrough [9, 10].

Professor Juran characterizes breakthrough as the creation of good or at least necessary change and the dynamic decisive movement to new higher levels of performance. Juran argues that successful management will be based in large part on the belief that survival and growth of an organization make it virtually mandatory for managers continually to 'break through' to higher levels of performance.

Apart from the top management itself, departments exist in most firms which also have responsibility for managerial breakthrough; departments such as, for example, Research and Development, Long Range Planning and Systems Development. However, an attempt should be made to state the key parameters for the management of change:

a) How is responsibility for managerial breakthrough organized within the management hierarchy of the firm.

b) How effective is the system which exists within the firm for the communication and implementation of change.

It is suggested that cybernetics and systems research theory make little mention of (*a*) above but all the applications of the systems approach mentioned in this Chapter are greatly concerned with both (*a*) and (*b*) although they rest on the simplest theoretical basis of Action Research.

Implementation

The key problem in the firm is therefore getting the basically laissez-faire, natural self-organizing core of the system of the firm to accept adjustment to and in fact to work positively for achievement of these higher goals, i.e., to accept change. The mechanism for attempting to obtain acceptance of change and dynamic adaptation to its goals will center round the communication system of the firm in its broadest meaning, and the decisiveness and relevance of the actions taken on communications (particularly at the top decision level).

The features of importance in the communication system of the firm include the nature of the feedback control mechanism both formal and informal which exists within the firm and between the firm and its environment; the openness, awareness, and sensibility to the personal communications of decisions, which take place at each level in the organization; the development of people within the organization; the explanation, education, degree of participation engendered. In practical applications of methodology to problem solving or organizational development in the firm it is these aspects of communication or implementation which account for the major part of the work of any project team.

Changes are difficult to implement in the firm. The firm itself is not, as already stated, a highly developed system at an advanced stage of evolution. Thus it is argued that the lifespan of the firm would be short without continual transformation of its central code, the principal impetus for which will come from the hierarchy of management within the firm. The central self-regulatory survival mechanisms of the firm are in a real sense therefore self-defeating as they are usually opposed to dynamic changes and adaptations to new goals.

The firm is an individual organism without family, which seeks to develop itself from within through the power of its leadership.

Much more valuable research could be undertaken on the problems of implementation of change. It is surely the most important element not only in the practical application of any methodology of cybernetics or systems research but also relating to the development of the theories themselves. It continues to be the Cinderella of research which often concen-

trates on mathematical theory or identifying and defining isomorphic relationships.

Modeling the decision progresses of a firm embedded in a complex dynamically changing environment

Effective problem solving or organizational development within the firm should encompass the following concepts or stages of development:

1. Recognition of the importance of the quality of management decision making on the survival and growth of the firm. Management must transform the objectives of the firm as proves necessary. They must provide the objectives for any systems study or development of the organization or alternatively transform the objectives of the firm in response to the results of a systems study.
2. An understanding of the firm as an open system within a complex dynamically changing environment leading to adoption of the systems approach to problem solving within the firm.
3. Where possible, the design of models of the internal structure of the firm and of the relationships of the firm with its complex environment, leading to design of improved feedback control mechanisms.
4. Improvements to the information and communication systems within the firm, providing the firm with systems which are adaptive and responsive to change.

Pertinent to all these stages is the implementation of change, the communication of proposals, and the use made of new methods of communication. At this stage it is proposed to briefly outline several applications which encompass these concepts and stages.

1. Dynamic analysis of an animal feedstuffs business

A firm buying raw materials such as soya or fishmeal from international markets, compounding them and selling to livestoch breeders, is contained within a particularly complex and dynamically changing environment. The export of raw materials from international markets is controlled by a limited number of suppliers and buyers, and operates within similar conditions to a currency or share market. Prices for raw materials fluctuate widely and are influenced by a number of factors which are extremely difficult to predict, including world availability of materials, and the policy of the major exporting and importing nations. On the other hand, demand for the finished products are subject to widely differing pressures,

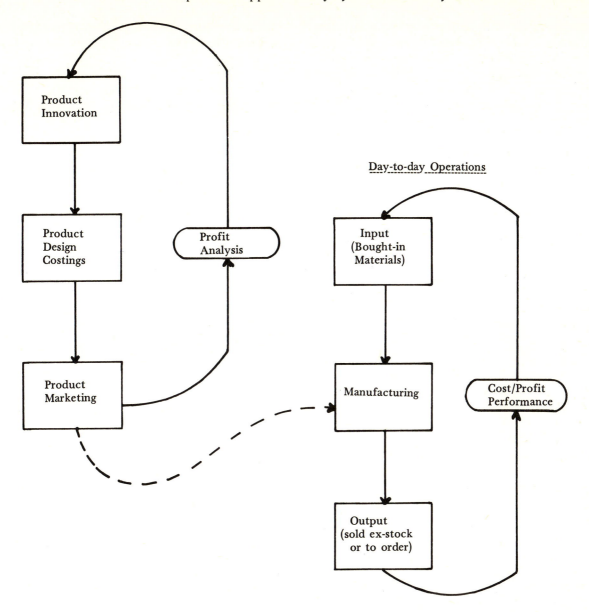

Fig. 2 Periodic Product Review.
Whilst long-term planning is important to any business, the product will remain basically unchanged for
long periods and thus product-review does not exist as a function affecting day-to-day control of profitability
of the business. Product innovation and manufacturing/sales are therefore largely separate functions.

including, for example, the pressures on the price of
meats, and foods in general from the government of
the particular market region and the effect of this
on livestock herd economics.

The animal feedstuffs business must be buying
materials for long but variable periods ahead, and
handling at least the following major variables
together with the complex interactions which take
place between them:

i. Forecast product sales for individual forward
months.

ii. The pattern of fluctuation of actual sales
about the sales trend.

iii. Distribution of errors in forecast product
sales.

vi. Forecast of raw material price trends.

v. The pattern of fluctuation of raw material
prices about the trend.

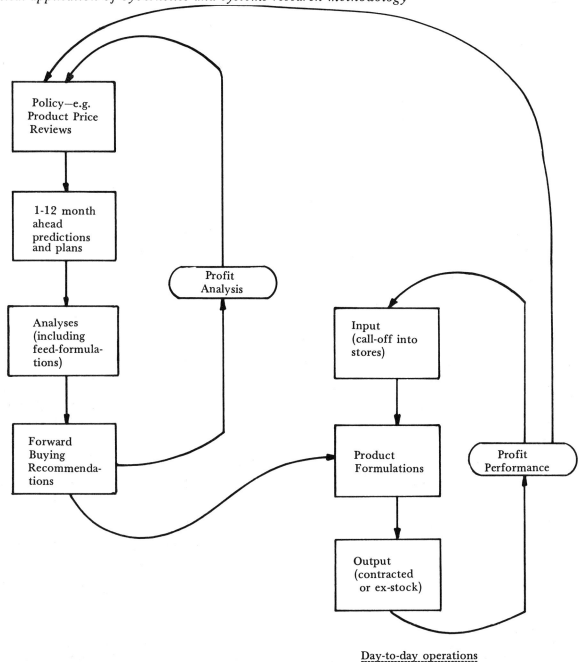

Fig. 3 Continuous Product Review
Such a business must be considered as a whole, and have long-term forward plans, which are *continuously* under review

vi.   The distribution of errors in the forecast of raw material price trends.
vii. The minimum lead time for further contract supply.
viii. The forward planning horizon required.
All of these and consequently the formulation of the finished products themselves are subject to continuous review.

To understand the dynamics of the situation, compare for instance the cycles of process steps of product design and manufacturing between a more typical manufacturing industry (Fig. 2) and on animal feedstuffs business (Fig. 3).

In most industries "product design" will remain

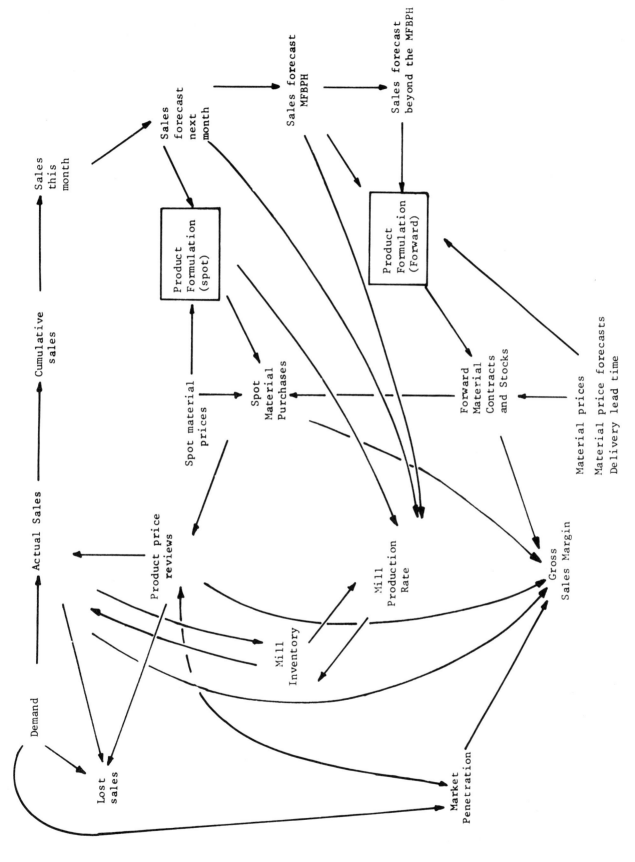

Fig. 4 Influence Diagram
All these 'influence' relationships are subject to continuous, ie., dynamic, change

unchanged throughout relatively long periods whereas in the animal feedstuffs business the product is changing continuously.

The approaches adopted to improving the system of operation of this business were therefore,

i. To instigate a practical systems study reviewing the organization of buying, production and marketing as a whole, both the planning methods used and the communication systems within the firm.

ii. To examine the possibility of constructing a dynamic model of the main functions of the business which would allow alternative short- and long-term planning methods, and alternative organizations to be compared. This dynamic model would have to cover at least the influence relationships described in Fig. 4.

2. A data management system designed for a pharmaceuticals company

This is an example of the application of systems thinking because the parameterized data management system was designed to meet particular communication system requirements of a single firm. Its design resulted from application of the systems approach to the very particular problems of an individual firm.

It had been established that a pharmaceuticals company has particular need for its production planning system to be flexible. Expressed simply, this was necessary to be both able to change the features of the system at short notice to meet dynamically fluctuating market conditions, and also to be able to amend and extend the system at relatively short notice to meet totally new conditions.

Because of the complexity of the types of planning problem to be solved, it was decided to design a parameterized data management system for the company. This system, known as PASS (Parameterized System Skeleton) provides a range of generalized input, output, file handling, and processing facilities designed to meet over 80% of system requirements for the production area within the facilities of the system.

It should be emphasized that it is not a generalized data management system of the type produced by computer manufacturers or software houses with such broad objectives as establishing company wide data bases. It was specifically designed to meet very particular needs of this pharmaceuticals firm for a flexible and adaptive planning system. The system has proved equally useful in other areas within the same firm, e.g. as a basis for marketing and commercial information systems.

The particular dynamically varying parameters governing the pharmaceuticals company or affecting its environment, which resulted in the requirement for the data management system included, e.g., the changes in demand which take place for antibiotics world-wide, which arise from the occurrence of epidemics and the essential need to be able to meet such demands whenever and wherever they occur, as people's lives may be at stake.

3. Dynamic analysis of industrial situations in the U.K.

The work of the systems research group at Bradford University in the U.K. (Director—Dr. R.G. Coyle), involves the practical applications of the principles outlined in this Chapter. They have been concerned with dynamic models of industrial situations, particularly with

a) The dynamics of production processes.
b) Commodities.
c) Corporate planning.
d) Economic dynamics.
e) Long-range forecasting.
f) Corporate structure analysis.

4. Recent applications of the systems approach to control system design in the U.K.

Another University department in the U.K., already mentioned in this Chapter, which has been actively applying in industry the systems approach is The Systems Engineering Department at Lancaster University. Examples of their practical projects are described in the Journal of Systems Engineering published by the University in the U.K., references to which are appended. Some at least are really practical applications of the principles outlined in this Chapter. The basic theme of this Chapter is that only the simplest conceptual theories of systems research or cybernetics can be practically applied to industrial systems at the present time, and that Action Research is the prime example of such an approach.

Conclusions

An objective of this Chapter was to provide some feedback to those engaged on theoretical work in the fields of systems research and management cybernetics from a practising manager of systems development in an industrial firm.

The author's final plea is that more of the theoretical work undertaken in universities and research centers should be based on empirical studies in industry. Too high a concentration on 'a priori' thinking and mathematical definition without parallel work on empirical studies will surely be counterproductive. Such theoretical work is unlikely to lead to early applications to the solution of real life problems within the firm.

References

1. BEER, S., Cybernetics and Management.
2. VESPER, V.D., 'Beyond the goals—the existence function of the firm', Proceedings of EMCSR *Advances in Cybernetics and Systems Research*, Transcripta Books, London (1973).
3. HORSMANN, W.B., 'Biological specialization and the communication system of the firm', Proceedings of 1st EMCSR, 1972, *Advances in Cybernetics and Systems Research*, Transcripta Books, London (1973).
4. JENKINS, G., *Journal of Systems Engineering* 2(2), 170 (1971).
   "I would go further. I find it difficult to see how the use of mathematical definitions can help at this stage in the development of the subject, which eventually will be judged by its ability to solve complex organizational problems. I agree that a more formal and rigorous approach in systems work is not only necessary but essential. However, I suggest that what is needed first is an attempt, by analysing a wide range of real-life systems, to determine which properties of a system are really important. Then, when this has been done, formalization can take place with greater confidence that the results will have widespread applicability."
5. JENKINS, G., p. 170, *op.cit.*
   "An analysis of the lessons learned from each project leads to a greater theoretical understanding of
   (*a*) the characteristics which efficient operational systems should possess,
   (*b*) the conceptual processes needed to design better systems, paying especial attention to the role of people.
   Finally, this improved theoretical understanding is applied to further problem solving, leading to yet further iteration."
6. JENKINS, G., p. 172, *op.cit.*
   (1) Sub-systems—which interact with each other.
   (2) Inputs—from its wider system and environment, which are transformed by the system into Outputs, which are fed to its wider system and environment.
   (3) Objectives—which may be in conflict but for which a compromise must be sought.
   (4) A Wider System, forming part of a hierarchy of wider systems—whose objectives govern the objectives of "the system" being engineered.
   (5) An Environment—over which it has no control but with which it may have important interactions.
   (6) Resources—to be manipulated in order to achieve the objectives.
   (7) A Performance Criterion—so that the extent to which the system is achieving its objectives can be assessed and its performance improved ("optimised").
   (8) A Decision Taker (or decision-taking process) —to manage, or manipulate the resources.
   (9) Boundaries—which must be clearly defined and which delineate the area over which the decision taker's power to manage must be exercised.
7. VON BERTALANFFY, L., 'General systems theory', in: *Gen. Syst.* 61.1 (1956).
8. CHECKLAND, P.B., 'Systems and science, industry and innovation', *Journal of Systems Engineering* 1(2), 16 (1970).
9. JURAN, J., 'Managerial Breakthrough'.
10. SCOTT, Sir Walter D., 'Management breakthrough and the conditions for its control', Proceedings of "Management & Growth" 14th CIOS International Management Congress, Rotterdam University Press (1966).
11. WRIGHT, R.D., 'An industrial dynamics implementation: growth strategies for a trucking firm', Sloan Management Review (Fall 1971).
12. COYLE, R.G., 'DMC Ltd. The Dynamics of a Production/Distribution System', Unpublished case study, University of Bradford, Systems Dynamics Research Group.
13. EMERSON, E.C., 'A systems study of Carribean transport', *Journal of Systems Engineering* 2(1) (Summer 1971).
14. POGSON, C.H., 'Defining the "right" problem: a production control problem', *Journal of Systems Engineering* 3(2) (Winter 1972).

Basic criteria in cybernetics: communication and organisation

FERNAND E. MAIRLOT* and DANIEL M. DUBOIS**
*Université Catholique de Louvain, St.-Niklaas, Belgium
**Université de Liège, Liège, Belgium

The concept of communication

The object of cybernetics is systems study. A system reaches its reality through its functioning, dynamism and behavior. The set of its constituent elements corresponds to a totality defined by an observer by its significance and by its action on the environment (Mairlot [1]). In any system the concepts of communication and organization are complex. Indeed a system is defined necessarily through a communication observed between its parts considered as constituent elements. This communication is the basic principle for organization.

As the communication is a complex process, simplified assumptions are often necessary. This is why models of communication are chosen in simple physical systems, which can more easily be studied, quantified and mathematically resolved. This reduction is made by the observer. A system is analyzed by the observer who projects himself into the process and decodes the communication, which corresponds for him to a message interpreted and transformed in mathematical language.

If a system is decomposed into N parts a first approach of knowledge of this system can be obtained by knowledge of the states of an information variable I_k $(k=1,...,N)$. These N components can be represented by a vector $\underline{I}$, such as

$$\underline{I} = (I_1, I_2, ..., I_N) \tag{1}$$

Moreover, this message represents information for the observer (Dubois [2]). Indeed, if $p(\underline{I})$ is the distribution of I_k's, the H-function (Shannon and Weaver [3]) can be calculated

$$H = -\int p(\underline{I}) \ln p(\underline{I}) d\underline{I} \tag{2}$$

with a normalization condition

$$1 = \int p(\underline{I}) d\underline{I} \tag{3}$$

where the integration is made in the $\underline{I}$-space.

However, contrary to this message which leads to an approach of a system, i.e., to information for the observer, the modification of the receptor by the communication may also be interpreted as information too (the receptor element is informed).

For the observer, the etymological sense of the concept of information is concerned with the modification of the form of the receptor by the integration of a message. From this elementary sequence of events, the basis or organization process is realized.

Progress in Cybernetics and Systems Research, Volume 2
Copyright © 1975 by Hemisphere Publishing Corporation

The communication between constituent elements is fundamental in systems theory. The dynamism of systems is induced by communication and a functional totality is realized through a certain behavior.

So it appears as a necessity to elucidate the instrument which is at the basis of the communication process. But generally this instrument of communication depends on the point of view of the observer and on the methods of measurement of phenomenons. Due to the communication process the receptor is not superposable to its previous state. This change may be a modification of form, a variation of frequency, etc., and generally this process is the result of work in relation to a thermodynamic gain through the concept of entropy. The relation between entropy, information and work appears to involve some unusual concepts.

Brillouin [4] gives the following distinction between them. Entropy relates the measure to the system and information relates the measure to the observer. This is, however, a rather artificial distinction since thermodynamics always implies the observer as establishing constraints on the system. (See the proposed model, below.) Microscopic information can be converted into work. Alternatively, work can also be converted into information since one can do work to place a system in a certain microstate or at least a group of microstates considerably more restricted than the equilibrium ensemble. Continuous work can therefore lead to the self-organization of systems.

Morowitz [5] gives an excellent explanation about the equivalence of information and negentropy (entropy decrease). In general, a system goes from a state of greater uncertainty about the microstate to a state of lesser uncertainty. Information is gained because in the second case the uncertainty about the microscopic description of the system is less than originally. Thus a decrease of entropy corresponds to an increase of information about the microstate. Entropy is proportional to a function which measures the lack of information about the microstate of a system. A high entropy means a great deal of information is necessary if the microstate of a system is to be known, but this implies very little knowledge as to which state it actually is in. As the entropy (S) decreases we are less unsure as to the state of the system, hence we have gained real information about the system. Therefore a decrease, $-\delta S$ of entropy does correspond to an increase in our actual knowledge about the microstate of the system.

Nevertheless, each point of view for the observer covers only one aspect of the processes, which is

not sufficient to describe the whole reality. The reduction of the reality to only one aspect is dangerous if this reduction corresponds for the observer to the sole reality. It is the reason why the concept of communication must be studied independently of the observer.

The concept of ENERSEAN

When a communication is established between two constituent elements, energy is emitted from one and received by the second. Liberation of a part of the available energy in the first element changes the form of this element. Liberation initiates the communication process in the first element. If the second element receives all or a part of this released energy, the change in form resulting from the integration of this energy is the process by which the second element is informed. Communication is a process which develops in emitter and receptor and modifies them. Although energy is required for communication, it is not information.

All forms of energy are not equally efficient for establishing a communication and inducing an integration process. Energy must, in addition, possess a specificity, i.e., the capacity to induce communication and inform. In order to affect an element, energy must be relevant to this element which changes and is informed. This capacity to act on the constituent element gives significance to this energy, a semantic value. This "semantic value" (Mairlot [6]) becomes the specific instrument for the communication process. This instrument of communication, defined as a "semantic energy", can cause some trouble: the specialists in physical sciences consider only the concept of energy and the specialists in human sciences do not use the concept of energy. It is the reason why a neologism based on the concept of "semantic energy" seems adequate: ENERSEAN (contraction of SEmANtic ENERgy) (Mairlot [7]). This concept indicates that in a communication, energy is always taken with reference to a receptor and possesses a capacity to inform this receptor. One could develop cybernetics beginning from this concept, because it represents what connects constituent elements. This specific instrument of communication is able to impart information both in natural and artificial systems. In a communication process, both energetic and semantic parts are necessary. However, the importance of each part is different following the nature of the receptor inside a system. In engineering systems, the energetic part is important, in human sciences the semantic aspect is predominant and in biological sciences both the two contributions are equally necessary.

Moreover, this concept is at the basis of systems dynamics which, owing to adequate organization, permits regulation and behavior.

The concept of organization

This concept of enersean is elementary in the sense that it constitutes a basis for others. To obtain a system, this enersean must be ordered in relation to the constituent elements on which it acts. From a formal point of view, a totality is obtained which is determined by the significance of the system. This totality is realized through an organization process which constitutes the second principle of cybernetics.

Organization appears, in its totality, as a harmony of spatial and temporal ordering of the constituent elements and of the enersean, the whole relation to the significance of the system.

From the mathematical point of view, organization could be considered as the information value of all the correlations in the system. Information would characterize neither the system itself nor the observer but would correspond to measurement operations by which the observer would know the system. Organization would be the characteristic of operations from which physical laws are established, a correlation between measurements.

With the concept of enersean, the system is decomposed into its constituent elements and an analytical method permits an understanding of the communication process. On the contrary, with the concept of organization, the system is looked upon as an ensemble of elementary parts which is studied as a whole. This duality part-ensemble leads to the question of uncertainty in cybernetics. Indeed, each theory starts with a certain arbitrariness in the choice of what kind of information the observer wants and how he chooses to coarse-grain or fine-grain his observations. Such a choice may be imposed mathematically by a constraint. If the constraint is defined by the mean square deviation σ^2 of the information variable I_k $(k=1,...,N)$, we can write

$$N\sigma^2 = \int p(\underline{I})(\underline{I}-\underline{I}_o)^2 \, d\underline{I} \qquad (4)$$

where $\underline{I}_o$ represents a reference state of $\underline{I}$. The greater N is, the more fine-grained will be the observation. It is evident that this value of σ^2 will be in a closed relation with the dynamics part of the system.

In both the kinetic theory of heat and communication theory, energy is directly proportional to the square of a variable—velocity in kinetic theory, voltage in communication theory, and so on.

If the information variable I_k represents the density in a certain volume of liquid (the total volume is divided into k-subsystems $k=1,...,N$), the variance will be in relation to the fluctuations of density inside the system. In a previous publication one of us has introduced an index of fluctuations D_o for ecological and biological systems (Dubois [2,8]) as a dynamic characteristic of the system and which is in narrow relation to a variance

$$D_o \sim D_o^* = \sum_{i=1}^{S} (p_i - \overline{p}_i)^2 / 2\overline{p}_i , \qquad i=1,...,S \qquad (5)$$

where p_i is the probability of species i and $\overline{p}_i$ the reference state of species i. It was also shown that this function is connected with the stability of the system.

Thus, Eq.(4) could represent the *dynamic part* of a system. Now it is necessary to point out its *structural part*, i.e., the general topology of the constituent elements inside the system. In analogy with statistical methods, a second constraint on the system is introduced which has the form of a potential energy V. This V function may be considered as an *organization potential*. For example, the structuralization of liquids and the crystallization of solids are well explained by the shape of the potential responsible for the forces between the atoms.

If Γ_k represents the potential existing in the k-subsystem $(k=1,...,N)$ and I_k the density, the potential energy may be written

$$V = \int p(\underline{I})(\underline{\Gamma}-\underline{\Gamma}_o) \times (\underline{I}-\underline{I}_o) \, d\underline{I} \qquad (6)$$

where $\underline{\Gamma}$ is a vector function of N components

$$\underline{\Gamma} \equiv (\Gamma_1, \Gamma_2,...,\Gamma_N) \qquad (7)$$

$\underline{\Gamma}_o$ is the value of $\underline{\Gamma}$ at the reference state and the cross represents a scalar product. Moreover, each Γ_k is a function of the corresponding information variable I_k:

$$\Gamma_k = \Gamma(\underline{I}_k) , \qquad k=1,...,N \qquad (8)$$

Equation (6) may be written

$$V = \int p(\underline{I})(\underline{\Gamma}-\underline{\Gamma}_o) \times \underline{I} \, d\underline{I} \qquad (9)$$

because of the properties of the reference state.

Now, in order to calculate the distribution $p(\underline{I})$, under to two constraints, Eqs (4) and (9), the extremum of H, Eq.(2), is calculated. Indeed, we assume that the system behaves efficiently: information theory arose in the communication theory where the amount of information transmitted in a communication channel is measured quantitatively. With such a measure, it would then be possible *to optimize the information per unit energy expenditure*. Here, information deals with the knowledge of a set of information variables *to an observer*.

In order to optimize Eq.(2), we apply the well-known method of "Lagrange multipliers" to these integrals (see, for example, Jaynes [9], Grossman [10]).

A necessary condition for the optimizing of H is

$$\frac{\partial H}{\partial p} - \lambda_1 \frac{\partial \phi_1}{\partial p} - \lambda_2 \frac{\partial \phi_2}{\partial p} - \lambda_3 \frac{\partial \phi_3}{\partial p} = 0 \qquad (10)$$

where ϕ_1 stands for the normalization condition [Eq.(3)], ϕ_2 the first constraint [Eq.(4)], and ϕ_3 the second constraint [Eq.(9)]. The Lagrange multipliers λ_1, λ_2, and λ_3 are proportionality constants that adjust their associated rates of change, in the differential equations, in accordance with normalization condition and the two constraints of their respective integrals.

Accordingly,

$$\frac{\partial H}{\partial p} = \frac{\partial(-p \log p)}{\partial p} = -(1 + \log p) \qquad (11a)$$

$$\lambda_1 \frac{\partial \phi_1}{\partial p} = \lambda_1 \frac{\partial p}{\partial p} = 1 \qquad (11b)$$

$$\lambda_2 \frac{\partial \phi_2}{\partial p} = \lambda_2 \frac{\partial((\underline{I}-\underline{I}_o)^2 p)}{\partial p} = \lambda_2 (\underline{I}-\underline{I}_o)^2 \qquad (11c)$$

and

$$\lambda_3 \frac{\partial \phi_3}{\partial p} = \lambda_3 \frac{\partial(p(\underline{\Gamma}-\underline{\Gamma}_o) \times \underline{I})}{\partial p} = \lambda_3 (\underline{\Gamma}-\underline{\Gamma}_o) \times \underline{I} \qquad (11d)$$

Summing,

$$-1 - \log p - \lambda_1 - \lambda_2(\underline{I}-\underline{I}_o)^2 - \lambda_3(\underline{\Gamma}-\underline{\Gamma}_o) \times \underline{I} = 0 \qquad (12a)$$

or

$$p(\underline{I}) = p_o \exp(-\lambda_2(\underline{I}-\underline{I}_o)^2 - \lambda_3(\underline{\Gamma}-\underline{\Gamma}_o) \times \underline{I}) \qquad (12b)$$

where

$$p_o = \exp(-1-\lambda_1) \qquad (13)$$

Substituting p back into the original integral equations, we obtain from Eq.(3)

$$1 = p_o \int \exp(-\lambda_2(\underline{I}-\underline{I}_o)^2 - \lambda_3(\underline{\Gamma}-\underline{\Gamma}_o) \times \underline{I}) d\underline{I} \quad (14a)$$

from Eq.(4)

$$N\sigma^2 = \frac{1}{2\lambda_2}\left(1 + \frac{\lambda_3^2}{2\lambda_2}(\underline{\Gamma}-\underline{\Gamma}_o)^2\right) \qquad (14b)$$

and, from Eq.(9)

$$V = -\frac{\lambda_3}{2\lambda_2}(\underline{\Gamma}-\underline{\Gamma}_o)^2 \qquad (14c)$$

Then, the H function

$$H = \lambda_1 + \lambda_2 N\sigma^2 + \lambda_3 V \qquad (15a)$$

is written

$$H = \ln p_o^{-1} + \frac{N}{2} + \frac{\lambda_3 V}{2} \qquad (15b)$$

If we define two quantities F_o and T_o

$$F_o \equiv T_o \log p_o \qquad (16a)$$

$$T_o \equiv 2/\lambda_3 \qquad (16b)$$

Eq.(15b) is written

$$F_o = -T_o H + \frac{NT_o}{2} + V \qquad (17)$$

Now, let us discuss the meaning of this Eq.(17) from the cybernetics point of view.

In the frame of the statistical thermodynamics theory, a free energy functional F is connected with energy E and entropy S by the following formula:

$$F = -TS + E \qquad (18)$$

where T is the temperature, S the entropy, and E the energy. The statistical definition of the entropy is in narrow relation to the information ones,

$$S = k_B H \qquad (19)$$

where k_B is Boltzmann's constant.

With the purpose of obtaining the same value for F_o and F, a relation between T_o and T is written

$$T_o = k_B T \qquad (20a)$$

and

$$T_o H = TS \qquad (20b)$$

In these conditions, Eq.(17) is written

$$F_o = -TS + N \frac{k_B T}{2} + V \qquad (21)$$

and we recognize the second term which is similar to the kinetic energy of a perfect gas and V the potential energy.

As we have characterized the system by the H-function, there naturally appears a temperature T_o associated with this H. It would be of some interest to connect this temperature with the concept of organization since the H function is connected with the global information of the system.

T_o can be considered *as the degree of organization of the system*, Prigogine and Lefever [11] have insisted on the concept of organization of a system.

"The evaluation of the enormous information content of biological molecules is rather useless as long as it does not give us any indication of the mechanism by which it has emerged. What must be taken into account is the fact that the purpose of biological structures is to accomplish certain functions with the best efficiency possible. In other words the degree of organization of a biological system is always appreciated with respect to what biologists would call "project", i.e., to see for an eye, to hear from an ear, etc...."

Moreover, Markowitz [12] considers a system defined by an assembly of oscillations representing the motions of biochemical reaction chains. The dynamical framework is supplemented by a statistical hypothesis that a complete state of a multichain system is specified by the set of probabilities with which each chain occupies its various oscillatory modes. A free energy functional is assumed to represent the major difference between "similar" biochemical systems *in vivo* and *in vitro*. General forces for energy and entropy are discussed. A parameter T_o, defined as *organization temperature*, multiplies the entropy term.

Conclusion

In the first part of this Chapter, the concept of communication is largely discussed and thus the concepts of message and information. Generally, a communication process can be considered as the result of work in relation to a thermodynamic gain through the entropy.

In the second Section, the concept of ENERSEAN is introduced with the purpose of studying a system independently of the observer. Moreover, this concept is always taken in reference to a receptor and possesses a capacity to inform this receptor.

Finally, the concept of organization is discussed in relation to a formal mathematical model. From an abstract point of view, an organization potential for systems is discussed in analogy to statistical mechanics. A temperature could represent the degree of organization of the system. It must be pointed out that the preceding considerations are of minor importance in classical thermodynamics, where large systems and macroscopic properties are only considered. But they become of greater importance where small systems and non-equilibrium systems are considered. Moreover, they are of very great importance in dealing with small, highly organized, far-from-equilibrium systems (such as biological and human sciences).

References

1. MAIRLOT, F.E., 'Principe de cybernétique, science de l'invariant', Association Internationale de Cybernétique (Namur), Série Documents (1973a).
2. DUBOIS, D.M., 'Mathematical aspect of invariant in cybernetics, Applications in ecology and in biology', *Cybernetica*, No.3, 161-176 (1973).
3. SHANNON, C.E. and WEAVER, W., *The Mathematical Theory of Communications*, The University of Illinois Press, Urbana, Ill. (1963).
4. BRILLOUIN, L., *Science and Information Theory*, Academic Press, New York (1962).
5. MOROWITZ, H.J., *Entropy for Biologists*, Academic Press, New York (1970).
6. MAIRLOT, F.E., 'La cybernétique, science de l'invariant et son impact sur la solution de problèmes réels', *Rev. des Questions Scientifiques*, No.144, 529-534 (1973b).
7. MAIRLOT, F.E., 'La définition de l'objet de la cybernétique et l'extension de son contenu', Rapport du VIIe Congrès International de Cybernétique (Namur, 1973), *Cybernetica*, No.1 (1974).

8. DUBOIS, D.M., 'Learning, adaptation and evolution of the ecosystem-environment couple', *Progress in Cybernetics & Systems Research*, Proceedings of the European Meeting in Vienna, Hemisphere Publishing Corp. and John Wiley & Sons Inc. (1974).

9. JAYNES, E.T., 'Information theory and statistical mechanics', *Physical Review* **106**(4), 620-630 (1957).

10. GROSSMAN, M., 'On the nature of information', *IEEE Spectrum* (December 1965).

11. PRIGOGINE, I. and LEFEVER, R., 'Stability and Selforganization in Open Systems' (preprint).

12. MARKOWITZ, D., 'Co-operativity model of cellular control: organization and complexity', *Journal of Theoretical Biology* **33**, 27-53 (1972).

The dynamic "Rocket" model of the management information and control system

GYÖRGY HORVÁTH
Ganz Measuring Instrument Works,
Budapest, Hungary

The Hungarian Ganz Instrument Works produces instruments serving to measure and control electric units. Moved by this kind of profile, the management felt morally obliged to search for possible applications of cybernetics. Many interesting technical books and review articles presented a number of cybernetical methods, effectively applicable in technical and economic practice, and the new ideas have stimulated—at least in a small degree—the experts of the company to realize them in practice.

1. Some characteristic data of the company

The present organization of the Ganz Instrument Works was formed in 1964, with unification of three, formerly legally independent companies. The central management of the Works was based on the management system of a factory, and in this way, the management of the *Works* and that of factory 1 was realized by the same organization and persons.

The general manager and his deputies (the technical, trade and economic managers, and also the chief engineer of production) as well as the middle-management, first of all the functional departments (for example, the planning, organizing and controlling departments), have a bilateral task, and, accordingly, they need two-levelled information.

The factories have maintained their earlier product range, i.e.,

Factory no. 1 produces innumerable types of electrical instruments,

Factory no. 2 produces metric gauges and control meters, while

Factory no. 3 produces instruments for vehicles.

All in all, we produce about 2500 variations of about 500 types within the framework of this profile. Some branches which produce component parts operate in a concentrated way in the largest factory of the Works—in factory 2.

The company has 6000 employees. Both the export—it is about 40% of its products—and the import of special electric components is carried on independently (without any connection with foreign-trade companies). The foreign and domestic sales organization is articulated according to the profiles of the various factories, but is concentrated in the center of the company. Moreover, the formation and distribution of resources and investments

Progress in Cybernetics and Systems Research, Volume 2

come to pass on the basis of the decision of the center of the company. Apart from this, the managers of the factories have a relatively great deal of independence, first of all in the field of preparation for production, purchase (except importation), management of production, development of products and technology of manufacturing—disregarding a few restrictions, for example, the licence and know-how contracts and standardization.

In the field of electronic data processing, the company made its first steps during the course of 1969, in factory 1, when we began to organize the computerized management of production. Last year, we began to extend this application to the management of production in factory 2.

The company has not its own computer yet.

2. The basic "Rocket" model of the information system

The management of the company has the opinion that establishing a dynamic model of management requires, by all means, a careful elaboration of an information, planning and decision system. Within the framework of this, however, the organization of an information system must be considered as the principal task, this being a basic condition of well-operating planning and effective decision-making. Therefore these subsystems of the company have been termed "primary systems", as opposed to other "secondary subsystems", for example, the coordinative, organizational, financial, accounting, and control systems. "Just as the flow of materials is of basic importance in the material sphere of producing plants, so in the same way the flow of information is of basic importance to the control sphere of the plant", writes Walter E. Schwitter in the review *Organisation und Betrieb*, No. 7/72. Having accepted this thesis we formed the "Rocket" model of the information system of the Ganz Instrument Works, paying particular attention to the above-mentioned peculiarities of the company.

Our information system is based on five information bases. In the basic model (Fig. 1), five bases are to be seen, i.e.,

Commercial base (CO)
Technical development base (D)
Production base (P)
Central base (C)
The management (M)

The connections and the flows of information are illustrated only in two dimensions in the figures presented. It would be an extremely awkward task

to illustrate these functions in space also (in three dimensions) though it was one of our objectives.

The central base has an extremely important and outstanding task in the establishment of an information system, as well as in management and coordination of the continuous operations of the special bases. This central base will direct the electronic data processing later, when it will be extended from the field of the management of production to the field of the other special bases, though in this respect the central base, providing the most important coordinative task, operates as not only the most significant central regulator of the information flow but as

- Special base of economical information, and
- Special base of social information (information on the personnel system and on the social sphere of the company and its environment).

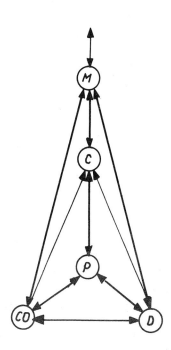

Fig. 1 The basic "Rocket" model of the information system

Progess of the "Rocket" model, respectively that of the "control sphere" of the company is determined, first of all, by information on the market situation, as well as on the technical and social environment. The information energies stream to the company through this base and in the process of production and under the continuous regulation of the central base, these energies finally appear as material values (benefits) and stream into the surrounding world. The principle of action and reaction prevails in this way, in consequence of which our "Rocket" model is in continuous movement. On the peak of the model is the management, the function of which is to determine the principal trend of progress, to realize it, and accordingly to control its realization.

Though the presented basic model is similar to a managerial pyramid, the activities are grouped not in compliance with managerial levels, but rather according to the special information. Accordingly, the commercial manager belongs to the commerical base and the technical manager to the base of development while practising their routine work, but on the other hand, as deputy-directors, these managers belong to the management information base.

In this way, some units of the company (which otherwise are related in the organizational structure) are separated in the model of information. For example, in the presented model the purchasing department may be classified in the commercial base, while the other departments of provision are classified in the production base. On the one hand, these bases of information mean cooperation between the units of the company under the informal direction of a center of information (i.e., department of information), but on the other hand, these bases also provide for the coordination of the managerial actions and functions in a certain special field, as is illustrated in the Figures presented later.

Therefore, the information needs of the management are developed not from one, but four centers of information. Fundamental changes are not planned in this respect, except the possible effect of changes which become necessary in the organization of information in consequence of the development of electronic data processing. Apart from this, we have an organizational task in connection with the reorganization of the central base, because of the mentioned bilateral tasks (in professional and regulatory fields), which resulted in a relative overcharge of this base.

3. Operation of the information bases

If we want to search for a comparison with the operation of the human organism, we may say that
- the commercial and development bases are the lungs,
- the production base is the heart, while
- the central base provides for the function of the brain.

We borrowed our comparisons from the technical field, but always kept in view the social aspect of the company and the characteristics of its operation arising from this aspect.

The tasks of the information bases are the following:
- formation and development (if necessary) of the base,
- obtaining of information, its evaluation, elaboration and transmission to planning, decision-making or to further elaboration.

The system concept necessitates a maximum co-ordination between the various bases. This complete harmony requires unified, homogeneous language for the information system.

In our "Rocket" model, the information bases operate almost in the manner of a wireless. Figure 2 shows the "wireless model", in which the waves (the information) stream naturally not only out of the center, as occurs in the case of real radio-waves, but also from the margin to the center. In this model, therefore, marginal information and central information are moving in both directions, and between them is placed the so-called "medium" information.

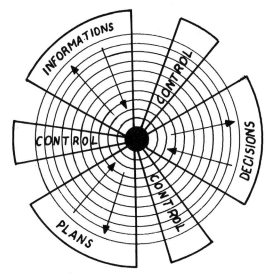

Fig. 2 The "radio-wave" model of the information bases

The greatest problem for us was to secure the unified wavelengths and wave-frequencies. These wavelengths and frequencies are destined to secure the accord of the managerial system (first of all the harmony of planning, of decisions and control). As all information on a given level has to reach the same level of decision, the management has the information grouped or typified according to the various managerial levels.

The Ganz Instrument Works has attempted to construct these kinds of tables, in the first place for the decisions on exportation and on development of products. The table presented in Fig. 3 prescribes the managerial levels, to which in the case of certain types (degrees) of development, the suggestions and decisions (S and D) have to be forwarded.

Managerial level	Types of information or decision					
	A	B	C	D	E	F
5. Engineer, or head of section	D	S	S	S	S	S
4. Head of department	–	D	S	S	S	S
3. Head of department (chief of No. 4)	–	–	–	D	S	S
2. Technical manager	–	–	–	–	D	S
1. General manager	–	–	–	–	–	D

Fig. 3 Categories of the information for development

The categories of demands for development are as follows:

a) Demand for a small modernization of an instrument (modification of some component, etc.).

b) Considerable constructional changes in a particular type of instrument.

c) Manufacture of an old instrument by new technology.

d) Utilization of new types of instruments for already well-known purposes.

e) Utilization of new types for presently unknown purposes (for example, in new industrial branches or in tropical regions, etc.).

f) Fundamental change in profile (manufacture of other engineering products besides instruments).

Using similar tables, one may realize the importance of collecting information in the place of decision, according to categories (wavelengths), and in case of it surpassing the given limits, to forward it to the next category. The limits of categories may be determined in monetary value, in natural or in other units of measure.

The operation of control and the feedbacks are organized, first of all, in the framework of the information bases. Figure 2 presents the control as operating almost as a moving controlling disc.

Figure 2 presents the operation of the informative bases according to managerial levels. This operation necessitates, however, connections between the departments and their chiefs. We may demonstrate it as well by the example of the information base for development.

According to Fig. 4, which presents the example of the development base, this base has five units (sub-bases) which are

– informative units, serving for the research and development of products,

– for research and development of technology,

– for development of energy supply,

– for investments,,

and finally, the central informative unit of the basis.

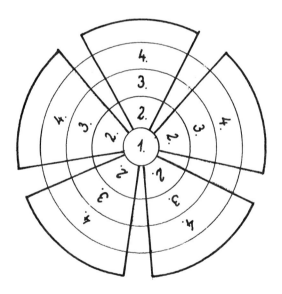

Fig. 4 Information base for development

As a person on the top managerial level, the technical manager was placed at the center, while widening from beginning to end, the lower managerial levels are situated from the center of the circle toward the margin.

Another Figure (Fig. 5) presents the production base in a form similar to a gear-box, in which
- the scheduling (programming) operates as the greatest wheel including the whole structure. It obtains directives from the central basis, while the concrete demands (information) are obtained and worked up through the commercial and development base.
- the second, smaller wheel operates as the co-ordinating and information-processing department,
- the smallest wheels (for example, departments of design, of technology, provision of materials, preparation for manufacturing and the producing industrial units) furnish information which is necessary for the preparation and accomplishment of production.

We do not present a separate Figure on the central base, as our ideas are not fully developed in this respect yet and depend on forthcoming development of the electronic data processing.

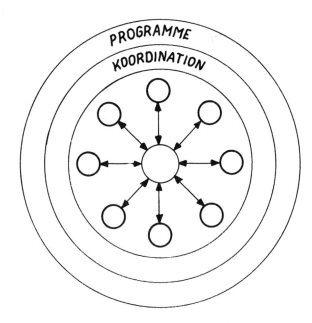

Fig. 5 Information base for production

4. Complex information models

In economic life, most companies are complex entities with more or less dependent units (affiliated firms, plants, etc.). The consequence of this is that our basic information model needs further development also in this respect.

Our task is to organize
- the model of the individual units,
- the connection of the partial models
on the basis of unified principles.

The structure of the models depends on the organizational structure, on the responsibility of management of the individual units, and on the degree of centralization or decentralization of functions. In spite of the plentiful possible variations, the initial point may be always the "Rocket" model.

Figure 6 presents the case of loose information links. In this case the management of the company was concentrated in one of the factories. The other factories are not legally independent any more, but

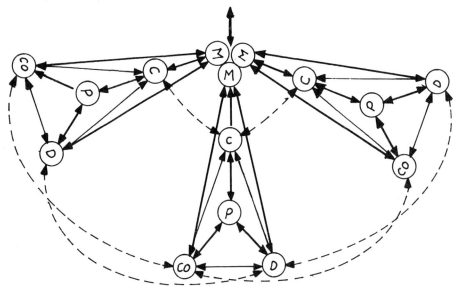

Fig. 6 The case of loose connection between informative systems

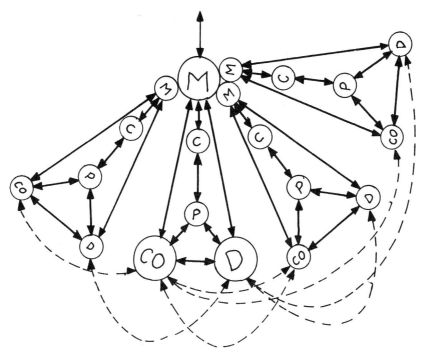

Fig. 7 Connection in the case of centralization of functions (degree I)

they preserved independence of informative connections with the external environment. Similar to this is the model of companies which
- operate as economically independent companies further on,
- are, at the same time, parts of a greater totality, for example, a merged (fused) large enterprise.

The incorporation of formerly legally independent companies raises new kinds of organizational tasks with respect to transformation of the information system. In the "Rocket" model, first of all, one has to connect the information bases of the management. The next task is to determine the level of independence of the professional bases, then to establish the connection of the bases to one another—in the first place, however, to establish their connection to the central base and the coordination of the operation.

Figure 7 presents this connection on the basis of the example of the Ganz Instrument Works. In this model the functions of the professional bases are clear-cut. The different profile of manufacture and the partly different sales areas make this partition possible. The proportion of production of the plants, measured against factory no. 1 are 1:2, respectively 1:0.5. This suggests that the forces, acting through the commercial basis and the basis for development, are not equal. From the point of view of the management, the knowledge of these forces is highly important, in order to maintain the balance of the "Rocket" model (consisting of three units) and also

in order to determine adequately the resultant force.

In the case where the units (factories) have lost their independence also in the fields of marketing, selling and purchasing, the development of products will also be centralized, and in this way only the production remains the main task of legally not independent units. Therefore, our "Rocket" model must be transformed again, and the model of the smaller units (factories) mutilated (Fig. 8).

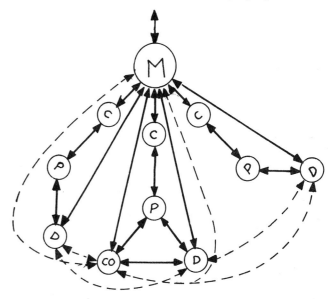

Fig. 8 Connection in the case of centralization of functions (degree II)

Finally, we present the model of a large enterprise in which a separate organization (general management or trust) directs the units. The basic principles of this kind of connection of information are consequences of the variation, made known beforehand.

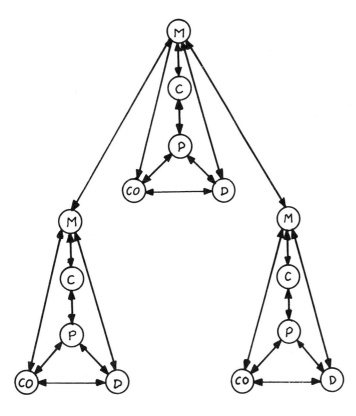

Fig. 9 Model of information in the case of units managed by a separate organization

5. Progress of the company in the surrounding world

An industrial enterprise exists and progresses in three spheres, namely

The technical sphere:
- economic systems (companies), producing with the same technology, including the partners for cooperation and the competitors.

The commercial sphere:
- the buyers and sellers (the latter may partly

be classified in the technical sphere).

The social sphere:
- the social systems, including the social norms and laws.

In reality, these spheres overlap one another (for example, the companies, producing in the same industrial branches may also appear as buyers, or: the social sphere includes the other two spheres as well, etc.).

Examining the progress of the company with the aid of the "Rocket" model for information, the management has the important task of controlling

a) The basic objectives.

b) The course of the progress and divergences from it, and

c) Needs to be informed on the force and speed of movement in an almost up-to-date way and to control it. It needs not only knowledge of information, containing the data of past, present and future within its own company, but also data of the other companies and institutes of the surrounding economic system.

The basic objectives are prescribed and if necessary are corrected by the owner, respectively by the management of the company.

Fixing the parabolic or rather hyperbolic trajectory of progress is an extremely difficult but interesting ballistic task, and needs plenty of information considering the force and speed of economic movement of the company.

As the people and economic systems cannot determine any more their sort and progress independently from one another, in the same way, industrial companies cannot successfully progress on their planned course without suitable economic or other kinds of cooperation and exchange of information with other companies.

Figure 10 demonstrates the above-mentioned ideas and presents the progress of the company as a model for information. Cooperation with other companies requires a common language, the same kind of coding or re-coding of information, as was mentioned during the presentation of the radio-wave model. The international political, economic and social organizations have recently made considerable progress toward realizing and developing this common language in the interest of exchange of information.

Examining the informative model, the companies have to be well acquainted with their own ballistic curve as well as with that of the other companies, to be able to determine and correct the suitable course of progress, the desirable speed and other parameters.

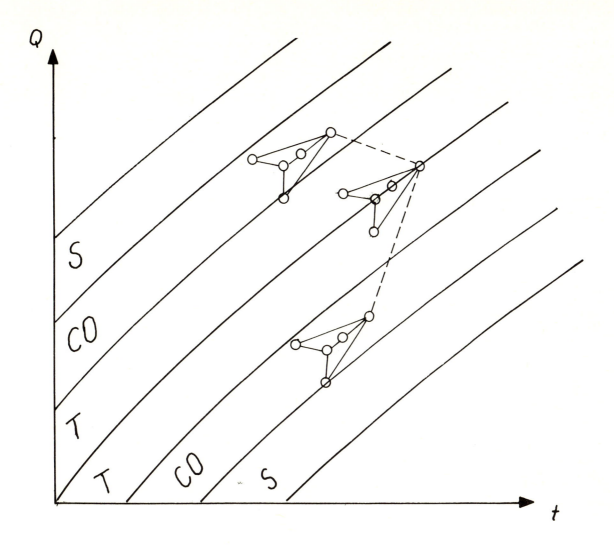

Fig. 10 Progress of the company in the environment

6. Conclusions

In organizational practice it is always one of the most difficult tasks to develop a well operating information system. To solve this problem, the management of Ganz Instrument Works also used the science of communication and control, i.e., cybernetics.

We attempted to learn the practice of an information system and the rules of management by use of a model closely paralleling astronautical techniques.

Dynamic simulation of a cattle farm

MANUEL GUTIÉRREZ, ANDRÉS F. GUTIÉRREZ, and ANDRÉS E. GUTIÉRREZ
Universidad de Carabobo, Valencia, Venezuela

General system

The general system was developed with four main parts:

(*a*) The dynamic simulator of a cattle farm: This is the heart of the work and through it all costs and profits are calculated monthly. The model was built with a set of finite difference equations that give the state of each variable in the following way:

$$X_{i+1} = X_i + \text{INPUT} - \text{OUTPUT}$$

To compute the next quantity of the variable X we add the input and rest the output, the input to the variable X is the output of some other variable, and the output of the variable X is the input to some other variable in the system.

In the Section about system dynamics is presented an analysis of each state equation of the model.

(*b*) The controller: This part of the system represents the policy to be followed running the cattle farm. Since this depends on the objectives and on the particular strategy used, it gives the need to develop several experiments in order to choose the policy that suits best under any conditions.

(*c*) Economic analysis: At the end of each run the rate of capital return is calculated using an iterative subroutine. The input to this subroutine is the flow of capital during the simulation, an estimate of investment and salvage value. This result allows the person conducting the experiment to make a rapid evaluation of the results.

(*d*) Information system: Most of the values of the parameters used in the model depend on the region where they are applied; therefore, an information system containing these values is required in order to make use of the simulator easy. The experimenter controls the flow of information to the system at the beginning of each run.

In Fig. 1 is presented the flow of the four parts described above showing the way in which they are related through the operator.

System dynamics

This part of the simulator represents the source of information for all other calculations.

In Fig. 2 is shown a flow diagram that presents the dynamic relationships between the different animal groups in the system. Each box represents a transfer function that relates the input to the group to the output and gives the aggregated measure of the particular state.

The model of the system was developed with 12 states.

1. Female calfs from 1 to 6 months.
2. Female calfs from 7 to 12 months.
3. Heifers.
4. Pregnant cows.
5. Post-pregnant rest cows.
6. Cows in lactation.

Progress in Cybernetics and Systems Research, Volume 2

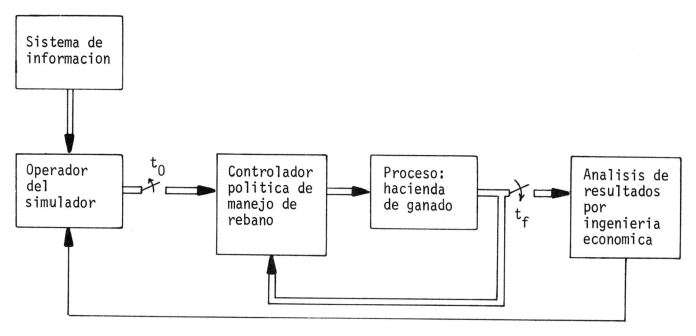

Fig. 1

7. Male calfs from 1 to 6 months.
8. Male calfs from 7 to 12 months.
9. Males from 1 to 2 years.
10. Males from 2 to 3 years.
11. Males older than 3 years.
12. Breeding males.

The states were chosen in the way presented above because they represent the natural way in which they are classified in a cattle farm.

Each iteration in the discrete state equations represents one month real time delay.

Young female dynamics
The first group of equations represents the females younger than two years. These equations are

BECEAS ← BECEAS + IENTR1 − ISALI1
MAUTAS ← MAUTAS + ISALI1 − ISALI2
NOVAS ← NOVAS + ISALI2 − ISALI3

where the variables BECEAS, MAUTAS and NOVAS represent the quantity of female calfs from 1 to 6 months, from 7 to 12 months and the heifers, that there are in the flock per month. The variable IENTR1 represents the new calfs that are born, while ISALI1 represents those that are 7 months old,

so that they go into their new classifications, and the same for the variables ISALI2 and ISALI3 with respect to their classification. Figure 3 represents the flow diagram of these equations where the symbol Δ stands for one month's delay.

Cow dynamics
This section classifies the cows in production into three classes: Pregnant cows indicated by VACPRE(I), cows in post-pregnant rest VACREP(I), and cows in lactation given by VACLEC(I). Within each group they are classified by the number of months they have been in it, and that is indicated by the subscript I, for example, for VACPRE(I), I is between 1 and 9, for VACREP(I), I is between 1 and 3 or 4, and for VACLEC(I), I is between 1 and 10.

Figure 4 shows the flow diagram of the finite difference equations of this part of the simulator.

Bull dynamics
This part of the model simulates the growing process of the males in the herd. The male calfs up to six months and up to 12 months are represented by the variables BECEOS and MAUTES. Those 1 to 2 years old are represented by the variable NOVOS1, and

367

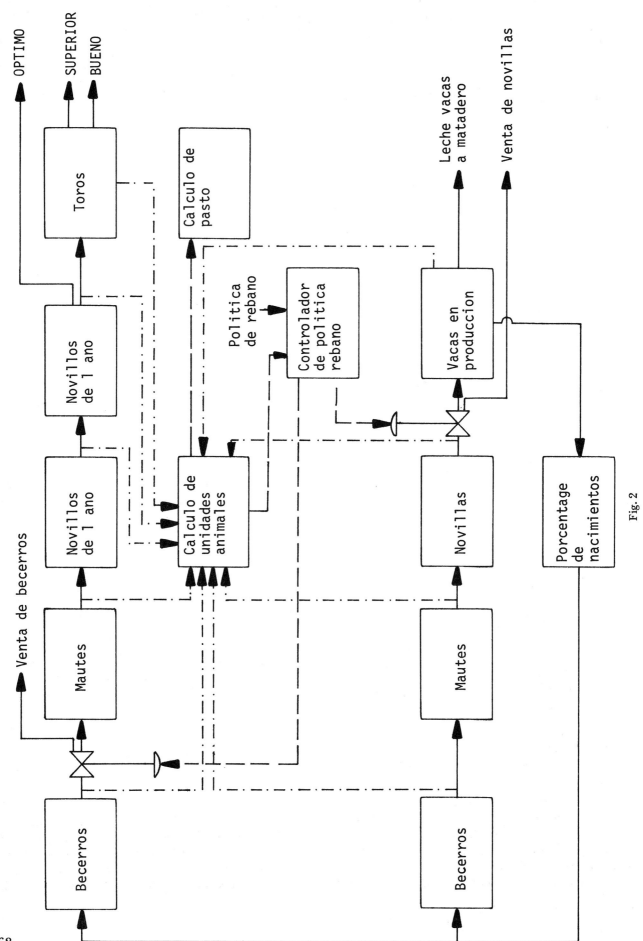

Fig. 2

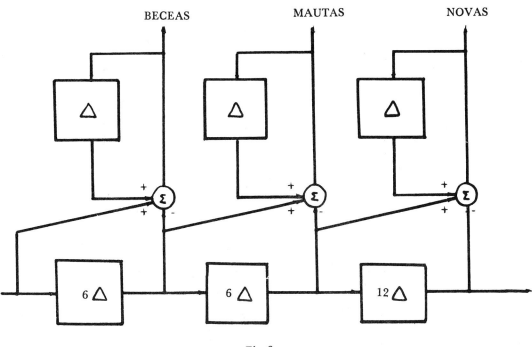

BECEAS   MAUTAS   NOVAS

Fig. 3

those 2 to 3 years old by NOVOS2. Figure 5 shows the flow diagram of the equations.

Some of the bulls are sold when they are three years old, depending on the weight they have gained by this time. In this simulator these bulls are classified as optimus, and those that did not obtain the desired weight are usually held for some period of time, after which they are sold as superior or as regulars. It was found that this is the most popular way of handling the males, but, again, there are some other possible strategies that could be used.

The parameter PTOOPT represents the percentage of optimus when the bulls are three years old, and PTOSUP represents the percentage of bulls that are superior when they are 4 years old. The flow diagram of Figure 6 indicates the dynamics of the equations that model this.

Breeding males dynamics
The philosophy used in the simulator was to hold a specified minimum number of breeding males for a determined quantity of production cows, the parameter VACSEM given indicating how many cows there are per breeding male. At the same time, these animals are held for some desired time, given in the

number of months by the parameter ITIEM. The flow diagram of Fig. 7 shows the dynamics of these finite difference equations.

Controller
When the cows are two years old we suppose that one of the main decisions to be made is to incorporate the new cows into the production group or to sell them. This depends on the desired production level or the maximum land available.

This is implemented by that part of the controller that calculates the hectares that are available, and from this decides to sell or to increment production. The flow diagram of this section of the controller is depicted in Fig. 8.

The first step is to determine whether the pasture is common or not. In the case where it is not, the maximum potential quantity of hectares HASM is the variable to use; otherwise subtract from HASM the hectares that are in use by the males. Afterwards, the maximum potential quantity of cows in production is calculated and compared with the actual quantity. From this the decision to sell or not is taken.

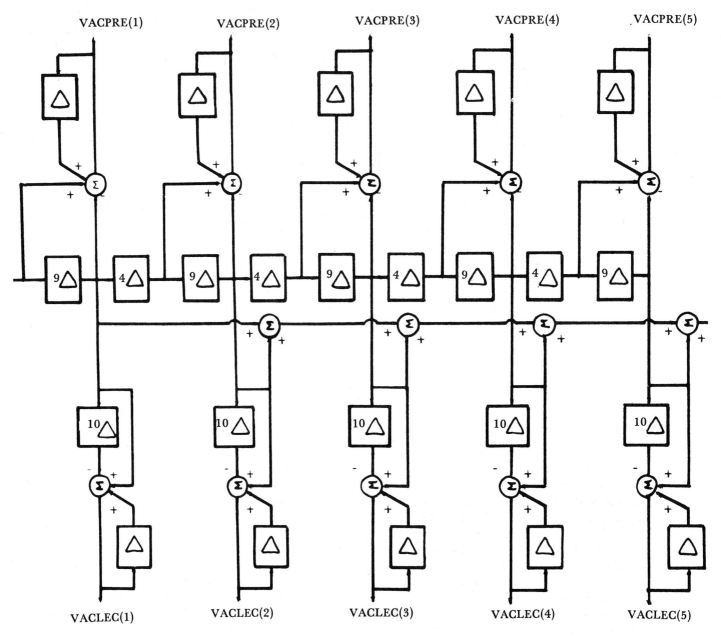

Fig. 4

Another function of the controller is to decide either to sell the males of 6 months, as is usually done in a farm dedicated to milk production, or to raise them until they are about 3 or 4 years old and have gained enough weight.

This is a special type of controller, which was implemented due to its universal popularity. However, in some farms a different strategy may be used at some other place in the flow. This is very easily implemented.

Cost computations
The cost of operating a cattle farm is divided into two classes: The variable costs, which depend on the production level, and the fixed costs. Both are affected, in the simulator, by an inflationary trend with rates specified by the user.

Variable cost
The variable costs calculated by the simulator are the following:

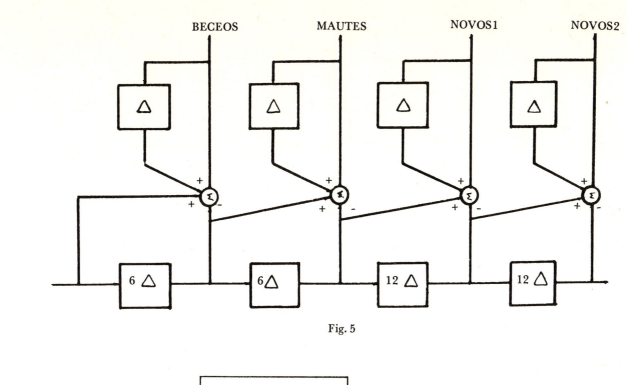

Fig. 5

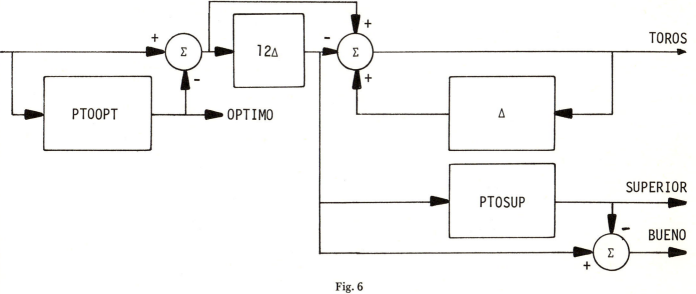

Fig. 6

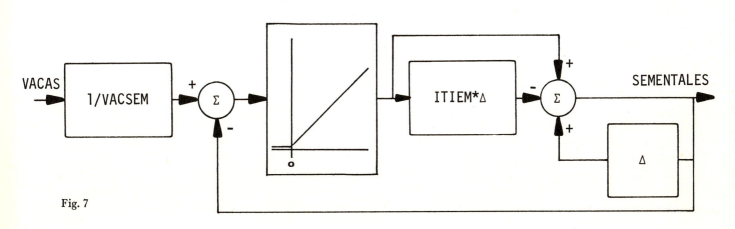

Fig. 7

371

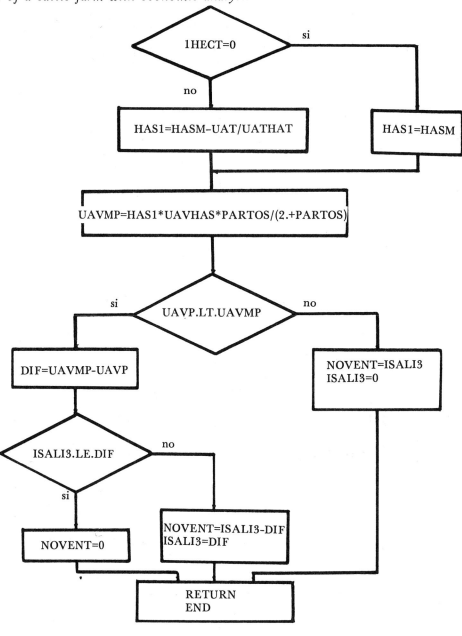

Fig. 8

(*a*) The variable cost proportional to the cows in lactation.

(*b*) The cost of putting more hectares of pasture into production, as required by the quantity of animal units. This is indicated in Table 2 by the columns CIHAS and CIHAT for the cost due to new hectares for females and males, respectively. For the case where the pasture is common to both, column CIHAT gives the results. In this same Table the columns HAS and HAT present the quantity of hectares available for females and males. For the case where they are common it is shown in column HAT.

(*c*) The cost of maintenance of hectares of pasture. This is indicated in Table 2 by the columns CMHAS and CMHAT for the pasture of female and males. Again, for the case where they are common, it is shown by column CMHAT alone.

372

Dynamic simulation of a cattle farm with economic analysis

MES	BECEAS	MAUTAS	NOVAS	VACPRE	VACREP	VACLEC	VACTOT	BECEOS	MAUTES	NOVOS1	NOVOS2	TOROS	TORTOT	UAV	UAT
1	0	0	100	0	16	16	116	0	0	0	0	0	0	92.0	0.0
2	0	0	90	14	12	16	116	0	0	0	0	0	0	95.0	0.0
3	0	0	80	28	8	16	116	0	0	0	0	0	0	98.0	0.0
4	0	0	70	42	4	16	116	0	0	0	0	0	0	101.0	0.0
5	0	0	60	56	0	16	116	0	0	0	0	0	0	104.0	0.0
6	0	0	50	66	0	16	116	0	0	0	0	0	0	107.0	0.0
7	0	0	40	76	0	16	116	0	0	0	0	0	0	110.0	0.0
8	0	0	30	86	0	12	116	0	0	0	0	0	0	113.0	0.0
9	0	0	20	96	0	8	116	0	0	0	0	0	0	116.0	0.0
10	0	0	10	106	0	4	116	0	0	0	0	0	0	119.0	0.0
11	5	5	0	102	14	14	121	5	5	5	0	0	5	123.3	1.3
12	10	10	0	88	28	28	126	10	10	15	0	0	10	124.5	2.5
13	15	15	0	74	42	42	131	15	15	20	0	0	15	125.8	3.8
14	20	20	0	60	56	56	136	20	20	24	0	0	20	127.0	5.0
15	24	24	0	64	52	66	140	24	24	28	0	0	24	128.0	6.0
16	28	28	0	68	48	76	144	28	28	32	0	0	28	129.0	7.0
17	27	26	5	72	44	86	148	27	26	36	0	0	32	130.3	8.3
18	26	25	10	76	40	96	152	26	25	40	0	0	36	131.5	9.5
19	25	24	15	76	40	106	156	25	24	44	0	0	40	132.8	10.8
20	24	20	20	76	40	116	160	24	20	44	0	0	44	134.0	12.0
21	26	24	24	86	30	102	160	20	16	44	0	0	44	134.2	12.2
22	16	28	28	96	20	88	160	16	12	44	0	0	44	134.4	12.4
23	12	27	32	102	10	74	165	12	13	36	0	0	44	136.6	15.1
24	13	25	36	88	14	74	165	13	26	40	0	0	49	141.6	19.1
25	14	24	40	74	28	78	170	14	25	44	0	0	54	145.0	23.0
26	15	20	44	60	42	82	175	15	24	44	0	0	59	148.5	27.0
27	20	16	44	64	56	86	180	20	20	44	0	0	64	151.3	30.2
28	28	12	39	68	52	86	184	24	16	39	0	0	68	153.9	33.2
29	27	13	39	72	48	86	188	28	12	39	0	0	72	156.5	36.2
30	26	14	39	76	44	86	192	27	13	39	0	0	76	160.9	39.5
31	25	15	40	76	40	96	196	26	14	40	0	0	80	163.7	42.7
32	24	20	40	86	40	106	200	25	15	40	0	0	84	166.6	46.0
33	20	24	40	101	30	116	204	28	20	40	0	0	88	167.8	47.2
34	16	28	40	116	20	102	204	27	24	40	5	0	88	168.0	47.4
35	12	27	40	117	10	88	204	28	28	39	10	0	88	169.7	48.6
36	13	25	40	108	14	74	209	29	27	39	15	0	88	173.4	52.3
37	14	24	44	108	28	74	214	28	25	39	20	0	93	178.4	57.3
38	15	20	44	98	42	78	219	25	24	40	24	0	98	184.8	62.2
39	20	16	44	88	56	82	224	20	20	40	28	0	103	189.5	67.0
40	24	12	39	96	52	86	228	16	16	40	32	0	108	193.5	71.0
41	28	13	39	104	48	86	232	12	12	40	36	0	112	197.3	74.8
42	27	14	40	111	44	86	235	13	13	40	40	0	116	201.1	78.6
43	28	15	40	110	45	86	237	14	14	40	44	0	120	204.2	82.7
44	29	20	40	105	50	101	243	28	15	40	44	0	126	204.7	87.2
45	30	24	44	100	55	116	249	29	20	44	44	0	132	208.1	91.0
46	28	28	44	105	50	131	251	30	24	44	44	0	138	209.8	92.7
47	25	25	44	116	39	122	247	28	28	44	39	1	136	210.5	89.4
48	22	28	39	127	28	112	243	25	27	39	39	2	133	207.5	86.9
49	23	27	39	124	27	102	243	22	27	39	39	3	130	206.4	86.8
50	28	28	39	106	27	106	245	23	28	39	39	4	133	207.0	88.4

Table 1

TIEMPO	CVPL	CIHAS	HAS	CMHAS	CMVAC	CIHAT	HAT	CMHAT	CMTOR	COSEME
0.100E+01	0.400E+03	0.000E+00	0.155E+03	0.465E+04	0.232E+03	0.000E+00	0.500E+01	0.250E+02	0.000E+00	0.600E+04
0.200E+01	0.400E+03	0.000E+00	0.155E+03	0.465E+04	0.232E+03	0.000E+00	0.500E+01	0.250E+02	0.000E+00	0.000E+00
0.300E+01	0.400E+03	0.000E+00	0.155E+03	0.465E+04	0.232E+03	0.000E+00	0.500E+01	0.250E+02	0.000E+00	0.000E+00
0.400E+01	0.400E+03	0.000E+00	0.155E+03	0.465E+04	0.232E+03	0.000E+00	0.500E+01	0.250E+02	0.000E+00	0.000E+00
0.500E+01	0.400E+03	0.000E+00	0.155E+03	0.465E+04	0.232E+03	0.000E+00	0.500E+01	0.250E+02	0.000E+00	0.000E+00
0.600E+01	0.400E+03	0.000E+00	0.155E+03	0.465E+04	0.232E+03	0.000E+00	0.500E+01	0.250E+02	0.000E+00	0.000E+00
0.700E+01	0.400E+03	0.000E+00	0.155E+03	0.465E+04	0.232E+03	0.000E+00	0.500E+01	0.250E+02	0.000E+00	0.000E+00
0.800E+01	0.300E+03	0.000E+00	0.155E+03	0.465E+04	0.232E+03	0.000E+00	0.500E+01	0.250E+02	0.000E+00	0.000E+00
0.900E+01	0.200E+03	0.000E+00	0.155E+03	0.465E+04	0.232E+03	0.000E+00	0.500E+01	0.250E+02	0.000E+00	0.000E+00
0.100E+02	0.100E+03	0.000E+00	0.155E+03	0.465E+04	0.232E+03	0.000E+00	0.500E+01	0.250E+02	0.000E+00	0.000E+00
0.110E+02	0.350E+03	0.000E+00	0.155E+03	0.465E+04	0.242E+03	0.000E+00	0.500E+01	0.250E+02	0.125E+02	0.000E+00
0.120E+02	0.700E+03	0.000E+00	0.155E+03	0.465E+04	0.252E+03	0.000E+00	0.500E+01	0.250E+02	0.250E+02	0.000E+00
0.130E+02	0.110E+04	0.000E+00	0.155E+03	0.488E+04	0.275E+03	0.000E+00	0.500E+01	0.263E+02	0.394E+02	0.000E+00
0.140E+02	0.147E+04	0.000E+00	0.155E+03	0.488E+04	0.286E+03	0.000E+00	0.500E+01	0.263E+02	0.525E+02	0.000E+00
0.150E+02	0.173E+04	0.000E+00	0.155E+03	0.488E+04	0.294E+03	0.000E+00	0.500E+01	0.263E+02	0.630E+02	0.000E+00
0.160E+02	0.200E+04	0.000E+00	0.155E+03	0.488E+04	0.302E+03	0.000E+00	0.500E+01	0.263E+02	0.735E+02	0.000E+00
0.170E+02	0.226E+04	0.000E+00	0.155E+03	0.488E+04	0.311E+03	0.525E+03	0.550E+01	0.289E+02	0.840E+02	0.000E+00
0.180E+02	0.252E+04	0.000E+00	0.155E+03	0.488E+04	0.319E+03	0.875E+03	0.633E+01	0.332E+02	0.945E+02	0.000E+00
0.190E+02	0.278E+04	0.000E+00	0.155E+03	0.488E+04	0.328E+03	0.875E+03	0.717E+01	0.376E+02	0.105E+03	0.000E+00
0.200E+02	0.305E+04	0.000E+00	0.155E+03	0.488E+04	0.336E+03	0.875E+03	0.800E+01	0.420E+02	0.116E+03	0.000E+00
0.210E+02	0.268E+04	0.000E+00	0.155E+03	0.488E+04	0.336E+03	0.140E+03	0.813E+01	0.427E+02	0.116E+03	0.000E+00
0.220E+02	0.231E+04	0.000E+00	0.155E+03	0.488E+04	0.336E+03	0.140E+03	0.827E+01	0.434E+02	0.116E+03	0.000E+00
0.230E+02	0.194E+04	0.000E+00	0.155E+03	0.488E+04	0.336E+03	0.189E+04	0.101E+02	0.528E+02	0.116E+03	0.000E+00
0.240E+02	0.194E+04	0.000E+00	0.155E+03	0.488E+04	0.347E+03	0.277E+04	0.127E+02	0.667E+02	0.129E+03	0.309E+04
0.250E+02	0.215E+04	0.000E+00	0.155E+03	0.512E+04	0.374E+03	0.290E+04	0.153E+02	0.843E+02	0.149E+03	0.000E+00
0.260E+02	0.226E+04	0.000E+00	0.155E+03	0.512E+04	0.385E+03	0.290E+04	0.180E+02	0 988E+02	0.162E+03	0.000E+00
0.270E+02	0.237E+04	0.000E+00	0.155E+03	0.512E+04	0.396E+03	0.238E+04	0.201E+02	0.111E+03	0.176E+03	0.000E+00
0.280E+02	0.237E+04	0.000E+00	0.155E+03	0.512E+04	0.405E+03	0.220E+04	0.221E+02	0.122E+03	0.187E+03	0.000E+00
0.290E+02	0.237E+04	0.000E+00	0.155E+03	0.512E+04	0.414E+03	0.220E+04	0.241E+02	0.133E+03	0.198E+03	0.000E+00
0.300E+02	0.237E+04	0.000E+00	0.155E+03	0.512E+04	0.422E+03	0.238E+04	0.263E+02	0.145E+03	0.209E+03	0.318E+04
0.310E+02	0.264E+04	0.000E+00	0.155E+03	0.512E+04	0.431E+03	0.238E+04	0.285E+02	0.157E+03	0.220E+03	0.000E+00
0.320E+02	0.292E+04	0.000E+00	0.155E+03	0.512E+04	0.440E+03	0.238E+04	0.306E+02	0.168E+03	0.231E+03	0.000E+00
0.330E+02	0.319E+04	0.000E+00	0.155E+03	0.512E+04	0.449E+03	0.917E+03	0.315E+02	0.173E+03	0.242E+03	0.000E+00
0.340E+02	0.281E+04	0.000E+00	0.155E+03	0.512E+04	0.449E+03	0.147E+03	0.316E+02	0.174E+03	0.242E+03	0.000E+00
0.350E+02	0.242E+04	0.000E+00	0.155E+03	0.512E+04	0.449E+03	0.880E+03	0.324E+02	0.178E+03	0.242E+03	0.000E+00
0.360E+02	0.204E+04	0.000E+00	0.155E+03	0.512E+04	0.449E+03	0.271E+04	0.349E+02	0.192E+03	0.242E+03	0.000E+00
0.370E+02	0.213E+04	0.000E+00	0.155E+03	0.535E+04	0.481E+03	0.380E+04	0.382E+02	0.219E+03	0.267E+03	0.000E+00
0.380E+02	0.224E+04	0.000E+00	0.155E+03	0.535E+04	0.492E+03	0.380E+04	0.415E+02	0.238E+03	0 282E+03	0.327E+04
0.390E+02	0.236E+04	0.000E+00	0.155E+03	0.535E+04	0.504E+03	0.364E+04	0.446E+02	0.257E+03	0 296E+03	0.000E+00
0.400E+02	0.247E+04	0.000E+00	0.155E+03	0.535E+04	0.515E+03	0.311E+04	0.473E+02	0.272E+03	0.311E+03	0.000E+00
0.410E+02	0.247E+04	0.000E+00	0.155E+03	0.535E+04	0.524E+03	0.291E+04	0.499E+02	0.287E+03	0.322E+03	0.000E+00
0.420E+02	0.247E+04	0.000E+00	0.155E+03	0.535E+04	0.534E+03	0.291E+04	0.524E+02	0.301E+03	0.334E+03	0.000E+00
0.430E+02	0.247E+04	0.000E+00	0.155E+03	0.535E+04	0.541E+03	0.311E+04	0.551E+02	0.317E+03	0.345E+03	0.000E+00
0.440E+02	0.290E+04	0.000E+00	0.155E+03	0.535E+04	0.545E+03	0.349E+04	0.581E+02	0.334E+03	0.362E+03	0.000E+00
0.450E+02	0.334E+04	0.000E+00	0.155E+03	0.535E+04	0.559E+03	0.288E+04	0.606E+02	0.349E+03	0.380E+03	0.000E+00
0.460E+02	0.377E+04	0.000E+00	0.155E+03	0.535E+04	0.573E+03	0.134E+04	0.618E+02	0.355E+03	0.397E+03	0.000E+00
0.470E+02	0.351E+04	0.000E+00	0.155E+03	0.535E+04	0.577E+03	0.000E+00	0.618E+02	0.355E+03	0.391E+03	0.000E+00
0.480E+02	0.322E+04	0.000E+00	0.155E+03	0.535E+04	0.568E+03	0.000E+00	0.618E+02	0.355E+03	0.382E+03	0.000E+00
0.490E+02	0.306E+04	0.000E+00	0.155E+03	0.558E+04	0.583E+03	0.000E+00	0.618E+02	0.371E+03	0.390E+03	0.000E+00
0.500E+02	0.318E+04	0.000E+00	0.155E+03	0.558E+04	0.588E+03	0.000E+00	0.618E+02	0.371E+03	0.399E+03	0.000E+00

Table 2

(*d*) The cost of maintenance of males and females. This is indicated by columns CMTOR and CMVAC, respectively. In this same Table the column COSEME indicates the flow of capital of buying or selling breeding males.

The sum of all the given costs is multiplied by a factor, estimated by the user, in order to have a security margin, and this total is indicated in Table 3 by the column CVARIA.

Fixed cost

The total fixed cost of operating the system is estimated by the user; to this could be added a monthly payment of a loan, after some time in the simulation.

```
****************************************************************************************
*          *          *          *          *          *          *          *          *          *
* TIEMPO   * CVARIA   * CFIJOS   * COSTOT   * GANBRU   * GANETA   * PR LEC   * PR CAR   * PR NVA   *
*          *          *          *          *          *          *          *          *          *
****************************************************************************************
* 0.100E+01* 0.136E+05* 0.350E+04* 0.171E+05* 0.336E+04* -.137E+05* 0.336E+04* 0.000E+00* 0.000E+00*
* 0.200E+01* 0.637E+04* 0.350E+04* 0.987E+04* 0.336E+04* -.651E+04* 0.336E+04* 0.000E+00* 0.000E+00*
* 0.300E+01* 0.637E+04* 0.350E+04* 0.987E+04* 0.336E+04* -.651E+04* 0.336E+04* 0.000E+00* 0.000E+00*
* 0.400E+01* 0.637E+04* 0.350E+04* 0.987E+04* 0.336E+04* -.651E+04* 0.336E+04* 0.000E+00* 0.000E+00*
* 0.500E+01* 0.637E+04* 0.350E+04* 0.987E+04* 0.336E+04* -.651E+04* 0.336E+04* 0.000E+00* 0.000E+00*
* 0.600E+01* 0.637E+04* 0.350E+04* 0.987E+04* 0.336E+04* -.651E+04* 0.336E+04* 0.000E+00* 0.000E+00*
* 0.700E+01* 0.637E+04* 0.350E+04* 0.987E+04* 0.336E+04* -.651E+04* 0.336E+04* 0.000E+00* 0.000E+00*
* 0.800E+01* 0.625E+04* 0.350E+04* 0.975E+04* 0.252E+04* -.723E+04* 0.252E+04* 0.000E+00* 0.000E+00*
* 0.900E+01* 0.613E+04* 0.350E+04* 0.963E+04* 0.168E+04* -.795E+04* 0.168E+04* 0.000E+00* 0.000E+00*
* 0.100E+02* 0.601E+04* 0.350E+04* 0.951E+04* 0.840E+03* -.867E+04* 0.840E+03* 0.000E+00* 0.000E+00*
* 0.110E+02* 0.634E+04* 0.350E+04* 0.984E+04* 0.294E+04* -.690E+04* 0.294E+04* 0.000E+00* 0.000E+00*
* 0.120E+02* 0.678E+04* 0.350E+04* 0.103E+05* 0.588E+04* -.440E+04* 0.588E+04* 0.000E+00* 0.000E+00*
* 0.130E+02* 0.759E+04* 0.385E+04* 0.114E+05* 0.908E+04* -.236E+04* 0.908E+04* 0.000E+00* 0.000E+00*
* 0.140E+02* 0.806E+04* 0.385E+04* 0.119E+05* 0.121E+05* 0.203E+03* 0.121E+05* 0.000E+00* 0.000E+00*
* 0.150E+02* 0.840E+04* 0.385E+04* 0.122E+05* 0.143E+05* 0.203E+03* 0.143E+05* 0.000E+00* 0.000E+00*
* 0.160E+02* 0.874E+04* 0.385E+04* 0.126E+05* 0.164E+05* 0.385E+04* 0.164E+05* 0.000E+00* 0.000E+00*
* 0.170E+02* 0.971E+04* 0.385E+04* 0.136E+05* 0.186E+05* 0.505E+04* 0.186E+05* 0.000E+00* 0.000E+00*
* 0.180E+02* 0.105E+05* 0.385E+04* 0.143E+05* 0.208E+05* 0.645E+04* 0.208E+05* 0.000E+00* 0.000E+00*
* 0.190E+02* 0.108E+05* 0.385E+04* 0.147E+05* 0.229E+05* 0.827E+04* 0.229E+05* 0.000E+00* 0.000E+00*
* 0.200E+02* 0.112E+05* 0.385E+04* 0.150E+05* 0.251E+05* 0.101E+05* 0.251E+05* 0.000E+00* 0.000E+00*
* 0.210E+02* 0.983E+04* 0.385E+04* 0.137E+05* 0.221E+05* 0.838E+04* 0.221E+05* 0.000E+00* 0.000E+00*
* 0.220E+02* 0.939E+04* 0.385E+04* 0.132E+05* 0.190E+05* 0.579E+04* 0.190E+05* 0.000E+00* 0.000E+00*
* 0.230E+02* 0.111E+05* 0.385E+04* 0.149E+05* 0.160E+05* 0.109E+04* 0.160E+05* 0.000E+00* 0.000E+00*
* 0.240E+02* 0.159E+05* 0.385E+04* 0.197E+05* 0.160E+05* -.371E+04* 0.160E+05* 0.000E+00* 0.000E+00*
* 0.250E+02* 0.129E+05* 0.420E+04* 0.171E+05* 0.174E+05* 0.247E+03* 0.174E+05* 0.000E+00* 0.000E+00*
* 0.260E+02* 0.131E+05* 0.420E+04* 0.173E+05* 0.183E+05* 0.958E+03* 0.183E+05* 0.000E+00* 0.000E+00*
* 0.270E+02* 0.127E+05* 0.420E+04* 0.169E+05* 0.191E+05* 0.229E+04* 0.191E+05* 0.000E+00* 0.000E+00*
* 0.280E+02* 0.125E+05* 0.420E+04* 0.167E+05* 0.191E+05* 0.247E+04* 0.191E+05* 0.000E+00* 0.000E+00*
* 0.290E+02* 0.125E+05* 0.420E+04* 0.167E+05* 0.191E+05* 0.243E+04* 0.191E+05* 0.000E+00* 0.000E+00*
* 0.300E+02* 0.166E+05* 0.420E+04* 0.208E+05* 0.191E+05* -.164E+04* 0.191E+05* 0.000E+00* 0.000E+00*
* 0.310E+02* 0.131E+05* 0.420E+04* 0.173E+05* 0.214E+05* 0.403E+04* 0.214E+05* 0.000E+00* 0.000E+00*
* 0.320E+02* 0.135E+05* 0.420E+04* 0.177E+05* 0.236E+05* 0.589E+04* 0.236E+05* 0.000E+00* 0.000E+00*
* 0.330E+02* 0.121E+05* 0.420E+04* 0.163E+05* 0.258E+05* 0.952E+04* 0.258E+05* 0.000E+00* 0.000E+00*
* 0.340E+02* 0.107E+05* 0.420E+04* 0.149E+05* 0.227E+05* 0.779E+04* 0.227E+05* 0.000E+00* 0.000E+00*
* 0.350E+02* 0.111E+05* 0.420E+04* 0.153E+05* 0.196E+05* 0.425E+04* 0.196E+05* 0.000E+00* 0.000E+00*
* 0.360E+02* 0.129E+05* 0.420E+04* 0.171E+05* 0.165E+05* -.623E+03* 0.165E+05* 0.000E+00* 0.000E+00*
* 0.370E+02* 0.147E+05* 0.455E+04* 0.192E+05* 0.169E+05* -.230E+04* 0.169E+05* 0.000E+00* 0.000E+00*
* 0.380E+02* 0.188E+05* 0.455E+04* 0.234E+05* 0.179E+05* -.550E+04* 0.179E+05* 0.000E+00* 0.000E+00*
* 0.390E+02* 0.149E+05* 0.455E+04* 0.194E+05* 0.188E+05* -.664E+03* 0.188E+05* 0.000E+00* 0.000E+00*
* 0.400E+02* 0.144E+05* 0.455E+04* 0.190E+05* 0.197E+05* 0.708E+03* 0.197E+05* 0.000E+00* 0.000E+00*
* 0.410E+02* 0.142E+05* 0.455E+04* 0.188E+05* 0.197E+05* 0.896E+03* 0.197E+05* 0.000E+00* 0.000E+00*
* 0.420E+02* 0.143E+05* 0.455E+04* 0.188E+05* 0.197E+05* 0.853E+03* 0.197E+05* 0.000E+00* 0.000E+00*
* 0.430E+02* 0.146E+05* 0.455E+04* 0.191E+05* 0.208E+05* 0.167E+04* 0.197E+05* 0.000E+00* 0.109E+04*
* 0.440E+02* 0.156E+05* 0.455E+04* 0.201E+05* 0.275E+05* 0.735E+04* 0.231E+05* 0.000E+00* 0.436E+04*
* 0.450E+02* 0.154E+05* 0.455E+04* 0.200E+05* 0.266E+05* 0.659E+04* 0.266E+05* 0.000E+00* 0.000E+00*
* 0.460E+02* 0.141E+05* 0.455E+04* 0.187E+05* 0.300E+05* 0.113E+05* 0.300E+05* 0.000E+00* 0.000E+00*
* 0.470E+02* 0.122E+05* 0.455E+04* 0.168E+05* 0.332E+05* 0.164E+05* 0.279E+05* 0.523E+04* 0.000E+00*
* 0.480E+02* 0.118E+05* 0.455E+04* 0.164E+05* 0.363E+05* 0.199E+05* 0.256E+05* 0.523E+04* 0.545E+04*
* 0.490E+02* 0.120E+05* 0.105E+05* 0.225E+05* 0.350E+05* 0.125E+05* 0.240E+05* 0.538E+04* 0.560E+04*
* 0.500E+02* 0.121E+05* 0.105E+05* 0.227E+05* 0.359E+05* 0.132E+05* 0.249E+05* 0.538E+04* 0.560E+04*
****************************************************************************************
```

Table 3

Profit computations

This simulator considers three basic possibilities of making a profit: That produced by selling milk which is indicated monthly in Table 3 by the col-

The fixed cost is indicated in Table 3 by the column CFIJOS, and the sum of variable costs plus fixed costs is given in column COSTOT of Table 3.

TABLA DE FLUJO DE CAPITAL

```
**********************************
*              *                 *
*   PERIODO    *  FLUJO DE CAPITAL *
*              *                 *
**********************************
*      0       *   -.2870E+06    *
*      1       *   -.8790E+05    *
*      2       *   0.4512E+05    *
*      3       *   0.3762E+05    *
*      4       *   0.5723E+05    *
*      5       *   0.1303E+06    *
*      6       *   0.1063E+06    *
*      7       *   0.1221E+06    *
*      8       *   0.4060E+05    *
*      9       *   0.1475E+06    *
*     10       *   0.5553E+05    *
*     11       *   0.1458E+06    *
*     12       *   0.1472E+06    *
*     13       *   0.1130E+06    *
*     14       *   0.1144F+06    *
*     15       *   0.6781E+06    *
**********************************
```

ITERACIONES PARA DETERMINAR LA RATA DE RETORNO

```
**********************************
*              *                 *
*  ITERACION   *  RATA DE RETORNO *
*              *                 *
**********************************
*      0       *     1.00000     *
*      1       *     0.86812     *
*      2       *     0.74580     *
*      3       *     0.63275     *
*      4       *     0.52894     *
*      5       *     0.43479     *
*      6       *     0.35152     *
*      7       *     0.28184     *
*      8       *     0.23059     *
*      9       *     0.20292     *
*     10       *     0.19561     *
*     11       *     0.19516     *
*     12       *     0.19516     *
**********************************
```

Table 4

INTERES DE RETORNO DE CAPITAL = 19.52

CREDITO=0.3290E+06 ,VALOR DEL CREDITO DESPUES DE 4 A#OS= 0.4709E+06

PAGO MENSUAL=0.5633E+04 ,RATA EFECTIVA DE INTERES ANUAL=0.9381E-01

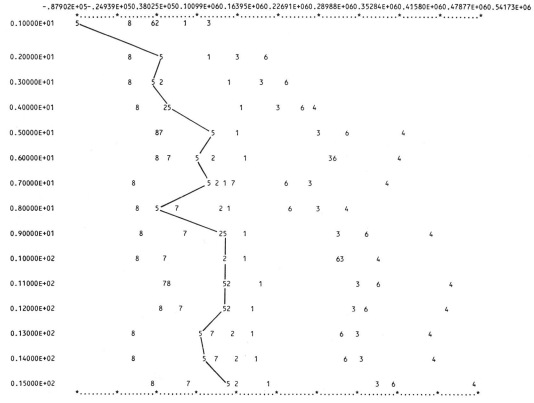

Graph 1

umn PRLEC. The sale of heifers of two years, indicated in Table 3 by the column PRNVA. And the sale of bulls, indicated in Table 3 by the column PRCAR.

Economic analysis

In order to make an economic analysis of the simulation, the output of Table 3 presents the total selling given by the column GANBRU, the total profit after costs given by column GANETA, and a graph for rapid evaluation. This graph presents in a sequence of equal numbers from 1 to 8 the independent variables, in the same order, as appears in Table 3. However, the values are aggregated by year.

Furthermore, Table 4 presents the capital flow per year. The capital investment is placed in the period zero, while the salvage value is included in the last period. The subroutine INGECO calculates the rate of return of the investment and is shown next to the Table.

Sensitivity analysis

The results of the simulator depend very much on the validity of the data used. A sensitivity analysis to the parameters will show those that produce a great change in the results of the simulator and which therefore should be reviewed.

In order to make a sensitivity analysis there is a subroutine that will make it on the cost parameters of the experiment and on the prices of the selling products. This routine analyzes the relationship of the particular change of each parameter, when the rest remain constant, to the changes in the over-all cost, over-all profit and changes in rate of return in one single run.

The outputs of this experiment are displayed in a Table that allows the person using the simulator to make his own conclusions. The data that give big changes in the outputs should be revised, and if the changes remain, then several experiments could be done, as for example

(*a*) To study alternatives of control on these variables.

(*b*) To study more stable alternatives in obtaining the same results.

(*c*) To develop a predictive model in order to study more closely future values of the parameters, and use it as part of the simulator.

Procedure for using the simulator

Throughout the main program of the system, the maximum capacity of the farm and the value of the different parameters as costs of maintenance, selling prices, etc., are given. All the values depend on each particular farm, and they generally depend on the region and objectives.

The simulator is built mainly around the subroutine SIMGAN which uses the subroutines DELAY1 and DELAY2 to solve the dynamics of the finite difference equations, and the subroutine CONTR1, which contains the controller of cows in production. For the outputs of data there are two subroutines SALDAT and PLOT1, the first one producing the output Tables and the second the graph. Finally, the subroutine INGECO calculates the rate of return.

Example

In order to demonstrate how to use the simulator, an example is presented here. This particular example is part of a project developed using this technique.

The main program contains all the data given to the simulator, which is self-explanatory, with comments in the Spanish language. With the data, all the control indicators of the simulator are given. However, an easier way to use the simulator is through a CRT, which displays the questions about the values of the parameters on the screen in order to be answered by the user.

The partial results of this particular example are shown in the Tables and the graph presented.

Conclusions

This simulator of a cattle farm can be used as a practical tool, mainly because it allows the making of experiments on the model, presenting clearly and rapidly the process behavior. It is important to note, however, that the results of the experiments through the simulator should not be the final word for the person who takes the decisions, although it could be a good guide for the user in helping him to establish the best strategy to follow.

The authors consider that the simulator can be used by government agencies, financial agencies or investors, dealing with beef or milk production, allowing them to predict the benefits obtained from their capital investment. The simulator could also be used to carry out experiments. By changing the parameters it is possible to evaluate different alternatives, including classes of pasture, classes of cows or bulls, etc. Finally, it could be used to evaluate different strategies of operating the farm.

The simulator is built so that changes can be made very easily. In that way, it can be tailored to any particular situation.

Ein Prognosemodell des Studenten- und Akademikerpotentials

Dr MAX STREIT
Institut für Wirtschaftstheorie an der
Universität Graz, Graz, Austria

In einem Simulationsmodell der Entwicklung des Studenten- und Akademikerpotentials stellen sich Hochschule und das akademische Arbeitspotential als Glieder einer offenen Prozeßkette dar. Als wesentliche exogene Variable fungiert dabei die Immatrikulationsbewegung, die sich selbst erst aus einem Komplex demographischer, soziologischer und ökonomischer Faktoren erklären ließe. Wir nehmen daher den Immatrikulationszeitpfad in verschiedener Weise gegeben an und studieren das daraus folgende Verhalten des betrachteten Systems.

Im folgenden Bild bedeuten:

$Im(t)$ ...die exogen bestimmte für die Vergangenheit gegebene und für die Zukunft mehr oder minder willkürlich angenommene Immatrikulationszeitreihe in einer bestimmten Fachgruppe oder Fakultät, z.B. Medizin oder Technik. Dabei sollen insbesondere die Auswirkungen logistischer und oszillatorischer Zeitpfade studiert werden.

$Gges(t)$ ...die endogen bestimmte Graduierungszeitreihe, die sich aufgrund des Modells ergibt. Diese Outputgröße des Systemelementes Hochschule ist selbst wieder Inputgröße des Systemelementes Akademikerpotential.

$Ges(t)$ ...die endogen bestimmte Zeitreihe der Gesamtstudentenzahlen einer bestimmten Fachkategorie.

$Akges(t)$ ...die von der Immatrikulationszeitreihe bestimmte Zeitreihe des Bestandes an Akademikern einer bestimmten Fachkategorie.

$Anz(t,j)$ ...die Zeitreihe der Verteilungen der Gesamtstudentenzahlen einer bestimmten Fachgruppe auf die einzelnen Jahrgänge (aus statistischen Gründen statt Semester).

$G(t,j)$ ...die Zeitreihe der Graduierungen in einer bestimmten Fachgruppe über die einzelnen Jahrgänge, wobei diese gesetzlich im allgemeinen frühestens nach Abschluß des 4. Studienjahres einsetzen.

$Dges(t)$ ...die Zeitreihe der gesamten Studienabbrüche in einer bestimmten Fachgruppe.

$D(t,j)$ ...die Zeitreihe der Jahrgangsverteilungen der Studienabbrüche.

$Akvert(t,j)$ ...die Zeitreihe der Altersverteilungen des Akademikerpotentials.

Als Systemparameter fungieren in dem Modell:

$DF(j)$ ...die Dropoutfrequenzverteilung über die Jahrgänge, d.h. der Prozentsatz der Student-

Progress in Cybernetics and Systems Research, Volume 2

en eines bestimmten Jahrganges, der am Ende des Jahres ausfällt. Diese Verteilung wird als Mittelwert vergangener Beobachtungen gewonnen und für den Prognosezeitraum als zeitlich konstant angesehen.

$GW(j)$ ...die Verteilung der Graduierungswahrscheinlichkeit über die einzelnen Jahrgänge. Diese Verteilung wird aus der Beobachtung der mittleren Studiendauer und aus der Streuung der Gesamtheit der Werte Studiendauer um diese mittlere gewonnen. Sie wird ebenfalls als für die nächste Zukunft fest angesehen, wenngleich das zu entwickelnde Programm durchaus in der Lage wäre, eventuelle Verschiebungen in dieser Verteilung zugunsten kürzerer Studiendauerwerte etwa aufgrund von Studienreform oder Hochschuldidaktikmaßnahmen zu berücksichtigen.

$VW(j)$ ...die Verlustwahrscheinlichkeitsverteilung des Akademikerpotentials über die Berufsjahrgänge.

Als Anfangsbedingungen des Modells fungieren:

$Anz(AJ,j)$ ...die Verteilung der Studentenanzahlen in der jeweils betrachteten Fachkategorie über die einzelnen Jahrgänge im willkürlich gewählten Anfangsjahr AJ.

$Akvert(AJ,j)$ ...die Altersverteilung des Akademikerpotentials der jeweiligen Kategorie

über die Jahrgänge der gesamten mittleren Berufsdauer im Anfangsjahr AJ.

Mit diesen Festlegungen ergibt sich Systemschema (Abb. 1) des zu betrachtenden Modells.

Die Güte der Prognose wird daran gemessen, inwieweit das Modell imstande ist, aus den gegebenen Anfangsbedingungen die unmittelbare Vergangenheit "vorherzusagen". Unseres Wissens wurden bislang nirgends in der Literatur quantitative Versuche, ausgewertet in dieser Richtung, auf diesem speziellen Problemkreis unternommen. Es existieren lediglich Ansätze zu einer Analyse der Retentionsraten [1].

Das folgene Model geht insofern weit über die erörterte Analyse Thonstads hinaus, als es von der Immatrikulation und nicht erst von der Graduierung als exogener Zeitreihe ausgeht und als es insbesondere auch die detaillierte Struktur der jeweiligen Studenten- bzw. der Akademikerpopulation zu erarbeiten vermag. Wie bereits dargelegt, wird ferner dem stochastischen Charakter der Dropout- und Graduierungsbewegungen durch Erzeugung von Zufallswerten innerhalb zulässig erscheinender Schwankungsbreiten der Dropoutfrequenz bzw. Graduierungswahrscheinlichkeit und darauf gegründeter, teilweise automatischer Auswahl der am richtigsten erscheinenden Strukturparametergrößen Rechnung getragen.

Wir entwickeln nun die Modellbeziehungen für die Entwicklung der Studenten- bzw. Akademikerpopu-

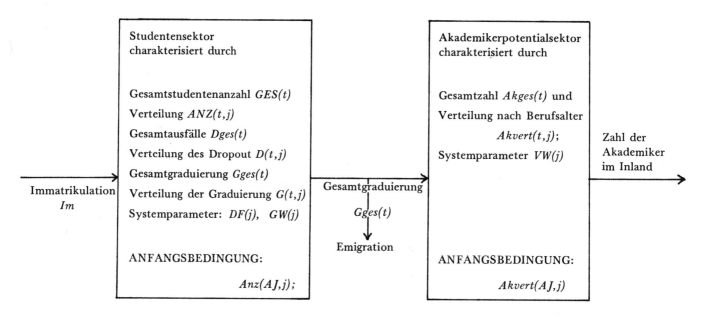

Abb. 1

lation. Die Entwicklung der Studentenpopulation ergibt sich als gewichtete Summe über die Immatrikulationszeitreihe bis zum betrachteten Zeitpunkt, wobei die Gewichtung durch die mittlere Retentionskurve über die einzelnen Jahrgänge ist.

Bedeute $\beta(t,\tau)$ den Retentionsprozentsatz eines bestimmten Immatrikulations-Jahrganges zum Zeitpunkt t, dann ergibt sich die Gesamtzahl der Studenten zum Zeitpunkt aus der Immatrikulation der Vergangenheit als

$$Ges(t) = \sum_{\tau=-\infty}^{t} \beta(t,\tau) \, Im(\tau)$$

$\beta(t,i)$ hat unter idealisierten Verhältnissen die Gestalt einer Rechteckverteilung

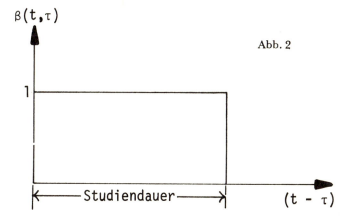

Abb. 2

Unter realistischen Annahmen sind aber vorzeitige Abgänge durch Studienabbrüche sowie die starke Streuung der Studiendauer zu berücksichtigen, so daß sich etwa folgender Retentionsverlauf über die Jahrgänge ergibt:

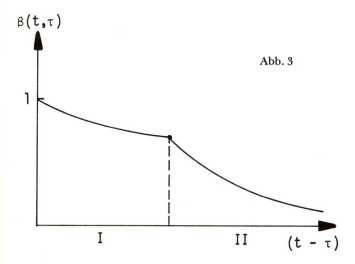

Abb. 3

Der Abfall in Phase I wird lediglich durch den Frustrationszerfall der Jahrgangspopulation bestimmt, der Abfall in Phase II zusätzlich und hauptsächlich durch den Graduierungszerfall. Bei der Auswertung der statistischen Daten bleibt allerdings die Größe des Einflusses von Umsattelbewegungen auf die Dropoutraten bzw. Graduierungswahrscheinlichkeiten ungewiß. Aufgrund der schließlich stark abnehmenden Gestalt von $\beta(t,i)$ braucht die Simulation für die praktische Berechnung nur bis zu einem gewissen Höchstjahrgang (EJG) geführt zu werden.

Aus der Faltungssumme der Studentenpopulation ergibt sich die Differenzengleichung

$$Ges(t+1) = Ges(t) + Im(t+1) + \sum_{\tau=-\infty}^{t} \{\beta(t+1,\tau) - \\ - \beta(t,\tau)\} Im(\tau) \qquad (1)$$

die sich im idealisierten Fall zu

$$Ges(t+1) = Ges(t) + Im(t+1) - Im(t-g) \qquad (2)$$

vereinfacht, wobei g die einheitliche Studiendauer bedeutet.

Gleichung (2) ist im wesentlichen der Ausgangspunkt des Thonstad-Modells, Gleichung (1) ist im Prinzip die Grundlage der folgenden Berechnung der Bewegung der Studentenpopulation in ihrer Gesamtheit.

Allerdings wird das System nicht in dieser geschlossenen Form behandelt, da dafür erst mit relativ großen Unsicherheiten behaftete Regressionsanalysen vonnöten wären. Es wird vielmehr ein direktes Verfahren entwickelt, das es erlaubt, die statistisch erfaßten Dropouthäufigkeiten und Graduierungsverteilungen unmittelbar in die Rechnung als Parameter einzuführen und dabei mögliche stochastische Schwankungen unmittelbar zu berücksichtigen.

Es folgen nun die Modellansätze in den Größen, die bereits eingangs festgelegt wurden:

$$Ges(t) = \sum_{j=1}^{EJG} Anz(t,j) , \qquad \text{für } t = AJ \qquad (1)$$

bzw. bei Vervollständigung um einen Restterm

$$Ges(t+1) = \sum_{j=1}^{EJG} Anz(t+1,j) + Anz(t,EJG) - \\ - D(t,EJG) - G(t,EJG) \qquad (1')$$

$$\text{für } AJ \leqslant t \leqslant EJ$$

Die Gesamtzahl der Studenten einer Kategorie zu einem bestimmten Zeitpunkt ist gleich der Summe über alle Jahrgänge der einzelnen Jahrgangspopulationen zu dem Zeitpunkt vermehrt um die Zahl jener Studenten des Jahrganges *EJG*, die im vorhergehenden Jahr weder graduierten noch ausgefallen sind, die daher im betrachteten Jahr wieder inskribieren; *t* läuft von einem bestimmten Anfangsjahr bis zu einem bestimmten Endjahr.

$$Anz(t+1, 1) = I_m(t+1) \tag{2}$$

Die Anzahl im ersten Jahrgang zu einem bestimmten Zeitpunkt ist gegeben durch die Immatrikulation.

$$Anz(t+1,j) = Anz(t,j-1) - D(t,j-1) - G(t,j-1) \tag{3}$$
$$j = 2,...,EJG$$

Die Anzahlen ab dem zweiten Jahrgang im folgenden Jahr sind gleich den Anzahlen in den um 1 erniedrigten Jahrgängen im vorhergehenden Jahr minus entsprechenden Dropouts und Graduierungen.

$$D(t,j) = DF(j) * Anz(t,j) \tag{4}$$

Die Zahl der Studienabbrüche eines bestimmten Jahrganges zum Zeitpunkt *t* ist gleich der Dropoutfrequenz des betrachteten Jahrganges mal der Größe der entsprechenden Jahrgangspopulation zum selben Zeitpunkt.

$$G(t,j) = GW(j) * (Anz(t,j) - D(t,j))$$
$$G(t,j) = GW(j) * (1-DF(j)) Anz(t,j) \tag{5}$$

Die Zahl der Graduierungen eines bestimmten Jahrganges zum Zeitpunkt *t* ist gleich der Graduierungswahrscheinlichkeit des betreffenden Jahrganges mal der um die Dropouts reduzierten Jahrgangspopulation.

$$Dges(t) = \sum_{j=1}^{EJG} D(t,j) \tag{6}$$

Die Gesamtzahl der Dropouts zum Zeitpunkt *t* ist gleich der Summe der einzelnen Studienabbruchszahlen über alle Jahrgänge.

$$Gges(t) = \sum_{j=1}^{EJG} G(t,j) + Rest(t) \tag{7}$$

Die Gesamtzahl der Graduierungen im Jahre *t* ist gleich der Summe der einzelnen Graduierungszahlen über alle Jahrgänge plus der Zahl der Graduierungen von Studenten eines höheren Jahrganges als *EJG*.

$$Rest(t) = P(Anz\{T{-}1,EJG\} - D\{T{-}1,EJG\} -$$
$$- G\{T{-}1,EJG\}) \tag{7a}$$

P Gewichtungsfaktor

Durch Zusammenfassung von (3), (4) und (5) ergibt sich:

$$Anz(t+1,j) = (1-DF(j-1))(1-GW(j-1)) Anz(t,j-1)$$
$$j = 2,...,EJG \tag{3'}$$

Die Dynamik des Akademikerpotentials ergibt sich einerseits aus der eben dargelegten Bewegungsgesetzmäßigkeit der Studentenpopulation, andererseits aus der jeweiligen Altersstruktur des Akademikerpotentials.

Wir betrachten wiederum eine "Überlebenskurve" *b(j)* der Population, die in diesem Fall etwa exponentiell mit einer konstanten Verlustrate abfällt.

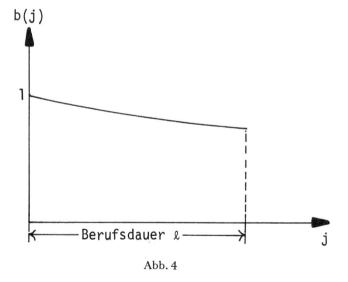

Abb. 4

Damit ergibt sich in analoger Weise zum vorigen:

Der Abfall der *b(j)*-Kurve läßt sich aus dem mittleren Ersatzbedarf der Akademikerpopulation erschließen, der sich ergibt, wenn man die Population auf konstanter Höhe halten will.

In weitgehend analoger Weise zum Studentenpopulationsmodell ergibt sich somit für das Modell der Bewegung des Akademikerpotentials:

$$Akges(t) = \sum_{j=t-l}^{t} Akvert(t,j) \qquad (1)$$

Die Gesamtzahl der Akademiker zum Zeitpunkt t ist gleich der Summe aller Alterskohorten über die gesamte Berufsdauer.

$$Akvert(t+1,1) = Gges(t+1) \qquad (2)$$

Die Alterskohorte 1 zu einem bestimmten Zeitpunkt $(t+1)$ ist gegeben durch die Gesamtzahl der Graduierungen.

$$Akvert(t+1,j) = Akvert(t,j-1) - V(t,j-1) \qquad (3)$$

$$j = 2,...,l$$

Die übrigen Alterskohorten zum Zeitpunkt $t+1$ ergeben sich als Differenz zwischen den Alterskohorten mit einer um 1 verminderten Jahrgangszahl zum Zeitpunkt t minus der Verlustzahl in dieser Kohorte zum selben Zeitpunkt.

Die Verlustzahl ergibt sich als Produkt von Verlustwahrscheinlichkeit eines bestimmten Jahrganges und Kohortengröße im betrachteten Jahr t.

Dabei bedeuten $V(t)$ den Gesamtverlust eines Jahres t, $VW(j)$ die jahrgangsabhängige Verlustwahrscheinlichkeit. Ferner führen wir die jahrgangsabhängige Retentionswahrscheinlichkeit $(KVW(j) = 1 - VW(j))$ ein.

Dann gilt:

$$V(t,j-1) = VW(j-1) * Akvert(t,j-1) , \quad j = 2,...,l$$

Zusammenfassend ergibt sich als Modell der Bewegung des Akademikerpotentials:

$$Akvert(t+1,1) = Gges(t+1)$$

$$Akvert(t+1,j) = KVW(j-1) * Akvert(t,j-1)$$

$$j = 2,...,l$$

$$(1-VW) = KVW \text{ "komplementäre Verlustwahrscheinlichkeit"}$$

Dabei läuft t wiederum von $t = AJ$ bis $t = EJ$.

Das vorgestellte Modell ermöglicht eine quantitative Analyse des Transformationsprozesses Immatrikulations-, Studentenpopulations- und Akademikerangebotsentwicklung, der durch das System Hochschule bewerkstelligt wird. Auf einer solchen Modellgrundlage lassen sich wesentliche Systemcharakteristika, wie Lag- und Gain-Größen ableiten. Ferner lassen sich auf diesem Wege durch Variation der für dieses Modell exogenen Immatrikulationsverläufe daraus resultierende Akademikerpopulationen entsprechender Größe und Struktur vorausberechnen. Das Modell ermöglicht somit eine Analyse der zeitlichen Entwicklung der Studenten- bzw. Akademikerpopulation.

Es wurde auf die akademischen Fachbereiche: Techniker einschließlich Absolventen der Montanistischen Hochschule, Mediziner, Juristen, Wirtschafts- und Sozialwissenschaftler, Absolventen der Philosophischen Fakultät, Veterinärmediziner und Absolventen der Hochschule für Bodenkultur, basierend auf österreichischen Daten, angewandt.

Literaturverzeichnis
1. Kneale T. Marshall, Robert M. Oliver, 'A constant-work model for student attendance and enrollment', *Operations Research*, S.193 ff (March-April 1970).

Abstract

Outline of student and academics' potential
Max Streit

A simulated model of the development of student and academic potential is described showing university and academic work potential as links in an open chain development. The period leading up to registration at university is assumed and a study made of the resultant functioning of the system observed. The study begins at registration, considering drop-out, duration of study and probability of graduation in relation to the discipline concerned and the year in which study was begun. The article includes a detailed study of the structure of student/academic population.

Support of regional planning processes by system simulation

WERNER F. PRAUTSCH
Fachbereich Kybernetik,
Technische Universität Berlin, Germany

1. Introduction

The city and regional planner today still depends largely on such information as is offered by the executive administration. The automation of administrative procedures in many fields of public administration has in the meantime reached such a stage of development that tangible consequences for the planner's information-based needs may also be deduced. Relevant data are far more easily available and faster to get. The properties of the data banks' software, developed in the meantime (aggregation and connecting possibilities), permit the routine-like inclusion of additional information, which on account of the cost arising from manual processing, had formerly been denied to the planner. Added to this, further possibilities of effective coordination and integration of the various planning fields, based on their organizational structure, are offered to the planner, due to the 'communal information systems' existing in many places as a result of the automation of public administration. Consequently, the planner may concentrate in increasing measure on the opening-up of additional sources of information and further development of his methodical instrumentarium. Both objectives lead him inevitably, among other things, to system simulation and the particular properties needed for his purposes.

The simulation of an 'actual environmental system' calls for a duplicate of this system; this will be labelled 'substitute systems' in the following descriptions. For the city and regional planning field, a duplicate of the system *Region* is required; this comprises relevant substitute systems and components of the various, planning projects. The applicability of simulation depends, therefore, largely on whether the planner has sufficient knowledge of the actual system, whose development he has to plan in order to convert it into such a substitute system.

The restrictions that come up here will be described below; they are based on several concrete planning fields.

2. Regional planning processes

2.1 General data

City and regional planning aims at guiding the processing of regional development. By regional development processing we mean the periodical progress of status-alterations within the infra-structure, demographic, economic, social, and ecological structure of a region. The planner specifies target statuses for these alterations and works out measures leading

Progress in Cybernetics and Systems Research, Volume 2

to the attainment of these objectives within the pre-determined period. The complexity of such a planning project is—even if one were to restrict oneself to only one of the mentioned structures—obvious, and it is usually considerably heightened by the need for long planning periods.

Besides this problem, the planner is confronted with purely, organizational difficulties. An additional complication in administrative planning, where the German Federal Republic (GFR) is concerned, lies in the fact that planning and decision authorities are not, as a rule, identical. Apart from the organizational problems mentioned above, this results in the planner often having different planning objectives in mind to those of the decider, since the latter doesn't possess sufficient knowledge of the former's intentions in policy.

All these facts compel the planner to adopt a flexible planning approach and indirectly to a constantly expanding and improving of his instrumentarium. Simulation models, better adapted to his needs, can help him here—at least in some of his tasks—far more so that the methods he had previously had at his disposal. Additional information of a special quality may be procured by the planner, should he be in the position to construct a model whose properties are adjusted to those of the actual system under survey. Simultaneously with the usual findings, the planner, aided by this substitute-system, can gain important knowledge as to the interdependency and dynamic behavior of the variables examined. Should he bring these together in relation to the model, to improve the quality of the model's adaptation to the actual system, then he can finally 'sample' alternative policies (according to the model's behavior) and their probable reaction to the actual system.

In a rough, diagrammtic delineation, the planner is depicted as a component of a planning system (Fig. 1) within which he takes up his typical functions: based on the planning data at his disposal (official statistics, administrative data, findings of quantitative economic and empirical research on social questions, reports of experts, etc.), he attempts to analyze the environmental field under his survey; to describe the behavior of relevant, influential factors in this field; to forecast; to specify planning objectives and to work out the required measures for their realization. In order to estimate, however, how far these functions may be supported by simulations, a few important, planning projects should at first be sketched and act as examples [1].

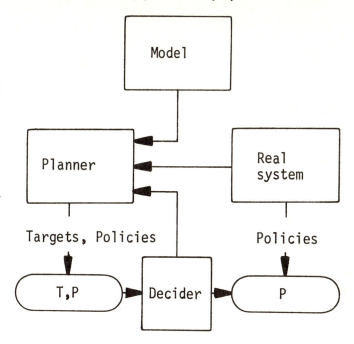

Fig. 1 Fundamental components of a planning system

2.2 *Planning functions*

Generally we can distinguish between *object planning* and *strategic planning*. Object planning endeavors to obtain a maximum, objective analysis (even independent of the main purpose) of the planning project—i.e., of the environmental area worked out by the planner—and from this analysis, to deduce the possible targets (designator system) plus the required means to reach them. Strategic planning endeavors to locate the optimal strategy by synchronizing the expected results with an optimal combination of the steps taken.

These classifications could be further broken down, taking specific regional or political features into consideration; but these particular cases may be dispensed with here.

If we were to interpret the planning project "region" as a system, then the operation of the planner could be roughly defined into:

- *analyses* of this system with reference to its structure and features, as well as its quantitative description;
- *prognosis* of future system-conditions, depending on either actual circumstances or on fictive measures;
- *development of adequate objectives* or goal-systems, as well as their realization, including assessment of their values.

This typology of planning projects is equally characteristic of the essential phases of the planner's work. In Fig. 2 these projects have been substantialized and described in a paper by H. Müller [2], who pointed out the above-mentioned difference in meaning. As a supplement here one should note that:

Structural investigations in economical, social, and population fields serve in

   a) deciding the structural variations in these fields;
   b) investigating indications regarding necessary and possible structural conversions;
   c) giving especially detailed descriptions of the actual condition of the region observed.

Furthermore, these investigations are to demonstrate the reasons for the conditions under observation, and to give a basis for an estimate of future developments.

The selection of regions to be furthered—serves to ascertain the justifiable claims for furtherance of regions or that of 'central areas' as a medium of space-planning policy.

Fig. 2 Representation of regional-planning projects

Projects	Object planning	Strategic planning
Structural investigations in economic, social and population areas	X	
Analysis of selected regions	X	(X)
Analysis of inter-sectoral relationship	X	X
Forecast of probable development in distinctive areas	X	
Designation for appropriate measures in regional-policy		X

The analysis of inter-sectoral relations—to demonstrate where interlocking regional structures exist and then to make a quantitative registration of sectoral dependence possible.

The predetermination of probable development— is deduced from forecasts of social and economic processes of development and serves especially to define objectives and select and estimate measures taken for their realization.

Finally, *the destination of regional-policy measures* —results from and with the aid of the differentiating cost-benefit-analyses; it is therefore primarily guided by the attempts at a rational calculation of the introduction of the available measures.

It is not necessary for our purpose to go into further details of these operations. In the following, however, the methical kind of 'instrumentarium' will be outlined for the processing of these operations, considering it possible to integrate the greater part of this so-called 'instrumentarium' in the relevant simulation models.

2.3 Planning instruments

Strictly speaking, we understand under *planning instrument* such a methodical instrumentarium, which is today actually in use within the frame of decision preparation and finding in an administrative board. Figure 3, moreover, gives a survey, where in the presentation the problem's classification of Fig. 2 was maintained. Especially such resources were admitted which were implementable and which would gain effectivity by implementation on a computer, e.g., which in principle qualify to be integrated in a planning-model.

Reference numbers are for nearly all planning fields the important orientation-aid. In most of these fields, reference numbers, coefficients, indices, etc., can be defined, calculated and used for purposes of spacial or temporal comparison. With a view to the quantitative description of the examined system, as well as for models of substitute systems, they have the character of system-parameters.

Statistical methods, especially, are able to work out in the analysis phase of planning, the gaining, evaluation and interpretation of the ascertained reference numbers. One should note here that, within bounds, the utilization of this method—at least in the practice of official boards—seldom goes beyond descriptive, statistical methods. With increasing availability of data processing machines and appropriate standard-software, especially utilization of this instrumentarium will become a matter of course.

Special methods, until now in certain cases applied in administrative management, are mathematical statistics as well as economic sciences (macro- and micro-economical appraisal procedure, linear and nonlinear optimization, and so on). Increase in complexity of demands, resulting from private as well as from official budgets and firms will make it indispensible in further developing such methods to

Fig. 3 Implementable resource-techniques

Methods-methodical resources	Application fields				
	Structure inquiries	Choice of promotion areas	Analyze inter-sectoral relations	Development prognosis	Determination of regional political measures
Reference numbers	Classification numbers Specialization coefficient Location ratio Growth indices Demographical numbers (migrations, commuter migrations)	Different indicators (i.e., population density, decrease in: population, real tax, gross national product)	Elements of the input-output table	Prognosis coefficient (depending on detailed prognosis methods)	Cost- respectively benefit-indices
Statistical methods	Description and analysis techniques of the descriptive statistic Calculation of indices for longitudinal and profile analysis (Shift-analysis)	Description and analysis techniques Discriminative analysis (for checking of factor-analytical index-factors	Aggregation techniques (for ascertainment of elements for the input-output matrix	Trend extrapolation Derivative methods Special forecasting methods	Aggregation-techniques for ascertainment of reference numbers for the cost-benefit analysis
Special methods	←——————————————— System Simulation ———————————————→				

specific planning instruments. But because of the constraint in "planning in legislative periods" too, these planning instruments become included in the planning process as steady components. From this background one may perceive the future system simulation's role, which, on account of its properties, could become a planning- and analysis-instrument of a very special quality.

3. System-simulation as a planning instrument

3.1 General data
Simulation then only becomes a planning instrument when it can effectively support the planner in his various functions. The functions and the planning project examples described above reveal, however, the difficulties one meets with should one try to back these miscellaneous kinds of functions and objectives with the help of adequate models. It is obvious, here, that the needs of planning experience are best solved if the planner were to be offered only as few such models as possible, i.e., if only a few *standard models* were to support the major part of his inquiries. Under the term, standard model, we mean a simulation model that, based on its structure and properties, supports one or more plan-

ning objectives; this means, therefore, one that is not restricted to either a special form of inquiry or limited to a particular region.

As far as we know, there is no such 'universal' or all-round model available in the GFR at present. We think it advisable, however, to assume that the development of such a model will sooner or later take place, and shall therefore attempt to describe the characteristics and assessment of the planning-aid, System-Simulation, starting from the idea of such an "ideal" model.

3.2 Model demands
A few global demands from an "ideal" model have already been mentioned. Bearing in mind the above-described tasks of the planner, these demands may be made concrete. Since the planner has to rely on such a model in his efforts to analyze a specific field and/or in forecasting or pre-determining future developments, as well as in the evaluation of steps to be taken, it must reveal differing characteristics in the various phases of the project. Roughly, they can be described as follows:
— At the analyzing stage, the model must procure information for the planner on the interactions of the system region's components. It must be applicable even with incomplete data on the examined

area, i.e., it must be able to replace estimated values with nonexisting material. It would in this place be useful should the findings reached at this stage of the simulation experiment—especially of the improved estimates of statistical, distinctive features—be integrated step by step into the model, so that the planner could in this way influence the model's adaptive quality and bring it to fit the actual system.

— Already, at this stage, by abstracting all the usual system variables, the model should be able to examine isolatedly the properties and time behavior of single variables, so as to obtain basic values for future forecasts.

— The semi-experiments of the analysis stage contribute a quantitative description of the actual system, as well as lead to a parametrical focusing (initialization) of the model on the region examined.

— Should the clearer focusing be adequately successful, i.e., if the substitute system shows approximately the properties of the actual system, then the planner may try to forecast in the subsequent stages future system statuses and, based on the model's behavior, 'sample' alternative policies and their reactions on the actual system.

In the forecast or estimate stage, inquiries arise that inevitably lie on different levels of aggregation. An 'ideal' model should, strictly speaking, be so shaped that it could take these different aggregation levels into account. It should, therefore, represent a mixture of an event-oriented and a continuous system and be able to suppress partly or completely one or the other components, according to the inquiries made.

It is definitely not practical to put so far-reaching a concept into the construction of a simple model. The model so far developed and tested in practice—adapted only to specific problems, usually only to a particular city or region—shows, however, that it will be possible (and therefore feasible) to develop at least something like a basic-type model that would at least partly solve the demands for differing extensive aggregation.

As for the rest, the model must be well disposed in its handling, therefore easy to manage, undemanding of any special EDP knowledge and relate to the available planning data of the individual planning fields. Furthermore, the supplementation of the substitute-system through additional modules developed by the planner, aided by a system-analyzer if necessary, should be possible without restrictions. The desire for a possibly uncomplicated input can be supplemented by the request for a convenient output, exactly tuned to the needs of the planner; a special significance should be given to the visualization of the findings in the shape of graphs, histograms, and charts (STAFF, SYMAP, etc.).

3.3 Types of models

Frequent mention has already been made of event-

Fig. 4 Types and functions of model-systems

	Systematic	
	Continuous Systems	Event-oriented Systems
Characteristics	High degree of aggregation Function: Macroanalysis	Detailed description of state and structure Function: Microanalysis
Analysis Phase	Temporal behavior of the process Dynamics of the process Properties of the process	Structure and structure's changing Sequences of events Possibilities in control of functional subranges
Prognosis- and Evaluation- Phase	Determination of critical system situations (unbalance, extreme constellations of system parameters) Reaction rate, i.e. sensibility of the system Global estimation of effects of alternative policies	Detailed forecast of values of different variables Estimates (evaluation) and optimization of measures Optimization of system flows Determination of optimal organization-forms

oriented, i.e., continuous systems, and we have imputed, according to the type of problem, that the one or the other system be more adequate for implementation. In order to clarify this claim, let us define and contrast them briefly (see Fig. 4).

Literary sources generally subdivide simulation in this case into *continuous* and *event-oriented* systems. The continuous system represents here a sequence of mutually-interconnected feedback loops. These interact continuously and constantly modify the state of the system. There are, therefore, no specifiable, individual events in such a system; the structure of the model especially is not altered during the experiment. On the other hand, in an event-oriented system, the system is represented by a sequence of events. Accordingly, the events that occur modify the state as well as the structure of the model. This happens through the generation, alteration, and destruction of activities, during the experiment. Both concepts, therefore, differ especially in that the (highly aggregated) continuous models only allow global outputs over the actual system state, i.e., of the dynamic behavior of the system. Event-oriented models offer detailed (but determined) descriptions of the state *and* structure of the system regarded.

According to these differing properties, both kinds of model are put to use for different problems. For models of continuous systems these problems are, above all,

a) Time-behavior of the system under observation, i.e., of its subsystems over longer time-periods in order to locate the process features.

b) Investigation of "critical" system states (after accurate description of the system), dependent on extreme constellations of system variables and system components.

c) The investigation of equilibrium states of the system.

d) The examination of the reaction-velocity of system-components and subsystems.

e) The global estimate of the effects in differential policies over long-range periods through systematic variation of the model parameters.

The high degree of aggregation in the model inevitably permits only global analyses of system-behavior. It assumes a thorough knowledge of the interdependences within the implemented regional systems. On the other hand, continuous models are easily put up and altered, not the least due to the implementation aids at their disposal. They can thus offer the planner helpful information especially in strategic planning fields, at slight expenditure—provided, of

course, that he has previously gathered knowledge of the system under observation.

The highly aggregated kind of observation of continuous models stands as against the possibilities which the simulation of event-oriented systems offer. This occurs in the analysis phase as well as in the forecast and evaluation phase. The following are typical applications:

a) Examination of the structural behavior and structural alternations of well defined regional field areas (subsystems) the components of which are already known or sufficiently descriptive.

b) Investigation and analysis of actual, event sequences within the system (in view of the investigation of "typical" event-sequences).

c) Forecast of the chronological course of individual system variables, based on investigated or theoretical, distributional functions.

d) Optimization of system flows.

e) Evaluation of alternative policies with reference to their relationship between expenditure and attainable effects.

Event-oriented systems are usually also deterministic models (the best known applications are, probably, found in the transportation field) and require accordingly detailed knowledge of the relevant variables in the system. These have to be indirectly described by way of the events flowing within the system. This inevitably directs the implementation of a complex system to a model of extensive proportions. Accordingly alterations in the model cannot be made so easily.

3.4 Application criteria

The criteria or tests that lead to system-simulation as an aid to planning consist in: the summing-up of the properties of an 'ideal' model, the planner's demands, as well as the problems that turn up with the construction of such a model—as already discussed in this Section:

1. Independent of the respective organization structure of the planning process that is to be assisted, the simulation model must, from the start, be *restricted* to the decision's preliminary preparations (analyses, forecasts, designational findings and evaluation). Its key function lies in the serving or feeding of additional information.

2. The system-theoretical concept of the model must lead to a highly, flexible structure that permits its parametrical adaption to the actual system just investigated and allows, simultane-

ously, the support of the planning phases mentioned above and on, say, nearly the same level of aggregation.

3. The model must be adapted to the computer capacity available in communal managements and must, therefore, make no unusual or exceptional hardware or software demands. (Should one not succeed in implementing such a model, in making it compatible and handy so that it may be used without incurring problems, then it would be useless for the daily 'routine' of the planner.)

4. Utilization has to be uncomplicated and must not require special knowledge of the EDP.

5. The input data required by the model must be adapted to the various planning fields. In no case should the model's applicability be dependent on the painstaking editing and conversion from the existing planning data, in order to obtain an adaptable form.

6. The results generated from the model must be easily surveyable and properly visualized. Furthermore, it should be possible in each phase to recall the results in varying detail. The effectiveness of this instrument depends, too, largely on the form and easy handling offered by the designing of the model output.

4. Notes on the current stage of application

System simulation, as a method for the solving of problems, has aroused great expectations in city and regional planning boards. The large number of developed models in the USA (in the middle-sixties in Europe, too) proves this in an impressive manner. Publications describing these models emphasize the unique possibilities of this new planning instrument and recommend it to the planner. Should one, however, test the practical significance that the simulation has for the planner, in that one tries to determine which models are regularly used by planning groups, then this estimate has to be drastically lowered.

Although there are in the meantime various cases in the GFR where simulation in this particular field could be applied the "successfully" worked-out problems here are largely restricted to the planning and guiding of local transport systems, whereby instead of always using the simulation-systems in a stricter sense, variants of different optimization models are applied.

Reichmann [3], in his comparative studies of some of the best known models of city and regional planning, arrives at a more sober estimate of the role simulation currently plays in the GFR. This estimate is enforced in a corresponding paper by Harbord [4], which has just been published. According to these studies, the conversions of the findings attained by various, examined models has nowhere advanced far enough yet in planning experience to permit one to speak today already of a 'planning instrument' simulation.

This is a surprising fact, if one considers that the system-simulation is currently, unanimously regarded by most authors as THE ideal instrument. (It has actually become so in other research fields, such as that of enterprises.) The author has been studying this question for some time and has reached the following conclusions about the present state of development:

– The administrative, planning processes are not all so consistently organizational that one may simply speak of and define the various planning fields as 'standard functions' that could be, or evidently are, supported by the system-simulations.

– Similarly, such detailed descriptions as those, for instance, given of many enterprising fields are currently not yet feasible for the region. A sufficiently formalized and detailed description of the complex system, region, is, however, a pre-condition for the conception of a substitute-system (model); this should then allow quantitative outputs about the behavior of the real system.

– The meagre communication between planning specialists, system-analysts and EDP specialists, has so far prevented further development of relevant material (deduced, gathered) from the copious experience in this—for the simulation, new—utilization field. The principal disadvantage of the method developed so far, lies in the fact that the models so far are usually adapted to a particular or specific problem. This has made it clear that for a broader application of simulation, a comprehensive, fundamental survey must first be made. As this, however, cannot be effected by individual sources or colleges, only a more encompassing cooperation of the interested parties may realize this part of the development.

– Accordingly, most of the models developed so far have not been put into practical use, for the simple reason that they have not come up to the level expected.

And here, as we point out in conclusion, are the starting points for the development of experience-justified, standard models.

5. Conclusion

The above sobering facts about the actual situation in the application of simulation to city and regional planning in GFR should not, however, lead to the conclusion that the problem-solving method of simulation is not suitable for this field. The significance that such a universally applied model could have (even for a single planning field) for the daily tasks of the planner as well as those of the municipal official is simply too far-reaching for one to be able to afford simply to dispense with its development. Another fact is that present computer technology is advanced enough for the realization of such an 'instrumentarium'. The main difiiculty lies first of all in the standardized description of the planning activities and in the model-theoretical registration of regional systems as described above.

6. References

1. For a definition and defining of this notion compare: STACHOWIAK, H., 'Grundriß einer Planungstheorie', *Kommunikation* VI/1 (1970); and MAIMINAS, E.S., *Planungsprozesse—Informationsaspekt,* Verlag Die Wirtschaft, Berlin (1972).
2. MÜLLER, J.H., *Methoden zur regionalen Analyse und Prognose*, Gebrüder Jänicke Verlag, Hannover (1973).
3. Representative for many other views are two papers which may be consulted: LOWRY, I.S., *Seven models of urban development: a structural comparison*, RAND-Sonderdruck P-3673 (1967); REICHENBACH, E., *Vergleich von Stadtentwicklungsmodellen,* Veröffentlichungen des Institutes für Stadtbauwesen, Braunschweig (1972).
4. Compare the statements by HARBORD, S., *Computersimulation in den Sozialwissenschaften*, Rowohlt, p. 282 ff. (1974).

Survey of some economic models with special reference to the problematic nature of data availability

CLAUS SEEGER
Fachbereich Kybernetik,
Technische Universität Berlin, Germany

Introduction

The city and regional planner is constantly faced with the problem of how to acquire the relevant information needed for the various planning projects in mind. As the solving of his plans depends largely on the completeness and value of the information at his disposal, he is compelled to rely on methodically-based auxiliary material or aid; the EDP (Electronic Data Processing) is a great help in preparing or processing data and analysis. Excellent results have, moreover, been recently obtained in statistical forecast processes and from the usage of planning models.

A considerable range of data material is specially required for the economic planning fields. Data of previous periods are needed for the realization of time-trend analyses and forecasts. Additional problems arise due to the constant extrapolation of these time-series.

The planner is dependent, where regional and city-planning is concerned, on such data as, for instance, basic and individual data, those of economic enterprises and further data from economic fields and such as cannot be obtained from statistical boards. In order to obtain such data, surveys of the region must be made so as to fit the required information needed by the planner. These surveys are considerably complicated and costly.

To get satisfactory results, the planner obtains his information out of the projects to be planned. In individual cases accurate data may be had; in others, however, they are not at first apparent.

In solving a problem, others not at first perceived appear, giving rise to the need for new sources of information. So, in order to solve economic problems, the complete data of the economic field, as well as related social and infra-structural data should be surveyed as a whole. The handicap regarding the availability of documentary data for planners, politicians and economists becomes evident here.

Further planning statistics from the "primary data" may be gathered by various analysis tests (regression, correlation). The purpose of these statistical surveys is to deduce forecasts for the future trend of the various factors of interest for the planner out of the historical data given.

One may consider the region as a "system" and

describe its distinctive features and characteristics by the particularities of its individual subsystems. A few models have been produced to describe the development and conditions of a region. Simulation models are, above all, used for the purpose of indicating forecasts and time-trends of individual subsystems. In the USA they are mainly used to determine the various planning projects in each region. In the German Federal Republic (GFR) they are, up to now, only used in isolated cases.

These models have been developed from various economic theories. Some of these resulting estimates will be discussed more fully and will be based on available data material.

One may distinguish the following model-types concerning their theories.

Econometric model

Until now, there has not been a great deal of theoretical work done on econometric models in city and regional planning. A few exceptions are I.R. Klein, C.C. Harris, R.J. Anderson, N.J. Glickman, and E. Olsen, who have built some theories and models.

These models will be applied mostly to short-run forecasting in the region as opposed to their application in the national economy.

We shall not introduce any specific hypotheses, as used in the development of regional econometric theories, since they cannot be tested. The applied equations led to good adaptions and were declared for predestination purposes, where the different relations between the available data-variables confer on the model an implicit theory, e.g., that the theory is rather derived from the data, than that data were used as a priori theory.

Economic models developed up till now, are essentially forecasting models. In the case of a high degree of structural stability in the growth process of the region and if knowledge of regional development (i.e., given by trends) is available, the distinction between growth- and long-run forecasting model is blurred [1].

The econometric analyses can be regarded as quite a new area. Before applying these models as auxiliaries there should be further progress made in two fields:
1. Development of regional economic theory, and
2. collection and construction of data-series of regional key-variables (i.e., regional investment).

One often observes this in different models and it can be considered as a great disadvantage. Often the model was adjusted on the variables, which were available or which led to a high correlation-coefficient and thereby the economic theory falls behind. Glickman [2], for example, gives a forecast of the change of population by an equation, which links the change in population to the change in employment in the time. There he is using time as proxy for the increase and the migration. Some hypotheses are made that seem to be unreliable and which regional economists cannot support. For the most part these econometric models rely on the basic-nonbasic concept, whereby data collection procures the main difficulties.

Data of employment are often the only data available in regular intervals. Sales, respectively output and population data can be estimated and assertions about investments are usually missing, although they are of great importance in such models.

Data restrictions lead to statistical problems. So data-series can exist yet as invariable annual time-series and reaching back only a few years. Therefore the model has too many exogenous variables relative to the amount of observations. But leaving out some variables leads to false results. It is therefore necessary to apply techniques to reduce the number of variables in order to attain a more compact form. This principal component-analysis is used by Glickman, for example.

Further difficulties arise with regional data, when the data basis is referring to a shorter period than the forecasting period.

Basic-nonbasic model

Using the Basic-nonbasic model (BNM) it is possible to determine the development of a regional economy and its population. Thereby, optimal regional political measures can be derived, in order to reach an optimal growth of the economy.

This concept is based on a fully developed growth theory of stages of development, where a so-called "regional multiplier" can be determined. This factor serves as a basis for promotions, annually given in the GFR, i.e., for industry- respectively economy promotions.

Let us assume, that the regional growth and the factor of the development level is determined by the division of labor, and that there is a relation between sectors and regions not only inside but also outside the region. This leads to a circle of goods, which determines the growth of the economy.

Proceeding from these considerations, one derives a regional income and thereby regional growth. An

393

increase of external trade leads to a higher income and the division of labor depends on the external trade of a region [3]. Rise in growth and thereby increasing income, is given by interregional exports and here one can see some measures leading to growth rising, i.e., investments, promotions and supports of branches and economic sectors, producing goods for export. Indirectly, however, all are connected with export by production.

This leads to a division in the "basic" sectors, which produce for export, and in the "nonbasic" sectors, that are those sectors producing goods and services not directed toward export.

Theory maintains [4] that employees working in the "basic" sectors imply by their higher consumption and higher demand for goods and services a greater employment number in the "nonbasic" sectors. This gives a multiplier process by the employees of the "basic" sectors, making a contribution to the regional income of the "nonbasic" sectors. By distinguishing export and local activities, regional income shall be defined [5]

$$Y_R = Y_{EX} + Y_L$$

Local income Y_L is dependent on income gained by exports and marginal consumption rate of local goods and services

$$Y_L = Y_{EX}\left(\frac{1}{1-b} - 1\right)$$

This yields regional income Y_R as a function of export income and marginal consumption rate of local goods and services *(b)*

$$Y_R = Y_{EX}\left(\frac{1}{1-b}\right)$$

When b is constant and if the change of export income is known, then change in gross regional income Y_R is given. Because of exports ascertainment for forecast purposes, the last formula cannot be used. Therefore this equation was remolded in order to forecast population development, which implies direct correlation between income and employment. These relationships can be specified by

$$B_R = B_{EX} + B_L$$

$$B_R = B_{EX}\left(\frac{1}{1-b}\right)$$

B_{EX} = number of employees in basic sectors,

B_L = number of employees for local sales
B_R = regional gross employees.

Since b is assumed constant in different regions, it is obvious that the gross employment depends on the development of export employment, where one can derive the ratio B_{EX}/B_L = constant. B_L and B_R can be determined if a ratio number is found empirically and the *decisive* variable B_{EX} is known.

Proceeding from the theory, that on each employee in the region depends a certain number of persons (children, women), the gross population can assert independence to gross employment. Andrews [6] found out some typical ratio numbers

basic-nonbasic rate	1:2
basic employment to gross employment	1:3
gross employment to gross population	1:2
basic employment to gross population	1:6

The BNM uses the income produced and obtained by working in different sectors. This information can only be obtained through additional inquiries and is not available as statistical data. That is the reason why employment numbers are used in both sectors. This material, which also is not listed in statistics, can be obtained by inquiries; thereby recalculations and further assumptions must be made. This is implied by the arrangement of statistics, since the BNM requires another data disposition and therefore other data preparation (see Fig. 1).

Further difficulties consist (i.e., at the retail) in that for different economic branches simple transfer from income- to employment relations cannot be derived.

One important variable for the planner is the development of the population. The quotient from "basic" and "nonbasic" employment yields a rate which describes this development. Thus the planners are again dependent on data for employment.

As a condition for the application of a planning method, the sectors must be marked clearly such that a region can be classified accordingly. Further, employment of "basic" sectors must be measurable and, if possible, income in this sector too. (Figure 2 shows the economic circle of the BNM.)

Harrod-Domar-model

Proceeding from the Keynesian system and from the Classists Domar's [7] growth model is derived. The income- and employment-theory of Keynes utilizes an investment multiplier, whereas the classists stress the rise of the production capacity. Domar's is described through [8]:

1. The decisive factor for growth is the net-

Economic group	Subdivisions	Income	Employment	etc.
Basic sectors	i.e.:			
	Mining	Y_{EX1}	E_{EX1}	Z_{EX1}
	Chemical industry	Y_{EX2}	E_{EX2}	Z_{EX2}
	Metal industry	.	.	.
	Electrical industry	.	.	.
	Machinery industry	.	.	.
	. . .			
	etc.	Y_{EXn}	E_{EXn}	Z_{EXn}
Nonbasic sectors	i.e.:			
	Energy economics	Y_{L1}	E_{L1}	Z_{L1}
	Food consumption tr.	Y_{L2}	E_{L2}	Z_{L2}
	Contract constr. tr.	.	.	.
	Wholesale trade	.	.	.
	Retail trade	.	.	.
	Services	.	.	.
	.			
	etc.	Y_{Lk}	E_{Lk}	Z_{Lk}

Fig. 1 Systematical description of a basic-nonbasic table

investment of the total economy. An increase of production capacity P_t leads to increase of capital stock by a positive investment I_t.

$$P_t = \frac{1}{k} \cdot K_t$$

k_t = capital-output-ratio
k = marginal capital-output-ratio

2. Net investment is decisive for economic growth. If investment has an equal effect on capacity and income, equilibrium growth is obtained:

$$\dot{Y}_t = \dot{P}_t$$

$$\dot{Y}_t = \dot{I}_t / s'$$

growth of income

s = saving rate
s' = marginal saving rate at constant time-run

$$\frac{\dot{I}_t}{I_t} = \frac{s}{k}$$

3. Written as a differential equation

$$\dot{I}_t = \frac{s}{k} \cdot I_t \quad \text{with the solution} \quad I_t = I_o e^{\frac{s}{k} t}$$

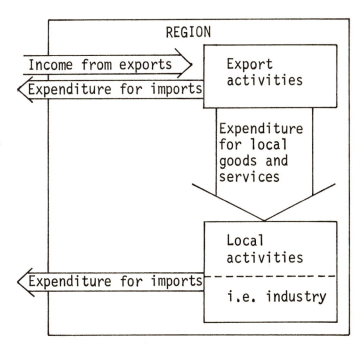

Fig. 2 Regional income flows in the basic-nonbasic model [18]

395

Survey of some economic models with special reference to the problematic nature of data availability

Harrod [9] proceeds from Keynesian theory. Autonomous investment is not considered. He explains the investment decisions by the acceleration-principle. Harrod's theory is described through [10]:

1. Demand of macro-economic variables is dependent on net investment I_t and C_t (consumption). If a behavior function for I_t and C_t is set up, demand can be derived. Saving decisions depend on real income, and investment decisions are influenced by changes of income.

$$S_t = s \cdot Y_t$$
$$I_t = v \cdot \dot{Y}_t$$

Real income is defined as

$$Y_t = I_t + C_t$$

2. Introduction of the Keynesian equilibrium condition

$$I_t = S_t$$

where

$$\frac{\dot{Y}_t}{Y_t} = \frac{s}{v}$$

follows.

3. Its solution is found in the real income function

$$Y_t = Y_o e^{s \cdot v/t} \quad \text{or} \quad Y_t = Y_o (1 + s/v)^t$$

4. Insertion of the acceleration principle in the Keynesian system leads to a dynamic system.

The basic equations of these two models are identical when equality of acceleration coefficient and capital-output ratio is given. Thereby both models united [11]:

With $I_t = \frac{s}{k}$; $\frac{\dot{Y}_t}{Y_t} = \frac{s}{v}$ and $k = s$ follows $\frac{\dot{Y}_t}{Y_t} = \frac{\dot{I}_t}{I_t} = \frac{s}{k}$

The introduction of difference equations gives for the Domar model

$$P_t - P_{t-1} = \frac{1}{k} \cdot I_t$$

$I_t = S_t$ \qquad equilibrium condition

$Y_t = P_t$

$S_t = s' \cdot Y_t$ \qquad behavior equation

and for the Harrod model

$$S_t = s \cdot Y_t$$

$$I_t = v \cdot (Y_t - Y_{t-1})$$
$$Y_t = I_t + C_t$$

there follows

$$Y_t = (1-s) \cdot Y_t + v \cdot (Y_t - Y_{t-1}) \quad \text{or} \quad Y_t = \frac{s}{v-s} \cdot Y_{t-1} + Y_{t-1}$$

From previous derivations and considerations, the Harrod-Domar model will be specified for a region [12]. This model was developed for regional growth analyses and considers inter-regional mobility of labor and capital.

The steady growth equilibrium conditions are

$$g = k = n \quad \text{with} \quad k = \frac{I}{K} = \frac{S}{K} = \frac{S \cdot Y}{Y \cdot K} = \frac{s}{v}$$

where g, k, n = rate of growth of output, capital, and population
v = capital-output ratio

Regions are open economies, whose static condition is

$$I + X = S + M \qquad \begin{matrix} X = \text{Export} \\ M = \text{Import} \end{matrix}$$

or

$$I + X = (s + m) \cdot Y$$

implying

$$\frac{I}{Y} = (s + m) - \frac{X}{Y}$$

The exports X_i of a region are given by the imports of other regions as

$$\sum_j M_{ij} = \sum_j m_{ij} \cdot Y_j$$

and its growth of output

$$g_i = \frac{s_i - m_i - \sum_j m_{ij} \cdot Y_j/Y_j}{v_i} \quad ; \quad v_i = \frac{K_i}{Y_i}$$

The equilibrium condition can be specified as

$$g_i = n_i \pm r_i \qquad r_i = \text{rate of migration}$$

Migration rate is a number of in- or out-migrants R_i divided by population E_i in a region

$$r_i = \frac{R_i}{E_i} = \frac{\sum_j R_{ij}}{E_i}$$

Domar's and Harrod's models are developed from

396

gross economy theory. Their model was derived from these models, which should be the reason that this is applicable to larger regions for which information exists about capital, investments, imports (respectively exports) and migrations.

Neoclassical model

Neoclassical models have as a basis the Domar model and consider the growth of population and the technical progress. The following assumptions are made [13]:

1. Introduction of the production function.
   There growth is investigated exclusively from the supply side derived from the production function. The development of full demand is not taken into account.
2. Saysche theorem.
   Thereby it is accepted that there is enough demand, to pick up the growing supply and guarantee full employment of all factors (Saysche's theorem).
3. Theoretical assumptions concerning production
   - Any divisibility of factors (production factors: tools, machines, labor, capital, etc.).
   - Substitution of factors (production factor labor and capital substitutable for each other).
   - Validity of the law of return (e.g., production coefficient increases).
   - Validity of marginal productivity (production factors are paid off with their marginal product).
   - Linear homogeneity of the production function (e.g., linear homogeneous interrelation).

The fundamental idea, which led to this concept lies in the assumption that growth of production Y depends on growth of labor potential A, of capital stock K and technical progress T.

$$Y = Y(A, K, T)$$

Real growth is attributed to
- growth of population and thereby of the factor labor, when capital stock and technical knowledge remain constant, or to
- growth of capital at constant population and technical knowledge, or to
- growth of capital stock and labor potential, or to
- growth of capital and technical knowledge at a constant labor potential, or to
- growth of technical knowledge at constant labor potential and capital stock.

Equilibrium growth is assumed. This means that the economy is growing at an equilibrium, if planned investments and savings and there the income, too, grow at the same rate.

Investments, and therewith investment rate, have no influence on equilibrium growth.

With assumption of time, the production function can be derived to

$$Y(t) = Y(t)[A(t),K(t),T(t)]$$

with $A(t)$ = production factor labor
$K(t)$ = production factor capital
$T(t)$ = technical progress (exogenous given).
Labor grows with the population and the rate w_A which is given exogenously.

$$A(t) = A_o e^{w_A \cdot t}$$

Investments are in proportion to national income

$$I(t) = s \cdot Y(t) \qquad s = \text{saving rate}$$

with the equilibrium restriction

$$S(t) = I(t)$$

With these theoretical considerations [14] a neoclassical model for a region is derived. Proceeding from the Cobb-Douglas function, further relations can be derived

$$y_i = a_i k_i + (1-a_i) \cdot l_i + t_i$$
$$k_i = {}^{s_i}/v_i \pm \sum_j k_{ji}$$
$$l_i = n_i \pm \sum_j m_{ji}$$
$$k_{ij} = f(R_i - R_j)$$
$$m_{ij} = f(W_i - W_j)$$

with

y,k,l,t = growth rate of output (production), capital, labor, and technical progress,
a = capital's share of income
s = saving rate
v = capital-output ratio
k_{ij} = annual capital flow from region i to region j, divided by the capital stock of region i
n = population's growth rate
m_{ij} = annual net-flow of migrations from region j to region i, divided by the population

of region i

R = rate of return on capital

W = wages

The disadvantage of this concept is that characteristics of regional economies are not included. Further, in the neoclassical model neither agglomeration economies at a locality and urbanization find any consideration, nor transport costs, which must be an integral part of any regional economic- model according to regional economists.

Also the Cobb-Douglas function has been criticized [14]. However, using this function, it is possible to take all return-effects into account although it might give growing returns to factors independent of technical change. By introducing a factor for the term *(1–a)*, all returns receive their own factor. Further condensation leads to the function

$$y_i = (a_i k_i + (1-a_i) \cdot l_i)^{g_i}$$

There the parameter g_i represents growing returns. Critical elements in the model are those equations which determine the capital flow of migrations. Thereby data for wages are easily obtained. More difficulties are encountered when data for capital stock or for rate of return on capital have to be assembled. This information one may get from special inquiries. The same is true for the saving, e.g., investment rates, which, however, can be found more often in regional statistics.

This model represents a further development of the Domar model. But in order to validate the criticism of the Cobb-Douglas function, additional data must be collected.

Post-Keynesian model

Proceeding from Keynesian theory, Kaldor derived a model considering short-run (*I/S* equilibrium) and long-run (constant profit rate *P/K* over the time) equilibrium. Kaldor [15], who has further developed the post-Keynesian theory, put up a saving function depending on profits *(P)* and wages *(W)* [16],

$$S_t = a \cdot P_t + b \cdot W_t$$

and the identity equation

$$Y_t \equiv P_t + W_t$$

Thereby a full employment situation results from the dynamics of the income distribution between profit and wage through adjustment of S and I.

Kaldor uses as short-run equilibrium condition

$$I_t = S_t$$

and a growth relation for labor potential L with

$$L_t^* = L_o \cdot e^{n \cdot t}$$

and an equilibrium condition in the system

$$L_t^* = L_t$$

where

n = max. population's growth rate

L_t = employment population

L_t^* = max. available employment population

The adaption process of short-run to long-run equilibrium growth is characterized by the change of capital-productivity *(Y/K)*, e.g., the capital-output ratio *(K/Y = v)* goes against zero

$$\frac{dv}{dt} = 0$$

If we assume that the profit-rate (long-run) will change in the same way as the long-run interest-rate r and risk factor z, we may conclude

$$\frac{P_t}{K_t} = r_t + z_t$$

The risk-factor is depending on capital-output ratio

$$z_t = f(v_t)$$

Kaldor characterizes the factor of economic development by
1. Permanent growth of production and labor-productivity (long-run).
2. Increase in capital-intensity.
3. Constant profit-rate over the time period.
4. Constant capital-output ratio over time.
5. Correlation of profit- and investment-rate.

As an application of this theory, Kaldor [17] defined a model for a region. Thereby he assumes that the behavior of production (output) and exports in a region depends on
1. An *exogenous* factor (growth of the world demand for a region's products).
2. An *endogenous* factor or quasi-endogenous factor (defining the movement of "efficient wages" in a region relative to other regions).

Movement in efficient wages results from
1. Change in money-wages, relative to change in

productivity (W/T with W = index of wage, T = index of productivity).

2. Wages and increase of wages-rate become similar for all regions.

Model:

$$t_i = f_i^1(y_i) \qquad f_i^1 \text{ is rising and} >0$$

$$(W_i/T_i) = f_i^2(y_i) \qquad f_i^2 \text{ is falling and} <0$$

$$y_i = f_i^3(W_i/T_i) \qquad f_i^3 \text{ is falling and} <0$$

$$W_i = \overline{W}$$

with

t = Rate of growth in productivity
$\overline{W}$ = national money-wages

Kaldor assumes that

1. The productivity growth-rate is an increasing function of output's growth rate.
2. The rate of money-wages grows constant in all regions.

He also uses in his model data for wages and rates of wages which are not available in all regions and branches of the economy. The same is true for output-data and the productivity index. Information about profits and investment and capital stock are rarely available on a regional level. Therefore, Kaldor developed a further-going theory and model. Its application, however, is possible only when heavy conditions are imposed.

Input-output models

Input-output analysis describes a process which estimates economic developments. By utilizing the input-output models for the regions to be examined, one may estimate and forecast their probable economic development. Increasing endeavors to determine and describe the cycle of political economics are nowadays a fact, and increasing use of the input-output analysis is the result. Starting with its application to the national or gross economy, attempts are now being made to make it available and use it in city and regional planning.

Limited use of this model has been made so far in the GFR with reference to planning objectives and planning-project purposes. Priority and considerable financial aid for future development and utilization is being given. First tests were made in various places. The results, which these models bring out, may easily stand comparison with the quality of other models; the former can be said to be on the same level as the latter. The use and propositional efficacy is, however, greatly dependent on the information-material needed for the construction of the model, that is, for the setting-up of the table. The insufficient support that these models have up to now offered is based on the fact that heavy demands are made on the statistical data-material. This is the main reason why the setting-up of the input-output tables is not feasible.

Due to efforts made regarding the setting-up of data banks for planning data, it becomes obvious that the input-output analysis methods will be used to an ever-increasing extent in the GFR.

Should a city or region have no statistical data at its disposal, then information data could be culled from that of larger regions (districts, states, provinces), meaning features common to both. A further possibility exists in the analysis of the region to be examined and of the statistical estimates at hand; this procedure would make the additional costs of further surveys superfluous.

The input-output tables themselves show the transactions between the various existing economic branches within a certain period of time (see Fig. 3). Application of this method of evaluation helps for short-run periods; estimates covering more lengthy periods, however, may be made, too. The starting point and basis for the input-output models is the regional gross evaluation. Through further disaggregation of single economic factors (for instance, of sales or production), that is, by closer study of the sectors of the total estimation and differentiated economic branches, one may indicate the inter- or intra-regional payments or deliveries made by a regional input-output table. These models may be divided into two groups

a) Inter-regional models:
   Study of the intersectoral interlacing within and between the various regions.

b) Intra-regional models:
   Study (or observation) of the intersectoral relationships within these single regions alone.

The actual input-output analysis is made in several stages,

a) Setting-up of a table for the input-output analysis.

b) Determining an interlacing balance for the input.

c) Specifying of exogenous variables.

The main difficulties with input-output models lie in their setting-up. These are difficult to overcome. In order, however, to make effective use of this model, a few criteria have to be complied with.

Input purchases from / Output sales to			Economic branches							l,k Enter sales Σ	Demand			m,o End demand Σ	$\Sigma(l+p)$
			Agriculture	Energy	Machinery industry	Retail trade	Wholesale trade	Services	Etc.		Investments	Private and official consum.	Exports		
			1	2	3	•	•	•	k	l	m	n	o	p	q
Economic branches	Agriculture	1	a_{11}						a_{1k}	A_1				D_1	X_1
	Energy	2	a_{21}							A_2				D_2	X_2
	Machinery industry	•												•	•
	Retail trade	•												•	•
	Wholesale trade	•												•	•
	Services	•												•	•
	Etc.	k	a_{kl}						a_{kk}	A_k				D_k	X_k
	Advance contributions	l													
	Depreciations	m													
	Income, wages, profits, rents	n													
	Imports	o													
		p													
	Gross input	q	IP_1	IP_2	•	•	•	•	•	IP_k					

Example [19]: Output (or production) can be computed: from

$$|X| = \underbrace{|A| \cdot |X|}_{\text{Gross input}} + \underbrace{|D|}_{\text{End-demand}} \qquad \text{we get}$$

$$|X| = (|E| + |A|)^{-1} \cdot |D|$$

with: $|X|$ = Detailed outputs of the economic branches; $|E|$ = Unit matrix;
$|A|$ = Matrix of input-coefficients for advance contributions; $|D|$ = Detailed demands (all).

Fig. 3 Input-Output table

They may be specified as follows:

a) Delineation possibilities of individual regions (economic).

b) Disaggregation of the economic sectors in individual branches.

c) Input and output of economic enterprises (trade) have to be filed under the respective sector of their classification group.

d) Statistical and systematic evidence of delivery relations in the sectors of the regions under survey.

e) Existence of required data material.

f) Delineation of the output flow in the input-output matrix.

Models are grouped into

a) Closed I-O models:
The interlacing balance is predetermined.

b) Open I-O models:
Individual sectors are taken from the matrix and substituted by exogenous variables that delineate the final demands.

The open I-O model can be used for city and regional planning and forecasts of developments; here several exogenous variables and interlacing balance for the input may be submitted. Should one wish, for instance, to estimate the GNP of a region, one may obtain this from the contributions of individual economic branches; indispensible, too, is the knowledge of the number of employees. The GNP in the various branches is determined in the individual economic branches, plus the addition of a specific key number. This key number is derived from the productive estimates within a branch; this, again, is determined by wages, rents, leasings, interest and profits. These facts are acknowledged only in fewest cases where a region has to be surveyed and data scarcely to be had, so that the planner is compelled to rely on data provided by the state or country, data which he has to transfer to the region under survey. One recognizes here already the difficulty of data collection and the uncertainty of the resulting factors obtained, as when studying the information on profits in enterprises. Also GNP, for instance, deriving from incomes, often cannot be ascertained, as derivation data in the detailed economy branches are not available.

The main difficulties confronting the use of this model lie in the setting-up of the matrix; statistical surveys, spot checks, estimates must be made that derive from other factors. These factors, summed-up, offer information of an uncertain kind.

W. Leontief [20] developed a different assessment by which the gross economy is divided into a hier-

archy of regions. This hierarchy consists of various stages to which material is allocated. Here Leontief has regional and international material under consideration. A classification such as this type of model requires, for statistical data is not available in the GFR and figures have to be converted, so that data pertaining to the gross economy may be made available for the region in question. This holds true, above all, for the interlacing balance that is applied to the region under survey within the gross economy; added to this, are the various measures to be taken in order to generate the model, as, for instance, that of regional distribution of production, etc.

Statistical material often exists only for certain sectors, so that in order to arrive at positive results, the model must be aggregated.

A further problem consists in the fact that, due to major disaggregation of individual economic branches and affiliations, the I-O tables increase considerably in size; thus, besides the complications of solving of the equation system, are added those of the memory capacity.

These constraints are confronted by propositional efficacy of the I-O model, plus a relatively simple possibility of the exogenous variables. Unfortunately, the necessary statistics of data material for this kind of model are not available in the GFR; this is the reason why methods for aiding and solving planning projects are seldom used.

Conclusions

These models only describe a small part developed for regional economies. However, one recognizes the basic theory in the latest models, which is sometimes further developed and additional spatial variables are taken into the models.

Most of these models are developed and applied in the USA for special regions and planning problems. A translation and application to planning problems in the GFR therefore is not possible without any modifications.

These models proceed from objective investigations and statistical inquiries in a region where it often seems that models are fitted to available data, and regional economic theory is not considered very much. Essential I-O models are used or they have as basis the basic-nonbasic concept.

These assessments and variables utilized in them, cannot be applied in the "Analysis and Prognosis Model (APROS)" as module. On one side, this model should be applicable for all regions and, on

Survey of some economic models with special reference to the problematic nature of data availability

Model	Input	Availability* 1	2	3	Output	Spatial Variable	Application	Remarks Criticism
Econometric Model	Manufacturing output		X		Manuf. output	Migration	Philadelphia Metropolitan Area	
	Nonmanufacturing output		X		Nonmanuf. output			
i.e.	Manufacturing employment	X			Manuf. employment		Analyses and Prognoses	
Glickman	Nonmanufacturing employment	X			Nonmanuf. employ-ment			
	Wages, Prices, Income		X		Wages, Prices, Income			
			X					
	Capital stock		(X)	X	Population			
	Governmental: Output	X			Local Government: Expenditures			
	Employment	X			Revenues			
	Wages	X			Investment			
	GNP	X						
Basic Nonbasic Model	Gross Income basic		X		Gross Income	–	In different regions of the GFR, i.e., for industry	Limitation between basic and nonbasic sectors must be possible
	Gross Employment b.	X			Gross Employment			
	Marginal Consumption Rate b.		(X)	X			Analyses and Prognoses of regional growth	
Neoclassical Model	Production (output)		X		Growth rate of: Production (output)	Migration	Analysis and Prognosis	General criticism against Cobb-Douglas function
	Capital		(X)	X	Capital			
	Wages		X		Labor			
	Return on capital		(X)	X	Capital flow			Additional Data Requisite
	Saving rate		(X)	X	Net-flow of migration			
	Population growth	X						
	Technical progress			X	Investment			
Harrod-Domar Model	Exports (Imports)		(X)	X	Labor rate	Migration	Analysis and Prognosis	For larger regions
	Saving Rate		(X)	X	Growth rate of:			
	Production (output)		X		Productivity			
	Capital		(X)	X	Population			
	Investment		X		Capital-output ratio			
	Population growth	X			Migrations			

(*) Definition: 1 Data available in official statistics
2 Available but not in all regions and economic branches
3 Data not available; necessity for special inquiries.

Fig. 4 Economic models

402

Model	Input	Availability* 1	Availability* 2	Availability* 3	Output	Spatial Variable	Application	Remarks Criticism
Post-Keynesian Model	Output (production)		X	(X)	Labor	–	Analysis and Prognosis	Only a theory
	Investment		X		Growth of:			Application in a region unknown
	Labor potential	X			Productivity			
	Profit			X	Wages			
	Capital		(X)	X	Output			
	Interest	X						
	Productivity		X					
	Wages		X					
Input-Output Model	Purchases from and sales to economic branches i.e.,				i.e.,		Analysis and Prognosis	i.e. City of Osnabrück
	Output		X		Output			
	Depreciations			X	Investment			
	Income		X		Consumption			
	Import/Export			X	Exports/Imports			
	Consumption			X	Depreciations			
	etc.				Income			
					etc.			

Fig. 4 continued

the other, no additional statistical inquiries should be made necessary. Until now, none of the investigated models fulfils these conditions. Stringent restrictions therefore become necessary, which harms the validity of the concept.

Figure 4 displays a partial result of the investigation. Thereby a survey is given on economic models, which contain the following points: Required input, availability of these key input data, further output, used spatial variables, application and short criticisms.

These results lead to the attempt of applying a vintage-model for a region, whose distinct features are: a small data base and a relatively large number of relevant output data. However, thereby one comes across considerable numerical problems, whose solution makes further investigations necessary.

References

1. RICHARDSON, H.W., *Regional Growth Theory*, pp 34-40, Macmillan (1972).
2. GLICKMAN, N.J., 'An econometric model of the Philadelphia region', *Journal of Regional Science* 11, 15-32 (1971).
3. Compare: RITTENBRUCH, K., 'Zur Anwendbarkeit der Exportbasis-konzepte im Rahmen von Regionalstudien', Schriften zu Regional- und Verkehrsproblemen in Industrie- und Entwicklungsländern (Hrsg. v. J.H. Müller u. Th. Dams), 4:15 pp, Berlin (1968).
4. Comp.: SCHMIDT, K.-H., 'Regionalpolitik und Betriebsgrößenstruktur', 'Göttinger Handwerkwirtschaftliche Studien 17' (Hrsg. W. Abel), Verlag Otto Schwarz & Co., Göttingen (1970).
5. RICHARDSON, H.W., *Elements of Regional Economics*, Penguin modern economics, Baltimore, P.19 pp (1969).
6. ANDREWS, R.B., 'Economic studies', *Principles and Practice of Urban Planning* (Hrsg. Goodman/Freund) Washington, D.C. (1968).
7. DOMAR, D.E.,'Capital Expansion, Rate of Growth, and Employment', E 14, 134-147 (1946), or DOMAR, D.E., 'Expansion and Employment,

AE R37, 34-55 (1947).

8. Compare: OPPENLÄNDER, K.-H., 'Die moderne Wachstumstheorie', Schriften des Ifo-Instituts für Wirtschaftsforschung, Duncken & Humbolt, Berlin-München, pp 32-36 (1963).

9. HARROD, R.F., *Towards a Dynamic Economics*, London (1948), or *Economic Essays*, London (1952).

10. Comp.: OPPENLÄNDER, K.-H., a.a., 37-41.

11. Comp.: OPPENLÄNDER, K.-H., a.a., 41-50.

12. RICHARDSON, H.W., *Elements....*, a.a., 47-50.

13. Comp.: SENF, B. and TIMMERMANN, D., 'Denken in gesamtwirtschaftlichen Zusammenhängen', Dürrsche Buchhandlung Bonn-Bad Godesberg, 1, P 189 pp (1971).

14. Comp.: RICHARDSON, H.W., *Regional...*, a.a., P 40 pp.

15. KALDOR, N., The Relation of Economic Growth and Cyclical Fluctuations, EJ 64, 53-71 (1954), and in: A model of Economic Growth, EJ, 591-624 (1957).

16. Comp.: OPPENLÄNDER, K.-H., 'Die moderne...', a.a., 205-216.

17. Comp.: RICHARDSON, H.W., *Regional...*, a.a., 14-34.

18. Comp.: RITTENBRUCH, K., 'Zur Anwend...', a.a., 19.

19. HASSELMANN, W., Stadtentwicklungsplanung, Grundlagen-Methoden-Maßnahmen, Institut für Siedlungs- und Wohnungs-wesen der Universität Münster, K.H. Schneider, p.73 (1967).

20. LEONTIEF, W. and SROUT, 'Die Methoden der Input-Output-Analyse', Allgemeines Statistisches Archiv, Bd.36, München (1952), and 'Interregional theory', *Studies in the Structure of the American Economy*, New York (1953).

A housekeeping model for urban EDP systems

PAUL E. MARTIN
INDUSTRA G.m.b.H.,
Zug, Switzerland

1. "Housekeeping" in EDP operations

Housekeeping in EDP goes beyond documentation in the sense of only registering data. It includes the synthesis of key data into meaningful decision formats and—if required—the corrective action follow-up.

Two prerequisites: we must first be in a position to quantify the dynamics of the system, and ensure the quality of the update of that system in order to be able to rely on the information content. Although these ideas are basic to any system, we have made a special effort to abide by these prerequisites in the EDP Housekeeping Model we are now building for the City of Vienna.

As regards the aspect of quantification, in a paper I gave at the First European Meeting of Cybernetics and Systems Research two years ago, I spoke about a micro-organizational concept for management information systems. This was based on the results of 8 years of study as to how to measure the flow of information in industrial information patterns.

We are aware that if we can learn to measure phenomena we can devise means to control them. Being a consultant for 15 years with an insight into some 100 enterprises, I have witnessed thousands of people, and hundreds of managers shunting about the elusive commodity of information. One thing struck me: the vast amount of energy expended in the process of generating, processing, distributing and focusing information—plus the effort to apply the regulatory feedback mechanism with all its shortcomings. *The waste factor in this process is enormous.*

The challenge was to learn more about the ephemeral substance of "information". To do so, we had to devise a means to trap it. This was done using a very pragmatic approach and tried in several firms under various conditions which enabled us to see:

- a) The total inventory of every segment and particle used in the information system.
- b) the interrelationships of the data (e.g., how a change of a data element in one part of the information system impacts throughout the system).

In this closed compound one can then measure the relative investment effort in each and every information circuit. The computer gives us the facility to monitor this with ease.

In the course of these experiments I came to look upon "information" as pulsations of energy. Its characteristics are akin to electricity. As such, it can be quantified, measured and channeled. It converts to other forms of energy. Uncontrolled, or poorly used, it can be dissipated.

But by knowing how to analyze, register, store, measure and direct information, we can do more than just control what we do; we can apply simulation techniques to improve any given system. Since information processing is a universal struggle, our application is equally beneficial to industry, government ministries or large cities.

It can be looked at as a tool for political leaders and administrators which holds out real hope to revitalize the service element to citizens by reducing the slothful lag time in bureaucratic circuitry.

Although the principles are universal, considerable effort must be invested to prepare the groundwork—mentally and physically—to "sell" the idea of a tightly controlled "housekeeping" function. Exact rules of implementation must be laid down, so that the job of installing "housekeeping" in our broad sense of the word must be treated like any other well defined project in its own right.

2. Modeling large systems

Housekeeping implies that we define and practise a certain routine to keep a system operating in an orderly, clean manner. The larger our system, the more involved the housekeeping tasks.

The relative accuracy we attempt to attain, and the degree of sophistication we build in to automate certain administrative functions, influences our design criteria. As the number of activities and their interdependencies increase, so grows the mass of data to be handled. As an antidote to the growing complexity, there is a tendency on the part of Systems Analysts to compromize quality for the sake of getting a job "running"——. But experience shows that every time we compromise on quality, the noise level in the system increases.

To avoid this error at the outset, a general pattern for EDP systems design must be followed. The pattern developed a decade ago by Professor C.S. Holling for the analysis of ecological systems seems to me to be universally applicable.

The chart (Annex A) depicts that a hypothesis for a system evolves in the mind in connection with certain elements of information (Stage a). Based on the projection of the data we have, related to the solution goal, we postulate a manner of manipulating the data. Initially this thought process is vague; the *principles* of information manipulation dominate the solution design. When we are satisfied that our pattern conforms to those principles, and we can envisage ready access to the data sources we need, our thinking as to how the model will function can

be formalized. At this point we concentrate on precisely *how* the model is to serve our purposes. This is where the model's rules of operation are defined (Stage b).

The model is then tested by feeding in the specific data processed in accordance with the rules we have set. The data fed in relates academically to the actual situations for which we created the model, so we are in a position to simulate a variety of conditions under which our model must work in real life. Simulation not only helps to test the adequacy of the organizational sophistication we have built into the model but also provides feedback which reveals whether or not we have missed any essential piece of logic or relevant linkage in formalizing the hypothesis. Finally, there is a cross-check on the veracity of our experimental input or output data.

This triple check we may call the "development control loop".

Once we have satisfied ourselves that our model meets all the solution goals for which it was designed, we pass it to Systems Analysts trained to mesh the requirements of the model with the realities of obtaining the data and training of people to carry out the required functions. We may call this work "Application Design" (Stage c). At this stage, the Systems Analyst can make certain specifications for results, or set certain predictions, by defining parameters within which he wants to control results to a certain degree of accuracy (Stage d).

We are now ready for field testing (Stage e) where we select one or more typical problem areas to which we apply the methodology, albeit in a restricted manner. Results are registered and are studied by the systems designers to check out the hypothesis and/or the model. We can call this the "preliminary execution control loop".

Provided that the field tests uphold the veracity of the model under real life situations, the results can be used by policy makers to motivate the institutions to establish the *legal and administrative preconditions* under which the model can function effectively. Generally, the policy makers will allow the system to be tested in one or more pilot areas. The results of these large-scale, fully supported system tests help to shape over-all policy so as to establish the environment for the model to operate in its broadest application. The pilot studies also substantiate the final organization plans for implementation.

As full implementation progresses, two final feedback control loops are established:
1. On the pragmatic side—the feedback of specified control data to key political and city officials.

SIMULATION
SYSTEMS ANALYSIS
INTENTIONS
MODEL
HYPOTHESIS
FIELD TESTING
PRELIMINARY EXECUTION
CONTROL LOOP
DEVELOPMENT CONTROL LOOP
EXPERIMENTATION DATA
SCIENTIFIC
FINAL EXECUTION CONTROL LOOP
IMPLEMENTATION
PRAGMATIC
PILOT STUDIES
POLICY FORMULATION
FINAL EXECUTION CONTROL LOOP
LEGEND of Stages
a) Idea generation
b) Idea formalization
c) Application design
d) Parameter definition
e) Test & Implementation
f) Tuning

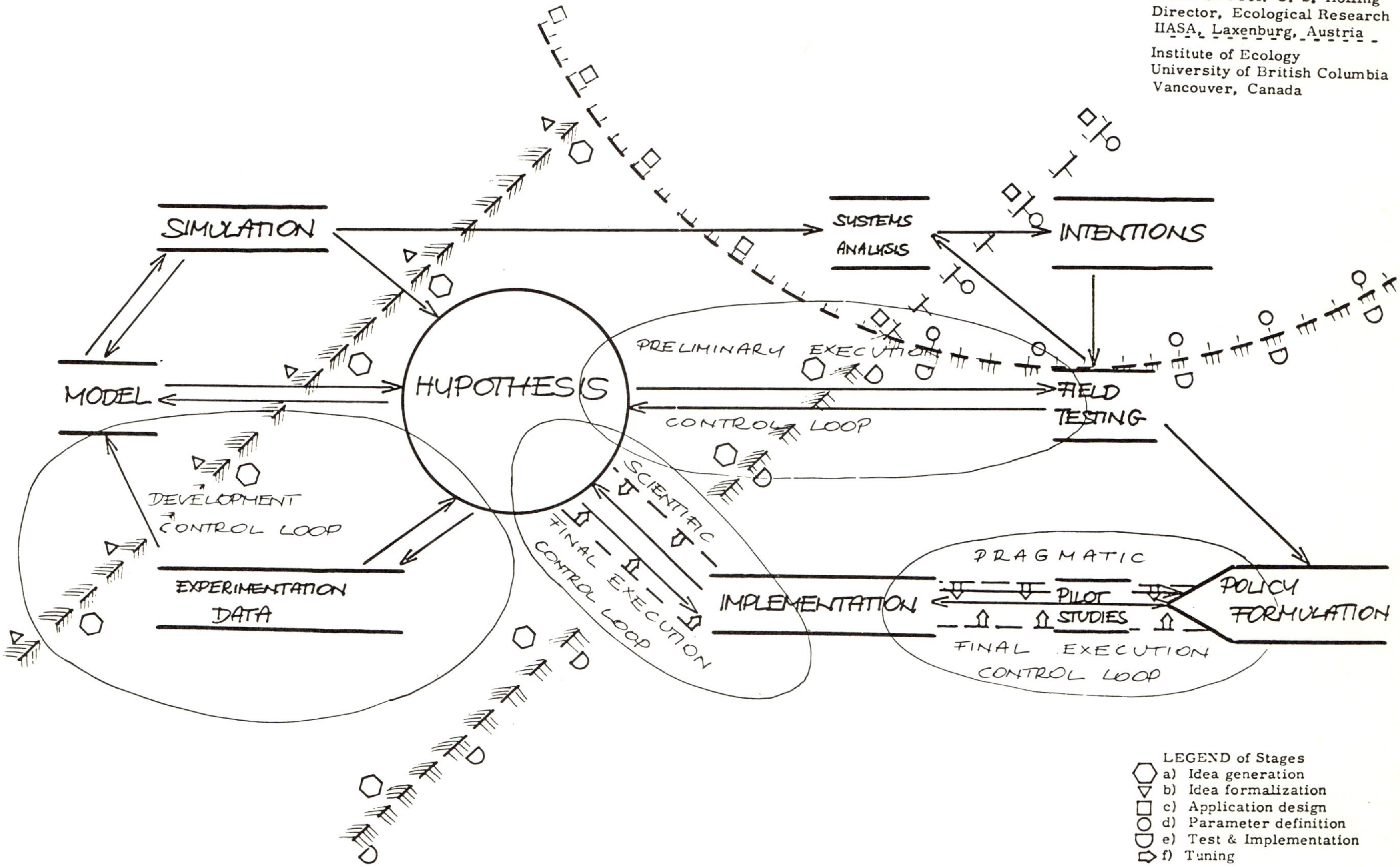

Based on Prof. C. S. Holling
Director, Ecological Research
IIASA, Laxenburg, Austria
Institute of Ecology
University of British Columbia
Vancouver, Canada

Annexe A A systems model

2. On the scientific side—the feedback of specific control data to the systems designers to ensure that the model remains valid by adjusting it to changing conditions in the real world.

This logic goes far in avoiding the sterilization of the model in time, stressed by Stafford Beer in his presidential address to the Society of General Systems Research in Philadelphia in December 1971.

3. Components of the Housekeeping Model

The review of systems modeling is intended to show how it fits into our "Housekeeping Model" project methodology.

At the outset mention was made of the immediate—visible—part of our systems goal—the cleanliness and the order in our shop. Beyond this, however, we are looking for a good planning aid which helps to answer the questions: "What will happen if—?" or "What influence does a change in quantity A have on XYZ?"

Two time dimensions are involved, as is generally known:

 a) The immediate information requirement for transparency of all present operations (MONITOR LOGIC).

 b) The "Gestalt" information requirement to support *future* operations (PLANNING LOGIC).

The challenge is to combine these two logic packages into an "all-seeing eye", as it were, by designing a practical minimal input with reasonable data security to achieve near optimal decision support output with economical machine usage.

Following a "Computer Audit" in 1973 the City of Vienna formed a small team with the mission to improve the entire communication concept of its computer center operations. This team then set about to define the key information and security requirements that the systems design had to meet. After months of work and close coordination with all management levels a general system was accepted by the EDP manager. It was named "VINCOS", an acronym for "Vienna's Internal Control and Organization System".

The study identified 7 major areas (subsystems) to be organized and monitored in order to ensure transparency of daily operations.

These subsystems are:
1. Planning—generative.
2. Human Guidance and Control.
3. Systems Control.
4. Machine Control.
5. Dispatching Support.
6. "No-Go" Support.
7. Communication—Structure Support.

Even though each subsystem is designed essentially as a "stand alone" entity, the advantages of integration are obvious. The function of each subsystem is briefly given below.

4. Functions of the model

ad 1—Planning-generative subsystem

This is the activity area of the long-range planning group—the "General Staff" which sets the strategic goals, issues priorities and authorizes the budgets. It provides the impetus at highest political and administrative levels which sets the other subsystems in motion. This policy group also lays down guidelines how EDP operations will best serve the city. The operation of this subsystem is critical, since its level of intelligence, discipline and relative degree of efficiency determines in large part the levels of efficiency which the other subsystems can attain.

Number 1 subsystem receives information from subsystems 2, 3, 4 in a standard report cycle to see how well the planning goals are being met. Specifically, the planners receive

- performance data on the systems analysts programmers,
- the impact of EDP mutations in the areas of application and data bank management (which reflect the systems dynamics),
- the performance of the hardware park (which reflects the machine dynamics).

ad 2—Human guidance and control subsystem

Here the data elements out of the planning activity (human and hardware capacity) as well as individual reporting against each assigned job are registered by Project, Human and Program Master files.

When new tasks are planned decisions are made on the basis of information from subsystem 2—viz., available manpower. Since the assigned load on each man is stored and updated, as is the performance by man and project, an overview of manpower availability is at hand. The system is so designed that slippage is spotted at 3 project levels at its earliest stage. Thus, depending on the urgency of the situation, manpower reallocations can be planned, deadlines modified, work packages redefined—all in good time. The reasons for all changes in planning are registered so that the learning curve of project management itself can be systematically improved.

ad 3—Systems control subsystem

Here all the mutations in Projects, Programs, Files, Tapes, and Mass storage units are registered on the respective master files. In principle this is a filter which monitors the mutations to ensure:

- conformity to key-lock criteria to meet data security requirements (who is authorized to update),
- conformity to certain check routine criteria (e.g., program changes are only accepted if change number is valid).

One of our main problems is turbulence. Many changes cause much confusion, especially since most changes beget a string of other changes. So we intend to employ "reason codes" to ascertain who is creating change turbulence and why. We shall register the source and the cost for use by the Internal Audit group which will look into justification.

This documentation allows for audit trails to all mutations, and where difficulties have to be traced, cuts trouble shooting time and effort to a minimum.

ad 4—Machine control subsystem

This data is the internal reporting by the machine on its own activities, known as "accounting routines" in EDP jargon.

The development of accounting software over the past years has been far more successful than teaching managers how to read, interpret and take action on the basis of the highly useful and available information. The experts of Vienna have given this problem a lot of thought. We shall make an extract of valuable data elements which register the use of the machine, and merge them on the update cycle with several of our master files—notably our files on personnel, projects and programs. This serves to quantify our events, which in turn aids the decision maker.

ad 5—Dispatching support subsystem

This subsystem is designed to aid the Work Preparation team to plan the best daily use of the machine in scheduling normal or ad hoc production jobs and normal and emergency tests.

Thruput efficiency of computers can be considerably influenced by scheduling jobs so that the best use is made of core allocation and peripherals. The size of the EDP installation of the City of Vienna (IBM 370/155—1,500 K with 1,600 million bytes online storage) on 3 shift operation warrants that as much aid as possible be given to the Work Preparation team.

To this end, standing jobs (recorded on a Schedule Master) are to be augmented with dynamic jobs which—coupled with control functions of checking accuracy of job requests with respect to projects, programs, files, tapes, and mass storage—will aid the Work Preparation team to schedule the work on the machine with a far higher degree of accuracy and sensitivity than has been possible to date.

ad 6—"No-Go" subsystem

In spite of all administrative precautions, filters and check points, EDP programs will still come to abnormal end (ABENDS). This subsystem aims to log in all "NO-GO's" with the correct reason (insofar as experts can ascertain) in order to systematically reduce both frequency and magnitude of failure to the absolute minimum.

Linking the master files in the system with some common sense, we have the means to analyze why jobs or programs fail. By cataloging no-go's and bringing them systematically to the attention of the management, the efficiency of all the other subsystems can be enhanced.

The data elements in our "No-Go" reporting concept gives management quantitative information as to which projects are having the most difficulty, who is involved, and how much human and machine effort has been expended. These reports inspire management to improve the quality of the staff by constant training effort for the people who need it most, so that the EDP personnel benefit from practical quality control measures.

ad 7—Communication-structure support subsystem

This subsystem can be likened to a target tracking mechanism. It compels us to quantify the communications network in the user's organization with a high degree of reliability, so that we can simulate new structures and patterns of communications, and see the magnitude of work when changes impact anywhere in the system.

To achieve this aim it is necessary that four further master files: DOCUMENTS, INPUTS, OUTPUTS and ELEMENTS link with the FILE and PROGRAM masters. This documents the human communications in the structure we are serving and gives management the first real grasp on the cost of the total information system by providing the means to:

- *control the growth rate* of each segment of our information system,
- *improve the methods* of communicating,
- *reduce lag time* in the system,
- *decrease the over-all cost.*

409

To explain in detail just how this subsystem will deliver these benefits goes considerably beyond the scope of this short Chapter. Suffice it to say, that by selective improvement of the quantitative side of the information system we gain qualitative advantages of:

- faster reaction time (improved viability of system)
- clearer transmission (less noise) = improved reliability re. information validity.

5. Plan for implementation

In terms of our general model we are now at the stages "Systems Analysis" and definition of "Intentions". We would like to implement the Planning-Generative Subsystem in parallel with the Human Guidance Subsystem first, followed by the other subsystems in the sequence given above.

One may ask: "Isn't this a lot of adminstrative effort just for housekeeping?" Maybe. On the other hand, compare this with the effort wasted every day by top notch specialists hunting bugs and patching endlessly because they have no reliable housekeeping method to aid them!! With the complexity of systems growing at fast pace—but the quality of human resources for coping with them remaining seemingly static (if not declining), do we honestly have an alternative to developing a good housekeeping system? Certainly not. Our experience in computer controls supports the contention that this approach —with its many innovations— will provide an interesting, practical solution to many organizational and operational problems which beset EDP managers of large urban communities.

SPECIAL ASPECTS

The application of general system theory to legal research

LEO REISINGER
University of Vienna, Austria

1. Introductory remark

The beginning of the scientific examination of the possible relationships between the computer and the law can be dated with 1949 when Lee Loevinger wrote his famous article 'Jurimetrics. The Next Step Forward' [1]. Since then this topic has been discussed under various headlines. In the USA the denotations 'Jurimetrics' [2], 'Lawtomation' [3], and 'Computer and the Law' [4] have been used. In France the expression 'Informatique Juridique' has been applied [5], followed recently by 'Cybernetique Juridique' [6]. In analogy to these denotations the Italian author Mario G. Losano uses 'informatica giuridica' [7] and 'giuscibernetica' [8]. Similarly the German speaking countries apply the expressions 'EDV und Recht' [9], 'Rechtsinformatik' [10] and 'Rechtskybernetik' [11].

This different usage can be explained by the historical development of the discipline and the different notions of 'informatics' and 'cybernetics' in the capitalist and socialist countries. Whereas Jurimetrics in its proper sense and the application of computerized data banks to law have originated in the USA, in Europe the traditional notion of 'legal system' has led to new developments of the discipline. Furthermore, in the European capitalist countries 'informatics' is usually a translation of the angloamerican 'computer sciences', whereas in the socialist countries it means a discipline concerned with the processing of scientific documents.

Until a conformity of nomenclature will be reached we propose the following preliminary definitions:

1. The term 'jurimetrics' shall be reserved for the attempts of formalization applied to the common law systems. A central problem of jurimetrics is therefore the attempt to formalize legal cases in such a way that predictions of judicial decisions may become possible.
2. By the term 'legal informatics' or 'law informatics' we shall understand the endeavors of applying computerized data banks (or information systems) to the law both in the countries of common law and continental Europe.
3. The term 'legal cybernetics' or 'law cybernetics' shall be reserved for the attempts of formalization applied to the legal systems of continental Europe.

2. The importance of General Systems Theory for Jurimetrics, Legal Informatics and Legal Cybernetics

Although the above-mentioned schools of thought differ considerably in their methods they can be united theoretically by applying the concepts devel-

Progress in Cybernetics and Systems Research, Volume 2

oped by General Systems Theory [12]. Especially the general notion of a system as a set of elements and a set of relations between these elements seems to be very fruitful as neither the elements nor the relations have to be specified beforehand. The concept of legal systems can therefore be analyzed by formal sciences. In doing so we can distinguish the following steps [13]:

1. Taxonomy. In the first step the elements of the concerned legal field are isolated and classified according to certain criteria.
2. Structuralistics. In the second step relations between these elements are defined.
3. Formalization in its proper sense. In the third step a formal system is chosen and the elements and relations are translated into terms of the formal system. In choosing a formal system, the rules by which the sequences of symbols can be transformed are established.
4. Algorithmization. In taking into consideration the chosen formal system an algorithm, i.e., a schematic procedure for solving certain classes of problems, is defined.
5. Automation. In the last step the algorithm is implemented on a computer.

The application of formal sciences in its proper sense only takes place during the steps 3 to 5. Taxonomy and Structuralistics have only a preparatory task by analyzing the legal field according to the methods of General Systems Theory. Nevertheless they determine the application of formal sciences considerably as the translation into terms of a formal system and the definition of an algorithm and implementation of this algorithm depend on the definitions of the elements and relations of the legal field.

3. The application of General Systems Theory to Legal Informatics

In the following part of the Chapter some of the above-mentioned steps of applying General Systems Theory to the law shall be illustrated by chosen examples from Legal Informatics, Jurimetrics and Legal Cybernetics. Let us consider Legal Informatics first. By applying General Systems Theory 'society' can be construed as a complex system consisting of different interactive subsystems. One of these subsystems is the 'Legal System' that is steering the whole social system by processing certain specified informations. An ordered set of decision elements is connected through a structure of information channels, the so-called 'Legal Information System', by means of which the decision elements exchange

messages. [14] Therefore, the Legal Information System is an integral part of the Legal System, any important change of the channels' properties alters the flow of information and thereby the production of legal information, i.e., the Legal System itself.

The analysis of the possibilities of applying automated data processing to the law has to start therefore by studying the decision elements, information channels and messages of the Legal Information System. The phase of taxonomy is in this case rather simple, the decision elements can be classified according to their roles in the Legal System. The roles of judge, plaintiff, defendent, etc., are defined by their functions in the Legal System. Although it is well-known that the actual behavior differs sometimes considerably from the prescribed roles, empirical studies on this subject have started only recently [15].

Especially important is the structural phase, i.e., the analysis of the channels of the Legal Information System. Each decision element selects information necessarily. In the traditional systems of documentation each user restricts himself to certain classes of documents (e.g., judicial decisions), certain senders (e.g., the supreme court), certain channels (e.g., official collections). This selection is partly defined by the prescribed function, partly by traditional behavior.

Related to the selection of information channels is the problem of determining the juristically relevant messages. In the continental European countries the traditional classes of documents are legal norms, judicial decisions and technical juristic literature. In the latter case and even more in the case of social data there exist no unanimously applied criteria of definition.

The aim of the analysis of elements, channels and messages is to formulate hypotheses of the Legal Information System's behavior. Comparing this behavior with the subsystems's functions in the Legal System it can be shown, that its efficiency may be increased considerably using automated data processing. For instance the actual selection of channels and messages raises the probabilities for certain documents to be used in legal decision processes whereas other possibly equally relevant documents have a probability of usage of practically zero. By using computerized data banks an approximate equality of chance for all relevant documents may be achieved.

The aforementioned analysis of the Legal Information System has so far been conducted without more than marginal help of the formal sciences. Doubtlessly a formalization of the Legal Information System would improve the analysis considerably but till now no attempts to formalize the jurist's information behavior have succeeded. Nevertheless, certain approaches in this direction can be noted in Jurimetrics and Legal Cybernetics. In both cases formal models are constructed to describe the decision elements' behavior after having collected the relevant information on which the decision is based.

4. A Jurimetrics' Model of Judicial Decision

According to the concept of common law a new case is to be decided from precedents, i.e., related cases that were decided in the past. Since 1957 jurimetrics has developed several formal decision models following the common law procedure [16]. These models are usually referred to as "predicting judicial decisions' as they are used for predicting the outcome of a case.

The general approach of these models may be described in the following way [17]:

1. Selection of a set of related cases.
2. Definition of a set of descriptors by which the selected cases can be described.
3. Indexing of the cases using the set of descriptors.
4. Definition of a correspondence function which relates the descriptors as independent variables to the judicial decision as dependent variable.
5. Evaluation of the results to gain criteria for the decision of the new case.

Applying these models to actual legal cases has given the following results. The selection of cases determines the definition of descriptors and the usefulness of the procedure. The more heterogeneous the cases the less concrete the descriptors and the less useful the model. An important assumption is usually that the descriptors compensate each other, that means no descriptor alone suffices to determine the decision. Each 'positive' value of a descriptor may be compensated by negative values of other descriptors. In most models the descriptors are binary variables: a certain condition applies to a given legal case or does not apply. The dependent variable, i.e., the judicial decision is usually also binary, that is pro or contra.

For the definition of a correspondence function different methods are used: multiple regression, discriminant analysis, linear programming, etc. A very simple but useful procedure is the so-called nearest neighbor method. Its basic assumption is that 'similar' cases are to be decided similarly.

Therefore a dissimilarity measure measuring the dissimilarity between legal cases is constructed.

The most simple model may be described formally in the following way:

Let $C_1, C_2, ..., C_m$ be a set of related cases. Each case C_i can be described by a vector $(x_{i1}, x_{i2}, ..., x_{in})$ with

$$x_{ij} = \begin{cases} 1 \text{ if the } j\text{th descriptor applies to } C_i \\ 0 \text{ else} \end{cases}$$

A simple dissimilarity measure between C_i, C_k is the Hamming distance

$$d(C_i, C_k) = \sum_{j=1}^{n} |x_{ij} - x_{kj}| .$$

To decide a new case C_o we seek $\min_i d(C_i, C_o)$, that is we look for the case that is most similar to C_o. The decision of this case is the best estimation for the decision of C_o.

As an illustration of the validity of the methods of predicting judicial decisions an investigation of 64 Canadian cases of capital gains dating from the years 1958 to 1968 may be cited [18]: of the 64 cases the number of wrong estimations was 4 using the nearest neighbor method, 7 using linear programming and 4 using experts' opinions. This investigation shows that the used formal models equal roughly the rate of precision derived from experts' opinions.

5. A Legal Cybernetics' Model of Judicial Decision

In continental Europe the standard procedure of judicial decisions is different. Here the judge compares the facts of the case with the legal norms laid down in statutes. Although the contents of a legal norm have to be clarified and made precise by applying judicial decisions and technical juristic literature nevertheless the primary source is the legal norm. Its standard form may be described as "if A then ought B". The condition A, referred to in German as 'Tatbestand' usually can be decomposed in several elements $A_1, A_2, ..., A_m$. The legal norm then becomes "if $A_1 \wedge A_2 \wedge ... \wedge A_m$ then ought B".

The judicial reasoning comparing the facts of the case (in German 'Sachverhalt') with the legal norm is usually termed 'subsumption'. In subsuming the facts of the case under the legal norm the following difficulty arises: The elements of the 'Tatbestand' are represented linguistically by predicators. That is to say, the standard form of a legal norm can be written in a more precise way as

"$\forall x$ if $(x \in A_1) \land (x \in A_2) \land ... \land (x \in A_m)$ then ought B",

where x represents the facts of the case.

Because of the general character of legal norms the predicators are often rather vague, e.g., 'darkness', 'noise', 'danger'. In these cases x cannot be said to be either A_i or be non-A_i, rather x may be, so to speak, 'more or less' A_i. The philosopher Carl G. Hempel uses in this context the term 'type' instead of logical concept to indicate the degree by which A_i may be fulfilled [19].

In formalizing judicial decisions as they take place in the continental European countries we have therefore to keep in mind that the predicators used in legal norms are frequently types. An adequate formalization can therefore not be found by using the ordinary theory of sets where there are only the possibilities of $x \in A_i$ or $x \notin A_i$.

A promising possibility is however supplied by the theory of fuzzy sets which has been developed by Lofti A. Zadeh since 1965 [20]. A fuzzy set may be defined in the following way: Let X be a set of objects then a fuzzy set A in X is defined by a characteristic function $f_A(x)$, which associates with each object in X a real number in the interval $[0,1]$, with the value of $f_A(x)$ at x representing the 'grade of membership' of x in A. Thus, the nearer the value of $f_A(x)$ to unity the higher the grade of membership of x in A. When A is a set in the ordinary sense of the term, its membership function can take on only two values 0 and 1, with $f_A(x) = 1$ or 0 according as x does or does not belong to A.

Every fuzzy set may be interpreted as the extent of a vague predicator. The elements x are facts of the case that are to be subsumed under an element A_i of the legal norm. The problem of practical application of fuzzy set theory to judicial decisions consists in the definition of interpersonal procedures to determine $f_{A_i}(x)$ and in the selection of a threshold a_i. Because of the necessity of binary judgement —an element of the legal norm A_i is fulfilled by x or not—a dichotomy is necessary, i.e.

$\forall x \, f_{A_i}(x) \geq a_i \quad A_i$ is 'fulfilled'

$\forall x \, f_{A_i}(x) < a_i \quad A_i$ is 'not fulfilled'.

The problem of selecting an appropriate threshold may be illustrated by the following example. Let us assume the predicator 'forest' is one-dimensional and may be measured by the number of trees [21]. If a hypothetical legal definition stated 'forest' means

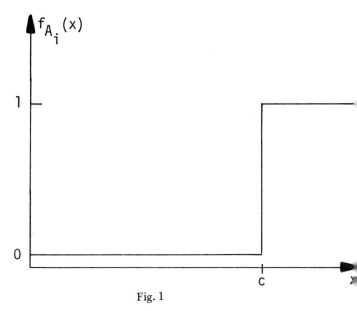

Fig. 1

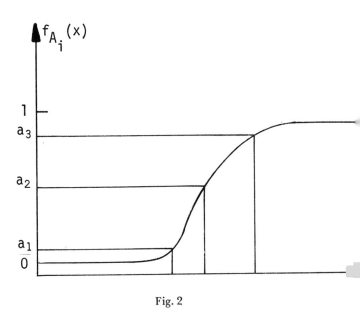

Fig. 2

'more than c trees' the corresponding characteristic function would be as in Fig. 1. If no such definition is available as it is in the general case the corresponding characteristic function is as in Fig. 2. Different thresholds a_1, a_2, a_3 lead to different decisions.

Considering the characteristic function and threshold for every element A_i the standard form of a legal norm becomes [22]

"$\forall x$ if $(f_{A_1}(x) \geq a_1) \land (f_{A_2}(x) \geq a_2) \land ...$

$... \land (f_{A_m}(x) \geq a_m)$ then ought B".

Let us end the discussion of this model by remarking that it is assumed here that the judge examines each element of the 'Tatbestand' separately and from this examination rules whether the legal norm applies to the facts of the case. Alternative strategies are possible. One would be the following. The judge weighs the importance of each element and defines a characteristic function for the 'Tatbestand' $f_A(x)$, e.g., $f_A(x) = w_1 f_{A_1}(x) + w_2 f_{A_2}(x) + ...$

$... + w_m \cdot f_{A_m}(x)$, with $w_i \geqslant 0$ and $w_1 + w_2 + ... + w_m = 1$.

The w_i would in this case be weights to indicate the importance of each element. In this model the legal norm would apply $\forall x \, f_A(x) \geqslant a$.

Which of these models corresponds better to reality has not yet been tested. It would seem that the first model would be suited better to explaining legal positivism whereas the second model would correspond to a hermeneutic point of view.

6. Concluding remarks

In this Chapter some examples of possible applications of General Systems Theory to legal research have been discussed. It is clear that at the present moment they are only tentative approaches. A lot of empirical research will have to take place until the formal models will help to guide actions to improve the functions of the Legal System. Nevertheless General Systems Theory seems to be an appropriate starting point for endeavors in this direction.

References

1. LOEVINGER, L., 'Jurimetrics. The next step forward', *Minnesota Law Review*, p. 455 (1949).
2. Cf. BAADE, H. (ed.), *Jurimetrics*, New York-London (1963).
3. The denotation 'Lawtomation' was proposed in 1963 by P.S. Hoffman. Cf. HOFFMAN, P.S., 'Lawtomation in Legal Research: some indexing problems', *Modern Uses of Logic in Law* 4 (1963).
4. Cf. Standard Committee on Law and Technology, Computers and the Law, American Bar Association, 2nd ed. (1971).
5. Cf. 'Pour une organisation nationale de l'information juridique', Rapport du groupe de travail pour l'informatique juridique constitué à l'initiative de l'unpl et du cnipe, Courbevoie, Paris (1970).
6. LOSANO, M.G., 'La juricybernétique', *Diogène* (1971).
7. LOSANO, M.G., 'L'informatica giuridica in Italia', *Il Ponte* 4, p. 600 (1969).
8. LOSANO, M.G., *Giuscibernetica, Macchine e modelli cibernetici nel diritto*, Torino (1969).
9. STEINMÜLLER, W., *EDV und Recht*, Berlin (1970). HAFT, F., *Elektronische Datenverarbeitung im Recht*, Berlin (1970).
10. FIEDLER, H., 'Automatisierung im Recht und juristische Informatik', *Juristische Schulung*, pp. 432, 552, 603 (1970); *Juristische Schulung*, pp. 67, 228 (1971). REISINGER, L., 'Rechtsinformatik. Die Probleme einer jungen Wissenschaft', *Mitteilungsblatt der österreichischen Gesellschaft für Statistik und Informatik*, p. 78 (1972).
11. PODLECH, A., 'Rechtskybernetik—eine juristische Disziplin der Zukunft', *Juristenjahrbuch*, p. 157 (1969/70).
12. Cf. especially BERTALANFFY, L.v., 'General systems theory', *General Systems* (1962). LANGE, O., *Wholes and Parts. A General Theory of System Behavior*, Oxford (1965). MESAROVIĆ, M.D. (ed.), *Views on General Systems Theory*, New York (1964).
13. Cf. REISINGER, L., 'Möglichkeiten der Gesetzesprognose', *Datenverarbeitung im Recht* 4 (1973). REISINGER, L., 'Überlegungen zur Formalisierung im Recht', *Datenverarbeitung in Steuer, Wirtschaft und Recht* 2 (1974).
14. Cf. ZIELINSKI, D., 'Das Juristische Informationssystem', *Datenverarbeitung im Recht* 1, p. 63 (1973). Bundesministerium der Justiz (ed.), *Das Juristische Informationssystem. Analyse, Planung, Vorschläge*, p. 32, Karlsruhe (1972).
15. Cf. for the German speaking countries STADLER, G., 'Benutzerforschung vor der Anwendung der EDV im Rechtsbereich', *Wiener Beiträge zur elektronischen Erschliessung der Information im Recht* (edit. by F. Lang and F. Bock), p. 73, IBM-Österreich, Wien (1973). Informationsverhalten und Informationsbedarf von Juristen. Eine Erhebung von Infratest Sozialforschung, München, im Auftrag des Bundesministeriums der Justiz und der Gesellschaft für Mathematik und Datenverarbeitung. Datenverarbeitung im Recht —Beiheft 2, Berlin (1974).
16. Cf. KORT, F., 'Predicting the Supreme Court decisions mathematically: a quantitative analysis of the "right-to-Counsel" cases', *American Political Science Review* 51 (1957). KORT, F., 'Analysis of judicial opinions and rules of law', *Judicial Decision-Making* (edit. by G.A. Schubert), New York (1963). LAWLOR, R.C., 'Fact content analysis and precedent—a modern theory of precedent', *Jurimetrics Journal* (1972).

17. Cf. MacKAAY, E. and ROBILLARD, P., 'Predicting judicial decisions: the nearest neighbor rule and visual representation of case pattern', Université de Montréal, p. 2 (1973). REISINGER, L., 'Überlegungen zur Formalisierung im Recht II', *Datenverarbeitung in Steuer, Wirtschaft und Recht* 3, p. 89 (1974).

18. LAWLOR, R.C., 'Fact content analysis and precedent', *op. cit.*

19. HEMPEL, C.G. and OPPENHEIM, P., *Der Typusbegriff im Lichte der neuen Logik*, Leiden (1936). HEMPEL, C.G., 'Typological methods in the social sciences', *Theorie und Realität. Ausgewählte Aufsätze zur Wissenschaftslehre der Sozialwissenschaften* (edit. by H. Albert), Tübingen, p. 194 (1964).

20. Cf. ZADEH, L.A., 'Fuzzy sets', *Information and Control* 8, p. 338 (1965). ZADEH, L.A., 'Quantitative fuzzy semantics', *Information Sciences* 3, p. 1 (1970).

21. Clearly in reality this is not the case as 'forest' has several dimensions. Cf. PODLECH, A., 'Wertungen und Werte im Recht', *Archiv für öffentliches Recht* 95, Heft 2, p. 214.

22. Cf. REISINGER, L., *Die automatisierte Messung juristischer Begriffe*, Berlin (1973).

Systemtheorie als theoretische Grundlage der Rechtsinformatik

HANSJÜRGEN GARSTKA and WILHELM STEINMÜLLER
University Regensburg, Germany

1. Zum Gegenstandsbereich der Rechtsinformatik

Aufgabe der Rechtsinformatik ist,

- Bedingungen und Folgen der Ersetzung bestimmter, beim juristischen Entscheidungsprozeß beteiligter, bislang vom Menschen wahrgenommener Funktionen von Automaten zu untersuchen,
- unter juristischem Aspekt die Veränderungen zu würdigen, die der Einsatz von Automaten an den gesellschaftlichen Informationsstrukturen bewirkt.

Eine Gegenüberstellung dieser beiden Aspekte zeigt, daß die Einheit des Gegenstandsbereiches der Rechtsinformatik nicht hergestellt wird durch ein einheitliches Vorgehen: beide Aspekte verlangen vielmehr eine kategorial verschiedene Argumentationsweise. Auf der einen Seite stehen Aussagen über das Vorliegen oder die Möglichkeit bestimmter Sachverhalte, mithin Beschreibungen, Erklärungen, Prognosen, auf der anderen Seite Alternativen juristischer Bewertungen von Sachverhalten, mithin normative Sätze.

Die Einheit wird vielmehr hergestellt durch einen einheitlichen Problemzusammenhang: die theoretische Bewältigung der Konfrontation einer technischen Entwicklung, hier der Verfügbarmachung von Automaten für einen Bereich geistiger Tätigkeit, mit einem Gesellschaftsbereich, dessen Funktion in einem engen Zusammenhang mit der Konstituierung der jeweiligen Gesellschaft selbst stehen.

Bereits aus diesem Ansatz ergibt sich, daß die Verbalisierung von Forschungsanliegen und -ergebnissen einen terminologischen Rahmen erfordert, der auf einer sehr abstrakten Ebene angesiedelt ist. Interpretiert mit informationswissenschaftlichen Inhalten, stellt die Systemtheorie unserer Meinung nach einen solchen Rahmen zur Verfügung.

Dies soll im folgenden an Hand einer präziseren Darstellung des Ausgangspunktes rechtsinformatischer Forschungen erläutert werden.

2. Recht als informationsverarbeitendes System

So verstanden, muß Rechtsinformatik zunächst einen Systemzusammenhang konzipieren, innerhalb dessen das Recht und die es konstituierenden Prozesse einerseits, die Automaten, die in rechtliche Zusammenhänge eingreifen, andererseits verortet werden können.

Das umfassende System, dessen Subsysteme an diesem Zusammenhang beteiligt sind, ist die Gesellschaft: dies bedarf keiner näheren Darlegung, Der Versuch, das Recht als Subsystem der Gesellschaft dazustellen, scheitert dagegen zunächst an der Vieldeutigkeit von "Recht": Von einer losgelösten "Idee" über die Menge aller Rechtssätze bis hin zu einer Menge von in der Gesellschaft durch besondere Stellung ausgezeichneten Personen können die verschiedensten Phänomene mit "Recht" bezeichnet werden.

Aus den beiden Möglichkeiten, den Gesamtkomplex dieser Phänomene, welche Wirklichkeitsbereiche auch immer er durchziehen mag, mit "Recht" zu bezeichnen, und der Auswahl eines einzigen Aspektes soll im folgenden die zweite gewählt werden: Recht soll das jenige Subsystem der Gesellschaft sein, das juristische Entscheidungen fällt und mit Hilfe solcher Entscheidungen auf die Gesellschaft (und damit auch auf sich selbst) regelnd einwirkt.

Damit ist zwar ein konkret festmachbares Subsystem der Gesellschaft gewonnen, die Frage seiner Abgrenzung aber auf die Frage verdrängt, was eine juristische Entscheidung ist. So elementar diese Frage ist, so ungeklärt scheint sie uns. Für die Rechtsinformatik wichtig ist jedoch ein unstrittiger Punkt: in die juristische Entscheidung geht ein besonderer Typ von Informationen ein, die sich um einen Kernbestand, den positiven Rechtsnormen, gruppieren, und deren Entstehung und Funktion sich nur mit Hilfe soziologischer Kategorien darlegen läßt. Für den Juristen stellen sich diese "juristischen Informationen" dar als ein Korpus schriftlich fixierter Regeln, die im Zuge bestimmter legitimierender Verfahren (z.B. Gesetzgebung, Rechtsprechung, wissenschaftliche Publikationen) erstellt werden. Manche dieser Verfahren unterliegen ihrerseits Restriktionen durch juristische Informationen, sind damit ihrerseits juristische Entscheidungsprozesse.

Entscheidungsprozesse sind Prozesse, in deren Verlauf Informationen verarbeitet werden—die Art und Weise dieser Verarbeitung unterliegt bestimmten Gesetzmäßigkeiten, die vom Entscheidungstyp abhängen: so weisen juristische Entscheidungsprozesse eine typische Struktur von Informationsverarbeitungsprozessen auf, die sich wiederum nach der konkreten Art der justistischen Entscheidung differenzieren läßt.

Damit kann Recht bestimmt werden als ein System einander überlagernder informationsverarbeitender Instanzen (Rechtsinstanzen), in die juristische Informationen als ausschlaggebende Größen eingehen (wobei unter Instanzen solche Elemente eines Systems verstanden werden sollen, deren Verhalten sich als Informationsverarbeitung charakterisieren läßt).

Rechtsinstanzen wirken aufeinander sowie auf die übrigen Subsysteme der Gesellschaft mit Hilfe der bei juristischen Entscheidungsprozessen gewonnenen Informationen (die ihrerseits wiederum juristische Informationen sind) ein. Diese Einwirkung läßt sich

darstellen als Regelungsprozeß: Die jeweiligen Entscheidungsergebnisse sind Stellgrößen, die bezüglich des beeinflußten Systems bestimmte Zustände herstellen. Diese Zustände lassen sich mit Hilfe einzelner Regelgrößen charakterisieren. Die Veränderung dieser Größen wird nach jeder Entscheidung beobachtet und als Grundlage einer evt. nötigen Korrektur der Entscheidung verwendet, die evt. auch von einer übergeordneten Instanz vorgenommen werden kann: das Regelungssystem des Rechts wird dadurch multistabil.

Recht als gesellschaftliches Subsystem wird auf dieser Grundlage faßbar für die Rechtsinformatik durch die Betrachtung der informationellen Koppelungen, die mit den anderen Subsystemen bestehen, und die auch die einzelnen Instanzen des Rechtssystems selbst verbinden. Das Verhalten des Rechtssystems läßt sich darstellen als Aufeinanderfolge einzelner Phasen der Informationsverarbeitung, deren konkrete Ausgestaltung Ausgangspunkt für die rechtsinformatischen Forschungen ist.

3. Recht und Informationssysteme
Automation im Recht bedeutet die Ersetzung bestimmter Informationsverarbeitungsprozesse, die bei juristischen Entscheidungen anfallen, durch die Funktionen von Automaten. Dieser Vorgang läßt sich darstellen als die Verselbständigung einzelner, bisher untergeordneter Systeme, zu Systemen gleicher Stufe. Der juristischen Instanz, die bisher als einheitliches System betrachtet werden mußte (z.B. der Richter, der Sachbearbeiter) tritt ein verselbständigtes System gegenüber, an das einzelne Funktionen übertragen sind.

Bei der Betrachtung dieser verselbständigten Systeme ist der Begriff des Informationssystem von ausschlaggebender Bedeutung.

Zwischen Entscheidungsinstanz und verselbständigtem System (Automat) bestehen informationelle Koppelungen derart, daß der Automat an die Entscheidungsinstanz bestimmte Informationen liefert, die im weiteren Verlauf der Entscheidung wieder durch die (ursprüngliche) Entscheidungsinstanz verarbeitet werden. Zweck des verselbständigten Systems ist damit die Bereitstellung von Informationen, die im Rahmen eines Entscheidungsprozesses benötigt werden. Solche Systeme werden Informationssysteme (i.e.S.) bezeichnet. Sind die Informationssysteme durch Automaten realisiert (automatisierte Informationssysteme; die Rechtsinformatik beschäftigt sich nur mit diesen), erfolgt diese Bereitstellung selbständig, d.h. das Informationssystem sucht ohne weitere Beeinflussung durch einen menschlichen Bearbeiter auf Grund einer bestimmten "Suchfrage" die benötigte Information aus der Menge der gespeicherten Informationen heraus.

Dieser Bestimmung steht eine weitere gegenüber. Sie berücksichtigt, daß die Bereitstellung von Informationen (und auch schon ihre Speicherung) nicht ohne Einbeziehung des Benutzers (desjenigen, der aus dem Informationssystem Informationen bezieht) untersucht werden kann.

Dies läßt sich aus der Funktion von Informationen überhaupt erklären: Informationen geben Sachverhalte wieder, die in bestimmten Entscheidungssituationen eine Rolle spielen. Informationen treten für den Entscheider an die Stelle des realen oder ideellen Sachverhalts. Sie konstituieren damit Modelle des wiedergegebenen Sachverhaltsbereiches, z.B. des jeweiligen Realitätsausschnittes. Jedes Modell muß im Zusammenhang mit dem Verhaltenssystem gesehen werden, für das es erstellt wurde; nur so kann seine Funktion erklärt, nur so kann ein Modell auch konstruiert werden. Dies gilt aber auch für Informationen.

In Informationssystemen (i.e.S.) werden Informationen gespeichert und zur Verfügung gestellt: es werden somit Modelle einer irgend wie gearteten Realität verwertet, die nicht unabhängig vom jeweiligen Benutzer gesehen werden können. Diese Abhängigkeit wird dadurch zum Ausdruck gebracht, daß Benutzer und Informationssystem (i.e.S.) als ein übergreifendes System, ein Informationssystem (i.w.S.) betrachtet werden, das wegen des Einbezugs eines (mehrerer) Automaten zu einem Mensch-Maschine-Kommunikationssystem wird.

4. Rechtliche Regelung von Informationsstrukturen in der Gesellschaft

Auch der zweite Aspekt rechtsinformatischer Forschungen läßt sich auf eine systemtheoretische Betrachtung gründen.

Sie geht davon aus, daß konstante Informationsprozesse, die zwischen einzelnen Mitgliedern und Subsystemen der Gesellschaft ablaufen, eine die jeweilige Gesellschaft kennzeichnende Struktur bilden, die Informationsstruktur.

Diese Informationsstruktur wird in entscheidendem Ausmaß vom Recht geprägt: zum einen unterliegt auch sie als gesellschaftliche Struktur der rechtlichen Regelung, ist also durch auf Grund juristischer Entscheidungen gewonnener juristischer Informationen konstituiert und gesichert; zum anderen trägt die Art, in der sich juristische Entscheidungen vollziehen,

zur konkreten Ausgestaltung der Informationsstruktur bei.

Der Einsatz informationsverarbeitender Automaten in der Gesellschaft führt zu einem tiefgreifenden Wandel der Informationsstrukturen. So macht z.B. der Aufbau umfassender Informationssysteme, in die sowohl die für die öffentliche Verwaltung als auch die für die Privatwirtschaft wichtigen Informationen tendenziell komplett eingehen können, eine Art der Informationsweitergabe und -sammlung möglich, wie sie bislang technisch nicht möglich war.

Das rechtliche Regelsystem muß auf diese Entwicklung reagieren: Dies ist aber insbesondere deswegen ein hochkomplexes Problem, weil die juristischen Entscheidungen selbst wegen der auch bei ihnen durchgeführten Automation einem analogen Wandel der Informationsstruktur unterliegen. Es erscheint möglich, diese Komplexität mit Hilfe systemtheoretischer Überlegungen begrifflich zu erfassen und damit auch die erstrebte rechtliche Regelung in die Wege zu leiten.

Abstract

Systematic theory as a theoretical basis of a system of processing legal information
Hansjürgen Garstka and Willhelm Steinmüller

The Chapter gives a theoretical discussion and definition of the aims of a system of processing legal information. Evaluation is made from the legal point of view of changes effected by the use of machinery to the social information structure. Examination is made of the conditions and consequences of the substitution of certain functions of machinery involved in the legal process. Presentation is made of the systematic theory with a precise description of the starting-point in the research of processing of legal information.

Consideration is given to law as a system for processing information.

Law and information systems are discussed.

Kritik systemtheoretischer Machtanalysen

Dr ERICH HOEDL
Institut für Makro- und Strukturplanung,
Technische Hochschule, Darmstadt, BRD

Die Leistungsfähigkeit systemtheoretisch-kybernetischer Analysen für die empirische Forschung ist kaum kontrovers. Darüber hinaus wird von der Systemtheorie jedoch nachdrücklich der Anspruch einer *universellen* [1] Anwendbarkeit auf alle sozial-ökonomischen Probleme gestellt und mit der generellen Übertragbarkeit des Systemkonzeptes auf beliebige Fragestellungen begründet. Daß dieser Anspruch methodisch und inhaltlich nicht eingelöst wird, läßt sich an einem Zentralpunkt der Sozialwissenschaften zeigen: dem *Herrschaftsproblem.*

Der Herrschaftsbegriff wird in der neueren Systemtheorie als veraltet und für die "Leistungsgesellschaft" als unbrauchbar erklärt. [2] Die Tatsache der Über- und Unterordnung in sozialen Systemen wird damit freilich nicht bestritten, sondern deren Analyse an partiellen Machtrelationen und nicht am System als ganzen vorgenommen. Soweit die Systemtheorie am Gesamtsystem—also an ihrem ursprünglichen Gegenstand—ansetzt, wird Herrschaft nur durch Beobachtung und Messung empirisch erfaßt und damit nicht erklärt. Der kategoriale Apparat reicht nicht aus um die Vorbedingungen der Entstehung individueller Machtpositionen aus dem Gesamtsystem kausal zu erklären.

Der "Herrschaftskonformismus" [3] der Systemtheorie besteht methodisch in der empiristischen und daher metatheoretischen Position, die eine strenge Trennung von Wissenschaft und Politik impliziert. Inhaltlich ergibt sich daraus eine "wertfreie" Analyse, obwohl die Parteinahme der Wissenschaft für den Fortschritt beteuert wird. Die Herrschaftsanalyse kann aber dieses verbale Zugeständnis nicht unbefragt lassen, weil sie—da Theorie auch ein Machtfaktor ist—gerade die streng theoretische Beurteilung zu liefern hat, in welcher Richtung bestimmte Forschungsarbeiten die Praxis beeinflussen. [4] Wenn von der hinreichend gesicherten Erkenntnis ausgegangen wird, daß eine höchst ungleiche Machtverteilung in der Gesellschaft vorliegt, dann müßte eine Parteinahme für die Beherrschten nicht problematisch sein. Die Verlagerung von mehr Macht zu den gegenwärtig Beherrschten muß mit dem Fortschritt zusammenfallen, weil deren Eigenbestimmung dadurch erweitert wird. Würden wissenschaftliche Analysen des Herrschaftssystems geliefert, dann könnte auch gezeigt werden, daß durch solche Forschungsarbeit keine diskontinuierlichen Entwicklungen eingeleitet, sondern eher verhindert werden. Die theoretische Analyse der Herrschaft ist von ihrem Gegenstand her notwendig parteiisch und dies mag ein Grund für die Ablehnung des Herrschaftsbegriffes in der Systemtheorie sein. Es läßt sich anderseits nachweisen, daß auch in der Umgehung der Herrschaftsanalyse durch partielle Machtanalysen die theoretische Frage der Parteinahme ausgeklammert wird, dadurch nicht nur erst recht eine Parteinahme erfolgt, sondern darüber hinaus auch im objektivistischen Sinne kaum etwas erklärt wird. Dazu sind der Macht- und Herrschaftsbegriff zu

Progress in Cybernetics and Systems Research, Volume 2

präzisieren.

M. Weber [5] hat Macht als die Chance definiert, seinen eigenen Willen auch gegen Widerstreben anderer durchzusetzen, gleichviel worauf diese Chance beruht. Herrschaft ist ein genauerer Begriff, der die Machtbeziehungen zwischen angebbaren Personen hinsichtlicher bestimmter Inhalte nennt. Sie kann also nur innerhalb eines bekannten sozialen Systems festgestellt werden. Wenn in einem sozialen System der Herrschaftsaspekt untersucht werden soll, dann kann dafür der Machtbegriff verwendet werden. Das Herrschaftssystem ist dann die Gesamtheit der Machtbeziehungen, die in dem System institutionalisiert sind. Die Herrschaftsanalyse kann also als Machtanalyse geführt werden, allerdings leistet die formale Machtdefinition erst etwas, wenn sie auf das *System* bezogen wird, d.h. die Analyse sich nicht auf Zweck-Mittel-Relation konzentriert, sondern auf die Interaktion der Subjekte und daher den Konfrontationsprozeß gegensätzlicher Machtinteressen. Die Analyse der Herrschaft mit Hilfe des Machtbegriffes ist nur durchführbar, wenn von den *Gegensätzen* ausgegangen wird. [6] Daraus ergeben sich zumindest 3 Aspekte für die Machtanalyse.

a) Die Macht*ausübung* eines Subjektes (Personen, Institutionen usw.) ist immer gleich der Macht*ausübung* der betroffenen Subjekte. Dieses dem physikalischen Kraft-Gegenkraft Prinzip analoge Verhältnis wird dadurch verkompliziert, daß zumindest ein beteiligtes Subjekt seine Macht nicht voll ausspielen muß um das Gleichgewicht zu halten. Die *manifeste* Macht ist für dieses Subjekt geringer als die *latente*. Die manifeste Macht entspricht der (ausgeübten) Gewalt [7] und die latente der Machtpotenz oder Macht im strengen Sinne.

b) Die Veränderungen der Machtbeziehungen können sich auf die Verlagerung unter den Herrschenden beschränken, ohne die Machtverhältnisse unter den Beherrschten zu berühren. Diese *horizontale* Verlagerung unterscheidet sich von der *vertikalen*, die die Positionen der Beherrschten gegenüber den Herrschenden verändert. Gesellschaftlicher Fortschritt im machttheoretischen Sinne kann sich nur durch eine vertikale Verlagerung nach unten vollziehen.

c) Subjekt und Objekt einer Machtbeziehung können nur *Menschen* sein und daher ist der Begriff der "Sachherrschaft" widersinnig. Sachen können zwar die Handlungen der Menschen einschränken, aber hinter diesen Sachen stehen immer Menschen, die aus der Sachkonstellation Vorteile ziehen, obwohl sie auch von den gleichen Sachen eingeschränkt werden können. Sobald die Sachkonstellation selbst den Herrschenden nur einen geringen Handlungsspiel-

raum läßt, ist das Herrschaftssystem irrational geworden und historisch überlebt.

Mit diesen Präzisierungen des Machtbegriffes läßt sich überprüfen, ob die systemtheoretischen Machtkonzepte das Machtproblem selbst und darüber hinaus das Herrschaftsproblem erfassen können.

Mit Hilfe der Kybernetik ist versucht worden, das Herrschaftsproblem unmittelbar zu analysieren, allerdings primär nur in Anwendung des Regelungskonzeptes. [8] Ziel der Analyse ist, mittels verbesserter Informationen eine *Stabilisierung* des Systems zu erreichen. Die kybernetische Analyse wird daher als Bewußtseinsanalyse verstanden, die in einem sich selbst kontrollierenden System auf die Verbesserung des "Selbstbewußtseins" zielt. Die "reflexiven Mechanismen" [9] bieten jedoch keine Gewähr, für eine systemrationale Stabilisierung, denn nicht nur das Bewußtsein, sondern auch die Organisationsform und die Eigentumsverhältnisse können einer Veränderung entgegenstehen. [10]

Die Herrschenden können zwar ein Bewußtsein über die Notwendigkeit systemrationaler Veränderungen haben, sind aber kaum bereit ihre partiellen zweckrationalen Handlungen darauf abzustimmen. Solange sie in einem Konkurrenzverhältnis stehen, würde ihre Macht ohnedies den Konkurrenten zufallen (z.B. Konzentration in der Wirtschaft) und das Gesamtsystem kaum verändert werden. Eine vertikale Machtverlagerung tritt nicht ein und die Konkurrenz unter den Herrschenden wirkt tendenziell auf die Erhöhung der traditionellen Leistungen (z.B. Notwendigkeit des Wirtschaftswachstums), die den Herrschenden selbst aufgezwungen wird. Unter diesen Bedingungen müssen die Herrschenden ihre Macht gegenüber den Beherrschten möglicherweise vorsichtig ausüben, damit deren Leistungsfähigkeit durch die Machtausübung nicht zu weit eingeschränkt wird, denn die Stabilität des Gesamtsystems hängt wesentlich von den Leistungen der Beherrschten ab. Die Macht*ausübung* der Herrschenden und Beherrschten ist dabei zwar gleich groß, jedoch die *latente* Macht der Herrschenden ist definitionsgemäß größer und deshalb liegt die Möglichkeit einer alternativen Stabilisierungspolitik primär bei den Herrschenden. Sofern die Differenz zwischen latenter und manifester Macht bei den Herrschenden größer ist als bei den Beherrschten bringt eine kybernetische Bewußtseinsanalyse vor allem den Herrschenden einen strategischen Vorteil. Die kybernetische Machtanalyse ist in diesem Falle also eine Theorie für die Herrschenden, die inhaltlich auch die Sollwerte festlegen können. Das Erkenntnisinteresse der Beherrschten kann sogar prinzipiell nicht an der Stabilisierung liegen, sondern nur an der Bestimmung ihrer latenten, also noch nicht ausgeschöpften Macht. Für sie ist die Stabilität ein zweitrangiges Ziel, das nach dem Interesse an einer vertikalen Machtverlagerung steht.

Die Bestimmung der latenten Macht gewinnt auch für die Herrschenden an Bedeutung, sobald ihr Handlungsspielraum geringer wird. In *Krisenzeiten* können sie das System gerade noch oder nicht mehr kontrollieren, sodaß für alle Subjekte eine unerwünschte Situation eintritt. Diese "Lernpathologie" des Systems ist nicht mit Hilfe der Analyse manifester, sondern nur der latenten Macht antizipierbar. Die rationale vertikale Umschichtung kann kontinuierlicher, wenngleich nicht ohne Konfrontationen erfolgen. Zur bewußten Steuerung dieser Machtprozesse kann die empiristische Analyse wenig beitragen, weil die an der Oberfläche erscheinenden manifeste Macht mit dem latenten Machtpotential nicht in Verbindung gebracht wird. Die Fixierung der Systemtheorie auf die manifeste Macht drückt sich am schärfsten in der Ablehnung der Klassenanalyse—die eine Analyse latenter Macht sein muß—zugunsten der deskriptiven Schichtenanalyse aus. Der empiristische Ansatz verschließt der Systemtheorie sogar ihr eigenes Ziel einer rationalen Stabilisierung.

Die Betonung der manifesten Macht führt notwendig zum Meßproblem. [11] Die Auswahl der Subjekte, deren Macht festgestellt werden soll wird aber wiederum nicht theoretisch aus dem gesamten Herrschaftssystem abgeleitet, sondern eine plausible Auswahl von Subjekten—oft nach politischer Opportunität—getroffen. Die Aggregatbildung kann zu einem statistischen Ausgleich von unterschiedlich Beherrschten führen oder machtrelevante Variable überhaupt vernachlässigen. Die Eigentumsverhältnisse sind beispielsweise in der Systemtheorie nahe vollständig ausgeklammert.

Die Messung von Macht wird vor allem auf die Veränderung in horizontaler Richtung eingeengt, worin sich die Vorstellung ausdrückt, daß die Machtanalyse nur dort geführt werden kann, wo Macht vorhanden ist. Daß es eher darum geht, Macht dorthin zu verlagern wo sie noch gering ist, wird durch die Datenorientierung verhindert.

Soweit die Messung der Veränderung der manifesten Macht von mächtigen Subjekten zur Diskussion steht sind einige geeignete Vorschläge gemacht worden. Die "wirksame" Macht eines Subjektes wird als Grad der Wahrscheinlichkeit der Beeinflussung eines anderen Subjektes hinsichtlich bestimmter Variabler verstanden. Die "wirksame" Macht ist dann die Differenz zwischen der Wahrscheinlichkeit der Be-

einflussung des anderen Subjektes und des eigenen. [12] In einer Konfrontation kann es vorteilhaft sein, die strategischen Variablen nicht voll auszuspielen oder zu wechseln. Die Konfrontation wird dann von den wichtigsten Variablen den sog. "Grundwerten" aus taktischen Überlegungen auf "Nebenwerte" verlegt [13] oder sogar ein Konsensus über die von den Kontrahenten erwünschten Vektoren von Grund- und Nebenwerten erreicht (Oligopolverhalten). Für alternative Vektoren können von den Subjekten Kostenüberlegungen [14]—diese schließen Kosten der Konfrontation und Gewinn durch die Ergebnisse ein—angestellt werden, aber die Akzentierung des Kostenaspektes zeigt, daß nur an mächtige Subjekte gedacht wird. Die Oligapolanalyse und insbesondere die Spieltheorie sind unter dieser Fragestellung konzipiert worden. Ein kostenoptimales Machtverhalten setzt einen Reichtum d.h. eine hinreichende Differenz zwischen latenter und manifester Macht voraus, die bei den Beherrschten nicht nur gering ist, sondern auch von den Herrschenden gesteuert werden kann. Restriktive Finanzierung oder mangelnde Ausbildung sind Beispiele machtpolitischer Variabler.

Die teilweise Verlagerung der Macht auf andere Variable ist in letzter Zeit unter einem anderen Aspekt erfaßt worden. Es wird nicht mehr der Vektor der Machtvariablen für ein Subjekt untersucht, sondern die mit einer Vektoränderung verbundene *Zirkulation* [15] der Macht. Obwohl das Modell als Fortschritt gepriesen wird, enthält es die bisher oberflächlichste Machtbetrachtung. Die Machtänderung wird nämlich von den Subjekten losgelöst und ganz analog behandelt wie in der ökonomischen Theorie die Warenzirkulation. Freilich wird die Entstehung der Macht, ebenso wie in der ökonomischen Theorie die Entstehung der Waren mitgedacht, aber dafür eben keine Theorie entwickelt. Der Hauptakzent liegt in der Analyse der Zirkulation, die nur mehr die *Folgen* der Machtprogresse erfaßt. Es werden weder die Konfrontationsprozesse analysiert, noch die bestehende Machtverteilung. Die Machtanalyse gibt nur die *Veränderungen* an und verfolgt das gleiche Ziel wie die Einkommensanalyse in der ökonomischen Theorie, die die Vermögenverteilung ausklammert. Die Machtanalyse endet also auch dort, wo das historisch vorgegebene Herrschaftssystem gar nicht mehr als Problem registriert wird.

Die Zirkulation von Macht kann überhaupt nicht ohne das dahinterstehende Herrschaftssystem verstanden werden. Macht kann nur in Bewegung geraten, wenn sich zumindest eines der beteiligten Subjekte im Herrschaftssystem hinreichend artikuliert hat und "abstützen" kann. Die Verankerung der

Subjekte im Herrschaftssystem ist einerseits die Voraussetzung zur Ausübung von Macht und andererseits konstituieren diese Subjekte das Herrschaftssystem. Weil aber die Subjekte ihre Macht nicht in jedem Falle ganz ausspielen, ist das Herrschaftssystem die Gesamtheit der latenten Macht. Der Begriff der latenten Macht läßt sich auf das Gesamtsystem nicht sinnvoll übertragen, weil hier Subjekt und Objekt zusammenfallen. Die Analyse der der Herrschaftsstruktur des Gesamtsystems läßt sich aber in gleicher Weise wie die der latenten Macht analytisch isolierter Partialsysteme durchführen.

In diesem einheitlichen Ansatz muß das Verhältnis der *Menschen untereinander* ins Zentrum gestellt werden. [16] Der begriff der Macht behält seine Bedeutung, weil sie nur zwischen Menschen ausgeübt werden kann. Die Vermengung von Menschen und Sachen, die in der Bildung von Aggregaten (Institutionen) konzeptionell angelegt ist, wird dann aufgelöst und die Hilfsfunktion der Sachen bei der Ausübung von Macht freigelegt. Von hier aus wird jede Sachkonstellation in bezug auf die Beherrschung von Menschen kritisierbar und durch die Analyse latenter Macht der Beherrschten deren Handlungsspielraum angebbar. Auch mit dieser Analyse wird nur ein Bewußtsein geschaffen und die tatsächlichen Veränderungen müssen von den Betrofenen selbst vorgenommen werden. [17] Der Ansatz ist aber mit dem der Systemtheorie nicht vergleichbar, weil dort nur von Partialsystemen ausgegangen und deren interne Herrschaftsstruktur als gegeben hingenommen wird. Jedes Partialsystem bezieht ihre Macht gegenüber anderen Subjekten nur von dieser internen Machtordnung und speziell von den Beherrschten. Diese haben in der Regel kein Interesse an einer Machtausübung gegenüber anderen Subjekten und werden durch die Herrschaftsstruktur diszipliniert.

Die Bedeutung der systemtheoretischen Machtanalyse liegt also in der Erfassung der von der Herrschaftsstruktur bedingten Macht*veränderungen*. Ihr Empirismus in bezug auf Machtprobleme schränkt sie vom Wissenschaftsbegriff her auf die Analyse der *Folgen* einer der Herrschaftsstruktur ein. Die Bestimmung des Ausmaßes der Macht und deren Verlagerung oder gar Zirkulation verdeckt die Beziehung zwischen den Menschen, zu deren Erfassung ein Konzept weitgehend ausgearbeitet ist: die *Arbeitswertlehre*. [18]

Wenn Arbeit eine Entäußerung des Menschen ist, dann lassen sich die Machtbeziehungen zwischen den Menschen an der Aneignung fremder Arbeit bestimmen. Historisch ergibt sich aus dieser Aneignung eine einseitige Akkumulation der "eingefrorenen" Arbeit, die dann als Sachkomplex zur weiteren Ausübung von Macht verwendet werden kann. Die Erklärung der Veränderungen der Sachkonstellation kann stets aus der, über die Arbeit definierten Beziehung zwischen den Menschen erfaßt werden und daraus auch die Machtausübung der Herrschenden auf die Beherrschten—stets am Maß der Aneignung fremder Arbeit, die im historischen Verlauf durch den Sachkomplex erschwert oder erleichtert werden kann.

Dieser Ansatz muß hier nicht weiter dargestellt werden. Es war nur zu zeigen, daß der systemtheoretische Ansatz nur an den historisch vorgegebenen Erscheinungen ansetzt, aber das dahinterliegende Herrschaftssystem, das nur von der Beziehung der Menschen untereinander erklärbar ist, ausklammert.

Fußnoten

1. HABERMAS, J., and LUHMANN, N., *Theorie der Gesellschaft oder Sozialtechnologie*, S. 378 ff., Frankfurt/M. (1971).
2. Ebenda, S. 398 ff.
3. Ebenda, S. 402 f.
4. Die Systemtheorie kann dazu nach eigener Einschätzung wenig Aussagen machen. LUHMANN, N., 'Die Praxis der Theorie', in: *Soziale Welt*, S. 129 ff.
5. WEBER, M., *Wirtschaft und Gesellschaft*, S. 28 f., Tübingen (1922).
6. Die Untersuchung der Beziehung zwischen der Machtanalyse und der dialektischen Methode steht noch aus.
7. BIERSTEDT, R., 'An analysis of social power', in: *American Sociological Review*, S. 730 ff. (1950).
8. SENGHAAS, D., 'Sozialkybernetik und Herrschaft', in: *Texte zur Technokratiediskussion* (edit. by C. Koch und D. Senghaas), S. 196 ff., Frankfurt/M. (1970).
9. LUHMANN, N., 'Reflexive Mechanismen', in: *Soziale Welt*, S. 1 ff. (1966).
10. HÖDL, E., *Das Problem sozial-ökonomischer Macht*, Darmstadt (1973) (Habilitationsschrift).
11. HARSANYI, I., 'The measurement of social power', in: *Behavioural Science* (1962/1).
12. DEUTSCH, K.W., *Politische Kybernetik*, S. 170 ff., Freiburg/B. (1970).
13. LASSWELL, H.D. and KAPLAN, A., *Power and Society*, S. 74 ff., New Haven (1950).
14. HARSANYI, I., The Measurement, a.a.O.
15. DEUTSCH, K.W., Politische, a.a.O., S. 178 ff. Eine ähnliche Perspektive enthalten die Elitetheorien.

16. Dazu vor allem die Diskussion um die "Techno-kratie": Koch, C., Senghaas, D. (Hrsg.), Texte, a.a.O.

17. MARX, K., 'Thesen über Feuerbach', in: *Marx-Engels I* (edit. by I. Fetscher), S. 139 ff., Frank-furt/M. (1966).

18. Zur Arbeitswertlehre und ihrer geschichtlichen Entwicklung: Stark, W., Die Geschichte der Volkswirtschaftslehre, Dordrecht/Holl. (1960).

ABSTRACT
Critique of systems-theoretical power and analyses
The paper cites 18 sources in this critique of power analysis. Efficiency of cybernetic approach to the problems is examined. Applicability to all social-economic problems and general transferrability of the systems concept is discussed. The social-power system is included in the paper and compared with other, newer concepts. Explanations delving into human relations are given.

Traffic noise, town planning and cybernetics

Dr A. SCHWARTZ and **Arch P. LEONOV**
Dr A. Schwartz & Co.,
Acoustical Consultants Ltd, Haifa, Israel

1. Introduction

Urban traffic and the noise nuisances it provides are in mutual relation with the general structure of the town: physical, social and demographic, economic, etc.

This study concentrates on the effects, both favorable and unfavorable, of motor traffic and its noises on urban activities.

The characteristics of traffic noises and their propagation, their sources, the ways of measuring them, their influence on human beings and the means of protection against them, are essential information for studying their effects.

These basic subjects were reviewed elsewhere [1, 2].

2. Dealing with traffic noise

The means to be adopted for reducing noise may be divided into three "levels":

1. Dealing with the source of the noise.
2. Treating the medium which conducts the noise from the source to the listener.
3. Insulating the listener.

In order to be able to act at any of these levels, various measures may be chosen such as the prediction of sensitive zones (the character of the traffic, noise levels, etc.), mechanical improvements and modifications (to vehicle parts, to the routing of roads, to the zone between the road and the buildings, to the fronts of the houses themselves, etc.), early specific and over-all planning (covering such subjects as through traffic, kinds of roads, separation of zones and their functions, screen construction, the layout of apartments and their orientation, etc.), or the enactment of laws and regulations (to limit vehicle noise, to circumscribe road traffic, to lay down maximum speeds, determine noise boundary values, impose fines, etc.). The most effective results will obviously be achieved by the simultaneous treatment of the three levels enumerated above.

2.1 Dealing with noise at its source

Attacking the problem by improving the vehicles involved will be the most promising procedure, since if successful this would damp the noise before it has had time to spread. However, long periods of intensive work are required for obtaining suitable modifications to different parts of the vehicles, so that this treatment is to be considered mainly as a long-term prospect. The principal systems to which such efforts are being directed are the engine, the air-intake and the exhaust of the burnt gases, and the braking system, with other mechanical parts following close behind, such as the friction between tyres and pavement, and aerodynamic noises.

When these items are being dealt with from the acoustical point of view, attention must be paid to the weakest link, that is to say the noisiest part, since any improvement achieved in the less obnoxious constituents will be of little practical value as long as the din from that one part blankets all the subsidiary ones.

Supervision of the traffic and the maintenance of its composition, density and speed, will be adjuvants in controlling the noise level. The aims mentioned are attained, among other means, by the control of points of departure and destination, the distribution of road junctions and traffic lights, the radii and banking angles of curves, facilities for stopping and parking en-route, the number of turnings from a given road, etc.

2.2 *The noise-conducting medium*
The treatment of the space intervening between the source of the noise and the person exposed to it usually involves the construction of the road along the bottom of a cutting, the utilization of the unbuilt zones lining urban highways (a proceeding that is not always practicable), and the exploitation of existing natural and other barriers or their creation for the purpose of inhibiting the propagation of the sound waves from their source to the ear of the listener.

The height of the road above the plane of the environment, or its depth below it, is a critical element in the magnitude of the noise spreading outward. The deeper the road below the general level of the environment, the smaller the noise propagated. The greatest effect is achieved by planting vegetation on the two slopes flanking the sunken road. Very poor results, on the other hand, derive from low parapets and the like along elevated highways.

Various factors affect the minimum clearance required between the roadside and an adjacent building. Of primary importance are such considerations as noise standards and the volume and speed of the traffic, while influences of the second order are exerted by such data as the height of the buildings, the type of development undergone by the environment, the layout of the soil and the plants, etc., on it, and other obstacles. These are factors usually determined by technical, economic and esthetic, considerations. The buffer zone must be increased

in width if the volume or the speed of the traffic increases or if the permissible noise level is reduced. Low houses protected by dense vegetation or other barriers to the propagation of sound may be placed nearer to the road than taller buildings the upper stories of which are exposed to the noise without intervening shields. When giving thought to the different alternatives of traffic noise protection to be provided for a high-rise building (such as distance, plantings, relatively low slopes lining the road, or a tall intervening structure), the closest proximity of the building to the road is, of course, achieved when a tall building serves as a screen between it and the road. In such tall buildings themselves, which are situated some distance from the road, the lower stories may benefit from lower noise levels thanks to the effects of noise absorption by the ground. Upper stories of high-rise buildings standing close to the roadside, on the other hand, will experience only a slight reduction in the noise level compared with that prevalent near the lower floors.

Seclusion from the effects of traffic noise may be achieved by certain earthworks, natural or artificial hills or slopes, existing buildings, masonry walls and, in certain instances, dense vegetation. The acoustical efficiency of the different sound barriers may reach considerable values—of the order of 20 dB(A), being a function of their mass, their height above the noise source and relative to the receiver, their distance from these two points, their continuity and length, the absorptive capacity for sound of their surfaces facing the source of the noise, the angle they form with respect to the source and to the receiver, and the existence of sound-reflecting objects in the area. When planning obstacles to sound propagation, certain characteristic data such as the stability of the structure, safety, a pleasing appearance, and the capacity to reflect sound back to the road, must be taken into account.

The over-all treatment of the environment from the aspect of acoustics will include the planned utilization of the different substructures in the town area and the consideration of given data, the direction of the traffic flow in accordance with such given conditions, the planning of the road network, road-widths, and the continuum of the vertical fronts alongside, and occasionally also a transfer of substructure utilization and its concentration in suitable localities, special treatment to be given to commercial centers where pedestrian traffic is particularly dense etc.

Since in a township most residential buildings are gathered in blocks or groups, the deflection of heavy vehicular traffic away from such areas will cause an immediate alleviation of the sometimes extreme inconvenience suffered by a multitude of people. In large cities, however, it is often well-nigh impossible to find alternative sparsely inhabited or uninhabited quarters for the passage of heavy vehicles. On the contrary, most of the major hotels, for example, are usually clustered round the much-frequented business districts; and it is difficult to prescribe rapid throughways for a city that will not adversely affect a certain percentage of persons in their quarters, whether of permanent or of temporary residence. Directing through-traffic around the periphery of a city will, in the final count, be the quickest way, despite the relative length of the road, to reach different parts of the urban area. Bypass and ring roads ("Beltways") do provide a certain amount of relief to inner-city traffic, but they are unable to present a long-term solution to the dynamic growth of urban traffic. Rerouting internal traffic to bypass and ringways may be likened to fire-fighting, and it is in any case effective only for a number of years; while a general improvement of the traffic network requires many years' planning and reconstruction and involves a huge capital outlay.

The intrusion of high-speed roads into the hearts of cities gives rise to serious acoustical problems in different quarters of the town, and it is imperative that the acoustical repercussions along the proposed route be foreseen and borne in mind. Their effects must be studied in detail, and the route, road surface, environment, and other items must be carefully planned. Meticulous design of walls, protective strips, and noise barriers, is essential if road planning in areas where noise levels must be kept to a minimum is to be successful. When the roads are being built, the construction of noise barriers suited to the specific requirements of the residents in the vicinity must be taken care of in advance (from the point of view of location, strength, etc.).

On the administrative plane, noise control involves the creation of special precincts with limits set to the permissible noise. The different zones must be brought to the notice of the public at large, to enable would-be purchasers of real estate, for example, to take the factor of acoustics into account.

Such division into acoustical zones is already being carried out in a number of countries, e.g., Switzerland, Austria, France, Japan, and others. In Israel, too, the problem is receiving active attention. Increasing night-time traffic is about to attain noise level values comparable to those met with during daylight hours, and supervision and control is ac-

cordingly needed during 24 hours of the day. The control of nocturnal traffic may include such provisions as speed limits, prohibition of the entering of certain areas, the enforcement of noise limitation by-laws (such as the elimination of sounding the horn), stringent special legislation regulating commercial traffic (e.g., limiting the hours during which goods may be loaded or unloaded). It will thus be possible to a certain extent, to reduce the disturbance caused to residents in their sleep.

In Israel the subject described has been treated under the "Prevention of Nuisances (unreasonable Noise) Regulations, 1973".

If, in spite of all the efforts, there still remain areas in which the expected noise level is likely to exceed the tolerable limit, having regard to local living conditions, an attempt should be made to substitute certain less noise-prone urban activities for those now prevailing. This means, in effect, a change in the existing utilization of the substructure, which may take place either in a natural fashion as a result of slow processes, such as the gradual take-over of the area by business and trades simultaneous with the withdrawal of residents from it, or under an intensified procedure encouraged "from above" by means of suitable financial compensation or the provision of fair alternatives.

2.3 The immediate environment of the "receiver"
If there is no way of silencing individual vehicles in a satisfactory manner or at least controlling its operation in a fashion conducive to minimizing the noise it makes, and if in addition it appears impossible or at least difficult to deal with the medium through which the noise has to travel, the only alternative remaining for influencing the exposure to traffic noise is that of introducing architectural improvements and modifications to the buildings. The means for that purpose include correct siting in order to have the building face the road in the most favorable manner, having regard to the shape of the building and its layout with a view to reducing sound-reflection and reverberation to a minimum, arranging the rooms with freedom from noise in mind, the insulation of those fronts of the building that face the road. Unlike the sound barrier, insulation only reduces the noise inside the building thus treated; but in many cases insulating the building is the only means or at any rate the most efficient one to control the internal noise level.

Where a building is situated on a busy thoroughfare, the shape and orientation of the building is of great importance. If, for example, the concave front of a building faces the road, the hollow will collect the sound waves and will have them reflected back and forth from one side to another. A convex shape, on the other hand, will scatter rather than gather the sound waves. Floors that recede from the road are well protected against traffic noise, provided only that the recess is adequate. Properly designed balconies with sound proof parapets, may serve as additional protective features for a building front.

When a building is in the planning stage, there is still time for seeing to it that the internal spaces most likely to suffer from noise are situated at the back of the buildings, while the service rooms—staircases, kitchens, wash-rooms, etc.—face the road.

Windows, are as a rule, the weakest link where the insulation of residents against external noises is concerned. The essence of any frontal insulation will therefore in the main boil down to a treatment of the windows. Their closures, weatherproofing, and reduction of surface area, as well as such means as the provision of double glazing. These measures require the modification of ventilation arrangements, which by themselves may cause a subsidiary noise problem arising from the operation of the pertinent machinery. Such are rotary fans and air-conditioners. In addition, noise from outside may be conducted along vents and other necessary openings.

Changes and events in traffic systems and their noise levels, as well as in other urban systems, are, as mentioned before, in mutual relationship.

These relations may operate in one or more directions, have favorable or unfavorable effects, and may originate in intentioned or spontaneous developments.

3. Mutual influences

Hereunder we describe some examples of mutual influence of the traffic system and its noise levels on the one hand and the general urban structure on the other hand.

1. Drastic changes in the noise levels along the thoroughfare of an area, caused *i.a.* by the increase in traffic density and speed, or by the intrusion of heavy vehicles, may determine significant changes in the environment, near and far.

Conspicuous changes in a built-up area are those originating from noise measures, such as modifications in the fronts of buildings for providing noise insulation, or the construction of fences, walls or earth embankments for screening purposes.

Other transformations not less significant but slower and less conspicuous, are changes in the demographic, social and economic stucture of the

area. People living close to the noise sources may leave their homes and move to other sections. The prices of their dwellings, which are exposed to noise and pollution, will decrease progressively and instead of the former inhabitants, there may occur an intrusion of a population of a lower socio-economic level and of land uses such as workshops or wholesale stores. This process is accompanied by the deterioration of building maintenance, leading to the creation of slums.

Commercial and social relations which developed normally between residents of the area, before its streets became noisy arterial highways, will progressively degenerate into a dismembered urban structure. This applies, of course, to high-speed traffic of special intensity. Traffic increasing to a certain volume only may, on the contrary, contribute to the commercial and social development of the area.

If, on the other hand, the area is intended for various land uses, other than residential, the process described above may be considered favorable and it may be encouraged by the authorities.

2. It may happen that the evolution of streets into arterial highways affects favorably other areas, as when the traffic is diverted from them to the area in question and relieves them from the nuisances of noise and pollution.

3. Changes can also develop from the opposite direction, when certain characteristics of the urban structure affect the level and quality of the noise in the traffic arteries and their environment.

High, flush and continuous house fronts along both sides of the street may increase the noise level by 3-6 dB(A).

4. On the other hand, low and scattered houses, with high and dense vegetation around them are favorable to the dispersion and absorption of the sound waves, thus decreasing the over-all noise level.

5. Protecting walls along the traffic artery from both sides may reverberate the sound waves, increase the noise level and, if they are not high and long enough, even allow the waves to pass them.

6. On the other hand, earth embankments with planted slopes along the traffic way absorb a certain part of the sound waves, stop the noise originating from the vehicles and keep the environment on their other side quiet.

7. Bends of the road affect considerably the noise level. In comparison with earth roads, which create dust clouds, but absorb a certain proportion of wheel friction noise, the hard and rough surface of a carriageway increases the noise level by about 10 dB(A).

8. The installation of a great number of traffic lights in the streets provides a good regulation of the traffic flow, avoids traffic jams and the need to operate horns, but they make stopping and starting more frequent, thus increasing the noise level.

4. Practical examples

There is a high probability that designers may not take into account possible unforeseen and generally unwanted consequences originating in modifications of one of the elements of the planning. On the other hand it may be expected that the knowledge of the influences and the interconnections of the noise sources and the measures to be taken for dealing with them will lead to the desired consequences, by a planned sequence of reactions, developing spontaneously.

Hereunder are described two examples, one unfavorable and one favorable, of the influence of treating noise problems on urban development.

Example A

In a densely built and highly motorized town, there is generally a serious disproportion between the number of persons wishing to move in and out on the one hand, and the available traffic system on the other hand, originating mainly in the insufficient traffic roads, their poor quality and the lack of proper traffic control.

In order to overcome these difficulties, multilane through roads are built inside the town in densely populated areas.

The following example illustrates the above-mentioned process.

The master traffic plan of Jerusalem foresees the building of an express-way through the heart of an old residential quarter.

The coherence of the quarter in question may suffer, the identity of the formerly homogeneous quarter may be lost and the separate sections may turn into satellites of nearby neighborhoods without proper integration.

The acoustic nuisance to the inhabitants may bring about—without proper guidance and assistance from the authorities—individual uncontrolled architectural changes.

Such developments may cause the people to leave the area which will progressively deteriorate.

An alternative solution which may prevent this process would be to build an underground tunnel for the part of the road crossing the center of the quarter, thus maintaining the connections between

its parts.

This is of course an expensive solution but in the long range it can prove worthwhile, by avoiding the evacuation of the area, which can require the payment of compensation and the erection of alternative housing.

Example B

An example of a favorable solution is the erection of the Central Bus Terminal of Tel-Aviv in the heart of a declining residential area.

The Terminal which reaches the last stage of construction, is designed for a daily turnover of 500,000 passengers carried in 12,000 buses operating on 200 interurban and 30 urban lines. It will house about 500 businesses, including two movie theaters as well as restaurants, supermarkets, etc.

There will be parking space for about 1,000 cars. The Terminal will have direct connection to interurban super-highways.

The Terminal complex and the adjoining streets, with their intense traffic, will generate noise levels of $L_{10} = 80 - 90$ dB(A). Noise and air pollution will make the area unfit for habitation.

The quarter in which the Terminal is being erected is destined, according to the Master Plan of Tel-Aviv, to become part of the area of factories and workshops and it is already being occupied by wholesale warehouses, industrial plants and workshops, which replaced progressively deteriorating housing.

The people who are still living in this area will certainly choose to leave it very soon and to move to the quieter outskirts of the town.

The process of the evacuation of the inhabitants and the penetration of users which are less sensitive to noise may lead naturally to the desired result.

(Difficulties may arise if the inhabitants demand, considerable compensation or alternative dwellings of a higher standard. In this case the intervention of the local authorities may be required.)

In addition to what has been said above, the commercial traffic that will be attracted by the area will release residential areas from the heavy traffic load. This may increase the value of houses in those areas and improve the social level of their inhabitants.

5. Conclusion

The above explanations and examples show the influences of actions taken in order to change the character of urban areas.

The relations between the different disciplines of urban development such as transport, social structure,

431

economy, etc., may cause a negative feedback process leading eventually to the deterioration or destruction of one or more of the elements involved.

The systematic knowledge of the complex connections and relations between the many fields of urban science, makes possible the development of a sound planning policy which takes future developments into account.

A thorough investigation of the many elements of the urban system and their integration in mathematical models will enable their effects to be analyzed, synthesized, simulated and evaluated with the aid of a computer.

This means a more rational planning process, which takes as many fixed and variable factors into consideration as possible and may be completed in a comparatively short time.

The noise forecasting and measurement in the project of ordinary and elevated roads in the Tel-Aviv Bus Terminal area [3] may serve as primary data in similar planning processes.

References

1. SCHWARTZ, A., 'Traffic noise, town planning and cybernetics', Paper presented at the 7th International Cybernetics Congress, Namur (September 1973).
2. SCHWARTZ, A., 'Traffic noise, town planning and cybernetic influences' (in Hebrew), Paper presented at Symposium of the Israel Ministry of Transport, Tel-Aviv (September 1973).
3. SCHWARTZ, A. and LEONOV, P., 'Traffic noise problems near the Tel-Aviv New Bus Station', Research Report presented to 'Ayalon Ways', (in Hebrew).

Author Index

Note: Numbers indicate the first page of the chapter in which the authors appear.

Subject Index